With our blessings
and best wishes to
Sri V. Jayaraman
on the occasion of his
Shastiapdhapoorthy on
October 29, 2001

RAJALAKSHMI
&
G.V. RAMAMURTHY

UNIVERSAL MESSAGE OF THE

# Bhagavad Gītā

*An Exposition of the Gītā in the Light of Modern Thought and Modern Needs*

**VOLUME 2**

*by*

**SWAMI RANGANATHANANDA**

Advaita Ashrama
(Publication Department)
5 Dehi Entally Road
Calcutta 700 014

*Published by*
Swami Mumukshananda
President, Advaita Ashrama
Mayavati, Champawat, Himalayas
*through its Publication Department, Calcutta*


First Edition, December 2000
3M3C

ISBN 81-7505-214-7

*Printed in India at*
Trio Process
Calcutta 700 014

# Contents


Hints on Transliteration and Pronunciation 4

Chapter Five 7

Chapter Six 107

Chapter Seven 188

Chapter Eight 275

Chapter Nine 335

Chapter Ten 399

Chapter Eleven 463

Index 515

# Hints on Transliteration and Pronunciation

In the book, Devanāgarī characters are transliterated according to the scheme adopted by the International Congress of Orientalists at Athens in 1912 and since then generally acknowledged to be the only rational and satisfactory one. In it the inconsistency, irregularity, and redundancy of English spelling are ruled out: f, q, w, x, and z are not called to use; one fixed value is given to each letter. According to this scheme

| | *sounds like* | | *sounds like* |
|---|---|---|---|
| अ | a o in s*o*n | ड | ḍ d |
| आ | ā in m*a*ster | ढ | ḍh dh in go*dh*ood |
| इ | i in *if* | ण | ṇ n in u*n*der |
| ई | ī ee in f*ee*l | त | t French t |
| उ | u u in f*u*ll | थ | th th in *th*umb |
| ऊ | ū oo in b*oo*t | द | d th in *th*en |
| ऋ | ṛ somewhat between r and ri | ध | dh theh in brea*the* *h*ere |
| ए | e a in ev*a*de | न | n n |
| ऐ | ai y in m*y* | प | p p |
| ओ | o oh | फ | ph ph in loo*p* *h*ole |
| औ | au ow in n*ow* | ब | b b |
| क | k k | भ | bh bh in a*bh*or |
| ख | kh ckh in blo*ckh*ead | म | m m |
| ग | g g (hard) | य | y |
| घ | gh gh in lo*g-h*ut | र | r r |
| ङ | ṅ ng | ल | l l |
| च | c ch in *ch*uckle | व | v in a*v*ert |
| छ | ch chh in cat*ch h*im | श | ś sh |
| ज | j j | ष | ṣ sh in *sh*ow |
| झ | jh dgeh in he*dgeh*og | स | s s |
| ञ | ñ n (somewhat) | ह | h h |
| ट | ṭ t | ं | ṁ ng |
| ठ | ṭh th in an*t-h*ill | : | ḥ half h |

*The following points may also be noted:*

(1) All Sanskrit words, except when they are proper nouns, or have come into common use in English, or represent a class of literature, cult, sect, or school of thought, are italicized.

(2) Anglicized Sanskrit words like 'kārmic', 'samsāric', 'Arhathood', etc., are romanized.

(3) Current geographical names, except in cases where their Sanskrit forms are given, or in special cases where the context requires it, and all modern names from the commencement of the nineteenth century are given in their usual spelling and without diacritical marks.

# BHAGAVAD GĪTĀ

## CHAPTER 5

## SANNYĀSA-YOGA
## THE YOGA OF RENUNCIATION

This evening, 12 February 1989, we are entering into the fifth chapter. As I said before, these chapters are all very very important, conveying a profound message to all humanity, and not for the people of India alone. Wherever the human being is there and is striving for fulfilment, he or she needs guidance from a rationally satisfying philosophy. It is that philosophy which is expounded in the *Gītā,* and the very essential parts of that philosophy you get in these chapters.

This fifth chapter, entitled *Sannyāsa-yoga,* starts with a question dealing with whatever Śrī Kṛṣṇa had said in the fourth chapter. Arjuna finds some confusing elements in those teachings. That is being brought up in the opening verse of the fifth chapter.

अर्जुन उवाच –
*Arjuna uvāca —*

*'Arjuna said:'*

संन्यासं कर्मणां कृष्ण पुनर्योगं च शंससि ।
यच्छ्रेय एतयोरेकं तन्मे ब्रूहि सुनिश्चितम् ॥१॥

*Sannyāsam karmaṇām kṛṣṇa punaryogam ca śamsasi;*
*Yacchreya etayorekam tanme brūhi suniścitam —* 5. 1

'Renunciation of action, O Kṛṣṇa, you commend, and again, its performance; which of these two is the better one? Do tell me this decisively.'

'O Kṛṣṇa, you have praised *sannyāsa* or renunciation of *karma—sannyāsam karmaṇām kṛṣṇa*—you have praised it in the fourth chapter'; *punaryogam ca śamsasi*, 'and you also praise *karma-yoga*, doing of actions'. *Yat śreyaḥ etayoḥ ekam*, 'between the two, which one is more excellent'; *tat me brūhi suniścitam*, 'tell me that decisively', is Arjuna's question.

Very often, even the clearest teaching can confuse people. That is what often happens in all types of education. Ādi Śaṅkarācārya refers to this in his commentary on the *Kena Upaniṣad* (II. i), in a beautiful Sanskrit sentence:

*Ekasmāt guroḥ śṛṇvatām* (*śiṣyāṇām madhye*), 'among a number of students listening to a teacher in a class'; *kaścit yathāvat pratipadyate*, 'some students understand exactly what the teacher has said'; *kaścit ayathāvat pratipadyate*, 'some understand it wrongly'; *kaścit viparītam pratipadyate*, 'some understand it just the opposite of what was said'; and *kaścit na pratipadyate iti*, 'some will not understand even a word'.

These are the four types of students every teacher has to confront with in his or her work of education. So, in the case of the *Gītā* also, these doubts come, in spite of using the clearest language; and the whole Indian mind, for the last thousand years, has been completely confused on these very questions. The thought of the people took this turn: If I am to improve my mind, and if that is superior, I shall sit quiet and improve my mind; why go about here and there working hard? And the whole nation became lazy, and the training of the mind also vanished. This wrong understanding of the philosophy had ruined the nation.

After four years of exploding Vedantic thought bombs suited to the Western people in U.S.A. and England, Swami Vivekananda returned to India in 1897, and in the very first full public lecture on the soil of India in Ramnad, he summoned our nation to wake up and face the challenges of the modern age (*Lectures from Colombo to Almora*, p. 50; *Complete Works of Swami Vivekananda*, vol. 3, pp. 145–46):

'The longest night seems to be passing away, the sorest trouble seems to be coming to an end at last, the seeming corpse appears to be awaking....India, this motherland of ours...from her deep long sleep. None can resist her any more; never is she going to sleep any more; no outward powers can hold her back any more; for the infinite giant is rising to her feet.'

We have to train the body, the senses and the mind; then we become great workers. That is the education of the whole man, not merely the thinking aspect. In the absence of this, we became mere intellectuals; we even failed to train our emotional faculties in the direction of human concern and human service. The whole body-mind complex became the servant of the tiny ego within the individual. And we can trace this happening in our recent history. In this modern age, fortunately, we got teachers like Swami Vivekananda and Sri Ramakrishna. Śaṅkarācārya taught us *samādhi* but he also lived the most active life. We all forgot his active side, and turned our attention to experience *samādhi*, which means, in our case, deep sleep or laziness. For centuries together, our nation went to sleep. When I watch people working, like digging the earth, I see them lifting the spade in a half sleep condition. Our people have yet to gain work efficiency and humanist concern. It was that half-sleepy India that Swami Vivekananda summoned to wake up and face the modern challenges by bursting Vedantic thought bombs suited to our nation.

Now comes Śrī Kṛṣṇa's answer to this question which has worried Arjuna and which has been nagging our whole nation. We have to clarify it once for all in this modern period.

**श्रीभगवान् उवाच —**

*Śrībhagavān uvāca —*

*'Śrī Bhagavān said:'*

**संन्यासः कर्मयोगश्च निःश्रेयसकरावुभौ ।**
**तयोस्तु कर्मसंन्यासात् कर्मयोगो विशिष्यते ॥ २ ॥**

*Sannyāsaḥ karmayogaśca niḥśreyasakarāvubhau;*
*Tayostu karmasannyāsāt karmayogo viśiṣyate —* 5. 2

'Both renunciation and *yoga* of action lead to freedom; of these, the *yoga* of action is superior to the renunciation of action.'

There is no equivocation in this sentence, but we as a people have tried to find equivocation. What did Śrī Kṛṣṇa say? *Sannyāsa* and *karma-yoga*, 'renunciation of action to realize the Atman and the path of detached action in the spirit of *yoga*', both these are capable of leading one to 'high spiritual development', *niḥśreyasa*. But, *tayostu*, 'between the two'; *karmasannyāsāt karmayogo viśiṣyate*, '*karma-yoga* is superior to *karma-sannyāsa*'. Renouncing actions is called *sannyāsa*. That is not so good. Engaging oneself in action and developing the spiritual awareness along with it, is far superior, *viśiṣyate*, 'is more excellent'. You may go to the forest, live in meditation, live a quiet life and try to realize the true Self. That is beautiful. But on the other hand, when you hear the cry of distress from thousands of people, if you go to serve them, make them better, you will still remain a spiritual seeker. This is certainly far better than that. We must remember that such a teaching has come from Buddha also. Though his teaching is essentially of the path of *jñāna* and monastic in application, yet when he went round the monastery and found in one cell a monk suffering from diarrhoea, he asked him, 'Did not any brother come to look after you, to serve you?' 'No Sir, they were all in meditation.' Buddha served him; then other brother monks came slowly. He asked them, 'Why did you not come to serve this monk; he was in distress.' 'Sir, we were all in meditation. And you have taught us meditation.' 'What foolish thing! You throw away your meditation. When you see a person in distress, you go and serve him!'

If a Buddha could say so, Śrī Kṛṣṇa says that hundred times more, because his teaching is essentially a teaching of practical spirituality—spirituality in action. See the language: spirituality in action. Behind every action is spirituality. But it does a double good. It gives me some spiritual strength; it brings peace and solace to people around me. 'Certainly that is superior,' *tayostu karma sannyāsāt karmayogo viśiṣyate*. That is the clearest exposition. In the third chapter also Śrī Kṛṣṇa had said, 'Nobody remains without any action; everybody does some action impelled by one's own nature. Even sitting in meditation is an action.' These are the words Śrī Kṛṣṇa had said at that time. So, better to do action for the good of all. Any ignorant person works for fattening one's own life and career. But the intelligent person, the wise person, the enlightened person, works for the good of all. Why don't you then be an enlightened person? That came in the third chapter. *Saktāḥ karmaṇyavidvāmso yathā kurvanti bhārata; Kuryād vidvāmstathā'saktaḥ cikīrṣurlokasamgraham,* to bring about *lokasamgraham,* 'welfare of the world'. You are a part of the world around you. You can't neglect all of them and remain quiet in your own way. That is not proper. That is called unenlightened attitude. This is enlightened attitude. *Avidvān* and *vidvān;* two types of people. The *avidvān* will be busy making enormous efforts to gain for oneself; the *vidvān,* on the other hand, will also work very hard; he or she has in view the welfare of people around. These are the two types. Śrī Kṛṣṇa has shown that, apart from these two, there is a third type who will be busy developing one's own spirituality, not at all doing any worldly action, ever concerned with only one's own salvation, one's own peace of mind. Such a person doesn't care if there are hundreds of people starving around. It was that philosophy which influenced our people for centuries together. And the result is so much of sufferings all over the nation. Nobody cares. Everybody going to temple, prays only for one's self, 'O God, save me!' Not once have our people prayed to God to give His blessings to someone else! What kind of religion is it? What kind of spirituality is it? This question came in the modern period, first from Sri Ramakrishna, and then from Swami Vivekananda. Sri Ramakrishna said, 'Religion is not for empty bellies'. And Swamiji said (*Complete Works of Swami Vivekananda,* vol. 5, p. 50):

'I do not believe in a God or religion which cannot wipe the widow's tears or bring a piece of bread to the orphan's mouth.'

These wails are going on all around us. Can't I go and look after them? Can't I wipe away the tears from the eyes of people? Is it not religion? Ask that question. The *Gītā* will tell you that it is true religion. Based on the Upaniṣads, the *Gītā* asks you to work. Why? Because, as prayer is a part of religion, work also is a part of religion. But we never understood this Upaniṣadic teaching. Today, Sri Ramakrishna comes and conveys to you that teaching. What is this world? The same Brahman, on whom you meditate in your heart, is also there in front of you in these millions of forms. They all have come from Brahman. The universe has come from Brahman, lives in Brahman, returns to Brahman. Sri Ramakrishna told Swami Vivekananda, 'Meditate closing your eyes on God within you, and when you open your eyes, the same God is in front of you in these forms. Serve them.' There are not two gods. Only one God, who is inside as well as outside. *Antarbahiśca tat sarvam vyāpya nārāyaṇa sthitaḥ.* In the *Mahā Nārāyaṇa Upaniṣad* comes this verse. 'Nārāyaṇa exists both inside the human being and outside also.' We don't have the concept of a devil in our Indian philosophy. Inside, it is all God; open your eyes, and it is only devil! We have no such idea. The same divine is in every being. So, service of man becomes worship of God. Sri Ramakrishna expressed it in a very beautiful language: 'every *jīva* is *Śiva*. Service of the *jīva* is worship of *Śiva*.' So, we get today pure Advaita, non-dualistic philosophy, leading to love, compassion and service. Formerly, by Advaita was meant, '*neti, neti,* not this, not this; this is all *samsāra* and Brahman is transcendental. That Advaita was what our people took to for centuries—a negative Advaita. We want to be alone, we want to realize our Self. We don't want this *samsāra,* and won't get involved in its troubles. That is the idea that came later. Some of the later books also mentioned the same thing. In the monastic community, we say in Hindi: *Duniā tīn kāl me nahīm hai,* 'this world doesn't exist in the three divisions of time; past, present and future'. Why worry about it?

A different approach came from the Advaita Vedanta of Sri Ramakrishna. A human being there is in distress. How can you ignore that? So, that Advaita has become transformed into real Advaita today; that there is only One; as when you close your eyes, Brahman is there, so also when you open your eyes, Brahman is there. That message had come in the *Muṇḍaka Upaniṣad* (II. ii. 11), which we studied here before we took up the *Gītā*. *Brahmaivedam amṛtam,* 'this whole world of manifestation is the same immortal Brahman'. See the words! *Idam,* a technical word in Vedanta meaning 'this manifested universe'. What is this universe? It is Brahman. What Brahman? *Amṛtam brahma,* 'that immortal Brahman' is this universe. *Purastāt brahma,* 'in front is Brahman'; *paścāt brahma,* 'behind is Brahman'; *dakṣiṇataścottareṇa,* 'on the right as well as left'; *adhaścordhvamca prasṛtam,* 'it is spread above as well as below'. Then finally, a tremendous statement: *brahmaivedam viśvamidam variṣṭham,* 'this *viśvam* or universe is only that supreme divine Brahman'. The *Gītā* teaching, and today, the Ramakrishna-Vivekananda teaching of Advaita, is based upon this idea that the divine is in the heart of all. We have to worship God by serving people around. We contracted this whole teaching later on. In our *bhakti* religion we saw Brahman only in the temple; outside the temple it is all *samsāra* or worldliness. That is why you find a person going to a temple, cutting grass there with great devotion, because that act has behind it the devotion to the divine, to that image of God that is there. You wash vessels, cut grass there, and when you return, you feel you have done a religious act. But you did not do so to human beings. You limited God only to that particular image. You couldn't feel the presence of God elsewhere. Therefore, you made your religion too narrow, so non-human and, also often, anti-human. That is what had happened to our religious ideas in the past centuries.

That is what is being corrected by Sri Ramakrishna's and Swami Vivekananda's teachings. This wonderful teaching is meant to make for a fulfilled humanity. We are here to reduce people's suffering. Life means also suffering; but there are people to help all such afflicted ones. Then they can bear their suffering better. Go to any village; if people there see that you are there to help them, they will be tremendously encouraged. Nobody has encouraged them. Everybody has gone only to exploit them till now. Go to the tribals, not to exploit them, but let somebody go saying, 'I am here to help you.' But merely saying so won't do. They will suspect you. You have to show by your living there that you are their friend. Once you demonstrate that, you open up their hearts. You are treated as their real friend. So, this kind of attitude must be pervasive in society, East or West. The developed nations, the developing nations, everywhere, we are one. That wonderful Advaitic vision can make for tremendous change in the world today.

The whole world has to be raised. You can't raise only one part of the world. We need a philosophy for it. We need a particular ideology for it. Not mere humanistic jargon; that won't do. That won't make you fully inspired. We must have a basis in truth before our action. That truth is what the philosophy and spirituality of Advaita proclaims. There is only one infinite Self in all. Differences are only on the surface, at the sensory level. Deep down there is perfect unity. You and I are one. Then love alone can come out of your heart. Service alone can come out of your heart. We need a philosophy of human unity, of human service. That philosophy will be very inspiring. Vivekananda preached it, and the world likes to hear it today. That is why his books are very much in demand even among the people of Soviet Russia today, where they have themselves started a Vivekananda Society. A group of intellectuals and scientists of Soviet Russia have started a Vivekananda Society in Moscow. They feel that the problems afflicting the world today need a philosophy to make it recover from them. A wrong philosophy has brought us to this trouble. A more comprehensive philosophy we need today. And Vedanta is that comprehensive philosophy, *a science of human possibilities,* if I can use the word coined by the late British biologist, Sir Julian Huxley.

So, that is why it is attracting more and more people. It is so rational; you can question, you can turn it upside down. Try to understand it, try to experiment, try to realize it for yourself. And the whole thing is directed not to mere belief but to experience, here, in this very life. It does not give a passport to heaven. Because of that wonderful quality of Advaita as expressed in the Upaniṣads, the *Gītā*, in many parts of *Rāmāyaṇa, Mahābhārata, Śrīmad Bhāgavatam,* and also in the wonderful original message of Buddha, that Advaitic vision out of which alone infinite compassion can come, even to the animals, it should dominate the world situation today. If in the twenty-first century more people understand this truth, this will be really a bright century. Everything is ready, but there is so much of distortion, so much of violence, so much of crime, so many weaknesses of the human mind. This cannot be removed by merely political methods. Even democracy itself can become a mobocracy, as I said earlier. A democracy that condemned Socrates to death in Athens became a mobocracy. The then Athenians couldn't understand the higher levels of life. So, they condemned this great man to death. That made Plato tremendously a hater of democracy. Plato said democracy is absolutely mobocracy. There is nothing high in it. If you want democracy to succeed, this element of ethical, moral and spiritual growth must come to the people. So, in Vedanta you will find, in the context of modern science, modern techniques, modern socio-political processes, this great spiritual orientation given to human life and human development. That appeals to many thinking people all over the world; to increasing number of people, including, as I said, people in the communist countries, to whom all this was anathema till now. Even Indian communists like the C.P.M. in Calcutta, West Bengal, have started praising Vivekananda recently in one of the articles in their journal. They have never done it before. The world is changing. People are seeking for a guidance, a philosophical guidance. They don't get it from mere political leaders. They can take you up to some distance and not more than that, just like the 18th and 19th century industrial revolution which took the Western nations some steps forward. They abolished poverty and many other things. But so many other evils have come. Some evils have gone.

Other evils have come. These evils are deep. For what you see as human distortions in the West today, there is no complete philosophy of life; there are only sectional philosophies. They are all in search of this complete philosophy. That is why the word holistic comes again and again in Western literature today: holistic medicine, holistic life, holistic health, holistic this and holistic that.

So, this is how this subject has become so important today for us in India, and for others elsewhere. And they are in search of it; they are not able to get it so easily; but, they understand things better than our people in India. We are not able to grasp it so much. The past static centuries' pressure is on our minds. We have not yet felt the real problems of life. When that feeling will come, then we will come to this practical Vedanta of the *Gītā*. We are satisfied when we go to a temple and ring the bell, and we feel that we have done everything. A few rituals are enough. That is our present condition. But wait! Life is becoming more complicated, more problems are coming, and the result, as it happened in the West, is that the traditional religious ideas can never make you face up to these challenges. We need something deeper, something strengthening, something heroic. That is what you get here in this great book. A hero's teaching to another hero; that is the *Gītā*.

Arjuna was a hero. Śrī Kṛṣṇa was a still greater hero. And he communicated this message not for any goody-goody purpose of a little bit of cheap religion; that is all what we understand by religion today. The lowest level of religious understanding in India, even among some intellectuals and pandits is: go to Hardwar, catch hold of the tail of a cow, pay five rupees to a priest, and you will go to heaven. That is all of religion to such people. That is the lowest level. So, such cheap ideas are plenty all over India. Even top people will do these things. Some government ministers will do this often when, in fact, they have plenty of other good things to do—to bring up the millions of common people, to serve the nation, to give people strength, to make them able to carry the nation on their shoulders as its enlightened citizens, etc. The people must be made the centre of democracy. Many of our politicians are fond of the cheap kind of religion. But for doing the work that is given to him or her, and for raising the nation from its sufferings and privations, they don't have the will to do. That is why, in spite of plenty of politics, there is so little human development, human welfare. The cry of distress comes from more and more hearts everyday. So, we have with us Gandhiji's prescription to some people who went to him and asked, 'what shall we do?' He said, 'before you plan to do anything, sit quiet for some time, and ask one question: will, what I plan to do, bring welfare to the weakest person in my country? Then, if you receive proper answer, go ahead with the project.' That is the most important thing today. He said, my life and work will continue till I wipe away the tear from the last sorrowing person. These are beautiful ideas, highly spiritual and truly political. Real politics is what makes a citizen stand on his or her own feet. They must hear the voice: this nation belongs to you; you are the strength of this nation. Today, our politicians want to *use* the people to get power. All political parties are engaged in *using* the people, making use of them as cattle, purchasing their votes for five rupees or hundred rupees. That is where the *Gītā* teaching has to come to help us, to correct our politics and administration. There is so much political strength, democratic strength in its teaching.

In fact, this chapter, the fifth chapter, contains an exposition of the 'philosophy of equality', *samatva, samadarśitva.* We are all one. We have to establish that sense of harmony, that sense of equality, in our country. What a beautiful theme! An ordinary person standing before an extraordinary person, does not feel small; he or she also has some greatness about him or her. This kind of human growth has to come to our nation in this modern age. The philosophy to help you to achieve it is here in this *Gītā* teaching. It is practical Vedanta, practical Advaita. And Vivekananda said, there is no new text book needed for practical Vedanta, because it is already there in its best form in the *Gītā*. So you have the answer Śrī Kṛṣṇa is giving: *Tayostu karmasannyāsāt karmayogo viśiṣyate,* 'between the two, *karma yoga* is superior to *karma sannyāsa*'. You may have peace of mind, you may be happy. You may be free from all trouble, but does it absolve you from your responsibility to help suffering people around you? They are also in distress. Don't you have a heart? Does not the heart feel for others? What is the use of human life and religion if the heart is completely dry? We unfortunately developed a dried-up heart in our country. Brilliant intellects, dried up hearts. Our hearts have never functioned for centuries together. Generally, we think women have a heart. But even the women's heart became so circumscribed to their own children that it never extended to anybody else. That is what happened to our country. So, Swami Vivekananda said, combine Śaṅkarācārya's intellect with Buddha's infinite heart. Then you will become a great person yourself.

That is the work we have to do in this modern period. Our intellect is bright, but our heart is very very narrow. Why all these evils like bride-burning and other things? All because the heart is not there. The brain is there. Heart is absolutely dead. That is the nature of our human situation. That is why this teaching needs to be converted to practical implementation. Our character must be shaped in the light of this teaching. A new type of humanity has to come up in the light of this teaching. Now Śrī Kṛṣṇa is going one step further. He said that between renunciation of actions through *sannyāsa* and doing actions in the spirit of *karma-yoga,* the second one is better, the second one is more excellent. He now goes still further in the next verse.

ज्ञेयः स नित्यसंन्यासी यो न द्वेष्टि न कांक्षति ।
निर्द्वन्द्वो हि महाबाहो सुखं बन्धात् प्रमुच्यते ॥ ३ ॥

*Jñeyaḥ sa nityasannyāsī yo na dveṣṭi na kāṅkṣati;*
*Nirdvandvo hi mahābāho sukham bandhāt pramucyate* —5. 3

'He or she should be known a constant *sannyāsī,* who has no personal likes, nor dislikes; for, free from the pairs of opposites, O mighty armed, that person is easily set free from bondage.'

Know that person to be a 'constant *sannyāsi*', *nitya-sannyāsī*. Who? *Yo na dveṣṭi na kāṅkṣati*, 'who has no hatred for anybody, and who is not greedy to possess everything for oneself'. That type of person is a *karma-yogi*. *Nirdvandvo*, 'free from the pairs of opposites' in society, like good and bad, happiness and misery. *Nirdvandvo hi mahābāho*, 'his or her mind is steady even in the midst of all these dualities'. *Sukham bandhāt pramucyate*, 'he or she gets freed from all bondages easily', when he or she develops this kind of mind. You are in the midst of work, in the midst of problems, but your mind is so trained, so as to be able to remain calm and steady and face all these challenges before you. Such a person is a *nityasannyāsī*, 'a constant *sannyāsi*'; what a beautiful expression! *Sannyāsa* is so great; everybody appreciates *sannyāsa* in India. But what does *sannyāsa* mean? Originally it meant giving up wife and children, or husband and others, and going to the forest and living all alone. They don't cook food, they get it by begging. *Niragni*, 'no handling of fire'; a *sannyāsi* is not expected to cook food for oneself. A Buddhist *sannyāsin* who is called a *bhikṣu*, is not permitted to cook food for himself. Suppose he goes to a house, and the housewife gives him raw rice and vegetables, he will say, 'Sorry.' 'Have you got any cooked food? Just a little?', he will ask. He will not ask also. Generally he will keep quiet. That is the rule for Buddhist monks. So also for Hindu monks. Monks are free from owning things and cooking food for themselves. They only live by begging, and that begging also is done a little from each house. They call it *mādhukari*, a wonderful term they have coined for it. Like a bee that takes honey material from various flowers, never disturbing a single flower, should be the monk who takes his food from seven or eight houses, and not from one house which would be a burden to that family; a small quantity is not a burden. This is the usual idea of *sannyāsa*.

Now, everybody can't be a *sannyāsi*. What about the others? O we are mere householders, that is the attitude. No, you are also a *sannyāsi*, is what Śrī Kṛṣṇa is going to tell everyone. As soon as you develop this quality as given in the verse, you become a *sannyāsi.* Whether you are living at home, or in the market, doing work, it doesn't matter. It is the mind that is a *sannyāsi,* the attitude you have developed. Your work is going on for the good of the world. That will continue. But your mind has become free. *Sukham bandhāt pramucyate,* 'you easily get freed from bondage', what you call worldly bondage. That is one step further than the previous verse. But that is not enough. The next *śloka* clinches the whole issue.

सांख्ययोगौ पृथग्बालाः प्रवदन्ति न पण्डिताः ।
एकं अपि आस्थितः सम्यक् उभयोर्विन्दते फलम् ॥४॥

*Sāṅkhyayogau pṛthagbālāḥ pravadanti na paṇḍitāḥ;*
*Ekam api āsthitaḥ samyak ubhayorvindate phalam* — 5. 4

'Childlike or immature people, not the wise, speak of Self-knowledge and *yoga* of action, as distinct; one who is truly established in one, gains the fruits of both.'

*Sāṅkhya* and *yoga* are the two paths. Of these two, the path of renunciation of all actions, going into the forest, trying to realize your Atman, was called the *Sāṅkhya* path. In the second chapter, Śrī Kṛṣṇa had referred to this path, and said there is another path called *yoga, karma-yoga.* Then he says here that, 'these two paths are different,' is said only by people of undeveloped minds. Undeveloped minds are described in the Sanskrit language as *bālāḥ,* 'immature children', babies. That these two are different, 'is babies' talk.' That is the language: *bālāḥ pravadanti, na paṇḍitāḥ,* 'but not by a *paṇḍitā*'; those who are highly intelligent and wise, they will never say that these two are different. Why? *Ekam api āsthitaḥ samyak ubhayoḥ vindate phalam,* 'if one is well established in one, he or she reaps the fruits of both'. That is the language. You are doing *karma-yoga,* be well established in it. You are as good as a *sannyāsin* who has renounced everything and gone to the forest. This is the great status that Śrī Kṛṣṇa gives to the householder who lives and works as a *karma-yogī;* the person who has human responsibilities to discharge and works hard. We have completely forgotten this teaching, and one of the most evil things today is a feeling of smallness on the part of our householders: 'I am nothing, I am a *samsāri.* I am only a *gṛhastha.* I am not fit for this and that.' That kind of degradation has come on the human mind. It is extremely bad to lose faith in oneself, and in one's way of life. Have faith in yourself. I may not be a very high householder, but I am a good householder, I carry out my family and social responsibilities properly. In that way, self-confidence must come to the householders who constitute 99.9 per cent of our population. Śrī Kṛṣṇa wants to infuse that self-confidence, *ātma śraddhā,* in people who have to face challenges, difficulties, and family and social responsibilities. This is the standard Indian idea of the householder. We have come down and fallen far away down from that idea, and we are feeling, 'We are nobody, we are nobody.' I have told our householders here and there to be somewhat more helpful to the weaker sections. But, 'we are only householders, we are not *sannyāsins,*' has been the usual response. I used to exclaim, 'What do you mean? Is it not a joy for you to serve people?' Look up into our *Manu Smṛti.* I often quote that famous law-book in which the *gṛhastha* or householder is given a very high position. There he says, among the four *āśramas—brahmacarya, gṛhastha, vānaprastha,* and *sannyāsa*—the *gṛhastha āśrama* is the 'pre-eminent *āśrama*' (3. 78):

*Yasmāt trayo'pyāśramiṇo jñānenānnena cānvaham;*
*Gṛhasthenaiva dhāryante tasmāt jyeṣṭhāśramo gṛhī* —

'Since the *gṛhastha* discharges the responsibility of educating and feeding the other three *āśramas,* the *gṛhastha āśrama* is the pre-eminent *āśrama.*'

A *brahmacārin* does not earn; the *vānaprasthin* also doesn't earn; so also, a *sannyāsi* doesn't earn. Who runs the whole society? This one single group called the *gṛhastha,* the householder. *Tasmāt,* 'therefore', *jyeṣṭhāśramo gṛhī,* '*gṛhastha* is called the *jyeṣṭhāśrama,* pre-eminent *āśrama*'. What a high status is thus given to the householder! But what is the nature of that householder? Its equivalent today is what you call a free and responsible citizen in a democracy. That citizen not only takes care of himself or herself, but takes care of the whole nation. That is where Śrī Kṛṣṇa's philosophy of *yoga* comes in. 'I am a simple *samsāri,* a worldly person, I have no status,' that kind of demeaning attitude is the opposite of the high status given to the householder by our ancient law-giver Manu. Today, our *gṛhasthas* must realize this truth. Whatever can be achieved by the *Sāṅkhya* path of *sannyāsa* and *jñāna,* can be achieved by the *yoga* path of action and day-to-day dedication. This is the language. *Yat sāṅkhyaiḥ prāpyate sthānam tadyogairapi gamyate,* 'whatever high state you achieve through *sāṅkhya,* exclusive path of Self-knowledge, that you achieve through *yoga* also.' This statement comes in the *Mahābhārata* and other places also repeatedly. We have forgotten all this. Why? Because a national decay had set in, the body became weak, mind became weak, and the will became weak; we mistook obstinacy as strong will. We have plenty of obstinacy. Will and obstinacy are not the same. Will can change if you know that it is not correct. Obstinacy can never change. We often mistake obstinacy for will. 'That person has a strong will,' that only means he or she is very obstinate. He or she will never change. If you suggest that the hare he or she has caught has no horns, it has only two ears, the reply will be, 'No! it has got two horns. I am sure, I am sure.' That is the expression of obstinacy in one of our languages. So, strength of will and clarity of thinking make for precision. We lack precision in thinking, speaking and action. Precision, we had destroyed long ago. What can be said in two sentences, we will take two hundred sentences, and yet in the end we do not know what we said. In many lectures you can see, after two hours you do not know what the speaker had said. There is no clarity; there is no precision. Now, these are highly trained intellectual products that our people are achieving slowly. So, today, if we want to develop our nation into a powerful one, we need to change the mind of the people, make it a trained mind, not a stuffed brain. Mostly it is a stuffed brain. Opinions it has in plenty, but not convictions. So, in all our Pañcāyats, Zilla Pariṣads, University Senates, and Assemblies you will find plenty of talk, but as to the work to be done, the action programme, there is very little of it, because the heart is not moved by the surrounding human situation. When you see a man in distress there, you can't go and deliver a lecture to him. You are there to remove his distress. That is the first work you have to do. What *Bhagavān* Buddha told: A man struck by an arrow and suffering from the wound, told a person who went to him. 'Now, tell me who shot this arrow at me? Tell me from what tree was the wood taken to make this arrow?' He went on asking such questions. Buddha took this example. 'By the time he replies to two or three such questions, the patient would die away. Get the arrow removed first,' he said. That is the first thing to be done; remove that arrow. Then you can discuss in plenty the theory of all these things. That is a wonderful example. And we in India need that teaching very much today. People are in distress, people are suffering. Remove that first; then you can have a discussion about other connected matters.

यत्सांख्यैः प्राप्यते स्थानं तद्योगैरपि गम्यते ।
एकं सांख्यं च योगं च यः पश्यति स पश्यति ॥५॥

*Yatsāṅkhyaiḥ prāpyate sthānam tadyogairapi gamyate;*
*Ekam sāṅkhyam ca yogam ca yaḥ paśyati sa paśyati* — 5. 5

'The goal which is reached by the *jñānis* is also reached by the *karma-yogis.* One who sees *jñāna* and *yoga* as one, alone sees.'

What is *yoga?* What is *Sāṅkhya?* They are really one. There is no difference between the two. That is real understanding. That, in reality, is seeing the truth. This is what Śrī Kṛṣṇa says here.

So, a householder, who wants to respect the *sannyāsin* who has given up the world and gone on a lonely life, does no harm in respecting such a person, but not at the cost of demeaning oneself. Don't demean yourself, while you respect somebody else. That is the first lesson we have to learn. Our self-respect must be maintained. Then only that respect for the other person has some meaning. But when you find, even in our politics, that people seeking a ministerial post go and touch the feet of a holy person, where is personal dignity? *Gītā* won't allow it. If you want to touch the feet of somebody else, do so, but as a product of your own dignity and self-respect. By doing that you must feel your own dignity enhanced. That can never happen unless the one whose feet you touch is a good person, is endowed with moral values. Then only will you feel dignified; otherwise, you simply go down in self-respect.

Once, I remember, in Chandigarh and in Amritsar, I was addressing the Medical College. The Principal, a Sikh gentleman, was a very fine person, very independent, and always in trouble with the authorities because of his very independent spirit. He did not mind that. I met him again in Kabul, where he was in charge of the children's hospital donated by the Government of India and run entirely by Indian personnel and Indian goods. They took me to that hospital. During that time he heard all lectures which I used to give in Kabul. After a few days, before I left, he came to me and said, 'I don't salute anybody, I am very independent, but I want your permission to bow down to you.' This was the language. I said, 'if by bowing down to me like that, you feel your own self-respect enhanced, then you may do so; don't do so under any other condition.' He was very happy. He was already a man of tremendous self-respect, he had nothing to lose, so he bowed down and was happy.

Now this is the truth that we must keep in view. Anything that demeans somebody else should not be done; also anything that demeans oneself, should not be done. Let everybody be raised in his or her own self-respect. Then only we can have a healthy human society. The householder and the *sannyāsin* have both a high status in society; it is this idea you get in Swami Vivekananda's famous book *Karma-yoga* composed of some of his lectures delivered in America. Its second chapter is entitled 'Each is Great in His Own Place'. Is a *sannyāsin* greater, or is a *gṛhastha* greater? Each is great in his own place. That is the subject, and a beautiful illustration is given there.

In what way is one or the other great? That is what our nation must learn today in a big way.

Then comes a wonderful statement, *ekam sāṅkhyam ca yogam ca yaḥ paśyati sa paśyati*, '*yoga* and *sāṅkhya* are one and the same.' Renunciation of action and trying to get *samādhi* in some cave or mountain, and doing actions in society in a spirit of *yoga,* with detachment and in a spirit of service and dedication, both these are the same. They lead you to the same goal. What a beautiful idea! This is the central stress in the *Gītā*. In no other book will you find this clarification, and this lifting up of the ordinary human life to such high level; that the highest spirituality can be had *here and now,* in the midst of work, in the midst of struggle, by the mind attuned to that *yoga* attitude.

In the *Hitopadeśa,* second part, there occurs this very luminous verse (*Sandhi*, 90):

*Vane'pi doṣā prabhavanti rāgiṇām*
*gṛheṣu sarvendriya nigrahastapaḥ;*
*Akutsite karmaṇi yaḥ pravartate*
*nivṛtta rāgasya gṛham tapovanam* —

'Even in the forest, if one has sensory cravings, he or she will have trouble to lead a spiritual life; people with sensory attachment will face evil problems even when they go to the forest to live there in meditation'. *Gṛheṣu sarvendriya nigrahastapaḥ,* 'but, remaining at home with disciplined sense organs is *tapas*'. Then, *akutsite karmaṇi yaḥ pravartate nivṛtta rāgasya gṛham tapovanam;* a very definite statement. *Akutsite karmaṇi yaḥ pravartate,* 'those who are engaged in blameless deeds'; *nivṛtta rāgasya,* 'those who are free from sensory attachments'; *gṛham tapovanam,* 'his or her own home becomes a forest retreat. The *gṛham,* a home, gets transformed into a *tapovanam,* a forest retreat.'

This tremendous emphasis is on not where you stay, but how you train your mind, how you shape it. You can do it here, or you can do it there. In fact, when you do it here, it is more successful, because in the midst of challenges you are strengthening the mind. If there is no challenge, there is nothing to strengthen. If the mind is not distracted by anything, there is no challenge to the mind. What you achieve is poor.

However, in the midst of challenges if you are able to pacify the mind, then it is wonderful. It is just like this: *Sannyāsins* do not carry money, that is the rule. Swami Vivekananda travelled all over India without touching money. That was the old system—without ever touching money, you have developed detachment for money. But, while handling money can you still be detached? That is a much greater achievement. A bank officer has to deal with crores of rupees. It passes through his hands. It doesn't stick there. But very often it sticks! And that is called corruption. But, the rule is, you pass it on, it is not yours, it belongs to the public. You are only handling it. That is also true with regard to a spiritual householder. He or she is only handling the money in a spirit of detachment. And, if one can do so, he or she is better than the one who says, 'I don't touch money, therefore, I am clean and pure.' You are handling money and still you are keeping clean and pure. What a beautiful idea! More challenges are there before you. You overcome them. Now these ideas come again and again in the *Śrīmad Bhāgavatam, Mahābhārata* and in the *Gītā* also.

This is what Śrī Kṛṣṇa is stressing because everyone can rise to the highest spiritual level. One has only to take into account this particular subject in the midst of one's day-to-day activities. He or she should not get lost in the day-to-day activities, pleasures, and comforts, forgetting to train one's mind to rise higher and higher. There are higher levels to attain.

So, the one clarion call of the Vedanta to every spiritual seeker is, *don't stagnate at the physical level, at the sensory level.* That is animal life. Human beings have the capacity to go beyond this level. So, continue to march on; don't stagnate. That is its only message; it doesn't condemn sensory life; it doesn't condemn our day-to-day actions for earning money, for running our households; not at all. There is no place for the devil in the whole of Vedanta. We are all great, we are all good, but don't stagnate. Stagnation alone is called *samsāra.* Don't be a *samsāri*; when you stagnate at the sensate level, then you are a *samsāri.* Otherwise, you are in *samsāra,* you are struggling, you are developing; just like a baby, interested only in eating, drinking, and comfort, slowly develops a desire for knowledge, goes to school, reads books, and progresses to higher levels of seeking knowledge and excellence. In that kind of life's march, you also find a stage where you go beyond sensory limitations, beyond all this *samsāra,* or stagnant sensory life. Then you begin to realize your own true nature and the tremendous possibilities hidden within you. God Himself is hidden within you, that knowledge will come to you.

*The whole of that process is called tapas.* That *tapas* can be done in the context of household life itself. It doesn't mean a dry asceticism; not at all. You are enjoying your day-to-day life, you have contact with society, you can smile, you can enjoy everything. But you are not stagnant at that level. You are going higher and higher. Even if you are an educated person, you can play with children with toys; there is no harm. You are encouraging the children thereby, so that you never become an ascetic of the dry type. Sri Ramakrishna always said, 'Don't be a dry ascetic. O Divine Mother, don't make me a dry ascetic.' That kind of asceticism, which we usually associated earlier with a very wry face, not even a smile, not even pleased to see a baby in front, that kind of asceticism has no place in Vedanta. Don't become a dried up ascetic. That is where this teaching has a tremendous significance. March on, march on, don't stagnate, don't stagnate. There are so many heights to conquer.

That is the clarion call of the *Kaṭha Upaniṣad* (I. iii. 14): *Uttiṣṭhata jāgrata prāpya varān nibodhata,* 'arise, awake and stop not till the goal is reached', as freely rendered by Swami Vivekananda. That goal is perfect realization of the divine hidden in all of us. And the divine in me is also the divine in you. There is only one divine, undivided, existing in apparently divided existences. That is the language of the *Gītā* in a later chapter (13. 16, *see also* 18. 20): *Avibhaktam ca bhūteṣu vibhaktam iva ca sthitam*, 'that infinite Atman is one and undivided, *avibhaktam*, but it appears to be divided in you, in me, in all'. This knowledge then comes to you, 'that I am one with all. I am the infinite Atman'. Just as space is undivided, even though it becomes apparently divided by raising a wall in it. Space itself does not know this limitation. That is why the Atman is compared to space. What a beautiful illustration! Space is ever clear, ever pure; nothing can taint it. The Atman is also the same. So, *ākāśa* becomes a symbol of the Atman in the Upaniṣads. It has all these qualities except consciousness. If consciousness is added to *ākāśa,* it is Brahman. So, in many places you find mentioned, Brahman is *ākāśa, ākāśa* is Brahman.

Vedanta prescribes short-term ideals and long-term ideals. In economic development, we have five-year plans; but in life, we need to have that as well as five hundred year plans. What type of human being is coming out of all these plans? Ask that question. Is he or she going to be selfish, money-mad and corrupt? Then the five-year plan will be dangerous for any nation. We need to develop decent human beings inspired by ethical values, humanistic values, who love other people, who try to lift up common people—that is the long-range plan. Now that is the subject which is going on all through this *Gītā*. And the *Gītā* says that it is the birthright of one and all, all over the world. Today or tomorrow, you will reach the end of this great struggle, this great adventure, and become free, here and now, in this very world. You may have to pass through many births; it doesn't matter. But you must feel that you are on the way. What are births and deaths in this spiritual adventure? Merely punctuations. Just like when you write a sentence, you put a comma, put a semi-colon, but no full stop. Full stop is where everything ends. That is *mokṣa,* absolute spiritual freedom. Till then it is a continuous march. I am in that great line of pilgrims towards that highest spiritual realization. So, Śrī Kṛṣṇa is telling in the next verse, the verse which we shall now study, verse 6:

संन्यासस्तु महाबाहो दुःखं आप्तुं अयोगतः ।
योगयुक्तो मुनिः ब्रह्म नचिरेण अधिगच्छति ॥६॥

*Sannyāsastu mahābāho duḥkham āptum ayogataḥ;*
*Yogayukto muniḥ brahma nacireṇa adhigacchati* — *5. 6*

'Renunciation of action, O mighty-armed, is hard to attain by one who has not passed through the *yoga* of action; the meditative person, purified by the *yoga* of action, quickly attains Brahman.'

Real *sannyāsa*, renunciation of action, cannot come without perfection in *yoga, karma-yoga.* That is the language. Real *sannyāsa*! Fake *sannyāsa* you can have, but real *sannyāsa* cannot come. *Duḥkham āptum*, 'is difficult to achieve'; *ayogataḥ*, 'for one who has not been disciplined in *yoga*'. First, discipline in *yoga.* Then you will know how to renounce your actions. That renunciation will be a spiritual renunciation, not a physical renunciation. Without fulfilling your citizenship responsibilities, how can you have real *sannyāsa*? You have a responsibility to the society. Never forget it. As Swami Vivekananda said using two terms, 'manhood' and 'sainthood': 'don't try to become a saint before you become a man in the true sense of the term.' Sainthood raised on manhood will be genuine. Sainthood without the manhood below will be fake sainthood. And in this country, we have been after that for centuries together. Fake sainthood; put on a dress, you become a saint. But here it is different. You have worked hard, you have struggled, developed high character, helped people, you have discharged your citizenship responsibilities. Then you will become a real saint. Develop this 'I', expand it, feel one with all. That is the first stage of human development. And the last stage is, renounce that 'I' once for all. God alone is, there is no 'I' at all. So, renouncing the 'I' cannot come without training the 'I' and strengthening it; otherwise, it will be a fake renunciation.

Swami Vivekananda said regarding some of our people: everybody wants to be a saint in India, nobody wants to be a man in India with good human relationship with others. He said, "a poor man comes to me saying, 'Swamiji, I want to renounce the world'. I ask him, 'What have you to renounce? Neither a strong body, nor a trained mind, nor money in the pocket. What will you renounce? Have something to renounce. When you have something to renounce, that renunciation is genuine.'" Therefore, the language here is, *sannyāsastu mahābāho duḥkham āptum ayogataḥ*, 'without this training in *yoga*, i.e. *karma-yoga*, by which one develops character efficiency and public spirit, spirit of service and dedication, none can achieve real *sannyāsa*.'

Bhāsa was a great poet like Kālidāsa. In his book *Avimāra*, chapter 5, verse 5, there is a very beautiful verse.

*Prājñasya mūrkhasya ca kāryayoge*
*samatvam abhyeti tanuḥ na buddhiḥ* —

'If a wise person and a fool are working, when we look at them at work, they do look the same; but in their minds they are different.'

As I said in the Andhra Government Secretariat lecture in Hyderabad two or three years ago, 'Do a clerk's work, not with a clerk's mind but with the mind of a citizen of free India.' In all departments this applies. The work becomes great, when done by a great mind. The work becomes small, when done by a small mind. It is not work that is great, it is the mind that is behind the work that makes it great. The mother cooks food for you, and the paid cook also cooks food for you. Cooking is the same, but the mind is so different between the one and the other. So, that is the most important thing so far as human beings are concerned. *Karma-yoga* deals with that subject. How to make this mind rich? How to make this mind pure? How to make this mind unlimited? That is the work we have to do. How, in the context of work itself, you are handling the mind? Normally, nobody cares to do so. When we are working, we are busy with the work. We neglect the mind. But, no. This work is meant to educate you, to train you.

What a wonderful thing it is! Work as a centre of education is a very important thing. It is not only reading books that is education. But the work that you do, the human relations that you have, they are all centres of education for you. That is how you grow. That makes for total education. We at once mark that this is meant for all—for children, for grown ups, for people in East or West, for atheists, agnostics, religious people, for all. As a human being how do you grow? How do you bring out the possibilities hidden within you? That subject must engage your mind. Then turn to the *Gītā* and you will find the guidance. Turn your life situation into a tremendous all-round education for yourself—physical, intellectual, spiritual and social. All education will come to you, provided you know how to manipulate your work and life situation. Let not the situation manipulate you. You manipulate your life and work situation. Then only you are free. Otherwise, you are an animal. An animal never manipulates its life situation. Life situation manipulates the animal. The bull is yoked to the plough; what has he to do? He goes on working till somebody stops it. In the case of the human being, he or she does all work, but he or she also does something more. He or she is training the mind, shaping one's inner life to make it richer, and going deeper into oneself to realize one's own infinite ever-free nature. That is how a big human being comes out of a puny human being. We have to build up our higher personality on the given personality.

That is what true education means, which is not confined to school and college or an institution, but life itself is the centre for that education. That is the real teaching of the *Gītā*. You erect yourself above yourself. This is a raw product. You have to process it, and something beautiful will come out of it. This human body-mind complex, when we are young, is a raw material. We have to transform it. But the whole transformation process is education, of which, religion understood as spiritual development, is only a higher part. But it is a continuous education. That is everybody's privilege and responsibility. If one neglects it, remains stagnant at a lower level, at the animal level, it is a matter of tragedy. All tragedies come from that kind of life. In all literature you can find tragedies centred on the human being who has become stagnant at the organic level. That should not be. Be great. Try to expand, grow. The word is expansion, growth; in Sanskrit we call it *vikāsa, ātmavikāsa.* Have I grown, have I spiritually expanded? That is the question each has to ask oneself. Physical expansion, strength of body; then mental expansion, strength of knowledge; and spiritual expansion, realizing our own infinite nature, feeling one with all. What a beautiful society will come when majority of people will be on that path of expansion from the physical to the spiritual. That will be a really well-developed society. 'Truth does not pay homage to any society, ancient or modern. Society has to pay homage to Truth or die,' is a sentence in Swami Vivekananda's lectures in London. (*Complete Works of Swami Vivekananda,* vol. 2, p. 84)

Then Śrī Kṛṣṇa says:

योगयुक्तो विशुद्धात्मा विजितात्मा जितेन्द्रियः ।
सर्वभूतात्मभूतात्मा कुर्वन्नपि न लिप्यते ॥७॥

*Yogayukto viśuddhātmā vijitātmā jitendriyaḥ;*
*Sarvabhūtātmabhūtātmā kurvannapi na lipyate — 5. 7*

'With the mind purified by devotion to performance of action in the spirit of *yoga*, and the body conquered, and sense organs subdued, one who realizes one's self, as the Self in all beings, though acting, is not tainted.'

*Yogayukto,* 'one who is well established in this *karma-yoga*'; *viśuddhātmā,* 'pure in mind'; *vijitātmā,* 'who has conquered the body'; and *jitendriyaḥ,* 'who has conquered one's sensory energy system'. Such a person who has used one's life situation to achieve these, *sarvabhūtātmabhūtātmā,* 'one who feels oneself spiritually one with all does not feel that he or she is being confined to his or her tiny organic system; he or she becomes expanded and feels one with all, being one with that infinite Self'. *Sarvabhūtātmabhūtāmā,* the language is *sarva;* it means all. Till now you were an isolated individual. With a little development of spirituality, one feels one's oneness with *others*, feels the desire to serve people and becomes, in its early stages, a good citizen. But its highest expansion comes, when one feels oneness with *all*. The sufferings and joys of all others become one's own sufferings and joys. There is only one infinite Atman; one realizes that truth. *Sarva bhūtātma bhūtātmā*, such a person, *kurvannapi na lipyate*, 'even though he or she is constantly performing actions, he or she will never be tainted'. That person is unique. The whole human evolution is seen by Vedanta to be in that direction. From the particular to the universal is the direction of human evolution. A baby begins its life by completely identifying itself with its body. It cannot think of anything else. It wants to protect its body. It wants to get the warmth of its mother's body and the touch of the skin of its mother's body. Mother's skin touch is very important for a baby, for its feeling of security and development. For a baby it is quite alright. But it should not remain in that state for long. As it grows, it knows how to detach itself from its body, how to grow, how to respect and love other people; all these expansions come.

What is the nature of that expansion? Psychic expansion. Actually, it is a spiritual expansion, *adhyātma vikāsa*, through the psychic system. A good citizen has spiritually expanded; he or she can feel the suffering of fellow countrymen; and it finds expression in the feeling, 'I have to go and help them'. That is called citizenship in a limited nationalistic sense; today, it refers to citizenship of the whole world. The entire world is one; we call it today the humankind awareness. In all these matters, when you go beyond your own ego, your own organic limitation, you expand your sense of 'I'. That first stage of expansion is social awareness, a concern for others. That is spiritual expansion, and this when you continue further and further, it becomes *sarva bhūtātma bhūtātmā*, 'I am the Self of all beings'. It is an extraordinary development; a few only—a Jesus or a Buddha—have realized this kind of highest unity with all. Their compassion had this as the base. Śiva, in our literature, is of this nature. He is one with all. He is full of compassion. And so, *kurvannapi na lipyate,* 'even though one is working, one will not be tainted'. Mind is pure; that is how one will experience more and more of this as one proceeds in this direction. Then, this is explained in detail in the next two verses.

नैव किञ्चित् करोमीति युक्तो मन्येत तत्त्ववित् ।
पश्यन् शृण्वन् स्पृशन् जिघ्रन् अश्नन् गच्छन् स्वपन् श्वसन् ॥८॥
प्रलपन् विसृजन् गृह्णन् उन्मिषन् निमिषन् अपि ।
इन्द्रियाणि इन्द्रियार्थेषु वर्तन्त इति धारयन् ॥९॥

*Naiva kiñcit karomīti yukto manyeta tattvavit;*
*Paśyan śṛṇvan spṛśan jighran aśnan gacchan svapan śvasan—5. 8*
*Pralapan visṛjan gṛhṇan unmiṣan nimiṣan api;*
*Indriyāṇi indriyārtheṣu vartanta iti dhārayan — 5. 9*

'The knower of Truth, (being) centred (in the Self) should think, "I do nothing at all"—though seeing, hearing, touching, smelling, eating, going, sleeping, breathing, speaking, letting go, holding, opening and closing the eyes—convinced that it is all the senses that move among sense objects.'

*Naiva kiñcit karomīti yukto manyeta tattvavit,* 'the knower of Truth, *tattvavit,* must think like this: "I do not do anything"'. Though a lot of work is being done, *I* am not doing anything. *Yukto,* 'a *yogī*'; *manyeta tattvavit,* 'a knower of Truth must think like this' in regard to what all things he or she is doing. What are the things included in such doing? Everything. So, in three lines *Gītā* gives a sample. What is that? *Paśyan,* 'seeing', *śṛṇvan,* 'hearing', *spṛśan,* 'touching', *jighran,* 'smelling', *aśnan,* 'eating', *gacchan,* 'going', *svapan,* 'sleeping', *śvasan,* 'breathing', *pralapan,* 'speaking', *visṛjan,* 'letting go', *gṛhṇan,* 'holding', *unmiṣan,* 'opening (the eyes)', *nimiṣan,* 'closing the eyes', *api; indriyāṇi indriyārtheṣu vartanta iti dhārayan,* 'thinking that the sense organs are functioning among the sense objects', being fully convinced that 'I do nothing at all'. One gets the capacity to detach from, and the capacity to attach to the sense objects, with a free mind. This double capacity must come to each one: the capacity to attach, and the capacity to detach. That is called freedom. If only one is there, it is not freedom. If both are there, there is freedom. So, here is a senior man in the house, he is very detached, but he can play with children, he can talk with people, he can enjoy everything, and yet essentially he is detached and free. That is called a fuller life. Otherwise, merely an ascetic attitude that, 'I am free, I am detached,' but cannot smile when others are smiling, that is not true freedom. It has gone into another type of stagnation. So here is that, *yogayukto viśuddhātmā vijitātmā jitendriyaḥ sarvabhūtātmabhūtātmā kurvannapi na lipyate,* 'though working you are not tainted by that work'. *Lepana* means 'taint' or some dirt attached to the body. The human being has the capacity to separate the Self from the sensory functions. That is the experience of freedom. We begin our spiritual growth from that level. The capacity to detach from the sensory system. No animal can do it, including a chimpanzee. And because the human being developed that capacity even a little, he or she is also able to dominate animals. This is what neurology says. Once I referred to it in Gray Walter's book: *The Living Brain*—capacity for image making or imagination. Before you act, you can picture to your mind the situation and *then* act. And you can change one action to another in imagination, before you actually act externally. This capacity only the human being has, and with that the human being dominates all nature. Gray Walter says: 'If you don't accept what I say, I will only ask you, suppose the tiger or the lion develops this capacity. What would be the result? We won't be here to answer that question.' Any animal that develops this capacity will dominate. That is the power of imagination. Detaching from the sensory system, and studying what is what, then reacting in an original way; it is not merely as an action-reaction programme, which is the normal way. Here between input and output, imagination intervenes. That makes a lot of difference. There you find the initial appearance of detachment. But it has to be developed further and further. Most people do not go beyond that; that is why they suffer. So, all that idea comes here in this wonderful statement. *Kurvannapi na lipyate*, 'even though you are working, you are not at all tainted by the work or its results'. And the next *śloka* is a consummation of all this that we have studied so far in this chapter.

ब्रह्मण्याधाय कर्माणि सङ्गं त्यक्त्वा करोति यः ।
लिप्यते न स पापेन पद्मपत्रं इवाम्भसा ॥१०॥

*Brahmaṇyādhāya karmāṇi saṅgam tyaktvā karoti yaḥ;*
*Lipyate na sa pāpena padmapatram ivāmbhasā —* 5.10

'One who does actions forsaking attachment, resigning them to Brahman, is not tainted by evil, like a lotus-leaf by water.'

This is a well-known verse of this chapter. *Brahmaṇyādhāya karmāṇi*, 'offering all actions to Brahman'. In the 24th *śloka* of the fourth chapter, we had read what we use as a prayer during meals:

*Brahmārpaṇam brahma haviḥ brahmāgnau brahmaṇā hutam;*
*Brahmaiva tena gantavyam brahmakarma samādhinā —*

'The offering, the fire, the human being who offers, the result of the offering, everything is Brahman.'

That is what Śrī Kṛṣṇa had said there. Here the tenth verse says, let all your actions go to Brahman. Everything has come from Brahman, from that one infinite spiritual Source. Everything has to be given back to Brahman. *Brahmaṇyādhāya karmāṇi saṅgam tyaktvā*, 'renouncing all attachment and offering all actions to Brahman'; *karoti yaḥ*, 'one who does so'; *lipyate na sa pāpena*, 'is never touched by sin'; *padmapatram iva ambhasā*, 'like a lotus leaf which is in water but is not touched by water at all'. That is a very famous example in all our literature. *Padmapatram iva ambhasā; ambhas* means water, *padma* means lotus, *patram* is leaf. So, a lotus leaf is never wet though it is always in water. Take it out, all water is gone. Similarly, this human being is in the midst of heavy work. Work doesn't touch him or her, doesn't taint such a one. What a beautiful idea! Anybody can try and realize for oneself whether this is true or not. These are all verifiable truths. Therefore, it is a science; a science of human being in depth. Anything that you can verify is scientific. A mere belief, without subjecting it to verification, cannot be science. Belief, when verified, then it is true, scientifically true. So, the *Gītā* teaches many truths about the human being, which are verified and verifiable. Some people have verified it before. And it is placed before you not for your belief, but for your verification. Try and see, one step, two steps, how far you are able to verify this particular truth. So, *brahmaṇyādhāya karmāṇi,* 'renouncing all actions in Brahman'; *saṅgam tyaktvā karoti yaḥ,* 'one who does work renouncing attachment'; *lipyate na sa pāpena,* 'such a person is never touched by sin'; *padmapatram iva ambhasā,* 'like a lotus leaf by water'. That is a great state of mind. That is the nature of this wonderful spiritual realization. This famous verse 10 is capped by the next verse, verse 11.

कायेन मनसा बुद्ध्या केवलैरिन्द्रियैरपि ।
योगिनः कर्म कुर्वन्ति सङ्गं त्यक्त्वात्मशुद्धये ॥११॥

*Kāyena manasā buddhyā kevalairindriyairapi;*
*Yoginaḥ karma kurvanti saṅgam tyaktvātmaśuddhaye*—5. 11

'Following the *yoga* of work, *yogis* perform action only with body, mind, senses and intellect, forsaking attachment, for the purification of the heart.'

'*Yogis* perform work', *yoginaḥ karma kurvanti; saṅgam tyaktvā,* 'giving up attachment'; *ātmaśuddhaye,* 'to purify the inner life'. This is the stress. Increased productivity is one aspect of work; inner purification is the other aspect of work. Śrī Kṛṣṇa had defined his message of *yoga* thus in the second chapter, verse 50. What kind of actions are referred to here? *Kāyena,* 'by the body'; *manasā* ,'by reason', by exercising reason; and *buddhyā,* 'by the discriminative faculty; not only so, *kevalairindriyairapi,* 'even ordinarily by the senses also'. The objective is *ātma-śuddhaye,* 'to purify the inner life', so that he or she can manifest one's divine nature. The divine nature is always there. Nobody can destroy it. This is the indestructible nature of the human being, the infinite Atman. That is the most inspiring message of Vedanta. The Atman is always pure, ever free, ever awakened. But in our day-to-day life, we neglect it; we are busy with the sensory world and the sensory reactions. The Atman is always there, neglected all the time. Now, no more neglect. 'I am going to recognize the profound dimension of my personality.' This is the constant stress in Vedanta. Even now, when I am ignorant of the Truth, the Truth is there. Ignorance doesn't abolish the Truth. Remember that expression in a scientific language: ignorance doesn't abolish the Truth. Even in civil life we say, ignorance of law is no excuse. You committed a crime against law. If you say, 'I didn't know that law,' it doesn't matter. Pay for that action that you did. So, in this way, there are profound truths about the human being. The profoundest is that you are the eternal Atman, ever-free, ever-pure, ever-awakened. Śaṅkarācārya puts this sentence in a fine place in his commentary on the *Brahma Sūtras: Nityaśuddha, nityabuddha, nityamukta, paramātman. Nityaśuddha* means ever-pure. Whatever impurities you may have, do not affect the Atman; they affect only the body, the senses and the mind. Never beyond that. So, *nityaśuddha,* 'ever-pure', and *nityabuddha,* 'ever-awakened', just like the sun, ever bright; a little cloud covering it temporarily does not affect the sun. Then *nityamukta,* 'ever-free'. I don't experience it, because I have not thought about it. I have not worked towards it. I have forgotten it. That is what we are doing. But your true nature is this. In no other literature will you find proclaimed this high status of the human being. Even in the state of ignorance, even in the state of bondage, you are ever-free, you are ever-illumined; that is your true nature. Let people realize this truth even a little; how great will life be then!

Śaṅkara's commentary in the first chapter of the *Bṛhadāraṇyaka Upaniṣad* contains a profound statement: *Prāk brahma vijñānād api sarvo jantuḥ brahmatvāt sarva bhāvāpannaḥ paramārtataḥ,* 'even before the realization of Brahman, every being is Brahman and therefore he or she is one with all.' Even before realization of Brahman, you are that Brahman. That is the nature of truth. The Upaniṣads will constantly say, 'You are That, you are That, *tat tvam asi, tat tvam asi*'. According to some of the modern scientists as well, this is a profound truth about the human being. You are free, you are free. If you are not free, you can never become free. You can't become what you are not. You have only forgotten this truth about yourself, only neglected it. Don't neglect it, don't forget it. Work towards it. That is the special emphasis in Vedanta, and in Vedanta alone you will find it. This tremendous statement, 'I am essentially free', we studied in the last seven verses of the third chapter, where it was said that evil and sin affect only the body, the senses, and the mind, but never the Atman. And so, try to manifest the Atman and overcome the evil that has afflicted your body, mind and sensory system. That salvation or liberation is built into yourself. You needn't depend upon anybody else for it or go to any far away heaven to attain it. The last verse in the third chapter said:

*Evam buddheḥ param buddhvā samstabhyātmānam ātmanā;*
*Jahi śatrum mahābāho kāmarūpam durāsadam —*

'Thus realizing the Atman beyond the *buddhi*, and controlling the rest of the body-mind system, overcome this enemy of lust which is difficult to conquer'. This is the great message given in the third chapter to all human beings.

So, in this fifth chapter, we have seen that with the mind, with the senses, with the body, great sages do work. A *karma-yogi* does the work, but he does it to purify oneself so that this Atman can find manifestation. Opaque, translucent and transparent are the covers that are covering us from the Atman. Swami Vivekananda defines religion as the manifestation of the divinity already in the human being. A matchstick contains fire; but touch it, it is cool; and strike it on the matchbox, fire comes out. But the matchstick must be dry. If it be wet, any amount of striking will not bring out the fire. So, certain conditions are to be satisfied for the divine to manifest itself. Those conditions are what Śrī Kṛṣṇa is telling here. Therefore, it is the privilege of every human being to manifest this divine within. That is the sole purpose of religion.

Man realizes one's own true nature, manifests it, and lives a life based upon that realization. Everything is here and now. Not going to some heaven in some particular place, here or there. Not at all. It is all *here and now*. In this chapter, a few verses later, you will get that word, *ihaiva,* 'here itself'. It is attained here itself. What can be more rational, what can be more practical, what can be more universal, than this message?

Even yesterday, a young man had come. His parents refused to take him back home, because he married somebody. He needs their help now. But they wouldn't help him. So, you can see the result of attachment, blinding one and narrowing one's area of sympathy. But Śrī Kṛṣṇa teaches only detachment. Love can flow from you when you are truly detached. That lesson we have to learn in a big way. Then everybody becomes free. Nobody is a slave to somebody else. What a beautiful idea of life is this—being free. *Saṅgam tyaktvā,* 'forsaking attachment,' they had to perform actions with the body, the senses, the mind, the *buddhi,* for what purpose? *Ātma śuddhaye,* 'to purify oneself'. With this pure mind only can we realize Truth. Let us purify our minds. The mind is the only instrument we have, to deal with the world or for dealing with spiritual life. Keep that mind fresh, pure, strong. That is the one great lesson Vedanta emphasizes again and again. I have said before, how every day, in every action, in every human situation, we can train this mind to become freer, purer, nobler. That is how life has to be utilized, so that we don't become a squeezed orange at the end of life. We become full, we become fulfilled in the true sense of the term. Now we come to the next verse.

युक्तः कर्मफलं त्यक्त्वा शान्तिं आप्नोति नैष्ठिकीम् ।
अयुक्तः कामकारेण फले सक्तो निबध्यते ॥१२॥

*Yuktaḥ karmaphalam tyaktvā śāntim āpnoti naiṣṭhikīm;*
*Ayuktaḥ kāmakāreṇa phale sakto nibadhyate* — 5. 12

'The well-poised one, forsaking the fruit of action, attains peace, born of steadfastness; the unbalanced one, led by desire, is bound by being attached to the fruits (of action).'

Two types of people are mentioned: the *yuktaḥ* and the *ayuktaḥ*. Those who have entered the path of *yoga*, of inner discipline to realize the Truth that is hidden, such people are called *yuktaḥ*. The other people are called *ayuktaḥ*. So, how does a *yuktaḥ* fare in this path? *Yuktaḥ karmaphalam tyaktvā*, 'the *yogī*, renouncing the fruits of action'; *śāntim āpnoti naiṣṭhikīm*, 'attains peace through such a methodical process'. The other one, *ayuktaḥ kāmkāreṇa*, 'the non-*yogī*, impelled by sensory pulls and desires'; *phale sakto*, 'getting attached to the fruits of actions'; *nibadhyate*, 'becomes bound'. So, two types of people are there: the free and the bound. Nobody can be forced to choose either of these paths. We can see these two types in the world. But the second type, *ayogī, ayuktaḥ,* have increased all over the world, increased in India also. *Karmaphale sakto,* 'attached to the fruits of action'; *nibadhyate,* 'becomes bound'. He or she doesn't realize that he or she is bound. That is the tragedy. Those who are bound do not realize that they are bound. If they realize it, then only they will try to change from that state of bondage. But they are happy with that bondage. They think this is the normal way. Many people today belong to this category.

In one of his very beautiful parables, Sri Ramakrishna illumines this subject. There are four types of human beings, Sri Ramakrishna said: *baddha, mumukṣu, mukta, nityamukta. Baddha* means the bound. *Mumukṣu* means bound, but struggling to be free. That is the second type. Then, *mukta,* free. By his or her struggle, he or she has achieved freedom. And the fourth category is *nityamukta,* the ever-free, never even once got into bondage. These are the four types. And Sri Ramakrishna gives an illustration. When fishermen cast their nets into the lake to catch fish, many fishes are clever enough never to be caught in the net. They are the *nityamuktas,* Sri Ramakrishna said, the ever-free. But quite a good number are caught. Among these, some struggle to get out. They know that they have been caught in some net. So, you can see the fish struggling to get out. The struggling one is called *mumukṣu,* 'one desiring to become free'. Among many who struggle, a few fishes escape out of the net, and the fishermen will sadly exclaim, 'O those are gone!' That is the *mukta,* free type. But, continues Sri Ramakrishna, there is one set of fish, who never feel that they are in bondage. They bite the net, and peacefully live under the mud, thinking they are safe. But, within a few moment, they would be taken away by the fishermen and sold away in the market. They are called the *baddha,* 'the bound', the first type in the list. These are the four types of human beings: *baddha, mumukṣu, mukta, nityamukta.* Pointing to Narendranath, the later Vivekananda, sitting there, Sri Ramakrishna said that he belongs to the *nityamukta* class. *Māyā* could not catch him. He is ever free. The Divine Mother casts Her net of *Māyā* to catch people. She could catch all people in Her net but not these few, those who are eternally free. And others belong to those whom She has caught in the net; some of them struggle to get out of the net of *Māyā;* and that is the sign of spiritual life.

That is a very illumining parable to deal with this subject of this *yuktaḥ* and *ayuktaḥ. Yuktaḥ karmaphalam tyaktvā śāntim āpnoti naiṣṭhikīm,* 'the *yogī* achieves real peace of mind, because of his or her renouncing the fruit of actions'; whereas the *ayuktaḥ,* the attached one, *kāmakāreṇa,* 'because he or she is carried away by sensory desires'; *phale sakto,* 'being attached to the fruit of actions'; *nibadhyate,* 'is bound'. His vision is short, he can see only a few feet ahead; what you call in English, 'he is under the tyranny of the immediate present'. This type of people, when they increase in a society, that society goes down. All values disappear from that society. We are passing through that state in our country now. It is this we have to reverse. If the *Gītā* becomes universally understood, and a struggle issues in us to live according to it, more and more people will come to that free state, that *yogi* state. We have to create more such *yogis* in our society, not *yogis* who have renounced actions and live in the Himalayas; a minority of such ascetics is an asset, but a majority of such in any society will lead to decay. Citizenship itself is a type of *yoga.* The *citizen-yogī* is more important today. We need millions of *citizen-yogīs.* That is why

Śrī Kṛṣṇa has given this kind of classification. They work, they run institutions, they run organizations. They work in factories, offices, everywhere. But their mind is being trained to pursue the path of *yoga*. Through all this they are advancing step by step towards their own spiritual goal and fulfilment. That is the type of humanity on the march, a productive march outward and an inward march towards the divine that is within all. This is the type that can create great culture, that can create great integration and harmony in society; less of crime, less of delinquency, less of exploitation you will have in society when this type of people increase. That is called real social progress. We have made a big mistake in evaluating social progress only in terms of better food, better dress, better conveyances, better houses, better this and better that. What about better men and women? We rarely consider that. As the British poet, Oliver Goldsmith, said in the 18th century England:

> Ill fares the land, to hastening ills a prey,
> Where wealth accumulates and men decay.

Wealth has accumulated in India. Plenty of money, here, there, mostly black money. But the real progress of the nation can be brought about only by education, and not by wealth. Men and women endowed with the humanistic impulse and the spirit of service alone can have the right type of education. The *śloka* that you recite in the beginning of each lecture refers to this necessity of making education the source of our all round progress: *saha vīryam karavāvahai*, 'let us get energy out of our education'. Not only so, *tejasvi nau adhītam astu*, 'let us become illumined as a result of this study'. So, energy and illumination, both must come through education. Then only, a nation becomes great. Therefore, these ideas have intimate relevance to our life today. Something has gone wrong. Humanity has lost its way. It has to be brought back to the correct way. Then advance, go ahead. *Uttiṣṭhata, jāgrata,* 'arise, awake' of the *Kaṭha Upaniṣad;* once awakened then every one can say this oneself. Swami Vivekananda spoke of India as this great national ship, in his Madras lecture on 'My Plan of Campaign' (*Complete Works of Swami Vivekananda*, vol. 3, p. 227):

'This national ship has been ferrying millions and millions of souls across the waters of life. For scores of shining centuries it has been plying across this water, and through its agency, millions of souls have been taken to the other shore, to blessedness. But today, ...this boat has become a little damaged, has sprung a leak; and would you therefore curse it? Is it fit that you stand up and pronounce malediction upon it, one that has done more work than any other thing in the world? If there are holes in this national ship, this society of ours, we are its children. Let us go and stop the holes. Let us gladly do it with our hearts' blood; and if we cannot, then let us die. We will make a plug of our brains and put them into the ship, but condemn it never.'

That is how he ends that great Madras lecture nearly a hundred years ago, in 1897. What far-sight he had, to see the new developments that will come, and how to guide it in the right direction; the *Gītā* gives us that philosophy of action, of endeavour, of collective life. How to build up a new India, stronger, purer than what we inherited from the past? So,

सर्वकर्माणि मनसा संन्यस्यास्ते सुखं वशी ।
नवद्वारे पुरे देही नैव कुर्वन् न कारयन् ॥१३॥

*Sarvakarmāṇi manasā sannyasyāste sukham vaśī;*
*Navadvāre pure dehī naiva kurvan na kārayan — 5. 13*

'The subduer (of the senses), having renounced all actions by discrimination, rests happily in the city of the nine gates, neither acting, nor causing (others) to act.'

*Sarvakarmāṇi manasā sannyasya*, 'renouncing all actions mentally', actually you are doing many actions, but mentally you renounce all these actions. That is the meaning of detachment. When you detach, you renounce actions mentally and yet you are working. You are doing everything. *Āste*, 'he or she remains'; *sukham*, 'very happily'; *vaśī*, 'the self-controlled one'. 'My senses are under my control;' that person is called a *vaśī*. Every human being must be a *vaśī*. Animals alone are not *vaśī*. We have control over our senses to some extent. We have to increase it a little more so that we know when to say 'yes' and when not to say so. This kind of discrimination comes to us by training. Such a person remains *sukham*, 'happily without tension, without peacelessness'. Where? In this body. He or she remains in this body. How? *Navadvāre pure dehī naiva kurvan na kārayan*, 'neither acting nor making others act, he or she remains within this body of nine gateways'; the body is compared to a city with 'nine gateways', *navadvāra;* such a city is the human body in which this Self is living, absolutely peaceful, doing all the work; no tension, no fear, no un-fulfilment. This conception of the body as a dwelling place, like a house, like a city, comes in the Upaniṣads. *Gītā* refers to it here. We are not the body, we *live* in the body. *Navadvāre pure dehī*, this has nine gateways to come and go; seven in the head, and two below. These are the nine *dvāras* or openings according to the *Gītā*. In the Upaniṣads, it is referred to as eleven *dvāras,* including the navel and the *brahma randhra,* the hole in the head. That is eleven, here it is nine. *Navadvāre pure dehī; dehī,* one who lives in the *deha* or body is the *dehī,* 'the embodied one'. I am not the body, I *live* in the body. I am not the house, I *live* in the house. Body is like a house to us. That is why we have to keep it clean. That is why unlike our recent misunderstanding, neglect of the body is never allowed in Vedanta; it is just like neglecting your house. If you don't keep it clean, if you don't repair it, attend to its maintenance, soon it will become unfit to live in. So also the body. Take care of the body. This is a house in which you live. Keep it clean. But don't get attached to it. Body is only a vantage, wherefrom you can go out, do your work and come. So also is the house in which you live. Don't get tied to the house. When you are tied to the house, the house becomes a prison. We are not free to come in, nor free to go out. That is called a prison. That is how persons who live in prisons are not free to come, nor free to go. Their house becomes a prison. If our body also becomes a prison, that will be very unhappy situation. Don't make the body a prison. Be free; you can go out, you can come in, freely. What a beautiful idea of human life and human freedom!

As I said earlier, ancient Chinese thought also stresses this point. Without doing any action, you are able to produce results. That action is mental. Mentally he or she is free. Physically he or she is acting in plenty. Therefore, he or she is said to be free from action. That is the high mystical thought in China as well as in Japan. Without excitement, without tension, without noise, without fuss, when you work, with a calm mind, it is as good as non-acting. This can be done, and the whole teaching of the *Gītā* regarding work is this: act without fuss. Live without fuss. Fussy action, fussy living, is not living at all. So, that fuss-free life can be lived by training the mind in calmness, perfect self-control and self-possession, aligning it with the Atman, which is one's true nature and which is always inactive and all-powerful, and yet doing all the work. All these verses refer to this tremendous possibility in all of us, by training our minds according to the teachings given in the *Gītā*. *Karma-yoga, karma* in the light of *yoga*—therefore, it is called *karma-yoga*. Mere *karma,* without any *yoga,* all animals do; men and women also do; but, only human beings can train themselves in doing *karma* in the light of *yoga.* That teaching began from the second chapter when Śrī Kṛṣṇa started to expound this wonderful new philosophy of 'work without attachment'; with that type of attitude known as *buddhi-yoga;* that type of *buddhi,* which is *sama,* equal, without any ups and downs in the *buddhi;* work is full of ups and downs, but the *buddhi* is absolutely free. This is possible. So, *buddhiyukta,* 'one who has that *buddhi*', is certainly a *karma-yogī*. Now comes a very beautiful idea of Vedanta in the next verse.

न कर्तृत्वं न कर्माणि लोकस्य सृजति प्रभुः ।
न कर्म फल संयोगं स्वभावस्तु प्रवर्तते ॥१४॥

*Na kartṛtvam na karmāṇi lokasya sṛjati prabhuḥ;*
*Na karma phala saṁyogam svabhāvastu pravartate* — *5. 14*

'Neither agency, nor actions does the Lord create for the world, nor (does He bring about) the union with the fruit of action. It is nature that does it all.'

The divine personality, the supreme divine Being, 'did not prescribe any agency of action', *na kartṛtvam. Na karmāṇi,* 'nor actions'. *Lokasya sṛjati prabhuḥ,* 'neither of these was prescribed by the divine Lord for humanity'. Then how does this action go on? *Svabhāvastu pravartate,* 'nature does it all'. As in the case of the animals, it is nature that is impelling us; nature that is outside has found a place within us also. Man is an outpost of external nature in many respects. Our digestive system, our reactions, are all the work of nature. So, *svabhāvastu pravartate,* '*svabhāva* or nature is acting in you and in me' as well as in the outer world. Here *svabhāva* means nature. That plain nature outside induces us to eat, drink, to rear families. All that is *svabhāva* acting through the human being. God did not tell me to do this or that. This is the language. That *svabhāva* or nature has entered into us and become part of our constitution. Impelled by it we do all these things. That is the truth about the human being.

I had occasion to refer to the book, *Modern Man in Search of A Soul,* by Karl Jung, the famous Zurich psychologist. He also makes a distinction between our actions impelled by nature, and our actions impelled by our own higher nature. Vedanta alone speaks of a higher dimension of nature, *parā prakṛti,* apart from *aparā prakṛti,* ordinary nature. The first is intelligence and the second is non-intelligence. Vedanta speaks of the dominance of the intelligent principle, *parā prakṛti,* over the *aparā prakṛti* or *svabhāva,* as the instrument of human freedom, as the goal of human evolution. Here Śrī Kṛṣṇa clearly puts it, *svabhāvastu pravartate,* '*svabhāva* or ordinary nature is acting in all of us'. It is like this: Somebody abuses me and I immediately give him a slap. What has happened? *Svabhāva* has taken charge and acted in me. I have another *svabhāva,* intelligence or *parā prakṛti,* by which I can check it. That *svabhāva* is silent, not functioning yet. Everything is *svabhāva,* or *aparā prakṛti.*

Raw nature is functioning in you and me. The other is my higher nature, my own true nature as the Atman helping me to check all these and making me behave in a better way. This higher nature rarely finds expression. In most people, only the lower nature, *aparā prakṛti* or *svabhāva,* is there; the external nature manifesting in our physiology, anatomy, neurology, and even psychology. Much of our psyche is controlled by this external nature. So, this is a fact to be understood. A human being is a combination of two natures: the external nature, and the higher nature, i.e. intelligence. The higher nature functions as a subordinate of external nature in most people. It cannot express itself because the other nature, *aparā prakṛti,* is very dominant in most people. That is ordinary human life out of which comes crime, delinquency, etc. But whenever that nature is slowly controlled, and the higher nature finds manifestation, then slowly spiritual culture comes. We evolve into better and still better human beings. Real civilization itself is the product of a little dominance of this higher nature over that lower nature. This is the meaning of Śrī Kṛṣṇa's telling us here, *na kartṛtvam na karmāṇi lokasya sṛjati prabhuḥ. 'Prabhu,* the divine Master of the world, did not prescribe either agency of action, or action, to any individual here.' Then he says, *na karma phala samyogam,* 'nor the bringing out the union with the fruit of action'. Then how does life go on? *Svabhāvastu pravartate.* '*Svabhāva* is acting'.

Having said this, the lesson we have to learn is that, that *svabhāva,* which is external nature, *aparā prakṛti,* which has found lodgement in our system, we shall control it, we shall go beyond it by expressing our true nature as pure intelligence, because we are a combination of both, what we call in Vedantic language, *cit-jaḍa-granthi.* Every human being is a knot of *cit* and *jaḍa. Cit* means consciousness. *Jaḍa* means inert nature. Both are there in a human being. In external nature it is all *jaḍa.* But when you come to living beings, you are in the realm of consciousness as well. And that too, with respect to a human being, a higher form of consciousness called self consciousness, the consciousness of the self as 'I, I, I' gets manifested. No animal can experience 'I'; only the human being has this awareness of being a subject and not an object. That is why we are asked to treat every human being as a subject and never as an object. Generally, when we exploit others, we treat them as objects. But when moral sense comes we think, 'no, everybody must be treated as a subject. I am a subject, you are also a subject. I should treat you as a subject and not as an object'. That is called moral sense. *To see the subject in a social object is called moral sense.* Human being is a social object, unlike material objects like tables and chairs. This human being, therefore, has a uniqueness. He or she has a subjective dimension also. So, we treat him or her as a subject, and never always as an object. In the treatment of ethics by the German philosopher Kant, you will find this idea. That is ethical sense according to Kant and according to Vedanta. By manifesting our higher nature, let us try to control and dominate that *svabhāva* or lower nature; the *jaḍa svabhāva* is to be controlled by the *cit svabhāva*.

That is called the human being's spiritual evolution. Out of that will come tremendous peace and harmony in the world. The human being will be the saviour of the whole world. Otherwise, if he or she is subject to the *jaḍa svabhāva* within, the human being will as well be the author of destroying the whole of nature and the whole of humanity. That is the situation in the world today. Most people are subject to the *jaḍa svabhāva.* They want to live according to that *svabhāva,* which I had referred to in the first volume in relation to the American youth movement as *impulse release* philosophy. Release all your impulses as they come. Don't check them, don't discipline them. That *jaḍa svabhāva* must be allowed to work freely. That is a dangerous philosophy that is going on now practically all over the world. We have to reverse it. Let the other higher *svabhāva* begin to function in you. There is something very precious in you. You are free, you are free. *Jaḍa* nature is not free, but you are free. You are a mixture of freedom and no-freedom. Assert the freedom part in you.

In this connection, I would like to mention one of the many experiences I had during my 18 months lecture tour of North and South America in 1968-69, one of which was at Portland Radio on 31 January, 1969. America was then passing through the Hippy and drop-out movement. Mr. Fenwick, of the drop-out type, was the interviewer. It was the most illuminating experience which I have recorded in my book, *A Pilgrim Looks at the World.* (Vol. 2, pp. 27-29: Bharatiya Vidya Bhavan, Mumbai)

'The interview began with his introduction of me to the listeners. As happens in all cases where yogis and spiritual teachers, especially from India, are interviewed, the introduction starts on a light note. So introducing me to the listeners, Mr. Fenwick said: Oh, here is another Swami in front of me! He is so and so, etc., etc. But, within a minute, the whole aspect changed, as I gently changed the subject into the problem of man in modern civilization and other serious topics. Mr. Fenwick immediately caught the inspiration of the new situation and shouted into the microphone: Oh, this is a new type of Swami! Please listen to what he says! All flimsiness vanished immediately and, from then on, it was earnest and serious discussion till the end.

'And in the course of the next few minutes of the interview, I had occasion to refer to the need for a measure of self-discipline on the part of modern man. No sooner had I uttered the word 'discipline', than Mr. Fenwick interrupted me and protested loudly into the microphone: Oh Swami, we don't believe in all this discipline! What is there to discipline? We believe in being *spontaneous, natural*.

'He uttered these words in a triumphant manner and with a touch of hilarity. But I was not put out, but at once grasped the whole background of thought behind his remark, and said: Mr. Fenwick, you were highly appreciating, just a few moments ago, Pundit Ravi Shankar's beautiful sitar music. How fascinating, how spontaneous, how natural, is his music! You had said. That is fine, I said, and continued: But did you ever stop to think even for a moment, Mr. Fenwick, that behind that spontaneity and naturalness of Ravi Shankar's music, there lie years and years of hard discipline? Did you ever give a thought to that?

'As soon as I had put it that way, Mr. Fenwick became excited and literally burst into the microphone to say: That is a wonderful idea! I had never thought of it that way! This is something new! I do realize the importance of discipline from that point of view. And he exclaimed into the microphone: All of you, listen to what the learned Swami from India has to say!

'By this time, the scheduled 20 minutes period was ending; but his interest in the discussion, on the other hand, was just mounting; and he asked me sweetly, and in the hearing of his listeners, for, the whole programme was a live transmission: Swami, are you tired? Can we continue the interview? No, I am not tired at all, I replied; I am ready to go on as long as you like. At this, he was happy, and announced it into the microphone, and the interview ended only at midnight!

'Continuing the theme, I said: Mr. Fenwick, I also appreciate naturalness and spontaneity. Human life should be natural, spontaneous. But I discern two types or two levels of spontaneity and naturalness; one lies below discipline, and the other lies above discipline. And, for the next several minutes, he was an absorbed listener, putting an occasional question or re-stressing a point I had made, as I was expounding this theme in the light of Vedanta and twentieth-century biological thought.

'The animal is spontaneous and *natural*, I continued; the cow or horse eases itself wherever it stays or moves. That is one type of naturalness. But do we not subject a human child to a bit of toilet discipline? That is the first lesson we give to all children, followed by other disciplines first given to children by parents from outside, then given by children to themselves, so that they may rise to the level of *human nature* and develop the human way. All culture is the product of discipline of the impulses; and culture is specifically a human phenomenon;

animals have no culture. By such judicious discipline, guided by reason and love of truth, *man manifests the higher and higher aspects of nature, first the human, then the divine,* from within oneself. And the whole of such discipline of impulses, and the manifestation of the divine within, *can be as natural and spontaneous a process* as the expression of impulses at the organic level, when we understand the wide range of the meaning of the words 'nature' and 'natural'.

'Two types of people, I continued, do not need discipline or do not experience tension and struggle, and are perfectly natural and spontaneous; and I quoted the following well-known verse from the *Śrīmad Bhāgavatam,* the greatest book on *bhakti*, or pure love of God, in the Indian tradition, to explain the point (III. vii. 17):

*Yaśca mūḍhatamo loke yaśca buddheḥ param gataḥ;*
*Tāvubhau sukham edhete kliśyatyantirito janaḥ —*

"Two types of people experience happiness and are free from all tension, namely, the uttermost fool among men (in whom the struggle for humanness has not yet commenced), and the one who has gone beyond *buddhi*, intellect or reason, (in the *experience* of the Atman, the infinite divine Self, and the transcendence of both animal and human nature). All others, in between, are in varying stages of tension and struggle."'

That is how Vedanta tells people that, don't take things as they are. You can make them better and still better. There is a progress from this to that. You can be the architect of your own destiny. No animal can be the architect of its own destiny. Nature is the architect there. In our case, *svabhāva* is not our architect, nature is not our architect. *We* are the architect, *we* can reshape our lives. This must be constantly kept in view. Because we forgot it after the independence of India, *jaḍa* nature is acting in its own way in India. Raw humanity, just selfish; quarrelling, fighting, killing; everything just as we do in a wild state. That is a great misfortune. Human dignity doesn't find expression there. I can easily kill anyone or, if I am a cannibal, I can eat him or her also. But in civilization, at least we don't eat human beings. Swami Vivekananda said, the old cannibals *ate* human beings; today we do not do so, but we *cheat* each other. The same cannibalism in a new way. That has to go. When you free yourself from that *jaḍa svabhāva,* that *svabhāva* which has got into your psycho-physical system, beyond which is the Atman, that Atman begins to find expression in you. Try to find its expression. A little expression is there when the baby develops the consciousness of 'I' and expresses, 'I want it, I want it'. That 'I' is like the tip of a tremendous rock that is below the water level. Only the tip you see. That is all we consider as this 'I'.

But that is not its true dimension. That dimension is infinite. That 'I' is really one with all. That is the truth which is going to be told by the *Gītā* a few *ślokas* later, that this concept of *yoga* will lead you to that realization. We are essentially one. There is only one Atman in all of us; that truth is going to be told. And therefore, let this 'I' be treated as the tip of a big rock projecting above the water level. Unless you probe deeper, you won't see that immense dimension. That little ego is the visible part of something immense, namely, the infinite immortal Atman. Depending only on the little tip, the ego creates all the mischief in human life. Treat it as a simple initial datum. Try to find its true dimension. As you begin to dive into it, you will find the ego is expanding and expanding, and ultimately, realizing that, 'I am one with all. We are all essentially one.' Then something great will happen. That is how this chapter is going to give us a profound message of human unity and equality. How we shall live in society as the equal of all? What a beautiful concept! Equality is an inspiring concept. We are one, we are all equal. So, that is being given to us a few verses later in this very chapter.

All these teachings are not just dogmas. This is meant to be thought about, meant to be applied, meant to be checked up, meant to be verified. The science of *yoga* in the *Gītā* is a verifiable science. That is what we are asked to do. Let us see how this will function in our case. No misty ideas are here.

Everything is clear; dealing with the human being, his or her possibilities, and how he or she can unfold these possibilities. So, in the next *śloka*, Śrī Kṛṣṇa continues this idea.

नादत्ते कस्यचित् पापं न चैव सुकृतं विभुः ।
अज्ञानेनावृतं ज्ञानं तेन मुह्यन्ति जन्तवः ॥१५॥

*Nādatte kasyacit pāpam na caiva sukṛtam vibhuḥ;*
*Ajñānenāvṛtam jñānam tena muhyanti jantavaḥ* — 5. 15

'The Omnipresent Divine does not take the merit and demerit of anyone. Knowledge is enveloped by ignorance, hence do beings get deluded.'

What a wonderful idea! This *vibhu*, the divine Master of the universe, does not take the sins of anybody, nor the merits of anybody. *Nādatte kasyacit pāpam*, 'doesn't take the sins of anyone'; *na caiva sukṛtam*, 'nor whatever good anyone does'. But what is the actual situation? *Ajñānena āvṛtam jñānam*, '*jñāna* is hidden by *ajñāna*', *tena muhyanti jantavaḥ*, 'thereby the creatures are deluded'. That is the situation.

Our *jñāna* is lying hidden by *ajñāna*. That makes us deluded. And we function in that deluded state. That is what we do everyday. This was referred to in the third chapter, towards the end (3. 38), dealing with the source of crime in society. There also Śrī Kṛṣṇa had said, *ajñāna* or spiritual blindness covers *jñāna*, just like ash covers fire. You find no fire at all. Fire is there, but covered by ash. Remove the ash, put a few faggots, you find again the flame coming. So also, this *ajñāna* is hiding *jñāna;* it means, being subject to that *svabhāva* referred to earlier, just like all animals which are subject to that *svabhāva* or nature. But in the case of human beings, we can redeem ourselves from this *svabhāva* by the power of the higher *svabhāva* in us which is called here *jñāna,* spiritual knowledge. That effort is being referred to here. But at present, *ajñānenāvṛtam jñānam, 'jñānam* is covered over by *ajñāna*'. *Tena muhyanti jantavaḥ,* 'thereby, beings are deluded'. When there is *ajñāna*, there is delusion. When there is *jñāna*, there is no delusion at all. We see things clearly. Just like when you drive in a foggy weather, you can't see your way. That is the state of *ajñāna* or delusion. So many accidents can take place. I remember my being taken from Paris airport to our Vedanta Ashrama in Gretz, a distance of 29 kilometres, in February 1961. So thick was the fog, we couldn't see one inch ahead of us. And the road was small. How slowly we had to go to avoid any kind of accident! So, this *ajñāna* is like that fog. We can't see the way at all. *Tena muhyanti jantavaḥ,* 'by that, beings are deluded'. But will it remain like this all the time? No. We can lift the fog. We can remove that *ajñāna*. That is the text of the next *śloka*.

ज्ञानेन तु तदज्ञानं येषां नाशितमात्मनः ।
तेषां आदित्यवज्ज्ञानं प्रकाशयति तत्परम् ॥१६॥

*Jñānena tu tadajñānam yeṣām nāśitamātmanaḥ;*
*Teṣām ādityavajjñānam prakāśayati tatparam* — 5. 16

'But whose ignorance or spiritual blindness is destroyed by knowledge (of the Self)—that knowledge of theirs, like the sun, reveals that Supreme (Brahman).'

What beautiful ideas, what beautiful illustrations you find here! *Jñānena tu tat ajñānam yeṣām nāśitam,* 'whose *ajñāna* or spiritual blindness is destroyed by *jñāna* or knowledge'; *ātmanaḥ,* 'of the Self'; that is, 'I have destroyed my *ajñāna* by my *jñāna;*' when that happens, *teṣām,* 'their'; *ādityavat tat jñānam param prakāśayati,* 'that knowledge of such a person reveals that Supreme Brahman, just like the sun in the sky,' which was once covered over by thick clouds, but is shining brightly now as the clouds have gone. The sun was there, but it was hidden by clouds. Similarly, here also, *jñāna* reveals to you your own infinite dimension. You are not a chip of that *svabhāva.* There is another profound dimension within you. This truth shines on you when *jñāna* removes *ajñāna* from your system. It was shining then also; it is shining now too; the cloud could not destroy the sun's effulgence; but it could make the sun invisible. In your case also, it is the same. *Prakāśa* means shine. Till now it was not shining. All human beings, proclaims Vedanta, are essentially pure and free. We are of the nature of pure consciousness. We are of the nature of light. The light of consciousness is our nature. But when we are deluded, that light becomes dim and we do all sorts of evil. Remove that delusion. Remove that *ajñāna*. Then *jñāna* shines in its own splendour. The British poet Robert Browning calls it 'the Imprisoned Splendour' in his poem *Paracelsus*. That wonderful splendour is in you, in me, in all. Even in the animals it is there. Vedanta speaks of the Atman as present even in the tiniest worm. It is there, but that body won't be able to discover this truth. Only in the human body, can this truth be sought after and discovered.

*That is the supreme uniqueness of the human being.* We are striving to understand this ever-present truth of the infinite Atman as our true nature. *Svabhāva* or external nature is controlling us. We have to develop additional strength to overcome that drag of *svabhāva* on us. Then we realize that *ajñāna* is gone, *jñāna* has come, like the sun shining when the clouds have departed. That is what is happening to you and to me in all our spiritual, ethical and moral development. *Tatparam,* 'when attuned to That', by making our mind attuned to the divine that is within, a human being is able to overcome *ajñāna* and realize one's own true nature thereby. This is a beautiful verse, verse 16. This term, *tat para,* will come in a full verse ahead. Complete dedication to that Divine truth that is hidden within us will be expounded in a verse to come.

This is the great truth about all human beings. We can call it the Science of Human Possibilities, just like we have the Science of Physical Nature's Possibilities. This wonderful human being can achieve such great heights. That little baby of today can become a Mohammed Ali or an Einstein or a Buddha tomorrow. All that possibility is sleeping in every human child. We have to help the baby to unfold these possibilities. That is the word *jñāna*. The human being alone has the capacity for *jñāna;* in animals *jñāna* is centred in the sensory system, never beyond it. You can see this in the behaviour of all animals. What the *Devī Māhātmyam,* that great book on the Divine Mother says (1. 47):

*Jñānam asti samastasya jantor viṣayagocare*

*'Samastasya jantoḥ,* 'of all creatures', their *jñāna* functions only at the sensory level. The bird can look and find out where its prey is. Also, other animals can do the same; all at the sensory level, never at the higher level. In the human being alone is there the capacity to go beyond the sensory level and discover knowledge in its true form. That is *jñānam;* scientific, ethical, and spiritual. A few verses later this idea will be developed still further and a new truth will be added, namely, the spirit of equality, equal-mindedness, equality of vision; that can be taken as the great message of this fifth chapter.

What is the significance of the word *svabhāva* or *prakṛti* or nature? The *Gītā* has referred to it in many places. Usually—and in the Western context too—it means only physical nature or external nature. But, from the Indian point of view, there is another approach to this subject of *svabhāva.* The whole of reality is *svabhāva,* but it has two dimensions. Ordinary *svabhāva* is *aparā prakṛti,* and higher *svabhāva* is *parā prakṛti,* as will be expounded in the seventh chapter fully. The word *prakṛti* also means the same, *svabhāva,* or nature. So, in the chapter that lies ahead, we shall study nature in these two dimensions, ordinary *prakṛti* and higher *prakṛti.* Both together constitute reality.

That is what the *Gītā* is going to tell us later on. So, this concept of *prakṛti, aparā* and *parā,* is treated as the Divine Mother, or the Divine *Śakti* or *Parāśakti* in Indian mythology and spiritual thought. What is dull, dead nature becomes the expression of that *cit-śakti* or energy of Consciousness, the *Parā-Śakti,* the Divine Mother. In the *Gītā* this is referred to several times but in the *Devī Māhātmyam, The Glory of the Divine Mother,* this is the central theme. The Divine Mother is everything. All energy or *Śakti* of the universe, whether it is physical, biological, intellectual, or spiritual, is the manifestation of that one Divine *Śakti,* the *Ādyā Śakti,* the 'Primordial Divine Energy'. That is what manifests as this universe; manifests it, withdraws it, again brings it out. And this Divine Mother is praised in that *Devī Māhātmyam: Prakṛtistvam hi sarvasya,* 'You are the

*Prakṛti* of everything'; *guṇa traya vibhāgini*, 'Your *Prakṛti* is of three-fold nature, *sattva, rajas* and *tamas'*; *kālarātriḥ mahārātriḥ moharātriśca dāruṇā*, 'that *Prakṛti* can make for a *moharātri*, a very terrible night of delusion'; for a *kālarātri*, 'a dark night'; and a *mahārātri*, 'a dense night of ignorance'. We are, everyone of us, a playground of the forces of this *Prakṛti*, *aparā* as well as *parā*. When we are selfish, violent, cruel, *aparā prakṛti* is functioning within us. When we are compassionate, loving and peaceful, *parā prakṛti* is functioning within us. It is for us to change from one to the other. *That is where human freedom comes.* No animal can do it. No nature can do it. But that higher nature which manifests in the human system, that can transform the operation of *svabhāva* from the ordinary to the extraordinary. *That is the uniqueness of the human being;* then, this body and mind will become the playground only of that higher nature or higher *Prakṛti*, not of the lower *Prakṛti*. This is our responsibility. In the *Devī Māhātmyam* this is beautifully expressed in many places. The Divine Mother is called that *Ādyā Prakṛti*, that *Parā Prakṛti*, and the whole universe is Her energy manifestation, *Śakti* manifestation.

Sri Ramakrishna used to say, whenever you are conscious of yourself and the external world, you are within the jurisdiction of this *Śakti*, this Divine *Prakṛti*. Whenever you go into deep *samādhi*, then alone you go beyond the *Śakti* jurisdiction. So, *Śakti* jurisdiction extends throughout the universe, everywhere, in external nature and in the human being at various levels. But when we come to the *nirvikalpa* state of *samādhi*, going beyond all duality, then we go beyond *Śakti* to that *Śiva* nature, which is eternal, without change, ever the same. But, till then all are within the jurisdiction of *Śakti*, *Ādyā Śakti*, or *Parā Śakti*. So, here three words are used: *Kālarātri*, *mahārātri* and *moharātri*. *Rātri* means (darkness of) 'night'. What is that darkness of night? Delusion. *Moharātri*, 'the dark night of delusion'. And *Mahārātri*, 'very dense darkness of ignorance and misunderstanding'. And then, *Kālarātri*, 'frightful night'. Sometimes we pass through frightful experiences, all due to delusion. All that is because of being in this type of *rātri.* There is no light. There is no knowledge. There is no illumination. That is also the same *Prakṛti* or Nature; for example, in a piece of stone, it is absolute darkness. There is no consciousness. There you can see that kind of darkness of delusion. In ourselves also, every now and then, we will find this darkness of delusion, and we do all sorts of evil in that condition. The Divine Mother is playing in that particular way in you and me. But, what we are asked to do is the other way. Let Mother's higher energy, the *Parā Prakṛti,* manifest in and through us. We have to do it. We have the freedom to do it. Let people realize this great truth. We are free to allow *Aparā Prakṛti* to play in us, or *Parā Prakṛti* to play in us. That must be the first truth we must realize. Don't say it is all destiny. I can change, I can change the play from one to the other. In the words of Sri Ramakrishna, *Avidyā Māyā* and *Vidyā Māyā,* are two aspects of *Māyā.* Let *Vidyā Māyā* be within me. When you try to help people, you are influenced by *Vidyā Māyā;* when you try to injure people, you are influenced by *Avidyā Māyā.* The heart is the playground for either of them. And we are responsible. The human being has a sense of ethical responsibility. Animals have no responsibility. They are not subject to ethical judgement. If you go near an ass and it gives you a kick; you can't say 'you are a bad ass'. It is an ass, that is all. There is no good, there is no bad; that is its nature. It does so just to express its own nature. In us also, there is that ass nature, and yet, a higher nature also. We can control that ass nature. If a person comes near me, I need not bump on him. I can shake hands, I can smile, it is up to me to do this way or that way. *Svabhāvastu pravartate—svabhāva* in this sense means that lower nature. That is activating us to do this and that. The higher nature of *svabhāva* also can activate us. Then great character comes, great spiritual development will come.

That is how the word *Prakṛti* or *svabhāva* is used in this *Devī Māhātmyam* and in much of Sri Ramakrishna's teaching. Brahman and *Śakti,* Brahman and *Māyā, Śiva* and *Śakti,* they are one and the same. But the *Śakti* aspect is what makes for the manifestation of this universe. When *Śakti* pulsates, the universe comes into being. When the *Śakti* becomes quiescent, the universe is withdrawn. In fact, one of the most beautiful truths of the Sāṅkhya philosophy is, whenever the three *guṇas* are in perfect equilibrium, there is no universe. This is similar to the modern Western astronomy's concept of the state of singularity. That is what is called *Pralaya.* The whole universe is withdrawn into its Primordial Nature. What a beautiful conception! And when does manifestation begin or creation begin? When there is a slight disturbance in the equilibrium of the three *guṇas*. The creative process, the manifestation process, starts. Then all the uniformity that existed before becomes diversity. What was one, becomes many. That is put into the Upaniṣadic statement by saying: Suppose that primordial Reality, that background material of modern astronomy, were to say what it experienced, then what would be its language? That is what the Upaniṣad says: *Eko'ham bahusyām,* 'I am one, let me be many'. That Primordial Background Stuff, which exploded and became the universe, that concept of the Big Bang as they call it in modern Western astronomy, is close to this conception.

These are beautiful ideas in our cosmology, which very much echo the great ideas of modern cosmology. Only, Indian cosmology had taken one step more. It found a high place for Consciousness behind this Background Material, which much of modern astronomy doesn't find a place for. But some Western astronomers *are* trying to find a place for Consciousness and thus coming to ancient Indian Cosmology. That is what I once before referred to in the first volume, namely, British astronomer Fred Hoyle's later book, *The Intelligent Universe.* Till now we were dealing with an un-intelligent universe. Now we are dealing with an intelligent universe. If modern astronomy continues in that line, it will come exactly to what the Sāṅkhyas and Vedantists have discovered here. In that primordial State, everything is one alone and non-dual. *Ekam eva advitīyam brahma,* 'Brahman, that ultimate Reality, is one alone, and not two'. That Brahman in its *Śakti* aspect, became manifested as this universe. Sri Ramakrishna said,

Brahman and *Śakti* are one, the Impersonal and Personal aspects of the ultimate Reality. Vedanta calls it *Parā Prakṛti, Parā Śakti* or ultimate Reality, a combination of *Parā* and *Aparā Prakṛti.* That subject will come up fully in the seventh chapter.

So, in this statement of verse 14, *svabhāvastu pravartate,* '*svabhāva* acts', we must not fail to realize the divine dimension of that *svabhāva.* That *svabhāva* which is very dull, dead matter, in ordinary physical terms, is entirely that Pure Consciousness in action, in the *Śakti* form. It becomes dull dead matter on one side, and consciousness and conscious beings, on the other. Therefore, *Prakṛti* has two dimensions, the unconscious and the conscious, the *jaḍa* and the *cit.* Both are there in *Prakṛti.* When *Gītā* refers to our activities, *Gītā* refers to that *jaḍa prakṛti, svabhāva. Svabhāva* is acting in you and me. But *Gītā* will assure us, don't be frightened by *svabhāva.* That very *svabhāva* is the manifestation of the Divine Mother in the form of lower nature and higher nature. That is how, in India, we developed the feminine aspect of the divine, the divine *Śakti.* From Her the universe has come. She maintains this universe. These ideas come in many verses in the *Devī Māhātmyam.* 'Eternal Feminine' is a beautiful phrase used by Goethe, the German poet and dramatist, in his book, *The Faust.* That last line of *The Faust* is simply wonderful. 'The Eternal Feminine leads us on and on.' Goethe must have read Indian philosophy and he admired Kālidāsa's *Śakuntala.* By that time lots of Indian books were coming up in Europe. So, this concept of the Eternal Feminine which leads us on and on, is exactly that Divine *Śakti, Parā Śakti,* which is behind this whole universe. What a beautiful conception! My divine Mother, as Sri Ramakrishna said again and again. Everything is under the jurisdiction of the Divine Mother. We call it Kālī. Many other names are there. These names are nothing.

'O Black Mother! Have none sung Thy praise? I shall sing Thy praise, O Mother.' This is written by Walt Whitman of America. We also sing similarly. Dark Mother, concept of Kālī.

So, you can view the universe as a combination of Brahman and *Śakti, Śiva* and *Śakti. Śakti* is feminine. So, we call it the Divine Mother, from whom the whole universe has come, who withdraws the universe unto Herself. That is how the concept of God as Mother came into Indian thought and that concept was pre-Christian thought, present in Europe and in many other primitive cultures. But philosophically and spiritually developed concept of God as Mother, is the product of Indian thought only, developed by the help of Vedanta. That is why even a high philosopher like Śaṅkarācārya speaks of the Divine Mother as supreme in many of his songs and hymns. So, the *Gītā* here has referred to that particular idea: God has not prescribed any work for you, nor any fruit of work. But *svabhāvastu pravartate. Svabhāva* that is in you is making you work this way and that way. This *svabhāva* is nature in its ordinary form. We are here to overcome this aspect of Nature and build up the higher nature that is waiting to find expression. That is *parā prakṛti,* superior *prakṛti.* And both together constitute the totality of the Cause of the universe. That is what the *Gītā* will say in the seventh chapter. *Śloka* 15 said that the Divine does not take the *pāpam* or sin of anybody, nor the *puṇyam* or merit of anybody. The truth is *ajñānenāvṛtam jñānam*, '*jñāna* is hidden by *ajñāna*', and the result is, *tena muhyanti jantavaḥ*, 'all beings are under delusion because of that'. And it is through this delusion that we commit all the evil deeds that we do. This must be overcome. How? The present *śloka* 16 says:

*Jñānena tu tadajñānam yeṣām nāśitamātmanaḥ;*
*Teṣām ādityavajjñānam prakāśayati tatparam —*

'Through *jñāna*, when this *ajñāna* is overcome within oneself, in such people the ultimate Reality is revealed by that *jñāna*, just like the sun shining in the sky lighting up the whole world.'

*Jñāna,* spiritual knowledge, is the theme. In the fourth chapter also it was the theme. Here also it is *the* theme. But, in all these, it means redeeming spiritual knowledge, not book knowledge. We may have any amount of scholarship. That doesn't make for even the slightest illumination. It is only scholarship and nothing else. Sri Ramakrishna speaks of a parable about this type of mere intellectual knowledge, how it cannot save you from this life of delusion. A number of people got into a boat to cross a river. Among them was a philosopher, an intellectual. So, when the boat was moving, he asked the boatman, 'My dear boatman, have you studied psychology?' 'No, sir'. After some time he said, 'then 25 per cent of your life is a waste!' Then after some time, he asked, 'have you studied biology?' 'No, sir.' '50 per cent of your life is a waste!' One by one he went on thus. Next time he asked, 'Have you studied philosophy?' 'No, sir.' 'Then 75 per cent of your life is lost!', he said like that. People in the boat were watching. Then came a storm. The boat started to rock. And the philosopher became very much worried about what was going to happen. Then the poor boatman gently asked the philosopher, 'Do you know swim-ology?' 'No, sir!' 'Then one hundred per cent of *your* life is gone,' said the boatman. Mere intellectualism is not religion. You have to realize the truth for yourself.

So, Sri Ramakrishna has compared great intellectuals and scholars to kites flying high up in the sky. But where is their attention? On some dead body lying below on the earth. That is the nature of mere intellectualism. So, this *jñāna* is spiritual illumination, awakening. That alone can destroy delusion. Delusion cannot be removed by book-reading, by scholarship. Not at all. In fact, it may increase also that kind of delusion; later on, pride is added, arrogance is added. So try to have realization, *anubhava*. What is needed is to rise from intellect to experience. Intellectually, I know so much about love, I may write a book and get a PhD degree, but if you ask, do you know *how* to love? 'That I don't know. I know *about* love, I can write a good deal, but I don't experience love at all.' Then what is the use of that scholarship? In all departments, this is true. You write a book on citizenship, but you yourself do not behave like a citizen. What is the use of that knowledge of citizenship? You know about law, but behave lawlessly all the time! What is the use of that knowledge of law? You study science, but don't have scientific thinking. You have no scientific attitude. What is the use of that science? In all these matters, 'be' is more important than mere 'know'. That is why Swami Vivekananda defined religion as *being and becoming*. *Jñāna* or spiritual knowledge overcomes *ajñāna* or ignorance, just like the sun illumines the whole world; the ultimate Reality is revealed to you through that *jñāna*. This is a very great statement in this 16th verse. Then comes verse 17, one of the most wonderful verses, full of meaning.

तद्बुद्धयः तदात्मानः तन्निष्ठाः तत्परायणाः ।
गच्छन्त्यपुनरावृत्तिं ज्ञान निर्धूत कल्मषाः ॥१७॥

*Tadbuddhayaḥ tadātmānaḥ tanniṣṭhāḥ tatparāyaṇāḥ;*
*Gacchantyapunarāvṛttim jñāna nirdhūta kalmaṣāḥ* — 5.17

'Those who have their intellect absorbed in That, whose self is That, whose steadfastness is in That, whose consummation is That, their impurities cleansed by knowledge, they attain to non-re-birth (*mokṣa*).'

This is a remarkable verse. *Tat buddhayah*, 'those whose *buddhi* or intellect or reason is devoted to That', that supreme Reality. *Tat ātmānaḥ*, 'who has That as one's own Self'. *Tat niṣṭhāḥ*, 'who have constant discipline in That'. *Tat parāyaṇāḥ*, 'whose final goal is That'. The word *Tat* comes in this verse four times in all. *Gacchanti apunarāvṛttim*, 'they will reach the state from which there is no rebirth'. To them there is no more *samsāra*. *Jñāna-nirdhūta-kalmaṣāḥ*, 'those whose evils of the mind, all sins and impurities, have been destroyed through *jñāna*'. *Kalmaṣāḥ*, 'evils', are *nirdhūta*, 'destroyed' or washed away. Therefore, he is able to achieve that Supreme State from which there is no rebirth. This constant birth and death, like a wheel going on, of which we are all helpless victims, that won't happen to them; they become free. This is a preliminary statement. In a later *śloka*, the greatness of that achievement is shown that you get it *here and now*, not in some future life, not in some heaven. Here itself, in this life, in this body, we can come to this state of realization, this state of non-birth, the state in which we are truly free. In birth and death, we are not free. A potter takes clay, puts it on his wheel, makes pots, and thus it goes on. Clay has no say in the matter. We are like that clay in the hands of the nature, putting it this way, that way. But that condition will end for you. Nobody can shake you then. You will become your own master, *svarājya,* as we call it.

This is a wonderful idea in Vedanta. Śaṅkarācārya refers to it as *svārājya-siddhi,* 'you become your own master'. No outsider is going to dictate to you. That is high spiritual freedom, spiritual realization. And the method is this: *Tadbuddhayaḥ,* the *buddhi* is fixed on That. *Tadātmānaḥ, tanniṣṭhāḥ, tatparāyaṇāḥ.* I am constantly aware of that. That is the goal; not these petty little achievements everyday. Such persons, *gacchanti,* 'attain', *apunarāvṛttim,* 'no repeated birth and death'. *Samsāra* means that which moves on, the state of birth and death, constantly like a *cakra* or wheel. That condition of life does not come to such a person. *Apunarāvṛtti* means also *mokṣaḥ,* real spiritual liberation. *That is the highest goal of human evolution, according to Vedanta.* A human being alone can achieve that perfect freedom, freedom of the spirit. Many other freedoms we seek. Freedom from hunger, freedom from thirst, from illiteracy, all these things we seek. These are all needed at our ordinary level of life. But even there, the supreme freedom is the freedom of the spirit. Suppose you are fed well, given good clothes and a good house to live in. But, in spite of these, you are a slave under a master. What fun is there? Those things have no value. The most important thing is freedom. I want to be free. That infinite urge in every human heart finds its consummation in this spiritual realization: I am the Atman, ever-free, ever-pure; that is my true nature. No delusion will make me fall down from that state. That delusion has been burnt away through *jñāna,* or washed away, *jñānanirdhūta kalmaṣāḥ.* All *kalmaṣāḥ* or evils have been washed away, destroyed, through *jñāna.* Then this freedom becomes a fact. Now, it is only an ideal: 'I *want* to be free'. But, in that state, it becomes a fact of experience. I realize I am free. Vedanta doesn't speak of salvation. It speaks of freedom. Are you free?

Are you free? Learn to be free. Even within the limits of day-to-day life, we can be free. You can express that freedom. What a beautiful idea! A free mind, a free life, if it is genuine, it will never harm somebody else's freedom. If it is not genuine, it may happen otherwise. But real freedom is what enhances freedom of others as well. Be free, be free, is the constant exhortation of Vedanta to all humanity. So, here is that great verse. I like it the way it is put:

*Tadbuddhayaḥ tadātmānaḥ tanniṣṭhāḥ tatparāyaṇāḥ;*
*Gacchantyapunarāvṛttim jñānanirdhūta kalmaṣāḥ —*

*Jñāna* fire destroys all *kalmaṣāḥ* or evils. Yesterday, I committed a sin. Ten years ago, I had committed a sin. All these will be destroyed when a bit of *jñāna* comes. What Sri Ramakrishna said, if a room or cave is dark for a thousand years, does it take a thousand years to light it up? Just strike a matchstick. Instantly, all darkness goes away; immediately it becomes lighted. That is the nature of knowledge. That is why our whole Indian culture praises knowledge very highly. And India was very devoted to knowledge! Every type of knowledge—worldly knowledge or spiritual knowledge. Up to 1000 AD, this country was very devoted to the acquisition of knowledge, and to expansion of human life. Later on, came a contraction of human life. A contraction which went almost to the point of death, national death, in the eighteenth and early nineteenth centuries. Out of that we have come out. Now we are again in that expansive state. This philosophy will sustain us in this great struggle. Knowledge, more knowledge, still more knowledge of all levels. Out of that will come excellence of character, excellence of work, excellence of conduct. This is how we build up a new destiny for ourselves. That is the importance of this wonderful statement. It may refer to the great *sādhakas* or those who undertake spiritual practices, who realize this truth, but it may refer to you and me also at our level. At every level, any greatness in any field, should depend upon this sense expressed in this verse. *Tadbuddhayaḥ tadātmānaḥ tanniṣṭhāḥ tatparāyaṇāḥ*. A burnt seed, if you put in the soil, won't sprout again. So also, *jñāna* burns away all *kalmaṣāḥ* or evils within the system. Then that entity cannot be reborn again, because all its evil tendencies inside have been burnt away through the power of *jñāna* or spiritual knowledge which has been compared to fire, *jñānāgni*, earlier. That is how this is constantly emphasized in Vedanta. Freedom, freedom—here and not in a future life. In many aspects of our earlier teaching, it had been often told in the beginning that you get freedom in a future life, after you die. Somehow you believed that in this life you have achieved some spiritual development, but for real freedom you will have to wait for a future existence. That became changed in the Upaniṣads and the *Gītā*. In Vedanta came this profound teaching of *Jīvanmukti*, 'freedom while being alive'. And that is what is being proclaimed in the *Gītā*, in the Upaniṣads, in Śaṅkarācārya's writings, and today, in Ramakrishna-Vivekananda literature also. What is the use of living a wretched life here, and getting a future blessed state later on? Why not now? Why not enjoy the best here? The immortal Atman is our very nature. That was the realization that motivated these great sages. So, having said this, the next *śloka* gives us a marvellous truth! That is the very *soul* of this *Gītā*. When do we attain that state? How do we express that state in life? These are expressed in this verse.

विद्या विनय संपन्ने ब्राह्मणे गवि हस्तिनि ।
शुनि चैव श्वपाके च पण्डिताः समदर्शिनः ॥१८॥

*Vidyā vinaya sampanne brāhmaṇe gavi hastini;*
*Śuni caiva śvapāke ca paṇḍitāḥ samadarśinaḥ* — 5. 18

'The *paṇḍitas* or knowers of the Self look with an equal eye on a *brāhmaṇa* endowed with learning and humility, a cow, an elephant, a dog, and an eater of dogs (low-caste person).'

You become a *paṇḍita*, one whose knowledge has grasped the truth of the Atman. A *paṇḍita* is a *samadarśī*, 'who sees all with an equal eye'. No high and low in his or her eye. Everybody is the same Atman. That is expressed with a little more detail by saying, *vidyā vinaya sampanne brāhmaṇe*, 'in a *brāhmaṇa* who is endowed with *vidyā* and *vinaya*, knowledge and humility'; *gavi*, 'in the cow'; *hastini*, 'in the elephant'; *śuni*, 'in the dog'; *śvapāke*, 'who eats the dog', who, in India was called in the earlier social thinking, a *caṇḍāla; paṇḍitāḥ samadarśinaḥ*, 'the *paṇḍitas* see as equal' all of them. That *brāhmaṇa* and that dog, he or she doesn't make any distinction. Why? Because, the same Atman is in all of them. So, distinctions vanish. In ignorance, you find difference between things; in knowledge, you find unity. That is a great truth in Vedanta. Ignorance leads to diversity. Knowledge leads to unity. This will be discussed later in the seventeenth and eighteenth chapters while dealing with *sāttvika, rājasika* and *tāmasika* knowledge. Our senses reveal diversity, but knowledge reveals unity. Even in physical science, take all the various items of experience in any particular scientific field. Everything is different from each other in the beginning. As you investigate, you find basic unity emerging between things. So, the world has come from Brahman; when one realizes that Brahman and looks out, he or she sees the same Brahman everywhere.

So, the statement: *vidyā vinaya sampanne brāhmaṇe*. It is easy to see God in a person who is holy and pure. But, how to see Him in a dog, in an ordinary person, even in a criminal, in a prostitute? How is it possible? Yes, this person has achieved that universal vision. In Sri Ramakrishna's *Gospel*, you read: he saw Brahman in dogs, in cats, in human beings, in the prostitute standing out there, in every one of them. And he saluted every one of them; this happened in our own time. These are not mere words, these are not theories, these have been demonstrated again and again. So, *samadarśitva*, 'seeing all as equal', is a profound message of the *Gītā*. And it is also the very soul of democracy. Any kind of hierarchical consideration goes against the spirit of democracy. *Samadarśitva* should be there. Here in the Vedanta, and in this chapter of the *Gītā*, this is a big theme. The physical eyes cannot reveal this *samadarśitva* or *samatva*. Eyes reveal only differences. But the mind, when it becomes pure, can penetrate through these appearances and discover the pulsing of unity behind all diversity. That is the unique human capacity. Such a person is called a *paṇḍita*. *Paṇḍā* means *ātmaviṣayā buddhiḥ*, '*buddhi* that has the Atman as its object of knowledge', says Śaṅkarācārya. One who has that *buddhi* is called a *paṇḍita*. What a high meaning this word has! But, today this word has lost that high status and has come to mean a language teacher or even a cook. Swami Vivekananda was very fond of this expression *samadarśi*. When he was in the Maharaja's palace at Khetri in Rajasthan during his wandering days, the Maharaja arranged for a singing session by a nautch girl; a good singer. The Maharaja sent word to Swamiji, 'Please come, you will love the music. She sings very well.' Swamiji said, 'I am a *sannyāsin*, why should I go to listen to a nautch girl's music?' That was Swamiji's first reaction. The singer was deeply grieved when she heard this, and sang, as it were in reply, a song of Surdas, the blind Vaishnava poet saint. The song's main theme was this *samadarśitva*. The first line is:

*Mere avaguṇa citta na dharo samadarśi ho nām tihāro —*

'O Lord, do not look upon my evil qualities, Your name is same-sightedness, i.e. *samadarśitva*.'

When Swamiji heard the song, he was deeply moved. And he said, 'I am a *sannyāsin*, I made a distinction between this person and that person, that this is a nautch girl, this is somebody else, etc. She has taught me real Vedanta today.' He forthwith went to the hall of audience and joined the party. When the music was over, she came to Swamiji to make pranams to him, and Swamiji blessed her. Swamiji himself has told the story of this event. Our whole country needs to understand this truth of *samadarśitva*, because all our social life is riddled through and through with its opposite. We never had *samadarśitva*, only *a-samadarśitva*, inequality, high and low, hierarchical considerations, etc.

However, in the modern age, Swamiji said, we shall make this Vedanta the sheet anchor of our society. A new society we shall evolve where this *samadarśitva* will be there. And when India became free, she adopted a Constitution, a democratic republican Constitution, of which this *samadarśitva* is the very soul. Distinction between one and another as a citizen is abolished. Every citizen is equal to every other citizen. We have to look at him or her in that attitude of oneness. Unfortunately, we do it now only during elections. We forget it immediately after the elections. A candidate will go to a poor old lower caste woman and say, 'Madam, please come and vote for me, you are all a part of our democracy, we are all one.' That is how democracy functions. But, I am sorry to say, it functions so only once a while. Afterwards, you are you, and I am I. That is the attitude later on. That will change when political democracy is strengthened by spiritual democracy, through the great spiritual teachings of Vedanta. When these teachings go to the people, they will realize that this is not a mere political arrangement. This is a constant spiritual attitude. We have to maintain it, cultivate it. That is how, I have every hope, with Vedanta as the great philosophy behind us, with Swami Vivekananda as the expounder of that great philosophy and its practical implications, our democracy will develop that soulfulness, that spiritual enrichment, which very few democracies in the world have. We have that opportunity this time.

So, the next *Gītā śloka* is going to be on this subject of *samadarśitva*. *Paṇḍitāḥ samadarśinaḥ*. *Paṇḍitas* are *samadarśis*. And we all have the organic capacity to understand that truth of *samadarśitva* and live according to it. If a leader follows a path, we all will also follow that. There is such a thing as mimetic tendency in society. Whatever great persons do, we also do. Because our leaders practised only inequality all this time, we all practise inequality. The *brāhmaṇa* practised inequality. And what is the result? Even the *caṇḍāla* is practising inequality with respect to still lower people.

In Bangalore, in the 1930's, I saw two types of *caṇḍālas: eḍakai mādiga* 'left handed *mādiga*' and *valakai mādiga*, 'right handed *mādiga*'; one will not touch the other, because they have all followed that long-standing teaching and practice, that example that was given to them by the higher castes. Now, if the example changes at the top, everything will change at the bottom also. There will be real equality everywhere. No superiority to anyone, except what is given to you by people's consent. A minister has a certain status. Prime Minister also has a status, both given by the Constitution, given by the people. There is no harm in that. But, even then, he or she should not think, I am someone superior. He must go to the people, become one with them. That is real democracy. So far as socio-poltical democracy is concerned, the Scandinavian nations are the most advanced in this matter. When I was on a four month lecture tour of 17 European countries in 1961, I observed that even the king of Norway or Sweden will go shopping, and no kind of traffic jam will be there. They are just like other citizens. There you can see social democracy as a fact. It will take quite a bit of time for us in India to come to that high level. But that is the goal in this modern age of India's history, according to Swami Vivekananda. And therefore, in the next verse this idea is put in a stronger language:

**इहैव तैर्जितः सर्गो येषां साम्ये स्थितं मनः ।**
**निर्दोषं हि समं ब्रह्म तस्माद् ब्रह्मणि ते स्थिताः ॥१९॥**

*Ihaiva tairjitaḥ sargo yeṣām sāmye sthitam manaḥ;*
*Nirdoṣam hi samam brahma tasmād brahmaṇi te sthitāḥ*—5. 19

'(Relative) existence has been conquered by them, even in this world, whose mind rests in sameness, since Brahman is the same in all and is without imperfection; therefore, they indeed rest in Brahman.'

This is a very great verse, the soul of this chapter. *Ihaiva*, 'here itself', in this world, in this body itself; *tairjitaḥ sargo*, 'they have conquered relativity'; *yeṣām sāmye sthitam manaḥ*, 'whose mind is established in this *sāmya sthiti*, this vision of equality, this oneness'. *Nirdoṣam hi samam brahma*, 'Brahman is free from all evils', and is equal in all. *Tasmād brahmaṇi te sthitāḥ*, 'therefore, they are established in Brahman'. The great importance is, *ihaiva tairjitaḥ sargo*, 'here itself they have conquered relativity, birth and death.'

*Sarga* means 'without our choice we are put into a body-mind complex.' We have no choice in the matter. We have no freedom. We become a creature. Just like a prisoner who has no freedom. He or she is put into a prison, and cannot come out. He or she is not free there. So, our birth is of that nature, we didn't choose it; it has come to us. Now, it is a challenge to us. This kind of birth—*sarga* means birth of this nature where helplessness comes in; that will end when you realize Brahman. That is the central theme of the *śloka*. If you freely choose a birth, that is beautiful. When a person is taken to a jail for some crime, he or she has no freedom to go in or to come out. But, if somebody goes to jail, freely, to do some great good to the people, that is beautiful. Gandhiji went to jail. Why? In order to secure release for millions of people from the jail of political slavery. In the nineteenth century, a British citizen, Canon Wilber Force, if I remember right, did a formal crime and went to jail; there he studied the wretched condition of the helpless prisoners. On release from prison, he gave wide publicity to this situation; and the result was prison reforms.

That *sarga* is welcome. This *sarga,* where we are helpless, is a challenge to us. Why are we here? How can we be free? We have to take up this challenge. That is what Vedanta speaks about in dealing with the human situation. So, this *śloka* says, when you struggle in this way and seek for freedom from being a creature of the birth-and-death process, you come ultimately to this realization. And in this very life one realizes it, 'whose mind is fixed in sameness, same-sightedness'. Why? 'Brahman, the infinite consciousness, is free from all evil and equal in all'. Brahman is *sama,* equal, in all. Therefore, those who realize this truth, 'they exist in Brahman'. Now, this word Brahman is a great word in Vedanta. Vedanta says that no word can explain, or indicate, the highest Reality. But, we have to use some word. The Upaniṣads therefore used two words: Brahman and Atman. So far as the infinite cosmos is concerned, they discovered its unity in Brahman, the infinite. So far as the human being is concerned, they discovered his or her true nature also as the Atman, the infinite pure Consciousness. And the next great discovery was that this Atman and this Brahman, being pure Consciousness, are one and the same. There cannot be plurality in consciousness. That was a tremendous conclusion arrived at by the great sages of the Upaniṣads. Plurality is impossible with respect to Consciousness. There is no evidence, there is no proof. That is why in modern times, nuclear scientist Schrodinger, particularly stressed this point by saying that Consciousness is a singular of which the plural is inconceivable. That plurality that you attribute to it is because of the different body-mind complexes in which Consciousness manifests. Consciousness is not plural, but the bodies, in which Consciousness manifests, are plural. And therefore multiplicity is wrongly attributed to Consciousness. Really, Consciousness is one and indivisible, just like space.

That is the great conclusion of Vedanta; and this conclusion of the infinite Consciousness, one and non-dual, which unites everything in this world, is slowly getting expounded more and more by Western scientists today. Physicists, psychologists, medical scientists, and those who deal with environmental problems, everyone of them is slowly coming to this unity behind the diversity. Intimate relationship of everything with each other, and that unity is something spiritual. The Atman is pure Consciousness, Brahman is pure Consciousness. So, the Upaniṣads speak of the world coming out of Brahman in one place and from Atman in another place. It is one in you, in me, in all. This subject is slowly becoming attractive to those people in the West today who deal with ecology and environmental problems. They see a unity behind all this diversity. And that unity is a spiritual unity. The word spiritual comes again and again in many books written by these great thinkers. So, they are travelling upon the road that have been travelled earlier by the great sages of the Upaniṣads, and they will come to the same conclusions.

What is the definition of Brahman? The *Taittirīya Upaniṣad* asks this question. And it answers (II. i. 1): *satyam jñānam anantam brahma,* 'Brahman is *satyam,* truth, *jñānam,* consciousness, *anantam,* infinity'. There are no two. It is infinite and non-dual. Now, this is the conclusion towards which modern Western thought is proceeding. They are advanced thinkers who are not tied down to the materialistic dogmas of science, and they are increasing in number. Any number of books are coming out. So, this *śloka* has tremendous significance from that point of view. When you realize this truth of Brahman or Atman, you become free. You are no more *a creature*. That is the idea of *brahmajñāna,* 'knowledge of Brahman'—a wonderful word in Vedantic literature. Some of the great utterances of the Upaniṣads refer to this great truth. In the *Muṇḍaka Upaniṣad* (II. ii. 11), there is this verse which is uttered with a sense of ecstasy after realizing this truth: *Brahmaivedam amṛtam,* 'this manifested universe is nothing but Brahman, the immortal'. Things and beings are mortal, but Brahman, that exists in all of them, is immortal. So, *idam* means 'this manifested universe'. Then the Upaniṣad expands it, *purastād brahma,* 'in front is Brahman'; *paścāt brahma,* 'behind is Brahman'; *dakṣiṇataścottareṇa,* 'right and left'; *adhaścordhvam ca prasṛtam,* 'it spreads above as well as below'. And finally, it ends up with a wonderful note: *brahmaivedam viśvamidam variṣṭham,* 'this whole universe is nothing but Brahman, the supremely adored one'.

Now, that is the Brahman referred to in this *Gītā* verse 19. Those who have realized Brahman, they realize the spirit of unity, the spirit of harmony. When we deal with the body, we find lots of differences. No two people are alike so far as body is concerned. The Vedantic search for the truth behind this world started from the sensory level, and at the sensory level we see nothing but differences. Everything is different, so much so that, diversity is the truth about the world viewed from the sensory point of view. Then out of this comes all the evils in society; evils of violence, crime, and one of those evils that afflict even today: human society's caste and racial superiority attitudes, including South African White's racial superiority attitude. Out of this the world is slowly evolving a human sense of oneness, a humankind awareness, obliterating these differences, which are not negated, but which are said to be only on the surface. Deep down, there is unity. Outwardly there are these differences, we don't deny. Even the difference between man and woman. But behind both is one infinite Self. That is our true nature. *Tat tvam asi,* 'you are That' as the *Chāndogya Upaniṣad* expresses it. Now, when this truth comes into operation in society, you will find greater integration of human beings with human beings and nature. And today that integration process is going to be international in scope. We are all one. Imagine what was man thinking fifty years ago and what it is today! Pre-war thought and, post-war thought. Pre-war was full of differences, full of superiority, inferiority and exploitation; all that was going on. But in post-war conditions, things have changed. A search for unity, giving up of racial superiority, or every other kind of superiority, even masculine superiority over women. When that is being banished, step by step, whereto are we moving? What is its direction?

It is that direction that Vedanta supplies to the entire movement of thought in the modern age. For, in these Upaniṣads and in the *Gītā*, you are in the presence of great sages who took up this problem ages ago, three to four thousand years ago, and discovered this profound truth of absolute spiritual unity and oneness, and the more you realize it, the happier you will be, the more fulfilled you will be. The more you stress on differences, the more sufferings you will have. So, human life has to be geared in this direction. *Ihaiva tairjitaḥ sargo yeṣām sāmye sthitam manaḥ*. 'If one is established in *sāmya,* he or she conquers relativity here itself;' not in any heaven but in this very world. We are all one and the same; you are a human being, I am a human being. Today, we speak of homo sapiens. Humanity is one. Biologically it is one. Modern biology describes humanity as a single inter-thinking and inter-breeding species. That unity has been discovered in biology; so we are essentially one. Therefore, develop that *sāmya* attitude. Don't look to the differences in wealth, power and position. Now this is still a speculative venture; but, it is the truth behind it that takes you to the idea of Brahman and Atman. Behind this body-mind complex is the infinite spiritual Reality called Atman, and it is one in all of us, 'existing undivided in things apparently divided'. That is the language of the *Gītā,* a few chapters later. Bodies are divided, but the Atman is undivided. We are all one. Love comes only when we realize this sense of unity. Wherever there is separateness, it is difficult to bring love into the picture. So, love, compassion, and all such positive virtues can manifest when we obliterate these external differences and stress the basic unity behind all this. That is the meaning of this *śloka,* and the world is going in that direction. Brahman is *sama;* in all beings it is present in 'equal measure'. Nobody has more of it, nobody has less of it. Remember this beautiful idea: Brahman's presence in all of us is equal. In none more and in none less. See the wonderful truth. *Brahma nirdoṣam,* 'free from all evil is Brahman'. Brahman is absolutely pure, ever-free, and it is equal in all of us. That is the most profound truth Vedanta conveys to all of us; whether it is the human being, whether it is an animal, insect, or trees and plants, or even rocks and minerals, everywhere the same infinite Consciousness is present in its wholeness. This is the truth which the Upaniṣads had discovered and all human beings can discover it. By that discovery, they reach the goal of human evolution. All this long evolution has a goal. This is that goal. Realize universality by realizing this Brahman which is *nirdoṣam,* 'free from evil', and *samam,* 'equal', in all beings. *Tasmāt,* 'therefore'; *te,* 'those who realize this truth'; *brahmaṇi sthitāḥ,* 'are established in Brahman'.

What a beautiful conception! We are established in the body as separate from each other. A few people are established in Brahman, and have realized their oneness with all. So, that is the difference between ordinary life and the highest spiritual attainment. In many places in the *Gītā,* this idea will be expressed from different angles, from different points of view. So, this is a *śloka,* which is in tune with the great urge in modern civilization. As I said, after the Second World War, we are proceeding in that direction. What a difference between 19th century and 20th century from this point of view! In the last century, what kind of differences we cultivated, how much exploitation of one person by another went on. That is why this new thought development, probably through the suffering of war and violence, has taken place, and we are on the road to human unity and harmony.

न प्रहृष्येत् प्रियं प्राप्य नोद्विजेत् प्राप्य चाप्रियम् ।
स्थिरबुद्धिरसंमूढो ब्रह्मविद् ब्रह्मणि स्थितः ॥२०॥

*Na prahṛṣyet priyam prāpya nodvijet prāpya cāpriyam;*
*Sthirabuddhirasammūḍho brahmavid brahmaṇi sthitaḥ*— 5. 20

'Resting in Brahman, with intellect steady, and without delusion, the knower of Brahman neither rejoices on receiving what is pleasant, nor grieves on receiving what is unpleasant.'

This person is established in Brahman, because he or she has that sameness in attitude. *Na prahṛṣyet priyam prāpya*, 'does not become over-elated when something advantageous comes to him or her.' *Nodvijet prāpya cāpriyam,* 'nor does one become depressed when something disadvantageous comes to him or her'. *Na udvijet,* 'don't get emotionally upset'. *Sthirabuddhiḥ,* 'with the *buddhi* which has become steady'. *Asammūḍho,* 'not at all deluded'; *brahmavit,* 'that knower of Brahman'; *brahmaṇi sthitaḥ,* 'is established in Brahman'. To be established in Brahman is the great objective of human life. That alone is where you are steady, you are free, and you are full. You are fulfilled only in that state. In every other state, you are not fulfilled, only partly fulfilled and many things remain unfulfilled. But once you establish yourself in Brahman, the all, you become the all. That is fulfilment. And I am using the word *fulfilment* here because it has come into biology in this century, in this post-war period; Sir Julian Huxley accepts that the goal of human evolution is fulfilment, not merely organic satisfaction which is the goal of animal life. But, at the human level, organic satisfaction is secondary; primary thing is fulfilment. Are you fulfilled? When you realize Brahman you can say, I am fulfilled. There is nothing more for me to attain.

*Kṛtakṛtya* and *kṛtārtha,* are the two words in Sanskrit to indicate that state. What ought to be done being born as a human being has been done, and being a fulfilled individual—these are the meanings of these words, *kṛtakṛtya* and *kṛtārtha*. *Bhagavān* Buddha, when he achieved spiritual illumination or *bodhi,* stood up and used the same word, 'I have achieved what ought to be achieved being born a human being. I am fulfilled. I am fulfilled.' That means he became full, and out of that fullness, he shared something with the world, that blessed millions of lives thereby. So, this is a great direction of human evolution. *Brahmavit brahmaṇi sthitaḥ,* 'such a knower of Brahman is established in Brahman'. What a wonderful idea! To be established in Brahman. We can establish ourselves in very many grounds which are shaky. That kind of life we have day-to-day, but here you are firmly based.

One example and parable given by Jesus in the *New Testament* is beautiful. 'A foolish man built his house on sand, and the rains descended, the floods came, the winds blew, and beat upon that house, and it fell. And great was its fall.' That is called *pratiṣṭhā*, or establishment, on sand; it is loose, it cannot sustain the house. 'But a wise man built his house on rock, and the rains descended, the floods came, the winds blew, and beat upon that house, and it fell not. Because it was founded on a rock.' Can this human life be founded on something like a rock which will never shake, which will never break? There is; and that state is called *brāhmīsthiti.* In the second chapter of the *Gītā,* the last nineteen verses refer to the *sthitaprajña,* 'one whose mind is constant and steady', because it has realized Brahman. That is a great series of verses at the end of the second chapter. Here also, the idea comes. *Brahmavit brahmaṇi sthitaḥ,* 'a knower of Brahman is fully established and steady in Brahman'. Even to think of this, to meditate on this, is a great experience. We are far away from it. What does it matter? That is the ideal. Much of human life today is full of suffering, because it has no goal. It has no direction. It is simply moving here and there. But here at last life gets a direction, and that too, towards fulfilment. Let me go in that direction. One step, two steps, as much as I can. That is how these ideals are to be preached to everyone. Place no barriers to neighbourliness. Feel your oneness with all. How can crime and delinquency ever come, or even tensions and breakdowns come, when such knowledge comes to children as well as to grown ups? So, this is how Vedanta exhorts humanity today: Place your life under the guidance of the highest philosophy—experiential, not speculative, and live as much of it as you can, and continue to progress step by step. Then Śrī Kṛṣṇa says, there are millions of normal human beings living at the sensory level. And that sensory apparatus controls them, limits them, and makes them separate from each other. They have to treat it as a challenge. That is a great Vedantic exhortation.

बाह्यस्पर्शेषु असक्तात्मा विन्दत्यात्मनि यत्सुखम् ।
स ब्रह्मयोगयुक्तात्मा सुखं अक्षयं अश्नुते ॥२१॥

*Bāhyasparśeṣu asaktātmā vindatyātmani yat sukham;*
*Sa brahmayogayuktātmā sukham akṣayam aśnute* — 5. 21

'With the heart unattached to external contacts, one realizes the joy that is in the Self; with the heart devoted to the meditation on Brahman, he or she attains undecaying happiness.'

Verse 21 gives us this great teaching: *bāhya sparśeṣu asaktātmā*, 'with the heart unattached to external contacts'; why should that external object be my master? Ask this question. For the animal there is no other way. They can't overcome that situation. But a human being can. He or she needn't remain a slave to all the external things that are there. The Self in him or her is of far greater value than all the values that he or she finds outside. This truth shines upon one's mind during war times. When refugees leave a war zone, observe what they do. They throw away one by one their priceless possessions in order to somehow save their body-mind complex; then the realization comes that life is more important than possessions. But, people forget this truth in peace time. *Bāhyasparśeṣu asaktātmā*, 'one who has no attachments to external contacts'. *Sparśa* is a great word meaning touch. There are five sense organs in a human being. One is for sight, the other is for hearing, there is one for smelling, the other is for tasting, and the last one is for touch. The most tangible of all the sense organs is the sense of touch. The word tangible itself comes from the word touch. When you touch a thing it is called tangible. And we generally consider a thing real if it is tangible. I can just touch it. Then it is real. So, reality is measured by tangibility by ordinary human minds. Things which are intangible are unreal to most people. So, extremely gross minds are very much conditioned by the skin touch. That is why it is said *bāhyasparśa,* 'external touch'; touching one's own body won't do. I want to touch something out there; that is the meaning of *bāhya.*

As a baby, it is a beautiful thing to enjoy *bāhyasparśa.* The baby needs it for its growth. The mother's skin touch to the baby is absolutely essential for the baby's sense of security and its mental development. But when we cease to be babies, we shall have to ask this question: how long shall I live at the lowest level of the sensory apparatus, at the skin touch level? Without touch, even by expressing through ear, nose, or eyes, we can still establish human relations. Touch is not that important. That is how we mentally grow one step, then another step, until the senses cease to exercise control over us. I can go beyond all of them. That is the high state of human evolution. These are all gateways. We are tied up with them, but we can go beyond them. Going beyond the sensory level is the beginning of human spiritual life. So long as one is tied up at the sensory level, one is still at the animal level only; to all appearances a human being, but actually an animal. So, *bāhyasparśeṣu asaktātmā,* 'one who is thoroughly unattached to all external contacts'; *vindati ātmani yat sukham,* 'what happiness that person enjoys in his own Self'; what I expect to get by all the sense touches, million times more than that I get from within. I didn't know this truth till now. Now I am realizing it. So, the *Gītā* says, whatever you get from outside touch, you get much more from your own Self. There is nothing to compare the joy of the Atman with the little joys that come from touch, sound, etc. That is a truth that we must realize as we become more and more mature. A baby cannot understand it. The baby lies entirely at the sensate level. As you go beyond the baby level, this truth must come to you. Without any external contact, if my mind is detached from it and inwardly touches the Atman, I enjoy an incomparable experience of bliss *within* myself. That is what Śrī Kṛṣṇa says here. The Atman is of the nature of infinite bliss. Even the joy from all external senses, says the *Taittirīya Upaniṣad*, is only a fraction of the bliss of the Atman coming through that particular sensory system.

The *Taittirīya Upaniṣad* says in its chapter on 'Enquiry into Bliss': Every joy you have in life is nothing but a little fraction of the infinite joy of the Atman which is your true nature and is *ānanda svarupa*. We don't condemn these ordinary joys; only treat all of them as a fraction of the *Ātmānanda*. *Bāhyasparśeṣu asaktātmā vindati ātmani yat sukham,* 'unattached to external contacts, what *sukham* or joy one enjoys within oneself'; *sa brahma yoga yuktātmā,* 'that person who has become connected with the source of all joy, namely, Brahman', what does such a person live by? *Sukham akṣayam aśnute,* 'such a one experiences imperishable happiness'. All types of sensory happiness are perishable; they come and they go. But this happiness is always there. That is your true nature. So, *sukham akṣayam aśnute. Sukham* means 'happiness', *akṣayam* means 'imperishable', *aśnute,* 'experiences'. This is the true direction of human evolution. We begin with joys coming from the external world, but slowly we reduce dependence on them when we begin to experience the ever-present pure joy of the Atman. That is what you see in great mystics of all religions and even in some ordinary human beings. When *Bhagavān* Buddha achieved enlightenment under the Bodhi tree, he experienced this ocean of bliss for several days under that tree. What else is freedom? Freedom is independence from the external environment. Suppose I call myself free. And somebody abuses me. And I become depressed, full of tension and depression. What has happened to my freedom? My freedom is in somebody else's pocket! He has held it there. He uttered a word and that made me unhappy and tense. Freedom is freedom from the pressure of external environment. You are established in yourself. Then you are free. Therefore, the *Gītā* says here. *Sa brahmayoga yuktātmā,* 'he or she is united with Brahman within oneself'. Such a person, *sukham akṣayam aśnute,* 'he or she enjoys imperishable happiness'.

A great teacher like *Bhagavān* Buddha, a Sri Ramakrishna; what joy they experienced welling up constantly within themselves! They did not enjoy anything outside. Wherefrom did they get this joy? If a person observes a fast on *Ekadaśi* day and remains cheerful throughout the day, that means he or she has got a little spiritual touch. Suppose one fasts and goes on complaining the whole day that he or she is being deprived of something worthwhile; such a one has not got anything new. So, whenever you give up anything outside, and remain cheerful, that shows you are in touch with the deeper Reality which is the source of all joy. That is why it is not an ascetic philosophy. It is a philosophy of fullness, of joy, of fulfilment. You give up something smaller for something better, something richer; and what is the richest? Your own infinite Self. Nothing can be compared to that. And we forget it again and again. *Today's consumerist civilization needs to understand this truth very much.* We always measure civilization in terms of consumption of goods and services; the more, the better. And that has come under criticism today. Consumerism will destroy the whole of nature. And violated nature will also violate humanity which did that violation. These are the truths that are being impressed by thoughtful minds upon the human minds today. So, they are thinking of ways to get out of this consumerist mania? It is a real mania. And our T.V. advertisements increase this mania. As soon as somebody sees some advertisement on the T.V., the whole family will say, 'O we want that.' This is what is happening all over the world, and so, it is a world problem today, this consumerism, by which the ecological balance is being destroyed. All these sufferings are coming; even cosmic disasters are expected, and the ozone layer is getting depleted; then total life will suffer here. These are the warnings given by great thinkers today.

However, how to control this consumerist mania? If I control all this, I become a dry ascetic. That is not what Vedanta wants. You must have another source of joy. Is there such a source? Yes, there is. You have never thought about it. There is something infinite about you. The joy that comes from that source within is something which has no comparison. That is real joy. When people begin to experience it, this consumerist mania will become automatically reduced.

In Vedanta, the five sense organs of human beings are called *śabda,* sound, *sparśa,* touch, *rūpa,* form, *rasa,* taste, and *gandha,* smell. Under restraint they are helpful and friendly; otherwise, they are harmful. Ādi Śaṅkarācārya refers to this in a thought provoking verse in his *Vivekacūḍāmaṇi* (verse 76):

*Śabdādibhiḥ pañcabhireva pañca*
*pañcatvamāpuḥ svaguṇena baddhāḥ;*
*Kuraṅga mātaṅga pataṅga mīna*
*bhṛṅgā naraḥ pañcabhirañcitaḥ kim —*

'By the sense of sound and the other four sense organs, each animal, like deer, elephant, moth, fish, and bee, tied down by their respective rope of one sense-attachment, experienced death; so, what to speak of the human being who is attached to all the five sense organs!'

Sri Ramakrishna, in one of his teachings, divided human joys into three categories: *Viṣayānanda, bhajanānanda, and brahmānanda. Ānanda* means 'joy or bliss'. *Viṣaya* means 'sensory objects'. All consumerism refers to these sensory objects. 'The joy that comes from experiencing sensory objects' is called *viṣayānanda.* Vedanta does not look down upon it. It is valid, but carried beyond a certain level, it can destroy you and destroy the world. That is what we are seeing today. *Because today's materialism says there is nothing higher, we are tied down to that level. But here is a philosophy that tells all that there are higher levels of joy. Try to know them today.* When I give up enjoying something of the consumerist material, I am not left joyless. I am in search of deeper levels of joy. That second joy Sri Ramakrishna calls *bhajanānanda*, 'bliss coming from *bhajana*', from repeating God's name, singing Divine Glories; it is a purer joy. Proceeding in this direction one reaches the highest level of human development, namely, coming in touch with the bliss of Brahman that is ever within us. That joy is million times more intense than all types of joys including *viṣayānanda.* People who have experienced it alone can tell how immensely different it is from all *viṣayānanda.* In between is *bhajanānanda,* a wonderful *ānanda* or bliss. You come back refreshed from a *bhajanānanda* session, whereas, you come back refreshed and happy from *viṣayānanda,* if it is moderate, and tired, if it is too much. Some of the examples given today in various magazines and newspapers are about this thirst for *viṣayānanda.* When you go out on a week-end trip to the sea-side on a Friday, you return on Monday or Sunday evening, more tired and exhausted than before. Many journals and papers in England and America discuss this problem. There is no space on the sea-side to which many go; on the road, there is traffic jam. The whole of *viṣayānanda* is thus defeating itself today.

But a little *bhajanānanda* can give you greater refreshment and joy. Why should I go out all the time? Let me sit quiet and be myself for some time. Let me read a beautiful book. Today, many people have lost the capacity to be alone and happy and to read great books. Similarly, let me sing the name of God, enjoy music, enjoy those beautiful things. They don't cost much. And how much joy you get thereby. Above all, when a devotee of God sings *bhajan,* what wonderful joy it is! Very often people are able to sustain themselves even though many *viṣayānandas* are not available. By a little *bhajanānanda* we feel refreshed. People forget this truth today. So, that is the second joy, *bhajanānanda*. Our country never had the problem of drunkenness. Most people never knew what is an inebriating drink, though unfortunately, after independence, we are learning it quickly and well, because the *bhajanānanda* idea is being forgotten. We used to take the name of God;

after a whole day's work, when we would come back home, we would repeat the name of God, sing *Rāmnām saṅkīrtan*. Our common people did not need this external kick coming from drinks and other drugs. That joy, *bhajanānanda*, is taken away from them today. So, they have to depend upon the external joy. And what is the result? Unhappy homes, break-up of marriages, etc. So, the human being must understand how to experience joy from within. Sitting quiet itself can then be a great joy for those who know how to enjoy aloneness, not loneliness. Aloneness is a great thing. Why should I run about all the time? Let me sit by myself for some time; let me meditate; let me think of God; let me sing *bhajan*. All that constitute the sources of *bhajanānanda*. It does not cost anything, but it refreshes every time.

And the third type of bliss is called *brahmānanda*, what is referred to in this verse here. When you actually realize that infinite Brahman, what infinite joy is yours! You can't measure it at all. Immeasurable, *akṣayam*, that is the language of the *Gītā*. That is the language of Sri Ramakrishna's parable. Every joy is welcome. Vedanta does not look down upon any sensory joy. But there are joys *and* joys. There is a passage from a lower joy to a higher joy. Don't forget that. That is the warning that Vedanta gives. So, from *viṣayānanda* you must learn to achieve *bhajanānanda*. And if one is fortunate enough, if there is the grace of God on him or her, one can achieve *brahmānanda* also. But, *bhajanānanda* is the via media; it is a beautiful experience; millions of people today are seeking that *bhajanānanda*. One of the things I saw while travelling abroad is the spread of Indian *bhajans* all over the world today. Any part of the world you go to, everybody wants *bhajan*. *Bhajan* cassettes can be seen everywhere. Divine singing, and finding joy in it—that is a wonderful new development. We in India need it very badly today to save us from the consumerist current which destroys the consumer as well as nature. That should not happen. That is why this teaching is needed. This *śloka* has that reference. *Bāhyasparśeṣu asaktātmā vindatyātmani yat sukham*. *Ātmani* means 'in one's own Self'. *Yat sukham*, 'whatever happiness' you enjoy. *Sa brahmayoga yuktātmā*, 'who has become one with Brahman'. *Sukham akṣayam aśnute*, 'experiences imperishable happiness'. From the sense of touch we get various types of pleasures and happiness. But, the real test of human maturity is getting free from the need for that happiness coming exclusively from touch. Go higher and higher. There are more subtle human relationships. It is like two types of people sitting together; one type constantly chattering. Without it there is dryness. There is another type of people living together for days and months without a word being exchanged. Yet their hearts are always pulsing together with joy. Now, these are all parts of human experience. We have forgotten these higher dimensions of human possibilities.

It is written in the life of Swami Brahmananda that he and another disciple of Sri Ramakrishna lived together for months in Vrindavan without exchanging a word. But they were all the while close to each other; their hearts were pulsing together. That state is absolutely possible. But in the early stages of one's life, we need to talk with others; the first few months after marriage, the husband and wife need a good deal of talking. But once the married life is well established, they don't need much of talking. That shows a maturity of mind that has come at that stage.

There are thus grades of human happiness. We must always try to go to the next grade. Vedanta never condemns any type of pleasure. It only says, there are still higher grades. If you stay put in one, you are depriving yourself of higher types of joys which are waiting for you. This is the language of Vedanta, which has been strengthened by the beautiful exhortation of the *Kaṭha Upaniṣad* as freely rendered by Swami Vivekananda: 'Arise, awake and stop not till the goal is reached'. There is so much to achieve. If you have achieved something, march on, something still greater is there. As a baby I played with toys. 'O! I enjoyed it immensely.' I remember, as a child, I used to be forgetful of the whole world when I played. But, if one continues like that, even though one is grown up, it is something unhappy, tragic. How many other joys are waiting for you! Go to the school, develop knowledge and understanding. That is a higher joy. Mental joy is something higher. Then the highest, experiencing the joy of realizing your own infinite Self, *Ātmānanda*. What a wonderful concept of human possibilities Vedanta presents in this context! So, Śrī Kṛṣṇa says in the next verse:

ये हि संस्पर्शजा भोगा दुःखयोनय एव ते ।
आद्यन्तवन्तः कौन्तेय न तेषु रमते बुधः ॥२२॥

*Ye hi samsparśajā bhogā duḥkhayonaya eva te;*
*Ādyantavantaḥ kaunteya na teṣu ramate budhaḥ* — 5. 22

'Since enjoyments that are skin-contact-born are sources of misery alone, and have a beginning and an end, O son of Kuntī, a wise person does not seek pleasure in them.'

This is the conclusion on this subject. *Samsparśajā bhogā*, 'pleasures coming from external contact', they are called *samsparśajā; samsparśa* and *sparśa* mean the same thing, 'external skin contact'. All such pleasures have one defect: *ādyantavantaḥ*, 'they have a beginning and an end'. You can't always have them. You miss them. Besides, *duḥkhayonaya eve te*, 'they become sources of pain or sorrow'. You can't have only pleasure; pain also will come. Life is a constant movement between pleasure and pain. The English poet John Keats has expressed it thus in his *Ode to Melancholy*:

Ay, in the very temple of Delight
Veil'd Melancholy has her Sovran shrine!

In one of the poems of the great Sanskrit dramatist, Kālidāsa, in his *Meghadūta*, 'Cloud Messenger', occurs this truth:(verse 113)

*Kasya atyantam sukham upanatam duḥkham ekāntato vā;*
*Nicaih gacchat upari ca daśā cakra nemi kramеṇa* —

'Who has continuous happiness? Who has got continuous sorrow? Our situation goes up and down like the *nemi* or rim of a wheel.'

That is a constant truth about human life. So, Śrī Kṛṣṇa is expressing that idea. *Ye hi samsparśajā bhogā duḥkhayonaya eva te,* 'pleasures coming out of sense contact are the sources of *duḥkha* or sorrow; *ādyantavantaḥ kaunteya,* 'Arjuna, they have a beginning, they have an end'. Therefore, what is the way to deal with it? *Na teṣu ramate budhaḥ,* 'a mature mind or a wise mind will not take delight in them'. All this is dealing with the actual human situation. When we study ourselves and our various reactions, we come to understand so many new things about oneself and one's possibilities. It is good to know what are the possibilities that are hidden within oneself. We need a science of human possibilities, said Sir Julian Huxley; and Vedanta is just that, very ancient and yet very modern. As mentioned before, *viṣayānanda, bhajanānanda,* and *brahmānanda,* all the three are human possibilities. Therefore, we should keep in view these various grades of joys that are there, and pass on from one to the other. Don't stay put too long at one particular level. Avoid stagnation. Don't stagnate, is the constant exhortation of the Vedantic teachings. Don't stagnate, says also modern biology about human evolution.

Now we shall take up the remaining verses in this chapter. What a beautiful chapter, and the next *śloka* 23 is a wonderful verse. I recite it in my mind so many times; anybody can do so, and gain great strength thereby.

Every creature is seeking happiness or bliss. Only a human being can seek this bliss at higher and higher levels. All other creatures, seek only at the physical level. That is why the word used was *sparśa. Bāhyasparśeṣu asaktātmā,* 'one who is unattached to the *bāhyasparśa* or external contact'; contact by the grossest sense organ in a human being, namely, the sense of touch, without control, reduces any human being to the animal stage. Above the sense organs we have the psychic system, much subtler than the sensory system. But the subtlest of all is the Atman, the divine Self that is within all. It is from there that all the happiness that we experience comes to us. We have to go up in that direction. That is progress. And that depends upon a certain discipline of the sensory energies in the human being. If one doesn't do so, he or she will be in trouble. We have to seek for something higher and higher, and that possibility exists; this is all what our Upaniṣads and the *Gītā* have said. As I said earlier, the only clarion call to humanity given by Vedanta is, march on, march on. Don't stay put at a particular level. There are higher possibilities waiting for you to unfold, within yourself. That is how we go beyond the sensory system, the psychic system, and beyond all this, discover the infinite Atman of the nature of pure consciousness. There, *in the Atman, all these subtlety, immensity, and inwardness reach their infinite dimension*. That is our true nature. This limited human being is limited only when you look at him or her from the sensory point of view. When you feel, touch, see or hear, you feel he or she is a very limited being. But if you can penetrate this external psychophysical structure, you will find something tremendous within that person. He or she will be found to be infinite, immortal.

This truth is proclaimed by a sage addressing all humanity (*Śvetāsvatara Upaniṣad,* 4. 3):

> *Tvam strī tvam pumān asi tvam kumāra uta vā kumārī;*
> *Tvam jīrṇo daṇḍena vañcasi tvam jāto bhavasi viśvato mukhaḥ* —

'You are the women, you are the man, you are the boy and you are the girl; you are the old man tottering on his stick, you are born in various universal forms.'

In the same Upaniṣad, a young sage addresses all humanity as *amṛtasya putrāḥ,* 'children of immortality' (*Śvetāsvatara Upaniṣad,* 2. 5). But at the sensory level, we are not *amṛtasya putrāḥ*. All the evils in life, along with its share of joy, come from the sensory level. But a human being must be able to rise above this to something deeper, more subtle and more steady. And the highest is to realize the divine that is within all of us. This truth is placed before us and we are asked to go in that direction for our own good, for the good of society. It is in such a situation only that there can be peace within and peace without. All crime and delinquency come from the sensory level of life, and partly from the psychic level. Along with pleasure, lot of evil also comes from that level. So, we have to go a little deeper. And having gone deeper, and got in touch with the deeper dimension of Reality within, then you can function again at the sensory level *in a masterly way*, doing immense good to society. That is how the *Gītā* places before us the total vision of our life, how to shape it, which we have to do ourselves. That is the main education that one gives unto oneself with or without the help of others. This is the importance of verse 22. In modern civilization, money plays the biggest part. Every physical consumption means more and more money. Since people want more and more consumer goods, so people want more and more money. Since you can't get that money in a normal way, you get it by cheating others, cheating the government, stealing or robbing, or in whatever way you can. Today that is one sad aspect of the human situation.

The only way to get out of this situation, to redeem humanity from this weakness, is to tell him or her, again and again, what tremendous possibilities are lying hidden within them, and direct his or her attention in that direction. That is what the *Gītā* is doing. Ours, today, is a highly consumer oriented world civilization. And all the problems arising from this civilization, we can see in plenty all around us. So, some way must be found to get out of it. The *Gītā* gives you that direction. It is the study of the human being in depth, and investing human energies for higher and higher stages of evolution. There is a direction of human evolution; that direction is fulfilment. That is what we have to achieve. That development is possible for all humanity through the spread of Vedantic ideas in the context of modern physical science. In modern philosophy of civilization, there is no direction at all. It is simply going round and round. Same thing again and again. That is what is happening today. Therefore, there is aimlessness everywhere. And men and women without aim, without direction, can be the sources of much tension, sorrow, unfulfilment, and they can project the same on to society. And we are having such a society even in our own great India, which has a fund of tested wisdom, and much of rational thinking available to uplift the whole human society. In verse 23, this subject will be presented in a remarkable way, which as I said previously, I often repeat in my mind and find out deeper and deeper meanings. That is the importance of this verse 23, where Śrī Kṛṣṇa says:

शक्नोति इहैव यः सोढुं प्राक् शरीर विमोक्षणात् ।
कामक्रोधोद्भवं वेगं स युक्तः स सुखी नरः ॥२३॥

*Śaknoti ihaiva yaḥ soḍhum prāk śarīra vimokṣaṇāt;*
*Kāmakrodhodbhavam vegam sa yuktaḥ sa sukhī naraḥ* —*5. 23*

'One who can withstand in this life, before the liberation from the body, the current arising from lust and anger, he or she is a *yogī*, he or she is a happy human being.'

A remarkable verse. *Śaknoti*, 'whoever is capable', *ihaiva*, 'in this very life', in this very body, not in some heaven; *soḍhum*, 'to withstand'. What do you withstand? *Vegam*, 'the tremendous current'. What kind of current? *Kāmakrodhodbhavam*, 'arising from *kāma* and *krodha*', sensory craving as well as anger. These are powerful forces which can take you off your feet; it can destroy a whole life. That is the nature of this current. Therefore, 'those people who can withstand this tremendous current of *kāma* and *krodha* here, in this very life, before the death of this body', *śaknoti ihaiva yaḥ soḍhum prāk śarīra-vimokṣaṇāt*. After death nothing can be done. Only before death we can achieve this. *Prāk* means 'before'. *Śarīravimokṣaṇa* means 'liberation from the body'. The *Gītā* asks all human beings to realize their own inner possibilities and learn to be free, learn to withstand all these various currents within us. What is the achievement thereby? *Sa yuktaḥ*, 'he or she is a *yogī*', *sa sukhī naraḥ*, 'he or she is a happy human being'. If happiness is to be sought after, you have to achieve this particular strength to withstand the currents that take us this way, that way, making us mere slaves of various forces acting within ourselves. Where is freedom? And where is happiness? 'Without tranquillity within, where is happiness?', *aśāntasya kutaḥ śukham?* Śrī Kṛṣṇa had said this in the second chapter of the *Gītā*.

Where is happiness for the mind that has not become peaceful and tranquil, which is shaken all the time like a wind blowing across a forest of trees, and trees are falling down here, there, everywhere? That kind of human life, how poor it is! But there is also the well-rooted tree; winds blow, but it can stand. If it is rooted in the surface, quickly it falls down. A similar teaching of Jesus we discussed a few pages earlier. So, there is such a thing as getting rooted in the truth that is hidden within us. That life is steady, that life is strong; we will see that person absolutely calm and steady even in difficult circumstances. Wherefrom does he or she get that energy? From a deeper level, from one's own true nature. And so, in this *śloka*, Śrī Kṛṣṇa tells us: *Śaknoti ihaiva yaḥ soḍhum prāk śarīra vimokṣaṇāt;* that is a wonderful expression. Much of religion promises only post-mortem achievements. That kind of religion has no place in the *Gītā*. It is all *ihaiva, ihaiva,* 'here itself, here itself'. Youthful energy has to be disciplined to rise to higher levels; energy is less and less in old age. If water flows in a river, you can put a dam, create a big lake, make hydel channels for electricity generation as well as agriculture; but if there is no water in the river, what is the use of putting a dam? And so, in old age, there is no energy. In youth there is energy. It is then that we need this tremendous channelization of human energy. First, to serve other human beings; second, to achieve spiritual growth and fulfilment.

*This is the picture of human development and fulfilment that the Gītā presents to all humanity*. When one is young, if that energy goes on pushing him or her here and there, making the person do bad things, anti-social things, then that way human life becomes very miserable, a tragedy. The human being has to discipline oneself to increase the quality and direction of his or her energy. The river needs disciplining by human beings; the river cannot discipline itself. It flows on. And when there is a flood, it destroys houses, destroys fields, destroys harvest, it brings so much calamity to humanity. So, the human being knows how to control rivers, which were wild before, and produce electricity and do irrigation. The same thing a human being must do with one's own energy system and one has to do it by oneself. In the verse, these two words, *kāma* and *krodha,* are used. Actually, there are six items; they are called the six enemies of human beings when unrestrained, and I have described them in the third chapter. They are called *ṣaḍripu* in Sanskrit. *Ripu* means enemy. *Ṣaḍ* means six. Six enemies of man; nowhere outside, all within. First is *kāma,* unrestrained lust; second is *krodha,* anger; then greed, *lobha;* then *moha,* delusion; *mada,* arrogance or pride; *mātsarya,* jealousy. These are the six enemies which are lodged in everyone of us. We have to handle them, make them friendly. They are all energies, and energies can be enemies or processed to become friends. Human animal energy needs a little purification, refinement, through self-discipline. Then something greater will come out of the individual. So, when this is achieved, *sa yuktaḥ sa sukhī naraḥ,* 'that person is a *yogī* and a happy one'. How much do farmers living near rivers suffer! Water comes up to the level of the house. All agriculture is destroyed, bringing so much suffering. Then comes a government project for channelizing all this energy into agriculture and electricity. It is then that you will find the people there happy! *Sa yuktaḥ sa sukhī naraḥ.* The same thing is our case also. We want to become *sukhī,* happy; we want to become *yuktaḥ,* spiritually disciplined. By this same method only this can happen. If we become subject to these pressures, we are blown away by those currents. Where are we then? We are lost in the crowd as it were.

Human literature is full of examples of men and women who have been blown away by these inner currents, by the six enemies lurking in every human being. What you call tragedy in literature comes from this particular source. And tragedies are beautiful to see in a drama, in a theatre, but terrible to experience oneself. Never forget, tragedy is not meant to be experienced. You can enjoy it in representation. You should not make your life a tragedy. And so, there is one famous dramatist and poet who has expressed his views on this question just like the *Gītā* has done in this chapter. That is the German poet Goethe in his book, *Faust*. I have mentioned this in the earlier part of this book where this idea came. Echoes of these ideas of the *Gītā* appear in such Western literature; in Browning, Shelley, in all these British poets including Tennyson and Wordsworth, and in the European continent Goethe and some others. These ideas had started moving from East to West and this process has been intensified since then.

So, in this way, in day-to-day life, we experience these things, and every minute we are subjected to these emotional energies within us, *kāma, krodha, lobha, moha, mada, mātsarya*. We have to handle them, and we have to do it ourselves. Nobody else can do it for us. Once attained, you will be happy and fulfilled, *sa yuktaḥ sa sukhī naraḥ*. Now, this is what we have to try and achieve by our efforts. Śrī Kṛṣṇa is giving us this insight. When we are sitting quiet, we must think of that. Here is a tremendous gush of energy coming, the energy of hatred. I must withstand it. Similarly, greed. It comes; left to itself it will go on up and up. But if you know how to check it, then you become the master of the situation. Thus you cease to be carried away by these six currents arising from within.

Even ambition, for example, can be a current; if you withstand it at a particular level, you will have achieved great things. But if you yield to that current of ambition, you lose everything. The story of Napoleon and Hitler is very important in this connection. If Napoleon had stopped Spanish wars in 1808, and had never gone to the invasion of Russia, he would have built up a stable united democratic Europe. Unlike Hitler, he had great ideas also. But his unchecked ambition failed him, and he had to die as a prisoner of Britain in St. Helena! In Hitler's case also you can see the same thing. Unchecked ambition destroyed him after he had inflicted great harm to his own people and the Jewish community. All unchecked ambition takes away our judgement, and we get destroyed. Here you can see, the self destroying the self, one becoming one's own enemy, as this *Gītā* will tell us in the beginning of the sixth chapter.

That is why we are asked to deal courageously with these tremendous forces lodged within each of us. We have to discipline and refine them *by ourselves*. That is how we become men and women of high character. What a beautiful society will be created, when men and women will do this kind of work themselves and build up beautiful characters with love and concern for others.

Śaṅkarācārya repeats it again and again in his *Viveka-cūḍāmaṇi* (verse 52):

*Mastaka nyasta bhārādeḥ duḥkham anyaiḥ nivāryate;*
*Kṣudhādi kṛta duḥkham tu vinā svena na kenacit —*

'If you are carrying a heavy burden on your head, somebody else can help you to remove it and give some relief. But, if you are hungry, nobody can relieve you by eating on your behalf. You must eat for yourself.'

Similarly he further adds in verse 54:

*Vastu svarūpam sphuṭabodha cakṣuṣā*
*svenaiva vedyam na tu paṇḍitena;*
*Candra svarūpam nija cakṣuṣaiva*
*jñātavyam anyair avagamyate kim —*

'The nature of truth must be realized by each person by one's own clear eye of knowledge, just like the rising full moon which each must see by oneself. Can somebody's description of it satisfy him or her?'

So, this kind of experience is what Vedanta stresses—experience of this higher life. It is possible for you to do so, if you know the technique of it. But experience it; don't merely talk about it; don't merely read about it. This is stressed in this *śloka* 23 of this chapter. It conveys a profound meaning for men and women today all over the world. We are having so many young people today, without any inner discipline, but plenty of animal energy, and you can see what happens in various fields. How quickly the rowdy element in the human being comes into the picture. All football and international games are getting spoiled today by a lot of youthful rowdy energy. Think of that unfortunate event that took place in Belgium when the British football players came and did tremendous havoc. So also in Germany. In India itself, plenty of such instances are coming on. And even our politics has become a playground of rowdyism. A democracy cannot function at its best if it is based on such people. If this energy is not diverted to higher purposes, democracy will suffer terribly. It is a warning for all of us. Everywhere you will find plenty of animal energy. But the whole thing is going to waste, destroying the peace of the people. That is what is happening today in society and in politics. Such things should not happen. You must listen to the great teachers who loved humanity, who will be giving us something that we *can* practise from our own level. There is nothing impossible in what they say. And what they say is quite sound and rational, dealing with a knowledge of the human being in depth, then placing before you this picture of a peaceful life, a fulfilled life. *Sa yuktaḥ sa sukhī naraḥ,* 'such a person is a *yogī* and a happy person'. That is why Śrī Kṛṣṇa puts it so beautifully. We have to withstand these currents in which thousands of lives are brought low everyday weakening many societies thereby. When you study Roman history as given by Gibbon, when the decaying process started from the second century onwards, you will find human character going down and down. The whole of the Roman system became subjected to the pressures of the external world, consumerist mania became high. The result was so much suffering for the whole population. Even Roman emperors became tools in the hands of the military soldiers. To please them, they had to pay special donations to them. Human taste became crude. Violent sports of animals killing human prisoners became attractive to Roman gentlemen and ladies. That is how the decay started in the Roman empire. Another two centuries it went on going down and down, limping as it were, and finally, the whole civilization decayed and died. The end of a civilization is marked by men and women being carried away by the strong emotional current from within, consisting of *kāma, krodha,* and the four other evils. This should be recognized and attended to. When you attend to it, you develop a healthy civilization, a healthy stable society. Today, we have to turn back to this kind of teaching to make India a progressive democratic order. That is the challenge before us. *As I often express the idea, we have plenty of maladies, but we are fortunate, we have also remedies to remove the maladies.* Apply the remedy, the malady goes. That is the situation with respect to our and of some other countries today. The next verse, verse 24, is a very beautiful continuation of the same idea.

योऽन्तः सुखोऽन्तरारामः तथाऽन्तर्ज्योतिरेव यः ।
स योगी ब्रह्मनिर्वाणं ब्रह्मभूतोऽधिगच्छति ॥२४॥

*Yo'ntaḥ sukho'ntarārāmaḥ tathā'ntarjyotireva yaḥ;*
*Sa yogī brahmanirvāṇam brahmabhūto'dhigacchati* —5. 24

'Whose happiness is within, whose relaxation is within, whose light is within, that *yogi* alone, becoming Brahman, gains absolute freedom in Brahman.'

That *yogi* achieves *brahma nirvāṇam,* 'complete realization of Brahman'; *brahmabhūtaḥ,* 'becoming one with Brahman'. What kind of *yogī? Yo'antaḥ sukho,* 'whose happiness is within'. He or she doesn't depend on anything external for his or her happiness. When we are children, we depend entirely upon external things for our happiness. When we become mature and more mature, that dependence becomes less and less. But in this case of the *yogī,* he or she becomes absolutely free. No dependence on any external factors. That is called freedom. Freedom means non-dependence on external factors. That is the truth of things. Says the *Manu Smṛti* (4. 160):

*Sarvam paravaśam duḥkham sarvam ātmavaśam sukham;*
*Iti vidyāt samāsena svarūpam sukhaduḥkhayoḥ* —

'Everything that makes you dependent on external factors is unhappiness; everything that makes you free from such dependence is real happiness. That is the nature of happiness and unhappiness; please understand in brief this truth.'

Any dependence on external factors is unhappiness. We want to overcome that. But mutual dependence is perfectly allowed; there is no actual dependence there. But more and more the stress should be—'I can do without it'. Such a person has found the Light of all lights within oneself, in the Atman, which is described in the *Muṇḍaka Upaniṣad* (II. ii. 9) as *jyotiṣām jyotiḥ*, 'the Light of all lights.' The *Kaṭha Upaniṣad* (II. ii. 15) also says, *tasya bhāsā sarvam idam vibhāti*, 'by Its light alone this whole manifested universe is lighted'. That is the Atman, a bit of that Light I have seen, therefore, I have become fully satisfied. That is the language. *Brahmabhūtaḥ*, 'one who realizes Brahman' becomes Brahman according to Vedanta (*Muṇḍaka Upaniṣad*, III. ii. 9): *Brahmavit brahmaiva bhavati*, 'the knower of Brahman verily becomes Brahman'. Knowledge and being are the same in the inner life of man. That is not possible in our external life. When you know a table, you don't become the table; but when you know you are pure, you become pure. When you know you are illumined, you are illumined. That is your true nature. By writing a book on purity, you won't become pure; you have to realize purity in yourself. *In all inner experiences, all knowing tends to being*, but not so in the external world. Verse 25 brings another important truth:

लभन्ते ब्रह्म निर्वाणं ऋषयः क्षीण कल्मषाः ।
छिन्न द्वैधा यतात्मानः सर्वभूत हिते रताः ॥ २५ ॥

*Labhante brahma nirvāṇam ṛsayaḥ kṣīṇa kalmaṣāḥ;*
*Chinna dvaidhā yatātmānaḥ sarvabhūta hite ratāḥ* —5. 25

'With imperfections exhausted, doubts dispelled, senses controlled, engaged in the good of all beings, the *ṛṣis* obtain absolute freedom in Brahman.'

*Labhante brahma nirvāṇam ṛṣayaḥ*, 'sages achieve *brahma-nirvāṇa*, oneness with Brahman'. What kind of *ṛṣayaḥ*? *Kṣīṇa kalmaṣāḥ*, 'whose sins and evils have been completely eliminated'. Then only can we realize our true nature. *Chinna dvaidhā*, 'one who has transcended the notion of duality'. The notion that things are separate from each other has gone away from him or her after realizing the basic oneness of everything in Brahman. *Yatātmānaḥ*, 'the person highly disciplined within'. Then, outwardly, *sarva bhūta hite ratāḥ*, 'interested in the happiness and welfare of all beings'. What a beautiful idea! When you achieve these things within, then your whole energy flows out in a positive form of bringing cheer and happiness to other people. How did a Mahatma Gandhi become a *Mahātmā?* All his energies flowed out to bring happiness and cheer to millions of other people. Today, in India, if we can achieve in our people even a fraction of this state, what great blessings will come! An administrator will say to oneself: 'Millions are starving; let me serve them. I am appointed by the government to look after the rural people in various forms. Let me make them happy.' For him or her to be able to say and do so, he or she must achieve a measure of this spiritual growth within themselves. If a measure of such growth comes, all our developmental plans will become successful. Without a little of that growth, all our developmental plans will become merely *garībi haṭāo* slogans, as we see everyday. All the money is wasted. No progress takes place.

So, this teaching is not merely for sages and saints. This is for everyone, so that, persons can get on to the road of their own spiritual development by taking one step, two steps, three steps, and so on, and bring happiness to millions. But some people may progress far and achieve very great heights; they are ones that are referred to here. *Labhante brahma nirvāṇam ṛṣayaḥ kṣīṇa kalmaṣāḥ; Chinnadvaidhā yatātmānaḥ sarva bhūta hite ratāḥ*. They are 'always interested to work for the welfare of all people', *sarvabhūta hiteratāḥ.* This is the state of mind that creates high character. A Gandhiji and a few others fall in this category. In small ways, there are thousands of people all over India who have this attitude. You don't see them in the open, but they are there. They are not entirely absent in our society or in any other society. But it must become an educational programme to put all our people on that road to total human development. That is real education. Swami Vivekananda calls it man-making, nation-building education and religion. What a beautiful concept of education! Through their words, we build up the life of the people. Banishing poverty, ignorance, exploitation, creating justice in society; how do you do so? From your heart comes an energy that flows in a man-ward direction, because it has already gone in a God-ward direction within. Now it gets a man-ward direction. These are the two directions of human energy. *Gītā* combines both of them. A God-ward energy is turned into a man-ward direction. Thus one becomes a blessing to humanity. That is the language of this particular concept: *sarvabhūtahite ratāḥ*. They are 'interested in working for the welfare and happiness of all people', irrespective of caste, creed, or gender. The next *śloka*, and whatever *ślokas* come later, are wonderful.

**काम क्रोध वियुक्तानां यतीनां यत चेतसाम् ।**
**अभितो ब्रह्म निवाणं वर्तते विदितात्मनाम् ॥ २६ ॥**

*Kāma krodha viyuktānām yatīnām yata cetasām;*
*Abhito brahma nirvāṇam vartate viditātmanām — 5. 26*

'Released from lust and anger, the heart well controlled, the Self realized, absolute freedom is for such spiritually disciplined people, both here and hereafter.'

*Kāma krodha viyuktānām,* 'those who are free form *kāma* and *krodha*'; *yatīnām,* 'to spiritually disciplined people'; *yata cetasām,* 'whose mind is fully under control'; to such people, *abhito brahmanirvāṇam vartate,* 'this unity with Brahman is an accomplished experience'. Such a person need not sit in meditation to get this kind of experience. Twenty-four hours, while dealing with human beings, dealing with administration, dealing with politics, dealing with business, he or she will be in Brahman. *Viditātmanām,* 'to one who has realized the Atman'. Therefore, their life is completely transformed *here and now.* That is the great statement here. That word *abhito* is very important. Every minute, whether you are alone, or in company, in meditation or in work, such a one is always in that atmosphere of Brahman. *Abhito brahmanirvāṇam vartate viditātmanām,* he or she has realized the infinite Atman or

Brahman in you, in me, in all of us. And therefore, they are able to work for the happiness and welfare of all people. That is a great ideal of work which the *Gītā* places before us: work for the good of all, for the happiness of all. *Bhagavān* Buddha proclaimed that idea when he started his preaching: *Bahujana hitāya, bahujana sukhāya,* 'for the happiness of the many, for the welfare of the many'. That is a great emphasis in the *Gītā*. The welfare of all, not merely of one person or of a small group. *Sarva bhūta hite ratāḥ* is the language. Then, in two verses Śrī Kṛṣṇa speaks of meditation. A little inwardness is needed to deal with all these problems of inner life.

स्पर्शान् कृत्वा बहिर्बाह्यान् चक्षुश्चैवान्तरे भ्रुवोः ।
प्राणापानौ समौ कृत्वा नासाभ्यन्तरचारिणौ ॥ २७ ॥

यतेन्द्रियमनोबुद्धिः मुनिः मोक्षपरायणः ।
विगतेच्छाभयक्रोधो यः सदा मुक्त एव सः ॥ २८ ॥

*Sparśān kṛtvā bahirbāhyān cakṣuścaivāntare bhruvoḥ;*
*Prāṇāpānau samo kṛtvā nāsābhyantaracāriṇau* — 5. 27

*Yatendriyamanobuddhiḥ muniḥ mokṣaparāyaṇaḥ;*
*Vigatecchābhayakrodho yaḥ sadā mukta eva saḥ* — 5. 28

'Shutting out contact with external objects; steadying the eyes between the eyebrows, restricting the even currents of *Prāṇa* and *Apāna* inside the nostrils; the senses, mind, and intellect controlled; with *mokṣa* or spiritual liberation as the supreme goal; freed from sensory desire, fear, and anger: such a person is verily free forever.'

Two verses compressing the whole subject of meditation, which provides an introduction to the next chapter which is called the *Dhyana Yoga* chapter, 'Meditation Chapter'. So, what is given in a nutshell here, becomes expanded in more detail in the next chapter. *Sparśān kṛtvā bahiḥ bāhyān,* 'shutting out all contacts with external objects'; when you sit in meditation, the sensory system is not expected to function; we take leave of them; they are of no use to you in this inner life. In the outer life, they are fully useful. So, the first thing we do is to take leave of the entire sensory system. They are of no use to me there. They can't reveal any truth of inner life. They can reveal only the changeable universe around you. *Cakṣuś-caivāntare bhruvoḥ,* 'steadying the eyes between the eyebrows'. Though not very necessary, it is just mentioned here: 'the two eyeballs come close together and meet at the centre of the two nostrils'; that is an indication of a concentrated state. Generally, we close the eyes. That is the best thing, because the eye is a sense organ disturbed by visual objects which disturb meditation. That is what every psychologist will tell, that something striking the eye can disturb the mind much more than striking the skin. Therefore, closing the eye is the early standard technique in meditation. Then, *prāṇāpānau samo kṛtvā,* 'breathing evenly *prāṇa* and *apāna* in the system'. *Nāsābhyantaracāriṇau,* 'moving within the nose'; it is the discipline of breathing to make for calmness of mind. Then, *yatendriya mano buddhiḥ,* 'the senses, the *manas* and the *buddhi* well disciplined'; *muniḥ mokṣaparāyaṇaḥ,* 'the sage, the *sādhaka,* the silent seeker, in search of spiritual liberation'; 'I don't want to remain a creature,' with that attitude the seeker is engaging oneself in this discipline of meditation. *Vigatecchābhayakrodho,* 'who has completely given up *icchā, bhaya, krodha,* desire, fear, and anger'. These three are very strong emotions. They can destroy one's life, and bring unhappiness to many others; the *Gītā* has referred to these three together. *Icchā, bhaya, krodha. Vigata* means without or free from. *Yaḥ sadā mukta eva saḥ,* 'such a person is always spiritually free'.

This is how meditation takes you into some inner development and that gives you that wonderful freedom which mere external life cannot give. This meditation, at every step, will have its happy repercussions in our external life, in our human relations, in our dealing with our human problems. The deeper we go, the better will be our external life, external work, external inter-human relation. So, this *yogī,* this *muni,* has given to oneself this discipline, and therefore 'he is ever free'. *Sadā mukta eva saḥ,* 'he or she is ever free'; that is an ideal. We are far away from it. But we can enter on that path, and go one step, two steps, three steps, as one develops one's capacity.

It is difficult, but it is not impossible. The next chapter will deal more with these problems of meditation, how difficult it is and all that. Arjuna will ask on our behalf, and Śrī Kṛṣṇa will answer.

During his lecture in a town of the west coast of America, Swami Vivekananda referred to the subject of meditation in a marvellous passage (*Complete Works of Swami Vivekananda,* vol. V, p. 253):

'Meditation is the one thing. Meditate! The greatest thing is meditation. It is the nearest approach to spiritual life—the mind meditating. It is the one moment in our daily life that we are not at all material—the Soul thinking of Itself, free from all matter—this marvellous touch of the Soul!'

We have now the last verse of the fifth chapter, verse 29, a very remarkable verse from the spiritual point of view. The verse says:

भोक्तारं यज्ञतपसां सर्व लोक महेश्वरम् ।
सुहृदं सर्वभूतानां ज्ञात्वा मां शान्तिमृच्छति ॥२९॥

*Bhoktāram yajñatapasām sarva loka maheśvaram;*
*Suhṛdam sarvabhūtānām jñātvā mām śāntimṛcchati —5. 29*

'Knowing Me as the receiver and dispenser of (the fruits of) sacrifices and spiritual practices, as the great Lord of all the worlds, and as the friend of all beings, one attains Peace.'

Śri Krsna is telling this as the Incarnation of the Divine, about which he had said in the fourth chapter. Know Me as *bhoktāram yajña tapasām,* 'receiver and dispenser of the fruits of whatever sacrifices and spiritual austerities are done'; ultimately these reach him, the one ultimate Reality. *Sarva loka maheśvaram,* 'the Lord of all this universe', the one infinite Divine behind this universe. Similarly, a third characteristic which is the most important, *suhṛdam sarvabhūtānām,* 'the *friend* of all beings'. God is described here as the friend of all beings. No cause for fear. The god of fear vanished from Indian religion long long ago. In its place came the God of love, and therefore, Śrī Kṛṣṇa said, 'I am the friend of all.' Knowing Me as such, a person attains Peace. That is the last line.

This is a very beautiful verse centred in *Bhakti* or pure Love; *bhakti* to the personal aspect of the Impersonal-personal God of Vedanta. This *bhakti* will become the theme of the seventh and other chapters. It has just come as an introduction here. 'Know Me as the friend of all beings'. What a beautiful conception! We are limited in power, limited in our energies, but there is one unlimited Energy behind us. We can always draw upon that Energy. Just like a small bank, if too many people rush to that bank to withdraw their deposits, the bank will fail. But, if it has the Reserve Bank behind it, it has nothing to fear. Similarly, in our human life, with all our weaknesses, if we have that intense faith that there is an infinite Reality behind this universe, behind me, closest to me, and is my friend, my own inner Self, ever ready to help me, we can get peace and freedom from tension.

In this world of tension, today, we have to, as one of the Western writers said, 'if there is no god, we have to invent one.' He is needed today. Have that tremendous faith in the Divine, but here you have not to invent. Our philosophy tells you there is a reality behind this changing universe. It is a *vastu,* a Reality. He is our own Self, the Self of all beings. That is our true nature. *Tattvamasi, tattvamasi* means that. You are That. Now, that truth is dawning on the minds of many more scientists today. Great thinkers, they feel that they cannot explain this universe without reference to an ultimate principle of consciousness. That is coming more and more into modern thought. It will lead them to what Vedanta has described as that *Saccidānanda Svarūpa paramātman,* the infinite Self, of the nature of Existence, Knowledge and Bliss, absolute. Whatever bliss we enjoy, is only a particle of the bliss of the Divine. That is infinite in dimension. And so we can participate in the life divine, and by doing so, we enrich ourselves. We become better and better.

Today, the stress is therefore on how to get qualitatively richer within. Quantity has been the whole theme of modern scientific thought and modern industrial civilization. Now there is a great need expressed by great thinkers in the West to bring in the concept of quality. What is the quality of your life? Are you peaceful? Are you happy? Can you live peacefully with others without strife, without tension? All these questions of quality are becoming more and more prominent, and it is that quality aspect that comes by believing in this divine Reality behind the universe, who is a divine Person, and because you are a person, God appears to you as a Person. And He can respond. So, in philosophy, we speak of an *ultimate* Reality. But in spiritual life, we speak of an *intimate* Reality. That is ultimate, this is intimate. *Bhakti* makes this Divine Reality intimate to us. He is one with us. He is not far away. He is here.

In the Upaniṣads, this language is used; enigmatic, paradoxical language. God is far away, God is near, nearest of the near; He is small, He is big; all this language you will find. Beyond the limitation of space, no language of big and small, distant or near, can stand with regard to that Reality, because it is only within spatial limitation that we can use these expressions. He is beyond space and time, the Infinite, the Immortal. That is our true nature. He is the Self of our self. He is the thread that runs through all of us, like the thread that unites a garland of flowers. That language Śrī Kṛṣṇa is using in the seventh chapter, that He is the thread that unites all beings into a unity. The more you touch that thread, the more firm, the more strong, the more peaceful, you will be. *Mayi sarvam idam protam sūtre maṇigaṇā iva;* we shall study this in the coming chapters. 'All this universe is threaded in Me like so many pearls in one garland'. Pearls are different, but they become one in the garland, because of the thread. That thread of Being is the Divine in me, in all.

Based upon this, this chapter, the fifth chapter, spoke of the feeling of equality. We are all equal. Brahman is equal, we are also equal. The presence of Brahman in you and in me, in the highest and the lowest, is always a unit; there is no fraction of the unit. Therefore, equality is the great ideal of human progress and development, based upon seeing the same Divine in all its fullness in every being. We have already expressed that idea in verses 18 and 19; idea of *samam, samatva*, the feeling of equality, of sameness, we are one, we are one, we are one. The senses reveal differences, but deep down, when you begin to think and investigate, you see unity. Live in that awareness. It is that idea that Śrī Kṛṣṇa expresses here again as God who is the friend of all. He is our own inner Self, nearer to us than anything else. There is a sentence in the *Koran*, where Prophet Mohammad says, 'God is nearer to you than the veins in your neck.' So near to us is He. That is the concept of the divine in great philosophies and religions. So, in the fifth chapter, you find the whole teaching ending with this wonderful note of assurance:

*Bhoktāram yajñatapasām sarvalokamaheśvaram;*
*Suhṛdam sarvabhūtānām jñātvā mām śāntimṛcchati —*

**इति संन्यास योगो नाम पञ्चमोऽध्यायः ।**
*Iti Sannyāsa yogo nāma pañcamo'dhyāyaḥ —*

The end of the fifth chapter, designated, *The Yoga of Renunciation.*

# BHAGAVAD GĪTĀ

## CHAPTER 6

## DHYĀNA-YOGA
## THE YOGA OF MEDITATION

The sixth chapter, as I said, is called *Dhyāna Yoga* chapter, 'Chapter on the *Yoga* of *Dhyāna*, Meditation'. In spiritual life, we need a certain training to achieve *samatva,* the sense of equality. One such training is meditation; the other is working with people in a spirit of harmony or co-operation; the third is inner life, by which you discipline your mental energies, and make the mind realize the divine that is within, by going closer and closer to it by inward penetration. Meditation depends upon this capacity for that inward penetration being developed. And so, when we enter into the sixth chapter, we have the very opening verses dealing with spiritual life; and a few verses later, the technique of meditation is expounded in a series of beautiful verses. Here it says in the very opening verse:

**श्रीभगवान् उवाच –**

*Śrībhagavān uvāca —*

*'The Blessed Lord said:'*

**अनाश्रितः कर्मफलं कार्यं कर्म करोति यः ।**
**स संन्यासी च योगी च न निरग्निर्न चाक्रियः ॥१॥**

*Anāśritaḥ karmaphalam kāryam karma karoti yaḥ;*
*Sa sannyāsī ca yogī ca na niragnir-na cākriyaḥ —* 6. 1

'One who performs one's bounden duty without depending upon the fruit of action—he or she is a renouncer of action as well as one of steadfast mind; not one who does not handle fire, nor one who is without action.'

In the very first *śloka* Śrī Kṛṣṇa tells us about 'who is a *yogī,* who is a true *sannyāsi,* or renouncer'. He is asking that question and giving the answer: *anāśritaḥ karmaphalam kāryam karma karoti yaḥ,* 'whoever does his or her duties, without expecting to get the fruits for oneself'—that is the attitude. The whole teaching of the *Gītā* is based upon the spirit of non-attachment—*anāsakti*—don't depend upon the fruits of the actions; it belongs to all, not only to you. So, *anāśritaḥ karmaphalam kāryam karma karoti yaḥ*, implies: you do what is to be done, in a spirit of dedication. The little 'I' is no more in the picture. The deeper 'I', which is one with all, is slowly being manifested. Therefore, we are able to renounce the fruits of actions coming to oneself—'we don't need it hereafter'. That attitude, *anāśritaḥ karmaphalam kāryam karma karoti yaḥ; sa sannyāsī ca yogī ca,* 'that person is a true *sannyāsi*, a true *yogī,* a man of true renunciation, a person of *yoga* in truth'*; na niragniḥ na cākriyaḥ,* 'and not those who undergo a *sannyāsa* ritually'. That is the meaning of *niragniḥ,* 'one who does not cook one's food in one's own fire-place'. Householders light a fire to use for worship, as well as for cooking. A *sannyāsin* doesn't cook for oneself, and so he or she is called *niragniḥ;* whatever food he or she gets by begging, he or she is satisfied with that; so, in Sanskrit we call him or her *niragniḥ*. But a mere *niragniḥ,* who doesn't touch fire or utilize the fire by himself or herself, doesn't make one a *sannyāsin;* but, that person who performs actions without attachment to the fruits is a real *sannyāsin. Na cākriyaḥ,* 'nor one who is without action'.

Why do we do anything? Because of the unfulfilled desire; therefore, we have to do. Desire impels us to do. When your desire is transcended, you have nothing to do; therefore, non-doing has become a characteristic of a highly spiritual person. But, giving up of activities is no high spirituality at all. So, that way you don't become a *yogī* or *sannyāsin. Na niragniḥ na cākriyaḥ. Kriyaḥ* means 'action'. Action is prompted by desire; first desire, then urge, and then action.

In psychology, you read that at first some desires arise in your mind. That becomes strong and becomes an urge. That impels you to action, and you receive the fruit of action, and the desire dies away. Then another desire comes up. In this way, the root of all actions is desire. This has been studied in the *Manu Smṛti* (2. 4):

*Akāmasya kriyā kācit dṛśyate neha karhicit;*
*Yad yad hi kurute kiñcit tat tat kāmasya ceṣṭitam—*

'There is no action for one who is desireless; whatever a person does, that is a product of a prior desire.'

And non-desire is of two types. One is of the ignorant person, the lazy person, who has no particular desire; the other is of the man or woman who has gone beyond all duality and become spiritually free. These are the two types of desirelessness. In most societies, especially in India, desirelessness is not a good quality. We want a little desire in people. 'Why should I live in dirt? Let me make life better and better.' That desire must be there. Only with that desire will people get education, improve their surroundings. And without that desire, none of these can come. So, what we want to do is to create desire in our people for a better life, more of sanitation, more of education, more of public service activities, religious life, etc. So, desire is to be induced in them. The desirelessness which you find in most of such people is not of a high type. But when you have achieved the knowledge of Atman, the knowledge of God, then you become desireless in a higher sense. You don't need anything; your mind doesn't go out at all. If it goes out, it is only to bless somebody, to help somebody, and for nothing else. That idea comes in the *Gītā* in several places (5. 25; 12. 4)—*sarva bhūta hite ratāḥ*, 'always interested to bring happiness and welfare to all people', that is the highest form of desirelessness. We want a human being to have desires so that he or she can make his or her quality of life better and better, and not remain in what you call a dismal life. So, have some desire for betterment. Today, we have to invoke such a desire in our people. But, the same desire will cease to operate once you achieve higher and higher development in the spiritual field—so we call it *akāmaḥ,* absolutely no *kāma*. So, *akāmaḥ* exists in two dimensions. One is the ordinary dimension, full of ignorance, delusion and laziness; the other is the *sāttvika* type of *akāmaḥ,* beyond these cravings for this or that, because one has realized the Atman. What more do you need? What can compare with God? If you get God, everything else is secondary and has absolutely no value. In many of the statements of the mystics all over the world—Christian, Sufi, Buddhist and others—you'll find the idea, 'I have got the most precious thing in the world, the Divine itself. I don't depend upon anything else.' Such a state is a state of desirelessness, and yet whatever desire is there in such persons is only to serve people, to make their life better and better. All great people belong to this category.

This idea is carried further in the next verse, a very important verse:

यं संन्यासमिति प्राहुर्योगं तं विद्धि पाण्डव ।
न ह्यसंन्यस्तसङ्कल्पो योगी भवति कश्चन ॥ २ ॥

*Yam sannyāsamiti prāhuḥ yogam tam viddhi pāṇḍava;*
*Na hyasannyasta saṅkalpo yogī bhavati kaścana* — 6. 2

'Know that to be devotion to *yoga* of action which is called renunciation, O Pāṇdava; for none becomes a *yogī* of action without renouncing *saṅkalpa*.'

'That thing what is called *sannyāsa*, the same thing is *yoga.*' *Yam sannyāsam iti prāhuḥ yogam tam viddhi pāṇḍava.* Not the mere giving up of this or that is *sannyāsa*. True *sannyāsa* and true *yoga* are one and the same thing. *Hi asannyasta saṅkalpo,* 'if you don't give up your *saṅkalpa*'; *na yogī bhavati kaścana,* 'you cannot become a *yogī*', or a *sannyāsi. Saṅkalpa* means the outgoing desire, 'I must have this, I must have that', endlessly going on, what I referred to earlier as the 'consumerist mania' of modern civilization. The mind is constantly formulating, 'I want this, I want that', that is called *saṅkalpa*. *Saṅkalpa* is the root of all desires. All desires come from *saṅkalpa*. In the *Mahābhārata* (Critical Edition: *Śāntiparva,* 171. 25) there is a wonderful story, towards the end of which, the man, who is the central figure of that story, says:

*Kāma jānāmi te mūlam saṅkalpāt kila jāyase;*
*Na tvām saṅkalpayiṣyāmi samūlo na bhaviṣyasi—*

'O, now I have understood. O desire, you are born of *saṅkalpa*. I shall not have *saṅkalpa*; then you'll not come and trouble me at all.'

So, *saṅkalpa* leads to desire, desire leads to various types of activity, including the delusive life we live very often in society which has been well portrayed by the German poet and dramatist Goethe in his book, *The Faust:*

'from desire I stumble to possession,
and in possession languish from desire.'

That is a wonderful passage in that famous drama.

So, whenever we are full of these *saṅkalpas*, we can't control them, we can't regulate them, we become slaves to them and they pull us this way and that way. And when you get something, you want something more; when you are not granted more, then you become unhappy. In this way, a human being is never fulfilled by running after things or expressing *saṅkalpa* through desires and desire-prompted activities. The only way is to divert some energy to something higher. That higher dimension is the spiritual development of the human being about which many Western scientists today are writing books. Number of books are coming out with the spiritual orientation of human life and human civilization.

And so, *na hyasannyasta saṅkalpo yogī bhavati kaścana*, 'you cannot become a *yogī* without giving up *saṅkalpa*'. That *sannyāsa* behind a *yogī*, is what makes him or her a *yogī*. *Saṅkalpa* is the thing which has to be controlled and disciplined. For example, how to stop this consumerist civilization from going in a wrong way. This consumerist mania must be controlled. This can be done by making a distinction between wants and needs: needs you fulfil, but check the wants; wants are endless. That is one great lesson we must learn; needs do not do any harm. We have forgotten the distinction between needs and wants. Everything is 'wants' now. All the 'wants' also become duly 'needs'. Therefore, the trouble has set in. I have earlier referred to wisdom that came to Yayāti, a great king in India who lived in the mythological ages, about five thousand years ago. He enjoyed a long life full of desires and their satisfactions, and, when he began to think about it, he found out this truth (*Śrīmad Bhāgavatam,* IX. 19.14):

*Na jātu kāmaḥ kāmānām upabhogena śāmyati;*
*Haviṣā kṛṣṇa vartmeva bhūya eva abhivardhate —*

'Desire is not quenched by satisfying the desire; it only gets inflamed like fire into which butter is poured (to put it out).' That is the language he has used there.

Just after the Second World War, as I have referred to earlier, a Hoover Committee commission was appointed to study the 'recent' economic trends in the United States. In the report of that Commission occurs this sentence:

'This inquiry has revealed that human desires are endless, that there are no new desires that will not make way for newer desires as soon as they are satisfied.'

Therefore, these endless desires go on and on, and, running behind them our lives become flimsy. It is just like the analogy found in our literature, of the donkey who makes the wheel in the oil mill go round and round. A little piece of carrot is held before it, and finding the carrot within its reach, the donkey tries to get it. That makes the donkey move, and the mill owner gets his work done through the donkey. But the donkey gets nothing! This human life is sometimes just like that. Running after this, running after that, and every day one becomes less and less as a human being. That is the result of consumerist mania. How to check it, how to divert it to higher levels? That question is central to all the discussions going on about human problems in modern civilization.

Vedanta discussed this subject ages ago and gave us some wisdom. It never said, 'don't enjoy'; it never said, 'don't satisfy your needs'; it said that, beyond a certain level, you should put a check on it, apply the brake. *Nivṛtti* is the word used for this; the other, running after things, is called *pravṛtti*. Putting a check on this craze of endless *pravṛtti* is called *niviṛtti*, 'withdrawal'—'I don't need it, I can do without it'. Only thinking people can take this stand, as they get a glimpse of transcendental spiritual life. But our thinking apparatus is very much affected today by television advertisements. As soon as you see an advertisement, you begin to feel you want this, you want that. Wants are *created* in you. Today, there is a protest in America by several writers against this work of the advertisers for getting people to purchase their goods, psychologically forcing them to purchase, as it were. And the advertisements being very costly, the price of that commodity is increased to pay for that advertisement! And you and I have to pay for it. We don't ordinarily know all these things. Slowly, you get to know that this is the situation: the more complicated the civilization, the less freedom men and women have to choose the things that one likes or needs. These are chosen for you by the advertisers concerned! So, these are the problems which we encounter in a consumerist society. What is the way out then?

We need a philosophy which sees men and women, not only as seekers of the sensory goods and satisfactions, but as seekers of higher values: music, art, ethical and moral values, spirituality; all these are part and parcel of human inheritance. We have the possibility within us to achieve all of them. Don't neglect them. Only concentrating on one level, the organic level, the sensory level, won't do. Never do that; you will suffer for it. That teaching has to come from the great philosophies and religions of the world. Vedanta prevails upon more and more people in this modern scientific age to take to this thinking.

Then we have a beautiful expression in the next verse:

आरुरुक्षोर्मुनेर्योगं कर्म कारणं उच्यते ।
योगारूढस्य तस्यैव शमः कारणं उच्यते ॥ ३ ॥

*Ārurukṣoḥ muneḥ yogam karma kāraṇam ucyate;*
*Yogārūḍhasya tasyaiva śamaḥ kāraṇam ucyate —* 6. 3

'For the person of meditation wishing to attain purification of heart leading to concentration, action is said to be the way. For such a person, when he or she has attained such (concentration), inaction is said to be the way.'

*Ārurukṣoḥ muneḥ yogam,* 'one who is striving to be a *yogī*'; he or she is striving; *ārurukṣoḥ* means 'desirous of climbing to'. *Karma kāraṇam ucyate,* 'action is said to be the means' to help him or her to climb to the high state of *yoga. Karma* or action has got a great role there: without doing something you can't climb to that state of *yoga*. But, *yoga ārūḍhasya tasyaiva,* 'for one who has achieved that *yoga*'; *yoga ārūḍha* means 'one who has already risen to the level of *yoga*'. Then what is that such a person will do? *Śamaḥ kāraṇam ucyate,* for him or her, 'inaction is the means'. He or she becomes perfectly inactive. All the commotion occurring within have vanished and absolute peace comes to the heart.

So, these are the two stages. At the time you are striving to be a *yogī,* you have to work hard. Once you become a *yogī,* all work ceases for you; you don't need anything; your mind doesn't go out at all—'I don't need, I don't need', that conviction comes to you because you have achieved something priceless in yourself.

Our philosophers never tell you to be dried-up ascetics. You give up something because you've got something better, something higher, something more valuable. And the highest value is spiritual realization. Complete fulfilment comes thereby and this fulfilment is the goal of human evolution, says 20th century biology—not organic satisfaction, not numerical increase, not physical survival—these are not the goal of human evolution. They were human goals according to 19th century biology, but in this century, due to great developments in science, men like Sir Julian Huxley presented this idea—the goal of human evolution is fulfilment. Are you fulfilled? If that is so, 'quality becomes enthroned over quantity', says Julian Huxley. Now, quality of your life and not quantity becomes a great criterion of evolution. Can you live at peace with yourself, with your husband, with your wife, with your friends? What a beautiful conception of quality! That is the goal of human evolution; through that only you become fulfilled. That fulfilment is considered the goal of evolution today. That is why Julian Huxley wanted physical sciences to develop into a higher science to deal with the subject of fulfilment, and he calls it *a science of human possibilities*. That is the exact status of India's ancient Vedanta—a science of human possibilities. All these possibilities are there in *every* human being; he or she can rise above tensions and become perfectly calm and steady. That possibility is there in you and me, says Vedanta.

The word *śamaḥ* means 'cessation of effort'—the heart is absolutely calm and quiet. When water in the lake is perfectly calm, without a single bubble or wave, that state is called *śama*. The mind is in that state of *śama*. That comes only when the sense of fulfilment comes to you. When you are truly fulfilled, you have that *śama* attitude. When you are hungry, you are full of tension within. Hunger makes you tense: 'I must eat, I must eat'; desire comes, activity comes. You cook, then you eat, then fulfilment comes. If thereafter somebody brings food, you say, 'No, I don't care, I'm full now, I'm absolutely fulfilled'. That is our daily experience, but it is only temporary. Philosophy and spirituality tell you that there is also a state of complete fulfilment when the mind will not run after anything else afterwards; that state is the realization of the Divine. That is the state of *yoga; yogārūḍha,* 'one who is well established in that state of *yoga*'. In a personality like Śrī Ramaṇa Maharṣi, for example, there is nothing to take him out of himself, except compassion; that compassion is always there. In a Buddha and a Jesus there was this tremendous compassion. With that compassion they spoke words which did so much good to people. Such persons are absolutely free, fulfilled persons: *kṛtārtha, kṛtakṛtya,* these are the words for fulfilment in Sanskrit.

So, this is the idea of *yogārūḍha*, 'rising to and being established in *yoga*'. The next *śloka*, verse 4, explains the nature of a *yogārūḍha*:

यदा हि नेन्द्रियार्थेषु न कर्मस्वनुषज्जते ।
सर्व संकल्प संन्यासी योगारूढः तदोच्यते ॥४॥

*Yadā hi nendriyārtheṣu na karmasvanuṣajjate;*
*Sarva saṅkalpa sannyāsī yogārūḍhaḥ tadocyate — 6. 4*

'Verily, when there is no attachment either to sense-objects or to actions, having renounced all *saṅkalpas*, then is one said to have risen to *yoga* state.'

A person is said to be a *yogārūḍhaḥ* when *na anuṣajjate*, 'he or she has not any interest'; *indriyārtheṣu*, 'in sensory objects'; *karmasu*, 'nor in actions' performed to appropriate those objects. Then *sarvasaṅkalpa sannyāsī*, 'a *sannyāsi* who has renounced all *saṅkalpas*'. Such a person is a *yogārūḍhaḥ*, 'one who has established himself or herself in the state of *yoga*'. This is a human possibility. You may not achieve it fully in one life, but it is good to go towards that even a little for getting at least a little joy out of this life, some real peace in this life of tension and struggle.

In the next two verses, verse 5 and verse 6, a great message comes from Śrī Kṛṣṇa to all people. These two verses are set in a beautiful language, and the sentiments expressed in these verses are sentiments which every father and mother can convey to their children. This is very important as you will see. Verse 5 says:

उद्धरेत् आत्मनात्मानं नात्मानं अवसादयेत् ।
आत्मैव ह्यात्मनो बन्धुरात्मैव रिपुरात्मनः ॥५॥

*Uddharet ātmanātmānam nātmānam avasādayet;*
*Ātmaiva hy-ātmano bandhur-ātmaiva ripur-ātmanaḥ—6. 5*

'Raise yourself by yourself; don't let yourself down, for you alone are your own friend, you alone are your own enemy.'

That is a wonderful utterance here. We always have the tendency to put our troubles as coming from somebody else.

And today, especially in modern civilization, this is a constant attitude of mind. Why am I like this? My father or mother was bad, or the society is bad, or God is bad. You put every blame on others, and assert inwardly that 'I am myself not responsible for anything.' As regards civilization, even children say today that, if anything is wrong with them, their parents are responsible. 'I have no responsibility, therefore, I can escape all blame.' As against it, it is good to have this new idea: *uddharet ātmanātmānam*, 'raise oneself by oneself'. Suppose you received some bad treatment when you were young. Well, you can overcome the bad effects. Have that positive attitude: 'raise oneself by oneself', and do not allow yourself to be jostled by others all the time. 'I had this misfortune; I have experienced it; now I have to overcome it. That strength is in me.' With that faith in oneself, those unhealthy ideas go away. Throwing the blame on everybody else! Why did you fail in the examination? Teachers did not teach! It is true these days in India, every teacher does not teach well; or the question paper was very heavy, and the questions were not covered by adequate teaching. All these answers are given, but there is also another answer, 'I did not study well.' That answer nobody gives. It is good for people to give that answer. 'I did not study well. I take the blame on myself. I shall correct myself.' That gives you strength; that gives you a sense of personal worth.

So, *na ātmānam avasādayet*, 'don't pull oneself down'. Why? *Ātmā eva hi ātmano bandhuḥ*, 'oneself is one's own friend', and, *ātmā eva ripuḥ ātmanaḥ*, 'oneself is also one's own enemy'. What a wonderful expression! *Ātmā eva hi ātmano bandhuḥ ātmā eva ripuḥ ātmanaḥ*. Verily true, 'I am my own friend, I am my own enemy.' Even if somebody troubles me, if I don't lodge it into my mind, it will not trouble me at all. If I take it, it will trouble me. So, my taking it, my accepting it, is responsible for this trouble. Don't take it. Try to keep it away from yourself. That strength we don't have. So, we are influenced by everything else. Hence, it is good to develop that inner strength. It is just like what we say in the medical language:

you may have a number of microbes around you which can cause disease in you, but if you are strong in physique, no disease will come to you, no microbe can do any harm to you. So, strengthen yourself. That is Śrī Kṛṣṇa's teaching.

When India was striving for political freedom, the first group of political leaders said, 'Please give us freedom as a gift.' Then came the real movement from Lokmanya Tilak of the Indian National Congress, who uttered that famous *mantra* 'Swaraj is my birthright. I shall have it.' It was that, when followed, which brought ultimately freedom to our country. Depend upon yourself, don't depend upon others. You are making yourself small by depending on others. Make yourself big in your own way. That is why it finally ended in Gandhiji's 'Quit India Movement' in 1942, and within five years the country became free.

So too, in personal life it is the same story. But then, we begin to question this idea: I can be my own friend, but how can *I* be my own enemy? My enemy must be somebody else! That is answered in the next verse.

बन्धुः आत्मात्मनः तस्य येन आत्मा एव आत्मना जितः ।
अनात्मनः तु शत्रुत्वे वर्तेत आत्मा एव शत्रुवत् ॥ ६ ॥

*Bandhuḥ ātmātmanaḥ tasya yena ātmā eva ātmanā jitaḥ;*
*Anātmanaḥ tu śatrutve varteta ātmā eva śatruvat* — 6. 6

'One becomes one's own friend when one has conquered oneself; but to the unconquered self, he or she is inimical, (and becomes) like (an external) enemy.'

These are all profound psychological insights embedded in these verses. When you discipline this sensory system, this psychic system, you develop great character-strength; then you become your own friend. But, the other way, *anātmanastu śatrutve*, 'when you leave the mind and the sensory energies to themselves, and you don't discipline them, you don't train them, then you become your own enemy'. This is the teaching.

How much it means to all of us in the development of character! Always complaining against others is not good. In fact, the complaining attitude is a very poor attitude for a human being, and many people have this complaining attitude: always complaining against this, against that, against that person or this situation, etc. And then comes resentment: resenting like this, 'O, this has been done.' I carry in my heart one resentment, a second resentment, and so on. I once read a sentence in an American journal, years ago; it said, 'blessed is the heart that doesn't collect resentments.' You go on collecting resentments from morning till evening. By the time you are forty or fifty, your heart is full of complaints, full of resentments. What has happened to you? You have become your own 'Enemy Number One'. Why did you collect those resentments and keep them within you? You could have just analysed them and thrown them away. So, who is your enemy? You yourself. Somebody abuses me and goes away. I take it in, I culture it in my system, and it makes me weak, it makes me depressed. That man is dead and gone; but, I am still cherishing the words he has thrown at me, because I took it in. Who is your enemy? You yourself. Because you didn't have any control over your mind, over your inner life.

You see children, for example. One child abuses another child. That child leaves and goes to its mother to complain. And we are like such children, constantly complaining about this, about that. Maturity has not come to us. Śrī Kṛṣṇa wants men and women to be psychically mature, that is, '*I* have to take the responsibility on myself; it is *my* responsibility.' When you do something wrong, for example, some punishment is given. 'Yes, I have done wrong, I take the punishment, there is nothing wrong in imparting that punishment to me.' That punishment may bring a trauma in the human mind is a modern fiction. From Freud onwards, such thinking has come. Any kind of punishment, even a scolding, can create trauma in the weak human mind; therefore, don't punish, don't scold. That is what has made the human mind very weak today. There is no need for it. 'Well, I have done wrong. I will pay for it. It is okay. The matter is over.' That is how inner strength comes from discipline. Such people alone can develop high character.

So, these two verses are important: *uddharet ātmanā ātmānam*—'raise yourself by yourself', because you are your own friend, you are your own enemy. How? When you discipline your own psychic and sensory energies within you, you become your own friend. If you don't do so, you become your own enemy.

If children bite their tongue, it pains them and they complain against their mother for if. If you have bitten your own tongue, lay the blame on yourself, don't lay it on somebody else. In this way, you have to build up your inner strength. The more you build up the inner strength, the less you will complain against others; the more you put blame on others, you become weaker and weaker. A little strength must come to the nation, to the people, by having faith in oneself. 'Yes, I have done it. I shall not do it again.' That's called manliness, a strong attitude. If I have done wrong, I have to pay for it by being punished; I am glad to pay the penalty.' It is not a mere theory; it can be implemented in life.

*Anātmanaḥ tu śatrutve varteta ātmaiva śatruvat*, 'don't become your own enemy by not handling this psychic energy packet that you have got'. Handle it, refine it, purify it, discipline it; then your whole system becomes your friend. Nothing can do harm to you.

Śrī Kṛṣṇa is introducing in these two verses this beautiful technique, 'raise yourself by yourself, don't let yourself down, for you are your own friend, you are your own enemy.' Those who can discipline their inner energies, they become their own friends. Those who do not do so, they become, as it were, their own enemy. So, don't be an enemy to yourself. That is the instruction Śrī Kṛṣṇa gives to all of us. This is how we build up our inner strength. And I personally feel that every child must be told, 'you are your own friend, you are your own enemy'. That will give them more and more inner strength. At present it is not there. Always the accusing finger points to somebody else. 'That person troubles me. This person or this child troubles me.' That must change, so that children develop their inner strength. If it is a very dangerous situation, if external things are very bad, you have to fight them, but for dealing with minor human interactions, in which you are often getting into trouble, you must find strength from within to withstand things yourself, and not become a *mimosa pudica* plant that breaks down at the slightest touch from outside. That should not be. *Mimosa pudica* is that plant which becomes half-dead if you blow at it; then again it comes back to life. It is a wonderfully sensitive plant. So, human beings should not be *mimosa pudica*. They must have some strength to stand the pressure that comes from outside. A child brought up at home, in familiar surroundings, when it goes to school or college, it sees a different world. So many pressures come upon the child. It must be able to withstand them and develop new strength. That is why we send children to school; they will be good-for-nothing if they stay only with intimate people at home. The wider world is there; they have to make their way in that situation also. What an amount of inner strength we need to stand the pressures that act on us in modern societies. The only solution is to strengthen yourself. Before you send the child out into the world, strengthen it, and that strength is, essentially, spiritual strength, not mere physical strength, not mere intellectual strength, but real spiritual strength. Children need some spiritual strength to understand the pressures of modern civilization. Without it, they can be simply consumed by civilization.

So, the *Bhagavad Gītā* tells every parent to give this teaching to one's children, boy or girl; before you go into the world, strengthen yourself. There are so many currents and cross-currents in this world. Children and youth will be washed away in that current. We don't want them to be washed away. We can enjoy the river if we know how to swim. If we are washed away by the river there is no fun in getting into the river. Modern society is like this. So, this teaching must be given to all children today, because the situation is getting more and more difficult day by day. In olden days, except on certain days, there was no such current outside. Today there is plenty of it. In five days a child can be completely ruined by the society outside. What is the remedy? The remedy is only here—*uddharet ātmanā ātmānam*, telling the child, 'stand on your own feet', develop strength, then you won't be carried away by whatever you experience. Develop a little spirit of discrimination. Through this inner discipline you develop tremendous strength in yourself, and that strength, as I said earlier, is not mere physical strength or even intellectual strength. A first class student can get into trouble much more quickly than a second class student. Intellectual strength is of no use here. Some awareness of the Divine spark that is within you can alone save you. Tell children of that awareness, that behind the body-mind complex there is a spark of the Divine. That is a source of infinite strength. 'Let me take recourse to a bit of that strength; then I can withstand the pressures outside.' If this kind of training is given to children, they will be able to withstand modern society's pressures; otherwise, forty to fifty per cent of children will be physically affected in the current of modern life.

So, this teaching of Śrī Kṛṣṇa is supremely significant for all children in today's society. It is useful for all times, but especially now, when there are so many troubles coming from outside, which can shake the mind of even the strongest people. That is the world we are living in. So, spiritual strength is the real strength. Any child who has got spiritual strength can face stress and strain; it can stand a little scolding or even a little caning, and it will not cause any trauma in the child. But, today, very few children have the power to withstand all this; they quickly develop trauma, various complexes in the mind, and they become apathetic, forget their duties and responsibilities, and sit quiet. All these difficulties will come. Society is like that today. And so, people should understand this truth of the ever-present spiritual strength in every human being, which is given to us in the Vedantic literature.

As I said earlier, there are three sources of strength in every human being. The first is muscular strength, *bāhu balam*, that is the most ordinary and the most palpable form of strength. The second is *buddhi balam*, intellectual strength. But, these two are very ordinary. The second is better than the first, but even the second is useless in the world in which we live. And so, there is a third source of strength in everyone, says Vedanta. That is called *ātma balam*, or *yoga balam*, strength coming from one's spiritual development, strength that comes only from the Atman; that is supreme strength. So, *bāhu balam*, *buddhi balam* and *ātma balam*. We do need to develop all these three *balams* in our children. Let them do exercise; let them play games; let the body be developed. Similarly, let them study books, think and develop their minds and intellect, be creative; that is very necessary. But, let them not stop at that. Let them try to get a little spiritual strength from within themselves. With a little bit of *ātma balam*, they can withstand the pressures from outside more and more.

These are the wonderful ideas that come out of the sixth chapter of the *Gītā;* these words, I personally feel, children must hear. Let them be given this thought at the age of six or seven; then onwards it must be given prominence. By the time they are twelve, they will be able to understand a little bit. 'Yes, I can depend upon my inner strength; I can develop some inner strength', that kind of thinking must come. By the time they are fully mature, twenty or twenty-one, it becomes a wonderful possession. This is what the world needs today. These two verses have a special significance, therefore, for humanity in today's civilization.

Śrī Kṛṣṇa now begins to expound the main subject of this chapter, namely, meditation. Preliminary ideas were given till now. We now come to the actual technique of meditation from the next verse onwards. Śrī Kṛṣṇa says here in verse 7:

जितात्मनः प्रशान्तस्य परमात्मा समाहितः ।
शीतोष्ण सुखदुःखेषु तथा मानापमानयोः ॥७॥

*Jitātmanaḥ praśāntasya paramātmā samāhitaḥ;*
*Śītoṣṇa sukhaduḥkheṣu tathā mānāpamānayoḥ — 6. 7*

'To the self-controlled and serene person, the Supreme Self is the object of constant realization, in cold and heat, pleasure and pain, as well as in honour and dishonour.'

*Jitātmanaḥ*, 'whoever has conquered one's own inner energies'; *ātman* sometimes means 'the body', sometimes 'sense organs' or 'the mind', and sometimes, used in its own sense, namely, 'the infinite Self'. So, the body also is *ātman*. So far as the chair is concerned, the body is the *ātman* which sits on the chair which is the *anātman,* not-self or object. So, from the body onwards, Vedanta uses the word Atman, to denote various constituents of personality, which are subjects in one context and objects in another context. But really, the pure Self is the real Atman, the Self within the self, the immortal Divine Self, the One in all, always the subject and never the object. So, in order to characterize It, there is another word *Paramātman,* the Supreme Self. The word Atman is enough, but sometimes *Paramātman*, the Supreme Self, is used. From various levels we understand the truth and so from a lower level if you understand the Atman, then the real Atman will be *Paramātman*, the Supreme Self, the Divine itself.

So, *jitātmanaḥ*, 'he who has conquered the Atman'. What is this Atman? The body, the sensory system, the *manas*—these constitute the Atman in this context; *jitātmanaḥ*, 'of one who conquers oneself by disciplining oneself'. *Praśāntasya*, 'of the tranquil person'; out of that disciplining will come real tranquillity, real peace. Peacelessness of the self is at the sensory level, at the mental level. Above that everything is full of peace. So, we have to concentrate at this level to discipline these energies; then you will become tranquil. *Paramātmā samāhitaḥ*, 'such a one becomes fully established and concentrated in the *Paramātman,* the Supreme Self'. By this method only we can achieve the Supreme Self. When there is a chaotic inner life, we can't have the experience of the Atman. This is a very beautiful idea!

So, *śītoṣṇa sukha duḥkheṣu tathā māna apamānayoḥ*, the mind remains steady all the time, even amidst the various changing aspects of our daily life, like 'cold, heat, happiness and sorrow, and honour and dishonour'. The external events are impinging upon us all the time; but the inner mind remains serene. That is the meaning of the word *praśāntasya.* When you are *praśāntaḥ,* you don't mind whether you are honoured or dishonoured, whether it is cold or hot, whether it is happiness or sorrow. That is the fruit of *yoga. Yoga* alone gives a man or women freedom. We are not free now. We are subject to nature's pressure, but when you take to *yoga,* you slowly experience, 'yes, I am free, I am free. I will not be at the dictate of the external forces.' This is a profound truth, which, in the modern age, is very much needed. We are so much controlled, directed, conditioned by the external forces. We have lost our own inner integrity of the Self. Therefore, *yoga* is very important for every human being. And fortunately, today, people all over the world are pursuing this subject increasingly.

Then, the next *śloku,* verse 8, says:

**ज्ञान विज्ञान तृप्तात्मा कूटस्थो विजितेन्द्रियः ।**
**युक्त इत्युच्यते योगी समलोष्टाश्मकाञ्चनः ॥८॥**

*Jñāna vijñāna tṛptātmā kūṭastho vijitendriyaḥ;*
*Yukta ityucyate yogī samaloṣṭāśmakāñcanaḥ —* 6.8

'Whose heart is filled with satisfaction through knowledge and wisdom, and is steady, whose senses are conquered, and to whom a lump of earth, stone, and gold are the same, that *yogī* is called steadfast.'

At this stage of life, when external things do not attract you, do not enslave you, you become free, you become steady within. Such a person is described here, 'he or she is truly a *yogī*'; *yuktaḥ,* means 'well established in *yoga*'. How? *Jñāna vijñāna tṛpta ātmā,* 'satisfied with *jñāna* and *vijñāna*'. *Jñana* here means merely the understanding of the pros and cons of things, the technical know-how of things. We study all about *yoga,* all about *brahmajñāna;* that is called *jñāna*. But, when you experience the truth contained in the study, that is called *vijñāna,* 'wisdom: the experience of it'. It is not enough that you know the theory. You must experience it. In spiritual life, that is the most important thing. The amount of technical knowledge, theoretical knowledge, is of no use at all. But an ounce of practice is far superior to tons of study and theory. Therefore, *jñāna vijñāna tṛpta ātmā,* 'who is satisfied with *jñāna* and *vijñāna*'; *kūṭasthaḥ*, 'who becomes steady', absolutely steady. As our teachers often express it, be like an anvil in the blacksmith's shop. How many unnumbered pieces are hammered and shaped, and sent out, but the anvil remains absolutely steady. This is the example given. So, *vijitendriyaḥ*, 'he or she who has conquered all the senses'. The senses can't do what they like; without *my* permission no sense organ will function. I am the master here; that situation is mentioned here. Nature also intended that the sense organs must be mastered by the man or woman concerned.

Otherwise, the cerebral system becomes a slave to the sensory system. That is very unfortunate, and today, that is the condition of most human beings. Their entire thinking power is controlled and directed by their sensory appetites; the senses are the master. The human being is only a servant. The situation is just like tail wagging the dog. And most people are in that condition. The sensory system controls and directs the cerebral system; it has no independence at all. But, according to neurology, the cerebral system is meant to make us independent of the sensory system, to take us to higher levels of life's development.

So, Śrī Kṛṣṇa says here, *vijitendriyaḥ*, 'such a person who has controlled the senses'; *yukta ityucyate*, 'is called a *yukta*, well-established in *yoga*', that is, a *yogī*. And his or her mind has a wonderful quality. His or her evaluation of things will be different from that of others who have not controlled their senses. We ordinarily evaluate the world on the basis of sensory attraction, sensory nourishment, etc. But a *yogī* has no sensory attraction, so he or she does not evaluate the world in that way. That is why it is said here, *sama loṣṭāśma kāñcanaḥ*; *loṣṭa* means 'mud'; *āśma* means 'a piece of stone'; and *kāñcana* means 'gold'; *sama*, means 'equal'; these three are just the same to him. That is the attitude. These are meant only for sensory satisfaction, and they have no value beyond the sensory level of the human life.

Therefore, at this stage, one develops that wonderful quality of *samatva*, 'even-mindedness'. Sri Ramakrishna practised it saying, *'ṭākā māṭi, māṭi ṭākā'*, and throwing them both into the river Ganges. *Ṭākā* means 'rupee', *māṭi* means 'mud'; *ṭākā māṭi, māṭi ṭākā* means 'rupee is mud, mud is rupee'. Its value is only for physical satisfaction. Money has no other value. Peace of mind, moral elevation, spiritual development, none of these can come through money. Only eating, drinking and pleasure; nothing else money can give. And so, this idea, *sama loṣṭāśma kāñcanaḥ,* comes again and again.

As soon as you step on the road of *yoga*, you develop this capacity to discriminate. These are ordinary things; you become indifferent to them; you don't need them much, just enough for the maintenance of life, a decent human life. That is the attitude that you develop once you go beyond the sensory level of life. That is called *yoga*. Going beyond the sensory level of life is called *yoga,* which also then helps to steady that sensory level of life. These are all natural to the practitioner of *yoga*. It is *not an external pressure* that forces a person to give up this or that. No sense of loss, even no sense of sacrifice is there. The whole thing is very natural. 'I am in search of something profound, something deep. Compared to it, these are very ordinary'—that attitude comes to such a *yogī*. When we achieve God, how can these little things attract a person? These are nothing, just a dust particle—that is the language used. This is the experience of such men and women; *bahavo,* 'many people', have experienced it.

You have to remember this: if there is evil in society today, it is entirely due to this over-evaluation of these ordinary sensory things. Thereby, all higher things have been completely eliminated or devalued. As the great devotee Hanumān said, 'I have got the great gem of Rāma in my heart, what do I care for these things?' That's what the *bhaktas* or devotees of God hold; that is not a mere theory; it is an experience. There is no struggle, there is no sense of privation; everything is done naturally.

Then comes another quality of such a person:

सुहृन्मित्रार्युदासीन मध्यस्थ द्वेष्यबन्धुषु ।
साधुष्वपि च पापेषु समबुद्धिर्विशिष्यते ॥९॥

*Suhṛnmitrāryudāsīna madhyastha dveṣyabandhuṣu;*
*Sādhuṣvapi ca pāpeṣu samabuddhirviśiṣyate* — 6. 9

'One who looks with equal regard upon well-wishers, friends, enemy, neutrals, arbiters, the hateful, the relatives, and upon the righteous and the unrighteous alike, attains excellence.'

That *sama buddhiḥ*, that 'equanimous vision', is highly praised in the *Gītā*. In the fifth chapter also (verse 18) we had reference to that *samadarśin*, 'person equal-minded in all situations'. *Suhṛt*, 'a friend'—one who is *always a well-wisher* is called a *suhṛt* in Sanskrit; and *mitra* means *merely* 'a friend'; *ari*, 'enemy'; *udāsīna*, 'an indifferent person'; *madhyasthaḥ*, 'one who is equal to both the sides in a dispute', something like an arbitrator; *dveṣyaḥ*, 'one who hates you'; *bandhu*, one's own 'relation'; *sādhu*, 'good people'; *pāpeṣu*, 'with sinful people'; *samabuddhiḥ*, 'one whose mind is equal in reaction'; *viśiṣyate*, 'that is the most excellent attitude to have'. This can come only by a little advance in the path of *yoga*, in the path of spiritual awareness. If somebody scolds you, or abuses you, it won't give you any kind of trauma if you are advanced in spiritual life. It will be just like a small flea bite. That strength comes from within, because you are in touch with something greater within you—the infinite Self. 'These events are not going to disturb me at all; my peace of mind will be unruffled.' But when I am intensely worldly, any one of these can upset my peace of mind. Once you step into spiritual life, these external pressures lose their pressure on you. They become powerless to disturb you. This can be experienced by everyone. How to reduce the impact of these external events on your mind? Not by physical power; that cannot sustain you for long. But, if your mind is riveted to something higher, these external impacts are as nothing. They are very ordinary to me. 'Let him speak, it doesn't matter'—that attitude you cannot have without taking the first step in *yoga*. Afterwards everything becomes steady.

This *sama buddhi* is highly praised in the *Gītā* where this idea finds mention in many places: in chapter 2, verse 15 as *sama duḥkha sukham;* in chapter 2, verse 48, as *samatvam;* in chapter 5, verse 18, as *samadarśin;* in chapter 12, verse 13, and in chapter 14, verse 24, as *samaduḥkhasukhaḥ;* in chapter 12, verse 4, as *sama buddhayaḥ;* and in chapter 13, verse 28, as *samavasthitam.*

Then, Śrī Kṛṣṇa says:

**योगी युञ्जीत सततं आत्मानं रहसि स्थितः ।**
**एकाकी यतचित्तात्मा निराशीः अपरिग्रहः ॥१०॥**

*Yogī yuñjīta satatam ātmānam rahasi sthitaḥ;*
*Ekākī yatacittātmā nirāśīḥ aparigrahaḥ —* 6. 10

'The *yogī* should constantly practise concentration of the mind, retiring into solitude, alone, with the mind and body subdued, and free from (all anxiety of) hope and possession.'

Having elaborated all the great achievements of *yoga*, the qualities that come out of the achievements, and the much-needed character-strength one gets thereby, Śrī Kṛṣṇa now introduces the technique of the specialized *yoga* practice—different from the *yoga* teachings of the previous chapters.

In verse 10 Śrī Kṛṣṇa advises such people: *yogī yuñjīta satatam ātmānam,* 'the *yogī* has to practise concentration of the mind constantly'. How to deal with this mind, how to shape it, how to make it pure, how to make it concentrated? One has to practise it 'constantly'.

How? *Rahasi sthitaḥ,* 'settled in a secluded place' in this specialized *yoga;* the mind can be handled nicely only in a quiet and secluded place, not in a place which is constantly disturbed by external forces. Not only so, *ekākī,* 'alone', not in a crowd. Once you try to go beyond the sensory level, there is no need of people at all. Even if somebody is sitting next to you, you are not in touch with the person. You are in a different world entirely; the other person is also in a different world. So, you become *ekākī* automatically when you sit in meditation. You might be in a crowd, but you are alone. This *aloneness* is a great quality of meditation. Husband, wife, children—all sitting together, but once you start your meditation, there is neither husband nor wife nor children. You are in a world of your own. That is aloneness, a wonderful experience. How to *enjoy* that aloneness? We shall realize then that we are not truly alone; through *yoga* we shall come in touch with the profound Divine being, hidden in our own heart. But this takes a long time and steady practice; and that technique is being expounded here.

Sri Ramakrishna used to sing:

*Jatane hṛdaye rekho ādariṇi śyāmā mā ke;*
*Mon, tui dekh ār āmi dekhi, ār jeno keu nāhi dekhe —*

'Hold the adorable Mother Śyāmā to your heart, O my mind, by means of your careful service; see Her yourself, and let me see Her, and take care that nobody else sees Her besides.'

In your heart you are just alone there, and there is the Divine Mother alone, and nobody else besides. This is the highest state of your mind. You are entering into it through steady practice. And through our moral life, we shall be able to advance in that direction.

So, Śrī Kṛṣṇa says, the *yogī* in this way should always try to discipline and control his or her mind and the inner forces. He should be a *yata cittātmā,* 'one who has disciplined one's body and mind'; *yata* means 'disciplined', and *yati* is 'one who has disciplined the mind'; it also refers to a *sannyāsin*. *Yata cittātmā* means that the *citta* as well as the *ātmā* should be controlled. Here *ātmā* means the body. He should also be a *nirāśīḥ,* 'desireless'; in him or her there should be no desire for the mind to go out. *Aparigrahaḥ* is 'taking no gift from others'. So many gifts are offered to you, and when you go on accepting all those gifts, then your mind is gone out. *Aparigraha* is a great virtue in *yoga;* it is so mentioned in one of the *Yoga-Sūtras* of Patañjali also (2. 30). When a person leads a worldly life, he or she needs help from people; but in this path of Self-realization, none of those things will be helpful to us at all. So, this wonderful virtue, this *aparigraha,* comes automatically to the spiritual aspirant when he or she realizes that, 'after all, others can give me only money or furniture, this and that.

But I don't find any use for them. I am not in search of them. I am in search of something higher.'

Then Śrī Kṛṣṇa continues:

शुचौ देशे प्रतिष्ठाप्य स्थिरं आसनं आत्मनः ।
नात्युच्छ्रितं नातिनीचं चैलाजिनकुशोत्तरम् ॥ ११ ॥

*Śucau deśe pratiṣṭhāpya sthiram āsanam ātmanaḥ;*
*Nātyucchritam nātinīcam cailājinakuśottaram — 6. 11*

'Having established his or her seat in a clean spot, firm, neither too high nor too low, and made of a cloth, a skin, and *Kuśa*-grass, arranged consecutively.'

That it is a science is understood from the subject described here. The whole thing is a science, precision as regards what to do, and how to do; everything is mentioned here. Select a clean place, *śucau deśe*; for what? For this meditation; *sthiram āsanam ātmanaḥ*, 'provide for oneself a steady seat'. The *āsana* must be steady. Then only the body can be steady, the mind can be steady. A shaky *āsana* is no use. And so, *śucau deśe pratiṣṭhāpya sthiram āsanam ātmanaḥ*. Then again, the details are given; very, very thoughtful observations are made; *nātyucchritam nātinīcam*, 'neither too high, nor too low'; both are harmful for meditation; you may fall down, or something might fall on you—all these are possible. Water may accumulate if you are in a pit-like place. Next, *cailājinakuśottaram;* three things are needed for the seat: first, an ordinary matting of grass; that is for protection from dampness; over that, a deer skin, and over that a piece of soft cotton cloth; *cailājinakuśa;* three things, one by one; the lowest one is *kuśa* and the highest one is *caila*, 'cloth'. What a beautiful detailed description is given! Having thus prepared the seat, now you are the experimenter in the science of *yoga*. This is just the preparation for it, like setting up a scientific laboratory.

Then, what will you do?

तत्रैकाग्रं मनः कृत्वा यतचित्तेन्द्रियक्रियः ।
उपविश्यासने युञ्ज्यात् योगं आत्मविशुद्धये ॥ १२ ॥

*Tatraikāgram manaḥ kṛtvā yatacittendriyakriyaḥ;*
*Upaviśyāsane yuñjyāt yogam ātmaviśuddhaye* — 6. 12

'There, seated on that seat, making the mind one-pointed, and subduing the action of the mind and the senses, let him or her practise *yoga* for the purification of the heart.'

Then, *tatraikāgram manaḥ kṛtvā*, 'there, trying to make the mind one-pointed'; *yatacittendriyakriyaḥ*, 'by regulating and controlling the activities of the *citta*, "mind", and *indriya*, "the sensory system"'; *upaviśya āsane*, 'sitting on that seat'; *yuñjyāt yogam*, 'you may practise *yoga*'. For what purpose? *Ātmaviśuddhaye*, 'to purify oneself'. You have not to bring about the Divine there; the Divine is already there, but these obstructions to Its manifestation are there also. You have to remove all those obstructions. Then the Divine manifests itself, like fire hidden beneath the ashes; the fire is there, but the ashes won't allow you to see the fire. Remove the ashes, and the fire will become manifest. Here it is only a question of manifestation; Vedanta holds that you don't have to create the Divine within; it is already there. Now, further instruction is being given. How careful the teacher of this science is! What a scientific approach to the subject!

**समं कायशिरोग्रीवं धारयन् अचलं स्थिरः ।**
**संप्रेक्ष्य नासिकाग्रं स्वं दिशः च अनवलोकयन् ॥ १३ ॥**

*Samam kāyaśirogrīvam dhārayan acalam sthiraḥ;*
*Sampreksya nāsikāgram svam diśaḥ ca anvalokayan*—6. 13

'Let one firmly hold his or her body, head, and neck erect and still, (with the eye-balls fixed, as if) gazing at the tip of one's nose, and not looking around.'

There, on that seat, keep your body straight; the three parts of the body, *kāya, śiras* and *grīvā*, 'body, head, and neck', must be straight and held steady. The entire spinal system should be straight and steady. Sitting in a bending posture is not proper. Therefore, this is emphasized, a steady body. This is a sign of alertness: *dhārayan acalam sthiraḥ*, 'absolutely steady, no movement at all'. *Sampreksya nāsikāgram*, 'the mind is being concentrated on the Atman. In that state the eyes will be absolutely steady'. Śaṅkarācārya explains the words '*as if* looking at the tip of the nose'. The tip of the nose is *not* the subject of meditation; the subject is the Atman.

*Diśaśca anavalokayan*, 'not looking about here and there to the four sides'; you should not allow the mind to wander. That means we are now *within* this human system, going inwards. The outer world is left behind. That is how we begin this science and technique of *yoga* practice.

प्रशान्तात्मा विगतभीः ब्रह्मचारिव्रते स्थितः ।
मनः संयम्य मच्चित्तो युक्त आसीत मत्परः ॥१४॥

*Praśāntātmā vigatabhīḥ brahmacārivrate sthitaḥ;*
*Manaḥ saṁyamya maccitto yukta āsīta matparaḥ* — 6. 14

'With the heart serene and fearless, firm in the vow of a *brahmacāri* or celibate, with the mind controlled, and ever thinking of Me, let him or her sit (in *yoga*) having Me as the supreme Goal.'

*Praśāntātmā*, 'one with a tranquil mind'; then, *vigatabhīḥ*, 'fearless'. We are going to achieve that state of fearlessness. As a creature in this world, we are subject to fear from animals, insects, birds and other human beings; all are subject to fear. But, here we are going to achieve the state of fearlessness. In no other way can we achieve fearlessness except by spiritual realization. *Brahmacāri vrate sthitaḥ*, 'engaged in the practice of *brahmacarya*'. *Manaḥ saṁyamya maccitto*, 'thus disciplining the mind and fixing it on Me', i.e. Śrī Kṛṣṇa, as the inner Self of all; *yukta āsīta matparaḥ*, 'one should sit becoming steady and established entirely in Me'. Śrī Kṛṣṇa is the goal of all the struggle that human beings are undergoing. Śrī Kṛṣṇa is called *Yogeśvara*, the Lord of *yoga*. We are in search of the *Yogeśvara* through *yoga*. In the last verse of the last chapter of this *Gītā*, you will get this word in *yatra yogeśvaraḥ kṛṣṇaḥ*, 'where there is Śrī Kṛṣṇa as the Master of *yoga*'. All the struggle is only for that, to become one with the Divine; that is a great achievement and that makes you one with all, because the

Divine is in all beings. This is the individual realizing its universality, here and now, in this very body.

When you practise thus, what happens?

युञ्जन् एवं सदात्मानं योगी नियतमानसः ।
शान्तिं निर्वाणपरमां मत्संस्थां अधिगच्छति ॥१५॥

*Yuñjan evam sadātmānam yogī niyatamānasaḥ;*
*Śāntim nirvāṇaparamām matsamsthām adhigacchati* — 6. 15

'Thus always keeping the mind steadfast, the *yogī* of subdued mind attains the peace residing in Me—the peace which culminates in *Nirvāṇa* (*Mokṣa*).'

*Yuñjan evam*, 'thus practising *yoga*'; *sadā*, 'always'; *ātmānam*, 'using oneself' as a great instrument to achieve this spiritual development through *yoga*; by doing what? *Niyatamānasaḥ*, 'with disciplined mind', you achieve *śāntim*, 'great peace'. What is that peace? *Nirvāṇa paramām*, 'peace that will lead you to *nirvāṇa*', complete spiritual realization transcending this world of duality and relativity—that is called *nirvāṇa*. When all this relativity is transcended, in that state which was achieved by Buddha and achieved by many great sages, one gets peace. *Nirvāṇa paramām śāntim*, '*śānti* that comes out of that *nirvāṇa*'; *mat samsthām*, 'that state of being established in Me'. In Me, one realizes one's fullness. So, *mat samsthām adhigacchati*, 'one achieves that state'. This is a brief description of the *yoga* practice from the beginning: preparing a seat, steadying one's body and mind, and then going deeper. All outlined in a short statement of a few verses.

Now, certain directions are given if you want to achieve success in this path. Our country has seen people doing all sorts of austerities—like fasting for a long time, standing on one leg in the hot sun, etc. Even Christian mystics in the early period have done a lot of such austerities, and the greatest teachers have said that these are useless and meaningless. There have been Christian mystics who have constantly beaten their body with sticks, just to go beyond body-consciousness. But, the greatest teachers never allowed this kind of senseless, physical mortification. So, a serene attitude in spiritual life has to come through *yoga*. It came through Buddha. He also did a lot of mortification like fasting, and became very weak. And then, after taking food given by a girl, Sujātā, he sat in meditation to realize the truth. Ultimately, we find in Buddha's address to his disciples: 'I found, in the beginning, everybody was undergoing physical mortification. I too fasted for long, and one day, I wanted to stand up; I had no strength and I fell down. I touched my belly here in the front and I could feel my backbone. So weak I had become. Then, the thought came to me. What a foolish thing I am doing! This body is the only instrument I have with which I can realize the highest truth. I am weakening it. I am doing something very wrong. No, I shall not do it.' Then came that great message, the *madhya-panthā*, 'the middle path'. Neither too much austerity nor too much sensory indulgence, but the middle path. Most of the time you have to devote yourself to spiritual practice; that is the *madhya-panthā*, which later on Buddha expounded to his five disciples at Saranath, in Benares, after his enlightenment.

The same idea comes here in the *Gītā*. In a healthy spiritual life, there is no place for senseless mortification, for useless dry asceticism. You can hear the language of Śrī Kṛṣṇa in this connection. He says in the very next verse:

नात्यश्नतस्तु योगोऽस्ति न चैकान्तमनश्नतः ।
न चातिस्वप्नशीलस्य जाग्रतो नैव चार्जुन ॥१६॥

*Nātyaśnatastu yogo'sti na caikāntamanaśnataḥ;*
*Na cātisvapnaśīlasya jāgrato naiva cārjuna* — 6.16

'(Success in) *yoga* is not for the person who eats too much or does not eat at all for long periods; nor, O Arjuna, for one who sleeps too much or keeps awake for long.'

One who eats too much cannot be a *yogī*. One who does not eat at all, such a one also cannot be a *yogī*. See, both are mentioned. *Nātyaśnatastu, ati* means 'too much'; *aśnataḥ* means 'for one who is eating'. Similarly, *na caikāntam anaśnataḥ*, 'not for those who practise fasting for long periods'; such persons also cannot become *yogīs*. Similarly, *na ca ati svapnaśīlasya*, 'not for one who sleeps too much'; such persons also cannot be *yogīs*. Then, *jāgrato naiva cārjuna*, 'O Arjuna, surely not for one who keeps awake all the time'; such men and women also cannot become *yogīs*. This is the negative side. The positive side is given to us in the next verse:

युक्ताहारविहारस्य युक्तचेष्टस्य कर्मसु ।
युक्तस्वप्नावबोधस्य योगो भवति दुःखहा ॥१७॥

*Yuktāhāravihārasya yuktaceṣṭasya karmasu;*
*Yuktasvapnāvabodhasya yogo bhavati duḥkhahā* — 6. 17

'To one who is temperate in eating and recreation, in the effort for work, and in sleep and wakefulness, *yoga* becomes the destroyer of misery.'

What a beautiful statement! How much of sane logic you find in this statement! *Yuktāhāra vihārasya*, 'moderate in *ahāra*, food, and *vihāra*, recreation'; *yukta ceṣṭasya karmasu*, 'moderate in engagement of work'. Always being engaged in work is not good, and laziness also is not good; *yuktasvapnāvabodhasya*, 'moderate in sleep and in waking'. To such a person, '*yoga* becomes the remover of all sorrow', *yogo bhavati duḥkhahā*. That is how we can achieve the fruit of *yoga*.

This is the wisest advice given to a practitioner in spiritual life. People have done all sorts of spiritual practices; even now people do, without knowing the truth expounded by great teachers like Buddha, Kṛṣṇa, Patañjali and others. They have their own inclination, and they follow that. Not much good can come through such practice. And so, this is the instruction given to us.

So, a true *yogī* is just a normal, healthy human being; only his or her search is for something deeper, and it is inward, not outward. Outward dimension one has finished. One has discharged all one's responsibilities; he or she had a family, gave in marriage all the children, and is free now; then one can resort to this *yoga* as the greatest experience of one's life. Or, those who from youth itself are devoted to this; they are wonderful! They had no attraction for worldly life and started from youth along this *yoga* path—both are welcome. Spiritual life and *yoga* can be taken recourse to at any time, at any stage of life; whenever you feel that you are fit for it, you enter into it. It is no use hurrying up on this matter. 'I am not fit for it now. I have got many other things to do.' Okay, there is no harm. When the time is ripe, you'll get it.

Sri Ramakrishna gives this parable. A boy told his mother while going to bed, 'Mother, when I feel the call of nature, please wake me.' Mother said, 'When the call of nature comes, that itself will wake you; I don't need to wake you then.' Similarly, when the hunger for the Divine comes, you cannot resist it. And it comes some time to everybody. And, when it comes, take hold of it. That's a great thing. Don't neglect it then. And so, this is how great teachers advise. Unnecessary physical austerities are not prescribed by the greatest of teachers.

Once two women came from Calcutta to Dakshineswar to see Sri Ramakrishna. They went to him and saluted him. They were fasting all this while for they had resolved to eat only after they see him. After giving certain instructions to them, Sri Ramakrishna learnt about the fasting they had and said: 'Why have you come here fasting? You should have come after taking food. Women are but so many forms of my Divine Mother. I cannot bear to see them suffer. You are all images of the Mother of the Universe. Come after you have eaten and you will feel happy.' Then he fed them with offerings from the temple and said: 'You have eaten something. Now my mind is at peace. I cannot bear to see women fast.' (*The Gospel of Sri Ramakrishna,* p. 432: 1996 edition: 24 May 1884). That is a very beautiful incident in the teachings of Sri Ramakrishna.

So, here in the present *śloka,* we have this achievement from *yoga,* namely, an end to all sorrow.

Now, Śrī Kṛṣṇa will take us through that process of meditation and tell us what spiritual achievement takes place through meditation. These form a series of beautiful verses.

In the verses 16 and 17 of the sixth chapter of the *Gītā,* a very important truth has been conveyed to us, that extremes must be avoided, and a middle path must be taken, that which Buddha called, *madhya-panthā*. Neither too much austerity, nor too much sense indulgence. That is how we can grow spiritually. Anything else may just be 'religious'. If you do some kind of austerity, you can be religious, but in spiritual life its value is minimum. Therefore, Śrī Kṛṣṇa said:

*Yoga* becomes the source of the destruction of all sorrow, if you follow the middle path of moderate eating, drinking, resting, working, etc. Not extremes; that is not good for the spiritual development. Buddha realized it from his own personal experience. Śrī Kṛṣṇa has given us that truth much earlier, in the *Gītā*.

Now, verse 18 begins to deal with the process and the technique of meditation. These are a few of the very important verses in the sixth chapter:

**यदा विनियतं चित्तं आत्मन्येव अवतिष्ठते ।**
**निःस्पृहः सर्वकामेभ्यो युक्त इत्युच्यते तदा ॥१८॥**

*Yadā viniyatam cittam ātmanyeva avatiṣṭhate;*
*Niḥspṛhaḥ sarvakāmebhyo yukta ityucyate tadā* — 6. 18

'When the completely controlled mind rests serenely in the Self alone, free from longing after all desires, then is one called steadfast (in the Self).'

The mind can be said to be *yuktaḥ*, 'established in *yoga*', when *viniyatam cittam*, 'the *citta* or mind, which has been disciplined'; *ātmanyeva avatiṣṭhate*, 'remains only in the Atman', not going here and there. Then, we can say that the mind is *yuktaḥ;* it has achieved *yoga*. This is the first statement. Then *niḥspṛhaḥ sarvakāmebhyaḥ*, 'no external desires come and disturb the mind'. It is absolutely established in itself. *Yukta ityucyate tadā,* 'then it is said to be *yukta,* united with God'. Then Śrī Kṛṣṇa gives an example, a very familiar one, from our literature:

**यथा दीपो निवातस्थो नेङ्गते सोपमा स्मृता ।**
**योगिनो यतचित्तस्य युञ्जतो योगं आत्मनः ॥१९॥**

*Yathā dīpo nivātastho neṅgate sopamā smṛtā;*
*Yogino yatacittasya yuñjato yogam ātmanaḥ* — 6. 19

'"As a lamp in a spot sheltered from the wind does not flicker"—even such has been the simile used for a *yogī* of subdued mind, practising concentration in the Self.'

As an oil lamp, which is kept in a place free from wind, is absolutely steady in its flame, such is the example of that mind which has become steady, i.e. without any fluctuation. The *yoga* state is compared to the state of a steady flame. When you see the flame moving all the time, it is because there is wind all around and it is influenced by all those wind currents. But, when it is put in a place where external influences cannot touch, it remains absolutely steady. That is the nature of the human mind in the state of *yoga,* absolutely steady. It is a very difficult process; a long training is needed, and yet it is not unattainable; it has been attained by people, and anyone can attain to *yoga*. And Śrī Kṛṣṇa will tell us in a series of verses the nature of that meditation, and the result of that meditation or *yoga*.

*Yathā dīpo nivātastho na iṅgate; iṅganam* means 'shaking' or in a wavy motion. It doesn't shake, it doesn't flicker; *sopamā smṛtā,* 'that is the well-known comparison to the state of the mind in *yoga*'; *yogino yata cittasya,* 'of a *yogī* who has disciplined his or her mind'; *yuñjato yogam ātmanaḥ*, 'of one who is practising concentration in the Self'.

In fact, sage Patañjali begins his famous aphorisms on *yoga* with this very truth: Two states of the human mind are there—the scattered state and the gathered state. The scattered state is the normal state of life. Mind is scattered among a thousand things. The gathered state is, what you call, sleep. You are gathered regularly, and then you are quiet, absolutely calm and quiet. But, the same gathered state can be of a new type; you deliberately gather the mind. That is the *yoga,* which Śrī Kṛṣṇa is going to expound in a few verses.

The gathered state requires an effort on the human part. Nature doesn't do it for you. Nature has given you the capacity, but you have to do it yourself. Therefore, this kind of unification and control of various states of the mind is what we are expected to do to become truly masters of ourselves.

When the mind is in perfect control, life is absolutely free. That is why it is needed for everyone, even a small measure of it. You may not have the whole of it, but even a little measure of the control of the mind is beneficial. When anger arises in the mind, one must will to be able to take cognizance of it, see that it is rising, and stop it then and there. A well-controlled mind can do this. You can feel that anger is rising slowly, that it is getting stronger and stronger. These subtle experiences of emotional states we can easily detect with a trained mind and we can stop its growth before it explodes on others in the world. This capacity is needed for everyone in day-to-day life; it is needed for a happy human relationship, and, above all, to realize the Atman, to become fulfilled; that is the main purpose of *yoga*—to realize our own infinite nature with the help of this mind by proper discipline and the whole of that discipline is being mentioned here in its technical aspect as *yoga*.

This *dhyāna*, or meditation, is only one chapter in the *Gītā*. *Yoga* of the *Gītā* is much wider than this *yoga* of meditation. It is only an accessory item among the total *yoga* of the *Gītā*, because the *yoga* of the *Gītā* contains emphasis on day-to-day work, human relationships, and so many other things. And meditation is added to this list because it helps you in achieving success in all those spheres; so *dhyāna* is only a part of the total *yoga* of the *Gītā*, not the whole thing. Some people may not be interested in meditation, but still they can be *yogīs*.

As Swami Vivekananda would say, 'A *karma yogī*, without the help of other *yogas*, can also realize the truth, realize the Atman; it is a path by itself.' But, it is helpful if it is accompanied by the training of the mind in meditation. So, Śrī Kṛṣṇa adds this teaching to the complete *yoga* of the *Gītā*. That is why, of the eighteen chapters, the sixth chapter alone is devoted to *Dhyāna Yoga*. That is the significance of *dhyāna* for spiritual life in general and *yoga* life of the *Gītā* in particular. And then:

यत्रोपरमते चित्तं निरुद्धं योगसेवया ।
यत्र चैवात्मनात्मानं पश्यन् आत्मनि तुष्यति ॥ २० ॥

*Yatroparamate cittam niruddham yogasevayā;*
*Yatra caivātmanātmānam paśyan ātmani tuṣyati — 6. 20*

'When the mind, absolutely restrained by the practice of concentration, attains quietude, and when seeing the Self by the self, one is satisfied in the Self.'

A series of verses are coming now, all beginning with 'when'. 'When this happens, when that happens,' and, at the end, Śrī Kṛṣṇa will say, 'this is going to be the result'. So, first *yatroparamate cittam niruddham*, 'when the *citta* or mind becomes inwardly drawn; *uparamate,* indrawn to itself'; *yogasevayā,* 'by the practice of *yoga*'; *yatra caivātmanātmānam paśyan ātmani tuṣyati,* 'when by seeing the Self in one's own self, you delight only in that Self'; that is a beautiful expression. By this withdrawing of the mind from external things, we are not going to some state of emptiness of mind. We are going to the infinite dimension of the Divine within and we find infinite delight in it. When that happens:

सुखं आत्यन्तिकं यत् तत् बुद्धिग्राह्यं अतीन्द्रियम् ।
वेत्ति यत्र न चैवायं स्थितश्चलति तत्वतः ॥ २१ ॥

*Sukham ātyantikam yat tat buddhigrāhyam atīndriyam;*
*Vetti yatra na caivāyam sthitaścalati tattvataḥ — 6. 21*

'When one feels that infinite bliss, which is perceived by the (purified) intellect and which transcends the senses, and established wherein one never departs from one's real state.'

*Sukham ātyantikam yat tat buddhigrāhyam atīndriyam;* 'supreme happiness', *ātyantikam sukham.* You begin to experience that *ātyantikam sukham*, infinite happiness; *yat tat buddhigrāhyam,* 'that which your *buddhi* can grasp'; *atīndriyam,* 'the sense organs cannot grasp it'. When the *buddhi* can grasp that wonderful joy that comes from the contact with the Atman, that joy is *buddhigrāhyam;* it is also *atīndriyam,* 'the sense organs can never go there'; their power is very, very limited. Even scientists ask, what is the speed of the nerve impulse? The sense organs work *through* the nervous system and the speed of the nerve impulse will determine how much the senses can do. Hardly some 200 kilometres per hour is the speed of a nerve impulse. How ordinary it is. How can it penetrate into the truth of things?

So, *atīndriyam* is constantly emphasized: this higher experience is beyond the sensory and nervous system. So, the sensory system has no value here. When you sit in meditation, you say good-bye to the sensory system. They stay outside. They don't function here. That kind of attitude you have to take towards the sensory system; not for it's own sake, but to go higher, to penetrate deeper. Even in physical science, very often, you have to go deeper, so that nature can reveal her mystery. But, these senses are useful only in the early stage of human life, particularly while dealing with the external world.

Therefore, *buddhigrāhyam atīndriyam*; here only *buddhi* or enlightened reason plays a role because, nearest to the Atman is *buddhi;* it is extremely subtle, and, when it is properly trained, it develops a high penetrating power. That is the language used in the Upaniṣads. Any energy can be made capable of deep penetration by giving proper training. Take radiation; you give it a training, high frequency training; then it becomes highly penetrating as an X-ray, though, by itself, it was a very flimsy radiation. Just a ray of laser can make high frequency radiation with the capacity to penetrate into the heart of things. That state, applied to the *buddhi,* is called *buddhigrāhyam.* That *buddhi* can capture this truth of the infinite joy coming from the realization of the Atman.

So, *buddhigrāhyam atīndriyam*. This idea comes from the *Kaṭha Upaniṣad,* (I. iii. 12)*: Dṛśyate tvagryayā buddhyā sūkṣmayā sūkṣmadarśibhiḥ*—this Atman is present in all beings, but it is lying hidden. Will it always remain hidden? No, we can discover it: *dṛśyate,* 'it is seen'. How? *Agryayā buddhyā*, 'when the ordinary *buddhi* becomes concentrated, one-pointed'; that is the nature of that expression. How do you get it? By training the *buddhi* in dealing with subtle, more subtle and still more subtle realities, the *buddhi* finally gets the capacity to realize the subtlest reality, the Atman. *Sūkṣma buddhi* is capable of realizing the subtle, and *sthūla buddhi* is capable of realizing only the gross. *Sūkṣmadarśibhiḥ*, 'by those who have trained themselves to perceive subtle and subtler truths'. Such people are called *sūkṣmadarśīs*. So, a *sūkṣmadarśī* can realize the Atman by his or her *sukṣma buddhi*; and one becomes a *sūkṣma darśī* because of his or her one-pointed mind. Let us make the mind as pointed as possible. That is the nature of the training of the human mind.

So, in that context, the Upaniṣad has said, *dṛśyate*, that the Atman 'can be realized', not by the senses, not by the *manas*, but by the *buddhi*. *Buddhi* is pure reason, as we call it in the modern language, but it is the purest of the psychic energy that you have. 'Psychic energies' mean all the energies in you. You go on training them, making it a little better; then it becomes the mind; making it still better, it becomes the *buddhi*. From the same energy, namely, that psychic force, the *buddhi* must be developed. Earlier in the *Gītā*, Śrī Kṛṣṇa had said so many times, 'develop *buddhi*, develop *buddhi*.' Through education you develop that *buddhi* which can discriminate between the real and the unreal, and penetrate into the heart of things. That is called *buddhi*.

So, *vetti yatra*, 'when one realizes this', in that state one will know this truth. And then, *na caivāyam sthitaścalati tattvataḥ*, 'one never falls down from the state of that truth'; *na calati*, mind 'doesn't fall down' from the state of truth. It is fixed on that. That is the state, absolutely steady.

**यं लब्ध्वा चापरं लाभं मन्यते नाधिकं ततः ।**
**यस्मिन्स्थितो न दुःखेन गुरुणापि विचाल्यते ॥२२॥**

*Yam labdhvā cāparam lābham manyate nādhikam tataḥ;*
*Yasminsthito na duḥkhena guruṇāpi vicālyate* — 6. 22

'Having obtained which, one regards no other acquisition superior to that, and where established, one is not moved even by heavy sorrow.'

*Manyate nādhikam tataḥ*, 'after attaining which you will not find anything better to achieve'. That highest state of joy you get there. *Yam labdhvā cāparam lābham tataḥ adhikam na manyate*, 'you don't consider at all that there could be something higher to achieve'. Your mind itself will tell you that you have achieved the highest. There is nothing higher than this. *Yasminsthito na duḥkhena guruṇāpi vicālyate,* 'established in which you are never shaken even by the heaviest of sorrow'. Even a little sorrow can shake us, but when established in the Atman, even the heaviest sorrow will not shake us. That is the expression: 'by even the heaviest sorrow'; *duḥkha* means 'sorrow'; *na vicālyate,* 'is not shaken'; one remains steady.

**तं विद्यात् दुःख-संयोग-वियोगं योगसंज्ञितम् ।**
**स निश्चयेन योक्तव्यो योगोऽनिर्विण्णचेतसा ॥ २३ ॥**

*Tam vidyāt duḥkha-samyoga-viyogam yogasamjñitam;*
*Sa niścayena yoktavyo yogo'nirviṇṇacetasā* — 6. 23

'Let that be known as the state called by the name of *yoga*—a state of severance from the contact with pain. This *yoga* should be practised with perseverance, undisturbed by depression of heart.'

*Tam vidyāt,* 'know that to be'; *duḥkha-samyoga-viyogam yogasamjñitam,* know that to be *yoga,* which is *duḥkha-samyoga-viyogam,* 'the disassociation of the association with pain, with sorrow'. See the language. *Duḥkha-samyoga* is one's normal life, 'associated with sorrow'. Just a pinprick in the skin and you get pain; that is called *duḥkha-samyoga; viyoga* means its absence; that association with pain is not there. Things that are painful happen, but you don't feel it, you don't worry over it; *yogasamjñitam,* 'this is known as *yoga*'; *sa niścayena yoktavyaḥ,* 'that must be practised with great determination'; *niścaya* means, 'certainty'; it is a possibility for everyone; it is not a mere theory, it is not a dogma, it can be realized, it can be achieved; so, *niścayena yoktavyaḥ yogaḥ,* 'this *yoga* must be practised with great determination'; *anirviṇṇacetasā,* 'without any kind of depression of mind'; steadily this *yoga* practice must be carried out. You may not achieve its results straight away; so, you may be inclined to give it up. No, continue, let it take a hundred years; what does that matter? Let me do something worthwhile; let me continue this wonderful search for my own true nature, my own true dimension. What is that dimension? What is that profound mystery? Let me try to understand it. This is the method by which we try to understand that truth. You found this type of determination, facing all privation and even death, during the early nineteenth century gold rush to the Western part of America.

So, here is just a couple of verses dealing with this subject. We can achieve *yoga* when we work hard for it. Remember that it is not a dogma or creed. That is why in India we scientifically analyse the whole world of religion. There are two classifications of religion. One is the ethnical classification based on dogma and creed; the other one is scientific classification. Ethnical is Hinduism, Buddhism, Christianity, Islam, etc. The other, the scientific classification, gives us *Karma Yoga, Bhakti Yoga, Rāja Yoga, Jñāna Yoga;* this is called the scientific classification. Here, *Gītā* deals with the scientific classification of religions, cutting across all these ethnical differences and limitations. And therefore, 'this *yoga* must be assiduously followed and some results gained in this very life', that is Śrī Kṛṣṇa's exhortation.

And now Śrī Kṛṣṇa says,

सङ्कल्पप्रभवान् कामान् त्यक्त्वा सर्वान् अशेषतः ।
मनसैवेन्द्रियग्रामं विनियम्य समन्ततः ॥२४॥

*Saṅkalpaprabhavān kāmān tyaktvā sarvān uśeṣataḥ;*
*Manasaivendriyagrāmam viniyamya samantataḥ* — 6. 24

'Abandoning without reserve all desires born of *saṅkalpa*, and completely restraining, by the mind alone, the whole group of senses from their objects in all directions.'

*Saṅkalpa prabhavān kāmān tyaktvā,* 'renouncing all the *kāmas* or desires, outgoing cravings, which are born of *saṅkalpa*'. When they are properly controlled; *sarvān aśeṣataḥ,* 'all of them completely'; *manasā eva indriyagrāmam viniyamya samantataḥ,* 'all the sense organs are slowly controlled and disciplined through the *manas* alone'. *Manas* or mind is the instrument for controlling the sensory system. *Manas* itself is a very subtle sense organ; they call it the sixth sense organ. And yet, it has the power to co-ordinate all the five sense organs. Through the *manas*, therefore, we gather all the energies of the sensory system.

In the third chapter of the *Kaṭha Upaniṣad*, *manas* is compared to the reins, the senses are compared to the horses, body is known as the chariot, and *buddhi* is the charioteer in whose hands the reins are held. This is a beautiful comparison. *Buddhi*, *manas*, sensory system, and the body—these are the four agents. Each one of these agents has its own function to perform. Here, the *manas* is to control the sensory system; the reins have to control the horses. If you want to control the horses, you must have the reins. So, that is why it is stated 'control the sensory system through the *manas*', and this controlling is done by *buddhi*, luminous reason-will; he is the ultimate master; he is the controller of the whole of life's journey. That is *buddhi*, the charioteer in the *Kaṭha Upaniṣad*. *Samantataḥ* means 'from all sides'. If there are five horses, and one controls only three horses, two are left behind to themselves. That will not do. You must control all the five horses. Then only the journey will be comfortable and capable of leading us to our destination.

**शनैः शनैः उपरमेत् बुद्ध्या धृतिगृहीतया ।**
**आत्मसंस्थं मनः कृत्वा न किञ्चिदपि चिन्तयेत् ॥ २५ ॥**

*Śanaiḥ śanaiḥ uparamet buddhyā dhṛtigṛhītayā;*
*Ātmasamstham manaḥ kṛtvā na kiñcidapi cintayet* — 6 .25

'With the reason or intellect joined with will, with the mind fastened on the Self, let one attain quietude step by step: let him or her not think of anything else.'

Now, the exact nature of meditation is described here. *Śanaiḥ śanaiḥ uparamet*, you can't attain quietude all at once; *śanaiḥ*, 'slowly, gradually'; *uparamet*, 'withdraw'. Great things can be done only slowly and gradually. They cannot be done quickly. If you try to do anything quickly, you will get into trouble. Either physical trouble or mental trouble will come. So, do it slowly, slowly; *buddhyā dhṛtigṛhītayā*, 'with will-power assisted by *buddhi*'—with all these energies gathered together.

*Ātmasamstham manaḥ kṛtvā*, 'making the mind slowly settled in the Self'; *na kiñcit api cintayet*, 'don't think of anything else'. What is the next step?

यतो यतो निश्चरति मनश्चञ्चलं अस्थिरम् ।
ततस्ततो नियम्यैतद् आत्मन्येव वशं नयेत् ॥ २६ ॥

*Yato yato niścarati manaścañcalam asthiram;*
*Tatastato niyamyaitad ātmanyeva vaśam nayet — 6. 26*

'Through whatever reason the restless, unsteady mind wanders away, let one, curbing it from that, bring it under the subjugation of the Self alone.'

The second advice is given in this verse, and we all need it whenever the mind goes out. *Yato yato niścarati manaḥ cañcalam asthiram*, 'whenever the mind, very fickle'; *asthiram*, 'never steady'; *cañcalam*, 'restless'; *niścarati*, 'goes out'; *tataḥ tato niyamya*, 'then and there, controlling it'; *ātmanyeva vaśam nayet*, 'bring it under the Atman alone'. This is a constant struggle, a war; for a long period it has to go on; there is no other way. But, Śrī Kṛṣṇa will say later on at the question of Arjuna, 'the mind is controlled by constant practice'. That will be one of the questions of Arjuna, which is also everyone's, which Arjuna asks on our behalf, later in the *Gītā*.

प्रशान्तमनसं ह्येनं योगिनं सुखं उत्तमम् ।
उपैति शान्तरजसं ब्रह्मभूतं अकल्मषम् ॥ २७ ॥

*Praśāntamanasam hyenam yoginam sukham uttamam;*
*Upaiti śāntarajasam brahmabhūtam akalmaṣam — 6. 27*

'Verily, the supreme bliss comes to that *yogī* of perfectly tranquil mind, with passions quieted, Brahman-become, and freed from taint.'

Such a *yogī* is *praśānta manasam*, 'whose mind is perfectly calm and tranquil', for, he or she has practised *yoga* for long. The mind of such a one slowly becomes calmer and calmer; now it has become perfectly calm. *Sukham uttamam upaiti*, 'supremely pure happiness comes to him or her'. Various types of happiness you can have, but this is *uttamam sukham*, 'the best happiness' that you can ever have. Eating delicious food is also happiness, but this happiness is quite different; this is *uttamam sukham*, it consists in being in your own Self; it doesn't depend upon something else. *Śāntarajasam*, 'all *rajas*, restless energy, has been completely eliminated from the mind'. What a beautiful state! Why is the mind disturbed? It is owing to its *rājasic* nature. That *rajas* element makes the mind run here and there. That is the meaning of *rajas*. *Tamas* and *rajas*, both these elements make the mind absolutely unfit for high purposes; when these elements prevail in the mind, the mind can then be used for very ordinary purposes only. So, in this case, the *rajas* element 'has been eliminated'; it has become *śāntarajasam*. There is nothing to shake it, nothing to make it jump about as it were. It is the *rājasic* mind that runs about all the time. Next, the *yogī* is *brahmabhūtam*, 'the mind has become one with Brahman', and *akalmaṣam*, 'free from all impurities', it is the purest mind; he or she is of this nature.

Sri Ramakrishna says, 'pure *manas*, pure *buddhi*, pure Atman are one and the same.' We use different words for various states of this inner life, but actually *śuddha* or pure *manas*, *śuddha buddhi*, *śuddha* Atman are one and the same. So, that *śuddha manas* which itself is *śuddha* Atman, which itself is *śuddhā buddhi*, is *akalmaṣam*, free from all impurities of the *manas;* when such a state comes within us, we become *brahmabhūtam*, 'one with Brahman'.

There is a famous passage by Plato, in his drama 'Freedom', in the *Republic of Plato*, his famous book. You will find there this beautiful statement:

'Thought is best when the mind is gathered into herself and none of these things trouble her, neither sound, nor sight, nor pain, nor pleasure; when she has as little as possible to do with the body, no bodily sense of feeling, but it is aspiring after a pure being, that is the state of mind which is the best.'

This is exactly the idea of Vedanta, speaking about the mind being controlled and disciplined and concentrated on the infinite Self in man. That is the state in which the mind is at its highest and best. This is the teaching of all the mystics—Sufi mystics, Christian mystics, and Hindu mystics. This mind needs its training and the turning towards the infinite Self. You turn the mind out and do work, produce wealth, improve economy. That is beautiful, but it is one side of human life. *Gītā* places great emphasis on that life of *karma,* action, *pravṛtti*. But, the *Gītā* also says, do this also, develop this capacity also, the capacity to withdraw, to unify the mental energies through meditation. These two must go side by side. Then only you will have complete efficiency in your life. That is what the *Gītā* wants to give to humanity. I have referred to this in the 'Introduction' earlier in the first volume.

In the second chapter of the *Gītā* (verse 50) you found efficiency defined as *yoga*, '*yoga* is efficiency in action', *yogaḥ karmasu kauśalam,* and by efficiency is meant a double efficiency, namely, outward work efficiency and inward spiritual efficiency. That is the speciality of the *yoga* of the *Gītā*.

So, Śrī Kṛṣṇa adds this idea of meditation also: trying to understand our own true nature. We don't let our minds become merely machine-like and get things done outside, and when the work is accomplished, throw the mind away on the scrap heap; that is how old machines are treated. Human beings should not be treated so. After heavy work you should become free, you should become pure, you should feel that you are up to yourself. *If that is to be attained, you have to follow this emphasis of the Gītā: external life* plus *internal life*. A human being is not a junk to be discarded. He or she has got an inner life; he or she has to achieve something within oneself, and not merely be a machine to be used by people for producing goods and services. That attitude of mind towards the human beings should be completely changed.

So here, in this verse, Śrī Kṛṣṇa says that, in this particular state, the mind of human beings becomes one with Brahman. We have achieved our fulfilment here on earth. We were working and will continue to work, but the whole work will become different. It is so full of the spiritual element that the work ceases to be work. It becomes *no work*. It is a teaching of

Taoist philosophy, Zen Buddhism, and Vedanta, which we have discussed in the fourth chapter.

These are a few verses dealing with this process of inner penetration.

युञ्जन्नेवं सदात्मानं योगी विगतकल्मषः ।
सुखेन ब्रह्मसंस्पर्शं अत्यन्तं सुखं अश्नुते ॥२८॥

*Yuñjannevam sadātmānam yogī vigatakalmaṣaḥ;*
*Sukhena brahmasamsparśam atyantam sukham aśnute* — 6. 28

'A *yogī*, freed from all taints, constantly engaging the mind thus, attains with ease the infinite bliss of contact with Brahman.'

*Sukhena brahmasamsparśam atyantam sukham aśnute; brahmasamsparśam*, 'the touch of Brahman, the touch of God, the touch of the Divine'. Devotees can understand this language. If you touch the feet of Śrī Kṛṣṇa once, what a wonderful joy it would give! Therefore, this *sukhena brahmasamsparśam aśnute*, 'one achieves the touch of Brahman very easily'; *atyantam sukham aśnute*, 'one enjoys infinite happiness'. By eating a nice meal we feel happy; getting a kind word, we feel happy. There are so many occasions when we get small measures of happiness. These are all little titbits of happiness in human life; but consider the ocean of happiness which is Brahman itself, *ānanda svarūpa*, of the nature of bliss; and these persons are in touch with That. We cannot even imagine it. But the truth is that, many of the books in our tradition have said that you will feel infinite joy in every pore of the body when you realize God. Those who have realized God have conveyed to us the infinite joy, because God is the essence of joy, 'the ocean of joy', *ānanda sāgara*; that is the language we use. So, little bits of *ānanda* we get here; it is only a little, truncated, *ānanda* derived from that infinite *ānanda* of Brahman. And so, you give up these little ones, go to the very source of *ānanda*, that is God itself. The *Bṛhadāraṇyaka Upaniṣad* (IV. iii. 32) says, *etasyaiva ānandasya anyāni bhūtāni mātrām upajīvanti*, 'every *ānanda* or bliss enjoyed by beings in this world is a little particle of that infinite *ānanda'*, which is *brahmānanda* or *ātmānanda*.

And now, this *yoga* gives you that *brahmasamsparśam*, 'the touch of Brahman, the infinite *ānanda'*; *atyantam sukham aśnute*, 'such people enjoy immense happiness'. Therefore, the *Gītā* said, 'we cannot achieve infinite happiness with our present state of mind.' We can only say, it is a very great joy, but we cannot appreciate its exact significance. In our present state, we are satisfied with the little joys that we get in our normal life. Even that itself is a great thing for us; we go into an ecstasy getting that little joy. If I have no employment, and I try hard to get a job, and after six months I get a job; I am in 'infinite' bliss. That is one human yardstick for joy. This is one type of human joy; various levels of human joys are there. So, just imagine, multiply these joys infinitely, and that is the joy of Brahman.

Now, this is the teaching Śrī Kṛṣṇa gives to Arjuna and to all of us through him.

सर्वभूतस्थं आत्मानं सर्वभूतानि चात्मनि ।
ईक्षते योगयुक्तात्मा सर्वत्र समदर्शनः ॥ २९ ॥

*Sarvabhūtastham ātmānam sarvabhūtāni cātmani;*
*Īkṣate yogayuktātmā sarvatra samadarśanaḥ —* 6. 29

'With the heart concentrated by *yoga*, with the eye of evenness for all things, he or she beholds the Self in all beings and all beings in the Self.'

A few more verses are there before you get to Arjuna's question, and in these verses Śrī Kṛṣṇa takes us through various subjects before Arjuna raises his question. Mind becomes calm and steady. One develops a spirit of equality, one has that kind of tremendous achievement when one becomes one with Brahman. That is described in these few verses as the achievement by the followers of *yoga*. So, in verse 29, Śrī Kṛṣṇa says what constitutes a high teaching in Vedanta.

With the heart concentrated by *yoga*, with the eye of evenness for all beings, (sameness, *samatva*, *samadṛṣṭi*), one beholds one's Self in all things and all things in the Self. To see everything in the Atman, and Atman in everything—that is the highest vision Vedanta promises to every human being.

*Sarvabhūtastham ātmānam*, 'the Atman existing in all beings', and, *sarvabhūtāni cātmani*, 'all beings existing in the Atman'; *īkṣate*, he or she 'sees' this kind of realization; *yogayuktātmā*, 'one who has achieved *yoga*', whose mind has become one in the spirit of *yoga*; *sarvatra samadarśanaḥ*, 'he or she sees equality everywhere', as the one infinite Atman; there is no high or low, no distinctions. The highest democracy comes here: we are perfectly equal with each other because one infinite Atman is present in all beings in its infinite fullness, not in fraction. *Samadarṣitva*, 'equality of vision', is a great teaching throughout the *Gītā*.

Our country needs this teaching more than any other country. We have always had this kind of differential way of looking at things and people. A person gets a little less money as salary, we look down upon him or her; one gets a little high salary, we look up to him or her. This kind of inequality is terrible in our society. This *Gītā* teaching will be a great blessing to us in the modern age: *Sarvatra samadarṣanaḥ*, 'one who sees equality everywhere'. He or she is a human being, whether in possession of more money or less money, why concern ourselves with that? That is not the main value of a human being, there is the infinite Atman within each. This teaching must inspire our people to make us part from caste and creed differences to true democracy in the socio-political field. A little bit of this *jñāna* of Brahman must come to us in the socio-political field. Then our democracy will be stronger and steady.

Then, Śrī Kṛṣṇa uses the word divine incarnation to mean Brahman; instead of saying 'he or she sees Brahman in all', Śrī Kṛṣṇa now puts it as 'he or she sees Me, an incarnation of God, in all':

यो मां पश्यति सर्वत्र सर्वं च मयि पश्यति ।
तस्याहं न प्रणश्यामि स च मे न प्रणश्यति ॥३०॥

*Yo mām paśyati sarvatra sarvam ca mayi paśyati;*
*Tasyāham na praṇaśyāmi sa ca me na praṇaśyati* — 6. 30

'One who sees Me in all beings and sees all beings in Me, such a one never becomes separated from Me, nor do I become separated from him or her.'

*Yo mām paśyati sarvatra sarvam ca mayi paśyati*, 'one who sees Me in all beings and all beings in Me'; *tasyāham na praṇaśyāmi sa ca me na praṇaśyati*, 'such a one will never be separated from Me, nor do I become separated from him or her'. We are always one, together.

सर्वभूतस्थितं यो मां भजत्येकत्वं आस्थितः ।
सर्वथा वर्तमानोऽपि स योगी मयि वर्तते ॥३१॥

*Sarvabhūtasthitam yo mām bhajatyekatvam āsthitaḥ;*
*Sarvathā vartamāno'pi sa yogī mayi vartate* — 6. 31

'One who, being established in unity, worships Me, who am dwelling in all beings, whatever his or her mode of life, that *yogī* abides in Me.'

*Sarvabhūtasthitam yo mām bhajati*, 'one who worships Me, who exist in all beings'; Śrī Kṛṣṇa exists in all beings like a thread that runs through all the pearls in a garland, uniting all the pearls into one garland, as he says elsewhere in the *Gītā*; similarly, the Lord exists in all of us as the central thread of beings. *Bhajati ekatvam āsthitaḥ*, 'worships Me being established in unity'; *sarvathā vartamāno'pi sa yogī mayi vartate*, 'whatever may be his or her way of life, he or she always lives in Me'. One may be selling various things, or may be making shoes, or breaking stones on the road side, or sitting in the chair of an administrator; whatever may be his or her mode of life, such a person always lives in Me; that is the language. What a beautiful idea! We can see the best devotees in the most unusual places. We have seen in our religious history that an ordinary shoe-maker has realized the Divine, a simple house-wife has realised the Divine. Her status in society is very ordinary, but spiritually it is very high. So, this can happen to everyone. Whatever be your station in society, or the nature of your work in society, you are always living in the Lord Himself in this particular achievement; *sa yogī mayi vartate,* 'that *yogī* lives in Me' all the time.

आत्मौपम्येन सर्वत्र समं पश्यति योऽर्जुन ।
सुखं वा यदि वा दुःखं स योगी परमो मतः ॥३२॥

*Ātmaupamyena sarvatra samam paśyati yo'rjuna;*
*Sukham vā yadi vā duḥkham sa yogī paramo mataḥ* — 6. 32

'One who judges pleasure or pain everywhere by the same standard as one applies to oneself, that *yogī*, O Arjuna, is regarded as the highest.'

*Ātmaupamyena*, 'as you feel about yourself', so feel about others also. What is painful to you, you want to avoid; therefore, don't inflict pain on others; as you feel for yourself, feel for others also. That is the universal maxim found in the Bible, Chinese thought, Indian thought, everywhere. Whatever is not pleasant to you don't inflict it on others—that is the language.

So, *ātmaupamyena*, 'see others as you see yourself'; *sarvatra samam paśyati yo'rjuna*, 'one who sees with the sense of equality everywhere O Arjuna'; *sukham vā yadi vā duḥkham*, 'whether it is happiness or sorrow'. If something gives you sorrow, see that that sorrow is not inflicted on somebody else. That attitude must be there. *Sa yogī paramo mataḥ,* 'that *yogī* is considered to be supreme'. He or she has realized oneness with all.

What a tremendous change will come in our society when a bit of this teaching gets into our mind and heart. We do so much evil to others not knowing that if that evil were to come to us, we would have become really miserable. We don't know how to feel for others. That feeling of oneness is not there. That is the great evil that has been afflicting our society for centuries together. Swami Vivekananda said that many of our people do not have a feeling heart; there is the intellect; the brain is there, the heart is not there, concern for others is not there. That is why we have brought our society to the lowest level.

Now our society must have a revolutionary change. And Vedanta gives you the way to get that inner change in yourself, by which this *samadṛṣṭi* will come to you; then society will become really a heaven. It will be happiness to live in such a society. You need not go to any heaven above. Here itself we can create a heaven. A *Satya Yuga,* a Golden Age, can come in this world when people will understand this truth and practise even a little bit of it. Great teachers came for that purpose only. Sri Ramakrishna came in our time. What an extraordinary personality was he, suffused with this spirit of oneness! Swami Vivekananda, Sarada Devi, and every one of the disciples of Sri Ramakrishna had the spirit of oneness. 'We are all one'. What a beautiful idea! That is why that Muslim revolutionary poet of Bengal, Kazi Nazrul Islam, when he wrote about Sri Ramakrishna, added this line: *Satya yuger puṇya smṛti kalite ānile tumi tāpas,* 'Hey *tāpas*, you brought the memory of *Satya Yuga* in this *Kali Yuga*'. What a beautiful idea! That Sri Ramakrishna has brought the memory of *Satya Yuga*. It is for us to assimilate this teaching and establish the *Satya Yuga* in society. That is our responsibility. He has shown us the way; he has given us the inspiration. That is a great contribution of Sri Ramakrishna.

So, here, Śrī Kṛṣṇa speaks of the *samadṛṣṭi, samatva*. Very difficult, but we have to achieve it. We have to give up our medieval heritage where everything was hierarchical. The king or aristocrat was there, enjoying nicely, having happiness all the time, surrounded by millions of people living in destitution and sorrow. That was our India. Even today, in many cases it is so. So many people working very hard so that a few, a handful, may live comfortably and happily! That will have to change thoroughly. That is the attitude the *Gītā* wants to develop in us and in all people all over the world.

This *samatā dṛṣṭi* is the sense of equality; and regarding this Arjuna will ask a question in the next *śloka:* 'it is a wonderful idea, this *samadṛṣṭi;* you have put it so nicely, but I find it very difficult to practise. Mind, I see, can never be in *samatva;* it always moves up and down; it is always wandering.

How can I control this mind?' So, that question will take us to the next *śloka*. Arjuna's question is on your behalf, on behalf of millions of people, because it is everybody's problem. Śrī Kṛṣṇa handles this important subject from the next verse onwards.

The four verses, 29 to 32, of the sixth chapter dealt with that capacity of the human being to see the same divine Reality in all beings. This was declared as a fruit of this inward meditation.

The *Gītā's* main *yoga* is connected with daily life and work. But meditation-*yoga* has something to contribute to this *yoga* of the *Gītā,* which is integral *yoga;* all aspects of spiritual life are combined together. So, one chapter is devoted to this great subject of meditation. We studied earlier the verses dealing with this subject. And the last four verses in this section, verses 29 to 32, refer to this great achievement of *samadṛṣṭi, samabhāva,* as a result of that meditation. This achievement can be had through *bhakti* and *jñāna* also, as through this *dhyāna* path specially developed by Patañjali in his *Yoga-sūtras*. So, we should keep in mind that this achievement can be had through all these paths. And in the fifth chapter we have already seen the spirit of equality, *samabhāva,* coming from *jñāna*. In the seventh chapter and in several subsequent chapters, you will get the same achievement through *bhakti*. So, the idea is this: to see the same Atman in every being and remove the feeling of separateness out of which comes evil, violence, hatred; everything evil comes from that sense of separateness.

So, this non-separateness, this *samatva-bhāva,* we have to achieve; and, for this, we have to go beyond the sensory level. At the sensory level everything is different. It is only when you go beyond the sensory level, that you find that supreme unity, pure consciousness, One and non-dual, behind everything in this universe. *And so, going beyond the sensory level is necessary in every path—bhakti, jñāna, karma* or *dhyāna;* the only difference is that, in this *dhyāna* or meditation path, and in this *jñāna* or spiritual knowledge, the path is rather difficult. But, in the *bhakti* path the same thing is achieved more easily. We don't do much violence to our own sensory nature. We go *with* it and this lower nature is *slowly* transcended. That will be told by Śrī Kṛṣṇa later on in the 12th chapter of this *Gītā* on *bhakti*. But, we should keep this in mind: the goal is this *samatva*, and this can be attained through all these various paths. But, in the *Gītā*, all these paths are blended together into one supreme spiritual path, which I call, 'a comprehensive spirituality of action and contemplation, *pravṛtti* and *nivṛtti*, blended together'. As I have dealt with this more fully in the 'Introduction', this is the philosophy for the modern age which has been emphasized today by Sri Ramakrishna also, *that God can be seen not only with eyes closed in meditation, but also with eyes open at the time of work*. This is a profound idea in Advaita Vedanta. Sri Ramakrishna has specially stressed the importance of this comprehensive spirituality of the *Gītā* based on that Advaitic vision. Meditation is a difficult art; everybody, who has tried it, will admit that it is not easy. For years you go on meditating, still meditation will not come to you so soon. When the mind has been accustomed in a particular way, we cannot change it so easily; if by concentration and meditation we have to get this sameness of vision or *samabhāva*, it is difficult, for our minds are always restless. This doubt has been voiced by Arjuna in verses 33 and 34, which we shall take up for study now.

**अर्जुन उवाच–**

*Arjuna uvāca —*

*'Arjuna said:'*

**योऽयं योगस्त्वया प्रोक्तः साम्येन मधुसूदन ।**
**एतस्याहं न पश्यामि चञ्चलत्वात् स्थितिं स्थिराम् ॥ ३३ ॥**

*Yo'yam yogastvayā proktaḥ sāmyena madhusūdana;*
*Etasyāham na paśyāmi cañcalatvātsthitim sthirām* — 6. 33

'This *yoga* which has been taught by you, O slayer of Madhu, as characterised by the vision of equality, I do not see (the possibility of) its lasting endurance, owing to restlessness (of the mind).'

Arjuna said: 'The mind is very fickle; I do not get that stability, that steadiness, to have this wonderful vision'. *Yo ayam yogaḥ tvayā proktaḥ*, 'this *yoga* which you expounded just now', *dhyāna yoga; etasyāham na paśyāmi*, 'I am not able to understand', *cañcalatvāt*, 'because the mind is very, very fickle'; *sthitim sthirām*, 'its lasting endurance'. We cannot concentrate easily. Such stability, such steadiness, we cannot get.

Then, the next verse expounds the idea further:

चञ्चलं हि मनः कृष्ण प्रमाथि बलवत् दृढम् ।
तस्याहं निग्रहं मन्ये वायोरिव सुदुष्करम् ॥३४॥

*Cañcalam hi manaḥ kṛṣṇa pramāthi balavat dṛḍham;*
*Tasyāham nigraham manye vāyoriva suduṣkaram* — 6. 34

'Verily, the mind, O Kṛṣṇa, is restless, turbulent, strong, and unyielding; I regard it quite as hard to achieve its control, as that of the air.'

Arjuna is putting forth the doubt which everyone has. He says, 'verily, O Kṛṣṇa, the mind is very, very fickle'. *Cañcalam hi manaḥ kṛṣṇa; hi* in Sanskrit means 'it is well known'. Wherever you find the word *hi*, it means 'it is very well known'. *Pramāthi balavat dṛḍham*, 'it pulls me powerfully this way, that way'. That is the nature of this mind; *tasyāham nigraham manye suduṣkaram*, 'its control and discipline I consider to be difficult'; *vāyoriva*, 'like trying to catch the air'.

So, these two verses convey the problem of dealing with the mind in the most luminous way. And it is good for us to know that it is not easy; it is hard. We cannot finish everything in six months and get away. And so Arjuna puts this question on our behalf, and Śrī Kṛṣṇa gives the answer, taking the subject to a wider dimension. Śrī Kṛṣṇa says, therefore,

श्रीभगवान् उवाच–
*Śrībhagavān uvāca* —
*'The Blessed Lord said:'*

असंशयं महाबाहो मनो दुर्निग्रहं चलम् ।
अभ्यासेन तु कौन्तेय वैराग्येण च गृह्यते ॥ ३५ ॥

*Asamśayam mahābāho mano durnigraham calam;*
*Abhyāsena tu kaunteya vairāgyeṇa ca gṛhyate* — 6. 35

'Without doubt, O mighty-armed, the mind is restless and difficult to control; but through practice and renunciation, O son of Kuntī, it can be achieved.'

*Bhagavān* says, 'you are right, Arjuna, this mind is very difficult to control.' Śrī Kṛṣṇa accepts this description of the mind by Arjuna; he doesn't contradict it. He says how we can yet manage to control the mind. *Asamśayam mahābāho mano durnigraham calam; asamśayam,* 'you are right, without any doubt'; *mano durnigraham,* 'mind is difficult to control'; *calam,* 'it is constantly flickering'. When Arjuna said I find the mind difficult to control, Śrī Kṛṣṇa gives the answer: *gṛhyate,* 'It can be controlled'. How? By two methods, *abhyāsena tu kaunteya vairāgyeṇa ca gṛhyate,* through *abhyāsa* and *vairāgya,* 'constant practice and a sense of detachment'.

In our daily life, not only in spiritual life, things which are impossible become possible when you do repeatedly the same thing. You get mastery over that thing. When you see somebody playing on the *tabla,* you think, 'O, it is impossible'. But, after six months of practice, you also get mastery over it. When I was a boy and saw people riding bicycles, I thought, 'how difficult it would be riding a cycle like this.' But when you try it for a few days, you also do it easily. So, it is a question of practice. *Abhyāsa* means practice. That is a very important word. And the next is *vairāgya,* a sense of detachment. Why does the mind run about? Because there are so many things to attract the mind. We shall develop a little detachment. That will help us in dealing with the mind better. So, *abhyāsa,* and *vairāgya* are important. And the same idea is expressed by Patañjali in his *Yoga-Sūtras,* dealing with the same subject about controlling the mind: *abhyāsa-vairāgyābhyām tan-nirodhaḥ,* 'the *cittavṛtti,* the action of the mind, its fluctuating nature, can be controlled by *abhyāsa* and *vairāgya*'. This confidence we must have. When you say that an achievement is impossible, then you will not be able to do that at all. You must first have the conviction that it is possible for you to achieve the goal, then only it becomes possible. What is impossible? Going to the moon was once thought to be impossible, but even that is possible today. So, there are many things, which we think impossible at one time; they become possible at another time. Therefore, don't say a thing is impossible. 'We shall do it, we shall do it'. This tremendous determination must be there.

This is expressed in the *Māṇḍūkya Upaniṣad Kārikā* of Gauḍapāda in a famous verse (3. 41) which says that, while dealing with the mind, you must have a tremendous determination. What is the type of determination? 'Taking a piece of grass, you try to empty the ocean, drop by drop.' With that determination you must control the mind:

*Utseka udadheryadvat kuśāgreṇaikabindunā;*
*Manaso nigrahastadvad bhaved aparikhedataḥ* —

Without depression, we must consistently pursue this work of dealing with the mind, just like a bird which had decided to empty the ocean because the ocean had destroyed the eggs the bird had laid nearby. The bird came, held a piece of grass in its beak and started emptying the ocean, drop by drop. A strange sight, but this is what we need to do in our daily life; we must have that determination, 'I shall succeed. I shall do it.' Climbing atop Mount Everest was difficult earlier; today, nearly everybody does it, women also do it. So, I say that there is a capacity in the human mind for achieving control over the mind and realizing the truth of the Atman. We must have faith in that power of the mind that, in our mind, there are hidden possibilities. A child finds a thing difficult; a young man of twenty will find it easy. In this example, you can see that our judgement regarding possibility or impossibility of things is very relative. So, don't go to an extreme assertion; though a thing is impossible, you can still say, 'at present it is impossible, but I shall do it, I shall do it.' That should be the attitude.

Consider an untrained tiger or lion in a circus party; on the first day a circus person goes to control it, he or she finds it impossible even to approach the animal. Such a terrible look and growling and roaring! And one gets frightened. But, we begin to train it slowly, and we succeed in training that terrible animal, till we can even just sit on its back. That is what we do. Just as with the wild animals around us, it is also the same with the wild mind. It can be trained; it can be made a servant of your purposes. Therefore, that faith must be there, 'I shall, I shall.' Let it take a number of years, even lives, but, we *shall* do it. Our concept of time is not confined merely to one physical existence. It is much wider, much vaster. What I fail to achieve now, I shall achieve later. But, I shall continue the struggle; I shall achieve something even in this birth. And I shall leave for the next birth to achieve the remaining. This vast canvas of time is given to all because one has got many things to achieve and one has many possible energies hidden within. And therefore, the scale of time which is given to us in Vedanta is so different from what is given to one in every other religion. Therefore, Śrī Kṛṣṇa will say later on, in this very chapter, about this wonderful time scale available to us for achieving things.

Śrī Kṛṣṇa said, *abhyāsena tu kaunteya vairāgyeṇa ca gṛhyate*, 'the control of the mind can be done through *abhyāsa* and *vairāgya*'. *Vairāgya* is 'the spirit of renunciation of a mere sensate life'. *Abhyāsa* is 'practice'. A wonderful idea is given here. You see a piece of rock there. A drop of water is falling from the top of that rock; falling drop by drop. After some years you will find that that rock has become eroded by the falling of those little water droplets. I have seen a rock where a person used to make *sāṣṭāṅga namaskāra*, salutation with the forehead touching that rock. I watched it for some years, and gradually, that rock began to develop a dent in it; that is the nature of repetition. A very tender touch of the skin, or a tender drop of water can make a dent on a hard rock. What a wonderful idea! So, we can do wonders with this mind; we can control it, though it looks very unstable and uncontrollable just now.

We shall have to make it strong and steady; that is the work we have to do in training the mind. This is the teaching that is given in this verse. All the great masters, who were produced in this country, have worked with patience and continued the struggle. 'We will win, we will win,' that is the language. Defeatism has no place in human life. You may get defeated once, but try again, and you will win. It is something like what I had said earlier about the British in the Second World War. Britain lost many battles, but she won the war. So, it is the same thing in our daily life; in dealing with the mind, we shall lose many battles, but eventually the war will be won, control of the mind will be achieved. That should be our attitude with regard to dealing with our mind. It is extremely difficult; in fact, this is so in the *Dhyāna yoga* and *Jñāna yoga* paths. In *Bhakti yoga* context also the same idea comes; we find our mind to be very difficult to control and a devotee prays, 'O, Lord, please do something to control my mind.'

Now, there is one *śloka* which is a prayer on behalf of the devotees of the world, because devotees know that their very weak minds can only be controlled through God's grace. The prayer is composed by Ādi Śaṅkarācārya, an extraordinary person, on behalf of you and I. He has dealt with this subject in his famous book, *Śivānandalahari*; the *śloka* 20 says in its second part:

*Kapālin bhikṣo me hṛdayakapim atyantacapalam;*
*Dṛḍham bhaktyā baddhvā śivā bhavadadhīnam kuru vibho* —

What a beautiful sentence! O *kapālin*, 'O Śiva'; Śiva is called a *kapālin* because he takes a skull from the cremation ground and uses it as a vessel for begging and eating food. It is a sort of begging bowl; *bhikṣo*, so he is being addressed as *bhikṣu*, 'a beggar'; *me hṛdayakapim*, 'the monkey of my heart'; *atyanta capalam*, 'extremely fickle' is this monkey; it never sits quiet; its eyes are always moving. You can see this nature of the monkey. What should Śiva do to you? *Dṛḍham bhaktyā baddhvā*, 'bind the mind strongly with the cord of *bhakti*'; but then, don't leave the mind here and there; *bhavadadhīnam kuru vibho*, 'keep it under your control', then there will be no fear. That is the prayer of Śaṅkarācārya on behalf of every devotee in the world.

So, Śrī Kṛṣṇa is telling us to have this positive attitude, 'I shall overcome, I shall overcome. How many difficult situations we have overcome; how many problems we have overcome! This also we shall overcome.' That should be the faith that must inspire our heart: *śraddhā*, 'faith', *ātmaśraddhā*, 'faith in oneself', faith also in the Divine that is within yourself. 'What is impossible when the Divine awakes in me?' That should be our attitude. This is called *śraddhā*, *a totality of positive attitudes*. Negative attitudes should not be cultivated for long periods; for a short period it may be there. The general attitude must be, 'I shall, I shall, I can, I can.' That is called *śraddhā* and Śrī Kṛṣṇa will say later in the 3rd verse of the seventeenth chapter, that 'a person is as good as the *śraddhā* that he or she has within himself or herself', *śraddhāmayo'yam puruṣo yo yacchraddhaḥ sa eva saḥ*. If you don't have *śraddhā*, you will be an absolutely good-for-nothing individual. Have that *śraddhā*; have that faith in yourself, have the faith that tremendous energies are hidden within you.

So, Śrī Kṛṣṇa says, *abhyāsa* and *vairāgya*. I have seen a boy in Rangoon, the son of a barrister. He was very weak and he had various evil habits like smoking, etc. So, when the barrister came to me one day and said, 'Such is the nature of the boy. He likes you, please give him some suggestion.' I said, 'Send him from Rangoon to Bangalore for physical culture training. There he should go and develop his body; the body has become very thin and weak; the mind is also weak; send him there.' And that had a miraculous effect. By the time the boy landed in Vizag from Rangoon, he gave up smoking by himself, without anybody telling him anything. Then he went to Bangalore, and developed his body; the change came, and he became, later on, a chartered accountant or some such thing.

This is how by a little effort, a new strength can come to us. We must be at it; that is why Śrī Kṛṣṇa is emphasizing this point. *Abhyāsa*—how many things we achieve through *abhyāsa*!

People learn music: how difficult it is to play on a harmonium, or a viṇa, or any such instrument! But, one achieves it all through practice. What is impossible at one moment becomes possible at another moment.

So, Śrī Kṛṣṇa says,

असंयतात्मना योगो दुष्प्राप इति मे मतिः ।
वश्यात्मना तु यतता शक्योऽवाप्तुं उपायतः ॥ ३६ ॥

*Asamyatātmanā yogo duṣprāpa iti me matiḥ;*
*Vaśyātmanā tu yatatā śakyo'vāptum upāyataḥ —* 6. 36

'*Yoga* is hard to be attained by one of uncontrolled self; such is My conviction; but the self-controlled, striving by right means, can obtain it.'

*Asamyatātmanā yogo duṣprāpa iti me matiḥ*, 'for one who has no control of the self or mind, there is no possibility of *Yoga*'; *asamyatātmanā* means, 'one devoid of control of the self or mind'; *samyata* means 'disciplined or controlled'; *asamyata*, 'without that control', when the mind is wandering here and there; *duṣprāpa iti me matiḥ*, 'such a one cannot get any kind of *Yoga;* that is My opinion', so says Śrī Kṛṣṇa here. *Vaśyātmanā tu yatatā śakyo'vāptum upāyataḥ*, 'but those who have some measure of control over the mind can achieve real *yoga* by adopting proper means'. Śrī Kṛṣṇa says, *sakyaḥ avāptum*, 'he or she can obtain *yoga*'; *upāyataḥ*, 'through proper *upāya* or means'. If you employ proper methods, you will achieve finally a complete control over the mind.

Then Arjuna asks another question:

अर्जुन उवाच –

*Arjuna uvāca —*

*'Arjuna said:'*

अयतिः श्रद्धयोपेतो योगाच्चलितमानसः ।
अप्राप्य योगसंसिद्धिं कां गतिं कृष्ण गच्छति ॥ ३७ ॥

*Ayatiḥ śraddhayopeto yogāccalitamānasaḥ;*
*Aprāpya yogasamsiddhim kām gatim kṛṣṇa gacchati —* 6. 37

'Though possessed of *śraddhā,* but unable to control oneself, with the mind moving away from *yoga,* what is the fate of one failing to gain perfection in *yoga,* O Kṛṣṇa?'

Consider a person who was struggling in the beginning; later on, he or she became a little amiss in the struggle, began to weaken his or her endeavour. Then such a one can be said to lose the *yoga* state. *Ayatiḥ,* 'unable to struggle'; *śraddhayopeto,* 'he or she has great *śraddhā:* "I must do."'; he or she has faith in oneself; *śraddhā* in *yoga* technique also is there, but, *yogāccalita mānasaḥ,* 'the mind has fallen down from the path of *yoga*'; a little bit of carelessness came and the mind has fallen down from that temper of *yoga. Aprāpya yogasamsiddhim,* 'not achieving the final goal of *yoga*'; *samsiddhi* means 'perfection' in *yoga. Kām gatim kṛṣṇa gacchati,* 'what happens to that person?' A person who is in this condition, he or she is on the deathbed and is to die. What will be his or her later state? The next *śloka* explains the question further:

**कच्चिन्नोभय विभ्रष्टः छिन्नाभ्रमिव नश्यति ।**
**अप्रतिष्ठो महाबाहो विमूढो ब्रह्मणः पथि ॥३८॥**

*Kaccinnobhaya vibhraṣṭaḥ chinnābhramiva naśyati;*
*Apratiṣṭho mahābāho vimūḍho brahmaṇaḥ pathi — 6. 38*

'Does such a person, fallen from both, and deluded in the path of Brahman, perish without support, like a rent cloud, O mighty-armed one?'

*Kaccinnobhayavibhraṣṭaḥ,* 'one who has lost both': worldly life and spiritual life; *ubhaya,* means 'both'; *vibhraṣṭaḥ,* 'fallen down' from both; *chinnābhram iva naśyati,* 'is he destroyed, just like the scattered cloud' by a strong wind; is the position of the seeker also of that nature? He or she has been practising *yoga,* had faith in it, but gave it up becoming amiss. Is such a one going to be destroyed just like the scattered cloud in the sky? *Apratiṣṭho,* 'without getting established' in the state of *yoga; vimūḍho brahmaṇaḥ pathi,* 'becoming deluded in the path of Brahman'. His or her mind has fallen down from there. What will happen to such a person who has failed to pursue this *yoga* path up to the end? This is Arjuna's question.

एतन्मे संशयं कृष्ण छेत्तुमर्हस्यशेषतः ।
त्वद् अन्यः संशयस्य अस्य छेत्ता न ह्युपपद्यते ॥ ३९ ॥

*Etanme saṁśayam kṛṣṇa chettumarhasyaśeṣataḥ;*
*Tvad anyaḥ saṁśayasya asya chettā na hyupapadyate—6. 39*

'This doubt of mine, O Kṛṣṇa, You should completely dispel; for it is not possible for any but You to dispel this doubt.'

*Etanme saṁśayam kṛṣṇa,* 'this doubt of mine, O Kṛṣṇa'; *chettum arhasi aśeṣataḥ,* 'you are capable of destroying this doubt completely'; *tvad anyaḥ,* 'other than you'; *saṁśayasya asya chettā,* 'remover of this doubt'; *na hi upapadyate,* 'I do not find'.

श्रीभगवान उवाच –
*Śrībhagavān uvāca —*

*'The Blessed Lord said:'*

पार्थ नैवेह नामुत्र विनाशः तस्य विद्यते ।
नहि कल्याणकृत् कश्चित् दुर्गतिं तात गच्छति ॥ ४० ॥

*Pārtha naiveha nāmutra vināśaḥ tasya vidyate;*
*Nahi kalyāṇakṛt kaścit durgatim tāta gacchati — 6. 40*

'Verily, O son of Pṛthā, there is no destruction for such a one, neither here nor hereafter for, the doer of good, O my son, never comes to grief.'

The first thing that Śri Kṛṣṇa does is to assure every person that if one has done good, he or she will never be destroyed. That is a great assurance coming from Śri Kṛṣṇa in the *Gītā,* in more than one place. Arjuna, I assure you that *na hi kalyāṇakṛt kaścit durgatim tāta gacchati. Kalyāṇa* means, 'what is good, what is auspicious'. It is a beautiful word in Sanskrit. *Kalyāṇa, maṅgala, śubha,* all three mean the same thing according to *Amarakośa.* Whoever does what is *kalyāṇa,* or *maṅgala,* or *śubha,* Śri Kṛṣṇa says, *tāta durgatim na gacchati,* 'my dear child, such a one will never come to grief', never come to any bad situation; *durgatim* means 'a bad state of life'. That degradation will never come to such a person. This is a promise. What will happen to that person then? Śri Kṛṣṇa explains it:

प्राप्य पुण्यकृतां लोकान् उषित्वा शाश्वतीः समाः ।
शुचीनां श्रीमतां गेहे योगभ्रष्टोऽभिजायते ॥४१॥

*Prāpya puṇyakṛtām lokān uṣitvā śāśvatīḥ samāḥ;*
*Śucīnām śrīmatām gehe yogabhraṣṭo'bhijāyate* — 6. 41

'Having attained the worlds of the doers of meritorious deeds, and dwelling there for long years, one fallen from *yoga* reincarnates in the home of the pure and the prosperous.'

*Yogabhraṣṭaḥ*, 'one who has fallen from the path of *yoga*', i.e. without completing the whole *yoga* process, because the mind became diverted due to carelessness; such a person will be born in the next life in a suitable environment to continue the unfinished task. That is the special teaching of the *Sanātana Dharma*. In no other religion will you find this idea, specially in the present day world religions. Earlier, primitive religions had this belief, but other religions hold that one has only one life, only the present particular physical manifestation, nothing else, neither before nor hereafter. But, in India all the great teachers of India's religions—Hindu, Buddhist, or Jain—have emphasized that this physical manifestation is only one such manifestation; many births have gone before this, many will come after this also. India's time and space scale is immense, like that of modern Western science. We are in search of something. If you can't get it in the present birth, you will get it in the next, or in a still later birth. You *will* get the opportunity. This is the concept of rebirth or reincarnation.

This coming and going will end when one realizes the infinite and immortal Brahman or Atman, the very source of the universe. Vedanta considers that realization as the one goal of human evolution. That knowledge of reincarnation came to us when we discovered that this human being has three personality levels. One is the gross personality of the human body, *sthūla śarīra*, within which there is a subtle personality of ideas, thoughts and impressions, etc. That is called *sūkṣma śarīra*, the subtle body, within which is the *kāraṇa śarīra*, the causal body, which is extremely subtle. So, one is gross, the other is subtle, and the last one is extremely subtle. At the time of death what happens is this: the gross body dies and is left behind; the subtle and causal bodies go away. It is compared to a snake leaving away its outer skin and getting a new skin. The gross has a limited frame of life. The time frame of each type of the body is different; for the gross, it is very limited, whereas the time frame for the subtle body is much vaster. Even now, much of our day-to-day life is conducted by that subtle body, through the physical gross body. It is only a continual expression of the subtle body through various gross bodies. Our conscious experiences are controlled by the unconscious and subconscious levels of the human mind. The subconscious and unconscious layers of the mind constitute the *sūkṣma śarīra*, containing all our impressions of actions performed in previous and present lives. When the seers discovered the *sūkṣma śarīra*, then they got this new idea that physical death is not the end of human life; only this particular manifestation ends here, and you are to continue in another life. So, death is treated not as a full stop, but only as a comma, or a semicolon. Life continues further and further, though physically you cannot verify it. It can be verified only spiritually.

So, the sages investigated the science of human possibilities; they could go deep into the human mind, could discover this type of existence beyond the physical manifestation. So, what is done in this life is not destroyed. We continue our march later. Death is just a kind of sleep and we wake up later and continue the march. A pilgrim going to a place of pilgrimage takes a night halt at a particular place and sleeps; but, the next morning, the pilgrim continues his pilgrimage again. And human life is like this. This a profound truth of our religion which is attracting the attention of increasing numbers of Western people, including a few scientists, even though it cannot be verified. There is no physical verification. This sensory system cannot verify it, because no quantity can be made out of it. And yet the whole idea has some profound truth in it; many people feel it.

It is this subtle body or *sūkṣma śarīra* that is the equivalent of 'soul' in the English language, and that forms the subject of rebirth or reincarnation. That this truth had been widely held by an impressive cross-section of humanity in ancient and modern times is revealed to us by a recent book: *Reincarnation: An East-West Anthology,* compiled by Joseph Head and S.L. Cranston, and published by the Julian Press, Inc., New York. The announcement over the cover flap reads:

'Reincarnation is frequently regarded as an oriental concept incompatible with Western thinking and traditional belief. The present encyclopaedic compilation of quotations from eminent philosophers, theologians, poets, scientists, etc., of every period of Western culture, and the thoroughly documented survey of Reincarnation Culture, and the thoroughly documented survey of Reincarnation in world religions, will serve to correct this error in thinking.

'This anthology deals with a subject which many philosophers have called the central issue of our time—the question of man's immortality.'

The announcement ends with the following comments of James Freeman Clarke:

'It would be curious if we should find science and philosophy taking up again the old theory of metempsychosis, remodelling it to suit our present modes of religious and scientific thought, and launching it again on the wide ocean of human belief. But strange things have happened in the history of human opinion.'

In the Preface to the book, the compilers state:

'Although a surprising number of distinguished thinkers of every period of history have either championed or on occasion favourably considered the idea of repeated existences upon earth, as this Anthology attests, such testimony hardly established reincarnation as a fact. It does suggest, however, that an idea that has occupied so many exceptional minds cannot be lightly dismissed, but is worthy of questioning, study, and investigation.'

We all live and one day we will die. Is everything over upon our death? That suspicion remains true. Every human mind has asked this question. *Astītyeke nāyamastīti caike,* as the

*Kaṭha Upaniṣad* (I. i. 20) says, 'some say there is, some others say there is not'. We may not see with these eyes, but something is there that transcends death. Based upon that truth of rebirth, Śrī Kṛṣṇa says, when that *yogabhraṣṭaḥ*, 'one fallen from yoga' dies, he or she has only lost the physical body, the *sthūla śarīra*, but the person with the *sūkṣma śarīra* continues and tries to get a new birth. All of his or her tendencies in this life will determine the type of birth that person will have in the next incarnation. *Yathā karma yaṭhā śrutam*, 'in accordance with their work and in conformity with their knowledge', as the *Kaṭha Upaniṣad* (II. ii. 7) puts it. What kind of birth will one have? Śrī Kṛṣṇa has given here two types of birth as examples. What is that?

*Prāpya puṇyakṛtām lokān*, first of all, that person has done much good work here, much *puṇyam* he or she has done here, so that person will go 'to subtle worlds of doers of meritorious deeds', *puṇyakṛtām lokān*. But that heaven is not eternal. When the merit capital which took that person there is exhausted, the person comes back to the human world, and is reborn; but, where? *Śucīnām śrīmatām gehe*, 'in a prosperous but pure family'; such a person will get birth there. He or she will be gravitating to that particular situation. After all, there is such a thing as affinity. This soul has affinity with that situation, with that environment. Therefore, he or she finds it possible to be born there. So, Śrī Kṛṣṇa says *śāśvatīḥ samāḥ*, 'having lived long in that heavenly enjoyment', when the *puṇyam* capital is exhausted, one may be born in a pure and prosperous family, *śucīnām śrīmatām gehe yogabhraṣṭo'bhijāyate*. And what happens thereafter? After one is born there, within a short time, the whole *samskāras* of the past come to influence that person. He or she starts the life's journey once again, where he or she had left off. Nothing of what you have done is lost.

*Tatra taṃ buddhisamyogam labhate paurvadehikam*, 'there he or she becomes associated with the entire totality of thoughts and aspirations that he or she had in the past life'. The fall that one had is overlooked and all these noble thoughts and aspirations come to him or her through various impulses from within. Then the seeker in the new birth says to oneself, 'now let me begin once again and continue the journey.' He or she may not remember all that was done in the past, but the subconscious mind takes the seeker in the right direction. *The only valid objection to the teaching of rebirth is that no one has any memory of last birth.* Vedanta says that this objection is not valid. *Memory cannot be the test of existence.* None has the memory of one's early childhood experiences.

This is just like what we see in our life today. What makes us choose a particular profession? Everybody born in the same family, with the same genetic constitution, does not live his or her life in the same way. Each child in the family chooses a particular profession: music, sport, science, or mountain-climbing, each according to his or her interest. *Where is this interest obtained from*? Not from this life; not from the genetic constitution which is common to all of them. In this life there has been no experience yet. So, *that impulse must be coming from the past*. Such a person will say, 'I don't know what it is, but it is impelling me. I must go for this, I must go for that.' You argue with that person, that boy or girl saying, 'No, don't do it. Go in for something else;' you may try your best, but no, he or she will come back to this and say firmly, '*this* is my choice, *this* is my choice.' This determination in a new life is based on all that one did in a past life. It gives you a particular impulse, a particular direction. First type of birth is *śucīnām śrīmatām gehe;* the second type of birth is in a *yogī's* own house as pointed out in the next *śloka,* 42.

अथवा योगिनाम एव कुले भवति धीमताम् ।
एतद्धि दुर्लभतरं लोके जन्म यदीदृशम् ॥४२॥

*Athavā yoginām eva kule bhavati dhīmatām;*
*Etaddhi durlabhataram loke janma yadīdṛśam —* 6. 42

'Or else one may be born into a family of wise *yogīs* only; verily, a birth such as that is very rare to obtain in this world.'

A very wise *yogī's* family, may not be a well-to-do one, but its members are fine, nice people, who practise *yoga;* there one may get one's next birth; that will stimulate the person all the more to strive for spiritual illumination. You can see it in India today in another context. Number of people apply for central services, particularly IAS and IPS. The largest number is from Delhi, because the whole atmosphere of the family there is governed by various types of services. So, the whole atmosphere gives a stimulus to a new-born child. In the beginning, Delhi dominated all these central services. Slowly, it is now spreading to the interior areas also. Because everywhere new *samskāras* are developing through social contact, people are coming to apply for central services today from far away places, even small towns, even villages. There is such a thing as a stimulus given to you by the atmosphere of the family, or society. This is easy to recognize. In the case of *yoga*, it is just the same. In a holy family, one will have the tendency to pursue what holy deeds one had done earlier; one may not know the why of it, but it is something that pulls him or her in that direction. One cannot say no to it, nobody can say no to it; that is the idea.

*Etat hi durlabhataram*, 'this is extremely difficult'; to get this option is not so easy. *Loke janma yadīdṛśam*, 'this kind of birth in the world' is rather very rare; only some cases are there of this nature. So, you are already in an atmosphere of *yoga*; there is already the impulse of *yoga* within you. These two, the family *yoga* atmosphere and the candidate's impulse of *yoga*, conspire to start one to continue the journey on the path of *yoga*.

Therefore, Śrī Kṛṣṇa says:

तत्र तं बुद्धिसंयोगं लभते पौर्वदेहिकम् ।
यतते च ततो भूयः संसिद्धौ कुरुनन्दन ॥४३॥

*Tatra tam buddhisamyogam labhate paurvadehikam;*
*Yatate ca tato bhūyaḥ samsiddhau kurunandana* —6. 43

'There, one is united with the intelligence acquired in the former body, and strives more than before, for perfection, O son of the Kurus.'

*Tatra tam buddhisamyogam labhate paurvadehikam; tatra,* 'there', by the time the child is four to eight years old, a certain impulse coming from the past birth, already working in its *sūkṣma śarīra* or subtle body, impels one to choose the spiritual path, the *yoga* path. He or she had left it off in a previous life; now, he or she will continue the journey towards spiritual perfection. *Paurvadehikam,* 'pertaining to the *pūrvadeha*' or 'the previous body' in which he or she had developed this *yoga* practice; *buddhi samyogam labhate,* 'that *buddhi* comes to him or her in a very forceful way', when he or she starts choosing a life career. And that *buddhi* will finally express in his or her mind thus: 'this is the career I will take up, this is what, this is where I left off in my earlier life.' *Yatate ca tato bhūyaḥ,* 'such a one continues spiritual practice again in that new life'; *yatna* means 'struggle, effort'; he or she continues the earlier effort; *samsiddhau,* 'to achieve *siddhi* or perfection in spiritual life'; *kurunandana,* 'child of the *Kurus,* i.e. Arjuna'.

This is the way one continues to struggle for what one aspires to be in one's present life, which could not be completed in an earlier life. In the next life the same impulse takes you to continue that struggle. That *buddhi,* that you had before, begins to influence you now. *Buddhi* doesn't die when the body dies. *Manas* and *buddhi,* both continue with all the impressions of life; all the *karmas* that we have done in previous life, its fruits, etc., are all there. So, that *buddhi* begins to assert in the new life. There is no other explanation why one child should choose to become a musician from the very beginning, while another child goes to the army, and another child goes for this or that. Born in the same family, genetically there is no difference at all, but why this difference in choosing? No genetics, by itself, can explain it.

Our people said, here is the truth: A human being is not merely the physical body, and therefore death doesn't mean the end of the human struggle. He or she has a subtle body. That body survives the death of the physical body, and that body, the *sūkṣma śarīra,* manufactures a new body for itself, suitable to its own purpose. This is the teaching given by all the teachers of various religions that had their birth in India. This truth cannot be arrived at by those who believe that the human being is only the physical body.

पूर्वाभ्यासेन तेनैव ह्रियते ह्यवशोऽपि सः ।
जिज्ञासुरपि योगस्य शब्दब्रह्म अतिवर्तते ॥४४॥

*Pūrvābhyāsena tenaiva hriyate hyavaśo'pi saḥ;*
*Jijñāsurapi yogasya śabdabrahma ativartate —* 6. 44

'By that previous practice alone, one is borne on in spite of oneself. Even the enquirer after *yoga* rises superior to the performer of Vedic rituals.'

*Pūrvābhyāsa*, 'the previous *abhyāsa* or practices that one had'; *hriyate hyavaśo'pi saḥ*, 'pulls one into the line of spiritual practice in spite of oneself'. You may not particularly very much choose it, but your inner impulses take you in that direction. Then a beautiful truth Śrī Kṛṣṇa conveys here: *jijñāsurapi yogasya śabdabrahma ativartate; śabdabrahma* means 'the Vedas', its ritualistic portions, the dos and don'ts about religion. Literally, it means Brahman, the Ultimate Reality, as *śabda* or sound; *śabda* means the Vedas. In the *Koran*, in the *Bible*, everywhere you will find that aspect of religion, the dos and don'ts of religion. The Vedas themselves say in its philosophical part that one transcends these dos and don'ts when one begins to experiment with religion. Till experimenting you are subject to the dos and don'ts, but once you start experimenting and experiencing, you go beyond the dos and don'ts of any religion. So, you transcend the *śabdabrahma;* who transcends? *Jijñāsurapi yogasya*, 'the very enquirer or investigator or experimenter with *yoga*'. When you begin to undertake *yoga* spiritual exercises, you don't need the help of these dos and don'ts at all. You are an experimenter, and *that* is real religion. Dos and don'ts are only very elementary; a child up to the age of five or six must abide by the 'do this and do not do that' of the parents, but afterwards one's own judgement comes to determine what is proper to do. One can then say, 'Yes, I like this, I like that', etc.

So, in spiritual life too, it is just the same. In the very elementary state of religion, you follow dos and don'ts. That is what you get in the Hindu *Smṛtis* and in the Islamic *Shariyat*, and in other various scriptures: do this, don't do this; we follow these injunctions, but it is not meant to be continued for long. You must transcend these and begin to experiment with the real subject of religion. We don't need these dos and don'ts at that time. That, Śrī Kṛṣṇa emphasizes in this great statement.

*Jijñāsurapi yogasya śabdabrahma ativartate*, 'even the inquirer into the nature of *yoga* goes beyond the jurisdiction of *śabdabrahma* or the Veda'; the *vidhi*, 'dos' and *niṣedha*, 'don't dos' of religion; 'I should do this, I should not do this'; you go beyond all this because you have become an experimenter. You are *in search* of truth. What a beautiful idea! To be limited by the Vedic injunctions is only like the limited application of dos and don'ts as when you were a child. When you are grown up, you think and act for yourself by yourself. Then you are going to enter into the field of search; you don't need these dos and don'ts any more. Before you start the journey, you consult the map. After consulting the map, you fold it, put it aside, and *start* the journey. According to the direction of the map, you go on to reach the goal yourself; you don't constantly keep looking at the map all throughout the journey. That is why this, the injunction, is secondary; and that, the quest, is primary; experience is primary, consulting books is secondary. *Consult with a view to experiment and experience*. That is a beautiful expression. In the *Sanātana Dharma* of India alone will you find this open admission that dos and don'ts of religions do not affect a person who has started experimenting with religion. When you live a spiritual life and start the struggle, you come to the science of religion. The other is the ethnical aspect of religion. 'I belong to the Hindu religion, so I have to do certain things; I belong to the Muslim religion, so I have to do certain things or avoid doing certain other things', etc. *But once you enter into the practice of religion, you come to the science of religion*. You will also discover the unity of all religions once you begin the actual practice. For instance, take all the mystics of religions—the Sufi, the Christian, the Hindu—you will find a lot of similarity, a lot of unity.

These are the universal truths experienced by the world's mystics of any and every religion. So, that is where pure religion begins: religion as a search, religion as a science. Science depends upon seeking. I am quoting Eddington, the famous mathematician-astronomer of England. He says, 'You cannot understand the spirit of true science or true religion without keeping seeking in the forefront.' Keep the idea of searching in front of you; then you are a scientist, then you are a spiritual person. Nobody is born a physicist; nobody is born an astronomer. One seeks astronomy, one seeks physics, therefore, one becomes a scientist or a physicist. In religion, we are born in a particular religion, in a particular set of dos and don'ts and we remain there. If you want to be a scientist in religion, you must begin to ask and seek; then you will become a scientist in religion. As physical science is universal—there is no American science or Indian science or Arabic science—so also is religion when approached as a science. *This is one great understanding upheld openly by Vedanta or Sanātana Dharma, which people must grasp today*. Permanent peace and harmony between religions will come when we understand this true dimension of religion. The first is only the beginning, but it must lead you to the second. Then only it will be a *science* of religion. And when there is a science of religion you are in search of truth, you are not in search of a dogma or creed. They have no value for you. 'Is this true?', you ask, and go to the truth of it; you continue your march, go ahead, and try to realize it for yourself. In this way, the whole of *Sanātana Dharma* is centred in this scientific understanding of religion. Have you realized the truth? What is the use of merely believing? Believing has no final status here.

Śaṅkarācārya speaks in his commentaries very often, 'any fool can say "I know, I know." Show what you know. Have you realized something? Let us see what you have realized.' That kind of testing and verification is needed. So many passages you will find in the spiritual literature of India, where this emphasis on *anubhava*, 'experience', is there. Belief has no high status in India. A man or woman may be exceptionally fine in character, though he or she may not have any beliefs at all, and yet we respect that person, for he or she is not merely a believer; a believer has no particular status.

So, Śrī Kṛṣṇa is giving the essence of a profound idea which is found only in the *Sanātana Dharma*. In every other religion, if you try to experiment, if you try to experience something outside the accepted dogma, you may be killed even. You may not go beyond orthodoxy, those particular dos and don'ts. You may never get beyond it all your life. How many great mystics have been killed for trying to go beyond dogmas. How many have been controlled by religious authorities in Christianity and Islam. In Islam there were many great mystics who had realized very high truths, and yet they had to face death.

So, this concept of going beyond the letter of the law, trying to get the spirit of religion, was emphasized by Jesus Christ also. Jesus also says, you must seek if you want true religion, 'ask and it shall be given, seek and you shall find, knock and it shall be opened unto you.' There you get the science of religion. But this was never popularized by the Christian Church throughout all these 1800 years. Today, we understand religion from the Indian point of view that it is a science of human growth and development, a science of human possibilities; that the Divine possibilities hidden within each one can be realized even in this very life. Nature has given the human being the organic capacity to do so. Therefore, today, more and more people are understanding religion from that point of view, as a science of human growth, development, and fulfilment, as a science of unfolding the infinite possibilities in every human being. When you do so, these dos and don'ts cease to have that appeal to you; they cease to exert control over you. That is what is expressed here in a brief sentence, *jijñāsurapi yogasya śabdabrahma ativartate*, 'even a *jijñāsu* of *yoga*, an inquirer into spiritual truths, goes beyond the control of all *śabdabrahma*, all Vedas, all scriptures.'

That is a wonderful truth. This subject is continued in the remaining few verses; all these verses are on the subject of *yoga*, on how one continues *yoga* practice life after life until, in the final life, one is spiritually ripe enough to achieve the highest realization. But, behind this final realization, there may be many failures that we don't mark, but they are there. That is what Śrī Kṛṣṇa is going to tell us; failures will ultimately lead one to success, if one persists; that is the idea.

This idea is very strongly upheld only in the Hindu tradition; not in the Christian, not in the Islamic. There the dos and don'ts are very very powerful. You cannot easily transcend them, and if you transcend them, you might be punished also, even with death. But, in the *Sanātana Dharma* tradition, when you transcend this and begin to *live* religion, *then* you are very much appreciated, because that is the soul of religion, because, in *Sanātana Dharma*, 'experience', *anubhava* is the test of religion, not belief. In all other religions, belief is very very central. But, in India it is different. That is why we don't harm even unbelievers, we don't burn or torture them. That is all due to this one single truth that is emphasized, '*religion is realization and not belief*'. And when you start experimenting with religion, with a view to realizing its truth, you go beyond all these little dos and don'ts.

The *sandhyā vandanā* that we have in our tradition, with *mantras* and all that, is a very formal ritual. The thing is, you don't get anything by the performance of *sandhyā vandanā*. But, if you don't do it, you get into trouble! *Akaraṇe pratyavāya doṣaḥ*, 'if you don't do it, you do a wrong'. That is the nature of this kind of ritual. And Sri Ramakrishna says '*Sandhyā* merges in *Gāyatrī*'. *Gāyatrī* is much higher spiritually than this ritual of *sandhyā*. So, when you find spiritual stimulus has come to you, you need not do the *sandhyā* at all; you can straightaway start with *Gāyatrī* meditation. *Gāyatrī* merges in *Om*, that Supreme Divine word, which is the symbol of the Absolute Reality. In this way, there is such a thing as progress in spiritual life. We do not remain static; we do not remain at that elementary stage, at the infant level, even at the age of eighty.

This concept is very strong in the Indian spiritual tradition. Wherever that emphasis is there, you have the science of religion: religion taking you to the experience of some profound spiritual truth. And the *Gītā* and the Upaniṣads are interested, not in confining people to these little dos and don'ts, but to give them a taste of the Reality hidden within each of them. You *must* realize this truth. Again and again this is emphasized in the Upaniṣads, in the *Gītā,* and in other great books of the Hindu tradition. In the Sufi tradition there is this emphasis, 'I am going beyond the rituals and the dos and don'ts of religion'; so also in Christian mystical tradition. But every time they have to watch for the reaction of the powerful orthodoxy. If you go a little more, orthodoxy will come upon you; the Church will come upon you. That is why they have to tread very carefully in the inner life. The finest spirits have been killed by orthodoxy in all these religions.

That is the speciality of the Indian tradition, that we don't kill people who take to religion seriously. We are happy that one has taken to religion seriously. Religion is not a matter for talk for humanity; humanity has to *live* it, has to *realize* it; it is this central idea of spiritual experimentation; it is those who have realized spirituality that have kept India strong and steady. That is the soul of religion. Other aspects of religion are sometimes to be ignored as we are doing today. How many dos and don'ts of religion, people in every religion, are ignoring everyday today! So many things which are prescribed by religion, they don't do. That doesn't make for loss to the Hindu religion, because it consists in a struggle to realize the truth hidden in one's own experience. Everybody can do it.

So, this is the importance of this statement in verse 44, where Śrī Kṛṣṇa says, *pūrvābhyāsena tenaiva hriyate hyavaśo'pi saḥ*. A yogī, if he or she falls down from that *yoga*-practice before attaining the end of *yoga* and later dies, in the next birth he or she starts from where one left off and continues the spiritual journey; and 'he or she is impelled by all those old spiritual *samskāras;* without knowing it, one is impelled to take to spiritual practice, and one soon becomes an experimenter in that new life and in that state becomes a *jijñāsu*, a questioner, a seeker.'

When Sri Ramakrishna started as a *pūjari* or a priest in the Kālī temple at Dakshineswar, he soon became a *jijñāsu* there. 'What am I doing? Worshipping a stone image? Is it true? Is it correct? Is there a Divine in this stone or in this Universe?' This kind of questioning you will find from the very beginning. That is the nature of the spiritual growth of men and women. Otherwise, we take it for granted. Every priest doesn't question all these daily acts. Whatever he has to do, he keeps on doing them like a machine. And if he gets his money, that is enough for him! But here it is quite different. Sri Ramakrishna started questioning, 'Are you true, O Mother? Or, are you a mere poetry, a mere imagination of people, a mere myth or legend?' All these questions came to his mind and out of this questioning came in the life of Sri Ramakrishna, that tremendous development of pure spirituality through various paths.

In the next *śloka,* verse 45, Śrī Kṛṣṇa says:

प्रयत्नाद्यतमानस्तु योगी संशुद्धकिल्बिषः ।
अनेकजन्म संसिद्धः ततो याति परां गतिम् ॥४५॥

*Prayatnādyatamānastu yogī ṣamśuddhakilbiṣaḥ;*
*Anekajanma samsiddhaḥ tato yāti parām gatim* — 6. 45

'The *yogī*, striving assiduously, purified of taint, gradually gaining perfection through many births, then reaches the highest goal.'

*Prayatnād yatamānastu*, 'when the *yogī* struggles with tremendous effort'; *yogī samśuddhakilbiṣaḥ*, 'in the course of that struggle, one is shedding one's sins, impurities, and other things of the mind'; *samśuddha kilbiṣaḥ* means 'one who has purified whatever is evil in oneself'. Thus, one goes on building up one's spiritual awareness step by step, in a series of births. Some part you do in one birth, then, continue it in the next birth, and so on. It is a long journey; it can't be finished just in a short time. So, *aneka janma samsiddhaḥ*, 'becoming perfected through many births'. *Tato yāti parām gatim*, 'then, in the last birth one achieves spiritual realization'. It can be done in one birth provided the spiritual assets are available. Otherwise, you have to build up these spiritual assets; and asset-building means living a good life based on ethics and morality, and trying to love God and to advance towards Him. A dynamic spiritual life is needed; not leading merely a stagnant life. In that way you start advancing. Even then, by the time you come to the end of your life, you may not have achieved much. Then, when you die with the thought of the divine, in the next life you continue your spiritual march.

Nārada, one of the greatest saints in the *Sanātana Dharma* tradition, devoted himself to spiritual life in his earlier birth, even from his mother's womb. He got spiritual instructions from the discussions of sages who came to his house; his mother was only a maidservant at that time. After his mother's death he struggled. He tells his own story in the *Śrīmad Bhāgavatam:* Then he heard a voice, saying, 'Nārada, you cannot achieve the highest in *this* life. There are still some weaknesses which have to be shed from you.' And, in his next life, we get a perfect Nārada, who becomes the great singer-messenger of God. Nārada's is a wonderful story we get in many of our *Purāṇas*.

*Prayatnāt yatamānastu yogī saṃśuddha kilbiṣaḥ*, 'through tremendous effort, the *yogī* becomes freed from all evil'; *aneka janma saṃsiddhaḥ*, 'having built up purity and spirituality life after life'; in the final life, *tato yāti parām gatim*, 'he or she achieves the supreme state' of perfection in spirituality. It is a very beautiful, elevating, encouraging truth for all of us.

In the next verse, Śrī Kṛṣṇa gives a comparison between various types of spiritual practitioners:

तपस्विभ्योऽधिको योगी ज्ञानिभ्योऽपि मतोऽधिकः ।
कर्मिभ्यश्चाधिको योगी तस्माद्योगी भवार्जुन ॥४६॥

*Tapasvibhyo'dhiko yogī jñānibhyo'pi mato'dhikaḥ;*
*Karmibhyaścādhiko yogī tasmādyogī bhavārjuna* — 6. 43

'The *yogī* is regarded as superior to those who practise asceticism, and also to those who have obtained knowledge (through the scriptures); the *yogī* is also superior to the performers of action (enjoined in the scriptures). Therefore, be you a *yogī*, O Arjuna.'

The best of *yogīs* is expounded here in the *Bhagavad-Gītā.* From the second chapter onwards, to present the highest *yogī* ideal, we have various thoughts and inspiration, including the great technique of meditation given in this chapter. We have Patañjali's idea of training the mind, making it calm and steady, all that is included in the *yoga* or practical spirituality of the Gītā; *Karma, Jñāna, Bhakti* and this *Dhyāna,* all these are included in Śrī Kṛṣṇa's teaching of *yoga*. That is the *Gītā's* idea of *yoga*. This *yoga* is very comprehensive; I call it 'a comprehensive spirituality'. During work, during leisure, during human relations, and during meditation, such persons are in that world of *yoga*. 'You are a *yogī*'; that is a beautiful idea to tell a housewife. People will be wondering, 'how can *she, a housewife,* be a *yogī*? A *yogī* is a specialized kind of human being, sitting somewhere in the Himalayas. No. Śrī Kṛṣṇa says, 'you *are* a *yogī*'; whatever one may be doing, Śrī Kṛṣṇa whispers into the ear of all working people: 'You are a *yogī*. You are all to be *yogīs*'. That is the nature of this comprehensive spirituality of the *Gītā*.

So, in this verse Śrī Kṛṣṇa says:

*Tapasvibhyo'dhiko yogī*, '*yogī* is superior to a *tapasvī*', one who practises austerities. Austerities are not of so much value. You can say, suppose I fast for five days; the only advantage you get out of it is that you can control your sensory appetites. That is one great gain. You get nothing else out of it. That is why a *tapasvī* is doing something good. But this *yogī* is superior to that. *Jñānibhyo'pi mato'dhikaḥ*, 'a *jñāni* who has studied all about philosophy and religion, what is God, what is soul; he knows everything *theoretically*, that *jñāni* also is inferior to this *yogī*'. You have known God, you have known the soul, but you have not experienced it and become one with it. That kind of *jñāni* is inferior to this *yogī*. And then, *karmibhyaścādhiko yogī*, 'those who do *karma* with attachment, with all the love-and-hate relationships, or *karma* involving rituals and ceremonies, that *karmi* is also inferior to this *yogī*'. Then, finally, comes a wonderful exhortation in the last part of verse 46: *Tasmād*, 'therefore'; *yogī bhavārjuna*, 'be a *yogī*, O Arjuna'.

If you ask what Śrī Kṛṣṇa is going to advise you, I will say this: He is whispering in your ear, and in everybody's ear, 'Be a *yogī*, be a *yogī;* that is your birthright. You are realizing what is already there, merely hidden within you. Spirituality is your birthright. Try to realize your birthright.' That is the message Śrī Kṛṣṇa conveys to every person.

There is no person who cannot become a *yogī*, as taught in the *Gītā*. Many people cannot perform various types of asceticism. But there is no need for it also. It is all mere waste of energy. Buddha discovered, after six years of ascetic life, that he had become thin, he had become lean, he had become weak. When he touched the belly, he said in his discourse, 'I could touch my backbone.' Such was the nature of his body due to leading an ascetic life. And when he tried to get up, he fell down. Then he sat and asked this question, 'What is this ascetic life? Where does it lead me to? Absolutely nothing. This body has to achieve the highest illumination, but I am weakening it all the time.' And so he said, 'Asceticism of this type is vulgar. Similarly, those who get merged in sensory life they also are vulgar. I shall follow the middle path.' What a beautiful expression—*madhyama pratipāda*, 'the middle path', which we saw already at the very beginning of the sixth chapter. 'Don't eat too much, don't starve too much, don't work too much, don't rest too much.' All these are told there. Those who take to the middle path, they achieve *yoga*.

I like this beautiful exhortation of Śrī Kṛṣṇa. To every child, in the ear you can tell, 'Be a *yogī*, be a *yogī*', as taught in the *Gītā*. You do good work, help people, serve people, bring happiness and cheer to one and all, develop peace of mind and strong detachment; all this is part of *yoga;* you will be leading a full life, as we call it. As Sri Ramakrishna enjoins, 'See God with eyes open at the time of work, and with eyes closed at the time of meditation'. That is the nature of this *yoga*. That is why you can bring in work as an important element of *yoga*. Usually, work is not considered an element of *yoga*. Work is just something that drags the mind to the external *samsāra* or worldliness. You are doing some work at home; you think it is *samsāra*. No, it is *not samsāra;* it is *yoga*. Śrī Kṛṣṇa is telling us in the *Gītā*, 'Every work is sacred, every work is holy. By itself work is neither good nor bad, but the attitude of the mind makes it good or bad.' In this way, work has been given a very high status in the *Gītā*, and *yoga* in the *Gītā* is based upon men and women at work, men and women who have to discharge their responsibilities in life, in the midst of which one can become spiritual, one can realize truth. That is the exhortation here to everyone—politicians, administrators, school teachers, professors and professionals, housewives, and to everyone else. If only we understand the *Gītā* correctly, we will be hearing a constant whisper that Śrī Kṛṣṇa is putting into the ears of people, every minute, *tasmāt yogī bhava*, 'therefore, be a *yogī*, be a *yogī*.' Slowly, steadily, advance; there is no need to perform quick march in this matter; you can walk at your own convenient pace. But it is a long road. Take one step. Be thankful that you have gained that one step; then take the second step; and, in this way, march forward according to your own strength.

So, this is a very practical philosophy. And when you adopt it, there is no need for any regrets such as: 'I have not gone fast enough.' You will go ahead according to your strength. To someone who is faster, you say, 'God speed, go ahead, I shall come behind you.' That attitude must be there. No jealousy, no pulling somebody down; say, 'You go faster. I will come behind you. I have got my own pace.' What a beautiful idea! High character comes out of this attitude. That is what we need very badly today.

In one of the speeches of Swami Vivekananda in London, the subject was Practical Vedanta; high character, most generous attitudes, all these are discussed in that context. Swamiji gave an illustration:

In the English newspapers of that day, a picture had appeared. The British Navy and the American Navy were having a joint manoeuvre in South Pacific. Suddenly, a storm came and the British Navy ship was shaking and slowly sinking. So, all the captains and all the other naval cadets, stood on the deck saluting the flag. In front, there was the American Navy ship going unaffected by this storm. 'And then', says Swamiji, 'these British Navy people, standing and saluting the flag, appreciated that American Navy people had escaped trouble and shouted to them, "go ahead, go ahead; all cheer, all cheer; we are happy that you have gone beyond this without trouble; we don't mind our ill fate." And they went down the ocean.'

As they were sinking, this was the attitude they took; high character is there behind it. We can see our weakness in this matter. If anybody escapes something bad, and we are in the middle of trouble, we will curse that fellow who has escaped. We don't have that high attitude. Also, when good has come to me, I go ahead without thinking of others. Why? Our minds are not big, character is not high; there is no *yoga* at all. In that event given above, there is a *yoga* attitude. Swamiji appreciated this very much. We need it very badly in our own country; we need this attitude, 'go ahead, go ahead. I will come behind you according to my own pace.' So this is the teaching, *tasmāt yogī bhavārjuna*, 'therefore, be a *yogī*, Arjuna.'

Then, Śrī Kṛṣṇa sings a new note on the subject of *yoga* which will become the main theme in the next several chapters. That note is *bhakti*. We were dealing with *karma*, we were dealing with education, we were dealing with meditation, so many things we have dealt with. At the end of the fifth chapter, there was just a gentle note of *bhakti* where verse 29 said:

*Bhoktāram yajñatapasām sarvalokamaheśvaram;*
*Suhṛdam sarvabhūtānām jñātvā mām śāntimṛcchati —*

A beautiful verse! Śrī Kṛṣṇa is telling us here about the Incarnation of the Divine as the friend of all. He says, *suhṛdam sarvabhūtānām*, 'those who know Me as the friend of all beings'. He accepts whatever you offer as worship to any god or to any deity; all these offerings ultimately go to Him; *bhoktāram yajñatapasām*, 'ultimately all these *yajña* and *tapas* reach Me, the universal Lord'; *sarvalokamaheśvaram*, 'the Supreme Lord of the Universe'. And then, *suhṛdam sarvabhūtānām*, 'the friend of all beings'; that is the language Śrī Kṛṣṇa uses there; *jñātvā mām*, 'knowing Me as such'; *śāntim ṛcchati*, 'they attain peace of mind'. Real peace will come in God, in the one indwelling Divine in all. That note Śrī Kṛṣṇa had struck at the end of the fifth chapter.

Now, in this last verse of the sixth chapter, a similar note of *bhakti* is being struck, so that the whole subject of *yoga* becomes richer and richer with new and newer ideas, newer inspiration, just as the Ganga becomes richer when other rivers join it as tributaries. So also is the state of *yoga*. It begins as a very elementary treatment of a philosophical theme; then every succeeding chapter adds a new meaning, a new strength, to that presentation. Here, in the last *śloka* of the sixth chapter, the new element that is introduced in *yoga* is *bhakti*, love of Personal God. When you work, if there is real love of God, that work becomes really a joyous experience. Therefore, you have first to put in that new element into the *yoga* of the *Gītā*.

योगिनामपि सर्वेषां मद्गतेनान्तरात्मना ।
श्रद्धावान्भजते यो मां स मे युक्ततमो मतः ॥४७॥

*Yoginām api sarveṣām madgatenāntarātmanā;*
*Śraddhāvānbhajate yo mām sa me yuktatamo mataḥ—6. 47*

'And of all *yogīs*, one who, with the innermost self merged in Me, with *śraddhā*, devotes himself or herself to Me, is considered by Me as the most steadfast.'

*Yogināmapi sarveṣām*, 'among all the *yogīs*'; *madgatenāntarātmanā*, 'whose inner self has been drawn towards Me, as the eternal Self of all, incarnate as Śrī Kṛṣṇa'; *śraddhāvān*, 'one endowed with faith and conviction'; *bhajate yo mām*, 'who worships Me'; *sa me yuktatamo mataḥ*, 'he or she is the supreme *yogī*, according to Me'. *Tamaḥ*, in Sanskrit, refers to the superlative; *taraḥ* and *tamaḥ*; *taraḥ* refers to the comparative; and if a thing is still better, we say, *tamaḥ*; it means superlative, the best. That is why *tāratamya* is the word for comparison in Sanskrit. *Sa me yuktatamo mataḥ*, 'among *yogīs*, he or she is *yuktatamaḥ*, the supreme *yogī*'. When *bhakti* enters into *dhyāna*, *jñāna*, *karma* and human relations, this *bhakti* becomes the base. So, a new element is entering into the exposition of the *yoga* of the *Gītā* from this verse onwards. And this is the last verse of the sixth chapter.

इति ध्यानयोगो नाम षष्ठोऽध्यायः ।
*Iti dhyāna-yogo nāma ṣaṣṭho'dhyāyaḥ —*

'Thus ends the sixth chapter, designated *The Yoga of Meditation.*'

# BHAGAVAD GĪTĀ

## Chapter 7

## Jñāna-vijñāna Yoga
## The Way of Knowledge with Realization

We now enter the seventh chapter. In this, you will find *bhakti,* or love of the Personal aspect of the Impersonal-Personal God, coming in a big way; and in chapters 8 to 12, it is all *bhakti*, strengthening this path of *yoga*, and enriching it in every sense of the term.

We have many aspects in our personality. Every aspect of personality is nourished by the comprehensive spirituality of the *Gītā;* otherwise, if there be only one side of spirituality, consequently, only some aspect of our personality will be developed, and the other aspects neglected. That should not be. Be all-sided by developing all aspects of your personality. And emotion is an important aspect. *Bhakti* is based on emotion and it concerns with handling that emotion intelligently and in a right way with the help of *jñāna*. That is why this is a great contribution to Śrī Kṛṣṇa's philosophy of *yoga*, which has been expounded from the second chapter onwards.

The seventh chapter begins with,

**श्रीभगवान् उवाच –**

*Śrībhagavān uvāca —*

*'The Blessed Lord said:'*

**मय्यासक्तमनाः पार्थ योगं युञ्जन् मदाश्रयः ।**
**असंशयं समग्रं मां यथा ज्ञास्यसि तच्छृणु ॥ १ ॥**

*Mayyāsaktamanāḥ pārtha yogam yuñjan madāśrayaḥ;*
*asamśayam samagram mām yathā jñāsyasi tacchṛṇu* — 7. 1

'With the mind intent on Me, O son of Pṛthā, taking refuge in Me, and practising *yoga*, how you shall without doubt know Me fully, that you hear from Me.'

Here is a very beautiful expression. *Mayyāsakta manāḥ pārtha*, 'with the mind intent on Me, O Arjuna'; *yogam yuñjan*, 'practising *yoga*'; *mad āśrayaḥ*, 'always depending upon Me', the one Infinite Self in the heart of all beings, who has become incarnate as Śrī Kṛṣṇa; that is His true dimension. *Asamśayam samagram mām yathā jñāsyasi*, 'how you will, beyond all doubt, understand Me in My fullness'; *tat sṛṇu*, 'that listen from Me', learn that from Me; *samagram*, know Reality in Its 'total aspect', and not in a segmental way.

Many people in religion are fanatic and intolerant. Why? Because they see Truth only in a piecemeal fashion, and they hold on to it thinking that everything else is wrong. And they come to fight and quarrel. Because India had a comprehension of the fullness of the Reality, India became the land of toleration, the land of this understanding that you can approach that Reality through various ways—not that what you have got alone is true. What, as they say in English, 'My doxy is orthodoxy, your doxy is heterodoxy; so, you must be punished.' That is the language. But here it is not so. We respect everybody's belief, everybody's spiritual path; we welcome them. That is the greatest glory of this great India and it started achieving this glory from the *Ṛg Vedic* period onwards.

The whole tradition of India, Swami Vivekananda used to say, the whole history of India, its real inner strength and spirit, can be understood by understanding that brief utterance of the *Ṛg Veda* of five thousand years ago: *Ekam sat viprāḥ bahudhā vadanti*, 'Truth is one, sages call It by various names.' Names are different, forms are different, but the Truth is one and the same. By this idea being deeply inculcated into the minds of her people, India became a land of harmony, a land of toleration. Compared to any country outside, no major persecution or killing—except for some occasional very minor incidents—have taken place in our history. Therefore, *samagram mām*, 'know Me (God) in its totality', in its fullness.

Because every personal experience will only deal with one aspect of the Divine, we are asked to practise respect and tolerance for other peoples' experiences as well.

That aspect of tolerance is expounded by our late President, Dr. S. Radhakrishnan, in his Oxford lectures in that famous book *Eastern Religions and Western Thought*. This is his definition of religion and toleration, as we understand in India.

'Toleration is the homage that the finite mind pays to the inexhaustibility of the infinite.'

The infinite is inexhaustible. If I have an experience of the infinite and if I say, 'I have taken the whole infinite into me,' it will be foolish; there is so much left over that, others can also have other experiences of the infinite. Because of that, not only do I tolerate other people, but I also respect and accept as true other peoples' experiences. That is India's attitude. That is a very beautiful idea. You take a vessel, go to the ocean, bring back the whole vessel full of water. Then if you say, 'I will exhaust the whole ocean next time. Nothing will be left there thereafter.' It will be very foolish! Any number of persons can take any amount of water from the ocean, and the ocean will still remain in its fullness.

Sri Ramakrishna gave this parable. An ant went to a huge mound of sugar. It took one grain and ate it; it took another grain in its mouth; and on the way back to its home it thought, 'next time I shall exhaust the whole hill of sugar!' What a foolish thought! Such statements are made in religion—in all non-Indian religions of the world. That is what creates intolerance, misunderstanding, violence and war. That could not happen in India because of this idea of not mere toleration but also acceptance. There is such a thing as partial knowledge of Reality and complete knowledge of Reality.

Here Śrī Kṛṣṇa says, I shall tell how you will know Me fully, *samagram;* that is the language used here; *samagram* means 'full', 'totality'; *asamśayam samagram mām yathā jñāsyasi tacchṛṇu,* 'listen to Me on how to understand Me without doubt and in My fullness'. That is the first *śloka* of this chapter.

Then the next *śloka* adds one more important aspect to this teaching:

ज्ञानं तेऽहं सविज्ञानं इदं वक्ष्याम्यशेषतः ।
यज्ज्ञात्वा नेह भूयोऽन्यत् ज्ञातव्यं अवशिष्यते ॥ २॥

*Jñānam te'ham savijñānam idam vakṣyāmyaśeṣataḥ;*
*Yajjñātvā neha bhūyo'nyat jñātavyam avaśiṣyate* — 7. 2

'I shall tell you in full, about theoretical knowledge, along with experience, knowing which, nothing more here will remain to be known.'

Śrī Kṛṣṇa says: *Jñānam te'ham savijñānam idam vakṣyāmi aśeṣataḥ,* 'I shall tell you fully all about *jñāna* along with *vijñāna*'. *Jñāna* is 'knowledge'; *vijñāna* is 'experience'. What a beautiful difference between the two—*jñāna* and *vijñāna*! *Vijñāna* is, 'intimate experience of the Divine'; *jñāna* is, 'understanding of the Divine, knowledge of the Divine'. So, *vakṣyāmi,* 'I shall expound to you'; *aśeṣataḥ*, 'all aspects of it'; *yajjñātvā neha bhūyo'nyat jñātavyam avaśiṣyate,* 'by knowing which nothing worth knowing will be left out'; everything worth knowing will be included; it is an all-inclusive knowledge.

Sri Ramakrishna gives a lucid description of *jñāna* and *vijñāna* (*The Gospel of Sri Ramakrishna,* 1942, New York edition, pp. 105–06):

'The *jñāni* gives up his identification with worldly things, discriminating, "not this, not this" (*neti, neti*). Only then can he realize Brahman. It is like reaching the roof of a house by leaving the steps behind, one by one.

'But the *vijñāni,* who is more intimately acquainted with Brahman, realizes something more. He realizes that the steps are made of the same materials as the roof: bricks, lime, and brick dust. That which is realized intuitively as Brahman, through the eliminating process of "not this, not this", is then found to have become the universe and all its living beings. The *vijñāni* sees that the Reality which is *nirguṇa,* without attributes, is also *saguṇa,* with attributes.

'A man cannot live on the roof for a long time. He comes down again. Those who realize Brahman in *samādhi* come down also and find that it is Brahman that has become the universe and its living beings. In the musical scale there are the notes, *sā, re, ga, ma, pa, dha,* and *ni;* but one cannot keep one's voice on *"ni"* a long time. The ego does not vanish all together. The man coming down from *samādhi* perceives that it is Brahman that has become the ego, the universe, and all living beings. That is known as *vijñāna*.'

That is the wonderful effort of the human mind in India from the time of the Upaniṣads; that is how these qualities of compassion, tolerance, and understanding have come. We have respected even atheists or agnostics all throughout our history because, when one has the complete knowledge of the Reality, one will find even in the agnostic or the atheist, a person who is *struggling to understand*. He or she may not have arrived at any conclusion regarding the ultimate Reality. Naturally, one feels sympathy for such a person; we respect him or her. But if one holds on to a particular theory only, one will be destroying other believers. That never happened in India in a big way. In small small ways, here and there, through the ignorance of certain people, only some little narrowness and intolerance have been experienced in our history.

*Yat jñātvā,* 'knowing which'; *iha,* 'in this world'; *bhūyo'nyat,* 'anything else'; *jñātavyam,* 'what is to be known'; *na avaśiṣyate,* 'will not remain'. Everything will be included—totality of Reality. True philosophy deals with Reality in its fullness. Various sciences deal with Reality from various segmental points of view. For example, chemistry or physics deal with certain aspects of physical reality. And when you go to botany or physiology, another aspect comes in. All these deal with the external aspect. And then psychology and ethics, etc., deal with the inner life. Now, take all these, external and internal aspects of Reality, together. Then only you get the totality of Reality. That is why many philosophers in Europe define philosophy as 'the summation of all knowledge.' All knowledge must be included in philosophy. Nothing should be left out. That is what we succeeded to do in Vedānta; that is what is being expounded briefly in this part of the *Gītā*.

And verse 3 is a great verse often repeated in our discourses by scholars and saints:

मनुष्याणां सहस्रेषु कश्चित् यतति सिद्धये ।
यततां अपि सिद्धानां कश्चित् मां वेत्ति तत्त्वतः ॥३॥

*Manuṣyāṇām sahasreṣu kaścit yatati siddhaye;*
*Yatatām api siddhānām kaścit mām vetti tattvataḥ* — 7. 3

'A few, among thousands of men and women, strive for perfection; and a few perchance, among the blessed ones striving thus, know Me in reality.'

'Among thousands of people only a handful really struggle for spiritual perfection', *manuṣyāṇām sahasreṣu kaścit yatati siddhaye; siddhaye* means 'for spiritual perfection'; *kaścit yatati,* 'a few only strive', others are not concerned with it. They are busy with eating, drinking and various other pursuits; that is the first line. But, *yatatām api siddhānām,* 'even among those who pursue the highest perfection'; *kaścit mām vetti tattvataḥ,* 'just a few really understand Me as I truly am'—to understand God as given in the New Testament's language, 'in spirit and in truth'. God is to be understood in spirit and in truth, not as a reflex of our own mind, an image of our own personality. That is not the fullness of understanding. You can *begin* with it; but end with what God is in Its fullness. What is the nature of that philosophy? It is the contribution of India's Advaita to the world thought—that philosophy of non-duality, ultimate oneness of existence. We all come from the One; we all return to the One. That One is, *ekam eva advitīyam brahma,* 'Brahman is one only and non-dual'. That is the Brahman which is the theme of Vedanta and there you will find the idea of completeness, fullness; nothing is left out.

So, here it is pointed out: many try, but a few only achieve. It is like our Olympics. How many people participate in the running, and a few only reach the finals, the destination, of which only one will get the first place because of the limitations of the others.

In spiritual life also, they all start together, but according to our capacities, our speed will be limited; so, it will take more time for some. But, having said this, the main truth is: everyone will attain the goal some time or the other, because that is one's own true nature. So, everybody is capable of achieving the highest.

In the New Testament, Jesus said, 'Many are called, but few are chosen'. This is like our employment business; out of ten thousand applications, ten will be taken, that is all. Similarly, in spiritual life, we all join the race, but because of the differences in capacity, endowments, etc., many are left behind; others go faster. In this condition, great are those left behind who say: 'Go ahead. I respect you. I will come behind. I know I will also reach there, but it will take a longer time for me. I don't mind it.' That kind of making peace with oneself is absolutely essential. Unnecessarily troubling the mind and weakening it by self-praise or criticism of winners is not allowed in Vedanta. Have faith! Have faith! Everyone will attain to it; that is the right attitude. So, this is an important verse which is true to life; in every department of life you can verify the truth of this statement: *Manuṣyāṇām sahasreṣu kaścidyatati siddhaye*.

Hundreds of parties stand in our elections. Many independents also stand and get defeated. Among hundreds of candidates of parties, many of them lose, some even their deposit money, but a few win. So, this is the nature of human life in every sphere. Similarly, it is the same in spiritual life; it depends upon our capacity, our energy; all these characteristics are not equal in every human being. Possibility of spirituality is common in all, but the capacity to express it is not common in all; it is differentiated between one person and another.

Now, Śrī Kṛṣṇa says that Reality can be divided into two departments: one is the reality revealed by the five senses; the other is what lies beyond the sensory level. If you want to achieve realization of the total Reality, you must take both these into view; not merely the external physical world revealed by the senses.

So, in this chapter, Śrī Kṛṣṇa is dividing the Reality into two categories. He calls both *Prakṛti* or Nature—*Parā Prakṛti* and *Aparā Prakṛti*. *Prakṛti* is the Sanskrit word for nature. In the West, nature means only physical nature. In India, nature or *Prakṛti* means everything, physical and super-physical; the whole of Reality is *Prakṛti*. Therefore, we don't have anything supernatural in Indian thought. In the West, because of the limited concept of nature, they have the supernatural in religion. But in science they don't accept it. There is thus a conflict between the two. We, in India, don't have that problem. Our concept of *Prakṛti* or nature is comprehensive; whatever exists is *Prakṛti*; whether it is inside or outside. So, we don't have or need the supernatural, but we have the super-physical, super-sensory, super-rational, or super-conscious. That is why our concept of nature does not conflict with the physical sciences, which do not accept anything supernatural.

So, Śrī Kṛṣṇa begins to classify two great departments of nature by which you can approach Reality. One is the sensory reality, revealed by the five senses, which is the subject of study for all the physical sciences; and the other, above the sensory level. Both are *Prakṛti*. The first one, Śrī Kṛṣṇa calls *Aparā Prakṛti*, ordinary or external *Prakṛti;* the second one, he calls *Parā Prakṛti*, 'superior, internal, or higher *Prakṛti*'. That is all. Two departments of *Prakṛti*—ordinary and extraordinary, with two types of sciences, according to the *Muṇḍaka Upaniṣad;* one is called *Aparā Vidyā*, 'ordinary science'; the other is called *Parā Vidyā*, 'higher science'. These are all well classified by our great sages.

So, what constitutes this *aparā* aspect of *Prakṛti*, that first part of *Prakṛti*, the *Prakṛti* that is revealed to you as perishable by the five senses? The next *śloka* deals with it:

भूमिरापोऽनलो वायुः खं मनो बुद्धिरेव च ।
अहंकार इतीयं मे भिन्ना प्रकृतिरष्टधा ॥४॥

*Bhūmirāpo'nalo vāyuḥ kham mano buddhireva ca;*
*Ahamkāra itīyam me bhinnā prakṛtiraṣṭadhā* — 7. 4

*'Bhūmiḥ* (earth), *Āpaḥ* (water), *Analaḥ* (fire), *Vāyuḥ* (air), *Kham* (space), *manaḥ* (mind), *buddhiḥ* (intellect), and *ahamkāraḥ* (egoism): thus is My *Prakṛti* divided eightfold.'

'Different and eightfold is My *Prakṛti*', *me bhinnā prakṛtiḥ aṣṭadhā*, says Śrī Kṛṣṇa, and that *Prakṛti* is what you find manifested as 'earth, water, fire, air, space, the mind, intellect and the ego' in human beings. All these are considered as My eightfold *Prakṛti* of the *aparā* type. That is the first sentence. *Bhinnā prakṛtiraṣṭadhā*, this is My nature. That means, in all the physical things I am present. Why? As pure Consciousness, He is present in all these things. That is the first statement.

The next statement is very interesting:

अपरेयं इतस्त्वन्यां प्रकृतिं विद्धि मे पराम् ।
जीवभूतां महाबाहो ययेदं धार्यते जगत् ॥५॥

*Apareyam itastvanyām prakṛtim viddhi me parām;*
*Jīvabhūtām mahābāho yayedam dhāryate jagat* — 7.5

'This is the lower *Prakṛti*. But different from it, know, O mighty-armed, My higher *Prakṛti*—the principle of intelligence or Consciousness by which this manifested universe is sustained.'

Consider, *aparā iyam*, 'this eightfold *Prakṛti* to be My inferior *Prakṛti*'; *itastvanyām viddhi me parām*, 'besides this, now try to understand that *Parā Prakṛti*, that higher *Prakṛti* of Mine, different from this inferior *Prakṛti*'; *jīvabhūtām mahābāho*, 'which is of the nature of intelligence or consciousness, O Arjuna!'; *yayedam dhāryate jagat*, 'by which this whole manifested universe is sustained'. Pure Consciousness sustains the whole universe; that is higher *Prakṛti* and the technique and science of understanding that *Prakṛti* is different from the technique and science of understanding this lower *Prakṛti*. This is *aparā vidyā*, lower science, physical; that is *parā vidyā*, higher science, super-physical or transcendental or spiritual; whatever is above the sensory system is called the transcendental; that is all what it means. Above the sensory level is the transcendental level. *Loka*, and above it, *lokottara*, as *Bhagavan* Buddha would say: this world is called *loka*, that transcendental is *lokottara*.

*Loka* plus *lokottara* is called 'the totality of Reality'. *Loka* alone cannot be the totality of Reality; *lokottara* alone cannot be the totality of Reality; *loka* plus *lokottara*, *aparā* plus *parā*—that is total Reality according to Vedanta. The whole world is dull dead matter from the starry system up to a lump of clay. *Jīva* is there in them, but not manifested; that manifestation will begin when cosmic evolution rises to organic evolution. From the Sanskrit word *jīva* comes the English words, gene and genetics. When the *jīva* appears on the scene, a new reality comes in, a new dimension comes in—*jīvabhūtām mahābāho yayedam dhāryate jagat*, 'Arjuna, Consciousness or Intelligence is what sustains this whole universe'.

This second aspect of reality was not there in modern physical science till now; only the first aspect was there; and they were telling us always, 'This is the whole of reality; there is nothing higher; matter is everything.' That kind of attitude is now slowly breaking down. In the West itself, many scientists themselves have begun to feel that this is only a limited aspect of reality; there is something higher. That something higher is consciousness, what you call intelligence. That is why, as new books come out from the press, you will find this classification of *Gītā* getting a corroboration.

The transition of scientific exploration from the external nature to the internal nature, which took place in India over 4000 years ago, finds a lucid exposition in Swami Vivekananda's lecture on *Vedanta* in Lahore, now in Pakistan, on November 17, 1897: (*Complete Works of Swami Vivekananda*, Vol. 3, pp. 393-94)

'Two worlds there are in which we live, one, the external, the other, internal. Human progress has been made, from days of yore, almost in parallel lines along both these worlds. The search began in the external, and man at first wanted to get answers for all the deep problems from outside nature. Man wanted to satisfy his thirst for the beautiful and the sublime from all that surrounded him; he wanted to express himself and all that was within him in the language of the concrete; and grand indeed were the answers he got, most marvellous ideas of God and worship, and most rapturous expressions of the beautiful. Sublime ideas came from the external world indeed. But the other, opening out for the humanity later, laid out before him a universe yet sublimer, yet more beautiful, and infinitely more expansive. In the *Karma Kāṇḍa* portion of the Vedas, we find the most wonderful ideas of religion inculcated, we find the most wonderful ideas about an overruling Creator, Preserver, and Destroyer of the universe presented before us, in language sometimes the most soul-stirring. Most of you perhaps remember that most wonderful *śloka* in the *Ṛg Veda Samhitā* where you get the description of chaos, perhaps the sublimest that has ever been attempted yet. In spite of all this, we find it is only a painting of the sublime outside, we find that yet it is gross, that something of matter yet clings to it. Yet we find that is only the expression of the Infinite in the language of matter, in the language of the finite, it is the infinite of the muscles and not of the mind; it is the infinite of space, and not of thought.

'Therefore, in the second portion of *Jñāna Kāṇḍa*, we find there is altogether a different procedure. The first was a search in external nature for the truths of the universe; it was an attempt to get the solution of the deep problems of life from the material world. *Yasyaite himavanto mahitvā*, "Whose glory these (mighty) Himalayas declare." This is a grand idea, but yet it was not grand enough for India. The Indian mind had to fall back, and the research took a different direction altogether, from the external the search came to the internal, from matter to mind. There arose the cry, "When a man dies, what becomes of him?" *Astītyeke nāyamastīti caike*, "Some say that he exists, others, that he is gone; say, O king of Death, what is the truth?" An entirely different procedure we find here. The Indian mind got all that could be had from the external world, but it did not feel satisfied with that; it wanted to search further, to dive into its own soul, and the final answer came.

'The Upaniṣads, or the Vedanta, or the *Āraṇyakās*, or *Rahasya*, is the name of this portion of the Vedas. Here we find at once that religion has got rid of all external formalities. Here we find at once that spiritual things are told not in the language of matter, but in the language of the spirit; the superfine, in the language of the superfine. No more any grossness attaches to it, no more is there any compromise with things of worldly concern. Bold, brave, beyond the conception of the present day, stand the giant minds of the sages of the Upaniṣads, declaring the noblest truths that have been preached to humanity, without any compromise, without any fear.'

The West developed philosophy, even from ancient Greek times, based on external nature. That is called speculative philosophy. Western religions also developed their theology, based on knowledge of external nature. Western physical science also is a study of external nature. Since it is a thorough investigation through scientific methods and has produced tangible results, it has overthrown the erstwhile dominance of Western philosophy and Western theology. This resulted in the growth of scepticism, agnosticism, and atheism in the world. Some years ago, an interesting item I read in a Western book. A Western philosopher was to deliver a public lecture; a Western Christian theologian was the President of the meeting. The theologian, in the course of his opening speech said: 'When I introduce to you our speaker, the philosopher, I shall take this opportunity to define philosophy for you; it is searching for a black cat in a dark room which is not there! I now request our philosopher to give his lecture.' He was embarrassed; and he began his speech by telling that, 'our friend, the theologian, has defined my subject, but he did not define his subject. I shall, however, define it for you all: theology is the searching for a black cat in a dark room which is not there, but *claiming that he has found it*!' There was a great applause!

This is the fate of all speculative philosophies and theologies. Is there not, can there not be a scientific, i.e. *experiential* approach to philosophy and religion? India gives the answer—Yes. The transition from speculative to experiential approach to religion and philosophy developed in India over 4000 years ago in the Upaniṣads when its brilliant minds turned their investigation from external nature to internal nature, to the study of the depth dimension of human nature.

This transition and its profound fruits are what the above passage from Vivekananda tells us. Today's physical science, especially nuclear physics and twentieth century biology, is slowly turning into that direction. The importance of the datum of the observer in dealing with nuclear phenomenon is the first step in that direction; if pursued further to enquire into the nature of the observer, physics will transcend its physical limitations and enter into a vast spiritual dimension. Biology has already entered into the spiritual dimension as cleverly hinted by Sir Julian Huxley in his book, most important as considered by him, *Evolution: A New Synthesis*, when dealing with the nature of evolution at the human stage. He says that, at the human stage, organic evolution has advanced into *Psychosocial* evolution; it is actually spiritual evolution, but he was afraid of using that word.

That spiritual evolution or psychosocial evolution has two steps, broadly speaking. First: ethical and moral; what is called today the value-orientation to integrate human beings into a peaceful and harmonious national and international world order. And second: the state which Vedanta calls *mukti* or complete spiritual freedom. *India's Vedanta, therefore, treats the science of values as a link between physical sciences and the science of spirituality*. Such an advance of human evolution in the modern age is an advance from knowledge to wisdom. If such an advance does not take place, and humanity continues at the current level of mere sensory satisfactions and ever-increasing consumerism, physical science and technology will turn out to be the enemy of humanity. The British agnostic thinker, the late Bertrand Russell, has given this warning in his post-Second-World War book, *Impact of Science on Society*, pp. 120-21):

'We are in the middle of a race between human skill as to means and human folly as to ends. Given sufficient folly as to ends, every increase in the skill required to achieve them is to the bad. The human race has survived hitherto owing to ignorance and incompetence; but given knowledge and competence combined with folly, there can be no certainty of survival. Knowledge is power, but it is power for evil as much as for good. It follows that, *unless men increase in wisdom as much as in knowledge, increase of knowledge will be increase of sorrow.*' (italics, not Russell's)

This is exactly the message that the *Gītā* conveys to humanity in the modern age.

Bertrand Russell's above statement is an echo of the challenge of the ancient *Śvetāśvatara Upaniṣad* to the modern space age (6. 20):

> *Yadā carmavat ākāśam veṣṭayiṣyanti mānavāḥ;*
> *Tadā devam avijñāya duḥkhasyānto bhaviṣyati —*

'Humanity may roll up space like a piece of leather, still there will be no end of sorrow without knowing one's (innate) Divinity.'

The same Upaniṣad says, in another verse, that the investigation into the human soul leads to the knowledge of the one infinite and Immortal Source of the universe (2. 15):

> *Yadātmatatvena tu brahmatatvam*
> *dīpopameneha yuktaḥ prapaśyet;*
> *Ajam dhruvam sarvatatvaiḥ viśuddham*
> *jñātva devam mucyate sarvapāśaiḥ —*

'When the self-controlled spiritual aspirant realizes, in this very body, the Truth of Brahman through the Truth of the Atman, self-luminous as light, then, knowing the Divinity which is unborn, eternal, and untouched by all the modifications of nature, becomes free from all sins.'

This profound truth is what we find in the great statements of Jesus in the *New Testament*: 'The kingdom of God does not come from observation, lo, it is here, lo, it is there; for the kingdom of God is within you'; 'blessed are the pure in heart, for they shall see God.'

This same teaching is also found in one of the sayings of Prophet Mohammad, known as *Hādith-e-Urufi* and *Hādith-e-Suidsi*, quoted and referred to often by Jalaluddin Rumi in his famous *Masnavi*:

*Man arafa nai sahū*
*faqo araba nab bahū* —

'He alone who recognizes his own Self can recognize God.'

Jalaluddin Rumi exclaims elsewhere:

'In each human spirit is a Christ concealed, to be helped or hindered, to be hurt or healed. If from any human soul you lift the veil, you will find a Christ there without fail.'

A few days ago, Fred Hoyle, astro-physicist of England, was here in Hyderabad speaking in the Birla Planetarium. I talked with him about his book written some forty years ago. Perfectly materialistic was that book. Now he has written a new book, *The Intelligent Universe;* that's a wonderful book in which intelligence has come in. He said, 'yes, we have changed our attitude; you can't explain the universe without that principle of intelligence.' What a wonderful idea! Even in biology, in all the subjects dealing with the living cell, many scientists, even today, will dispense with all concepts of intelligence. Everything is mechanical, chemistry and physics, nothing else. That is the view of some people. But other scientists are finding, 'No, that cannot be.' The behaviour of the living cell—what a wonderful behaviour: it develops, it grows, it multiplies, it replaces itself, it doesn't need external material to repair itself; from itself it finds material to repair itself—what a wonderful thing it is! And so also, the little cell becomes multiple and variegated, and becomes a living child! What a wonderful growth it is in biology! So, in all these fields, many scientists have begun to feel that mere mechanical explanation cannot explain the events and things within the living being. You *do* need that second category called intelligence or consciousness. All goal-oriented actions need consciousness to direct the activity. A particular cell, or a particular gene in the cell, goes to a particular target in the development of the embryo. What a tremendous directional movement we find there! All these cannot be treated as merely physical, or mechanical, though many scientists still stick to the mechanical theories of the nineteenth century. They are called reductionists, who reduce everything to the physics and chemistry of the world. They are not respected. Slowly, slowly scientists are going beyond that reductionist attitude.

So, Śrī Kṛṣṇa tells here, 'know this to be my inferior *Prakṛti*; there is also My superior *Prakṛti*, by which the whole universe is animated'. *Yayedam dhāryate jagat*, 'by which the whole world is sustained', namely, 'by intelligence', *jīvabhūtām*. The same divine Reality has two dimensions: *aparā* and *parā*. This *aparā* is *jaḍa* or 'inert'; this *parā* is 'consciousness' or *cit*, as we call it in Sanskrit. *Cit* and *jaḍa* are the two aspects. *Jaḍa* is what you see all around you. Only in the living self will you find the *cit* manifested. According to our philosophy, even in the *jaḍa*, the *cit* is there. The *jaḍa* is not developed enough to manifest its *cit* dimension, but when it becomes developed, slowly that manifestation comes. So, all evolution, according to Vedanta, is manifestation of something hidden deeply within, and so Vedanta calls it *evolution of structure and manifestation of Consciousness*. The material structure evolves. The main Consciousness is there, but it finds it easier to manifest through the structure that is evolved. In a single living cell, only a little Consciousness can find manifestation because it is not fully evolved. But, when the cells multiply and become diversified, they become integrated into an organism, and then Consciousness is manifested more and more there. The same thing happens when it develops a cerebral system in a human being. Consciousness is much more manifested there. What is manifesting? Consciousness. What is evolving? Not Consciousness. Consciousness has *no* evolution; it is always the same. Evolution is only in the structure, and by the structural evolution you manifest more and more Consciousness. What a beautiful idea! A baby's body has only a very elementary structure; by the time he or she is twelve or thirteen, new values begin to manifest in the child; for example, sex maturity comes at twelve or thirteen and the body evolves by which it is able to manifest it. When you fully develop the structure, i.e. the body-mind complex, and make it pure, then you will find the Divine manifesting in you, in me, in all.

This is how Vedanta explains evolution, which is a continuous process of manifestation from ordinary piece of matter to the Self, to the highest Buddha, and other great spiritual luminaries. The *cit* manifests through the *jaḍa* or lifeless matter; that *jaḍa* undergoes changes to manifest more and more of the *cit*; that is the language of Vedanta on the subject. The human being is described in Vedanta as *cit-jaḍa-granthī*, 'a composite of *cit* and *jaḍa*'. Both are there in us, *jaḍa* element and the *cit* element. How the *cit* handles the *jaḍa* is our responsibility. Very often, in many people, the *jaḍa* handles the *cit*, and controls it. That is very unfortunate. That means regression. Real progress is when the *cit* becomes more and more prominent in your life, and *jaḍa* becomes your servant as Swami Vivekananda said in the 1893 Chicago Parliament of Religions: 'matter is your servant, not you the servant of matter'. In today's civilization, matter is the master, and the human beings, who developed matter into consumer goods, are the servants of matter, because they don't know anything about the *cit* aspect of Reality. This is the importance of this *Gītā* classification.

When I handle the next few verses, you will find a wonderful commentary of Śaṅkarācārya on verses, 4 to 6. There you will find the scientific mind at work—how Reality is presented in a comprehensive way. Nothing is left out, and so science becomes complete. That is the language also of the *Muṇḍaka Upaniṣad*. What is *brahma-vidyā* or the science of Brahman? It is *sarvavidyā pratiṣṭhā*, 'the basis of every *vidyā* or science'. The totality of Reality is called Brahman, the Infinite, Immortal Consciousness, which is the one source of the whole universe, and *brahma-vidyā* is the Science that consummates all other sciences; it is the Science of sciences.

That principle of Consciousness, which is the totality of all experiences and of all existence, is the highest Reality called in Vedanta, Brahman or Atman. It is of the nature of pure intelligence, pure consciousness, *jñānam*. That is the language used in the *Taittirīya Upaniṣad*. What is Brahman? It is *satyam jñānam anantam brahma*, 'Brahman is Truth, Intelligence, and Infinity'. That is what sustains the whole universe. This is what Śrī Kṛṣṇa is telling here.

Having said this, in the next *śloka* Śrī Kṛṣṇa says:

**एतत् योनीनि भूतानि सर्वाणि इत्युपधारय ।**
**अहं कृत्स्नस्य जगतः प्रभवः प्रलयस्तथा ॥ ६ ॥**

*Etat yonīni bhūtāni sarvāṇi ityupadhāraya;*
*Aham kṛtsnasya jagataḥ prabhavaḥ pralayastathā* — 7. 6

'Know that these (two *Prakṛtis*) are the womb of all beings; I am the origin and dissolution of the whole universe.'

*Etat yonīni bhūtāni sarvāṇi iti upadhāraya*, 'please understand that all things in this world are the products of these two sources'. In the universe, you can see nothing outside of these two: *cit* and *acit*, consciousness and matter. You can see everywhere either *cit* or *acit*; nothing else. *Yoni* means 'source'. *Aham kṛtsnasya jagataḥ prabhavaḥ pralayastathā*. Śrī Kṛṣṇa says therefore, 'these are my two natures; through these two natures, I am the origin and dissolution of the whole universe.'

The commentary of Śaṅkarācārya on this verse is very beautiful and thought-provoking: *Prakṛti dvaya dvāreṇa aham sarvajñaḥ īśvaraḥ jagataḥ kāraṇam*, 'I, the all-knowing Lord, am the cause of this universe through the twofold nature.' What is the cause or source of this world? We ask this question: what is behind this world? The word 'cause' is used in the sense in which it is used in Sāṅkhyā philosophy, and also in modern scientific thought. Cause and effect are non-different; that is the idea of 'cause'. The cause continues in the effect; it is not external. And therefore, 'I am the cause of this universe, through the twofold nature': ordinary nature, which you study in physical science; and extraordinary nature, which you study as intelligence, as consciousness, is the science of spirituality. These are two aspects of one single Reality. Whatever exists has come from these two, from one or the other. When we study cosmology, we deal only with the physical aspect of things. When we study consciousness, when we study the nerve impulse, when we study the ways of the mind, we are dealing with another subject; a new value has come in, namely, intelligence or consciousness. We have to explain what exactly is the source of this consciousness that we find here. It is a tremendous datum which evolution has thrown up here. Swami Vivekananda, in his lecture in England about 90 years ago, said: 'A little worm is sitting on a railway track. From a long distance a train is coming. There is vibration on the railway track. A little stone on the track does not, cannot move away and is crushed. That little worm has the intelligence to protect itself; so it quietly moves aside.' That little worm has this tremendous datum called consciousness. Goal-directed action can come only through life and consciousness. And therefore, this language which Śrī Kṛṣṇa uses here, this second datum, namely, consciousness, *yayā idam dhāryate jagat,* is 'what is fundamental and sustaining the whole universe'. This is Śaṅkarācārya's commentary upon this verse. God in Vedanta is that Reality which is the cause of this universe through its double nature, *aparā* and *parā*. These two aspects of the Divine constitute the cause of the universe. That is why, in the Upaniṣads, they often mention creation as, 'the Lord *projected* this world and entered into it and remained there, like a spider that creates its web out of itself and lives in that web.' So, the Lord projected this universe; the world is not a *creation,* but it is a *projection*. In Sanskrit, *sṛṣṭi* means projection. There is no mention of creation in Vedanta. Therefore, Vedanta says, 'He projects this universe and lives in it, as the Self, as you and I, as consciousness', *tat sṛṣṭvā tadeva anuprāviśat*. In a cosmological sense, you cannot discover Him here because He is deep within the whole thing that you call *acit* or not-Self, though, according to Vedanta, even in *acit*, *cit* is there; everything is *cit*, but not palpable, not capable of being experienced. Only when *acit* develops into the living cell, does consciousness begin to appear. Before that you can't trace consciousness in anything in the universe. In the far distant galaxies, you can't trace consciousness. Consciousness is a tremendous value thrown up from within evolution, and as I said earlier, this evolution is only an evolution of structure; there is no evolution in consciousness. Consciousness is one and non-dual; by structural evolution, consciousness manifests more and more. Today, this fact has to be emphasized again and again. In the Vedantic language we say: evolution of structure and manifestation of what is ever present within it as consciousness; that is the nature of evolution. This was not accepted by modern physical science till recent decades; they were absolutely materialistic in outlook; only matter, dull dead matter is there according to them. We can explain everything through that dull dead matter. That was the rigid materialism of the 19th century, being carried over to the 20th century by some scientists even today. But fortunately, some scientists have swung over to this understanding, that this dull dead matter cannot explain the whole aspects of the experiences in this world. You must have something else.

That something else is exactly what Śrī Kṛṣṇa says here: *apareyam itastvanyām prakṛtim viddhi me parām*, 'this is ordinary nature; listen to Me about My *parā prakṛti*, higher nature'; *jīvabhūtām*, 'of the nature of consciousness'. The little cell exhibits a new dimension of reality; you can find that *parā prakṛti* manifested there in a very elementary form. It was there earlier, but it was not tangible, not manifested. When evolution progresses to the living cell level, then it finds manifestation. That is why the living cell has the capacity to duplicate itself; matter duplicating itself is called the living cell. So, there you find a new datum appearing. That datum is what Śrī Kṛṣṇa refers to here as *parā prakṛti*, 'of the nature of intelligence', *jīvabhūtām*. Those scientists today, devoted to materialism, will say that we can explain consciousness—this behaviour of the cell, the behaviour of the human being, the behaviour of a Shakespeare, behaviour of even great spiritual teachers—in terms of dull dead matter. That is called a very rigid type of materialism—*reductionism*, as mentioned earlier. Whatever great thoughts you have, you can explain them in terms of the genetic constitution, the chemistry and physics of the body. That is the extreme reductionist view of several scientists in India as well as abroad. But the hopeful sign is that a number of great scientists are breaking away from this reductionist attitude, truly recognizing a second principle apart from the dull dead matter principle. That second principle Śrī Kṛṣṇa refers to as *jīvabhūtām*, the presence of consciousness, intelligence. You can't do without it to explain this world. It will be highly reductionist and therefore unscientific in any sense of the term. That is why today's materialism is getting a break by the new developments in physical science itself.

Śrī Kṛṣṇa says here, 'I am the cause of this universe as the eternal Self of all, as the Lord of the Universe, through my twofold nature as *aparā prakṛti* and *parā prakṛti*; both are part and parcel of My nature.' In America there are any number of scientists who are pursuing this new line of thinking that dull dead materialism cannot explain all aspects of the universe. We must have the second aspect of nature—that *jīvabhūtām*. The place of consciousness is being increasingly recognized, and it is the subject of research in modern neurology. This is also a very big subject of controversy today. Fortunately, outstanding neurologists have accepted the idea that you cannot explain human behaviour based only on one item, namely, the brain; you have to have the second item, namely, consciousness or the mind; the mind and the brain. Brain alone cannot explain everything. Therefore, here you have a centre of thought which has become very crucial for the development of science; the whole of modern science will undergo a tremendous revolution, leading to spiritual development, if this thought gets prominence in physical science: that the brain cannot explain all aspects of neural behaviour, that there is a place for the mind. What the Vedanta has declared ages ago is being explained with great scientific precision by many aspects of modern science. For the last hundred years, every aspect of physical science has been to confirm what Vedanta has said ages ago. Not one single thought has gone against the teachings of Vedanta; moreover, modern physical science gives all such thoughts a more secure experimental basis. Our sages had realized the truth through their own internal spiritual experiences, but the modern scientists are showing it through external physical and psychological experiments as well.

In this connection, it is good to know those neurologists, who are supporting the idea that behind the brain there is a mind and both are needed to explain human behaviour. That is a crucial observation and we have some of our great neurologists who are now affirming this truth.

Until a few decades ago, psychology and neurology were both highly materialistic. It did not need any non-material reality to deal with human behaviour. But, as I said, several neurologists are breaking away from this crude materialism. They are trying to experiment and demonstrate the truth of the mind behind the brain. So, brain study of a new type is going on all over the world; formerly, it was only the study of a dead man's brain, a dead man's nervous system; *but now it is the study of the living brain, the living nervous system.* That is a wonderful change that has come in neurology, and a further development has come. They used to put people in the unconscious state when they studied the brain; now they keep people conscious, and you can hear the conversation between the scientist and the patient when the brain surgery is going on. That is a new development that is giving you a new knowledge of the true nature of the human psyche. Among such scientists, one was the late Wilder Penfield of Montreal Neurological Institute. He put a patient on the table, removed the bone cover of the head, and started operating on the brain. The brain feels no pain, and, therefore, one could operate on a patient who was conscious as well. And then there was a conversation between the doctor and the patient. From this study, Wilder Penfield realized that one can't explain human behaviour on the basis of neurone action alone—action of the neurones which constitute the various segments of the brain.

You need to understand that there is a mind behind the brain; that conclusion he has given in his book. I will just read presently that portion of his book where the subject is expressed. Earlier, we had the pioneer in modern neurology, Sir Charles Sherrington. In his early book, *The Integrative Action of the Nervous System,* he had not found much place for mind, though he knew that there must be something like the mind, but neurology could not vouch for the truth of the mind.

As I said earlier, Vedanta has said ages ago that this human being is a *cit-jaḍa-granthī*; a beautiful expression, 'the integration of *cit* and *jaḍa*'. What is consciousness is *cit* and what is inert matter is *jaḍa*; these two are combined in the human system. They are both there, the physics and chemistry is there; there is something higher also there; that is the Vedantic way of putting it—*cit-jaḍa-granthī*. This idea comes through writings of both Sir Charles Sherrington and Wilder Penfield. Here is a passage from Wilder Penfield:

'I started as a materialist. That is all that we can handle, but sheer fact began to stare me in the face, and I found I can't explain this phenomenon in terms of mere brain; I was compelled to consider the reality of the mind behind the brain.'

That was the change similar to that which came to Sherrington.

It is almost like repeating what Śrī Kṛṣṇa is saying in the *Gītā*. That is why I want to share these passages with you. There is so much of similarity. Śrī Kṛṣṇa tells that 'by the twofold nature, I am the cause of the universe'; not a one-fold nature, but all nature, both lower and higher; that is the language he has used here.

In June 1937, Sir Charles Sherrington wrote a Foreword to his book, *The Integrative Action of the Nervous System,* which was then being republished in his honour by the Physiological Society. The last paragraph of his Foreword expresses his conclusion on it all. Here is the passage:

'That our being should consist of two fundamental elements offers, I suppose, no greater inherent improbability than that it should rest on one only.'

There is *parā prakṛti;* there is also *aparā prakṛti*; it is not improbable at all. That is what Sherrington means. But when you come to the great neurologist, Wilder Penfield, he summarises all his discoveries during his long years of neurological surgery etc., in his book: *The Mystery of Mind – A Critical Study of Consciousness and the Human Brain: Relation between the Two.* I am reading out just two paragraphs from there. I quoted this in my inaugural lecture on *Neurology and What Lies Beyond,* at the All India Neurological Conference in Hyderabad in December 1987. It is a small book published by the Bharatiya Vidya Bhavan, Mumbai.

Wilder Penfield says:

'For my own part, after years of striving to explain the mind on the basis of brain action alone, I have come to the conclusion that it is simpler and far easier to be logical if one adopts the hypothesis that our being thus consists of two fundamental elements; if that is true, it could still be true that the energy required comes to our mind during our waking hours through the highest brain mechanism: our nervous system and the brain. They supply energy even for our consciousness. So far as the awakening system is concerned, that is not eliminated by this new discovery because it seems to me certain that it will always be quite impossible to explain the mind on the basis of neurone action within the brain.'

All the various neurones in the brain and their action can explain consciousness according to materialistic neurologists. Penfield says about this:

'No, this cannot be done. And because it seems to me that the mind develops and matures independently throughout the individual's life, as though it were a continuing element, and because the computer, which the brain is, must be programmed and operated by an agency capable of independent understanding, I am forced to choose the proposition that our being is to be explained on the basis of two fundamental elements. This, to my mind, offers the greater likelihood of leading us to the final understanding towards which so many...scientists are striving.'

What a wonderful way of putting it! *Many scientists are striving to know what is the truth about this.* If your mind is free to accept new facts and modify old theories in terms of new facts, that's called science. There is a theory; there is a contrary fact; one single contrary fact can break a theory. That is what is happening with the mechanical physics of the Newtonian period in modern nuclear physics. Nuclear physics has overturned many of the conclusions of mechanistic physics. Similarly, in neurology, we have certain old theories; we want to stick to the theory and twist the facts which don't suit the theory; that is not science. A fact is the greatest thing you have to respect; theory must be altered in terms of the facts. That is what these scientists are doing and, when they do so, they just repeat what Śrī Kṛṣṇa said in the *Gītā* ages ago in verse 5 quoted before.

In evolution, these two aspects of nature, *parā* and *aparā*, both appear; but the *parā* nature became manifest much later. When the living cell began to appear, *parā* nature appeared; until then it was completely submerged in the *aparā* nature. The whole of evolution is this kind of liberation of *parā Prakṛti* involved in *aparā Prakṛti*. Thus, we want to release the grip of lower nature on our higher nature, i.e. consciousness, to make it attain 'spiritual liberation', i.e. *mukti*, in the Vedantic language. This is the struggle of consciousness or intelligence to return to its own original state and discover that the whole world is nothing but an ocean of Pure Consciousness. 'Everything in this manifested universe is Brahman, the Immortal,' *brahmaivedam amṛtam* (*Muṇḍaka Upaniṣad*).

One English word we use, namely, 'experience'; in Sanskrit we call it *anubhava*. Now, in materialistic cosmology you do not find this factor called *anubhava*, or experience, throughout cosmic history. The sun has no experience; so also the stellar system; none of them has experience. But when evolution came to the level of the living cell, this new datum came into view—experience; the cell has experience. Wherever there is a subject, i.e. *dṛk*, and an object, i.e. *dṛśyam*, the subject knowing the object, that makes for experience; that experience was not there throughout cosmic evolution; that is an important factor. But, from the living cell onwards, experience becomes a profound datum of the cosmos; and that datum becomes gradually clarified as evolution advances. In subject-object relations, much of the subject is caught in the object itself! And we, at the human level, are trying to separate the subject from the object; it is highly mixed up in our system. As I said, though we are *cit*, we are, in the beginning, *cit-jaḍa-granthī*, consciousness and matter mixed together in a binding; that is called the human system. We are asked to separate the two, to realize our true Conscious nature as the Atman, pure Immortal Consciousness. That is why that great Upaniṣadic dictum from the *Chāndogya Upaniṣad* says: *tat tvam asi, tat tvam asi*, 'you are That, you are That'. You are not this lump of matter, you are that infinite Consciousness caught up in this matter. *Tat tvam asi*, 'you are That'; what a profound utterance it is! This is the understanding that is meant for human development and fulfilment. A nuclear scientist like Schrodinger appreciates this *Tat tvam asi* truth.

Man's evolution is the liberation of the source of all values, namely, Pure Consciousness embedded in the physical system or material system. That is the language of Vedanta. That is how we study the nature of evolution, cosmic, as well as organic, as well as human—three levels of evolution. First is the cosmic evolution; then you get organic evolution, beginning from the living cell; and from human life you start a new type of evolution, the spiritual evolution: how to release this Pure Consciousness from the clutches of this material world and the physical body?

We must be free; we must be free. Everybody is struggling to be free. That freedom is the freedom of Consciousness from the clutches of matter; and when you succeed, you become free, *here and now*; you are fully developed, you are enlightened. The one who has realized the infinite Atman has become completely free from the clutches of matter. Matter is his or her servant, not he or she the servant of matter. But today's civilization makes the human being completely a servant of matter, submerging him or her in matter; and this has developed into what is called unchecked consumerism with its evil effects on nature and the human being. The new scientific discoveries are going to release men and women from that condition. It is in that context that books like the *Gītā* and the Upaniṣads will become books of tremendous world significance. Upaniṣads, the *Gītā*, and Swami Vivekananda's literature—in all these you find this truth expounded: how to save humanity from its submergence in matter. Men and women have become slaves of matter, and this is what finds expression as unchecked consumerism today. They have forgotten their own divine nature. This is the greatest Truth, and not dogma, that men and women have to learn today.

That is what Swami Vivekananda did when he went to the 1893 Chicago Parliament of Religions where, in his Address, he quoted the *Śvetāśvatara Upaniṣad* and said that our sages address all humanity as 'children of immortal bliss'—*amṛtasya putrāḥ,* not a child of darkness, not a child of matter, but 'a child of the immortal'; you are all children of the immortal. That is what the Indian sages call you. Swamiji said that. It was a new message to them. They had never heard this before. But it is very fascinating. This remark I heard from a questioner when I spoke at the Moscow State University and again from a youth when I addressed a public meeting in West Berlin. This message is now catching up all over the world. The dignity of human beings, their greatness, their glory, comes from this infinite Divine nature. One doesn't know it, but not knowing it doesn't abolish the truth of it; the sooner you know, the better.

So, Śrī Kṛṣṇa describes 'My lower nature' in the fourth verse, and 'My higher nature' in the fifth verse; and the sixth verse combines these two. These two together constitute the totality of nature through which He, the Divine Incarnation, is the cause of the projection, maintenance, and dissolution of the universe. The world came from Pure Consciousness, the world is Pure Consciousness, the world will return to Pure Consciousness; that is the nature of this universe, according to the Upaniṣads.

Śaṅkarācārya gives a wonderful definition of the nature of the ultimate Reality; 'that is ultimate Reality from which the universe cannot be separated at any time—past, present, and future'; then only it is ultimate Reality. Consciousness is the ultimate Reality because from it nothing can be separated; everything is always part and parcel of that Consciousness, sometimes hidden, i.e. not manifested, or sometimes manifested; but Consciousness *is*; that is what we call Brahman. Brahman is not a thing, Brahman is Pure Consciousness. In the most beautiful verses in the Upaniṣads this subject is expounded and Śaṅkarācārya says in his commentary on the *Bṛhadāraṇyaka Upaniṣad*: 'the word Atman and the word Brahman have no particular meaning; you can use any other word; it doesn't constitute the name of Reality. Some word has to be used, therefore, we use the word Brahman or Atman'. Atman and Brahman are one. The Consciousness that is caught up in your body-mind complex, and the Consciousness that is behind the universe, both are one and the same. *Ātamaiva idam sarvam* and *brahmaiva idam sarvam,* 'Atman alone is all this universe' and 'Brahman alone is all this universe'. The whole universe is nothing but Pure Consciousness.

'The human being, thus, is essentially the immortal Atman; all the rest about him or her is lower nature or *aparā prakṛti*.'

While commenting on verse 4, Śaṅkarācārya says:

'The earth (in the verse) refers to the rudimentary earth element, and not to the gross earth; ... similarly, water, etc., also refer to the rudimentary elements of water, fire, air, and space. Mind refers to the cause of the mind, viz. the ego-sense; intellect also refers to the cause of ego-sense, the *mahat* (of the Sāṅkhya philosophy).'

The ever-present light of the immortal Atman behind makes the mind, intellect, and *ahamkāra* or ego-sense, intelligent and active; but they are essentially, says Vedanta, subtle evolutes of matter which can reflect the light of the Atman. The separation of the mind from the brain by advanced modern neurologists is only the forerunner to finally reaching the only principle of intelligence, namely, the Atman in the innermost core of the human being and in the whole universe. Śaṅkarācārya sings thus in his *Nirvāṇa Śatakam:*

*Mano-buddhyahamkāra cittāni nāham*
*na ca śrotrajihve na ca ghrāṇa-netre;*
*Na ca vyomabhūmi na tejo na vāyuḥ*
*cidānandarūpaḥ śivo'ham śivo'ham —*

'I am not the mind or intellect, or ego-sense or *citta* the mind-stuff, ... I am Śiva, of the nature of *cit,* Consciousness or Knowledge, and *ānanda* or Bliss.'

Not only the human body but also the whole universe is lighted by the Light of the Atman (*Kaṭha Upaniṣad,* II. ii. 15):

*Na tatra sūryo bhāti na candratārakam*
*nemā vidyuto bhānti kuto'yamagniḥ;*
*Tameva bhāntam anubhāti sarvam*
*tasya bhāsā sarvam idam vibhāti —*

'There (in the Atman) the sun does not illumine, nor the moon and the stars; nor do these lightnings illumine (there); and what to speak of this (domestic) fire; when That shines, everything shines after That; by Its light, all this (manifested universe) is lighted.'

Now, therefore, in the seventh chapter, Śrī Kṛṣṇa took up this idea: 'I shall tell you *jñānam* along with *vijñānam*', *jñānam te'ham savijñānam,* 'knowledge along with experience'; *vakṣyāmi aśeṣataḥ,* 'I shall tell you in its entirety.'

Sri Ramakrishna gives a beautiful illustration: the fruit of the *bel* tree, or *vilva* tree. Generally, people take the pulp from within, make *sherbat* or a drink out of it and drink it; that's called *bel* fruit; the pulp is the most useful part of the *bel*. But if you want to understand the totality of the *bel*, you must take also the fibre, the seed, and the outer cover; all these put together is the *bel,* though for eating, only the flesh is essential. So, in this universe, there is such a thing as totality of Reality. There both *aparā prakṛti* and *parā prakṛti* are to be taken into account; then you get the totality of Reality. That is what Śrī Kṛṣṇa has been telling from the beginning of this chapter. This chapter is important from that point of view.

Then he says *yat jñātvā neha bhūyo'nyat jñātavyam avaśiṣyate,* 'by knowing which there will be nothing else left to be known'. What a challenging statement it is! In fact, the word *brahma vidyā* is explained in the *Muṇḍaka Upaniṣad* as *sarva vidyā pratiṣṭhā,* 'the basis of every science'. The essence of every knowledge is *brahma vidyā,* Brahman standing for totality. Even the etymology of the word is that it expands and fills everything; that is the meaning of Brahman. So, that is called the totality. In modern Western cosmology you have, as totality, a background material, and into that small material the whole universe was compressed. That background exploded, and there is a study of what happened after that explosion. From that explosion, slowly, the universe began to unfold. In the beginning it was a singularity, as they call it in astro-physical language. There was no differentiation into atoms, molecules, electrons, etc.; nothing material was there; everything was simple energy. Then slowly diversification came; from unity to diversity, to greater and greater diversity. Vedanta also says all evolution is a transition from uniformity or unity, to diversity; it is put in a very simple language. Suppose that background material could speak. What it would have said? *Eko'ham bahusyām,* 'I am one, let me be many'; that is what the Upaniṣads say. If the background material could express its own intention, it would have said: 'I am one, let me be many'. The one becoming the many, nature undifferentiated becoming nature differentiated, that is called creation, or truly, manifestation; that is called evolution. This is common to Vedanta and modern cosmology, except that in the case of modern cosmology, the background material is a dull dead piece of matter. Modern science has no conception of Consciousness behind this universe. That conception will come, as I said earlier, through further developments in modern neurology, when it finds that mind is separate from brain. If this becomes confirmed, then the whole background of the modern cosmology will undergo a revolutionary change and that change will be exactly what has been expounded in Vedanta—*satyam jñānam anantam brahma*, 'Brahman or Atman is Truth, Knowledge and Infinity'. From That, the whole universe has come. So, we say, from God we came, in God we live, and to God we return, using the word God in a Vedantic sense, not an extracosmic God as we have in monotheistic religions. That is the language used in the second aphorism of the *Brahma-sūtras*: *janmādyasya yataḥ*, 'from Whom is the origin, sustenance and dissolution of the whole universe'. That is Brahman, that is the Reality we are devoted to; that is the principle of religion. That is also the principle we study in physical science in the manifested state as the universe. There is no conflict between the two; because of the unity behind this diversity, there is no conflict between science and religion in India. It would be the same in the West also when the West realizes that that background material is the principle of Consciousness, which becomes concretised as the manifested universe. There is plenty of scope for this kind of change in modern cosmology, when this new truth becomes available to investigators in neurology: that we can't explain the human system based only on one factor; we do need the second factor. And once you accept the second factor, the whole cosmology also will have to change because this factor must be there in the original background material as well. Ultimately, when we recognize this conscious principle in the ultimate Reality, then the whole of nature will appear in a new light, the concept of God and the Divine will appear in a new light. After all, what reveals this universe? That background material. Even the tiny movements of the body are regulated by that energy that is in that cosmic background material. If that is so, it becomes God. As it is, we cannot call it God; it is dull dead matter. The whole thing will be transformed when these truths, which Western neurology is trying to discover and expound, become generally accepted. We can expect a tremendous revolution in that direction in modern scientific thought in the next century.

So, let me repeat the sentence which Swami Vivekananda uttered in the Chicago World Parliament of Religions in 1893 (*Complete Works of Swami Vivekananda,* vol. 1, p. 15). Welcoming the tremendous advances in modern science, Swamiji said,

'Manifestation, and not creation, is the word of science today, and the Hindu is only glad that what he has been cherishing in his bosom for ages is going to be taught in more forcible language, and with further light from the latest conclusions of science.'

We discovered these truths through our own spiritual experiences; they are discovering through real external investigation, from the known to the unknown. They are coming through sense-data, but reaching the same point. That is what is happening today to Vedanta versus modern science. It will take some more time; a lot of prejudice is there in scientific minds, just like the control of dogma in the human mind that you find in religion. Materialism is one such dogma bedevilling physical sciences. When this crude materialism is eliminated, some new developments will come. Religion will be recognized as a tremendous scientific discipline for human development and human fulfilment; that is what Vedanta developed ages ago.

So, one simple truth Śrī Kṛṣṇa has conveyed here: there is nothing supernatural in the whole thought of Vedanta, everything is natural, but natural from two dimensions—*aparā* and *parā*; and that is also one of the important convictions of physical science; physical science cannot tolerate anything supernatural; everything must be natural. And we accept it. Vedanta has nothing supernatural; everything is natural, but nature understood in its full connotation: *parā vidyā* and *aparā vidyā,* higher science and ordinary sciences; *parā Prakṛti* and *aparā Prakṛti*. If you accept both, then there is no problem so far as explaining the events of the universe is concerned.

That is the importance of these three verses in the seventh chapter of the *Bhagavad-Gītā*. Similar things will come later in the 13th chapter also and, in the Upaniṣads, you have plenty of such passages. In Śaṅkarācārya's commentary on the

*Brahma-sūtras,* he begins with this statement, referred to earlier, that we are a combination of *cit* and *acit,* of *viṣayī* and *viṣaya,* 'of subject and object', and all *lokavyavahāra,* 'activity in the world', are based on this mix-up. Consciousness and dull dead matter are mixed up in our system; we have to separate them; we have to discriminate between one and the other. Sri Ramakrishna said: if you put sand and sugar together, the ant will come and take only the sugar, and separate the sand. The ant has the power of *viveka* or discrimination; we don't have that much discrimination; we need that discrimination today. So, in the first sentence itself, Śaṅkara refers to this natural state of the human mind: we mix up Consciousness and dull dead matter; we have to separate them and realize our own true nature as that pure Consciousness. We are *nitya, śuddha, buddha, mukta svabhāva paramātman,* 'eternal, pure, enlightened and free Supreme Atman', that is our true nature, says Śaṅkarācārya in the above commentary. So, the commentary begins with the need for *jijñāsa* or investigation. Because *cit* and *jaḍa* have got mixed up, there is need for investigation. The *Brahma-Sutra* expression is *brahma jijñāsā,* 'investigation into the nature of Brahman'. Why *jijñāsā*? Because everything is mixed up. You need to investigate, question, enquire. So, in all departments of our life, there is need for investigation. There is so much of mix-up of things in the world. So, what is science? Investigation. Science investigates, discriminates and then says, 'this is the truth'.

So, this is the meaning of these wonderful early verses of the seventh chapter—*parā Prakṛti* and *aparā Prakṛti* constituting the total Reality of the universe. With that we can explain everything. That is how Śrī Kṛṣṇa expounds this great subject.

If you see a wave on the ocean, you can ask this question, 'What is this wave? It comes and goes.' By the time you say it is a wave, it has gone away; it has a particular name; it has a particular form; but what *is* the wave? The truth is, it is the ocean; the ocean and the wave. The wave came from the ocean, stayed for a second, and returned to the ocean. The ocean is the truth. The wave is only a manifestation of that ocean for a temporary period. So, that ultimate Reality of Brahman is the Truth of this universe. It has manifested itself as the universe of living and non-living beings, and these objects are nothing but the infinite one, from which the universe rises, stays for a time, and goes back again.

*Taittirīya Upaniṣad*—a very profound Upaniṣad we studied here two years ago—defines the truth of the word Brahman thus (III. i. 1): *Yato vā imāni bhūtāni jāyante*, 'from which these various beings and entities are born'; *yena jātāni jīvanti*, 'by which, when born, they live'; *yat prayanti abhisamviśanti*, 'and when they cease to exist, they go back to the same Reality; try to realize that Truth; that is Brahman.' That is the utterance; and Śaṅkara gives the most scientific definition of cause: 'cause is that from which the effect is never separated', either today, tomorrow, or yesterday—in the present, future or past. The whole universe is taken as one; Brahman is that cause. So, we find Him at the time of manifestation; we find Him at the state of actual existence; we find Him again at the state of dissolution; that is the unchanging infinite Reality which appears in this gross form, and goes back to the original state. That is how Vedanta explains the nature of the ultimate Reality, which is of the nature of pure Consciousness, not just a lump of matter in its densest form, as modern cosmology tells us.

So, here is a beautiful idea which emerges when you study Vedanta from this point of view. Any subject which is studied by rational investigation, which is subject to questioning, which is subject to any amount of enquiry, that study alone has a scientific status. As soon as you put forth an idea, either you don't question it, or the idea is destroyed if you question it, in both these cases there is no science there. That is called dogma. No dogma can stand questioning; dogma is good for one's own private belief; keep it with you, don't question, and there is some place for it in human life.

Truths are things which shine; the more you question, the more they shine; just like gold, when put in fire, shines better and better. That is the closest approximation of scientific truth and Vedantic truth. Both are science; the only difference is you have got mathematics as essentially an integral part of physics and chemistry. But, in this science, mathematics has no place, what you call *quantity* has no place; we are dealing with *quality*; the higher the human being goes in evolution, the less becomes the place of mathematics. In any society, in any kind of study, quantitative measurement can be done only at very gross physical levels; at higher levels, quantity is displaced by quality; at the human level, quality is supreme; quantity has a place, but quality is supreme.

Now, this is also the conclusion of twentieth century biology; there is a lot of advancement in biology. When the Chicago University celebrated Darwin Centenary in 1959, there was a seven-day seminar on 'Events and Issues in Evolution–100 Years of Evolution'. There, speakers like Sir Julian Huxley spoke that, up to the human level, quantity was the criteria of evolution, but from the human level it is all quality. Quality enthroned over quantity; mind enthroned over matter; these are the words he has used. Now this has to become current coin in physical science and in our own understanding. When that happens, these words of the *Gītā* and the Upaniṣads will become very luminous, becoming strengthened by the contribution of that wonderful discipline of the modern period, namely, physical science which Vedanta treats as a friend and not as an enemy, unlike Western religion which treated and still treats physical science as an enemy. Vedanta treats physical science, in fact any enquiry into the truth of things, as a friend, as a fellow seeker in the world of truth; that is how this idea is expressed. I am very happy to find that, as I said before, this idea is getting strengthened through the advances in modern neurology. Wait for another few decades; this will go onward, forward; more and more truths will be expounded from the physical side to confirm the truths expounded by spirituality through Vedanta.

In 1981, Vivekananda Vedanta Society of Chicago held a public meeting to celebrate its golden jubilee; I was a speaker there along with that distinguished scientist and astrophysicist, Dr. Chandrasekhar of Chicago University. Dr. Chandrasekhar spoke on 'Search for Truth in Science', and I spoke on 'Search for Truth in Vedanta'. We had a large gathering at that time. The subject is so beautiful; both are search for truth, science at one level and Vedanta at another level. Dr. Chandrasekhar said frankly, 'I don't know anything about Vedanta; I know only my physics and my astro-physics and nothing else.' He was very open. But he found this subject also very interesting. 'I can't put it in my scientific language; my science cannot contain that thing', he admitted. My lecture has been brought out as a book by Advaita Ashrama, Calcutta. This will be the development in the next century; even in the remaining years of this century many more things will come to light.

So, the greatness of *Sanātana Dhurma* based on this profound rational philosophy of Vedanta will be appreciated by the whole world in course of time. Swami Vivekananda has predicted that Vedanta will be the religion of thinking humanity in the future.

Posing the question how the West, which has undoubtedly been in the forefront of advance in several fields of knowledge from the time of the Greeks, could lag behind India in this field of inquiry these thousands of years, Professor Max Muller answers (*Three Lectures on the Vedanta Philosophy*, London, 1894, p. 7):

'But if it seems strange to you that the old Indian philosophers should have known more about the soul than Greek or medieval or modern philosophers, let us remember that however much the telescopes for observing the stars of heaven have been improved, the observatories of the soul have remained much the same.'

The *Gītā* will further strengthen this subject in its thirteenth chapter by using the terms *kṣetra* and *kṣetrajña*. *Kṣetra* means 'the field'; *kṣetrajña* means 'the Knower of the field'. The field alone is not enough; somebody who knows it is also needed. The word 'field' is today a very important word in quantum physics. The whole world is a field of energy. That field of energy is observed by a self-conscious *observer*. There you will get the second factor, which is coming more and more into modern science; and, as I said earlier, in the next few decades this investigation will become well established: that there is an observer along with the observed universe. And that observer is a unique entity; it is infinite in nature, though within the body it looks very finite, very limited. That is why in the Upaniṣads they made the equation 'Atman is Brahman'. The Atman in you is the Atman of the universe; they are one and the same. Today, science, through neurology, will come to that conclusion when it begins to recognize the importance of the factor of consciousness or mind in our experience.

Having said this in verses 4 to 6, we go on to the 7th verse of the seventh chapter. Śrī Kṛṣṇa makes a great utterance here which has inspired our Indian thinking. Śrī Kṛṣṇa, identifying himself with that supreme Reality, uses the words, 'I, therefore, exist in all things'. We are limited; we are separate from each other, but *Bhagavān* Śrī Kṛṣṇa can say that He exists in all things. Therefore he said:

मत्तः परतरं नान्यत् किञ्चिदस्ति धनञ्जय ।
मयि सर्वमिदं प्रोतं सूत्रे मणिगणा इव ॥७॥

*Mattaḥ parataram nānyat kiñcidasti dhanañjaya;*
*Mayi sarvamidam protam sūtre maṇigaṇā iva* — 7. 7

'Beyond me, O Dhanañjaya (Arjuna), there is nothing higher. All this is strung in Me, like a row of pearls on a thread.'

A very profound verse. There is nothing higher than Myself, that ultimate Reality, the infinite pure Consciousness, which you call Brahman. There is nothing *paratararn*, 'superior', 'higher'; *na anyat kiñcit asti*, 'there is nothing other than that Reality'. That is why, in the beginning of the chapter, he said: 'I am going to tell you of the totality of the Reality; nothing outside of it is there'. That consists of these two factors—object and subject or *kṣetra* and *kṣetrajña*, 'the known and the knower', or, as we say in physics, quantum phenomena and its observer. Therefore, this unity is the ultimate, beyond which there is nothing; *mattaḥ parataram nānyat kiñcit asti dhanañjaya,* 'nothing else exists superior to or beyond Me, O Arjuna'. The next line is marvellous: *mayi sarvam idam protam sūtre maṇigaṇā iva,* 'the whole universe is strung in Me like pearls in a string'; that string runs through all the pearls to make a garland. You cannot see the string; you see only the pearls. That 'string' is Me, the *antaryāmi,* 'the one that is in the heart of all things', extremely subtle, not visible to the senses.

So, *mayi sarvamidam protam; idam* mean 'this', this manifested universe; *sarvam* means 'all'. We have this teaching in Vedanta and that makes a tremendous difference. The universal outlook of Indian culture comes from this teaching. We can see a human being from outside; you can judge him or her from his or her colour or height; many other variable attributes of individuals are there. They are all visible, but there is one invariable invisible attribute in all individuals in the world. What is that? The thread that runs through all of them, the Divine Inner Self; there we are all one. So, judge a person from that point of view.

That truth came to India very early in our cultural history—the ancient period characterized by the universality of our culture and outlook. Throughout the ages, we produced outstanding sages and thinkers, who applied this idea of universality, non-separateness. We are all separate from the sensory point of view, but deep down we are all one. That is the *Advaitic vision* that came to us very early in history. That made India a land of universal sympathy, a land of toleration and understanding. We cannot sufficiently thank these great sages who gave such a profound vision to the people belonging to not a tiny island, but to the subcontinent of this great country. And today, the world is searching for this very vision of human unity and harmony.

*Mayi,* 'in Me'; *sarvam idam protam sūtre maṇigaṇā iva. Maṇi* means 'gem' or pearl; *maṇigaṇā iva,* 'like so many pieces of gems', 'all strung together as a garland on a thread'. *Sūtra* in Sanskrit means 'thread'. The divine Reality is called by various names like *sūtrātman, antarātman, antaryāmin,* etc.; the one inside all. We are all separate, but the thread unites all of us. In the political language we say, we are all separate, but as citizens of India we are all one, belonging to one republican state. Otherwise, physically speaking, we are all separate. This was a profound discovery you find in the Upaniṣads. One of the great passages of the *Bṛhadāraṇyaka Upaniṣad,* in its *Antaryāmi Brāhmaṇa,* is on the Supreme Divine as the *antaryāmin,* 'the inner Self of all', regulating everything from within. Take a cell; what regulates a cell? Something from within itself. You are trying to find out what is that thing. In genetics, we say it is DNA, RNA. These are all observable phenomena; but go deeper, still deeper if you can, and you will really find nothing but the divine as the inner energy that manipulates the processes in that living cell, in this body, in this universe, everywhere; that is the one ultimate Reality. That is the idea that Śrī Kṛṣṇa expresses here in a small verse.

In the *Antaryāmi Brāhmaṇa* (III. vii. 3), this idea is stated in a whole para; its first line is:

> *Yaḥ pṛthivyām tiṣṭhan pṛthivyā antaraḥ, yam pṛthivī na veda, yasya pṛthivī śarīram, yaḥ pṛthivīm antaro yamayati, eṣa te ātmā antaryāmi amṛtaḥ —*

Very majestic utterance Yājñavalkya makes here:

'He who exists in the earth, but is within it, whom the earth does not know, whose body is the earth, who remaining in the earth regulates all the activities in the earth, that is the *antaryāmi*, that is the immortal Self'.

Every other aspect of the earth is mortal; but this one thing inside is its immortal dimension. Similarly, the example of *vāyu* or air and of other things are taken, and finally, the last line (ibid, III. vii. 15): *yaḥ sarveṣu bhūteṣu tiṣṭhan,* 'one who exists in all beings', 'that which though existing in all beings, they don't know Him, who, sitting within, regulates all beings'; *eṣa te ātmā antaryāmi amṛtaḥ,* 'this is your Atman, the *antaryāmin,* inner Self, *amṛtaḥ*, the immortal one.'

That is the famous *Antaryāmi brāhmaṇa* of the *Bṛhadāraṇyaka Upaniṣad*. Śaṅkara's commentary on these passages is marvellous. Such deep penetration you will find there in simple beautiful Sanskrit prose. This passage is highly prized by the next Vedantic teacher, Rāmānujācārya, expounder of Vedanta in its Viśiṣṭādvaitic form.

You get in the *Śvetāśvatara Upaniṣad* (4. 3), a beautiful statement, when the sage discovered this truth within, and, when he looked around, he found that infinite Reality is also there in every being, and declared:

> *Tvam strī tvam pumān asi tvam kumāra uta vā kumārī;*
> *Tvam jīrṇo daṇḍena vañcasi tvam jāto bhavasi viśvato mukhaḥ —*

*Tvam strī*, 'you are the woman'; *tvam pumān asi*, 'you are the man'; *tvam kumāra*, 'you are the boy'; *uta vā kumārī*, 'as well as a *kumārī*, a girl'; *tvam jīrṇo daṇḍena vañcasi*, 'you are also the old man tottering on a stick'; *tvam jāto bhavasi viśvatomukhaḥ*, 'you are manifest in this universe in millions of forms'. It is all You that we find in all of them; that is the highest vision expressed in spiritual poetry.

In the *Muṇḍaka Upaniṣad* passage (II. ii. 7) you find this idea: a sage discovered that Atman within himself and he looked out and he found the same Atman everywhere. So, he described it as *ānandarūpam amṛtam yat vibhāti*, 'of the nature of infinite bliss, immortal, that manifests in everything in the world around you'. The word *kavi* or poet, in Sanskrit, is also the name for God. God is described as *kavi*. In the *Gītā* (8. 9), you will get it: *kavim purāṇam anuśāsitāram*, 'God is the *kavi*, the supreme poet, he can see far ahead'. Śaṅkara's definition of *kavi* is: *krānta darṣī*, 'one who can see far away and ahead'. Such a person is called *kavi* and that is why we respect poets and their poetry. The higher the poet, the deeper is his or her penetration into human experience and the way he or she communicates the same thing. I like that particular verse in English, characterizing the greatness of Shakespeare. Why is Shakespeare so much respected? All over the world people study him. Even now, after 500 years, we study him; we enact his dramas, we quote his words, some of the most precious expressions you get in Shakespearean literature. What is the speciality about Shakespeare? Someone has put it into a small verse. It says:

The poem hangs on the berry bush,
when comes the poet's eye;
The street begins to masquerade
when Shakespeare passes by.

There is also Shakespeare's own poem about the poet (*A Midsummer Night's Dream,* vol. 2):

The poet's eye, in a fine frenzy rolling,
doth glance from heaven to earth,
from earth to heaven,
and as imagination bodies forth
The forms of things unknown,
the poet's pen turns them to shapes
and gives to airy nothing
A local habitation and a name.

So, we need to develop a little bit of that poetic vision. God is the supreme Poet and these poets have got a bit of that poetic vision of the Divine. The greater the poet, the more he or she will be taken up into that Divine vision. This is what we understand in India. The Upaniṣads themselves call God *Kavi* or Poet.

In the coming decades, we will be getting more and more of reconfirmation of this profound vision of the Vedic sages, and that is what is the current thought tendency today. It never becomes old, is always fresh. Truth is never old; truth is always fresh. If there is a dogma or a creed, that is at some later time thrown away as absurd, as being not at all relevant; it has then no currency value; but truth is always the same, universal. This is how the Vedas discovered some profound truths about human beings and the universe. When you speak of Veda, it means a set of knowledge discovered by profound investigation into the heart of human beings and the world. The sages discovered these truths and proclaimed them, and they are still current after four to five thousand years. These truths are always there; so, we gave it the name *Sanātana Dharma*, Eternal Dharma; it is called Perennial Philosophy by Aldous Huxley in his book of that name.

Now Śrī Kṛṣṇa goes on to expound this beautiful truth: in what way He is present in everything in this universe? A few samples are given in this chapter. A few more are given in the 10th chapter, called *Vibhūti Yoga, Bhagavān's vibhūti* or powers. He is present in all the manifested universe. So, a few samples of that presence is given in the present chapter from verse 8:

रसोऽहमप्सु कौन्तेय प्रभाऽस्मि शशिसूर्ययोः ।
प्रणवः सर्ववेदेषु शब्दः खे पौरुषं नृषु ॥८॥

*Raso'hamapsu kaunteya prabhā'smi śaśisūryayoḥ;*
*Praṇavaḥ sarvavedeṣu śabdaḥ khe pauruṣam nṛṣu* — 7. 8

'I am the sapidity in water, O son of Kuntī; I am the radiance in the moon and the sun; I am Om in all the Vedas, sound in *Ākāśa*, and manhood in men (or humanity).'

*Rasaḥ aham apsu*, 'I am the sapidity in water'; *rasaḥ*, means 'taste'. *Rasaḥ*, in Sanskrit, is a word with different meanings according to context. Its most important meaning is aesthetic delight associated with drama, poetry, music, and spiritual delight, especially in the path of *bhakti* or devotion to the Personal aspect of the Impersonal-Personal God. Secondly, *prabhā'smi śaśisūryayoḥ*, 'I am the radiance in the moon and the sun'; *praṇavaḥ sarva vedeṣu*, 'among all the Vedas I am the *Omkāra* or *praṇava*'; *śabda khe*, 'in *ākāśa* or space, I am sound'; sound is propagated through space and there I am the sound; *pauruṣam nṛṣu*, 'among human beings I am that *pauruṣa*, that kind of strength and manliness, courage, etc.'; and in anybody who has this, know that a touch of the Divine is there. That idea Śri Kṛṣṇa will say later on in another great verse (10. 41).

And then:

पुण्यो गन्धः पृथिव्यां च तेजश्चास्मि विभावसौ ।
जीवनं सर्वभूतेषु तपश्चास्मि तपस्विषु ॥९॥

*Puṇyo gandhaḥ pṛthivyām ca tejaścāsmi vibhāvasau;*
*Jīvanam sarvabhūteṣu tapaścāsmi tapasviṣu — 7. 9*

'I am the sweet fragrance in earth, and the brilliance in the fire am I; the life in all beings, and the austerity am I in ascetics.'

*Puṇyo gandhaḥ pṛthivyām ca*, 'I am in the earth in the form of auspicious smell'; 'in the earth the principle is *gandhaḥ*, good smell'; *puṇyo gandhaḥ*, 'very auspicious smell'; *tejaścāsmi vibhāvasau*, 'in fire I am brilliance', *tejas;* then, *jīvanam sarvabhūteṣu*, 'among all beings, I am the principle of life, principle of intelligence'; and, *tapaścāsmi tapasviṣu*, 'among those who are practising *tapas*, I am the very principle of *tapas* or austerity', that inspires one to practise *tapas* to achieve great things.

बीजं मां सर्वभूतानां विद्धि पार्थ सनातनम् ।
बुद्धिर्बुद्धिमतामस्मि तेजस्तेजस्विनामहम् ॥ १० ॥

*Bījam mām sarvabhūtānām viddhi pārtha sanātanam;*
*Buddhirbuddhimatāmasmi tejastejasvināmaham —7. 10*

'Know me, O son of Pṛthā, as the eternal seed of all beings. I am the intellect of the intelligent, and the heroism of the heroic.'

*Sanātanam bījam*, 'eternal seed'; *mām viddhi*, 'know Me'; *pārtha sarva bhūtānām*, 'of all beings, O Arjuna'; *buddhiḥ buddhimatām asmi*, 'among intelligent people, I am the very principle of intelligence'; *tejaḥ tejasvinām aham*, 'among the brilliant or heroic people, I am their brilliance or heroism'. In that way, we can feel the presence of God, as expressed in Vedanta, in the manifested universe. Thus, not only is He transcendental, He is also immanent.

बलं बलवतां चाहं काम राग विवर्जितम् ।
धर्माविरुद्धो भूतेषु कामोऽस्मि भरतर्षभ ॥ ११ ॥

*Balam balavatām cāham kāma rāga vivarjitam;*
*Dharmāviruddho bhūteṣu kāmo'smi bharatarṣabha — 7. 11*

'Of the strong, I am the strength devoid of sensual desire and attachment. I am, O bull among the Bharatas, that sensual desire in beings unopposed to *Dharma*.'

*Balam balavatām cāham*, 'I am the strength in those who have strength', but with this qualification—*kāma rāga vivarjitam*, 'free from sensory craving and attachment'; that strength that makes for the good of the people, that makes people elevated, I am that strength in such people. The next statement is also very remarkable: *dharmāviruddho bhūteṣu kāmaḥ asmi bharatarṣabha. Kāma* or sensory craving, is a habit of animals and humans; that *kāma* is usually condemned in all ascetic type of books, but not in Vedanta, not in *Sanātana Dharma* and not in the *Gītā*. *Kāma* has been given a high place. And in this case Śrī Kṛṣṇa says, 'I am that *kāma* in all beings which is unopposed to *dharma*'. 'I am that *kāma* which doesn't destroy other peoples' welfare'. Therefore, *kāma* has been given a very high status, but that must be a very disciplined type of *kāma* that doesn't destroy other peoples' enjoyment of the good things of the world. *Dharmāviruddho kāma*, 'desire unopposed to *dharma*'.

Then,

ये चैव सात्त्विका भावा राजसाः तामसाः च ये ।
मत्त एवेति तान्विद्धि न त्वहं तेषु ते मयि ॥१२॥

*Ye caiva sāttvikā bhāvā rājasāḥ tāmasāḥ ca ye;*
*Matta eveti tānviddhi na tvaham teṣu te mayi —* 7. 12

'And whatever states pertaining to *sattva*, and those pertaining to *rajas* and to *tamas* are there, know them to proceed from Me alone; still I am not in them, but they are in Me.'

This is a very remarkable verse where Śrī Kṛṣṇa says: *ye ca eva sāttvikā bhāvā rājasāḥ tāmasāḥ ca ye*, 'Whatever states, pertaining to *sattva, rajas* and *tamas*'; *matta eveti tān viddhi*, 'know that every one of them has come from Me only', even the *tāmasik* state comes only from Me. For example, when we are sleepy and yawning, you can see plenty of *tamas* there. We don't condemn it. This is a part of our life; it also comes from the Divine. So, *rajas, tamas* and *sattva*, all these, Śrī Kṛṣṇa says, *matta eveti tān viddhi*, 'know that they have come from Me only'; but, *na tvaham teṣu*, 'I am not in them', I am not imprisoned in them, but they have come from Me; *te mayi*, 'they are in Me'.

This is the language. God projects the universe out of Himself. The universe is of many varieties, and good and bad are also there in the universe; and so too, God is in the Universe. The universe is also in God, but God is not in the universe in the sense of being caught up there. He is ever free. He cannot be caught up in anything. Just like space which cannot be caught up in a pot, or in a building; it comes out of all this, as it is ever free; similarly is the Divine.

And with the next *śloka* begins the treatment of the subject of *māyā*, that these three *guṇas* constitute *māyā*, which is the cause of the manifestation of the One as the many:

त्रिभिर्गुणमयैर्भावैः एभिः सर्वमिदं जगत् ।
मोहितं नाभिजानाति मां एभ्यः परं अव्ययम् ॥ १३ ॥

*Tribhirguṇamayairbhāvaiḥ ebhiḥ sarvamidam jagat;*
*Mohitam nābhijānāti mām ebhyaḥ param avyayam* — 7. 13

'Deluded by these states, (which are) the modifications of the three *Guṇas* (of *Prakṛti*), all this world does not know Me who is beyond them, and is immutable.'

*Tribhiḥ guṇamayaiḥ*, 'this whole universe is constituted of the three *guṇas*'—*sattva, rajas* and *tamas; ebhiḥ sarvam idam jagat mohitam*, 'by these all this world is deluded'; *nābhijānāti*, people in the world are deluded by these three *guṇas*, and 'therefore they don't know Me', as existing in the *guṇas*, as the very soul of all these. They are carried away by the *guṇas;* so, they are not able to see Me who is within the *guṇas*. This Divine Consciousness is ever free there. *Mohitam*, 'because they are deluded'; *nābhijānāti mām*, 'they don't understand Me'; *ebhyaḥ param*, 'superior to all these', above all these; and, *avyayam*, 'imperishable'; is My nature; that one infinite Reality has become manifested as this universe. How?, through these three *guṇas*.

Some of the statements in Sāṅkhya philosophy and some of the statements in the *Gītā* look so alike. Indian cosmology tells us that when these three *guṇas* are in a uniform state, absolutely inactive, that is a state when the world doesn't exist separately. Then, a little disturbance takes place in these *guṇas*, and it becomes diverse. From that time manifestation begins; then permutation and combination of the three *guṇas* occurs, and the whole universe comes out of that. The ground material, Brahman, is the infinite Consciousness behind the three *guṇas*. So, all over the universe that Consciousness is there, but this medium of the three *guṇas* deludes the human mind and makes it unable to know Me, the supreme imperishable Reality, *mohitam nābhijānāti mām ebhyaḥ param avyayam. Ebhyaḥ param,* I am 'beyond all these'; I am the *avyaya; vyaya* means expenditure, *avyaya* means non-expenditure, i.e. ever the same; that's My true nature.

Having said this, now comes a tremendous statement which has been often quoted by spiritual teachers in India all these centuries; that is verse 14.

दैवी ह्येषा गुणमयी मम माया दुरत्यया ।
मामेव ये प्रपद्यन्ते मायां एतां तरन्ति ते ॥१४॥

*Daivī hyeṣā guṇamayī mama māyā duratyayā;*
*Māmeva ye prapadyante māyām etām taranti te* — 7. 14

'Verily, this *Māyā* of Mine, constituted of the *guṇas*, is difficult to cross over; those who devote themselves to Me alone, cross over this illusion.'

This *māyā* constituted of the three *guṇas*, He says, is divine; *daivī hyeṣā*, 'this (*Māyā*) is divine', belonging to the Lord Himself; *duratyaya*, 'difficult to cross', difficult to overcome. Once you are caught in *Māyā*, it is very difficult to escape from this *Māyā;* that is the nature of *Māyā*. That is a remarkable statement in the *bhakti* religion. If you ask, 'how the One became the many?', the answer is, 'through *Māyā*'. One has not become the many, and yet the many is there. In all these, you will find the One. Even now it is all that One only, behind all this diversity. As Swami Vivekananda said in his *Jñāna Yoga* lectures in England, '*Māyā* is not a theory. *Māyā* is a simple statement of facts, what we are and what we see around us.' We feel we are free, but we cannot express that freedom. This *Māyā* comes in between. Everywhere you see *Māyā* working. The whole manifested universe is in *Māyā*. Therefore, this is the Divine *Śakti*. We call it the *Śakti* of Brahman. Brahman and *Śakti* are identical.

In Sri Ramakrishna's teachings this has been so beautifully explained. It is a great help to our practical life. Everything is in *Māyā*, but *Māyā* has two dimensions; one is called *Avidyā Māyā*, the other is called *Vidyā Māyā*—*Māyā* of ignorance, and *Māyā* of knowledge. The first *Māyā* drags us down, towards the sensory level and even further down; that's called *Avidyā Māyā*. All the evils you find in society, all crimes, all corruption, they have come from the predominance of *Avidyā Māyā*. As soon as *Vidyā Māyā* sets in, you become pure, you become moral, you become ethical, you become concerned with others; high character comes; that is called *Vidyā Māyā*. So, both are within *Māyā*, the good life and the bad life. Both are in *Māyā*, but it is human responsibility to cultivate *Vidyā Māyā* within oneself in place of *Avidyā Māyā*. You have the freedom; animals have not that freedom; every man or woman has that freedom. If you don't exercise that freedom to change from *Avidyā Māyā* to *Vidyā Māyā*, your life will be a failure; you become caught up in this net of *Māyā*.

*Daivī hyeṣā guṇamayī*, 'composed of the *guṇas* is this divine *Śakti*'; *mama māyā*, 'my *Māyā*'; *duratyayā*, 'difficult to cross', difficult to overcome. But you *can* overcome it. How? *Mām eva ye prapadyante māyām etām taranti te*, 'those alone cross it who take refuge only in Me', whose *Māyā* is this. People are unable to overcome this tyranny of *Māyā*. Take refuge in the Lord whose *Māyā* this world is; then you can become capable of overcoming it. So there is *Māyā*, and the Lord lies above *Māyā*, as the *māyāvī*, 'the controller of *Māyā*'.

Sri Ramakrishna says very beautifully, 'when you see a magic—you have magic shows here several times—you are fascinated. You think it is all real, absolutely real and you are deluded by the *Māyā*. But look at the magician, watch him. Then you will find this *Māyā* is his magic only; it is all magic; it is not real. So, when you concentrate on the magic, you are caught. When you concentrate on the Magician, you are never caught. That is what is expressed in the passage: *mām eva ye prapadyante māyām etām taranti te*, 'you are able to cross over this *Māyā* by the help of that to whom the *Māyā* belongs'. That is what Śrī Kṛṣṇa says here. In all our *Purāṇas* you will find this wonderful idea of *Māyā* by which people are deluded, and some people get rid of this *Māyā* through *bhakti*, through *jñāna*, through developing this spiritual awareness of the Divine.

So, this is a truth about the human being: why did I do this evil? Why do I do that good? *Māyā* is working in me: one to pull me down, one to push me up; both are *Māyā*. When you go and kill somebody, that is *Māyā*. When you go and save somebody, that too is *Māyā*; but this latter is a divine *Māyā*, *Vidyā Māyā*, 'knowledge *Māyā*'. The other is *Avidyā Māyā*, '*Māyā* of ignorance'; that pulls you down. So, in this way, human choice is there to make one's heart the playground of either *Avidyā Māyā* or *Vidyā Māyā*. Everybody should realize this truth that it depends upon me and nobody else. 'I want to convert my heart into a place for *Vidyā Māyā*.' Yes, you can do it. Or, if you are satisfied with *Avidyā Māyā*; you continue there. In this way, everyone has the freedom to remain in or to overcome this *Māyā*.

People, all over the world, are not afraid that the sun may move from its location because it is absolutely fixed there. Everything in the world is fixed, deterministic, but in the human being alone is that freedom to escape from *Māyā*, to realize what is beyond *Māyā*. When you start exercising that freedom, you will see a new aspect of *Māyā*, *Vidyā Māyā*, the uplifting aspect of *Māyā*, which is more luminous, with more of the *sāttvik* element. *Tamas* pushes you down; *rajas*, more or less, keeps you down; but when *sattva* becomes predominant, you start living freely, you slowly become free. *Sattva* is also *Māyā*, but it is a *Māyā* which helps you to get rid of *Māyā*.

Sri Ramakrishna tells: 'when a thorn enters your foot, you take another thorn, remove it and throw both the thorns away.' So, if *Māyā* has caught you, then what will you do? You take one aspect of that *Māyā*, i.e. *sattva*, and remove this evil, the *rajas* and *tamas*, and then throw that *sattva* also away. *Sattva* also must be given up; it is relativity; it is not the highest. That is why beyond the *guṇas* is the Divine; *sattva* is only the highest part of this *Māyā* system.

So, there are many stories in our *Puraṇas* about this *sattva*—how this *sattva* can help us to overcome this *Māyā* by cultivating it in our mind. And *rajas* keeps you intensively active and tied to the world; *tamas* makes you wicked and lazy as well. So, wherever there is a predominance of *tamas*, you will find a lower level of life. Then comes *rajas*—activity, energy, but very often selfish, self-centred, etc. Then a little *sattva* enters—high character, and concern for others come; energy is still there, but purified energy—energy working for the good of all, that is called *sāttvic* energy. In this way, we can manipulate the energies of *Māyā;* we can do it ourselves. When we do so, we start evolving upwards. At a particular stage in our life, we get the capacity to go beyond *Māyā* and realize that Divine which is behind all this *Māyā*. That is freedom, absolute freedom for human beings. But *Māyā* is difficult to cross, as Śrī Kṛṣṇa says: *guṇamayī mama māyā duratyayā*, 'difficult to cross is My *Māyā* consisting of *guṇas*'.

There are many stories told about this *Māyā* and its power to delude man or woman; and some of them are very fascinating from this point of view. Sri Ramakrishna tells one such story. Nārada, the great sage, is ever free, ever pure, almost like a messenger of God. But, Nārada told Śrī Kṛṣṇa one day, 'I want to see what is Your *Māyā*. I want to experience it a little.' Śrī Kṛṣṇa said, 'Don't try it; it is very dangerous. Once you try to experience it, you will be caught in it. It is a very difficult thing.' Exactly the same language as used here—*mama māyā duratyayā*. But, Nārada was really very anxious. They were both walking in a field. At that time, when Nārada pressed Śrī Kṛṣṇa for the experience, Śrī Kṛṣṇa said, 'Okay, you can have a little experience of *Māyā.*' A little later Śrī Kṛṣṇa said, 'Nārada, I am very thirsty. I want a glass of water. Go to the neighbouring village and get me a glass of water.' Nārada went to the village and to a particular house in that village. A young daughter of that family brought a glass of water to Nārada. Nārada looked at her. Suddenly he became fascinated by her. Then he spoke to the father of that girl, 'Can I marry this girl?' 'Of course, we shall arrange a marriage for you', said the father. And so, Nārada married that girl, set up a family, children were born to them. After some time, a flood came; one by one the children were carried away; even the house was swept away. And the last one, his wife, with great difficulty was holding on; even she was carried away. Nārada was in great distress, in great sorrow. Just then somebody tapped on his back: 'Nārada, where is my water?' 'What? Water?', asked Nārada. 'For the past half an hour I am waiting for a glass of water,' said Śrī Kṛṣṇa. 'Half an hour! A whole life has passed here. I have had enough. No more do I want to see Your *Māyā,*' said Nārada. Now, if a highly spiritual Nārada can come into such a difficulty, how true is the statement *duratyayā mama māyā,*'My *Māyā* is difficult to overcome'. Try to overcome it, try to go beyond it, that is the real and right endeavour.

That story is so far as Nārada is concerned. But once the Lord Himself came into trouble! That is another story of Sri Ramakrishna. When Lord Viṣṇu incarnated as a boar to lift the earth, he finished his work; the earth was lifted, but he continued to be in the boar's body! He found it very pleasant. He had a boar wife; he had children, and very fine they were. So, he remained in that boar body. And the gods became frightened: 'What has happened to Lord Viṣṇu? He is no more in *Vaikuṇṭha,* the highest heaven of Viṣṇu.' So, they went to Lord Śiva and prayed, 'Please remove this delusion from him; let him give up his boar body and come back to *Vaikuṇṭha.*' So, Śiva told Viṣṇu, 'Your work is over, throw away this body and come.' 'No, no, I am quite okay', said Viṣṇu, and with a grunt he went away to another side. 'I am very happy here. What is the matter? Absolutely pleasant; there is no problem.' Then, Śiva said to himself, 'It is a serious matter. Viṣṇu took on the body of the boar and now he is attached to it, and he is feeling very pleasant!' So, Śiva found Viṣṇu is really in difficulty now. What did he do? He took his trident and pierced it through that body. As soon as the body was broken, Viṣṇu came out laughing and said, 'Ah, how did I get caught up in this? I didn't know that I was really caught up in this boar body.' Then he came back to his own *Vaikuṇṭha*.

The story, when I read for the first time, made me amused. But later, I saw the truth of it. One day, I found a huge pig lying on the pavement side, very happily snoring, pig children were drinking its milk, seven or eight of them drinking the milk of their mother, and she was very happy and very peaceful. Then I could see, what Lord Viṣṇu said was correct. In that body there is immense joy and pleasure.

Now, these stories tell us this fact: that *Māyā* is a reality of experience; it is very difficult to get rid of it, but, by effort and struggle, we can overcome *Avidyā Māyā* by *Vidyā Māyā*, and *Vidyā Māyā* will be overcome by itself. Thus we will go beyond *Māyā*. That is the possibility for all people. If that is so, we have to transcend *sattva, rajas* and *tamas*—we have to rise from *tamas* to *rajas*, from *rajas* to *sattva*, then go beyond *sattva* also; *sattva* also is to be overcome.

To illustrate that, Sri Ramakrishna narrates another beautiful parable. A person was going through the forest. Suddenly, three robbers came upon him and tied him hand and foot; they robbed him. The three robbers are *sattva, rajas* and *tamas*. Then one of the robbers said, 'Why leave him? We shall kill him and go away'. That is called *tamas*. *Tamas* said this, 'Let us finish with him.' Then one of the other two robbers said, 'Why kill him? We have already robbed him. Let us tie him hand and foot, leave him here, and go away.' *Rajas* said this. And so all of them went away leaving him in that condition. After some time, the third robber, *sattva*, came to him and said, 'So sorry, you have suffered so much.' He removed his bondages and released him. He said, 'Come, go to your house, I will show you the way.' He took him towards his town and showed him, 'There is your house. You go that way. You are free.' Then this man said, 'You have been so kind to me. Please come with me. I will entertain you in my house.' That robber said, 'I can't come. I am also under police's surveillance. I am also a thief, but I can show you your house.' And therefore, this robber, *sattva,* went away after showing him the goal.

That is what Sri Ramakrishna said. *Tamas* does lot of harm, *rajas* also does lot of harm, *sattva* releases you from the bondage. But *sattva* is not the highest state; it can only point out where the highest Reality is. You go there yourself. So, go beyond the *guṇas.* So, in the *Gītā* we read earlier (2. 45) *nistraiguṇyo bhavārjuna,* 'Arjuna, go beyond the three *guṇas,* to that very high state of mind.' It is very good to proceed in that direction.

So, this subject of *Māyā* comes again and again in our literature, not only in the path of *jñāna,* but also in the path of *bhakti.* In the *Śrimad Bhāgavatam* (XI. iii. 1) you will find this passage: *parasya viṣṇoḥ īśasya māyinām api mohinīm māyām,* 'that *Māyā,* the divine power of the supreme Lord Mahāviṣṇu, which can delude the minds of others'. People do this, people do that. All this is the play of *Māyā,* in you and in me; that is a fact. But, as I said again and again, we are not entirely subject to this *Māyā.* We can free ourselves from it. We are essentially Divine. We have the freedom, only we don't exercise it; we don't struggle. When we struggle, we become a playground of *Vidyā Māyā,* instead of *Avidyā Māyā.* Sri Ramakrishna wants people to understand this truth and set about freeing themselves from that negative *Māyā* so that the positive *Māyā* will take them beyond this *Māyā* itself. This is our own responsibility and our privilege; no animal can do it, only the human being can do it. So, that is the importance of the *śloka* 14.

'Those who take refuge in Me, they go beyond all this *Māyā;* they become free'. In *bhakti* path, there is the spirit of resignation to God, surrender to God. What a wonderful idea! And many had become free through that type of *bhakti* experience—Christian devotees, Sufi devotees, Buddhists, Hindus, all. In every religion you will find that those who became free from *māyā* by their own efforts finally depended on the Divine grace that came upon the individual at a particular moment of his or her life. So, this is the importance of *śloka* 14 of chapter seven. Then,

न मां दुष्कृतिनो मूढाः प्रपद्यन्ते नराधमाः ।
मायया अपहृतज्ञाना आसुरं भावमाश्रिताः ॥१५॥

*Na mām duṣkṛtino mūḍhāḥ prapadyante narādhamāḥ;*
*Māyayā apahṛtajñānā āsuram bhāvamāśritāḥ* — 7. 15

'They do not devote themselves to Me—the evil-doers, the deluded, the lowest of men, deprived of discrimination by *māyā*, and following the way of the *Asuras* or evildoers.'

Why do not people overcome this *Māyā*? *Na mām prapadyante*, 'because such people do not come to Me, do not devote themselves to Me'. Who? *Duṣkṛtino*, 'those who do evil deeds', they are so deep in *Māyā*, they can't even think of anything better; *mūḍhāḥ*, 'those who are deluded'. They are fools but they think they are intelligent. Actually they are fools subject to this blinding effect of *māyā*; *narādhamāḥ*, 'they are the worst among men and women'. Śrī Kṛṣṇa says further: *māyayā apahṛtajñānā*, 'their understanding has been completely carried away by the power of *Māyā*'; then, *āsuram bhāvam āśritāḥ*, 'they depend upon the *asura's* qualities of wickedness'. In chapter sixteen, Śrī Kṛṣṇa will give us a list of *āsurī* qualities, *āsurī sampat*, while discussing *daivī sampat* or divine qualities versus *āsurī sampat*. What a beautiful classification! There are people who have so many *daivī sampat* in them: compassion, love and concern for others, ever trying to help—that is called *daivī sampat*. The other is *āsurī sampat:* trying to trouble people, exploit them, destroy them, that is called *āsurī sampat*; both are there. So, these people, who are not devoted to the indwelling God, belong to the *āsurī* class.

Then Śrī Kṛṣṇa speaks in the next verse 16: Four types of people worship Me. This *āsurī* type, mentioned above, will not worship Me; they are satisfied with that *Māyā* in which they live. They are happy in it. But most human beings who worship God belong to four categories. This is also a fine classification in the *Gītā*:

**चतुर्विधा भजन्ते मां जनाः सुकृतिनोऽर्जुन ।**
**आर्तो जिज्ञासुः अर्थार्थी ज्ञानी च भरतर्षभ ॥ १६ ॥**

*Caturvidhā bhajante mām janāḥ sukṛtino'rjuna;*
*Ārto jijñāsuḥ arthārthī jñānī ca bharatarṣabha* — 7. 16

'Four kinds of virtuous human beings worship Me, O Arjuna—the distressed, the seeker of knowledge, the seeker of wealth, and the spiritually wise, O bull (greatest) among the Bharatas.'

*Caturvidhā*, 'four types (of people)'; *bhajante mām*, 'worship Me'; *janāḥ sukṛtino'rjuna*, 'those who are virtuous, O Arjuna'. The other is *duṣkṛtinaḥ*, 'vicious', mentioned in the previous *śloka*. But here we are talking about those who are *sukṛtinaḥ*, 'those who do virtuous deeds'. Among them also there is a classification. What is that? They are of four types: *Ārtaḥ jijñāsuḥ arthārthī jñānī ca*: One is *ārtaḥ*, 'one who is in trouble, in difficulty'. Whenever we are in trouble, we think of God; and even that is good. At least the mind goes to something higher, beyond this *Māyā*. *Ārtiḥ* is the word meaning 'suffering, trouble, tension'. So, when we are in *ārtiḥ*, then we think of God. That is one way of thinking of God, one motivation for thinking of God. Second is *jijñāsuḥ*, 'seeker of knowledge'. 'I want to know.' A seeker also is a devotee; the seeker of knowledge is a devotee of the Divine. Next is *arthārthī*, 'people in search of wealth'; such a person also thinks of God, though they are all of the worldly category, yet it doesn't matter. They are slowly connecting themselves from *Avidyā Māyā* to *Vidyā Māyā*. So, this little movement upwards must be encouraged. These are the first three: *ārtaḥ jijñāsuḥ arthārthī*. This only shows the highly generous character of the Teacher and His teaching that is given here. Then, *jñānī ca*, the last is *jñānī*, 'the spiritual seeker and knower', the wonderful human being who loves God for love's sake. He or she knows fully the nature of the

Divine; his or her whole heart is given to the Divine. Such a person is called a *jñānī*.

Here *jñānī* includes also *bhakta*. The highest *jñāna* and the highest *bhakti* are the same, perfectly free from the clutches of *Māyā*. Therefore, the word *jñāna* is used here not in the usual technical sense, but in the general sense. These are the four types of devotees of the Divine.

In the *Srīmad Bhāgavatam*, in the eleventh book, there is one famous *śloka* (XI. xx. 8). How does a man become God's devotee? There Śrī Kṛṣṇa says: By chance, a very worldly person heard a talk about the Divine, and a little interest in God grew in him or her at that time. He or she is still very attached to the world, attached to power or money, etc. But a little love of God entered into the mind. He or she has not the spirit of renunciation, but he or she is not over-attached also to the world. Such a person is a candidate to the path of *bhākti*:

*Yadṛcchayā matkathādau*
*jātaśraddhastu yaḥ pumān;*
*Na nirviṇṇo nātisakto*
*bhaktiyogo'sya siddhidaḥ* —

*Bhakti Yoga* leads one to the highest perfection! How? *Yadṛcchayā matkathādau jātaśraddhaḥ*, 'by chance, going on the road, he or she hears there is a talk going on, or a *bhajan* going on. He or she just enters the place and hears the spiritual talk without any particular objective. Some higher thought arises in his or her mind; a little spiritual awakening, a little spiritual feeling'. That person has started his or her march on the path of *bhakti*. Such a person, who is still full of worldly attachment, has very little renunciation, but still he or she has entered that path of *bhakti* which will take him or her finally to realization. Even *yadṛcchayā;* the word *yadṛcchā* is very important, 'by chance'. Sometimes, in an unplanned way you get spiritual inspiration. So many stories are there how lives were changed by some chance experiences.

There is the story of the father of poet Rabindranath Tagore, namely, Debendranath Tagore. He was a good scholar and a very rich zamindar. He was just sitting—he tells in his autobiography—I think, in Darjeeling or in his estate enjoying the quiet evening. A wind brought a small piece of paper towards his feet. He just picked up that paper, read in it something which turned out to be the famous first verse of the *Īśā Upaniṣad.* He read it, became inspired by it, and his whole life changed. What was that verse?

*Īśāvāsyam idam sarvam yatkiñca jagatyām jagat;*
*Tena tyaktena bhuñjīthā mā gṛdhaḥ kasyasviddhanam —*

'Everything in the manifested universe should be filled with the divine.' This is the first line. This inspired him to conduct further studies. And he gave that Vedic background to the Brahmo Samaj Movement of Calcutta of which he was a leader of that time after the death of Raja Rammohan Roy whom he had helped in founding the movement. That is the story of Debendranath Tagore. There are many further instances of this *yadṛcchayā matkathādau jātaśraddhaḥ*—by chance you hear a story about the Divine and faith in the Divine is born in you. Then something stirs in your mind. You never expected it before, you never sought it, and yet it came. That puts you on the road of *bhakti.* With that *bhakti* you go step by step to the highest level of spiritual development.

Here Śrī Kṛṣṇa says that among these four categories, the *jñāni*, the fourth one, is something special. He or she loves God in spirit and in truth. That is why that person is the highest. In the next *śloka,* Śrī Kṛṣṇa gives the highest tribute to that category.

तेषां ज्ञानी नित्ययुक्त एकभक्तिः विशिष्यते ।
प्रियो हि ज्ञानिनोऽत्यर्थं अहं स च मम प्रियः ॥१७॥

*Teṣām jñānī nityayukta ekabhaktiḥ viśiṣyate;*
*Priyo hi jñānino'tyartham aham sa ca mama priyaḥ — 7. 17*

'Of them, the *jñāni,* the wise person, ever-steadfast, (and fired) with devotion to the One, excels; for supremely dear am I to the *jñāni,* and he or she also is dear to Me.'

*Teṣām jñānī nityayuktaḥ*, 'among all of them the *jñānī* is *nityayuktaḥ*, constantly a *yogī*'; not a five-minute *yogī* who then gives it up. Just like an *ārtaḥ*; *ārtas* are generally religiously inclined when they are in trouble. When the trouble is over, they no more think of God. That is called *ārtaḥ* type. Even in respect of them, Śrī Kṛṣṇa is very generous. 'Even he or she is good because he or she also thought of the higher Reality beyond *Māyā*. *Ekānta bhaktiḥ, ekabhakti*, these are wonderful expressions in the science of *bhakti*. The great book on *bhakti*, the *Nārada Bhakti sūtras* (verse 67) says: *bhaktā ekāntino mukhyāḥ*, 'among all *bhaktas*, the *ekānta bhaktas*, one-pointed devotees, are supreme'. *Viśiṣyate*, 'is most excellent' among all the four; *priyo hi jñānino'tyartham aham*, 'to the *jñānī* I am very very dear'. Śrī Kṛṣṇa, as an incarnation of the Divine, uses *aham*, 'I'. *Sa ca mama priyaḥ*, 'he or she also is very dear to Me'. I love such a person very much, he or she also loves Me very much; there is no separation between us.

So, that is the nature of the highest *bhakti*, or the highest *jñāna*. For example, a boy like Prahlāda, whose story is narrated in the *Śrīmad Bhāgavatam* (seventh book), never wanted anything from the Divine. He wanted only pure love; love for love's sake only. The Lord was very pleased with that little child of five years old. In the presence of the Lord who incarnated as the Narasimha, or man-lion, everyone was frightened seeing the form of Narasimha. The only person who was absolutely fearless and calm was this boy, Prahlāda, because his heart was free from all evil, from all *Māyā*, and was absolutely pure. The merciful *Bhagavān* Narasimha offered a boon to Prahlāda because his father Hiraṇyakaśipu had troubled this boy very much. So, Narasimha said, says the *Śrīmad Bhāgavatam* (VII. ix. 52), 'Prahlāda, ask a boon from me. I am pleased with you': *prahlāda bhadra bhadram te prīto'ham te'surottama*, 'O, Prahlāda, may good betide you, may good betide you, I am very pleased with you, the best among the *asuras*.' Then he said, 'Ask any boon from me, I will be happy to give you.' And this boy says, 'I am not a business man to trade in love and *bhakti*. My *bhakti* is one-pointed. I don't ask anything in return.' He uses the word, 'I am not a *vaṇik* or merchant or a trader in *bhakti*.' That is why Prahlāda dominates the *bhakti* thought of India as a pure devotee of God.

So here, *priyo hi jñānino'tyartham aham, sa ca mama priyaḥ*, 'he is also dear to Me; I am also dear to him'; that is the language Śrī Kṛṣṇa has used regarding the fourth category, the *jñānī*. But the next *śloka* shows the generosity of the heart of Śrī Kṛṣṇa:

उदाराः सर्व एवैते ज्ञानी त्वात्मैव मे मतम् ।
आस्थितः स हि युक्तात्मा मामेवानुत्तमां गतिम् ॥१८॥

*Udārāḥ sarva evaite jñānī tvātmaiva me matam;*
*Āsthitaḥ sa hi yuktātmā māmevānuttamām gatim* — 7. 18

'Noble indeed are they all, but the *jñāni* or wise person I regard as My very Self; for with the mind steadfast, he or she is established in Me alone, as the supreme goal.'

All these four are *udārās*, 'noble-minded'; *udāratā* is noble-mindedness, a wonderful word in Sanskrit. A famous Sanskrit *śloka* says:

*Ayam nijaḥ paro veti gaṇanā laghucetasām;*
*Udāra caritānam tu vasudhaiva kuṭumbakam* —

'This is one's own, that is another's, is the attitude of the small-minded. But, to the noble-minded, the whole world is one's own family.'

This spiritual unity of all humanity makes the whole world, or *vasudhā*, a *kuṭumba* or a family. This is an ancient idea repeated again and again in our literature from the Vedas up to Sri Ramakrishna's time: *Yasya viśvam bhavati ekam nīḍam*, says the Vedas, 'for whom the whole world becomes one nest or home'.

Here Śrī Kṛṣṇa says: all these four devotees are noble-minded, *udārāḥ*, though the first one is selfish and wants God only to get something from Him, i.e. he *uses* God, he does not love Him. Even then, Śrī Kṛṣṇa says, 'you are noble-minded.' What a wonderful idea! *Udārāḥ sarva evaite*; but, *jñānī tu ātmaiva me matam*, 'so far as *jñānī* is concerned, he is My very Self.'

*Āsthitaḥ sa hi yuktātmā mām eva anuttamām gatim,* 'the *jñānī* is steadfast, he or she is established in Me alone as the supreme goal'. That is the status of the pure *jñānī* or of the pure *bhakta;* and I repeat once again what Sri Ramakrishna said, 'pure *bhakti* and pure *jñāna* are one and the same'. All differences vanish there. The Lord alone is; that is the nature of highest *jñāna* and *bhakti*. This is a great truth.

The next *śloka* gives you a wonderful thought: how do you get this highest attitude? You may have to work for it in many lives; struggle, struggle, eventually you will get to that state. It doesn't come straight away; it is not by magic one gets to that state. So, I just read the next *śloka* which introduces us to this idea: 'build up the spiritual life little by little'. What a beautiful idea it is! From boyhood or girlhood, a boy or a girl of ten tries to be spiritual, little by little, like those insects, those particular creatures in the ocean in the coral islands; from the bottom of the sea up to the top, these coral creatures have built up the coral islands.

बहूनां जन्मनां अन्ते ज्ञानवान्मां प्रपद्यते ।
वासुदेवः सर्वमिति स महात्मा सुदुर्लभः ॥१९॥

*Bahūnām janmanām ante jñānavānmām prapadyate;*
*Vāsudevaḥ sarvamiti sa mahātmā sudurlabhaḥ* — 7. 19

'At the end of many births, the man or woman of *jñāna* or wisdom takes refuge in Me, realizing that all this is Vāsudeva (Śrī Kṛṣṇa or the one innermost Self of all); very rare is that great soul.'

After repeated births, struggling, struggling to perfect oneself, in the final life one realizes the supreme truth, *vāsudevaḥ sarvam iti,* 'that everything is Vāsudeva, the Lord is there in everything'; but such a devotee is verily rare. That is the language here, *sa mahātmā*, 'he or she is a *mahātmā*'; *sudurlabhaḥ*, 'very difficult to come across'. It is a very high state of perfection, but everywhere there have been somebody or the other to achieve this perfection, just like what we find among those climbing the Mount Everest; only a few have succeeded so far. Similarly, there is a Mount Everest of spiritual experience, seeing the Lord in everything, inside and outside, and that is what this *śloka* says.

After defining four types of devotees: *ārtaḥ, jijñāsuḥ, arthārthī* and *jñānī*, Śrī Kṛṣṇa says, they are all fine, they are all noble-minded. *Udārāḥ sarva evaite*, even those who worship Me for getting worldly advantages, 'even they are *udārāḥ*, noble-minded'; *jñānī tu ātmaiva me matam*, 'but the *jñānī* is My very Self'; *āsthitaḥ sa hi yuktātmā mām eva anuttamām gatim*, 'ever fixed in Me, a *jñānī* achieves the higher state of existence'.

Having said this, in verse 19 Śrī Kṛṣṇa says: When you practise spiritual life, you gain something by the time life is over. You are dead and gone, but your *samskāras* or innate tendencies in your subtle body remain. Then you get another birth, continuing the struggle, building up something more. Therefore, the Lord says:

*Bahūnām janmanām ante*, 'at the end of many many births'. In life after life he or she has been striving to achieve the highest realization, and the *jñānī* comes to this realization in the final stage, in the last birth. What is the realization? *Vāsudevaḥ sarvam iti*, 'the whole universe is Vāsudeva', that primordial, divine Pure Consciousness, whom we call Brahman, Atman, Viṣṇu, or *Ādyāśakti*, or by various other names; but the truth is one and the same, and the whole universe is nothing but the manifestation of that absolute Reality. We call it Vāsudeva in the *bhakti* religion. Vāsudeva, Nārāyaṇa, all these are various words meaning the same Reality. This is the highest realization. Such a person is rare.

Swami Vivekananda said, if a society has not produced any such people, that society is doomed; it has no direction; it will slowly decay and disappear. But if there are a few such, they will show you the way. Then you can be sure that the culture in the society will be permanent and steady; such a society knows how to renew itself because it has the living example before it. This is the concept of this particular expression *vāsudevaḥ sarvamiti*, 'everything is Vāsudeva'. The whole world is *brahma mayam*, 'filled with Brahman'. In our time, you find Sri Ramakrishna saying in *The Gospel of Sri Ramkrishna:* 'I see everything in front of me as Nārāyaṇa.'

Every wave in the ocean is a pulsation of the ocean. The ocean is real, these pulsations come and go, but knowledge of the ocean is the supreme truth about the ocean and about the wave. In this universe of ours, that infinite Brahman, that Vāsudeva, that Pure Consciousness, has manifested in these millions of forms. Among other manifestations, there are these human forms. In the *Śrīmad Bhāgavatam* (XI. ix. 28) it is mentioned that, after creation, there came many types of entities in the universe in the course of evolution—cosmic as well as organic. Finally, Brahman, that supreme Consciousness, evolved the human form and then *mudamāpa devaḥ,* 'The Divine Reality was very happy'. The *Śrīmad Bhāgavatam* gives this reason for this happiness: 'Because in this form, there is the organic capacity to realize Brahman, the very source of the universe and human beings'—*brahmāvaloka dhiṣaṇam. That is a very wonderful statement*! That speaks of the *highest* uniqueness of the human being.

One whole book, written by Sir Julian Huxley, the biologist, has this title, *The Uniqueness of Man,* and the author says there: 'Man is unique in more ways than one.' That uniqueness understood by Western biology has been carried to the highest level by Vedanta. He can know the universe, he can ask questions, he can know the very source of the universe. That is why this sentence, *vāsudevaḥ sarvam iti,* is important. That realization comes to us in our last birth. By perfecting ourselves life after life, in the last birth, everything is ready. Just a little last effort and realization comes. That is called the last birth of a human being. He or she then realizes the supreme truth. 'Such great people are very rare', *sa mahātmā sudurlabhaḥ*. Every time there is somebody like that living in this great country, but we may not be able to recognize him or her; sometimes we can, mostly we cannot. Śrī Kṛṣṇa himself will say so later on (9. 11) . *Sarvam brahma mayam, sarvam vāsudeva mayam,* 'everything is Brahman, everything is Śrī Kṛṣṇa' these are the words we use in our literature. So, in this *śloka,* we have got the highest type of spiritual realization. Everything is Brahman, everything is that ultimate truth. This particular human being, giving up this particularity, the ego, could realize it; that is the ultimate realization. The last word in spiritual realization is this, says Sri Ramakrishna also.

कामैस्तैस्तैर्हृतज्ञानाः प्रपद्यन्तेऽन्यदेवताः ।
तं तं नियममास्थाय प्रकृत्या नियताः स्वया ॥२०॥

*Kāmaistaistairhṛtajñānāḥ prapadyante'nyadevatāḥ;*
*Tam tam niyamamāsthāya prakṛtyā niyatāḥ svayā* — 7. 20

'Others again, deprived of discrimination due to this or that sensual desire, following this or that rite, devote themselves to other mythical gods, led by their nature.'

People are carried away by their own *prakṛti,* by their own nature. There are *samskāras* which we have accumulated and which give us a particular direction in our own life. And so, in this case, people are drawn by various desires, *kāmaistaistairhṛtajñānāḥ,* 'the knowledge of oneself is covered up and one is drawn towards various desires and cravings'. And to satisfy those desire and cravings, apart from the striving of heart and mind, he or she also worships gods: 'Let me get something from Him. He may be able to give'. So, they say, 'All right, I shall worship this god, or worship that god'. Out of lots of mythical gods and goddesses, people create a religion and worship these particular gods drawn by their *kāma* or desire of the heart. *Kāmaistaistairhṛtajñānāḥ,* 'real *jñāna* is drawn away by these various cravings'; therefore, *prapadyante'nya-devatāḥ,* 'they worship various other gods'. Why not worship that supreme Divine from whom everything has come, in whom we live, and to whom we return? Why go to all these various gods? Because the heart is full of cravings. 'He may help me.' So, we have got a big calendar of mythical gods and goddesses and their worship in our religion. In other religions also, there are various types of gods and goddesses. This drawing the heart away from the One Supreme Divine to various lesser deities is in all religious practices.

*Tam tam niyamam āsthāya*, 'following the disciplines of those religions'; *niyamas* means 'rules and rites'; if one wants to worship a particular deity, there is one set of *niyama;* similarly, for other deities—gods and goddesses. We perform various rites, not knowing that these gods are only different forms of the one infinite Divine Brahman. That knowledge is not there. We separate these gods from the main divine Reality because the heart is dominated by *kāma* or desires. Heart's cravings have 'drawn away our *jñāna*', *hṛtajñānāḥ.* By discrimination (*viveka*), we are able to understand that there is only one infinite Divine; these different gods are merely different names and forms of that one Divinity. That truth can come only by the use of discrimination. Most people do not have this discrimination. What destroys discrimination? The predominance of sensory cravings. They destroy that power of discrimination. Therefore, they worship these various gods thinking they are all separate: 'This god will give us something, that god will give us something, etc.', generally with a worldly calculation. Now, this is called popular religion, and popular religion is everywhere the same. Very few people seek true religion, which has spiritual growth, development and realization as the theme.

So, here is one verse in which Śrī Kṛṣṇa refers to most people in the world. Having said that four types of people worship the Divine, He also said that they are all *udārās*, 'generous'; further, Śrī Kṛṣṇa is explaining their behaviour by saying that this is their difficulty: their nature drags them in a direction away from the Supreme Divinity.

In the Upaniṣads, this whole mistaken idea has been subjected to severe criticism. The English translation of Śaṅkarācārya's commentary on *Bṛhadāraṇyaka Upaniṣad* by Swami Madhavananda reads (I. iv. 10): 'because you are the Atman, what can these gods and other powers do to you?' Nothing. For *there is no difference as regards Brahman or the knowledge of It, between (spiritual) giants like Vāmadeva and the human weaklings of today*! The gods seem to keep the human beings under their control. Human beings are treated as 'cattle to the gods', *paśurevam sa devānām*; that is the exact language used in that *Upaniṣad*. And the example given is: A cowherd has about hundred cattle under him, and he is doing well. A tiger comes and snatches away one cattle. The cowherd is very unhappy because his property is being destroyed. Now, we are as such cattle to the gods above. They do not want anyone to give up rituals and deviate from their control; this is what is overthrown by the Upaniṣads. Looks like very modern! But this thinking is so ancient. Why do you remain like cattle to the mythical gods? Are you not infinite in your true nature? That infinite one from which this universe has come is your own true nature. Why don't you strive to know it? But if you try to know it, gods may put obstacles in your way. They don't want you to go beyond their control. See the language in the Upaniṣad and Śaṅkarācārya's commentary; both are masterly expositions of this infinite and free nature of the human being.

Śaṅkarācārya quotes a verse from *Mahābhārata* (XIV. xix. 54, Bhandarkar edition) in this connection, the second line of which says: *na ca etad iṣṭam devānām martyaih upari vartanam*, 'this is not liked by the *devas* that men or women should live above them.' This is reflected in human feudal societies where aristocrats do not like common people to rise above them.

A wonderful orientation to our religion was given by Swami Vivekananda in the modern period. We believe in hundreds of mythical gods and goddesses. Not much blessing came to us, only foreign invasion, again and again. Vivekananda said: 'First, have faith in yourself; then have faith in God and in other human beings.' We had no faith in ourselves, and therefore, all this trouble came. That Vedantic idea is coming to our people for the first time. Have *ātmaśraddhā*, the attitude of 'I can, I can. There are enormous energies within me. The divine is sleeping within me.' This is the new attitude. So, he boldly said, 'The old religion said he is an atheist who does not believe in God; the new religion tells you, he is an atheist who does not believe in himself.' First, have faith in yourself; then only can you have faith, solid, dynamic faith, in God or in other human beings. We have been too much carried away by the idea of being the slaves of all sorts of gods and goddesses.

So, our people must learn to realize the one infinite Divine as the Self of all; and everyone loves the Self, the most. Other loves are only the derivatives of this love, and that Self is the infinite Atman, the Self of your self. Turn your attention to the same Self in all; then you will love others also. This is the basic philosophy which Swami Vivekananda preached from the Upaniṣads for the modern period. It cuts through all limitations of nature, creed, race, etc.; it is universal. That Atman is your true nature. Atman is the nature of men and women in Russia, China, everywhere—the infinite Atman. What a beautiful conception! All slavery goes away; all kinds of fears go away. That religion of fearlessness is the great teaching of the Upaniṣads. That is the only literature in the world, Swamiji said, which always preaches fearlessness and strength, *abhaya* and *śakti*. It is the first lesson we have to learn. 'Each soul is potentially divine, the goal (of life) is to manifest this Divine within', is the first statement of the Vedantic truth given by Swami Vivekananda (*The Complete Works of Swami Vivekananda*, vol. 1, p. 124). One must base one's religion on this truth; then he or she can worship other gods if one likes, but with this knowledge that all worship is ultimately of the one Divinity. Don't quarrel about names, like, our Father in Heaven, Allah, Viṣṇu, Brahmā, Śiva. All these names also are of the one infinite Reality.

Therefore, do not quarrel, for truth is one. So, Śrī Kṛṣṇa is telling us here: 'When the heart is drawn by various cravings, the first thing that happens to you is that your power of discrimination gets destroyed; knowledge gets destroyed; then we become weak and behave like cattle to the gods. 'Don't behave like cattle to the gods!' That is the message of the Upaniṣads. There must be no more that sense of weakness, and self-hypnotising that people have practised for ages. Don't hypnotise yourself any longer; become strong, manifest the divine within, and every effort must be made in that direction.

Śrī Kṛṣṇa is telling that great truth in verse 20 and in the next verse:

यो यो यां यां तनुं भक्तः श्रद्धयाऽर्चितुमिच्छति ।
तस्य तस्याचलां श्रद्धां तामेव विदधाम्यहम् ॥२१॥

*Yo yo yām yām tanum bhaktaḥ śraddhayārcitumicchati;*
*Tasya tasyācalām śraddhām tāmeva vidadhāmyaham* — 7. 21

'Whatsoever form any devotee seeks to worship with *śraddhā*—that *śraddhā* of his or her I make unwavering.'

Śrī Kṛṣṇa is so generous: *yo yo yām yām tanum bhaktaḥ śraddhayā arcitum icchati,* 'Any devotee who wants to worship with faith any particular god or goddess', I help him or her to worship with great *śraddha* or faith. *Tasya tasyācalām śraddhām tāmeva vidadhāmyaham,* 'that very *śraddha* I strengthen in him or her'. That is the way he or she is expressing one's religious faith. If I disturb him or her now, that person may loose everything. Therefore, I don't disturb him or her now. One must come to the divine slowly, through experience and discrimination. This is the next teaching Śrī Kṛṣṇa is giving, namely, generosity—'don't condemn'. In the literature of Swami Vivekananda, we find this idea, 'don't condemn anyone'. If you can show anyone something better, show, but don't condemn. Strengthen each in his or her own faith, in his or her own belief, and later on, there will be some change in that person. 'Don't condemn' is a great command in religion which Swami Vivekananda uses. Sri Ramakrishna also used it and usually the Hindu religion has that generous attitude. Don't condemn any particular practice.

One day, Naren himself, the future Swami Vivekananda, condemned a particular religious sect of Calcutta of those times, in the presence of Sri Ramakrishna. After hearing everything, Sri Ramakrishna gently said: 'Naren, welcome them. They practise according to their understanding. Every house has a back door to enter, not only the front door. Some people will like to enter the house through the back door, where toilets are there; some people come from the front door. But, there is a back door also; it also allows you to enter.

Therefore, 'don't condemn.' That was an echo of this teaching, 'don't condemn', which we have to follow. It is important, especially in the modern age, with respect to children. If you start condemning when children commit small mistakes, they will lose faith in themselves; they will become weaker and weaker. Encourage them, join with them. Play with them and then they will grow higher and higher. That is the true attitude of education and the same thing is in religion also. For us, education and religion are earlier and later phases of human development. So, 'don't condemn' is a great expression. If you can't show something better, and that too with gentleness and sympathy, and if you just constantly condemn a particular person for his or her work or life, that is very bad; it would destroy one's faith in oneself.

So, 'that *śraddha* I strengthen in him'; how does that person benefit? The next verse answers:

स तया श्रद्धया युक्तस्तस्याराधनमीहते ।
लभते च ततः कामान्मयैव विहितान्हि तान् ॥२२॥

*Sa tayā śraddhayā yuktastasyārādhanamīhate;*
*Labhate ca tataḥ kāmānmayaiva vihitānhi tān* — 7. 22

'Endued with that *śraddhā*, one engages in the worship of that, and from it, gains one's desires—these being verily dispensed by Me alone.'

*Sa tayā śraddhayā yuktaḥ tasyārādhanam īhate*, 'endowed with that *śraddhā*, he or she engages in the worship of that particular form of the Divine'; *labhate ca tataḥ kāmān*, 'whatever fruit one hopes to get, he or she also gets it'. But, who gives this fruit to the worshipper? 'It comes from Me alone, the one infinite Source', *mayaiva vihitān hi tān*; not from the gods, but from Me. Therefore, whatever worship you do, whatever fruits you get, ultimately comes only from that one infinite Source.

Then the next verse says: but, if discrimination is used, you will realize that these are all limited advantages to get. You can see that those who worship the deities get limited advantages only; nothing very high; neither high spiritual development, nor knowledge, nor realization. What results will you get either by worshipping the gods or the one infinite Source? The next verse answers it:

अन्तवत्तु फलं तेषां तद्भवत्यल्पमेधसाम् ।
देवान्देवयजो यान्ति मद्भक्ता यान्ति मामपि ॥ २३ ॥

*Antavattu phalam teṣām tadbhavatyalpamedhasām;*
*Devāndevayajo yānti madbhaktā yānti māmapi* — 7. 23

'But the fruit (accruing) to these men and women of little understanding is limited. The worshippers of the *devas* go to the *devas* and My devotees come unto Me.'

*Antavattu phalam teṣām*, 'their fruits are all of temporary nature'; after some time they end, whatever blessing you will get, they are all of temporary nature. *Tatbhavati alpa medhasam*, 'that is because their intelligence is very ordinary'. Their worldly intelligence may be very high, but 'spiritual intelligence is very very limited in them', *alpa medhasām;* because they can't pierce through the delusion that is in them, and their discrimination has been carried away by so many sensory cravings. Then, people must ask themselves and find their answer. What is the result that we get by worshipping the gods, or by worshipping the infinite Divine Being? Śrī Kṛṣṇa says, *devān deva yajo yānti*, 'worshippers of the *devās*, gods, go to *devās*'; and, *mad bhaktā yānti mām api*, 'My devotees come to me'.

Here the words *mām api* are used; 'they come to Me (Śrī Kṛṣṇa) alone' as a human incarnation of the Supreme Divinity. Likewise, *Bhagavān* Buddha, Jesus Christ, Śrī Kṛṣṇa, Sri Ramakrishna or Śrī Rāma; they are all human incarnations. So, everybody cannot see that this person is that Divine Being in reality, because he or she is deluded by the external appearance. Śrī Kṛṣṇa said this in the fourth chapter, verses 6 to 8. Here Śrī Kṛṣṇa goes one step further to clarify the situation, to explain why everyone does not recognize a Divine Incarnation.

अव्यक्तं व्यक्तिमापन्नं मन्यन्ते मां अबुद्धयः ।
परं भावं अजानन्तो ममाव्ययं अनुत्तमम् ॥ २४ ॥

*Avyaktam vyaktimāpannam manyante mām abuddhayaḥ;*
*Param bhāvam ajānanto mamāvyayam anuttamam* — 7. 24

'The foolish regard Me, the unmanifested, as come into manifestation, not knowing My Supreme State, which is immutable and transcendental.'

'I am,' says Śrī Kṛṣṇa, 'really speaking, *avyaktam* or unmanifested, beyond these manifestations as the world; that is My true nature'. But now, as a human being, I have become *vyaktam*, a manifestation, an individual; that infinite has become a finite human being. In the latter form only, ordinary people look upon Me. They don't see My *avyaktam* dimension; they see only the *vyaktam* dimension. *Manyante mām*, 'they look upon Me'; *abuddhayaḥ*, 'those who have a low intellect'; *abuddhiḥ*, 'not a sufficiently intelligent person'; *param bhāvam ajānanto*, 'not realizing My higher nature'; this what you see is human nature, but there is also a divine nature in Me; that they cannot understand, they cannot see; *mama avyayam anuttamam*, 'My changeless, transcendental nature'. I am the Supreme Reality, above all the beings. I am the one Lord of the universe. That aspect they cannot see. They see what their senses tell them and conclude that, 'they are limited human beings. Like us, therefore, Śrī Kṛṣṇa also eats and drinks, he also lives like us. So, he is also one of us, nothing higher is there in him.' That is why people cannot appreciate greatness. Appreciating greatness needs a little greatness in oneself. This is a beautiful idea and I wish we understand it in our society. We always judge people in society. It is natural for us to judge people, but how do we judge? We judge according to the measure of our own experience; beyond that we cannot see that there is a higher dimension and that tremendous energy is concentrated in the person of that dimension.

When Gandhiji appeared in India as a political leader, many people looked at him and asked, 'what is there in him?', and when one national Congress leader, Mrs. Sarojini Naidu, referred to his thin body as a Mickey Mouse in all its humour, Gandhiji appreciated it. Soon our people knew that this

Mickey Mouse contains so much energy, so much power for influencing the whole nation, the whole world, as it were. So, this is a lesson other people must learn; we are so facile in judging people and holding on to our judgement. A little doubt is good: 'This is what I think, but I may be wrong.' That is a very good idea, and yet life has to go on based upon the judgement. But whenever you find a change is needed, do not hesitate to change. That is a great mind which can change quickly when the situation demands it.

So, regarding the highest manifestation of the Divine as an *avatāra,* Śrī Kṛṣṇa says that we can't measure him with our human skill. It is something extraordinary. Romain Rolland describes Sri Ramakrishna in the very Introduction to his book, *Life of Ramakrishna*. A man like Romain Rolland can see through the physical form and see the power working within—an artistic vision and a spiritual vision, different from a dull, prosaic vision. So, describing Ramakrishna, he gives us a wonderful sentence in that Introduction:

'Ramakrishna's external life was set in a very limited frame, far away from the currents and cross-currents of the contemporary world.'

Perfectly true! In a corner of the Dakshineswar Temple, living there, somewhat illiterate; he was a priest before. Externally there is nothing in him, we can say. Then comes the next sentence:

'His inner life embraced the whole multiplicity of men and gods.'

Similarly, Buddha was looked upon as a *mahā śramaṇā* or a great monk only; but he shook the whole of Asia, inspired millions and millions of people. Wherefrom did that power come? That power was there, but at that time people couldn't understand it; he looked so ordinary. That is why sometimes it is better not to see a great person from near, but see him from a distance in time.

Now this idea has been beautifully expounded by Sri Ramakrishna in a parable. A person took his diamond and asked a vegetable seller: 'how much will you give me for this diamond?' 'Only ten pounds of potatoes; nothing more.' Then he went to a cloth merchant. He offered nine yards of cloth and nothing more. Finally, he went to a diamond merchant and asked him, 'How much will you give?' He replied, 'Ten thousand rupees I shall give you'. So, in spiritual life, it is the same. When we try to judge others, always keep in mind this truth that that judgement is conditioned by the range of one's experience. Within that range only, does one estimate a person. So, it is good to have a little doubt, so that we don't become fanatics. It is fanaticism to think that whatever we estimate is correct and nothing else. 'What I understand is this; that is what I can say now; if I see more, I certainly may change my opinion.' That is a scientific attitude. Say, 'according to the present data available, this is the truth of it; but, if more data comes, some of them contradictory, I will change my conclusion.' That is called a scientific mind. So, in society, we need that scientific mind, that scientific temper, as we call it. We are in search of truth, we are not going to glorify our own opinion. We shall subject our opinion to the test of truth. When the whole nation is educated in this scientific temper, a beautiful human development will come. That is what we need very much in our society.

So, Śrī Kṛṣṇa says: *Avyaktam vyaktim āpannam*, 'the undifferentiated has become differentiated, the unmanifest has become the manifest'; *manyante mām abuddhayaḥ*, 'those who have no intelligence, they think like that about Me'; they think Śrī Kṛṣṇa is just a limited person like others in this world; *param bhāvam ajānanto*, 'not understanding My higher nature'. Some contemporaries of Jesus similarly remarked: 'Is he not a carpenter's son?' Verse 11 of chapter 9 is similar to this verse; only a slightly different phraseology is used there:

*Avajānanti mām mūḍhā mānuṣīm tanumāśritam;*
*Param bhāvam ajānanto mama bhūta maheśvaram —*

*Mām avajānanti mūḍhāḥ,* 'foolish people deride Me'; *mānuṣīm tanum āśritam,* 'who has assumed a human body'; *param bhāvam ajānantaḥ,* 'not understanding My higher form';

*Mama bhūtamaheśvaram,* 'My supreme state as the Lord of this universe'.

That is the meaning of this *param bhāvam ajānanto mamāvyayam anuttamam.* This is My true form. I am the Master of the universe. I assumed this human body to do some work, to save this world, but these people don't understand what is the truth about My nature. They will put the incarnation into trouble because of the lack of insight. In foreign countries, they will be crucified, as Jesus was. Here in India, at least we don't crucify them; we just speak ill of them from the beginning, and yet, slowly we understand, 'Yes, they are correct.' In Calcutta, some people used to say about Sri Ramakrishna, 'Who is that priest in Dakshineswar? Sometimes he goes into some sort of nervous sickness, and loses his consciousness.' But those who could understand, understood the greatness of the man. Men like Keshab Chandra Sen—he was a devotee of God leading a spiritual life—started to spread the glory of Sri Ramakrishna, 'he is not of an ordinary type, but extraordinary.' That is what made the people of Calcutta understand the greatness of Sri Ramakrishna and brought to him all the serious devotees, including the young devotees, who became, later on, Swami Vivekananda and others.

So, we have the next verse 25, which says:

**नाहं प्रकाशः सर्वस्य योगमायासमावृतः ।**
**मूढोऽयं नाभिजानाति लोको मां अजं अव्ययम् ॥२५॥**

*Nāham prakāśaḥ sarvasya yogamāyāsamāvṛtaḥ;*
*Mūḍho'yam nābhijānāti loko mām ajam avyayam — 7. 25*

'Veiled by the *yogamāyā,* illusion divine, I am not manifest to all. This deluded world knows Me not—the Unborn, the Immutable.'

*Nāham prakāśaḥ sarvasya,* 'I am not manifest clearly to everybody'. Why? *Yogamāyāsamāvṛtaḥ,* 'covered as I am by My own *yogamāyā*', that wonderful *Māyā* by which I can assume any kind of expression; *mūḍho'yam nābhijānāti loko mām,* 'this foolish world doesn't know Me'; *ajam avyayam,* 'I am the *ajam,* unborn, *avyayam,* imperishable.' That dimension of Mine *mūḍhaḥ ayam lokaḥ*, 'this foolish world'; *nābhijānāti*, 'they do not understand'. This is what Śrī Kṛṣṇa is telling here. That is why he had to suffer so much. Even somebody complained that Śrī Kṛṣṇa has stolen the *syāmantaka* jewel, that he was a thief, and some people began to think that Śrī Kṛṣṇa was indeed a thief. And he had to justify himself, go and find the *syāmantaka*, and hand it over to its owner, Satyajit. He is the divine himself. Even He, as a human being, had to pass through all these difficulties. Sri Ramakrishna and Buddha also had problems. Sri Ramakrishna suffered from throat cancer and passed away. So, when you see all these things, you may feel, 'how can this man be a God? This cannot be. He is an ordinary person'—that thought will come to many people. But those who know spiritual realities, they will be able to see through the external and see the real worth of the person concerned.

So, Śrī Kṛṣṇa says, 'I cover myself with My *yogamāyā* to make people see an ordinary person in Me, where there is really something infinitely deeper.' They can't see the infinite; they can see only the finite. That is the nature of *Māyā*. *Māyā* makes the infinite appear as finite, the immortal to appear as the mortal; and we are all within that *Māyā*. So, we are not able to understand the divine dimension of the incarnation. This is a wonderful statement Śrī Kṛṣṇa gives here in this verse 25.

In the next verse and the other remaining three out of four verses, some beautiful truths are given, and the scientific attitude is expounded in verses 27 and 28.

**वेदाहं समतीतानि वर्तमानानि चार्जुन ।**
**भविष्याणि च भूतानि मां तु वेद न कश्चन ॥२६॥**

*Vedāham samatītāni vartamānāni cārjuna;*
*Bhaviṣyāṇi ca bhūtāni mām tu veda na kaścana* — 7. 26

'I know, O Arjuna, the beings of the whole past, and present, and the future, but none knows Me.'

*Vedāham samatītāni bhūtāni vartamānāni ca arjuna*, 'I know the beings of the past, O Arjuna, and of the present'; *bhaviṣyāṇi ca,* 'and of the future too'; *mām tu veda na kaścana,* 'but none knows Me'; none knows My real dimension. That is what Śrī Kṛṣṇa is telling in this verse 26.

After that comes the definition of the scientific attitude, scientific mind, in two famous verses; verses which were commented upon by Śaṅkara to bring home some scientific truths that are some of the many contributions of India. Scientific thinking and search lead to scientific truth. As long as our nation stuck to science, it was great. As soon as we left science and began to entertain superstitious ideas, all sorts of mythologies, the nation became weaker and weaker. You can see that sometime from about the 9th century AD, this weakness came upon the national scene. We are getting out of it today. So, in today's science, we are really re-studying science. We had studied it before; it is not new to us. India is entering into a new era of scientific development after forgetting it for a few centuries. That is what is happening today all over this great country.

Now we enter into verses 27 and 28. I would like to point out the importance of these two verses; how Śaṅkarācārya brings out in his *Gītā* commentary, the scientific mind, the scientific temper, the scientific attitude of the *Gītā*, and stresses it. The *Gītā* merely says:

**इच्छा द्वेष समुत्थेन द्वन्द्व मोहेन भारत ।**
**सर्वभूतानि संमोहं सर्गे यान्ति परन्तप ॥ २७ ॥**

*Icchā dveṣa samutthena dvandva mohena bhārata;*
*Sarvabhūtāni sammoham sarge yānti parantapa* — 7. 27

'By the delusion of the pairs of opposites, arising from desire and aversion, O descendant of Bharata, all beings fall into delusion at birth, O scorcher of foes.'

O Arjuna, all beings are deluded from the very beginning because of the two passions of the human mind, *icchā* and *dveṣa.* The first is *icchā*: 'I want this, I want that, I desire this, I desire that'. The other is *dveṣa*: 'if I don't get it, I will get angry, I will destroy everything.' These are called *icchā* and *dveṣa.* 'Due to these two delusions', the human being is not able to know the truth. *Dvandva mohena,* 'from this twofold delusions', desire and aversion or anger—delusions which are always together; where there is desire, there is also aversion or anger. When an obstruction to fulfilling desire comes, anger comes automatically. These are the two *mohas*, 'delusions'; *bhārata*, 'O Arjuna'; *sarvabhūtāni*, 'all beings'; *sammoham sarge yānti*, 'at the time of creation, become subject to this tremendous delusion'; *parantapa*, 'O scorcher of foes, i.e. Arjuna'. Men and women suffer when they are subjected to these two delusions—*icchā* and *dveṣa*. Now, from this particular idea of the *Gītā*, Śaṅkara brings out the implication, *and that is something marvellous*: that, not only in the spiritual life you suffer when you are under the delusion of the *icchā* and *dveṣa*, even in day-to-day life, dealing with external nature, dealing with other human beings, we always suffer when we are subjected to these two delusions—*icchā* and *dveṣa*. That concept he puts in a fine sentence in Sanskrit:

> *na hi icchā dveṣa doṣa vaśīkṛta cittasya yathābhūtārtha viṣayajñānam utpadyate bahirapi—*

*Bahirapi* means 'even in our external life'; *jñānam*, 'right knowledge'; *na utpadyate*, 'does not come'; *icchā dveṣa doṣa vaśīkṛta cittasya*, 'of the mind which is subjected to the evils of desire and aversion or anger, in the mind completely controlled by these two'; *yathābhūta artha viṣaya jñānam na utpadyate*, 'there does not arise what is the truth of a thing as it is'; *bahirapi*, 'even in the external world'.

That is why the scientist tells us to train the mind in objectivity. Don't be carried away by your own passions and emotions. Suppose you are experimenting on a particular thing. You have a particular desire that this particular conclusion must be found in the results of the experiment. If the desire dominates you, you will certainly find that in the experiment, but it won't be true. That desire must go. 'I shall see the truth and then believe it. That will be science.' So, in this way *icchā* and *dveṣa*, 'desire and aversion', are to be eliminated from the mind. They make for wrong judgement of things and persons. Just like, in the High Court, if the judge has a particular preference about a particular accused, his judgement will go wrong. If he has no preference, he will try to be true to the facts before him and then give a judgement. That will be true justice.

That is how the scientific mind develops and discovers the truth of things; not what you *want* to see, but what *is* there—what Śaṅkarācārya calls in his commentary on the *Brahma-sūtras*, in the second *sūtra*: *vastu tantra jñāna*, 'knowledge flowing from an existing truth'. What a beautiful expression! *Vastu tantra jñāna. Vastu* is the technical Sanskrit word for 'a thing as it is'. *Tantra* means 'based upon'; *jñāna*, 'knowledge'—'knowledge based upon the thing itself'; that is called *vastu tantra jñāna*. Science wants to discover Truth, which is Truth for *all*. The other type of knowledge is *puruṣa tantra jñāna,* 'knowledge arising from personal preferences'. This truth is 'very personal', *puruṣa tantra.* 'I like mango. I like this particular type of fruit.' These are all our preferences. It has a place in human life. But, in science, when we search for the truth of things, we will have to purify the mind from all attachments and aversions. Anyone who judges other human beings must remove from the mind attachment and aversion. Then only he or she can judge him or her as he or she is in reality.

*Sarvabhūtāni,* 'all beings'; *sammoham sarge yānti,* 'in the manifested world, become subject to this delusion'. Śaṅkara says in his commentary *bahirapi,* 'even in the external world'; as it is difficult to discover truth even in the external world, when influenced by these two delusions, it is still more difficult to discover truth in the inner world. In the inner world, it is your mind that seeks, and your mind is also what is being studied; so it is very difficult to decide. First, Śaṅkara said about the difficulty of seeking truth in the external world, as referred to earlier. Then comes:

> *kimu vaktavyam tābhyām āviṣṭabuddheḥ sammūḍhasya*
> *pratyagātmani bahu pratibandhe jñānam na utpadyate*
> *iti—*

*Kimu vaktavyam*, 'what then can be said?' *Tābhyām āviṣṭabuddheḥ*, 'for the mind that is under the control of these two'; *sammūḍhasya*, 'of the deluded'; *pratyagātmani*, 'in dealing with our own inner Self'; *bahu pratibandhe*, 'which is full of obstacles'. Understanding our own true nature is full of obstacles. And therefore, *jñānam na utpadyate iti*, 'knowledge doesn't come to us'. Why? Because of these two obstacles that are there. So, whether it is in physical science or inter-human relationships, or realizing our own true nature as the Atman, we need to purge the mind of these two passions—*icchā* and *dveṣa;* then you will understand the truth yourself. *This is a beautiful commentary on these two important verses.*

The next verse will say, 'those who have overcome these evils, they realize God. They realize the truth clearly, because the Truth is there; it is a *vastu*, and we have only to discover it, recognize it. It is your own likes and dislikes that have to be removed from the mind.

**येषां त्वन्तगतं पापं जनानां पुण्यकर्मणाम् ।**
**ते द्वन्द्वमोहनिर्मुक्ता भजन्ते मां दृढव्रताः ॥२८॥**

*Yeṣām tvantagatam pāpam janānām puṇyakarmaṇām;*
*Te dvandvamohanirmuktā bhajante mām dṛḍhavratāḥ*—7. 28

'Those men and women of virtuous deeds, whose sin has come to an end, they, freed from the twin delusions, worship Me with steadfast devotion.'

'Those people who have overcome these two evils of *icchā* and *dveṣa*, realize Me truly, within, as the Self of all.' They have no difficulty, as their minds are pure. This is how the mind becomes pure. One's own likes and dislikes are thrown away. The mind wants nothing but the truth, nothing but the true Self that is in all. And for knowing this truth, one needs to train the mind.

In fact, in our Indian society, we need a good deal of this training. We are not interested in truth. We are interested in opinions; even prejudices are plenty. But, for one generation or two, children should be trained in the method of searching for truth; that is knowledge, and through that, they must develop some convictions. Opinions have their due place in human life, but not on serious subjects. Swami Vivekananda has said: 'Great convictions are the mothers of great deeds'. Knowledge is seeking for the truth. 'What is the truth of that or this thing?' I see a thing but I don't know whether it is true, or what is the truth of it. That questioning mind can create tremendous mental energy in a nation. You don't accept a thing unless you know it is true. You don't want merely an opinion, but the truth with that kind of thinking. Our politics and our society will be completely transformed, if we give this education to our people from their primary standard onwards.

So, *yeṣām tvantagatam pāpam,* 'those whose evils of mind have come to an end'; *pāpam* means 'evils, sinfulness of mind'; *antagatam,* 'have ended'; *janānām,* 'of people'; *puṇya karmaṇām,* 'those who have done good deeds'; when you have done good deeds, when these evil forces—attachment and aversion—have become less and less. The concern for others is a tremendous discipline for training the mind. Then, *te dvandva moha nirmuktā,* 'they who have become freed from these two delusions'; *bhajante mām dṛḍhavratāḥ,* 'worship Me in spirit and in truth with great firmness and determination'. That is the real worship of the Divine.

As the previous *ślokas* have said, we have so many desires. So, in some book you will get, 'worship this mythical god, and he will fulfil the desire', and thus we go on changing gods. This is one thing very characteristic of some of our people. We change gods when we find that this god has not given what we sought from him. Long ago, I had a friend in Bangalore. He was a member of many religious committees. One day, I asked him, 'Why did you become a member of so many religious bodies?' 'Swamiji, don't you know?' he replied, 'if one bank fails, the other bank will help me!' That was the attitude, and some of our people have that kind of attitude. That, *bhajante mām dṛḍhavratāḥ,* 'idea to worship God in spirit and in truth' doesn't come. Behind all these various *devās* and *devīs,* 'Brahman is the only one infinite divine and non-dual'—

*ekam eva advitīyam brahma*. That is pure religion; that search is the way of pure spiritual development.

So, in these two verses 27 and 28, very inspiring ideas are there, in tune with modern scientific training. In fact, there is a tremendous scientific training component in the Vedantic discipline. We are in search of truth; that is why Śaṅkara used the words, *vastu tantra jñānam*, '*jñāna* based upon the *vastu*': 'what is it in itself', and not as what it appears to you. That is the great quest of the Vedantic mind. The Upaniṣads are full of these, 'What is the truth?' There is this great utterance in the *Muṇḍaka Upaniṣad*: *satyam eva jayate*, 'Truth alone triumphs.' *Satyam* is the supreme virtue, supreme value. In the *Mahābhārata*, and everywhere in our literature, you will find stress on truth. Make your life true, do not take to a false life; go for true knowledge, not for false knowledge. In this way, *samyak jñānam* is stressed: the language used is 'true knowledge'. Similarly, we purify our mind by removing all that is adventitious there. Mind has to be trained in the power of penetration. What helps it to penetrate into the heart of truth is the cleaning away of *icchā* and *dveṣa*—these various likes and dislikes that fill the mind of human beings.

So, this kind of discipline must come to us from the very beginning. I want the truth of things. I don't want merely the appearance of things. So, a search for knowledge must become a search for the truth of things. That can be in the external world, and we call it *physical science*; it can be in the inner world, and we call it *the science of spirituality. Śrī Kṛṣṇa combines both here in these two verses giving the beautiful idea of the scientific training of the mind.* We have to emphasize this point often. We have so little *training of the mind* in our education. *It is mostly stuffing the brain* instead of training the mind. These are two different things. Stuffing the brain doesn't increase the power of the mind; it only becomes a sort of the Pandora's box to accumulate things. That is all. But the versatility of the human mind comes from the capacity to think, the capacity to question. That is how you train the mind. There you get precision in thinking. When you have precision in thinking, you have precision in speaking also. I have watched people giving the vote of thanks in various meetings. The same thing is said many times, and a lot of time is taken. The whole thing could be said in two minutes. It goes on for thirty minutes. Why? There is no training of the mind. Precise, to the point—that kind of thing comes only through good education. We have to train our own minds by searching for knowledge, for precise knowledge, neither more nor less but exactly, not indulging in vague speculations. At present it is not so. Mind is flimsy now; it has no power of impact upon the world around us. That is why this kind of training is absolutely essential.

You carry this same scientific attitude from the external to the internal; then religion will not become encrusted with superstitions. Today, there is plenty of superstition in the name of religion because the scientific mind is not there, that rational mind is not there, that truth-seeking mind is not there. It should not be so. You will then understand Vedanta better, which is the subject of tremendous scrutiny by brilliant minds. It is very simple and once you try to apply it in your life, a tremendous energy will come to you. High character will come to you. All that development has to come in our nation in the next few decades by understanding first, the scientific frame of mind and then approaching *Sanātana Dharma* from that point of view, approaching Vedanta from that point of view. This is a profound philosophy based upon the search for truth. That is the language of the Upaniṣads themselves, and when you search for truth you can question; others can't question. If you are in search of dogma, you cannot question; no dogma can be questioned, or can stand questioning; but truth can be questioned. The more you question, the better. Vedanta invites the whole world today to question its conclusions and try to see the truth for themselves. *That is the place of Vedanta in the thought world of today*. It accepts modern physical science; it is not afraid of modern science. It also takes you beyond physical science. When physical science is ended, it takes you gently by the hand to realize the truth hidden within you. Physical science deals with perishable external nature. Vedanta deals with the Imperishable in the internal nature *and* in human beings. What is that profound mystery in the human body? Now, this kind of subject is developed scientifically in the Upaniṣads, in Vedanta. And *Gītā* is conveying that message here. This nation will be completely transformed with tremendous resources of mind and spiritual values to inspire the nation. That is the bright future. Swami Vivekananda's literature will be a tremendous source of strength for our people, where he has shown the similarity between modern scientific method and thought, and Vedantic method and thought. So, this nation will become scientifically strong, and also spiritually strong. A complete civilization will come thereby. That is Swami Vivekananda's great hope for the future.

So, the next *śloka* says:

**जरा मरण मोक्षाय मामाश्रित्य यतन्ति ये ।**
**ते ब्रह्म तद्विदुः कृत्स्नं अध्यात्मं कर्म चाखिलम् ॥२९॥**

*Jarā maraṇa mokṣāya māmāśritya yatanti ye;*
*Te brahma tadviduḥ kṛtsnam adhyātmam karma cākhilam*—7. 29

'Those who, taking refuge in Me, strive for freedom from old age and death, know Brahman, and also the whole of *adhyātma*, and *karma* in its entirety.'

In order to free oneself from *jarā* and *maraṇa*, one takes refuge in the divine. *Jarā* is 'old age' and *maraṇa* is 'death'. Today, we have a word in English which is exactly a modification of the Sanskrit word *jarā*—geriatrics. Dealing with the problems of old age is called geriatrics. That is called *jarā*. *Jarā* and *maraṇa* are the two big problems of modern society. *Jarā maraṇa mokṣa* means 'freedom from old age and death'. That is a very special contribution of Indian thought. Ancient Greek thought, following the wise dictum of their oracle of Delphi, namely, 'Man, Know Thy self', knew one part of that oracle, the external sociopolitical part, not the internal spiritual part. They knew life but they didn't know what is *jarā* and *maraṇa*. They, excepting Socrates, never investigated that subject. We investigated the subject and discovered the truth that *jarā* and *mṛtyu* apply only to the body and not to the Atman within. Within the body is the infinite Atman, ever free, beyond change and beyond death; that is a wonderful truth! The Atman in every being is described in the *Vivekacuḍāmaṇi* of Śaṅkarācārya in these words (verse 256):

*Ṣaḍbhirūrmibhiḥ ayogi yogihṛt*
*bhāvitam na karṇaiḥ vibhāvitam —*

'The Truth of the immortal Atman is free from the sixfold waves of change, but it is available by the heart of *yogis*, and unavailable by the senses.'

There are six *ūrmis* or 'waves of change' affecting everything in this world, but not affecting the Atman. *Ūrmi* or wave is the Sanskrit expression used by Śaṅkarācārya in his *Vivekacūḍāmaṇi.* First is: *jāyate,* 'a thing is born'; then he gives it the attribute, *asti,* 'it exists'; till then it was not. Then, *vardhate,* 'grows'; a baby grows; within five years how active a little baby becomes! Then, *vipariṇamate,* 'evolves', lot of transformations take place from childhood onwards. Then begins the downward movement: *apakṣīyate,* 'goes on decaying', and finally, *naśyati,* 'dies or ceases to exist'. These are called the 'sixfold waves of change' affecting everything in this world, including the solar system, and all galactic systems. They all have a birth, have a growth, have a development, have a decay, and finally death.

But, behind this world of change is the changeless, the eternal, the immortal. That was the scientific discovery of the Indian sages pursuing the science of human possibilities or the science of human resources and finding expression in the Upaniṣads. That is what made them strong; that is what made Indian culture also immortal. By discovering the immortal, the Upaniṣads made themselves immortal and the culture sponsored by them also immortal. *Nowhere else in the world will you find that kind of 'Mount Everest' of thought and experience.*

The Vedas declare that 'life and death are the *shadows* of the One Supreme Reality,' *yasya chāyā amṛtam, yasya mṛtyuḥ* (*Ṛg Veda samhita*, X. viii. 121). They developed this depth dimension by studying the phenomenon of not only life, but also of death. Phenomena of old age and death the Greeks never knew, except, as referred to before, Socrates and Plato. This is the opinion of the British scholar Lowes Dickinson in his book: *The Greek View of Life*.

So, here Śrī Kṛṣṇa says, *jarā maraṇa mokṣāya*, 'in order to get liberated from *jarā* and *maraṇa*'. Those who know that it is the body that dies, that the Atman is ever the same, when such people face death, they face death with the greatest sense of assurance, greatest sense of peace of mind, than others. 'I have finished my journey; so far as this body is concerned, it has become useless; *jarā* has come to it, and the next stage is *maraṇa*, disappearance.' With this understanding, he or she faces death like a brother, like a friend: 'Yes, you have come, I am ready. I am ready to face this.' This attitude comes from knowledge, because we know that the true Self is beyond the sixfold waves of change. Whatever is material, whatever is physical, is changeful; not the one which is Pure Consciousness, the Atman. Śaṅkara puts it in his *Brahma-sūtra-bhāṣya*: *nitya śuddha nitya buddha nitya mukta paramātman. Nitya śuddha*, 'eternally pure'; *nitya buddha*, 'eternally awakened or illumined'; *nitya mukta*, 'eternally free'. That is the nature of the Atman. Atman is never subject to any condition. Because we don't know the truth, we feel we are conditioned. Therefore, when we understand this truth, our attitude towards death will be, 'Well, death has come. I will face it.' We hear, all over the world, beautiful examples of people dying with the spiritual knowledge strengthening them. It is not a matter to be frightened at, but we have to face it. Wherever there is birth, there is death. That knowledge is given to us in the second chapter of the *Gītā*. There again, you find this idea expressed: *vināśam avyayasya asya na kaścit kartum arhati*, 'nothing can destroy that imperishable Reality which is the Atman', and Śaṅkara comments, 'even God cannot destroy it'. See the language: 'even God cannot destroy the infinite Atman which is our true nature'.

And so, here Śrī Kṛṣṇa is saying: *mām āśritya yatanti ye*, 'those who struggle depending upon Me'; *āśritya* means 'depending upon'. Whom? Me, the One who is the infinite Self of all. Śrī Kṛṣṇa is identifying himself as the *antaryāmī*, 'the one Atman in the heart of all people', the deathless, immortal Self. *Mām āśritya yatanti ye*, 'who struggles in that direction depending upon me'; *te*, 'they'; *viduḥ*, 'understand'. What? *Te tat brahma viduḥ*, 'they understand that Brahman, that infinite Reality'. Then, *tat kṛtsnam adhyātmam*, 'the complete truth about the inner Self;' *karma ca akhilam*, 'also all about *karma*'. In the beginning itself, Śrī Kṛṣṇa had told that I am going to tell you the totality of Reality, with nothing left out, and therefore, he spoke of *aparā prakṛti* and *parā prakṛti*, 'ordinary nature and higher nature' as constituting the totality of Reality. That knowledge you will get in that state. *Adhyātmam karma ca akhilam*, 'also the knowledge of all spirituality and of all actions'. They will understand all this truth, *akhilam*, in its entirety, says this particular verse.

The body doesn't get that freedom; it will always be subject to *jarā* and *maraṇa*. If anybody wants to prolong this body, it will be very bad; in fact, nature won't allow it. This law was understood by ancient Indian thinkers; they also discovered that the death of the body is not the end of the story. There is something profound left at death.

In fact, I am putting it purely from a psychological point of view. If all changes including the final end, namely, death, is an experience, somebody must be there to observe it; otherwise how can any one say that there is death? But, the living alone sees the death of another; that living one also will die; the whole phenomenal world will die. But, that observer, eternal observer, the *sākṣi*, or witness, which is always there, is our true nature. We are essentially the eternal *sākṣi* of all the changes taking place in the world. Unless there is a changeless one, change cannot be perceived at all. That is the challenge of Vedanta. You can think for yourself. How can you perceive change, unless there is something that is changeless? You sit in a room. Somebody comes to visit you and goes away. You also go away with him. Another man comes there, meets another person; they also go away. But who can say that these various meetings took place unless there was one sitting there all the time, seeing the coming and going of all the people? Then only can one say that there is change. So, behind this world of change, there is the observer, the *sākṣi*, the witness, the changeless. That word *sākṣi*, meaning 'witness', is a very beautiful, philosophically significant word. In fact, the waking ego dies when one is in the dream state; the dream ego will also die in the dreamless state of deep sleep. Who understands the forming and going out of the two egos? That One is the *sākṣi* or witness, the ever-existing Reality. That is the logic and language of Vedanta—that which witnesses all change in the universe, who is also the universe, and who is also beyond the universe. The Sun is the *sākṣi* of the entire solar system. This Truth is beautifully expressed in one verse in the *Śrīmad Bhāgavatam* (VIII. iii. 3):

*Yasmin idam yataḥ cedam yenedam ya idam svayam;*
*Yo'smāt parasmāt ca paraḥ tam prapadye svayambhuvam* —

'In Whom is this universe, from Whom also is this universe, by Whom is this universe, Who Himself is this universe, Who is also beyond the highest in the universe, I take refuge in Him.'

It is infinite and immortal Consciousness, which has just begun to be mildly recognized in modern nuclear science. When it will pursue it further and further, it will come to the same conclusion. Consciousness is one and non-dual. There are no two or more Consciousness, as explained by nuclear scientist, Schrodinger: 'It is a singular of which the plural is unknown.' *Śāntam śivam advaitam caturtham manyante sa ātmā sa vijñeyaḥ*, says the seventh verse in the *Māṇḍūkya Upaniṣad*, describing this as *turīya*, 'the fourth', beyond the states of waking, dreaming and dreamless sleep. *Śāntam* means 'unchanging'; *śivam*, 'all that is auspicious'; *advaitam*, 'non-dual'; *manyante*, 'is considered as'; *caturtham*, 'the fourth'; *sa ātmā*, 'that is the Atman'; *sa vijñeyaḥ*, 'That is to be realized'. That is how the Upaniṣad puts it.

So, Śrī Kṛṣṇa tells here, 'I am that infinite Atman, of the nature of pure Consciousness. I am in the heart of all beings.

Depending upon Me, you can face the challenge of death.' Then you will understand all about *adhibhūta, adhidaivam* and *adhiyajña*. Three words are used here. What are these? That will be the subject discussed in the opening verses in the next chapter, chapter 8.

So, here in the last verse, verse 30 of chapter seven, Śrī Kṛṣṇa says:

साधिभूताधिदैवं मां साधियज्ञं च ये विदुः ।
प्रयाणकालेऽपि च मां ते विदुः युक्तचेतसः ॥३०॥

*Sādhibhūtādhidaivam mām sādhiyajñam ca ye viduḥ;*
*Prayāṇakāle'pi ca mām te viduḥ yuktacetasaḥ* — 7. 30

'Those who know Me along with the *adhibhūta, adhidaiva*, and *adhiyajña*, (will continue to) know Me even at the time of death, with a steadfast mind.'

Those whose mind is *yuktaḥ*, i.e. trained in the spirit of *yoga*, such persons understand these things; what are they? *Sa adhibhūta adhidaivam adhiyajñam*, 'that which presides over material elements of nature; then, that which presides over the divine beings called gods or "the luminous realities in nature"; and finally, that which presides over rituals, sacrifices, etc.'—all these are nothing but the Divine. *Yajñā*, as a name of Viṣṇu, occurs in the *Viṣṇu Sahasranāma*. Viṣṇu's name is *yajña*. *Yajño vai viṣṇuḥ*, that is the language used by Śaṅkarācārya. So, behind all this is that infinite Reality. *Sādhibhūta adhidaivam mām sādhiyajñam ca ye viduḥ*, 'those who understand this truth behind *adhibhūta, adhiyajña* and *adhidaiva*'; *prayāṇakāle'pi*, 'even at the end of life, just before passing away'; *mām*, 'Me'; *te viduḥ*, 'they understand', they realize Me; *yuktacetasaḥ*, 'with the mind well disciplined in the spirit of *yoga*, in the spiritual path.' These three words can stand for the physical dimension, i.e. *adhibhūta*, the moral-ethical dimension, i.e. *adhiyajña*, and the spiritual dimension, i.e *adhidaiva* respectively.

That is the last verse in the seventh chapter, and these words used here become the beginning of the eight chapter. There Arjuna will ask such questions as you and I will ask. He will ask this question: 'What are these *adhidaiva, adhibhūta*, etc.?'

Our thinkers have made a study of these. Here is a human being. He is surrounded by nature and, far into the heart of nature, some luminous powers are there. So, we call them *adhibhūtam; adhidaivam*, 'the Self that is within us'. I as the Self dealing with this, i.e. all the adjuncts, is called *adhidaivam*. The last one is *adhiyajña*, 'some ethical and moral values impacting upon the collective human world'. *Deva* is a beautiful Sanskrit word. It merely means that which is luminous; that is all. But, later on, it began to mean mythical divine personalities in heaven etc.—Indra, Varuṇa, all these mythical *devas*. But it is very interesting that today this ancient Indian *deva* concept is coming into modern experience. There is an American book called *The Secret Life of Plants*—and we have a copy of it in the library—written by an American, or two Americans, I think. I have forgotten the names. There, when they deal with plants, they bring the concept of *deva*. The *deva* energy makes the plants grow better; there is a method of doing it. And if you go to a plant with a view to burn it, there you will find some sensation going on in the plant which you can study through microscope, etc. So, all sorts of things like these are put together in that book. And this kind of research is going on both in Russia as well as in America. So, the *adhidaiva* concept is slowly coming into our own day-to-day life. This nature around us is not dead; it has a higher dimension, *parā prakṛti*. The old physical science stated that these are all dull dead matter. But no; everywhere there is a life principle inspiring everything here. To that conclusion more scientists are coming today, through various experiments and various studies. I had referred earlier to Fred Hoyle, the British astro-physicist, a materialist before, writing his new book, *The Intelligent Universe*. There the word and concept of *deva* comes in. That idea is inspiring more and more people in the modern age.

इति ज्ञानविज्ञानयोगो नाम सप्तमोऽध्याय: ।

*Iti jñānavijñāna-yogo nāma saptamo'dhyāyaḥ —*

'Thus ends the seventh chapter, designated *The Way of Knowledge with Realization.*'

# BHAGAVAD GĪTĀ

## CHAPTER 8

## AKṢARABRAHMA-YOGA
## THE WAY TO THE IMPERISHABLE BRAHMAN

This chapter begins with a question by Arjuna.

अर्जुन उवाच –
*Arjuna uvāca—*

*'Arjuna said:'*

किं तद् ब्रह्म किं अध्यात्मं किं कर्म पुरुषोत्तम ।
अधिभूतं च किं प्रोक्तं अधिदैवं किं उच्यते ॥ १ ॥

*Kim tad brahma kim adhyātmam kim karma puruṣottama;*
*Adhibhūtam ca kim proktam adhidaivam kim ucyate* — *8. 1*

'What is that Brahman, what is *Adhyātma*, and what is *Karma*, O best of persons? What is called *Adhibhūta* and what is called *Adhidaiva*? '

We came across a few of these words earlier; a few more are added here. Arjuna continues the question:

अधियज्ञः कथं कोऽत्र देहेऽस्मिन् मधुसूदन ।
प्रयाणकाले च कथं ज्ञेयोऽसि नियतात्मभिः ॥ २ ॥

*Adhiyajñaḥ katham ko'tra dehe'smin madhusūdana;*
*Prayāṇakāle ca katham jñeyo'si niyatātmabhiḥ* — *8. 2*

'Who, and in what way, is *Adhiyajña* here in this body, O destroyer of Madhu? And how are You known, at the time of death, by the self-controlled persons?'

*Adhiyajñaḥ*, 'the one who presides over the sacrifices, rituals'; *katham ko'tra dehe'smin madhusūdana*, 'in this body there is *adhiyajñaḥ*? How, and who is that *adhiyajñaḥ*, O Śrī Kṛṣṇa?';

*prayāṇakāle ca katham jñeyo'si niyatātmabhiḥ,* 'how can a well-disciplined mind realise You at the time of death?' *Prayāṇakāle* means 'at the time of final departure'. Actually *prayāṇa* means 'departure'; here it means 'final departure, namely, death'. In usual departures, we go and also return. In this departure, there is no return at all; so it is called 'a final departure'. *Niyatātmabhiḥ,* 'by minds that have been disciplined'. Mind has been disciplined, but still how can we understand You and realise You at that critical moment? Please tell us all these things. In this way Arjuna puts questions containing many expressions.

श्रीभगवानुवाच –
*Śrībhagavān uvāca —*

*'Śrī Bhagavān replies:'*

अक्षरं ब्रह्म परमं स्वभावोऽध्यात्मं उच्यते ।
भूतभावोद्भवकरो विसर्गः कर्मसंज्ञितः ॥ ३ ॥

*Akṣaram brahma paramam svabhāvo'dhyātmam ucyate;*
*Bhūtabhāvodbhavakaro visargaḥ karmasamjñitaḥ — 8. 3*

'The Blessed Lord said:'

'The Imperishable is the Supreme Brahman. Its dwelling in each individual body is called *Adhyātma*; the offering in sacrifice which causes the genesis and support of beings, is called *Karma*.'

*Brahma paramam,* 'the Supreme Reality, Brahman'; that is *akṣaram,* 'imperishable'; *svabhāvaḥ,* 'that very Brahman existing as the Self in men and women is our *svabhāva*'; that is our nature. *Svabhāva* means *sva bhāva,* 'our own nature'. *Adhyātmam ucyate,* 'that is called *adhyātmam,* the Self that is within us'. When you say, 'I saw', it is 'I' who am seeing. Suppose you say merely 'saw', it has no meaning. When you say, 'I saw', then another aspect comes in, namely, a subject—*somebody* who saw. Otherwise, there can be no seeing by itself. Somebody must see. An animal or a person, somebody must be there to see. So, the self that sees, the self that experiences, must be there.

*Bhūtabhāvodbhavakaro visargaḥ karmasamjñitaḥ*, '*karma* is the various processes of producing and changing things in this world'. There is one creation or projection at the beginning of the cosmic evolution. Within that evolution, there are so many other activities going on—of creating, of shaping this and that; that is called *visargaḥ* based on *karma* or activity—what is called 'process' in modern technical language. There are processes going on initiated by beings; that is called *karma* leading to *visargaḥ*. This is the first definition.

The second thing is:

अधिभूतं क्षरो भावः पुरुषश्च अधिदैवतम् ।
अधियज्ञोऽहमेवात्र देहे देहभृतां वर ॥४॥

*Adhibhūtam kṣaro bhāvaḥ puruṣaśca adhidaivatam;*
*Adhiyajño'hamevātra dehe dehabhṛtām vara* — 8. 4

'The perishable aspect of things is the *Adhibhūta*, and the Indwelling Self is the *Adhidaivata*; I alone am the *Adhiyajña* here in this body, O best of the embodied.'

*Adhibhūtam kṣaro bhāvaḥ*. What is *adhibhūta*? That which is possessed of 'plain nature'; *kṣaro bhāvaḥ*, 'subject to change.' Whatever is subject to change, subject to destruction, that is called *adhibhūta*. All *bhūtas*, all nature around us, are 'subject to change', *kṣaraḥ*. Brahman is *akṣara*, the Imperishable. This *adhibhūtam* is *kṣara*. *Puruṣaḥ ca adhidaivatam*, '*adhidaivatam* is the *puruṣa*, the Self.' *Adhiyajño'hamevātra; adhiyajñaḥ*, 'presiding over all sacrifices, rituals, etc.'; *aham eva*, 'I am Myself, as the Divine Self of all; I am that Reality;' *atra dehe*, 'within the body'; *dehabhṛtām vara*, 'O best among embodied beings'. I am the one that is called *adhiyajña*. *Atra*, 'in this very world'. I am the one who presides over all the things here in this world.

So, quoting scriptures, Śaṅkarācārya says, *yajño vai viṣṇuḥ*, '*yajña*, verily is Viṣṇu', that Divine Reality. When you just see it in a particular context, you will merely see *yajña* or fire sacrifice, but when you look at it from a deeper perspective, you will find ultimately it means that infinite Divine reality.

So, we see that the eighth chapter begins with Śrī Kṛṣṇa answering a few questions asked by Arjuna. Many of these terms are technically used in our Vedantic tradition—*adhyātma, adhidaiva, adhibhūta,* etc.; all these are certain technical terms. So, based on these words, Arjuna is asking some questions and these questions were prompted by Śrī Kṛṣṇa's reference to these very ideas in the last verse of the seventh chapter.

*Kim tad brahma,* 'what is that Brahman?' Śrī Kṛṣṇa used this word 'Brahman'; what is that? That is the first question. *Kimadhyātmam,* 'what is the inner self?' *Adhyātma* is *adhi* plus *ātma. Kim karma,* 'what is work or *karma*?' *Puruṣottama,* 'O, Best among men'. *Adhibhūtam ca kim proktam,* 'what is *adhibhūtam?' Bhūtam* stands for both nature inside and nature outside. The eleventh chapter will be describing the Vedantic God as *bhūtabhāvana* and *bhūteśa,* 'creator of beings and Lord of beings'. *Adhidaivam kimucyate,* 'what is that which is called *adhidaivam*', those divinities in nature whom our people saw; what is this *adhidaivam*?

Then, *adhiyajñaḥ katham ko'tra,* 'what is *adhiyajña?' Yajña* is sacrifice; what is that which presides over sacrifice. *Dehe'smin,* 'within this body'; *madhusūdana,* 'O Kṛṣṇa'; *prayāṇakāle ca katham jñeyo'si niyatātmabhiḥ,* and finally, 'how do people with discipline over inner life know You at the time of death?' *Prayāṇakāle,* 'at the time of death', how do they remember the Divine? These were the questions of Arjuna in two verses.

Śrī Kṛṣṇa begins the answer. First, what is Brahman? *Akṣaram brahma paramam,* 'the Supremely Imperishable Reality is Brahman.' There is this perishable universe. There is also the Imperishable behind the perishable; that is Brahman.

This is expounded in a beautiful passage in the *Bṛhadāraṇyaka Upaniṣad*—Yājñavalkya expounding the subject in a conference of scholars. Gārgī was a woman philosopher. Yājñavalkya says to her, *etat akṣaram gārgi,* 'O Gārgi, this is the great Imperishable Reality'. *Akṣaram* also means alphabets *a, b, c, d;* that is also *akṣara*. But the real meaning is, 'that which is without *kṣara*'; *kṣara* means 'destructibility'; the infinite one is indestructible; that is the ultimate Reality or Brahman. Then, *svabhāvo'dhyātmam ucyate,* 'that Brahman existing in you and me as the Self is our *svabhāva* or inner nature, and that is called *adhyātmam*'. That very Brahman is existing in you and me as the Self. *Bhūta bhāvodbhavakaro visargaḥ karmasamjñitaḥ*, '*karma* is action, a primordial, original process, by which this vast universe comes into manifestation'; the many coming out from the One. That whole process is known as *karma*. In English, philosophically they use the word 'process'. The world is a process; that means a continuous change is going on; that is called a process. So, *karma* is used in the sense of process. 'Process' and 'Reality'—Reality is the imperishable One. In process, it becomes the manifested universe, all the various galaxies, and later on, the planets, then nature and human beings, all come into being. That projection of all this is called *karma*. Each one of these elements is perishable. Therefore, it is called *adhibhūta*, which physics, chemistry, and all positivistic sciences study—the environment in which you and I live, including our body. Body also is an environment from the point of view of the Atman, as you will see when we will deal with the subject of death. That is why, in the *Taittirīya Samhitā*, Viṣṇu is called the *yajña*. *Yajṇo vai viṣṇuḥ*, 'Viṣṇu is *yajñaḥ*'. Viṣṇu and *yajña* are the same. So, in the *Viṣṇu Sahasranāma*, the name of Viṣṇu is given as *yajña*. So, *aham eva adhiyajño*, 'I am indeed the *adhiyajña*'; *asmin dehe*, 'in this body'; these were the various items asked for by Arjuna.

Then comes the question: at the time of death, how do people with self-discipline, fix their minds on You and achieve spiritual liberation? The answer is given here in verse 5:

अन्तकाले च मामेव स्मरन्मुक्त्वा कलेवरम् ।
यः प्रयाति स मद्भावं याति नास्त्यत्र संशयः ॥५॥

*Antakāle ca māmeva smaranmuktvā kalevaram;*
*Yaḥ prayāti sa madbhāvam yāti nāstyatra samśayaḥ — 8. 5*

'And he (or she) who at the time of death, meditating on Me alone, goes forth, leaving the body, attains My Being: there is no doubt about this.'

Whoever *antakāle*, 'at the time of death'; the last moment is called *antakāla; māmeva smaran*, 'thinking of Me alone'; *muktvā kalevaram*, 'casting away one's body'. The nature of death in India means 'the soul casting away the body': 'I am the soul; I am the Self; I am not the body; I am *in* the body; the body is *my* instrument.' So, death in India means the soul casting away its body—very often a troublesome body, which is useless for the purpose of life. Therefore, it is time to drop it away. That is the nature of death. So, *antakāle ca māmeva smaran*, at that moment of death, 'that person is thinking of Me'—Śrī Kṛṣṇa or Viṣṇu. *Muktvā kalevaram*, 'then he or she forsakes the body'. What happens next? *Yaḥ prayāti*, 'one who dies like this'; *sa madbhāvam yāti*, 'he or she attains to My being'. Whatever we think at the last moment of our life, that has a tremendous determining power for the future. So, in this case one who thinks of Me at the last moment, will certainly come to Me. *Nāstyatra saṁśayaḥ*, 'there is no doubt in regard to this matter'. This is a belief in every religion. The Christian, the Hindu, the Buddhist, all treat the moment of death as a very creative moment. All our future is based on that. You may not know clearly what the future is, but this much we know that if we keep our mind fixed on the highest, the Divine, that future is going to be bright. That is the belief. That is why at the time of death people think of God, recite *mantras*, or sing *bhajan*. We do all these, so that, that person passes away with a tremendous impression of the Divine within. Often the question is asked, how is it that that last moment *alone* determines the future? But, we must know that the capacity to lift the mind to the Divine at the last moment comes only from long experience through life. We train the mind throughout the life for the last moment; otherwise we fail to fix the mind on the Divine when we are not interested in that subject at all. So, that training makes us fit to fix the mind on the Divine at the last moment.

Sri Ramakrishna also said so, giving this illustration: An elephant, when it is given a bath, as soon as it comes out of it, sprinkles dust on its own body. That is the nature of the elephant. Similarly, we take the name of God, we become clean, and immediately after that, we start doing evil things.

So, that is the nature of the human being also. But, said Sri Ramakrishna, you bathe the elephant, put him in the stable, then he won't get dusty and unclean again. At the time of death that is what happens. We are not any more embodied thereafter to commit evil; this body is not there to commit any evil; we are just clean and pure at that moment when we reject this body, and we achieve the highest. That is the belief in every religion. So, the time of death is very important. We are not afraid of death. If our philosophy is properly understood, we will not be afraid to face death, because we know really the Self has no death, and the Divine, the *akṣara*, the Imperishable Brahman is there. We are a spark of that Divine Reality. Because of this understanding, that great practice arose in India from the Vedic times of burning the body as soon as the person is dead. That dead body has nothing more to do. The sooner it is reduced to its own chemical elements, the better. Nowhere else will you find this philosophical background of cremation. The body has done its work. It was a chemical laboratory, brought together for some life's purpose. It is no more useful. We discard it, just break it down to the elements through the touch of fire. Fire can reduce all aspects of the body back to their original elements. That is the concept of death in Indian thought.

In fact, this is a tremendous development of human thought. We think of human philosophy usually as studying only life—life and its various forms. But, very few philosophies study the nature of death. And we can't become perfect unless we know both; one must know life, and one must know death as well. That philosophy alone has depth which has probed into the nature of death. In India, from the *Ṛg-Vedic* times, we diverted our attention to the study of death also—and not only of life, and we declared the Ultimate Reality as 'that Light whose shadow is life and death', *yasya chāyā amṛtam, yasya mṛtyuḥ* (*Ṛg Veda samhita,* X. viii. 121). What a beautiful expression does one find in this *Ṛg-Vedic* utterance: whose shadow, *chāyā,* is death and immortality. That is Brahman. The same Brahman has appeared in the form of life, and in the form of death. That is why the word *kāla* means 'time'. *Kāla* also means death; the whole universe is under the control of *kāla*. Everything in this world, the world of manifestation, is subject to time and death. That *kāla* is an expression of the Divine itself. When we have this understanding, the fear of death becomes less. Normal fear in respect of death we all have, but that obsessive fear will not be there. That is the weakness of ancient Greek thought. Several writers on Greek culture have mentioned this. L. Dickinson in his *Greek View of Life* refers to this: the Greeks loved life, loved action, loved energy; everything dynamic they loved, but they could not reconcile with old age and death. And the vital energy was squeezed out of them by a force which they did not know. They remained forever unreconciled to death; that is the limitation of the Greek thought. That is why they couldn't appreciate Socrates who understood the nature of death, that he is truly immortal, that the body alone dies and not the Self. That understanding came to Socrates, but the Greeks never understood Socrates. They threatened him, charged him with misleading the youth of his days, and made him drink poison. And that noblest Greek died at the hands of his own countrymen. Therein you see that the classical Greek culture could not understand the nature of death, could not understand that dimension which Socrates spoke of, that essentially the Self is immortal. And he expressed this truth at the time of drinking the poison. With an absolutely calm mind, serene mind, he drank the poison, consoling the people, young and old, around him. One of them, Crito, an old friend, put a question to Socrates just when he was drinking the poison. In *Dialogues of Plato* you get this picture: Crito asked Socrates, 'Socrates, how shall we bury you?'. Socrates smiled! The man who is going to die wore a gentle smile and said, 'You must first catch *me,* the *real me,* before you ask this question'. That was the first sentence he spoke. The second sentence was, 'Be of good cheer, Crito. You refer to the body; as to the body do with it as you do with other people'. The same idea you find here. When you face death, understand that death is only of the body; we merely reject the body. That means we, the Self, reject the body which has been with us as a temporary instrument of our life. So, that is the full understanding in Indian culture. In Greek culture and in modern Western culture, the subject of death was very little understood. But that is being corrected now. With the spread of Vedantic ideas, people are realising more and more the Indian thinking in regard to death. Though in Christian religion there is the thought of the soul, it has not been philosophically presented. When people die they like to have religious ceremonies, so that their mind will attain to higher levels. That has been beautifully done, but the philosophical background of this whole process is found only in India, in its Vedantic tradition.

And so, this śloka says here:

*Antakāle ca māmeva smaran muktvā kalevaram;*
*Yaḥ prayāti sa madbhāvam yāti nāstyatra samśayaḥ* —

'One who passes out of life, by consciously thinking of Me at the last moment, will certainly reach Me'; *nāstyatra samśayaḥ*, 'there is no doubt on this question.'

I have heard of many people dying with great calmness of mind, without any fear, because of their devotion to the Divine. Even in recent times, we have had many examples. One patient was lying in the bed for three months in a Calcutta hospital. He couldn't get up; so weak was he. Doctors couldn't diagnose the disease, but he was very weak and could not eat anything; he was just lying down. All on a sudden, at night, at about three o'clock, he managed to sit up on the bed. How he managed it is a wonder; even the nurses couldn't explain it. And then, looking left and right, he said, 'Are you awake, any of you?' In Bengali he continued, 'I'm going, I'm going', he said. Then he looked around and said, 'Mother, you have come, you have come. I am coming, I am coming.' Saying thus, he dropped down and died. It impressed all the nurses who were still awake and working there. What a beautiful way of dying! And such cases of death are plenty.

So, there is such a think as living the life. That is beautiful. We are not going to run after death all the time; we are running after life. But death also is a fact of life. We must reconcile to it. We must understand it. Don't be frightened by it. That is a great idea. The heroic attitude to life will accept both life and death.

In Swami Vivekananda's literature, you find this idea that one who can hug the bosom of death, to such a one the Divine Mother comes. If you only take life and not death, you see only half of the Reality. The full Reality needs life and death. Those people who have understood the nature of death and have the courage to face death, only they can become great. Those who run only after life, their life will be only half well-lived, with the other half of life absolutely untouched.

Here is the statement therefore: live a life of activity, working hard, like the Greeks, and yet understanding that, really there is no death for oneself; it is the body that dies. So, the crucial time has come, I am going to face death. O, Death, you have come! I am here to greet you as a friend. That kind of attitude and fearlessness will come out of this kind of understanding of the nature of life and death. In the *Īśā Upaniṣad,* the last four verses refer to the death of a sage who had lived a good life. Now, he is facing death. His words are uttered there in that section. 'Let me realize that Supreme Reality, behind the Sun, behind the universe. I have lived my life. Now death has come. Let this body be dissolved into its components through the agency of fire. O, mind, think of the good deeds you have done.' Saying this, he quietly passes away. So, from very ancient times, this attitude towards the problem of death has been with us and we have got so many stories also in this connection. We have also made Time a person! *Kāla,* also called Yama, means 'the one who takes away life at the time of death'. *Kāla* actually means time, but it has been made mythical in the form of a particular person who comes to everyone. Nobody is left out at all. So, take account of *kālā*. *Kāla* is a Reality. The sun, the moon, the stars, all of them are subject to *kāla*. *Kāla* rules everything. And in the eleventh chapter, when Śrī Kṛṣṇa shows His universal form, He himself will declare (11. 32), *kālo'smi lokakṣayakṛtpravṛddho,* 'I am the mighty world-destroying Time, I am here to destroy this world.' Every moment it is running to destruction. It is going on all the time; only we don't understand it; we don't look at it in that light; we are afraid of it, and therefore, we avoid it. That is how we have been viewing it; that makes us weak. Why don't we face facts as they are? Death is a fact. Why not face it? That makes for heroism. A nation afraid of death can never be a nation of heroes. One alone who can face death can become a hero. You can see this in the West, though they never understood this higher dimension of death, but they have shown fearlessness with respect to death. They are prepared to die for the glory of their people, of their nation. Therefore, they built up great empires and became powerful. We in India lost that greatness in our society. So afraid of death are we that we are not allowed even to mention the word 'death' in our society, in our families, etc. That is why we became smaller and smaller. When I was a boy, whenever I referred to the word 'death' my people would say, 'Shut up, don't say anything about it!' They were closing their eyes to Reality; that is not the way to become great. Face the truth, face the fact; it is a proven fact in front of you.

Therefore, this Vedanta includes not only life but also death. That is why it has a completeness; it has comprehended Reality in its fullness. Otherwise, it becomes one-sided. The weakness of Greek culture was that one-sidedness. We understood death and the result was, we began to run after it in various ways neglecting life that was in front of us! We neglected life, and the result was that we became politically weak, socially weak, economically weak. So, we shall have to emphasize both life and death. Greek culture and Indian culture must play together to create a total culture, a human culture, under a comprehensive philosophy and spirituality, which is our Vedanta. That is the work that Swami Vivekananda did in the modern age: inaugurating a wonderful harmony of East and West. And so, these are beautiful ideas which refer to many aspects of human life and destiny, to various aspects of human culture.

Similarly, others may think of other Divine aspects. After all that Brahman is One, but It can assume any number of forms to satisfy the craving of the devotees. So, Śrī Kṛṣṇa doesn't stop with saying, 'those who think of Me, they achieve Me.' You may think of any Divine Reality, and still you will achieve that Reality. That is why in Sanskrit they say, *bhaktānām hitakāmyayā brahmaṇo rūpa kalpanā*, 'Brahman has no *rūpa* or form, but in order to serve the welfare of devotees, that Brahman assumes many forms'.

So, in verse 6, that subject comes up:

यं यं वापि स्मरन् भावं त्यजत्यन्ते कलेवरम् ।
तं तमेवैति कौन्तेय सदा तद्भाव भावितः ॥६॥

*Yam yam vāpi smaran bhāvam tyajatyante kalevaram;*
*Tam tamevaiti kaunteya sadā tadbhāva bhāvitaḥ — 8. 6*

'Remembering at the end of life, whatever object (Divine Form), one leaves the body, That (Ultimate Reality) alone is reached by him or her, O son of Kuntī, (because) of one's constant thought of that object.'

Whatever may be the Divine Form that a devotee meditates upon at the time of death, he or she attains that particular Form. So, in any religion, whenever there is this kind of the lifting of the mind to a higher level and concentrating on some Divine Truth, the same result occurs. So, it is a general statement. *Yam yam vāpi smaranbhāvam tyajatyante kalevaram*, 'those who forsake the body at the time of death by thinking of a Divine form—whatever might be the form of Divinity in front'; *tam tamevaiti kaunteya*, 'they achieve that very divinity'. Why? *Sadā tad bhāva bhāvitaḥ*, 'by constantly thinking of that particular *bhāva*', the mind becomes impressed by it, and therefore, in the next life, he or she achieves that Divine Unity. This is the faith of all devotees in every religion. Therefore, that being true, in order to prepare our minds to be able to orient at the time of death in that direction, we have to practise it quite early enough. A wise person will not depend upon a chance remembrance of the Divine. He or she will try to remember Him in life always, so that he or she will remember the Divine at the time of death.

So, Śrī Kṛṣṇa said:

तस्मात् सर्वेषु कालेषु मां अनुस्मर युध्य च ।
मय्यर्पित मनो बुद्धिः मां एवैष्यस्यसंशयः ॥७॥

*Tasmāt sarveṣu kāleṣu mām anusmara yudhya ca;*
*Mayyarpita mano buddhiḥ mām evaiṣyasyasamśayaḥ* —8.7

'Therefore, at all times, constantly remember Me and fight. With the mind and intellect absorbed in Me, you shall doubtless come to Me.'

*Tasmāt*, 'therefore'; *sarveṣu kāleṣu*, 'at all times'; *mām anusmara*, 'think of Me'; *anu* means 'continuously'; *mām smara*, 'think of Me'. I am the Self behind your own little self, I am the Infinite One, I am that *akṣara puruṣa*, that Imperishable Reality hidden within you. So, *tasmāt sarveṣu kāleṣu mām anusmara* and *yudhya ca*, 'and carry on the battle of life!' These two will have to go together. Thinking of the Divine, carrying on the battle of life. You are active in life; you have got plenty of work to do; *that* cannot be an excuse for not remembering the Divine. Remember the Divine is *within* you. He is the Self of your self. He is the Inner Self of *all* beings. That Divine Consciousness must be there at least a little bit in everyone; along with it, there must be the hard work going on in this world, the struggle, the endeavour, that wonderful 'battle of life'! *Yudhya ca*. So, this is a very important exhortation in the *Gītā*: *mām anusmara yudhya ca*, 'meditate upon Me and carry on the battle of life'. That is the language. *Anusmara*, 'continuous remembrance'; *smaraṇam* is 'remembering'; *anu smaraṇam* is 'continuous remembering'. Like oil poured from one vessel to another; that oil flows in a continuous stream. That is the example given by our spiritual teachers to have an understanding of this *anu smaraṇam;* the mind flows towards the Divine continuously. A portion of the mind is always devoted to this Consciousness. Sri Ramakrishna gave the example of a person suffering from toothache. Such a person is busy with the day-to-day work, but a part of his or her mind is always on that ailing tooth. Similarly, *mām anusmara yudhya ca*, 'meditate upon Me and carry on the battle of life'. They are not opposed to each other. They can be carried on together. *That is the special message of the Gītā*. That is why it is a message for all people. We are all working people. In the midst of work can we realize the Divine? Yes, we can. The Divine is our own nature. Realizing Him is our birthright. Everybody can realize Him. That is how the supreme Divinity has been presented in the *Gītā*.

*Mayyarpita mano buddhiḥ māmevaiṣyasyasamśayaḥ;* 'one whose mind is fixed on Me, whose *buddhi* is fixed on Me'. *Manas* and *buddhi* 'have been fixed on Me', *mayyarpita; māmevaiṣyasi*, 'reach Me only'; *na samśayaḥ*, 'there is no doubt on this question'. As your thoughts are, so will your life be. Thought very much modifies life, influences life; it is a great truth, and in this case, it is perfectly true. Thinking of the Divine, we become Divine. As Sri Ramakrishna said, 'one who always thinks that he or she is a sinner, he or she will become a sinner; one who thinks that he or she is a child of the Divine, such a one will become Divine.' Mind plays a great part in building up our life one way or the other. You go on suggesting to yourself, 'I am sick, I am sick', and one day you will fall sick, because you are suggesting that to yourself. Mind has the great power to shape our destiny. Therefore, never think of negative thoughts; take always to positive thoughts. And the greatest positive thought is of the Divine hidden in the heart of all, the Imperishable in the midst of the perishable.

How do we do so?

अभ्यास योग युक्तेन चेतसा नान्यगामिना ।
परमं पुरुषं दिव्यं याति पार्थ अनुचिन्तयन् ॥८॥

*Abhyāsa yoga yuktena cetasā nānyagāminā;*
*Paramam puruṣam divyam yāti pārtha anucintayan* — *8. 8*

'With the mind not moving towards anything else, made steadfast by the method of habitual meditation, and dwelling on the Supreme Resplendent *Puruṣa,* O son of Pṛthā, one goes to Him.'

This is the way to achieve that Highest Reality. *Abhyāsa yoga yuktena,* 'through *abhyāsa yoga, yoga* of constant practice'. With that *abhyāsa yoga; cetasā,* 'with such a mind'; *nānyagāminā,* 'with the mind not going elsewhere'. *Paramam puruṣam divyam yāti,* such a one 'achieves that supreme *Puruṣa,* the Divine'. How? *Anu cintayan,* 'by constantly thinking of that Reality'. We begin in a small way, but by habit and practice we make it a pervasive life-endeavour. Mind is always connected with the Divine; a portion of the mind rests in the Divine. That is what Sri Ramakrishna said, 'You have two hands. With one hand do the work of the world; with the other hand hold on to the feet of God. When the work at hand is over, with both hands hold on to the feet of God.' That is the language he used.

Then a beautiful description of the Divine is given in the next two verses, 9 and 10:

Śrī Kṛṣṇa says:

कविं पुराणं अनुशासितारं
अणोः अणीयांसम् अनुस्मरेद्यः ।
सर्वस्य धातारं अचिन्त्यरूपं
आदित्यवर्णं तमसः परस्तात् ॥९॥

*Kavim purāṇam anuśāsitāram*
*aṇoḥ aṇīyamsam anusmaredyaḥ;*
*Sarvasya dhātāram acintyarūpam*
*ādityavarṇam tamasaḥ parastāt* — 8. 9

प्रयाणकाले मनसाऽचलेन
भक्त्या युक्तो योगबलेन चैव ।
भ्रुवोर्मध्ये प्राणं आवेश्य सम्यक्
स तं परं पुरुषं उपैति दिव्यम् ॥१०॥

*Prayāṇakāle manasā'calena*
*bhaktyā yukto yogabalena caiva;*
*Bhruvormadhye prāṇam āveśya samyak*
*sa tam param puruṣam upaiti divyam* — 8. 10

'The Omniscient, the Ancient, the Over-ruler, more minute than an atom, the Sustainer of all, of form inconceivable, self-luminous like the sun, and beyond the darkness of *Māyā*, one who meditates on Him thus, at the time of death, full of devotion, with the mind unmoving, and also by the Power of *Yoga*, fixing the whole *Prāṇa* betwixt the eyebrows, such a one goes to that Supreme Resplendent *Puruṣa*.'

These are very beautiful verses meant for daily prayer. Very often people use this in their prayers. In the first word, the Divine is described as *kavi*, 'a poet'. Actually, it means a *krānta darṣī*, 'one who can see far and deep'; it means 'the omniscient One'. Why Brahman is called omniscient? Because Brahman is the all, therefore It is omniscient. See the language. If I am not the all, how can I know the all? Because I am the all, I am omniscient; that is the nature of God. Take for example, the sun in the solar system. We can say the sun is omniscient with respect to the entire solar system. His radiation penetrates everywhere revealing what is what; nothing is hidden from the sun. Similarly Brahman, which is the Light of all lights, the Light of pure Consciousness, is the all. It is in everything. Naturally, It knows everything. So, omniscience is possible only because of being that One in all. That is the idea. It is exactly as we speak in respect of the sun. Even in the most remote corner of a rocky cave, there is the sun's penetration. It knows what is going on there. If you credit sun with consciousness, you can say that the sun knows everything. Sun is everything; therefore, it knows everything. Similarly, Brahman is everything, Brahman knows everything. The word *kavi*, therefore, is a very beautiful word applied to the Divine. In the *Īśā Upaniṣad* also, this word occurs when dealing with the ultimate Reality. *Kavi* and also *kāvya*, 'the poet and the poetry'. In our day-to-day life, the poet is also great because of that. A poet can penetrate much more than an average mind. *Kavi* can go deeper, and therefore, he is called a poet; he is called a *kavi*, a *krānta darṣī*. Men like Shelley and others will say poets are the unacknowledged legislators of the world. They can see things clearly, and then present things beautifully, and so they attract us. Even today how deeply poetry attracts the human mind in every language. Sanskrit is full of such beautiful poetry. Upaniṣads themselves are full of such poetry. Take for example, this verse in the *Kaṭha Upaniṣad* declaring Brahman as 'the Light of all lights', *jyotiṣām jyotiḥ.* The light of the electric light gives us light here, but behind it we have got the solar energy. Then there are also the other stars. These are all lights, but there is a Light that lights up all this universe. The Light of all lights—that is how Atman or Brahman is described in that verse (*Kaṭha Upaniṣad*, II. ii. 15):

*Na tatra sūryo bhāti na candra tārakam*
*nemā vidyuto bhānti kuto'yam agniḥ ;*
*Tameva bhāntam anubhāti sarvam*
*tasya bhāsā sarvam idam vibhāti—*

'In that infinite Atman, the sun does not illumine, nor the moon, nor the stars, nor the light in our own household; that Light shines and, following It, these lights shine. Through that Light the whole world is lighted.'

It is 'the Light of all lights'. What a poetic expression of a profound truth: *tasya bhāsā sarvamidam vibhāti*, 'by Its Light, the whole world is lighted'. The sun and the moon get light only from Brahman. It is the Light of all lights. Now this is how poetry uses not only the knowledge of fact, but also knowledge of meaning and value. It makes us penetrate into the heart of things, and not merely see the surface. Because of the Light of all lights, *kavita* or poetry finds a little expression in the *kavis* or poets in our mundane world. Poetry in every language is highly commended. In fact, early literature in all languages was all poetry. Prose came much later. Even in prose what appeals to you is the poetical element. A beautiful prose is poetic, truly speaking. The only literature which is entirely prosaic is the law court registration material; the most prosaic literature you find there. But in every other type of prose, if there is anything attractive to you, there is a poetic element there.

So, *kavim*, is the first word, then we have *purāṇam*, 'the most ancient'. The most ancient is the Divine. Everything else came later. Śaṅkarācārya also gives the meaning to the word *purāṇa* as *purā api nava eva iti purāṇaḥ*, 'though ancient, it is always fresh', always new. That is another meaning of *purāṇam*. Take India for example. An ancient culture but every time it is new, ancient and yet not old, but new. What a beautiful idea! Dr. Brajendranath Seal of Calcutta, a fellow student of Swami Vivekananda, and the author of the book: *Positive Sciences of the Ancient Hindus,* has described India as ever-ageing, but never old. That is India, that is called *purāṇa*.

Next, *anuśāsitāram*, 'the ruler of the whole universe'. Through His law, the whole world is regulated. Then it goes on circling around; so also the galaxies and everything else. The law of nature is coming from that Reality that is behind nature. *Aṇoraṇīyāmsam*, 'smaller than an atom', subtle and subtler among all subtle things. *Anusmaredyaḥ*, 'one who meditates upon this truth'; *sarvasya dhātāram*, 'the base of everything in the world'. That which supports everything in the world is this Reality. As Sri Ramakrishna said, God is like the '1' that gives value to '0'. Put a number of '0's but without the '1' there is no value. That '1' gives value. One gives value to many. Take the one away and there is nothing but zero. So, that is why God is called *sarvasya dhātāram*. *Acintyarūpam*, 'unthinkable'; you cannot bring it to the realm of thought; beyond thinking is this Reality, because it is pure being. *Āditya varṇam*, 'luminous like the sun', glorious and luminous like the sun. *Tamasaḥ parastāt*, 'beyond all darkness and delusion'.

Such a Reality, *prayāṇakāle*, 'at the time of *prayāṇa* or death'; *manasā acalena*, 'with an unshakeable mind'. We fix the steady mind on this Reality at the time of death. *Bhaktyā yukto*, 'endowed with devotion'; *yogabalena caiva*, 'also with the strength of *yoga*' which also supports a steady mind. *Bhruvoḥ madhye prāṇam āveśya samyak*, 'concentrating all the bio-energies that are inside, between the eyebrows, in that state'. What happens to him or her? *Sa tam param puruṣam upaiti divyam*, 'such a one realizes that supremely Divine Person'. This is a two-verse statement on this subject.

The nature of Reality has been expounded as clearly as possible in Vedanta—Brahman, from Whom the universe has come, in Whom the universe exists, and to Whom the universe returns in the end. From the One, the many came. The many exist in the One even now, and the many go back to the One in the end. That One is of the nature of pure Consciousness, infinite and non-dual. That is how the *Taittirīya Upaniṣad* very rationally presents that ultimate Reality, Brahman. No word can express Its nature fully, but some word has to be used. Therefore, the word Brahman is used, and the word Brahman has the meaning of infinite expansion, something big, *bṛhatvāt brahma*, something big. So, the best word they found for the all-pervading Reality is the word Brahman or the word Atman, which is a spark of It in all of us. When the finger points towards you, that is called the Self. When the finger points outwards, that is called nature. So, this truth within is *pratyak*, and that truth outside is *parāk*. *Pratyak* means 'towards your own Self'. So, this is called the Atman or also *pratyagātman*, and Vedanta says, Atman and Brahman are one and the same Reality. That One caught up in the mind-body complex is the Atman; really, It is that infinite Brahman. So, Vedanta and Swami Vivekananda presents this knowledge with as much rational presentation as possible, because It is not *entirely* presentable to reason or to sensory verification. However, a good deal can be done to make one realize that there is such a Reality. The essential thing is realization: 'I have realized Brahman; I have realized the Atman'. That is the nature of this truth presented by Vedanta. *Śṛuli, yukti, anubhava,* Śaṅkarācārya says, when dealing with the ultimate Reality. We need three sources of knowledge. One is *śruti*, the experience of earlier sages, collected in books like the Upaniṣads; *yukti*, our own clear reason, reasoning on these various experiences; and finally, our own *anubhava*, our own experience to confirm, 'yes, that is true; I also have realized that truth'. *Śruti*, *yukti* and *anubhava* go together in our philosophy and spiritual life.

So, *sa tam param puruṣam upaiti divyam,* 'such a one achieves that supreme *Puruṣa,* the Divine One' at the time of death, because he or she has trained the mind in appreciating this truth. The whole life has been lived with a spiritual orientation. Religion can be done as a weekly affair! But, spirituality cannot; it is a constant affair. Our own true nature is constant, but religious acts and rituals one can do occasionally. That is why one is asked to go to church on Sundays; all the other six days we are not concerned with the church. We also have the same idea, going to a temple for a particular occasion. All that is religion, but spirituality is different— one's awareness of one's own true nature as a spark of the Divine. Behind the body-mind complex, behind the muscle, behind the nervous system, behind the psyche, is that infinite Atman, ever pure, ever free. That is our nature. This has been expressed again and again in the *Gītā* and the Upaniṣads and in Śaṅkarācārya's writings also. Today, in the Vivekananda literature, you get plenty of this message. Religious books describe this ritual and that. One may or may not do the prescribed rituals; it is up to you to do or not to do. Still you are a member of that religion. But spirituality is what essentially pertains to you, your own true nature, your real 'I'. That is where this teaching becomes absolutely relevant. Nobody is beyond spirituality, everybody is spiritual. We say in India, therefore, 'I don't believe in a God sitting in the sky, creating the world; I am an atheist.' We never condemn such people because he or she may be spiritual, though may not be religious. He or she may not believe in a particular idea of God, but may have high character, have compassion, may be doing service to people. These show that he or she is aware of the presence of the Divine within, behind the tiny ego. *That* is spirituality. Whenever you go one step beyond this ego, you are one step nearer to the Lord. That is spirituality. So, a life of service and dedication is spirituality. Therefore, none is beyond the domain of spirituality. One can easily go beyond the dos and don'ts of religion, and be on the road to spirituality. So, Swami Vivekananda said in this context, 'I do not call anyone a Hindu who is not spiritual.' You may not be religious, but you must be spiritual; that is the nature of this growth and development. This genetically centred ego or self of mine is transformed into my larger Self, which feels one with you and one with all. That is spiritual growth, the beginning of spiritual life. That is how a person, towards the end of his or her life, will be able to experience all these beautiful truths which are mentioned here. Work, joy and comfort, everything remains, but all in the context of this wonderful truth.

Śaṅkarācārya says in his Upaniṣad commentary: 'take away the Atman from the world, the world becomes a zero', *tat ātmanām vimuktaḥ jagat asat sampadyate*. I shall not separate the Atman from the world. That is called spirituality; the One behind the many in every action, every endeavour, every relationship. I stress this awareness of the Atman that makes me capable of establishing happy relations with other people, because it is the same Atman in every being; therefore, this is called spirituality. There is nothing magical or mystical about it. It is a living experience for every human being. It is *anubhava svarūpa,* 'of the nature of *anubhava*'. You can experience it in day-to-day activities. The housewife, who remains busy the whole day in the house, can be deeply spiritual with the awareness of the Divine within. We are not thinking of some gods sitting in the sky far away.

So, this is what Śrī Kṛṣṇa mentions here: we build up our life in this way, then finally death comes, the mind becomes easily fixed on that infinite Reality, Brahman, and we realize our oneness with It when the body is cast away; this is the language. We are *not* the body, we *have* a body. The second chapter already told us that: when the cloth becomes old and torn, we throw it away and put on a new cloth. That is the nature of the human body with respect to our own true Self. These are two beautiful verses, often used for prayer and meditation.

And so, in the eighth chapter, we are dealing with these subjects. Later on, will come cosmology, the infinite age of the universe, which will be echoed in modern cosmology. That we shall come to later on.

Then Śrī Kṛṣṇa says in the tenth verse, what happens when you realize this truth at the time of death.

*Prayāṇakāle manasā'calena*
*Bhaktyā yukto yogabalena caiva;*

At the time of *prayāṇa*, 'death'; *manasā acalena*, 'with a steady mind'; *bhaktyā yukto*, 'endowed with devotion'; *yogabalena caiva*, 'and also with *yogabala*'; due to the practice of concentration throughout life, you develop *yogabala*. It is a remarkable concept of *bala* or strength. *Mahābhārata* speaks of three types of strength available to human beings. First is *bāhubalam*, physical strength; by pushing and pulling things, children develop *bāhubala*. But that is very ordinary, the bull has more *bāhubala* than we have; the horse has more than that; a rocket has still more. So, *bāhubala* is the first stage of human strength, human power. Second is unique to human beings: *buddhibalam*, strength from thinking, from the mind, from the intellect, from reason. There the human being is supreme; but that is not the highest. There is something higher still; and that is the greatest contribution of Indian thought. *Buddhibalam* is not the highest; brilliant minds might be very ordinary in normal day-to-day human life. A third source of strength is there. That we call *yogabalam* or *ātmabalam*. *Bāhubalam*, *buddhibalam* and *yogabalam*. That *yogabalam* comes from realizing one's own spiritual nature, which is a source of infinite strength. Even the strength at the body level and at the *buddhi* level generally comes from the Atman. So, when you realize the Atman, your strength becomes infinite. This is *yogabalam* or *ātmabalam*. If, from our childhood, we can develop daily all these three strengths together, it will be ideal growth. We do need physical exercise and nourishing food by which you develop *bāhubalam*. Strong, steady human beings we become; what Vivekananda called 'muscles of iron and nerves of steel'. We need young people like that in India and everywhere else. He said, 'we have weakened our body a good deal; we have neglected it'. So, we need today *bāhubalam*. Along with it must come *buddhibalam*. Go to school, get education;

study, *think for yourself*, strengthen your intellect, your reason, your mind. And, along with these, try to realize a bit of the spiritual nature within you. Manifest that strength also. Little by little, from childhood onwards try to develop the spiritual side also. That is what Śrī Kṛṣṇa meant here when he said, *yoga balena caiva. A total education will help a human being to develop all these three dimensions of strength.* And that last dimension—*yogabalam* or *ātmabalam*—is the real strength. It alone can make you withstand the pressures of human life, and those pressures are plenty in today's society, breaking our nervous system, our psychic system, resulting in high tension, high stress. All that can be conquered only by a bit of that *yogabalam* or *ātmabalam*. And high character can come only from *ātmabalam*, not through *buddhibalam*. *Buddhibalam* is extremely susceptible to corruption, but, with a little *ātmabalam*, you can overcome all these weaknesses and develop an incorruptible character. So, children must develop all the three strengths. This third is needed only in small doses. The lower the type of energy, the more quantity you need. The higher the energy, the less the quantity you need. You don't need spiritual energy in much quantity. It is the quality which we value. Therefore, when we develop a little spirituality, we are able to stand and face the world. We become truly free. Nobody can frighten us; nobody can enslave us any more. That is spiritual freedom. A child must experience that spiritual freedom and respect the same freedom in others as well. That is the importance of that third strength—*yogubalam*. A little of it is enough to stabilise a human life. Remove all the pettiness, these quarrels and fights we find in our society. And make for a peaceful social order. What a beautiful conception! Inter-human cooperation, happy relations with each other, happy family life, all these can come only with a little bit of that *yogabalam*. Not by brain power only, *buddhibalam*. The brainy people are the worst people today. All the evil and weakness of the society come from brainy people. All corruption, most social conflicts, come from brainy people. From that alone we can realize that we have to go deeper than *buddhi* (which Śaṅkarācārya describes as *nediṣṭham brahma,* 'nearest to Brahman') to get a new source of strength which can stabilise our external life. That is the theoretical and practical significance of *yoga balam* or *ātma balam.*

In the body there are many organs. A big organ is the liver; much secretion the liver and other organs produce, but the pituitary and some other internal glands, situated in the brain somewhere, produce only a little trace secretion, but that trace secretion makes for the balance of this physical system and the mind! The beautiful harmony within this physical system comes from a bit of this and some other trace secretions. That is why quantity is not important, quality is. So, muscle is quantity, *buddhi* is quality and Atman is supreme quality. That is why this word *yogabalam* is used here. Śaṅkarācārya's commentary says, 'when you practise this kind of *yogabalam* from childhood, at the time of death it will stand you in very good stead; the tremendous power of *yoga* will sustain you there by not getting the mind drawn to everything around. That strength is available to everyone. If you don't do it from the beginning, from childhood itself, it will not be so easy to get it just towards the end at the time of death. Don't wait, therefore, for the end. Begin with *yoga* practices at the beginning of life itself. A parallel development of *bāhubalam, buddhibalam,* and *yogabalam* is needed.

*Bhruvoḥ madhye prāṇam āveśya samyak,* 'concentrating all the *prāṇas* in the body between the eyebrows', that is the *ājñā cakra,* the sixth centre of psychic consciousness. If you pass away in that state, you realize the highest. *Sa tam param puruṣam upaiti divyam,* 'he or she attains oneness with that Supreme *Puruṣa,* that imperishable Reality called Brahman. That is the meaning of these two verses; and now we enter into verse eleven.

यदक्षरं वेदविदो वदन्ति
विशन्ति यत् यतयो वीतरागाः ।
यदिच्छन्तो ब्रह्मचर्यं चरन्ति
तत्ते पदं संग्रहेण प्रवक्ष्ये ॥११॥

*Yadakṣaram vedavido vadanti*
*viśanti yat yatayo vītarāgāḥ;*
*Yadicchanto brahmacaryam caranti*
*tatte padam samgraheṇa pravakṣye — 8. 11*

'What the knowers of the Vedas speak of as the Imperishable, what the self-controlled (*Sannyāsins*), freed from attachment enter into, and to gain which goal they live the life of a *Brahmacārin*, that I shall declare unto you in brief.'

'I shall now tell you that supreme state', that is qualified by all these other statements here. What is that supreme state? *Yadakṣaram vedavido vadanti,* 'one syllable which the knowers of Vedas declare'. That is *Om,* the *praṇava. Viśanti yat yatayo vītarāgāḥ,* 'attained by those who overcome *rāga* or attachments'. Similarly, *yadicchanto brahmacaryam caranti,* 'in order to realize which, people live as *brahmacarins*' under their *gurus* in the *gurukula*. Their aim is this: 'I am a *brahmacārin*. Why? Because I want to attain to that highest Truth.' *Brahmacarya* has no meaning unless it is a means to this great realization. *Tatte padam samgraheṇa pravakṣye,* 'that state I shall tell you in brief'. That is what we call *Om.* A similar verse occurs in the *Kaṭha Upaniṣad,* adding *om iti etat,* 'this is *Om*' (I. ii. 15). What is *Om?* It is the supreme symbol of the Divine, the best symbol of that ultimate Reality, which is both *nirguṇa* and *saguṇa,* Impersonal as well as Personal. It is a symbol. It is called a symbol (*pratīka*), just like an image (*pratimā*). You worship the *Īśvara,* the Personal form of Reality, in an image. It is *not* the *Īśvara;* it is the best image you can have to denote that wonderful Reality. So, Śaṅkarācārya calls it, *om śabda vācyam, om śabda pratīkam ca,* in his *Kaṭha Upaniṣad* commentary. *Om śabda* is the *vācyam,* just the word to express the meaning; the meaning is something else. It is the word only. And it is the *pratīka,* only the symbol of that ultimate Reality. This *Om* is taken up in all our traditions in India. Every religion that developed in India has *Om* as the supreme Name of the Divine. The *Guru Granth Sāhib* of Guru Nanak begins with this *Omkāra,* that Supreme *Puruṣa* who is *Omkāra.* All the spiritual traditions in India take *Omkāra* as the best symbol of the Supreme Reality. It is slowly entering into Indian Christianity also, though with some difficulty. Some opposition is there. Orthodox people are against it. Other Christians, the mystical-minded Christians, take *Om* as a symbol of the highest Reality, both Personal and Impersonal. And they have this justification for it: because in Saint John's Gospel it is expressed as 'the Word'. 'In the beginning was the Word'; that Word for the Supreme Brahman is *Om*. 'In the beginning was the Word, and the Word was with God, the Word was God, and the Word became flesh', became incarnated as the Divine. Because of this John's Gospel, which is a mystical-oriented Gospel, Indian Christians, who are developing a spiritual attitude, are slowly introducing this universal symbol of the highest Reality, *Om*. Of course, in the West they are very fond of it. All those who have studied Indian literature are very devoted to this word *Om* as the supreme Name and Symbol of the Divine. And so, this is how we try to realize that which is beyond speech, beyond thought, beyond name and form. And the minimum name we give to That is *Om*. We also call it *praṇava*. The whole universe has come from this *Om*. It is called *śabda brahman*, 'Brahman in the form of sound'. What a beautiful expression, *śabda brahman* and *para brahman,* Supreme Brahman. *Śabda brahman* expresses *para brahman*. You realize *para brahman* through *śabda brahma*. The next two verses describe how one should depart at the time of death:

**सर्व द्वाराणि संयम्य मनो हृदि निरुध्य च ।**
**मूर्ध्न्याधायात्मनः प्राणं आस्थितो योग धारणाम् ॥१२॥**

*Sarva dvārāṇi samyamya mano hṛdi nirudhya ca;*
*Mūrdhnyādhāyātmanaḥ prāṇam āsthito yoga dhāraṇām—8. 12*

**ओमित्येकाक्षरं ब्रह्म व्याहरन् मां अनुस्मरन् ।**
**यः प्रयाति त्यजन् देहं स याति परमां गतिम् ॥१३॥**

*Omityekākṣaram brahma vyāharan mām anusmaran;*
*Yaḥ prayāti tyajan deham sa yāti paramām gatim — 8. 13*

'Controlling all the senses, confining the mind in the heart, drawing the *prāṇa* into the head, occupied in the practice of concentration, uttering the one-syllabled "*Om*", the Brahman, and meditating on Me—one who so departs, leaving the body, attains the Supreme Goal.'

In verses 12 and 13 you find this teaching given: *Sarva dvārāṇi samyamya mano hṛdi nirudhya ca*. How to meditate on the Divine and realise that Divine? All the various 'doorways', *dvārāṇi,* in the physical system are called the sense organs; they are called *dvāras,* 'openings'. Here is a door, it is an opening to the world outside. The human body is called 'a city'. It has so many openings leading out into the world. Eyes, nose, etc., all these *pañca* or five *indriyas* are called *dvāras*. So, *sarva dvārāṇi samyamya,* 'disciplining all the five *dvāras*'; you *have* the power to do it. All character, morality, ethics, all these come when men and women exercise their capacity to discipline these sensory *dvāras* or openings. *Mano hṛdi nirudhya ca,* 'and fixing the mind in the heart', in the lotus of the heart. Heart is a particular area in the yogic language. There are in this body in its spinal system seven lotuses or centres, *cakras,* as they are called. The third *cakra* is below the navel, and two others are further below. The fourth *cakra, anāhata,* is the heart *cakra.* That is the place for meditation. So, fix the mind in that lotus of the heart which is called the *anāhata cakra*. *Mūrdhnyādhāya ātmanaḥ prāṇam,* 'all the *prāṇa* energies within the body are to be concentrated between the eyebrows', in the *ajñā cakra; āsthito yoga dhāraṇām,* 'in that state you are in *yoga*'; you have perfectly centred all the psychic energies in that state.

*Omityekākṣaram brahma vyāharan,* 'reciting this single word Brahman, *Om*'; *mām anusmaran,* and along with that 'meditating on Me', the one Divine Self in all, as Śrī Kṛṣṇa is telling here; *yaḥ prayāti tyajan deham,* 'one who thus leaves the body'; *sa yāti paramām gatim,* 'he or she attains the highest state'. People *can* give up body through *yoga*. So many instances are there, but it cannot be done easily. A long practice is needed. So, in a state of *yoga,* the body is thrown away. Actually, we renounce the body because it is unfit to serve life's purposes. That is why we always speak of *tyajan deham*, 'renouncing the body'. You are not the body. You have it for a temporary purpose; now that it is done, you throw it away. So, the capacity to die in a very peaceful steady manner is a capacity we develop throughout our life so that, at the last moment, we are not at all in distraction but steady in the thought of Brahman.

'The world may weep, but I shall be smiling', that will be the attitude of such a dying person. That is the expression uttered by, I think, the Hindi poet Tulsi Das, telling the mind, 'when you were born, you wept and the world laughed; when you die, you will smile and the world will weep for you'. You have lived such a great life, the world will weep for you, but you depart smiling absolutely. That is what happened in the case of Socrates also.

अनन्यचेताः सततं यो मां स्मरति नित्यशः ।
तस्याहं सुलभः पार्थ नित्ययुक्तस्य योगिनः ॥१४॥

*Ananyacetāḥ satatam yo mām smarati nityaśaḥ;*
*Tasyāham sulabhaḥ pārtha nityayuktasya yoginaḥ — 8. 14*

'I am easily attainable by that ever-steadfast *yogī* who remembers Me constantly and daily, with a single mind, O Pārtha.'

Verse 14 tells that: *Ananyacetāḥ satatam yo mām smarati*, 'those who remember Me with a one-pointed mind'; *ananyacetāḥ*, 'mind goes only towards Me', nothing else. That is called *ananyacetāḥ. Satatam*, 'constantly'; *mām smarati nityaśaḥ*, 'remembers Me daily'; *tasyāham sulabhaḥ pārtha*, 'to such a person, O Arjuna, I am easy to realize'; *sulabhaḥ* means 'easily available'. Why? *Nityayuktasya yoginaḥ*, 'he or she is a *yogī* who is *nityayukta*, constantly in *yoga* state'. Not occasionally. By long and continued practice, the very life becomes a *yoga* practice. Some people have attained that kind of state. We study about them in some ancient and modern books.

Then, verse 15 says:

मां उपेत्य पुनर्जन्म दुःखालयं अशाश्वतम् ।
नाप्नुवन्ति महात्मानः संसिद्धिं परमां गताः ॥१५॥

*Mām upetya punarjanma duḥkhālayam aśāśvatam;*
*Nāpnuvanti mahātmānaḥ samsiddhim paramām gatāḥ—8. 15*

'Reaching the highest perfection and having attained Me, the great-souled ones are no more subject to rebirth (in the world)—which is the home of pain, and is ephemeral.'

*Mām upetya*, 'when you attain Me'; *punarjanma*, 'this rebirth', ceases for you. What is this rebirth? *Duḥkhālayam aśāśvatam*, 'the home of pain and ephemeral'. That is the nature of human life—so much sorrow along with some pleasure and comfort. Because we do not know anything higher, we think this is first class living. But when we know there is something higher, we understand that this is not first class at all. We are satisfied with what we are; we don't want to change. In this human body we get pleasure. In a pig body also there is pleasure. Ask a pig, 'do you want to change your body?', and it will say, 'no, I am very fine here!' Everybody is caught up in that particular attitude, not knowing that infinite freedom is awaiting us from the realization of the Atman behind the body.

The word *duḥkhālayam* does not mean there is no joy. There is joy, there is pleasure. In fact, there has been a study on this subject in both East and West. Is life more pleasure or more sorrow? Lokamanya Bal Gangadhar Tilak, in his scholarly two-volume book, *Gītā Rahasya,* discusses this subject. People say, 'if you think the world is full of sorrow, you are a pessimist!' The opposite is 'optimist'. But, if you know the truth of life, there is no question of pessimism or optimism; it is just *the* truth about the nature of the world and of human life.

In the course of the discussion on the subject in this book, Tilak says (vol. 1, p. 145):

'It is stated in Mohammedan history that, during the Mohammedan rule in Spain, a just and powerful ruler named Abdul Rahiman the Third, had kept a diary of how he spent his days and, from that diary, he ultimately found that, in a rule of 50 years, he had experienced unalloyed happiness only for 14 days. ...'

Tilak also puts the subject in the form of a ratio (144–5):

$$\frac{\textit{enjoyment of happiness}}{\textit{desire for happiness}}$$

'But this is such a queer fraction that its denominator, namely, the desire for happiness, is always increasing in a greater measure than its numerator, namely, the enjoyment of happiness. So that, if this fraction is, in the beginning 1/2, it becomes later on 3/10, that is to say, if the numerator increases three times, the denominator increases five times.'

I have earlier referred to the American Hoover Committee Report saying, there are no new desires which will not give way to newer desires as soon as they are satisfied. On the other hand, all progress comes only from dissatisfaction, says Queen Vidula to her princely son, Sañjaya (*Mahābhārata, Udyoga Parva,* 132–33): *Santoṣa vai sukham hanti,* 'contentment destroys worldly happiness'.

British thinker, John Stuart Mill, also refers to this subject in his book *Utilitarianism* (p. 14, 1907):

'It is better to be a human being dissatisfied that a pig satisfied; better to be Socrates dissatisfied than a fool satisfied. And if the fool, or the pig, is of a different opinion, it is because they only knew their own side of the question.'

Many people say, if you calculate pleasure and pain in society, pain and sorrow predominate, and not joy or pleasure. Joy and pleasure are there, but what predominates is sorrow. A young man or woman cannot understand that. After seventy or eighty, when he or she looks back, he or she can ask that question, 'What was the nature of my life? Was it all joy or sorrow, or more of joy or more of sorrow? Thinkers have done it. So, it is not pessimism or optimism. What is the truth about life? The truth is what you find mentioned by the *Gītā* here in *duḥkhālayam aśāśvatam.* When you have this body, you have so many pressures. The whole world is pressing upon you. You are trying to resist it, to be yourself. So, joy comes, sorrow comes, suffering comes, tensions come, all sorts of problems come. All these put together is what we repeat in our society as, *samsāra* is *tāpatraya,* 'worldly life is made of threefold misery'; that is the language. Every Hindu knows these words, *samsāra* and *tāpatraya;* everybody utters it. But the truth is: Yes, there is a majority of suffering, less of pleasure and comfort and happiness, but yet it is worth living; that also comes in our teaching. It is worth living because, as Vedanta puts it, through pleasure and pain, we can achieve our spiritual evolution; sometimes pain will help you better than pleasure in spiritual evolution. That is a wonderful teaching.

In Swami Vivekananda's lectures, you find this subject discussed: that the Hindu sages placed before men and women this great objective, that life's objective is not pleasure, is not pain, but spiritual knowledge—gaining knowledge by squeezing pleasure and pain. You try to get knowledge by discriminating, by thinking about it, by reflecting on it; then you get knowledge out of it. And, very often, pain gives you more knowledge than pleasure. That is human experience also. In this way, we go beyond pain and pleasure. Whether there is more pain or more pleasure is not the question. The human mind is set to a high purpose; it takes one beyond both pain and pleasure and then makes one realise the infinite Atman, the Divine, which is beyond all these dualities of pain and pleasure. You go beyond them both as Śrī Kṛṣṇa will say. These are all related to each other, pain and pleasure. If you have one, you must have the other also. Life cannot be all pleasure; there will be pain. Life cannot be all pain; there will also be pleasure. These are dualities, *dvandva,* in the *Gītā's* language. If you have one, you get the other also. You can't expect only one to be with you. Heat and cold, for example, always go together. If you have heat, you will have cold also. Both opposites are there around us.

And so, Vedanta teaches all to take life *as it is.* Life is a combination of pleasure and pain. Whether one is more, or the other is more, is just a theoretical question. We are passing through life which involves both pleasure and pain. Don't get stuck up in either of them, that is the Vedantic teaching. Squeeze both of them and get knowledge out of them. Experience *alone* can give you knowledge. Without the experience of pain you can't understand the world and sympathise with humanity. Unless you have starved a little, you can't understand that three hundred millions of our people are half-starving all the time. You can't have sympathy, you can't have understanding. So, utilize occasions of pain and pleasure to achieve knowledge and compassion—that spiritual expansion of the human personality. That is the Vedantic teaching. Swami Vivekananda expresses this beautifully in the first chapter of his *Karma Yoga,* which you get in the first volume of *The Complete Works of Swami Vivekananda.*

So, *mām upetya punar janma duḥkhālayam aśāśvatam; nāpnuvanti,* 'once you realize Me, no more will you be in this uncertain world of pleasure and pain', in this world of birth and death; *mahātmānaḥ,* 'such people are *mahātmās*', those whose Self is more than what is contained in the body; it has expanded and become one with all. Such a person is called a *mahātmā.* God Himself is declared to be a *mahātmā* in one of the Upaniṣads. This person also has achieved that infinite expansion of Self-awareness. *Samsiddhim paramām gatāḥ,* 'he or she has achieved supreme perfection in this very life; that is the language of the 15th verse.

The next verse deals with cosmology, the millions of years that have gone by since cosmic evolution started:

आब्रह्मभुवनात् लोकाः पुनरावर्तिनोऽर्जुन ।
मां उपेत्य तु कौन्तेय पुनर्जन्म न विद्यते ॥१६॥

*Ābrahmabhuvanāt lokāḥ punarāvartino'rjuna;*
*Mām upetya tu kaunteya punarjanma na vidyate — 8. 16*

'All the worlds, O Arjuna, including the realm of Brahmā, are subject to return, but after attaining Me, O son of Kuntī, there is no rebirth.'

This entire universe is characterized in Vedantic terminology as *ābrahmabhuvanāt lokāḥ,* 'all the worlds from

Brahmā up to a clump of grass'; all this is called *bhuvanāḥ*. That context in which things and beings exist and live, that is called *bhuvanāḥ*, 'the world'; you can say, 'the *particular* world in which a thing lives'—one is terrestrial, next is celestial, the third is stellar—these are all *bhuvanās*. So, from Brahmā—the first product of evolution—up to a clump of grass, a very ordinary thing, all this is called *bhuvanās*. *Ābrahmabhuvanāllokāḥ*, 'beings in all these *lokās* or worlds', Śrī Kṛṣṇa says, are *punarāvartinaḥ*, 'subject to rebirth', they return again and again. Everyone of these worlds, including Brahmā, are of this nature. Imagine such a great state called Brahmā, but Brahmā also has to change; it is only a temporary position. When God projects the universe, the cosmic mind, the first product of evolution, is Brahmā; that is the language used about Brahmā, the four-headed Brahmā. But, even his position is temporary!

Our mythology presents him as a god with four heads, and he is the embodiment of the whole Veda. Veda means knowledge, the science of everything—physical and non-physical; he is the *veda-mūrti;* he is *aja*. These are our beautiful ideas, highly philosophical and spiritual, put into a mythical language; that is all. That pure Consciousness was *unmanifest* before; it became manifest first as Brahmā. He was to continue this evolution of the universe. From him the whole world is manifesting. He is also called *Hiraṇyagarbha*, 'the Golden Womb'; many worlds are there in it. So, from that Brahmā, the first manifested Reality of the universe, up to a clump of grass, all these are subject to birth and death—*punarāvartinaḥ*. But, *mām upetya tu kaunteya punarjanma na vidyate*, 'once you attain Me, the One beyond this manifestation, that *akṣaram*, that Imperishable Brahman which I am, O Arjuna, no more of rebirth is there for you'. That will be the end of rebirth, this coming and going. You go beyond cause-and-effect relation. This world is a world of cause-and-effect relation. Today we call it the world of relativity; we believed in determinism. That is the world we are caught up in. We want to go beyond it. There is a tendency in each of us to go beyond it. Why? That is our true nature. That freedom is our true nature. That finds expression in this struggle to break through this kind of determinism. 'I must be free; I must be free.' *The call of freedom is the supreme call that has come to the human being and the struggle to be free is the greatest effort of human life*, and the highest freedom is spiritual. We talk of freedom from hunger, freedom from starvation, as well as of freedom from illiteracy, ignorance, or political bondage; all these freedoms are wonderful, but the supreme freedom is spiritual. Are you spiritually free? That is what we have to seek and attain.

So, the highest freedom comes when we realize that infinite Divine which is our true nature beyond this world of relativity, beyond the world of manifestation.

Now a little more of ancient cosmology comes in verse seventeen.

सहस्र युग पर्यन्तं अहर्यद् ब्रह्मणो विदुः ।
रात्रिं युग सहस्रान्तां तेऽहोरात्रविदो जनाः ॥१७॥

*Sahasra yuga paryantam aharyad brahmaṇo viduḥ;*
*Rātrim yuga sahasrāntām te'horātravido janāḥ — 8. 17*

'They who know (the true measure of) day and night, know the day of Brahmā, which ends in a thousand *yugas*, and the night which (also) ends in a thousand *yugas*.'

We have a time scale in India which is something extraordinary. No other ancient nation had this extraordinary vision of the infinity of time, as also the infinity of space. We were never narrow and small in thinking, that the world began in 4000 BC. Our minds went beyond millions and millions of years and, in modern cosmology, we accept the same idea. Time is relative; this is a situation in which you will find yourself. We are on a tiny planet called the earth and we measure time watching the rotation of the earth on its own axis and the revolution around the sun. So, we have a day, we have a night, we have a year, all these things we have, but we don't think that it is the same thing everywhere. What you call a day and night here, might be just a second in another plane. So, we call this terrestrial time. Then we move on to celestial time. Now, the earth goes around the sun in one year, but the sun itself is going around the galactic system. That takes two hundred million years. So, this kind of differences of year from different points of view was developed by the Indian sages in ancient times and now comes the statement that for Brahmā, that cosmic mind, that first product of evolution, his time is different from your and my time. Our time unit is very ordinary, just one year, and our life time is 100 years maximum. Brahmā also has 100 years, but his hundred years are different from our hundred years. What is his hundred years? Consider his one day: the day is divided into two halves, a day and a night. In Brahmā's day, the universe begins to evolve. And for the whole day, the evolution proceeds, and when the Brahmā's evening comes, evolution returns to its original source. The whole return story is called *pralaya,* 'the end of cosmic manifestation'. That cannot be certainly 100 years or 500 years or a 1000 years of our terrestrial time. So, Brahmā's one day is called a *kalpa,* a technical term for it. Hundreds of astronomers have discussed this subject; in the *Mahābhārata* also it is discussed; in the *Puraṇas* also it is discussed. We have called it a *kalpa*. Brahmā's one day is one *kalpa* and one night is another *kalpa*. So, this *kalpa* will constitute quite a large chunk of human years; about 432 crores of human years will constitute just a single *kalpa* of Brahmā. That is the expansive view of time.

So, the *śloka* says there is a night when the whole universe returns to the state of non-manifestation. The whole cosmos exists in two states: 1) the undifferentiated state or the unmanifested state, and 2) the differentiated state or the manifested state. That is also, to a large extent, the theory in today's cosmology. Today's astrophysics tells you that in that primordial background material, highly dense matter occupying very little space, the whole universe was contained. Then it exploded and with that explosion began the evolution of the universe. That evolution is going on still. That power of explosion is still acting upon some of the systems in the outer universe and you can study them by studying the various radio waves that come from them. So, everywhere, you will find radio astronomy developing. You cannot see them with telescopes but radio wave sensing devices can go farther than the telescope. So, that is how today's astronomy is developing the concept of time. What is the history of the universe? Not like your history, or my history; these are very ordinary. It is just like a man's hundred years life as against that of a small mosquito which lives for a day or two and dies. The mosquito's life is so ordinary. This human life is a little extraordinary but this also is ordinary when you deal with the cosmic time scale.

So, Śrī Kṛṣṇa says *sahasra yuga paryantam*, 'one thousand *yugas* of ours'; *brahmaṇaḥ ahaḥ*, 'is a day of Brahmā'; *rātrim yuga sahasrāntām*, 'one thousand more *yugas* is called the night of Brahmā'; *te'horātravido janāḥ*, those who know these 'they are the knowers of day and night'. So, two thousand *yugas* mean one whole day of Brahmā. And 365 days like that make one year of Brahmā; then a hundred such years make for a lifetime of Brahmā. The present Brahmā, according to ancient Indian calculation, is now 51 years old. Imagine we are given the age of Brahmā, that wonderful cosmic Reality. And all this belief is a part and parcel of our day-to-day life. In all *samkalpas*, before you perform a holy act, you repeat, 'I am doing this in the 51st year of this Brahmā, with this particular name'. That means we had an amazing mind that could go beyond the little limitations of space and time and see the vastness of both.

Everything is rotating around something else. Earth along with the other planets is rotating around the sun, but the sun also is rotating within this galaxy; the galaxy is rotating too. But what is the centre of all these rotations? We do not know. That is where we discovered the unmanifested Reality, the Brahman, the Absolute. That is what is being referred to here. And that time scale goes on up to Brahmā; time ends at the Brahmā level. If you go beyond Brahmā, you go beyond time. So, we have *both* time and eternity; eternity is the *akṣara* Brahman, the imperishable Reality of Brahman. The whole of Reality includes time *and* eternity. Time is where evolution goes on, activities go on, processes go on, beyond which is the One absolutely imperishable, changeless Reality. So, we have got *both* time and eternity as Reality; time is one aspect of it and timelessness or eternity is the other aspect. That is how we study Reality. *Kāla* is the word for time. *Kāla* is an expression of the Divine; *kāla* is therefore highly praised. Time is highly praised in the *Purāṇas*.

In the next verse Śrī Kṛṣṇa says:

अव्यक्तात् व्यक्तयः सर्वाः प्रभवन्त्यहरागमे ।
रात्र्यागमे प्रलीयन्ते तत्रैवाव्यक्तसंज्ञके ॥१८॥

*Avyaktāt vyaktayaḥ sarvāḥ prabhavantyaharāgame;*
*Rātryāgame pralīyante tatraivāvyaktasamjñake* — 8. 18

'At the approach of (Brahmā's) day, all manifestations proceed from the unmanifested state; at the approach of night, they merge verily into that alone, which is called the unmanifested.'

A very beautiful expression. *Avyaktāt*, 'from the unmanifested'. *Vyakta* means 'manifested'; *avyakta* is 'unmanifested'. From the *avyakta* has come all this *vyakta* or manifest universe. All manifested things have come from the unmanifested state. That is a wonderful idea in our Sāṅkhya and Vedanta philosophies. Two aspects of Reality—manifested and unmanifested.

Take a piece of wood. You find fire in it if you rub it vigorously; you can't see the fire, you can't touch it when it is unmanifested, but the fire *is* there. By rubbing it, you will find fire coming out. So, fire unmanifested is ordinary wood, fire manifested is the fire which you and I handle. So, the whole universe has these two dimensions—*avyakta* and *vyakta*—*avyākṛta prakṛti* and *vyākṛta prakṛti*, or simply *prakṛti* and *vikṛti*. *Prakṛti* is primordial nature; *vikṛti* is modified nature; *vikāra* is *vikṛti*. So, these are all technical terms which Sāṅkhya and Vedanta developed to deal with cosmic phenomena. So, *avyaktāt vyaktayaḥ sarvāḥ prabhavanti*, 'all *vyakti* or manifestations came out at that time from *avyakta* or unmanifested'. When? *Aharāgame*, 'at the beginning of the day' of Brahmā. *Aha* means 'day'; *āgame* means 'at the arrival of'; at such a time, these *vyakta* realities appeared from the *avyakta* Reality. Then what happened? *Rātryāgame,* 'when (Brahma's) night approaches', Śrī Kṛṣṇa says, *pralīyante,* 'the manifest universe becomes dissolved'; *pralaya* means 'dissolution'; *tatraiva avyakta samjñake,* 'in that same *avyakta*'.

So, these are the two aspects of creation. A pulsation taking us out, a pulsation taking us in. How does the solar system get imploded and go back to that primordial state? That we study in today's cosmology. At a certain future time—now it is 10 to 11 thousand million years of time since the explosion; after another 5 or 6 thousand million years—the sun will expand itself and swallow each one of these planets. A wonderful happening of swallowing all these planets one by one, and finally becoming a dead star. That is the future of the sun. It has been evolving like this now; hereafter it will be involving like this. This kind of study is going on in modern astrophysics. Astronomers in ancient India understood *pralaya* or cosmic dissolution correctly. *Laya* means dissolution. When a human body dies it is dissolving—dissolving back into the chemical elements from which it came. Everything goes back to its source; that is all; that is called *pralaya.* The whole world goes back like that to its source.

In a passage in the *Śānti Parva* of the *Mahābhārata* it is said, *adarśanāt āpatitaḥ, punaśca adarśanam gataḥ,* (you and I) 'have come from an unseen state, and (we will) return again to that unseen state'. In between we are in the seen state. The seen is something in between the two unseen. Past is unseen, future is unseen, the present is there for everyone to see; that is all we have. *Adarśanāt āpatitaḥ,* a baby appears from nowhere and *punaśca adarśanam gataḥ,* the old man also disappears; we don't know wherefrom it came or whereto it goes.

Let us live our lives in the light of this truth, that is what Vedanta says, and not in any make-belief world, not in some superstition. The truth is this: We have to live in this world, in this *vyakta* condition, for a short time. How will you live your life here? You can try to understand the whole truth about life and make the best of this life here. That is why these ideas also are part of our spiritual understanding. These are not mere cosmology to us. The presence of the sun is not mere cosmology to us. It nourishes every being every second. Everything in this life comes from the sun. So, it is not merely an objective cosmology. We are interpenetrated by the cosmos in which we live. That is why the concept of ecological unity is so strong in India in all our philosophy. We are only learning it today in modern Western experience, that the whole world is interrelated and interconnected. Some of the Western scientists have said the same thing: that any evil happening anywhere in the universe affects the whole universe. That is the interconnectedness or solidarity of things. That unity we are slowly coming to recognize by penetrating the *apparent* diversity on the surface of our experiences. So, here is a beautiful idea. The remaining verses of this chapter, about ten verses, are very beautiful. More of *bhakti* comes in at this stage.

In Vedanta, we imagine that background material saying to itself, *eko'ham bahusyām,* 'I am one; let me be many.' That Cosmic Mind which is called Brahmā here, is the first product of evolution. Just like when you put a seed in the soil, the seed is still undifferentiated within itself. The first differentiation comes when the sprout appears. From then on it is all differentiation. That is Brahmā, the first sprout—*prathamajā,* 'the first born'; that is the language used to describe Brahmā. We use a little mythology to deal with profound scientific truths. Our astronomers knew that it is only a mythical language, but that it makes it easier to understand the subject. In today's cosmology also, a lot of mythical language is slowly entering. But once intelligence is recognized as an integral part of evolution, the whole language of modern Cosmology will change. It will be nearer to our language in Vedanta—*eko'ham bahusyām,* 'I am One, let me be many.'

The previous *śloka,* verse 17, refers to this length of lifetime of Brahmā. As I said earlier, the present Brahmā is now 51 years old. He has got another 49 years to go. Thereafter, another person will go there as the commander of the whole universe. So, our time scale and Brahmā's time scale are quite different. So, there is a popular story, a funny story, that a devotee performed severe *tapasyā,* and God, in the form of Brahmā, asked him: 'What can I do for you? What blessing do you want?' And the devotee said, 'Give me this; give me that.' And Brahmā said, 'Please wait a minute. I shall give you all you want.' And the devotee waited for days, months and years! 'What is this?', that devotee asked. Brahmā replied: '*My* minute I meant, not *your* minute!' This subject of time, therefore, is a subject of very serious study in modern science. Several books are written today on the theory of time. We have studied time; we have *also* studied timelessness, eternity.

So, here in the *Gītā,* you hear the word *avyakta* or undifferentiated. There is no time idea in the undifferentiated; there is no process; there is no movement; time has dissolved back to that unmanifested state. As soon as manifestation begins, you get this *vyakta* or manifested universe. So, there is this *avyakta* of the nature into which the whole universe is resolved at the time of dissolution. There is another *Avyakta,* the Supreme Brahman of the nature of Pure Consciousness, of which Śrī Kṛṣṇa is going to tell us later on. That is always beyond time; that is eternity. That is the language we shall be hearing a verse or two later.

We have been studying verse 18 of this chapter. Very important ideas occur here; and very interesting also. *Avyaktādvyaktayaḥ sarvāḥ prabhavantyaharāgame. Ahaḥ* means 'morning'; *āgame,* 'in the beginning', i.e. in the beginning of the morning of Brahmā; *avyaktād,* 'from the unmanifested; *vyaktayaḥ sarvāḥ,*'all the manifestations'; *prabhavanti,* 'begin to appear'; cosmic evolution starts. *Rātryāgame pralīyante,* and 'at the beginning of night, all these get dissolved'; *tatraiva avyakta samjñake,* 'in that Reality known as *avyakta*'; into that *avyakta* the whole manifested world is dissolved at the beginning of the night of Brahmā. This is how day and night have been discussed here in terms of Brahmā, not in terms of you or I. In our own little time also, there is the waking time, and when night comes, we return into ourselves in deep sleep. Exactly the same experience. All these vast universes, all these powers, are gone as Brahmā goes into sleep.

So, this concept of *avyakta* plays a great part in our psychology, in our philosophy, and in our cosmology. Similar words are used in modern science also. The unmanifest is a beautiful idea; it *is* there but *not* manifest. That is the meaning of the unmanifest. In a banyan seed, the whole banyan tree is there, but you can't detect it. With these senses, you cannot discover a banyan tree in the seed. It is extremely subtle, undifferentiated. But, when it grows into a mighty banyan tree, then you realize, 'O! The banyan tree has become manifest now; it was unmanifest before.' *Avyakta* before, now it has become *vyakta*. A baby has so many energies within, but as a baby very little of it is manifest. Extremely tender, very weak is the baby, but slowly that baby may grow into a Mohammed Ali, or any other powerful person in course of time. It was all there in the baby. Slowly, it is evolving or manifesting. This is the way we study the world, both in its microscopic aspect and in its macrocosmic aspect, in both ways. The small as well as the big. This division is very relevant. *Avyakta* and *vyakta prakṛti;* nature is called *avyakta* in our philosophy—non-differentiated nature. That very non-differentiated nature becomes differentiated nature.

The next *śloka* says:

भूतग्रामः स एवायं भूत्वा भूत्वा प्रलीयते ।
रात्र्यागमेऽवशः पार्थ प्रभवति अहरागमे ॥१९॥

*Bhūtagrāmaḥ sa evāyam bhūtvā bhūtvā pralīyate;*
*Rātryāgame'vaśaḥ pārtha prabhavati aharāgame —8.19*

'The very same multitude of beings (that existed in the preceding day of Brahmā) merge, in spite of themselves, O son of Pṛthā, at the onset of night, and come out again at the onset of day.'

Here are two ideas. That is very revolting to many western people; though science compels them to accept it, they find it difficult.

One idea is that of *bhūtagrāmaḥ*, 'the entire world of cosmic entities and beings'; *sa evāyam*, 'these are the same;' these, *bhūtvā bhūtvā pralīyate*, 'get into existence and get dissolved back into primordial state'. When? *Rātryāgame*, 'at the onset of the night of Brahmā'. Śrī Kṛṣṇa uses the word *avaśaḥ;* that is a very difficult word meaning, 'without having any say in the matter'. It is all done by nature, our *avyakta*, without consulting us; that is called *avaśaḥ;* we are helpless in the matter. The sun is helpless in the matter of its dissolution or of projection. You and I are helpless in the matter. For example, your birth was not in your hands. 'Birth and death are in nobody's hands', Sri Ramakrishna used to say. We are thrown into the world. And then we are carried about here and there. Some will power is there; we are exerting it here and there. But in the larger sense, we cannot express our freedom at all, we are not free. Lot of things are happening from outside. The word *avaśaḥ* means 'helplessly'. People or beings come into the world helplessly, and go back out of this world helplessly. That is one idea which many Western people don't like. But the fact is that we are *avaśaḥ*. We can't make plans on these matters. Many things we can plan, but not everything. As Sri Ramakrishna said, 'we are like a cow tied with a thirty feet rope to a post. Within that 30 feet, the cow is absolutely free to move and graze or lie still. Beyond that, the cow is not free at all. The cowherd must come and shift it to another place.' So, freedom and necessity go together in our life. *Avaśaḥ* means that *some* freedom is there, but not much. Very limited it is.

The other idea, difficult for many Western minds, is: the same beings repeatedly manifest in every cosmic manifestation, in every creation. Many Western people say that this is the Hindu idea, repetitive; everything is the same as in the previous cycle. But they do not realize they are dealing with millions and millions of years of existence. Then you go back to primordial state, and come back. Do you think it is the same thing? You are not there to understand it at all. There are two technical terms in Sanskrit: *vikāsa*, expansion, and *saṅkoca*, contraction; it is going on eternally. Where is the element of creativity then? Within this infinite expanse of existence, there are little areas of creativity which you and I can experience.

Really, it is the same creative energy that repeats itself again and again, but it repeats for such a long time that you don't know that it is a repetition; it is going on; that is the language. 'Why should I be made to repeat my life again and again?', they ask this question in the West. You can't find an answer. Unless you can prove that new things are coming every time. It is like playing cards; you shuffle them and distribute them to the players again and again. Where is the 'new' thing? Existence is a totality now; it is now in an undifferentiated state. It comes into a differentiated state through millions of years of evolution and then it goes back again—*sa evāyam bhūtvā bhūtvā pralīyate*, 'that same *bhūtagrāmaḥ* comes, plays its part and goes away'. What about something 'new'? All these look like new, but is the same. Everyday you can see that life is a repetition: getting up in the morning, washing, taking breakfast, going to work, then lunch, then this and that, and last going to sleep. The same repetition day after day; everyday we are repeating, and *that* doesn't trouble you. When it comes into a cosmic existence, you feel it is bad. But here it is said, *sa evāyam bhūtvā bhūtvā pralīyate*. This *bhūtagrāmaḥ* constantly comes into manifestation and, after millions and millions of years, the whole universe goes back to that *avyakta* state, *rātryāgame*, at the time of night of Brahmā, the period of withdrawal of all activities. Brahmā is all active during the day. So, creation goes on. He begins to withdraw himself into himself during night. The creation returns to him. That is called *rātryāgame pralīyate*. *Avaśaḥ*, we have no say in the matter, we are helpless! The whole universe is helpless! It comes and it goes. That is the meaning of the word *avaśaḥ*. *Prabhavati ahar āgame*, and early morning again the manifestation starts, evolution starts! This is the nature of the cosmos. There is a discussion in modern cosmology: when the second creation will take place, whether that second creation will be original? They want it to be original, but you may try your best. You can make it original in a limited sense only. Thus, variety is there; there is provision for creativity; but, overall there is absolutely the same thing coming and going, the same *avyakta* getting *vyakta* and going back to *avyakta* state—*prabhavati ahar āgame*.

In verse 18, Śrī Kṛṣṇa had spoken of one *avyakta* into which the universe enters at the time of dissolution and from which it comes out. But, there is another *avyakta: avyakto'kṣara ityuktaḥ* (verse 20-21). That second *avyakta* is not of this nature. That is the pure Consciousness, namely, Brahman. That is a second category of *avyakta* which modern cosmology doesn't understand, doesn't accept or doesn't feel the need for. But, we in Vedanta speak of this *avyakta* which is Brahman, the Absolute, the eternal, not subject to time. Brahman and *Māyā. Avyakta, Māyā,* these are also common words. Due to *Māyā,* the *avyakta* becomes what you see here—the *vyakta* universe. The same *Māyā* takes it back also. These are all time-bound; but, there is another *avyakta*, beyond time, Eternity itself—*nityaḥ, sarvagataḥ, sthānuḥ, acalo'yam, sanātanaḥ*—as *Gītā* has said earlier (2. 24): 'Changeless, all-pervading, unmoving, immovable, this Self is eternal'.

So, in verse 20 Śrī Kṛṣṇa says:

**परः तस्मात्तु भावः अन्यः अव्यक्तः अव्यक्तात् सनातनः ।**
**यः स सर्वेषु भूतेषु नश्यत्सु न विनश्यति ॥२०॥**

*Paraḥ tasmāttu bhāvaḥ anyaḥ avyaktaḥ avyaktāt sanātanaḥ;*
*Yaḥ sa sarveṣu bhūteṣu naśyatsu na vinaśyati — 8. 20*

'But beyond this *avyakta* or unmanifested, there is that other *avyakta,* the Unmanifested, Eternal Existence—that which is not destroyed at the destruction of all beings.'

This verse gives a great truth which modern astrophysics is ignorant of. *Paraḥ tasmāt tu bhāvaḥ anyaḥ avyaktaḥ avyaktāt sanātanaḥ*, 'there is another *avyakta* superior to this *avyakta*'; that *avyakta* is *sanātanaḥ*, 'eternal'; *paraḥ*, 'supreme'. *Yaḥ sa sarveṣu bhūteṣu naśyatsu na vinaśyati*, 'which doesn't get destroyed when all these beings in the world become destroyed in that dissolution state'. These things have destruction, they come and they go, but this supreme pure spiritual Principle, which is called Brahman, remains ever the same. All modifications come only through nature, which is the power of Brahman, *Śakti* of Brahman; we call It *Śiva* and *Śakti*, Brahman and *Śakti*, Brahman and *Māyā*. Through *Māyā*, you find all these manifestations coming and going, etc., but behind this is the supreme Brahman, of the nature of Pure Consciousness, which, Śrī Kṛṣṇa says, *saḥ sarveṣu bhūteṣu naśyatsu*, 'when all the beings are dissolved', *na vinaśyati*, 'It is not destroyed'. There is the supreme spiritual Principle which is ever-pure, ever-free, ever-eternal. This is very difficult for modern scientists to accept. It will take a good deal of time for scientists to understand the nature of Consciousness—probably, in another few decades of scientific development, they will be able to understand the One behind the many, the One, ever the same, eternal, though It appears here as the many. This knowledge is slowly gaining acceptance by some scientists. It will take time, but this is what Vedanta has said. Behind the world of change is the world of the changeless, eternal, Brahman. That is why there is God in the universe. A changing God is not God at all. That is why even Brahmā is not treated as a God in that sense. Nobody worships Brahmā in the whole of India. We have only one Brahmā temple in Ajmer in Rajasthan. I don't think anybody will worship Brahmā as the one deity who wrote your fate on your forehead. Here, you can see the idea of the timeless behind time. This is the eternal nature of God. A God who dies is not a God at all. But, in the West, God was presented through mere dogma, not through rational investigation or from the depth of experience—an extra-cosmic God, outside the universe, by whose order the universe goes on. That kind of extra-cosmic God was presented in the West against which the Western thought revolted, until you came to the nineteenth century. There was a German philosopher, Nietzsche, who spoke of a superman, a superman appearing in the world with violence 'of deed and demeanour', exactly as Hitler who came later on. That is the story of the superman in Nietzsche. It was Nietzsche, therefore, who said, 'God is dead'. Why did God die? He wept and wept because he could not do anything for the world. He wanted to do but he had no power to do anything. Therefore, he wept and died. So, God is dead; that is the theory that started from that time. So, many Western writers speak of God as dead. The *Time Magazine* wrote ten pages on, 'Is God dead?' In 1968, when I was passing through South and North America, in several places, they took this subject of 'God is dead' for my lectures. I gave the Hindu view. Yes, that extra-cosmic god is dead. But the eternal Self of all is ever there. It is like the saying: king is dead, but long live the King! It is beyond life and death, beyond yes and no. That is the nature of the supreme Reality, the witness of everything. If there is a death, he witnesses it. The Self can never die; It is eternal. That is how we developed this truth of the eternal Divine behind the changing universe.

And in my correspondence with Sir Julian Huxley, given in the appendix of my book *The Message of the Upaniṣads*, this subject has been discussed. He had written in his book that God is increasingly becoming 'the fading smile of a cosmic Cheshire cat'. The smile still continues even after the cat is dead. That is the place of God today in the Western scientific thought. So, I wrote there, 'That might be true of an extra-cosmic God believed in by the Western people, but India's God is quite different.' There I quoted Śaṅkarācārya's *Vivekacūḍāmaṇi*, verse 572, in that letter:

*Astīti pratyayo yaśca yaśca nāstīti vastuni;*
*Buddhereva guṇāvetau na tu nityasya vastunaḥ —*

'The affirmation (of the theist) that the *vastu* or God is, the negation (of the atheist) that God is not, both these are nothing but pulsations of the human mind; it never touches the eternal Reality (behind the mind).' That is the nature of God presented in Indian cosmology, which is referred to here.

So, verse 20 says: *Parastasmāttu bhāvo'nyo'vyakto'vyaktāt-sanātanaḥ*, 'other than this *avyakta*, there is a *paraḥ sanātanaḥ avyakta*.' That is Brahman. *Yaḥ sa sarveṣu bhūteṣu naśyatsu*, 'which when the whole universe of beings gets destroyed'; *na vinaśyati*, 'It doesn't die'; It is always there. There we discovered the Reality of God, the eternal Self of the universe, eternal Self within men and women. The Atman and Brahman are one and the same. The same Brahman is in you, in me, as the eternal Self. Many scientific writers today refer appreciatively to this concept of India. I met two or three scientists who believe that the Atman is one with Brahman. The Atman, of the nature of Pure Consciousness in you and I, is one with Brahman which is the Pure Consciousness behind this universe. These are one and the same. This is a profound truth and it is admitted today by more than one scientist in their newly published books.

So, Śrī Kṛṣṇa is telling, *na vinaśyati*, 'that *sanātanaḥ*, eternal Reality, doesn't get destroyed'. 'The One remains, the many change and pass', is the famous passage in *Adonais* by Percy Bysshe Shelley, the British poet:

> The One remains, the many change and pass;
> Heaven's light forever shines, Earth's shadows fly;
> Life, like a dome of many-coloured glass,
> Stains the white radiance of Eternity,
> Until Death tramples it to fragments.

That is a famous line by Shelley, very much influenced by Vedanta. Browning and Shelley are two British poets greatly influenced by Vedantic ideas.

The next verse says:

अव्यक्तः अक्षर इत्युक्तः तमाहुः परमां गतिम् ।
यं प्राप्य न निवर्तन्ते तद्धाम परमं मम ॥ २१ ॥

*Avyaktaḥ akṣara ityuktaḥ tamāhuḥ paramām gatim;*
*Yam prāpya na nivartante taddhāma paramam mama—8. 21*

'What has been called Unmanifested and Imperishable, has been described as the Goal Supreme. That is My highest state, having attained which, there is no return.'

*Avyaktaḥ akṣara ityuktaḥ*, 'this *Avyakta* about which verse 20 said, "It is *sanātanaḥ*", that is, it remains when all the other entities are destroyed; it is *akṣara*, imperishable.' *Kṣara* means perishable, capable of getting destroyed. This is *akṣara*, 'imperishable'. *Tam āhuḥ paramām gatim,* 'that is considered to be the supreme Goal (of everyone)'. To realize Brahman beyond the *Prakṛti,* beyond *Māyā,* is the goal of human life. Ever-pure, ever-free and immortal, is the nature of that Reality.

So, we have in this *śloka* the wonderful idea: 'Reaching which there is no return'. Earlier we had come across that word *avaśaḥ,* 'helpless' in verse 19. That helplessness will disappear when you realize this great truth, the supreme Reality or Brahman. This *Avyakta* is *sanātanaḥ. Tam āhuḥ paramām gatim,* 'that is called the supreme *gati* or Goal'; *yam prāpya na nivartante,* 'by reaching which one does not return' to the cycle of birth and death. *Taddhāma paramam mama,* 'that is My supreme *dhāma,* i.e. Abode'. Śrī Kṛṣṇa is saying thus, identifying Himself with the supreme Divine Reality: that is My supreme Abode.

पुरुषः स परः पार्थ भक्त्या लभ्यः त्वनन्यया ।
यस्यान्तःस्थानि भूतानि येन सर्वमिदं ततम् ॥२२॥

*Puruṣaḥ sa paraḥ pārtha bhaktyā labhyaḥ tvananyayā;*
*Yasyāntaḥsthāni bhūtāni yena sarvamidam tatam* — 8. 22

'And that supreme *Puruṣa* is attainable, O son of Pṛthā, by whole-souled devotion to Him alone, in Whom all beings dwell, and by Whom all this is pervaded.'

This truth is called *Puruṣa,* the supreme Person, Impersonal-Personal God, the God of Vedanta. In one sense it is Impersonal; in another sense it is Personal. As Personal, it manifests as this universe, guides this universe, and does everything. And behind It is the impersonal Absolute, transcendental state of the *Puruṣa.* So, *Puruṣa sa paraḥ pārtha,* 'this *Puruṣa* is the supreme, O Arjuna'. This will be summed up in high language in chapter 15. The word *puruṣottama,* Supreme *Puruṣa,* will come there also.

How to achieve union with Him? *Bhaktyā labhyaḥ tu ananyayā,* 'only through *bhakti* can one reach Him'. What kind of *bhakti*? *Ananyā bhakti,* 'which is one-pointed devotion'. Mind doesn't go to anything else. That kind of devotion. *Ananyā bhakti, ekānta bhakti,* these are various terms and mean one-pointed devotion. Through that devotion alone can one realize this supreme *Puruṣa. Parā* means supreme; beyond all nature is the supreme *Puruṣa*. This comes in the *Kaṭha Upaniṣad* also. You have various categories of existence beyond which comes the highest. Beyond *Prakṛti* or nature, beyond *avyakta* or the unmanifested, is *Puruṣa*, and that *Puruṣa* is says the *Kaṭha Upaniṣad* (I. iii. 11): *sā kāṣṭhā, sā parā gatiḥ,* 'that is the *kāṣṭhā*, that is the highest'; *sā parā gatiḥ*, 'that is the supreme state'. We are studying gross things; then we go to subtle, and still subtler. The subtler the thing, the more universal it is. In that kind of study, we come out of this world of name and form, out of this outside world which is gross, and go through various stages like *manas, buddhi,* etc. Ultimately, we come to *Puruṣa* which is supremely subtle, supremely universal. *That is the consummation of subtlety, immensity, and inwardness*. Everything becomes universal there. So, that is the language of the Upaniṣads: *sā kāṣṭhā, sā parā gatiḥ*. That *Puruṣa* can be attained through pure *bhakti*, unmotivated *bhakti*. That is the meaning of *ananya bhakti*. 'I don't want anything else except love'. And this idea of *bhakti* has been illustrated in the *Purāṇas*, in the lives of various saints; and the most glorious story is that of Prahlāda; that five year old boy whose *bhakti* was absolutely pure and unmotivated. His story comes in the *Śrīmad Bhāgavatam*. He got the realization of the Divine and when Narasimha, that man-lion incarnation of God, pleased with this boy's devotion, said, 'Prahlāda, I am very pleased with you. Ask a boon of me, whatever you like,' Prahlada smiled and said, 'I am not a business man to ask a boon. I love you, that is all. I don't want anything in return.' That is why Prahlāda is praised in all our literature as the highest example of a *bhakta*. And *Nārada Bhakti Sūtras* will say, *bhaktā ekāntino mukhyāḥ*, 'devotees who are *ekāntis* (one-pointed) are the best among devotees'. One-pointed devotion can't be shaken by this or that.

In the same *Śrīmad Bhāgavatam*, seventh book, where you get this story of Prahlāda, you also get the story of Dhruva in the fourth book. A wonderful boy, a wonderful life also. But when he actually realized the Divine, he wanted to get a high position and God blessed him. With that he became *Dhruva nakṣatra*, the Pole Star. After his passing away he became the Pole Star. God had said to him, 'I shall give you that high state where even the *saptarṣis* will be with you all the time. You will be in the centre, constantly at the same place. That will be the highest place. I shall give that place to you.' He was satisfied. And God disappeared. After some time he began to think, 'What a fool I was. Coming to this great Divine, I asked for a little status. I am a fool.' He became very much regretful afterwards. This is the story of Dhruva in the fourth book and further comes in the seventh book the story of Prahlāda. There he was absolutely free. 'I do not want to ask anything. I am not a trader, I am not a business man.' I give you this; you give this in return. That's called business; exchange. Here there is no exchange. It is one-pointed devotion. 'Love for love's sake', as Swami Vivekananda said. This idea is highly commended in much of our spiritual literature. It is a very high state, but it is good to *know* that it is a high state. Otherwise, we will bring everything down to our own present state as some of the devotees do in India. He goes to one god, say Gaṇeśa. If he or she doesn't get what was prayed for, he or she goes to Kārtikeya , then to Śiva, then to another. He or she *must* get what was sought. God must be a servant and give him or her this and that. Dr. S. Radhakrishnan said, 'We don't love God, we use God.' That is not the type of *bhakti* in Prahlāda. Pure love is there. *Love for love's sake.* Vedanta calls it *ahaitukī bhakti.* Hari, Viṣṇu, or Śiva are various names of one Divine Person who is of such a nature that He draws the hearts of men like the young sage Śuka, who had already realized his own nature as the infinite Self. They have no cravings at all. Even then they worship Hari because God has this quality of drawing even their hearts. Here is a great verse in the *Śrīmad Bhāgavatam* (I. vii. 10). Men like Śuka and Prahlāda love God. What must be the greatness of that Divine Reality that even these people, who don't seek anything, love Him?

*Ātmārāmāśca munayaḥ*
*nirgranthā api urukrame;*
*Kurvanti ahaitukīm bhaktim*
*itham bhūtagaṇo hariḥ —*

'They take delight in the infinite Self, Hari'; *nirgranthā*, 'they have no bondages at all'; 'yet they constantly practise this kind of *ahaitukīm bhakti*, motiveless devotion. That is the nature of Hari'. So great is Hari, that He draws to Himself the hearts, not of ordinary people, but of extraordinary people like Śuka and Prahlāda.

That subject is coming up in the *Gītā* from now onwards. As I said, more and more of this wonderful teaching of *bhakti* will find expression in the later verses of the *Gītā*.

*Yasyāntaḥsthāni bhūtāni*, 'that *Puruṣa*, Supreme Person, in whom is this whole universe'. See the mythology. Today you can understand this mythology better. There are certain Western writers who have tried to interpret the myths and legends of the Hindu religion. Prof. Zimmer of France, a famous scholar who passed away some years ago, in his famous book, *The Myths and Symbols of the Hindu Religion*, beautifully brings out the truths behind some of these Hindu myths and symbols. For example, take the case of Viṣṇu: He lies on the serpent called *śeṣa;* see the name of the serpent. *Śeṣa* means 'what remains'; after all the universe dissolves what remains is *śeṣa*. On that, this infinite Consciousness is resting, absolutely calm and quiet, in a little *yoganidra*, '*yoga*-sleep'. When the time for creation comes, a lotus comes out of His navel. On the lotus appears Brahmā. That is the story in the *Śrīmad Bhāgavatam*. And Brahmā wonders, 'what am I to do?' He looks around, and finds nothing there. He goes through the lotus' stalk into Viṣṇu Himself. Then he understands. 'Yes, I must have some work to do, the Lord is omniscient.' Then he comes out and hears a sound, '*tapa, tapa*'. 'Do *tapas*, do *tapas*'. Not physical *tapas* but *jñānamayam tapaḥ*, 'knowledge *tapas*'. Through that *tapas* he understood the entire world of knowledge—every law, every theory, everything connected with the universe to come—he knew it all. So, he is called

*Vedamaya* or *Vedamūrti*, the embodiment of Veda. Veda means knowledge inclusive of the science of physical nature and the science of human possibilities which is the science of spirituality. Thorough knowledge is called Veda. When Brahmā heard this word '*tapa, tapa*', he got this profound message, and he engaged himself in *tapas*. What kind of *tapas*? Intense concentration to understand 'what is this work in front of me'. After that *tapas,* the universe came out.

The creative act of any creation is preceded by *tapas*. Without *tapas* there is no creativity. An artist is in *tapas;* then he or she gets creativity. Behind every creative action there is this *tapas*. That *tapas* Brahmā did, an 'exploding' *tapas*.

Now, in that story, we also read about the withdrawal of the whole universe and its also being taken back into Viṣṇu at the end of creation. There it remains dormant for thousands of millions of years. Then again occurs another act of creation. Viṣṇu opens the eyes and then creation begins. Viṣṇu closing the eyes, that is called dissolution. What must be the cosmic dimension of that Person? When we speak about it as a story, we think it is only children's story. But, when we study the subject in depth, we see it as a profound truth through a mythological language, anthropomorphic language. That is what our Zimmer has written about—several aspects of our Indian myths. Some of our myths are simply myths. But some myths expressed great truths. Take the myth of Śiva's bull, Nandi. Why does Śiva go on a bull? Bull stands for that energy, the pride of physical strength, mental strength, the strength of the ego, and Śiva controls it. It is perfectly under Śiva's control. The myth of Śiva's dance as the Naṭarāja, depicted in Tamil Nadu at Chidambaram temple, was used by scientist Capra in his *Tao of Physics* as illustrative of nuclear forces. That is what many Western scholars are doing today—investigating the philosophy and spirituality of the myths of the world. *Parabola* is coming here for some months; it contains a very rich description of Mexican and other myths of the world. Our myths also used to come in it. So, I am telling that you can put the same scientific truth through a myth. But very often some of the Western writers criticise our myths saying, 'this is the Hindu's belief that the earth is held by some elephants'. They take up only the children's stories and declare that this is all what the Hindus know. But today many are understanding the Hindu myths better. They are going to the truth behind all these stories. The land of India is famous for its creation of myths, creation of stories. In fact, children all over the world are indebted to India for the best of animal stories. The story of *Gajendramokṣa,* which I had referred to earlier, is so popular all over India. I was very happy to find it beautifully sculptured in Indonesia, in Cambodia, and in many other places. It is beautifully depicted in art, because it had appealed to the human mind outside India also.

The remaining verses will take up the subject again. Certain religious practices and beliefs tormented our minds at certain times. When new values came in, those things were quietly set aside, and new ideas came forth. That idea will come in the next few verses in this very chapter. There is such a thing as evolution of religious ideas. Spirituality is one, but the ways of expressing it can be different. Consider *śrāddha* or obsequies for the departed. We have a particular way of doing *śrāddha*. Today, many people don't like *that* particular ritual of doing *śrāddha.* They say, 'let us feed poor people in some orphanage; it is much better for the soul of my father than anything else.' Beautiful, you can change your method. You have the right to change. Nothing is stagnant, nothing is stationary, except the one infinite Reality. Everything else will change. That is the Hindu wisdom in respect of religion and religious practices; and, because we change, we are still alive. If we had been rigid, we would have died long ago. That is how our religion, as early as the *Ṛg-Veda,* declared this Truth: *ekam sat, viprā bahudhā vadanti,* 'Truth is One; sages call it in various names', which we hold on to even today. Essentially the spirit is the same, the expression alone is different. That is what makes a tremendous renewal in India age after age.

The remaining verses of this chapter deal with, what you call in Philosophy, eschatology or what happens to the soul after death. Many religions have many beliefs on this subject. So, here you have a statement of eschatology which obtained in the Vedic period. That is referred to by Śrī Kṛṣṇa in this chapter in the course of dealing with the main theme of the chapter.

After death people go to higher spheres; and in the Upaniṣads, specially the *Chāndogya Upaniṣad*, there is a reference to a twofold path: *devayāna*, 'the path of the gods', and *pitṛyāna*, 'the path of the ancestral spirits'. These are also called the Northern Path and the Southern Path corresponding to the sun's movement to the Northern hemisphere and to the Southern hemisphere. Even in the *Ṛg-Veda* there is mention of these two paths—*pitṛyāna* and *devayāna*. But a detailed description of the passage of the soul after death to that final state through stages along each of the paths, is not there in the *Ṛg-Veda*. Tilak in his *Gītā Rahasya* and in his earlier book, *Arctic Home of the Vedas*, studied the subject from the point of view of the climate and the situation. If our ancient home was somewhere in the polar area then we must have had the experience of six months of darkness and six months of light. Even today when you go to Sweden, Norway, far North, or the Arctic Circle, you will find this experience. Day continues for six months, night also continues for six months. Hardly for a few hours you will get a little sunlight in the winter season. Similarly, you will get very little darkness in summer. In fact, when I went to a little town Kiruna in Northern Sweden in 1961 during my lecture tour of seventeen European countries, it was 12 o'clock at night, and I was sitting in a car reading a book without any lamp. The sun is there, just below the horizon! It goes from this side of the horizon to the other side of the horizon. That is all its movement; that is the experience in the North Pole. In the opposite side, there is the South Pole. But when it became winter, there was long hours of darkness. Even in Holland, at ten o'clock in the night, it was just like 6 pm. here. Even at night at ten o'clock, I could sit in a park and take my dinner, because sun's light was still lingering. So, that is the nature of that experience. And when you come to the *Chāndogya Upaniṣad,* these two paths become paths for the souls to take after death. That is what is being discussed in the next four verses.

यत्र काले त्वनावृत्तिं आवृत्तिं चैव योगिनः ।
प्रयाता यान्ति तं कालं वक्ष्यामि भरतर्षभ ॥ २३ ॥

*Yatra kāle tvanāvṛttim āvṛttim caiva yoginaḥ;*
*Prayātā yānti tam kālam vakṣyāmi bharatarṣabha* — 8. 23

'Now I shall tell you, O great among the Bharatas, of the time (path) travelling in which, the *Yogis* do not return, (and again of that, taking which) they do return.'

First is the Northern Path which is mentioned here:

अग्निः ज्योतिः अहः शुक्लः षण्मासा उत्तरायणम् ।
तत्र प्रयाता गच्छन्ति ब्रह्म ब्रह्मविदो जनाः ॥ २४ ॥

*Agniḥ jyotiḥ ahaḥ śuklaḥ ṣaṇmāsā uttarāyaṇam;*
*Tatra prayātā gacchanti brahma brahmavido janāḥ* — 8. 24

'Fire, flame, daytime, the bright fortnight, six months of the Northern passage of the sun—taking this path, the knowers of Brahman go to Brahman.'

Śrī Kṛṣṇa says, 'Fire, flame, daytime, the bright fortnight, the six months of the northern passage of the sun—*uttarāyaṇam,* i.e. the northern passage; taking this path the knowers of Brahman go to Brahman'. This idea comes in our later theologies as the *krama-mukti*, 'slow and gradual emancipation'. You get a little high, stay for some time, climb still higher, still higher, without returning to the world of birth and death. You go to achieve realization of Brahman through *krama-mukti,* i.e. gradual liberation; that is one path. This is called *uttarāyaṇam* path. Then the second path is *dakṣiṇāyanam.* How?

धूमो रात्रिः तथा कृष्णः षण्मासा दक्षिणायनम् ।
तत्र चान्द्रमसं ज्योतिर्योगी प्राप्य निवर्तते ॥ २५ ॥

*Dhūmo rātriḥ tathā kṛṣṇaḥ ṣaṇmāsā dakṣiṇāyanam;*
*Tatra cāndramasam jyotiryogī prāpya nivartate* — 8. 25

'Smoke, night-time, the dark fortnight, the six months of the southern passage of the sun—taking this path the *Yogī*, attaining the lunar light, returns.'

The second path is through the south. Fire has both smoke and fire. Therefore, smoke also is a part of fire. So, that was the fire path mentioned earlier; this is the smoke path. Smoke, night-time, dark fortnight, six months of the southern movement of the sun—*dakṣiṇāyanam;* taking this path, the *yogī*, attaining the lunar light, returns. These are two paths mentioned in the *Chāndogya Upaniṣad* also, in much greater detail.

When Vivekananda dealt with this subject in a lecture abroad, he made this observation: 'I don't know what all these mean. Everybody says something or the other; since it is there, I am presenting it to you. I can't make head or tail of it!' Everything that is there is not to be taken in. Beliefs have changed in the course of time. Just like in scientific thought: when you know some aspects of nature, you follow some particular method, when you know more of that nature and probe to a deeper level, our approach changes. In philosophy it is just the same. So, when the Upaniṣads came, they retained some of the old ideas, but they had something more important to give to humanity. That is rational. That you can discuss, that you can experience also. These other things cannot be experienced. Nobody can say, 'let me die, go by that path and come back and tell what happened'. You can't do that. So, this is not meant for verification. But, in the Upaniṣads, the profound truths are those that are meant to be verified in life, verifiable and verified. You can check them up. Try to find out whether it is false. You are free to falsify it, according to one of the writers on the methods of science. You can say that, in this method of the real teaching of the Vedanta, you can verify it, you can falsify it if you can, but it is a challenge to everyone. It is *vastu tantra-jñāna*, 'knowledge of Truth as it is', says Śaṅkarācārya in the beginning of his *Brahma-Sūtra* commentary. That is the main teaching of the Upaniṣads. Many philosophical and spiritual truths you get there, but it contains also old un-testable beliefs and this is one such. Even something about sacrifices you will find in the *Bṛhadāraṇyaka Upaniṣad*. But that is only in the beginning. When the Upaniṣad proceeds, its own truths begin to come out. That is pure spirituality; the infinite nature of men and women; our oneness with all. You can realize this truth, not in a future life, not in a heaven far away, but *here and now*. The words *iha eva,* 'here itself', come again and again. If the truth is hidden in you, there is no need for you to go about to the sky to get realization; you can do it here, you can do it as a labourer, as a housewife, as anybody else. That teaching came later on in the Upaniṣads and subsequent literature as Vedanta with its two great spiritual paths, namely, *jñāna* and *bhakti*.

When these two paths of *jñāna* and *bhakti* were formulated, these Northern and Southern paths lost their attraction and relevance, and millions of our people began to follow these spiritual paths. In the *Mahabhārata,* you read about Bhīṣma waiting for the northern journey of the sun to discard his body. Lying on a bed of arrows without minding the difficulty he said, 'I shall pass away when the sun starts the northern journey, *uttarāyaṇa,*' and then he gave up his body at that time. *Mahabhārata* describes it very vividly. After that we don't hear of the paths of *uttarāyaṇa* and *dakṣiṇāyana*. As astronomical phenomena they are there, but as eschatological phenomena very few people hear of it or believe in it now. Through *bhakti* and through *jñāna,* we brought religion closer to people. All these un-understandable mysteries were quietly eliminated. Eschatology took a new form. Śrī Kṛṣṇa is referring to this because it is there in our Upaniṣads. But He Himself says at the end, that this is not the highest. The last *śloka* of the chapter will tell us that after referring to this old eschatology in the last but one verse:

**शुक्लकृष्णे गती ह्येते जगतः शाश्वते मते ।**
**एकया यात्यनावृत्तिं अन्ययावर्तते पुनः ॥२६॥**

*Śuklakṛṣṇe gatī hyete jagataḥ śāśvate mate;*
*Ekayā yātyanāvṛttim anyayāvartate punaḥ —* 8. 26

'Truly are these bright and dark paths of the world considered eternal: one leads to non-return; by the other, one returns.'

*Śuklakṛṣṇe gatī hyete jagataḥ śāśvate mate*, 'these two paths —*śukla* and *kṛṣṇa*, white and dark—they are eternal paths for people to take after death'. *Ekayā yātyanāvṛttim*, 'by one path when you go, you don't return to this world again'; slowly, slowly you achieve Brahman. *Anyayā āvartate punaḥ*, 'in the other path, you go, but come back again to this world' after enjoying the fruits of your good actions in some heaven. That is the characteristic of *pitṛyāna* or *dakṣiṇāyana*. Here there is a return journey. The other one is *devayāna*, which has no return journey. Now, having spoken about these two paths, Śrī Kṛṣṇa is giving in verse 27, a very interesting and inspiring spiritual truth which will constitute an introduction to the 9th chapter, where it will be stated that, through *bhakti* you have spiritual experience *here itself*. There is no going about here and there. That language will come later. Here it is just introduced:

नैते सृती पार्थ जानन् योगी मुह्यति कश्चन ।
तस्मात् सर्वेषु कालेषु योगयुक्तो भवार्जुन ॥ २७॥

*Naite sṛtī pārtha jānan yogī muhyati kaścana;*
*Tasmāt sarveṣu kāleṣu yogayukto bhavārjuna — 8. 27*

'No *yogī*, O son of Pṛthā, is deluded after knowing these paths. Therefore, O Arjuna, be you steadfast in *yoga*, at all times.'

The *yogī* is expounded by the *Gītā* in this verse. The word *yogī* is applied to anybody and everybody who has lived the spiritual life even a little. But, the *Gītā* has given in the second chapter, two wonderful expositions of *yoga*—*yogaḥ karmasu kauśalam*, '*yoga* is efficiency in action' (2. 50); and *samatvam yoga ucyate*, 'equanimity is called *yoga*' (2. 48). Many other such definitions will come later on. The *Gītā yogī* is quite different. How?

*Naite sṛtī pārtha jānan*, 'O Arjuna, knowing the nature of these two paths', the *yogī* of the *Gītā*, *na muhyati kaścana*, 'is not deluded at all'. By this path you go slowly and you reach the goal. By the other path you go and return—the *Gītā yogī* is not deluded by either of them. *Tasmāt* 'therefore', *sarveṣu kāleṣu yoga yukto bhavārjuna*, 'Arjuna, be a *yogī* at all times'. That is the *central theme of the Gīta*. That through work, through human relations, realizing the truth in the heart of all, you realize the truth *here* itself. You take the Name of the Divine and at the time of death, you achieve the highest human experience thereby. None of these eschatological paths are necessarily there. So, that is the greatness of the next chapter, the 9th chapter, which is very famous. And as we enter it, we shall see that the language used also indicates its special nature.

So, *tasmāt sarveṣu kāleṣu*, 'therefore, at all times', don't be deluded by all these paths; and *yogī bhava arjuna*, 'be a *yogī*, O Arjuna', live a spiritual life. God is not far away, He is nearer than the nearest. Islam's *Koran* says, 'He is nearer than the vein in your neck.' That is a wonderful idea; it is not going about here and there. That is not the way of religion. Realize Him here and now—*iha eva, iha eva*—as Śrī Kṛṣṇa will say later on. We have already heard it in verse 19 of the 5th chapter. Now He says in the last verse of this chapter:

वेदेषु यज्ञेषु तपःसु चैव
दानेषु यत् पुण्यफलं प्रदिष्टम् ।
अत्येति तत्सर्वमिदं विदित्वा
योगी परं स्थानं उपैति चाद्यम् ॥२८॥

*Vedeṣu yajñeṣu tapaḥsu caiva*
*dāneṣu yat puṇyaphalum pradiṣṭam;*
*Atyeti tatsarvamidam viditvā*
*yogī param sthānam upaiti cādyam* — 8. 28

'Whatever meritorious effect is declared (in the scriptures) to accrue from (the study of) the Vedas, (the performance of) *Yajñas*, (the practice of) austerities and gifts—above all these rises the *yogī*, having known this, and attains to the primeval, supreme Abode (*here and now*).'

This is the last verse of the 8th chapter. Whatever meritorious effect is described in the scriptures to accrue from the study of the Vedas, performance of the *yajñas*, practice of austerities or *tapas*, knowing all these, the *yogī* rises above all of them; see the language. That is the *yogī* of the *Gītā*. The *yogī* rises above all of them, having known them, and attains to the Primordial Supreme Absolute, *here and now*—that is written in brackets; it is not there in the text; that will come in the next chapter. This verse is like an introduction to the next chapter.

The *yogī, atyeti tat*, 'transcends all of them'; *sarvam idam viditvā*, 'after knowing all these paths'—that this path goes this way, that path goes that way, knowing this—he or she has no more delusion and has realized this truth. *Yogī param sthānam upaiti*, 'the *yogī* achieves the highest Primordial state' here itself. This is what came later on as the truth of *jivanmukti*, 'freedom while alive'. A *jivanmukta* has no bondage at all—he or she is liberated *here and now.*

So, this kind of going about here and there is not necessary. Everything is here. And Sri Ramakrishna tells us in our time, '"there, there" is ignorance, "here, here" is knowledge'. Whenever you think something is 'there', that is *ajñāna* or ignorance only. Everything is 'here, here'—*ekhāne, ekhāne jñān, śekhāne, śekhāne ajñān*. In Bengali *śekhāne* means 'there', *ekhane* means 'here'. That is what he said. So, that wonderful truth is the highest spiritual discovery in the Upaniṣads; and from that time through *bhakti, jñāna, karma* and *dhyāna*, we try to achieve the Divine here itself. If you fail, you will have a reincarnation to work it out. That truth came later on. This is how the *yogī param sthānam upaiti cādyam; ādyam* means 'the Primordial state'. How this universe was, what it was in the beginning? Brahman. That state we reach. After all these evolutionary steps, we realize through the human body itself that supreme truth, says this verse.

**इति अक्षरब्रह्मयोगो नाम अष्टमोऽध्यायः ।**

*Iti akṣarabrahma-yogo nāma aṣṭamo'dhyāyaḥ —*

'Thus ends the eighth chapter, designated *The Way to the Imperishable Brahman.*'

# BHAGAVAD GĪTĀ

## Chapter 9

### Rājavidyā-Rājaguhya-Yoga
### The Way of the Kingly Knowledge and the Kingly Secret

Now, we enter the ninth chapter. Its name is *Rājavidyā-rājaguhya-Yoga* chapter. It is described in the second line of the opening verse as a combination of *jñāna* and *vijñāna*, knowledge and direct experience. The first two verses refer to the chapter in a wonderful language. *Bhagavān* Śrī Kṛṣṇa continues his exposition without any need for Arjuna to ask a question.

श्रीभगवान् उवाच –
*Śrībhagavān uvāca* —

*'The Blessed Lord said:'*

इदं तु ते गुह्यतमं प्रवक्ष्याम्यनसूयवे ।
ज्ञानं विज्ञानसहितं यज्ज्ञात्वा मोक्ष्यसेऽशुभात् ॥१॥

*Idam tu te guhyatamam pravakṣyāmyanasūyave;*
*Jñānam vijñānasahitam yajjñātvā mokṣyase'śubhāt* — 9. 1

'To you, who are not of a carping mind, verily, I shall now declare this, the most profound knowledge along with experience or realization, knowing which, you shall be free from whatever is evil, i.e. worldliness.'

This is very simple, straightforward Sanskrit. *Idam tu te guhyatamam pravakṣyāmi*, 'Here, now, I am going to tell you the profoundest truth'. Because you are *anasūyave*, 'you have no *asūya*, you are free from jealousy'. Your mind is free.

Spiritual truths cannot enter into the heart of the people and stay there if it is full of *asūya,* jealousy, meanness, pettiness. That must go. In hundreds of places, in our spiritual literature, this has always been emphasized: Don't communicate this truth to one who is full of *asūya,* because that is a very low mind. No great truth can be understood by such people. So, *anasūyave,* 'one who is free from jealousy'. Also, in the end of the *Gītā,* in the eighteenth chapter, Śrī Kṛṣṇa will say this: 'don't teach this to one who is full of *asūya,* because they won't understand it at all.' It is sowing wild oats without any harvest coming out of it. So, Śri Kṛṣṇa is telling Arjuna, 'you are free from *asūya;* therefore, I am going to communicate to you this profoundest truth.' *Guhyam* and *guhyatamam* means, 'profound and profoundest'. '*Tamam*' in Sanskrit indicates superlative degree; '*taram*' indicates comparative degree. So, *guhyam, guhyataram* and *guhyatamam. Pravakṣyāmi,* 'I am going to tell you.' What is its speciality? *Jñānam vijñānasahitam,* 'it contains *jñāna* along with *vijñāna,* "knowledge and experience".' Suppose you say, 'take a glass of milk and make a good study of milk'; that is *jñāna.* You know all about milk. But, you drink it, get nourished by it, that is *vijñāna,* something more important than merely knowing the nature of milk. So, spiritual knowledge combined with spiritual experience, spiritual realization; the first must rise to the second stage. British thinker, the late Bertrand Russell says in his book, *Impact of Science on Society:* 'Unless we increase in wisdom as much as in knowledge, increase of knowledge will be increase of sorrow.' Both are needed: *jñānam vijñānasahitam. Yajjñātvā mokṣyase aśubhāt,* 'by knowing which you will be freed from all that is evil'. *Śubha* is good, *aśubha* is evil. You will be free from all evil. That is the promise in the first verse. And the second one expounds it and makes it still more explicit:

राज विद्या राज गुह्यं पवित्रं इदं उत्तमम् ।
प्रत्यक्षावगमं धर्म्यं सुसुखं कर्तुं अव्ययम् ॥ २॥

*Rāja vidyā rāja guhyam pavitram idam uttamam;*
*Pratyakṣāvagamam dharmyam susukham kartum avyayam — 9. 2*

'Of sciences, the highest; of profundities, the deepest; of purifiers, the supreme, is this; it is realizable by direct perception, endowed with ethical and moral values, very easy to perform, and is of an imperishable nature.'

Every word is full of deep meaning. The first word is *Rāja vidyā,* 'among *vidyās,* this is the royal *vidyā*'. *Vidyā* means 'science', knowledge. In fact, the word science also means knowledge. There is no mystery about it. Science means verified and verifiable knowledge. So, here *vidyā* means science. *Rāja vidyā,* among all the *vidyās,* this is the *rāja vidyā.* Chemistry, physics, astronomy, and many other *vidyās* are there. Among all these, this is *rājavidyā. Rāja guhyam,* 'the royal profundity'. *Guhyam* means 'profound, mysterious, or secret'. But, in the spiritual context, it means 'profound, deep'. *Guha* means a cave. Something is in a cave which you search, and with difficulty you find what you are seeking. All scientific truths lie hidden; one has to seek and discover them. You can't see with your eyes nor touch with your hands. In that sense the word *guhyam* means 'extremely profound'. You have to dive deep to get it. Just like the pearls which lie deep in the ocean; you have to dive and then get the pearl. This is like that. So, *rājavidyā, rājaguhyam.* Then, *pavitram idam uttamam,* 'supremely purifying is this (royal science)'.

Then comes a wonderful word: *pratyakṣāvagamam,* 'you can realize it in your own day-to-day experience'. *Pratyakṣa* means 'before the eyes'. Direct perception is called *pratyakṣa. Pratyakṣāvagamam* means, you can realize this truth even as you realize a *pratyakṣa vastu* in your experience. See the language: *pratyakṣāvagamam;* no going about millions and millions of light years into space to find out some particular heaven there. Here it is; open your inner eyes and see it. That is the language. In everyday life, during everyday activity, you can realize this truth. That is the meaning of *pratyakṣa.* You need not have a separate life to realize the truth. As a housewife, as a labourer, as a worker, as a politician, in every state of life you can realize the truth which is present in every one. That is the meaning of *pratyakṣāvagamam.* Not *śekhāne,*

*śekhāne,* 'there, there', but *ekhāne, ekhāne,* 'here, here' as Sri Ramakrishna expressed it in Bengali. This adverb is very important for us to understand and to appreciate and to benefit from. Not only so, *dharmyam,* 'it is inseparable from *dharma*'. That means, this particular spiritual message will strengthen society, will strengthen the human bonds in society. Some religious practices can harm society, can cause breaking away of human relations. All sorts of cheap mystical philosophies are there that can harm society. The mother gets visions every now and then, goes to some *bhajan* party. Who will look after the baby that is at home? Mother doesn't care! There you have *adharma* attitude. Society suffers. You may get some experience, but the society is suffering much from that experience. Where the society doesn't suffer, such a teaching is called *dharmyam.* And the teachings of great spiritual teachers are always *dharmyam.* They strengthen society, strengthen the human bonds. The *Gītā* repeatedly mentions this *dharmyam* along with *amṛtam,* i.e. the quality of being immortal. In the twelfth chapter we will come across this idea combined in the last verse. Śrī Kṛṣṇa tells there: 'My teaching is both *dharmyam* and *amṛtam*'. It makes you a unit of a healthy society; it strengthens the human bond. Along with it, it gives you the experience of the immortal, the divine in yourself: *dharmyam* and *amṛtam.* Some religions may stress only *amṛtam.* Mystical, other-worldly religions belong to that category. Others will stress only the worldly aspect, *dharmyam:* a good citizen, a good society. No higher experience. But, *My* message is *both dharmyam* and *amṛtam,* says Śrī Kṛṣṇa again in the last verse of the twelfth chapter of the *Gītā.* A comprehensive spirituality will include *dharmyam* and *amṛtam.* You are working in society, discharging your responsibilities, and while doing so, you are slowly realizing your own divine nature. What a beautiful conception and combination! Your outer journey is done along with an inner or inward journey. That inward journey is towards your own true nature as the infinite Atman. This combining of inner and outer journeys is called *dharmyam* and *amṛtam.* By your work, you strengthen society, you enrich it. By your inward penetration, you realize your own immortal dimension. One is *dharmyam*; the other is *amṛtam*. So, Śrī Kṛṣṇa is saying: 'I am going to teach you a philosophy which is *pratyakṣāvagamam dharmyam*.' If the path has so many beautiful characteristics, it must be extremely difficult. Not at all, *susukham kartum*, 'easy to do'. No kind of *abracadabra* is given in the name of this religion. Some people want a religion which is mysterious, un-understandable. They will say that if you give me something understandable, that is not religion; I will go to another teacher, and he will tell me something truly mysterious; then I will be satisfied; *that* is their idea of religion. I have seen this type in many situations. Anything straight and simple, we don't want. They are just like our village people who come to the doctor. If the doctor gives a small tablet, some patients will say: 'no, we want injection.' Some people behave like that in religion also. Here, Śrī Kṛṣṇa says that a mature mind understands and appreciates a path which is *susukham kartum*, 'easy to do', very simple. But, it is also *avyayam*, the fruit is 'infinite', 'imperishable'. Though it is simple, it will give a *phalam* or fruit which is *avyayam* or imperishable.

This is the introduction to this great subject which Śrī Kṛṣṇa is expounding in the ninth chapter: *spiritual realization, here and now, in the context of life and work and inter-human relations*. That must be a universal philosophy for all people.

I wish to give the story of my experience of people seeking magical and mysterious religion. I went to Kashmir from Karachi in 1944 with a friend. We spent quite a bit of time in Srinagar during which we met a person who was a disciple of a guru. In the course of talking while taking tea with him, he asked me a question. He said, 'My guru has given me a *mantra* and a method of meditation, and he told me: "when you meditate, you must have 35,000 cycles in meditation." Swamiji, I am trying my best, I have got only 25,000 cycles.' I couldn't make head or tail of what he said. What is the cycles in meditation? Some scientific jargon has been given by the guru to his disciple, and the disciple was very happy with it. I could not give any reply. After some talk, we took leave of him and went away. On the way, near the Śaṅkarācārya hill, children were throwing stones on a tree and a big beehive was disturbed. Bees started flying here and there. We thought we were quite safe. But, one bee came and stung me and another stung my friend in the back of the neck. We drove the bee away and started walking as if nothing serious had happened. First minute, there was no trouble. But after the first minute, both of us had a severe pain and there was headache. Then my friend turned to me and said jokingly: 'now it has become 35,000 cycles!'

So, this expression *susukham kartum* and *avyayam* means, 'easy to do but the fruit is infinite.' Love of God is a simple matter, and the fruit is infinite. Why don't you do so? Realizing one's own nature as the Atman is simple. There is nothing mysterious about it. But no! Many people want religious life to be as complicated as possible. For them, what one doesn't understand is *brahmavidyā*! What one understands is not, because it has nothing mysterious in it. That is ordinary people's general understanding of the subject. Even the word *brahmavidyā* is translated as 'something un-understandable' in many expositions in our country. But actually, *brahmavidyā* is simple. Śrī Kṛṣṇa is going to tell it here that it is extremely simple. But, people go on listening and saying that they do not understand it, but they also say that it is wonderful. What one does not understand is wonderful! But what do you mean by 'wonderful'? Many traditional presentations of religion are like this. But the *Gītā* and Śrī Kṛṣṇa present the subject in an easily understandable style: *pratyakṣāvagamam* and *susukham kartum,* as the second verse puts it. Magic and mystery, these have nothing to do with the science of religion.

We have associated all this with religion during our superstition-steeped period of history. Today, we are living in an age of science. Verifiable, communicable truths are there in science; so also, in the world of religion as expounded in the Upaniṣads and the *Gītā*. Nowhere else in the world will you get this teaching of the spiritual nature of the human being as the Atman, the ever free, ever pure Self of the human being, which all can realize. That is what the *Bṛhadāraṇyaka Upaniṣad* also says: *aupaniṣadam puruṣam pracchāmaḥ*. The student asked the teacher: 'We are asking you about the *puruṣa* taught in the Upaniṣad'. And Śaṅkara comments: *upaniṣadsu eva vijñāyate, na anyatra*, 'this teaching is found only in the Upaniṣads, nowhere else'. And today, it is appealing to millions of people in India and in the other parts of the world as well. That is why it is a simple spiritual teaching which says, 'manifest the ever-present divine within'. And this teaching is being given to Arjuna who is free from jealousy, *anasūyave*, 'to you who has no jealousy'—such a mind can manifest the Atman. When fire is covered by ashes, fire doesn't manifest. When you remove the ashes, fire manifests itself. Let me do that. If I start on that road, it is simple: *susukham kartum*. Effort is required, but it is worth trying. You find results. You see yourself becoming better, and still better. One can have a happier relationship with wife or husband and with all other people when this change comes in a person. That is the thinking by which we experiment on this teaching. We try to verify the teaching, and we see the fruit of the teaching: more happy human relations, more peace, more strength of mind, more compassion. So Śrī Kṛṣṇa says here: *pratyakṣāvagamam, dharmyam, susukham kartum, avyayam*. The fruit is infinite. What a beautiful description of the teaching that is coming hereafter!

Some years ago, I gave a parlour talk in Calcutta before a group of people. The subject I chose was, *Ecstasy in daily life*. It was a very beautiful evening. All enjoyed it. How can we get ecstasy in daily life? Now, ecstasy is a wonderful experience. You lose gravitational pull through ecstasy. You can get it through wine or other inebriants. That is also ecstasy. But, that is a dangerous and eventually harmful ecstasy. However, there is a spiritual method to develop that ecstasy. That is called *bhakti* as taught in this particular chapter. Here and now, let me love the Divine who is within me and in all others. Let me dedicate all my actions to him. In this way, when we practise spirituality, we live in ecstasy throughout the day. The housewife, though attending to so many activities of the household from morning till evening, is full of a sense of joy within. That joy comes from *bhakti* to the divine that is within which we have touched a little through our spiritual practice. Even a momentary touch can give us a great sense of elevation. That is the meaning of the subject, *Ecstasy in daily life.* The great teaching of *bhakti* in India was meant to give us that ecstasy. A *bhakta* is always ecstatic. How they sing! What a beautiful ecstasy comes out in the songs composed by our great poets and singers of religion, north and south, east and west! You will find real ecstasy in those wonderful songs which they composed. They poured out what they experienced within themselves. And so, these are the things which must inspire us today. A change of character, a change of attitude, a change of personality has taken place, because one great truth has come into our life: that is the all-loving God Himself, the most universal presence has come in me and into my life. Everything has changed. What Sri Ramakrishna said: 'you put a series of zeroes, they have no value at all; as soon as you put a "1" behind them, everything becomes full of value.' Every new zero adds to the value of the number.

That is how ecstasy in daily life becomes possible by clearly understanding the great teachings given by the *Gītā*. *Gītā* will convert everyone of us into such a centre of spirituality, of joy. God is *ānanda svarūpa,* of the nature of joy; we get a touch of that joy. *Raso vai saḥ* is a wonderful teaching in the *Taittirīya Upaniṣad.* What is God? 'He is verily *rasa* or bliss', and a little of that *rasa* makes all of us in this world very happy. We live because of that *rasa.* Now, Śrī Kṛṣṇa invites us to be in search of that *rasa* directly. Till now it was coming through various sources like the food we eat or the sensory objects we enjoy. The same *rasa* coming through these in small driblets. Śrī Kṛṣṇa asks us to go directly to the source of all *rasa,* the Lord Himself. That is why it is an intensely practical proposition. When Śrī Kṛṣṇa showed His universal Form to Arjuna in the eleventh chapter—we shall come to that in due course—Śaṅkarācārya introduces the last verse of that chapter, verse 55, thus: *adhunā sarvasya gītā śāstrasya sārabhūtaḥ artho niḥśreyasārthaḥ anuṣṭheyatvena samuccitya ucyate,* 'In order to convey the essence of the entire *Gītā śāstra* which leads one to spiritual freedom here and now, *Bhagavān* Śrī Kṛṣṇa says':

> *Mat karmakṛt mat paramo madbhaktaḥ saṅgavarjitaḥ;*
> *Nirvairaḥ sarva bhūteṣu yaḥ sa mām eti pāṇḍava —*

What a simple statement it is! 'O Arjuna, one who does all works as a dedication to Me, who makes Me his or her supreme Goal, who is My devotee, who is free from attachment, who cherishes no hatred towards anybody, such a one will realize Me.' Now, that is a teaching that one can practise in life. For this, one can get plenty of inspiration from our literature, from our *purāṇas,* and from our various hymns. Instead of running after magic and miracles, this is something that we should now concentrate upon; and the *Gītā* is a wonderful guide from that point of view. Here we have studied two verses giving us the introduction to this wonderful path. How can it be? *Pratyakṣāvagamam*—'it can be lived in day-to-day life', a realization that will inspire our day-to-day life. That is the challenge that *we* have to take, and verify or falsify. If I falsify it, very often it may be so because *I* am not up to the mark. Every scientist is not equally capable. One may falsify a scientific truth. But that may be only because the method adopted has been wrong. Other scientists, much more thoroughgoing, may say it is quite correct. So, falsification effort is also necessary for a test of scientific truth. Yes, but verification is the more important method. So, in this matter you can either verify or falsify; it is up to you. But, consider well whether you have been competent enough to either verify or falsify this truth. If you are truly capable, you will only verify it because many others before you have verified it already. Thousands, Śrī Kṛṣṇa has said earlier in the fourth chapter: *bahavo jñānatapasā pūtā madbhāvam āgatāḥ,* 'many have realized this truth, have gone beyond relativity, through the *tapas* of *jñāna*'. *Tapas* of *jñāna, tapas* of *bhakti*; at the highest level both are the same. And this is the promise in the beginning of this ninth chapter, the *jñāna-vijñāna* chapter.

The most important stress in the second verse is on that term *pratyakṣāvagamam,* 'which can be experienced in day-to-day life'. That God can be a constant awareness in day-to-day life because He is our own innermost Self. This has been verified by many saints—Hindu, Muslim or Christian. That is the main thrust of the whole verse. Therefore, as Sri Ramakrishna said: 'there, there'—that is how many people speak of God or religion, as something far away—that is *ajñāna.* 'Here, here', that is *jñāna.* In Bengali he said, *śekhāne, śekhāne ajñān; ekhāne, ekhāne jñān.* That is the importance of this phrase: *pratyakṣa avagama.* Any working person can have spiritual awareness. It is the birthright of all. Only, we must take this fact into account that something is hiding in this body-mind complex. The eyes and all the senses go *out* and see the reality outside. They must also be able to find out what is the reality *within* themselves. That is where pure spiritual development takes place. With this, that outer life will be richer and richer. That is the importance of this statement, *pratyakṣāvagamam.* If a God is 'there', far away in the universe, we can never make Him a subject of *pratyakṣāvagamam. But because God is presented as the one inner Self of all, of the nature of pure Consciousness, we can experience Him here and now in day-to-day life.* This is the importance of the message of the *Gītā.* It is meant for all: working people as well as for all those ascetics who have no work to do. But, this is specially meant for the working people. 'Universalisation of the spiritual life', this understanding must come to us. Those who do not have this understanding, they live an ad hoc life, day to day and minute to minute, without any far-sight and foresight, without any goal towards which the whole of life-activities are to be directed. That is the theme of the next verse, verse 3:

अश्रद्दधानाः पुरुषा धर्मस्यास्य परन्तप ।
अप्राप्य मां निवर्तन्ते मृत्यु संसार वर्त्मनि ॥ ३ ॥

*Aśraddadhānāḥ puruṣā dharmasyāsya parantapa;*
*Aprāpya mām nivartante mṛtyu saṁsāra vartmani* — 9. 3

'Persons without *śraddhā* or faith in this *dharma*, return, O scorcher of foes, without attaining Me, to the path of rebirth fraught with death.'

Those who have no *śraddhā* in this teaching, no conviction about this teaching, nihilistic type of people, extremely worldly-minded people to whom things which can be touched and handled alone are true, to all such people, who do not have any faith in this wonderful reality that is hidden within all of us, *aśraddadhānāḥ puruṣā*, such 'people lacking in faith'; *dharmasyāsya*, 'of this *dharma*', of this philosophy; *parantapa*, 'O Arjuna'; *aprāpya mām nivartante*, 'without realizing Me, without attaining Me, they return'; return whereto? *Mṛtyu samsāra vartmani*, 'to this path of *samsāra* which is fraught with *mṛtyu* or death'. This is the idea of all spiritual teaching. There is this ordinary human life. Many people feel that this sense-bound life is only a surface life. There is a deeper dimension to life. It is that investigation which the sages undertook in the Upaniṣads. What is the depth dimension of this human personality? On the surface, it is this little ego centred in this genetic system, seeking organic satisfaction. That is the human being on the surface. But a deeper enquiry reveals some infinite spiritual dimension in every one. To achieve the experience of that is the purpose of this human life. In a verse of the *Hitopadeśa* (*Mitralābha*, verse 25) you will find this statement: 'eating, drinking and sense pleasure, a human being shares with animals.' The human being may do it with a little more refinement; that is all. But otherwise, it is just common to all: human beings and animals. What is the uniqueness of the human being? It is *dharma*. Searching for some deeper dimension of human beings and nature. That is his or her uniqueness. If that uniqueness is taken away, human beings and animals are just the same. *Dharmeṇa hīnāḥ paśubhiḥ samānāḥ*, 'take away *dharma* from human life, he or she is equal to any other beast', *Hitopadeśa* concludes. That should not be. Though endowed with this profound brain, we find plenty of men and women today who remain a beast, often a beast of prey; cheat other people, kill animals and destroy nature. If they had only directed a little energy to investigate this higher spiritual dimension within, they would have been constructive and creative. Many people want to consume more and more of material goods in what we speak of today as a consumerist civilization; and the result is that the world is becoming bereft of many things, including forests and even animals and birds. Thus, the human being becomes the enemy of nature, and eventually one's own enemy as well. We are destroying the whole of nature. No animal destroys nature. They live in it, they are part of it. Human beings alone have the capacity either to destroy or to improve; but because one is concerned with this organic system alone, one becomes a destroyer of nature. How many birds have been destroyed all over the world so that men and women may have a feather to put on their heads or adorn their caps! So, Śrī Kṛṣṇa says here: *Aśraddadhānāḥ puruṣā dharmasyāsya parantapa,* 'O Arjuna, those people who have no faith or conviction in this great *dharma*'; this *dharma* that tells us that we have a dimension higher than this mere psychophysical system, that our true dimension, true nature is spiritual, and that dimension is one and the same in all, that God is hidden in all of us. What happens to those who don't have faith in this? *Aprāpya mām,* 'they don't attain to Me', the one Self in all, the pure infinite Consciousness; and, *nivartante mṛtyu samsāra vartmani,* 'they return to *samsāra* which is *mṛtyu*, which is of the nature of change and death.' They return again and again to this transmigratory existence. This is the language of this third verse. Then Śrī Kṛṣṇa continues:

मया ततं इदं सर्वं जगद् अव्यक्तमूर्तिना ।
मत् स्थानि सर्व भूतानि न चाहं तेष्ववस्थितः ॥४॥

*Mayā tatam idam sarvam jagat avyaktamūrtinā;*
*Mat sthāni sarva bhūtāni na cāham teṣvavasthitaḥ* — 9. 4

'All this world is pervaded by Me in My unmanifested form; all beings exist in Me, but I do not dwell (exclusively) in any one of them.'

I am pervading this entire universe. *Mayā tatam idam sarvam,* 'this manifested universe, in its entirety, is pervaded by Myself.' *Tatam* means 'pervaded', 'pervaded by that infinite pure Consciousness'. You may ask this question: is the solar system pervaded by some background material? Even according to modern cosmology, that background material which exploded and became this universe, that material is *still there* in this universe. The universe is pervaded by that material which was there. If it was not there, then it would not be here also. What is not in the cause cannot appear in the effect. Something cannot come from nothing. Only from something can something come. So, in this way, our teachers discovered this truth, that the whole world has come from Brahman, of the nature of Pure Infinite Consciousness. He is the inner Self of everything. Take a living cell; inside it the infinite Consciousness is present. It directs all the activities and processes in that living cell. So, it—the Consciousness—is *tatam,* meaning 'pervading everything'. This is a profound idea and I had said before that modern scientific thought is slowly progressing in this direction—to discovering that primordial reality behind the universe as consisting of Consciousness, not dull dead matter. That is the Vedantic way of putting it. And so, *mayā tatam idam sarvam.* Śrī Kṛṣṇa identifies Himself with that infinite reality and assumes a human form as the Divine Incarnation to do good to the world. 'Everything is pervaded by Me', *mayā tatam idam sarvam.* What is My nature? *Jagat avyakta mūrtinā,* 'I am in the world as an unmanifested form'. You cut open a thing, but you won't see infinite Consciousness there; but it is present there, unmanifest; the language is *avyakta mūrti.* No sense organ can detect it. That is the meaning that Śaṅkarācārya gives. That is the search of all science. What is that *avyakta mūrti* hidden in a piece of matter? Scientists are struggling, they are seeing many new and still newer realities within a piece of matter. And the latest is that they have discovered in nuclear science that consciousness also is part and parcel of this physical world *as the observer*. That is just the beginning. As they continue the investigation, they are bound to come to this great truth that Śrī Kṛṣṇa says in this verse. This *avyakta mūrti*, i.e. 'supreme infinite unmanifested Consciousness', is there in everything. We can detect it only with some inward penetration, both into the nature as well as into the human being. It is more easy to penetrate into human beings and discover it there than to discover it in the nature. The search into external nature will yield only hints and suggestions. But you cannot actually detect it there. That is the situation in physical science, even in biology. How do the organs develop? How do the features develop? Everything is well organized, well integrated, well related to everything else. There is a unity in the midst of diversity there. That unity is centred in the spiritual Consciousness that is present in everything. This is how the idea of this *avyakta mūrti* is understood; other things are tangible. We can see and handle them. This one you can't see, you can't handle, but you *know* it is there. It has left its footprints on the various events of the physical world. So, *mayā tatam idam sarvam jagat avyakta mūrtinā. Jagat* itself means 'the constantly changing universe'. 'I' am there in this universe. 'I' pervade the entire universe. *Matsthāni sarva bhūtāni,* 'all beings and things exist in Me'. *Na cāham teṣu avasthitaḥ,* 'but "I" am not in them'. 'They are in Me, I am not in them,' in the sense that 'I' am not *exclusively* in any one of them. 'I' am absolutely free. So, *matsthāni sarvabhūtāni,* 'all beings exist in me'; without Me they cannot exist. But none of them can contain Me in itself in fullness. That is the nature of that infinite reality. The next *śloka* will say something more, even contradicting the statement here:

न च मत्स्थानि भूतानि पश्य मे योगमैश्वरम् ।
भूतभृत् न च भूतस्थो ममात्मा भूत भावनः ॥५॥

*Na ca matsthāni bhūtāni paśya me yogamaiśvaram;*
*Bhūtabhṛt na ca bhūtastho mamātmā bhūta bhāvanaḥ—9. 5*

'Nor do beings exist in Me (in reality), behold My divine *Yoga!* Bringing forth and supporting the beings, My Self does not dwell in them.'

*Na ca matsthāni bhūtāni,* 'things are not in Me at all'; *paśya me yogamaiśvaram,* 'see My *īśvarīya yoga,* My divine *yoga* power'. What is the nature of that *yoga* power? *Bhūtabhṛt na ca bhūtastho mama ātmā,* 'My Self sustains all beings and yet I am not caught up in any one of them'; *bhūta bhāvanaḥ,* 'I am the one that nourishes and cherishes all the beings in this universe.' The more subtle the reality, the more will these characteristics become manifest; the more gross the reality, it can not reveal these characteristics. For example, this physical body can be only in one location. It cannot be in two locations. The grosser the thing, the more is it limited by space and time. The subtler a thing, it transcends that limitation. And so, *na ca matsthāni bhūtāni paśya me yogamaiśvaram.* Śrī Kṛṣṇa will say later on: This *prakṛti* or nature is *Māyā.* I take hold of that *Māyā* and create all this in this way, so that I am ever-free and yet animating everything, and through those things one can slowly come to discover My true nature. The whole universe is there for you to study and to discover My true nature. There is, in particular, the human being in this universe in whom this reality finds more expression. It has left more imprints on human experience than on external nature. By tracing those prints, you can discover Him. The words 'tracing those footprints' is a unique Upaniṣadic expression. When a cow is lost in the forest, the cowherd will search for the cow. And one method of searching is, tracing the footprints of the cow. By tracing the cow's footprints, he finds that the cow has gone to a reservoir of water. From there, the cowherd brings his cow back. Similarly, this Atman has left Its footprints on human experience; tracing the footprints, one can discover the reality that is there. So, in this way, *mama ātmā bhūtabhāvanaḥ,* 'My Self sustains everything in the universe'. An example is given in the next verse:

यथाकाशस्थितो नित्यं वायुः सर्वत्रगो महान् ।
तथा सर्वाणि भूतानि मत्स्थानि इत्युपधारय ॥६॥

*Yathākāśasthito nityam vāyuḥ sarvatrago mahān;*
*Tathā sarvāṇi bhūtāni matsthāni ityupadhāraya* —9. 6

'As the mighty air, moving always everywhere, rests ever in the *Ākāśa* or space, even so, do understand that all beings rest in Me.'

Air is there in the atmosphere; wherever you search you find air. Similarly in religion, you do not have to go here and there, or far away, to see God. Wherever you are, the divine is there, just like oxygen. Wherever you are, you can develop the scientific mind. It is not like telling, 'I want to go *there* to breathe oxygen'. Oxygen is *here* also. Just breathe, that is all. In the same way, this *ākāśa* is all-pervading, all-containing, in which the *vāyu*, i.e. air which is *sarvatrago mahān*, 'always moving everywhere and immense in range' rests. Probably, for a few hundred miles above the earth we find air, though thinner and less dense it becomes as you go higher up and very dense at lower levels. But it is there; even far up you will find it there. But there is a limit beyond which there is no air at all. In free space there is no air. Air is only an earthly phenomenon. Even in the planets of the solar system, scientists have not found air; it is only here on earth. But the main point is, I, Śrī Kṛṣṇa, am like that *ākāśa*. *Yathākāśasthito nityam vāyuḥ sarvatrago mahān.* Just like the air which is *sarvatraga*, 'which goes everywhere'; and is *mahān*, 'immense, great'; *ākāśasthitaḥ*, 'rests in *ākāśa*'; *tathā*, 'similarly', *sarvāṇi bhūtāni matsthāni iti upadhāraya*, 'understand that all beings are similarly established in Me.' As air moving everywhere, immense in nature, is established in the *ākāśa* or space, so also all beings are established in Me. Please understand this truth. *Avadhāraya* means 'please understand correctly'.

सर्वभूतानि कौन्तेय प्रकृतिं यान्ति मामिकाम् ।
कल्पक्षये पुनस्तानि कल्पादौ विसृजाम्यहम् ॥७॥

*Sarvabhūtāni kaunteya prakṛtim yānti māmikām;*
*Kalpakṣaye punastāni kalpādau visṛjāmyaham — 9. 7*

'At the end of a *kalpa* or cosmic cycle, O son of Kuntī, all beings go back to My *Prakṛti;* at the beginning of another *kalpa*, I send them forth again.'

All beings, O Arjuna, attain to My nature at the end of a *kalpa.* A *kalpa* is Brahma's whole day. At the end of the *kalpa,* all beings are absorbed back into Me. At the beginning of the *kalpa,* they are sent out once again. This is the idea in all astronomy; ancient Indian or modern astronomy, and in Indian Vedanta. In Semitic thought, where there is no concept of vast ages or of vast space, the concept is very much limited. However, the Indian concept is 'infinite'. In fact an infinitesimal fraction of a second is called *truṭi* in Sanskrit. The ancient Indians have spoken of that kind of an infinitesimal fraction of time. They are useful only in dealing with atomic phenomena. But even in ancient Indian thought you will find this one-by-twelve-thousandths of a second, and all such things, in concepts like *truṭi.* Similarly, in terms of large duration, we speak of millions and millions of years. And *kalpa* is one such concept, a day of Brahmā, at the beginning of which this entire universe gets manifested, and, after a long time, at the night of Brahmā, the manifest universe returns to its original state of *avyakta,* non-manifestation. That is called a *kalpa.* And so, at the end of a *kalpa,* this is what happens. At the beginning of a *kalpa,* the whole manifest universe comes out once again. *Prakṛtim yānti māmikām. Māmikām,* 'My *prakṛti*'. That *prakṛti* into which the universe dissolves is My nature, My own nature, My own *prakṛti. Kalpakṣaye,* 'at the end of a *kalpa*'. *Kalpādau punaḥ tāni visṛjāmyaham,* 'at the beginning of the *kalpa,* again I *project* them', as the Upaniṣads express it, *visṛjāmi,* 'project', like a spider projects its web out of itself, not from something external. That is one unique creature that we find as an example of cosmic creation in Indian philosophical thought.

From Brahman the world has come; in Brahman the world exists; and unto Brahman the world returns. This concept of a unity behind the universe, a unity at the beginning, middle and end of the universe, is common in Vedanta and modern science.

प्रकृतिं स्वां अवष्टभ्य विसृजामि पुनः पुनः।
भूतग्रामं इमं कृत्स्नं अवशं प्रकृतेर्वशात् ॥८॥

*Prakṛtim svām avaṣṭabhya visṛjāmi punaḥ punaḥ;*
*Bhūtagrāmam imam kṛtsnam avaśam prakṛtervaśāt* — *9. 8*

'Animating My *Prakṛti* or Nature, I project again and again this whole multitude of beings, helpless under the sway of *Prakṛti*.'

Thus, taking hold of My *Prakṛti*, I bring forth this universe again and again, *prakṛtim svām avaṣṭabhya visṛjāmi*, 'I project', *punaḥ punaḥ*, 'again and again'. How many universes have been there before, how many will be there hereafter as well! We are only in one universe, behind which there were, and after which there will be many such universes. We cannot conceive of them now. This is only one episode in the entire creation of the universe. *Bhūtagrāmam imam kṛtsnam*, 'this entire *bhūtagrāmam*, conglomeration of things in this world', I project and take back also. *Avaśam*, 'they have no say in the matter'; the sun has no say in the matter; the stars have no say in the matter; we also have no say in the matter. That we are born of some particular parents, we had no say in the matter. We are absolutely *avaśam*, means 'dependent'. Why are we not independent? Because *prakṛter vaśāt*, we are 'in the hands of *prakṛti*'. *Prakṛti* does this for you. That is the nature of the universe. *Prakṛter vaśāt*, 'helpless under the sway of *prakṛti*'. A little thinking will make us clarify this idea. What is this? I had no say in the matter when I came into being, I shall have no say in the matter when I leave also. But, now for some time, I have some say. Not entirely, but only a little freedom is there. The human being has been given a little freedom; animals don't have even that much. Human beings alone are a little free, beyond which one is absolutely *avaśam*, 'helpless', under the control of nature. That is the present situation.

The challenge of this situation, when faced, is what makes for spiritual development: 'I want to be free, I want to be free, I don't want to be a plaything in the hands of nature.' A *katputali* as they call it, just like a doll in the hands of nature. That is what animals are, what the sun is, what the stars are. But, a human being *can* be different. That is why this spiritual knowledge is needed—to give us that sense of freedom. 'I am free'. Where are you free? Not in your body; the body is subject to all the laws of nature. Nature's laws outside are also found in my body. They are all determined. Even psychically we are not entirely free. But, spiritually we can be free, absolutely free. That is our true nature. In this way, we are *avaśam,* helpless, just like the cattle which a cowherd takes this side, or that side, make them eat, drink or go about. *Avaśam,* 'absolutely without any independence'. Nature taken as a whole makes its products *avaśam.* All the items in nature are *avaśam,* 'subject to nature's control'. This is the challenge which the human being *alone* can face. Why should *I* be *avaśam*? No animal can question this situation. But a human being *can* question, *has* questioned and *has* found the answer: 'I can be free, I can be free', *āzād, āzād.* Swami Vivekananda used to say, 'I am free, I am free'. That truth must be realized. I am not a mere plaything in the hands of nature. Nature says: 'weep', and you weep! Nature says: 'smile' and you smile! Why is this so? Can't one determine this for oneself? One can, provided one struggles to manifest one's divine nature. So, the word *avaśam* has a great meaning. It is a fact of daily experience, but this experience can be eliminated. When we get rid of this *Māyā,* then we become free. Śrī Kṛṣṇa will say this later on that one can get rid of this *Māyā,* and realize one's true nature—one's affinity to that infinite reality which is beyond *Māyā*. Our real affinity is there, and not in this world of *Māyā*.

न च मां तानि कर्माणि निबध्नन्ति धनञ्जय ।
उदासीनवत् आसीनं असक्तं तेषु कर्मसु ॥९॥

*Na ca mām tāni karmāṇi nibadhnanti dhanañjaya;*
*Udāsīnavat āsīnam asaktam teṣu karmasu* — 9. 9

'These acts do not bind me, sitting as one neutral, unattached to them, O Dhanañjaya.'

I am doing all this: projecting the world and taking the world back inside. Do I suffer through all these actions? Not at all. They do not bind Me at all. I am ever-free because I am unattached. *Nibadhnanti* means 'make for bondage'. It does not make for bondage for Me. Why? *Udāsīnavat āsīnam,* 'I am indifferent to all these actions.' Actions are going on, but I am not very much involved in it. That sense of detachment is there. *Asaktam teṣu karmasu,* 'I am unattached to those actions'. That is Śrī Kṛṣṇa's own example, the divine example. We can also have the same situation. We can do plenty of work without any sense of attachment, and without feeling any tension of work. Śrī Kṛṣṇa told this even in the third chapter, giving his example: if you can work in a spirit of detachment, you become free, work will not bind you. Normally, work binds; the more you work, the more you get into bondage. But it need not be so. There is another dimension in us where everything is freedom. If you develop spiritual awareness, then work also ceases to be an instrument of bondage. So, Śrī Kṛṣṇa says: *udāsīnavat āsīnam asaktam teṣu karmasu,* 'in all these actions that I do, I am not attached at all'.

In the *Mahābhārata,* you will find Śrī Kṛṣṇa's story. He was perfectly unattached. He was very active, involved in hundreds of events, but He was always absolutely free, with no attachment at all—even without attachment to his own people, namely, the *Yādavas*. When they became power-mad and very wicked, Śrī Kṛṣṇa said: these fellows will give trouble to the whole world. So, He saw before his very eyes the whole *Yādava* race being destroyed by mutual killing in the last chapter of the history of the *Yādavas.* And so, there was perfect detachment. Kings came down from their throne at his word, but He did not want to be a king. He remained absolutely free. That kind of a detachment you can see in Śrī Kṛṣṇa's life, and what He says here is what He was in his life. If this is the nature of the Divine, you and I can be of that nature by a little effort.

मयाऽध्यक्षेण प्रकृतिः सूयते सचराचरम् ।
हेतुनाऽनेन कौन्तेय जगत् विपरिवर्तते ॥१०॥

*Mayā'dhyakṣeṇa prakṛtiḥ sūyate sacarācaram;*
*Hetunānena kaunteya jagat viparivartate — 9. 10*

'By reason of my over-all power, *Prakṛti* produces all this, the moving and the unmoving; the world wheels round and round, O son of Kuntī, because of this.'

I am presiding over the activities of My *prakṛti. Prakṛti* is part of Me as My *Śakti.* In fact, in modern Vedantic expressions, this is called Brahman and *Śakti,* or *Ṣiva* and *Śakti,* which together constitute the Ultimate Reality. One is active, the other is not active. But they are one and the same. A serpent in motion is *Śakti;* the serpent coiled up is *Śiva.* That is Sri Ramakrishna's way of putting it. Two aspects of the same Reality. Still water is *Śiva;* water thrown up in waves is *Śakti.* And these two are one; *Śiva* and *Śakti* are one; *nitya* and *līlā* are one. This is the language. *Nitya* means 'eternal Reality'; *līlā* means 'manifested universe'. Both are one and the same. That is the God of Vedanta. Impersonal plus Personal, that is the *nirguṇa-saguṇa* combination. So, *Śiva* and *Śakti,* Brahman and *Śakti* or *Māyā,* are one and the same. You see the same Reality in two aspects. So, Śrī Kṛṣṇa says here: *Mayā'dhyakṣeṇa prakṛtiḥ sūyate sacarācaram,* 'this entire world of moving and unmoving things, *cara* and *acara, prakṛti* creates, *prakṛti* projects out of herself; but, I am there only as the presiding power'. That is all, I don't do it; I am just there. Something like our President of India; the whole administration is done in his name, everybody is doing it, he himself does nothing. His very presence makes for the administrative stability. That is called *adhyakṣa. Mayā udhyakṣeṇa prakṛtiḥ.* We say in our political language, the Speaker is the *adhyakṣa* of the Parliament or the Loka Sabhā. And the Speaker is one who speaks very little. All the speaking is done by the people occupying the benches, but not the Speaker. By his presence, things go on in the Parliament. Not so in India always, isn't it? In spite of the Speaker, things can go very bad. That must change and will change for the better in course of time. And so, *mayā adhyakṣeṇa prakṛtiḥ sūyate,* 'projects', gives birth to; that is the meaning of *sūyate; sacarācaram,* 'all this *cara,* moving, and *acara,* unmoving, entities of the world'. *Hetunā anena,* 'by this reason'; *kaunteya,* 'O Arjuna'; *jagat viparivartate,* 'the entire evolution of the world takes place'. That is the nature of this *viparivartana* or evolution. *Viparivartana* or *viśeṣeṇa parivartana;* how many types of evolution are taking place constantly. We have cosmic evolution, organic evolution, human evolution; all these are going on. How? By this *anena hetunā,* 'by this cause'. The One and the many are one and the same. The many are not separate from the One. From the One, the many have come. Unto the One, the many return. And the unity of the One and the many is the unity of the supreme Brahman. So, Brahman is One, Brahman is many. You can apply both the terms, *ekam* and *bahu,* to the Reality. In the manifested, it is *bahu;* within itself, it is One. Take for instance, solar radiation; these are separate, various, different. But the sun itself is a unity by itself. In this way, *hetunā anena kaunteya jagat viparivartate,* 'the world goes on transforming, evolving due to this'. This is called *jagat viparivartate,* behind which is the action of *prakṛti* stimulated by Me, the infinite Self, the infinite Divine.

**अवजानन्ति मां मूढा मानुषीं तनुं आश्रितम् ।**
**परं भावं अजानन्तो मम भूतमहेश्वरम् ॥११॥**

*Avajānanti mām mūḍhā mānuṣīm tanum āśritam;*
*Param bhāvam ajānanto mama bhūtamaheśvaram—9. 11*

'Unaware of My higher state as the great Lord of beings, fools disregard Me, when dwelling in a human form.'

This is in relation to that topic that was first expounded in the fourth chapter: divine incarnation. That infinite Brahman can appear as a divine personality. That is called *avatāra.* His external physical system is a very poor expression of what is immense within Himself. Don't measure Him in terms of the body. The body is not the measuring rod for what is inside that person. Even in ordinary people, body cannot be the measuring rod. Sometimes you will find a very simple ordinary looking person. But when you begin to talk to him, you will find that he is extraordinary. I once went to the house of a primary school teacher in Bangalore. There, I found him to be a very lean person; getting a salary of fifteen or twenty rupees. A small lighted oil lamp was there. The house was very ordinary. But, that man had immense brain and intelligence! A scholar in Sanskrit; he could speak and write beautiful Kannada, English and Sanskrit. But he looked very ordinary. So, even in ordinary human life, the externals can deceive us. Some look fine, but they may be empty within; some look ordinary, but they are extraordinary. If that is so with regard to ordinary people, how much more true it must be with regard to a Buddha, a Jesus, a Śrī Kṛṣṇa, or a Sri Ramakrishna. They look ordinary. Śrī Kṛṣṇa is saying here: *avajānanti mām mūḍhā,* 'foolish people deride Me, do not understand Me'; *mānuṣīm tanum āśritam,* 'who has taken this human body', they treat Me like anybody else. Why so? *Mama param bhāvam ajānanto,* 'not knowing My higher nature'. What is that higher nature of Mine? *Bhūtamaheśvaram,* 'the supreme Lord of the entire universe'. That dimension people are not able to grasp. Therefore, they speak ill of Me, they insult Me; *avajānanti* means 'insulting'. This is why great teachers have to suffer. Jesus had to suffer, Śrī Kṛṣṇa had to suffer, Śrī Rāma had to suffer. So many accusations are there against these great personalities, great within and ordinary without; and naturally, people misunderstand. Ordinary people misunderstand, but not great sages, not spiritually inclined people. They understand the dimension of this remarkable human being in front of them. So, Śrī Kṛṣṇa says: *avajānanti mām mūḍhā,* 'foolish people deride Me', *mānuṣīm tanumāśritam,* 'when adopting the human body'. Why? *Param bhāvam ajānanto mama bhūtamaheśvaram,* 'I am that infinite reality behind all this universe; that dimension they cannot understand.'

One day, Sri Ramakrishna was walking in the rose garden in Dakshineswar. One Babu (gentleman) came and saw Sri Ramakrishna there. He took him to be the gardener. 'Will you please pluck a rose flower for me?' Sri Ramakrishna gently plucked a flower and presented it to him. After some time, Sri Ramakrishna came to his room and sat; many devotees were sitting there, and he was talking with them. The Babu entered the room because he had come to Dakshineswar to meet Sri

Ramakrishna. And he found that gardener sitting there! He was so exasperated. What did I do! But Sri Ramakrishna said: it is a great privilege to serve; you wanted a flower, I gave it to you. See the language there. So, that is how we mistake great people. They look ordinary, but they are extraordinary. I myself have come across some people, extraordinary within, but outwardly very ordinary. Therefore, we should not judge people from merely their appearance. There may be tremendously great people among them. Just like what we find in Śaṅkarācārya's life. He walked all over our vast India. How could anyone understand his greatness? Vivekananda walked through the whole of India. How few could understand his greatness! They saw in them a *sādhu* or a monk. How can we go deep into their greatness unless we are great ourselves? So, Śrī Kṛṣṇa says here: to discover an *avatāra* is extremely difficult. And, to discover even an ordinarily great person is also difficult, because we cannot measure that inner dimension. We measure the external dimension which we can really calculate. The height, length, size, appearance, all these we can study. But their mental level, we cannot study. It is good, therefore, to keep an open mind in judging other people. A poor man comes to a house for alms; he looks poor, but he may be a great poet and devotee like Purandara Dāsa of Karnataka. Purandara Dāsa was a rich man. One day, he distributed all his riches, became a poor *dāsa* or wandering minstrel, going from house to house singing his divine compositions before the people. They took him to be a beggar. Actually he was a prince. But he looked like a beggar. He knew that he had the Divine Reality within him. In this way, Śrī Kṛṣṇa speaks of the Divine Incarnation as a subject of still more difficult comprehension. It is like Jesus Christ being referred to as a carpenter's son! *Param bhāvam ajānanto mama bhūtamaheśvaram.* What kind of mentality do they of the *mūḍhā* or foolish type have?

मोघाशा मोघ कर्माणो मोघज्ञाना विचेतसः ।
राक्षसीं आसुरीं चैव प्रकृतिं मोहिनीं श्रिताः ॥१२॥

*Moghāśā mogha karmāṇo moghajñānā vicetasaḥ;*
*Rākṣasīm āsurīm caiva prakṛtim mohinīm śritāḥ* — 9. 12

'Of vain hopes, of vain works, of vain knowledge, and senseless, they verily are possessed of the delusive nature of *Rākṣasas* and *Asuras.*'

Such people have *moghāśāḥ,* 'vain hopes', all sorts of vain hopes they cultivate in their minds. Similarly, *mogha karmāṇaḥ,* 'doer of vain actions'; *moghajñānaḥ,* 'of vain knowledge'; and *vicetasaḥ,* 'senseless', without any kind of real understanding. *Rākṣasīm āsurīm caiva prakṛtim mohinīm śritāḥ,* 'they are really possessed of the delusive nature of *Rākṣasas* and *Asuras.*' Such people have no faith in higher values. If a great person like a Śaṅkarācārya goes to anybody's house, such people would think: 'he is only a beggar'.

There is a beautiful episode in Buddha's life. There is much charm and poetry in that episode. When Buddha, with a clean shaven head, was going from one village to another, once slight rains descended. He stood under the eaves of the hut of a farmer. Then a conversation between the two took place (*Daniya Sutta, Sutta Nipāta,* vv. 18–34; according to scholars, the *Sutta Nipāta* contains some of the oldest parts of the Pāli Canon):

'Cooked is my rice, milked are my kine', said Dhaniya, the herd, 'And here on Mahī's bank I dwell with them that are my peers. Thatched is my hut, well-fed the fire. Rain down, God, if Thou wilt!'

'From anger free, with every bar removed,' the Lord replied, 'A dweller here on Mahī's bank I sojourn but one night. Roofless my hut and quenched my fire. Rain down, God, if Thou wilt!'

'No gadflies here are to be seen,' said Dhaniya the herd, 'Amid the marshland grasses there my kine a-roaming go. The rain that comes they can endure. Rain down, God, if Thou wilt!'

'I made a raft to cross the stream, of logs well put together. Now have I crossed and gone beyond, by stemming on the

Flood. So now I need my rafts no more. Rain down, God, if Thou wilt!'

'My wife she is a loyal one—no wanton,' said the herd. 'Full many a day she's dwelt with me, and she is kind and dear. I hear no man speak ill of her. Rain down, God, if Thou wilt!'

'My mind is a docile one, set free,' the Lord replied. 'Full many a day I tamed it down and shaped it to my will. No evil now is found in me. Rain down, God, if Thou wilt!'

'By the labour of my hands I live,' said Dhaniya the herd. 'My children, they all dwell with me and they are stout and strong. Of them I hear no word of ill. Rain down, God, if Thou wilt!'

'I too, I am a slave to none,' the Exalted one replied, 'And by the powers I have won I roam through all the world. I have no need for service more. Rain down, God, if Thou wilt!'

'Kine have I, yea, and calves that suck,' said Dhaniya the herd, 'and cow in calf, and they shall carry on their breed for me. And a bull, the lord of all the herd. Rain down, God, if Thou wilt!'

'I have no kine, I have no calves that suck,' the Lord replied. 'I have no cows in calf to carry on the breed for me. No bull, the lord of all the herd. Rain down, God, if Thou wilt!'

'Well-set the pegs that hold my kine; shaken they cannot be. My tethers, made of *munja* grass, brand new and twisted well. No sucking calf can break 'em. So rain down, God, if Thou wilt!'

'But I, the Bull, have burst the bonds that bind,' the Lord replied. 'Have burst them as a tusker rends the twisted creeper-cords. Never again shall I be born. Rain down, God, if Thou wilt!'

Forthwith the mighty rain poured down and filled the hills and plains. When he heard the raining of the God, Dhaniya thus spoke his mind:

'No little gain is ours that we the Exalted One have seen. In Thee we take our refuge, Thou that hast the eye to see. Be

Thou our teacher, mighty sage. The good wife and myself, Docile, will live the holy life with Thee, O happy one, and passing over birth and death an end of suffering make!'

How difficult it is to understand greatness! Don't rush to make a judgement. We often do so; but we must learn to treat everyone with respect. Who knows that he, who in the form of the beggar has come to my house, may be a Buddha. He may be a Śaṅkarācārya. We don't know. That kind of respect is good so that we do not commit a blunder through misjudging another human being and showing disrespect. When these *Rākṣasī* and *Āsurī* qualities come, then we commit all these mistakes. We judge a man only in terms of money. We don't judge him in terms of his brains, in terms of his spiritual quality. How much money you have? You are poor! Okay, get out! We don't want you.

That is what king Drupada did to Droṇa as described in the *Mahābhārata* Epic. Droṇa was a classmate of Drupada. He was very poor. Drupada became a king of Pāñcāla. Droṇa said to Kṛṣṇa: 'Let us go to Drupada. He may give us some help. There is not enough in the house. I can't feed my children with a glass of milk even.' And that story is so tragic. Droṇa goes to Drupada, calls him his friend, and Drupada becomes very proud. 'What! You call me a friend! Friendship is only between equals. You are a beggar. I am a king. How can there be friendship between the two? Go away. I can't do anything for you.' He uttered the most dangerous words. This created the tragedy of the Kurukṣetra war later on. This is one of the tragic beginnings. This is how evils go on multiplying until a big conflagration takes place. That is the story in the *Mahābhārata*.

In this way, this verse says: whenever we are subject to pride, vanity, arrogance, selfishness, we are in the grip of *Āsurī sampat*. Chapter 16 will be discussing *Āsurī sampat* and *Daivī sampat*. Here in chapter 9 just a reference is made to *Āsurī sampat*. Those who have the *Āsurī sampat*, they are of this nature. Deluded they are, *prakṛtim mohinīm śritāḥ*, 'possessed of *Māyā* or *Prakṛti* which has a *mohinī* quality, deluding quality'.

Sri Ramakrishna has said: *Māyā* has two dimensions, *Avidyā Māyā* and *Vidyā Māyā*. *Avidyā Māyā* is what makes for delusion and delusive actions. *Vidyā Māyā* lifts one to higher and higher levels. One can choose between *Vidya Māyā* and *Avidyā Māyā*. A heart can become the playground of *Vidyā Māyā*. Then, *Daivī sampat* manifests; compassion, love, a spirit of service, truthfulness, all these will come. When there is *Avidyā Māyā* playing in the heart, then selfishness, pettiness, violence, hatred, exploitation, all these will operate. So, *prakṛtim mohinīm śritāḥ*, 'that is the *prakṛti, Māyā*, which is *mohinī*, which is of delusive nature'. What a wonderful idea! *Mohinī* is the form that Viṣṇu took to lure away the *Asuras* during the *samudramanthan* (churning of ocean) episode when *Amṛta* (nectar) came out. That is *mohinī*; very delusive. And therefore, in this life also, nature appears to you as a *mohinī* to delude you. Be careful about that delusion. Try to develop *Vidyā Śakti, Vidyā Māyā*, and then that delusion will not overpower you. Even if something comes to delude you, you won't be deluded. You will be free. You will be above it. That is how we win our freedom. We are free to accept the delusive *Māyā* or that elevating *Māyā*. We are all in *Māyā*. When you do evil, you are in *Māyā*. When you do good, you are in *Māyā*. When you sit in meditation, you are in *Māyā*. *Māyā* pervades everything. That is the divine *Śakti* in the two forms of *Avidyā Māyā* and *Vidyā Māyā*.

The next *śloka* explains the action of *Vidyā Māyā* or *Daivī Sampat*. How does it operate in you and in me? These are very practical ideas. They give us hints and suggestions to make our life really progressive, really pure and good, so that we can live at peace with others and within oneself. The next *śloka* deals with that positive side of life, *Vidyā Māyā, Māyā* which has no delusive power, which has the power to lift you up to higher levels. This is extremely practical and productive of great results. You want a happy family. I wish we have millions of happy homes. How can happy families come unless the members of the family are motivated by *Vidyā Māyā*? If they are motivated by *Avidyā Māyā*, there will be no peace in the family. So, this is a question which everyone must ask oneself. Every boy and girl must ask this question: Do you want your heart to be a playground of *Avidyā Māyā* or *Vidyā Māyā?* The answer must come: '*Vidyā Māyā.*' Then, struggle for it. When such persons enter into married life, they will have the happiest family life; the real joy of a householder's life one will get in that condition. That is the practical utility of this great teaching.

There is one type of people who deride Me, not knowing My higher nature, says Śrī Kṛṣṇa. They can't see through this physical form of Mine. They are the ordinary people, steeped in ignorance, with vain hopes and vain actions, etc. But there is another type of people, who are *sāttvika;* they can understand these things. The next verse, verse 13, says:

**महात्मानस्तु मां पार्थ दैवीं प्रकृतिं आश्रिताः ।**
**भजन्ति अनन्य मनसो ज्ञात्वा भूतादिं अव्ययम् ॥१३॥**

*Mahātmānastu mām pārtha daivīm prakṛtim āśritāḥ;*
*Bhajanti ananya manaso jñātvā bhūtādim avyayam—9. 13*

'But the great-souled ones, O son of Pṛthā, possessed of the Divine *Prakṛti,* knowing Me to be the origin of beings and immutable, worship Me with single-mindedness.'

*Mahātmānastu,* 'but those who are *mahātmas,* whose self is not exhausted within this body; they see the same Self in all'. They have become really great and big; so they are called *mahātmas.* They know Me as the supreme Divine Reality; how? *Daivīm prakṛtim āśritāḥ,* 'they are under the control of *Daivī sampat*', the higher *sāttvika* attitudes, which will be detailed later on in the 16th chapter as referred to earlier. When *Daivī sampat* predominates, everything is positive, everything is creative, going onward on the path of higher and higher moral and spiritual evolution. But, *tamas* and *rajas* which are called *Āsurī sampat,* when these predominate, one is absolutely worldly, petty-minded and quarrelsome. Very often one will find plenty of such people in any society. They want to pick up some quarrel, and wait for an occasion to do so. That type of people are highly controlled by *rākṣasī* and *āsurī* attitudes.

So, *mahātmānaḥ* are controlled by *daivī sampat; daivīm prakṛtim āśritāḥ.* What do they do? *Bhajanti,* 'they worship' Me; they understand My higher spiritual dimension; *ananya manaso,* 'with a one-pointed mind'; *jñātvā bhūtādim avyayam,* 'knowing Me to be *bhūtādim,* the origin of the whole universe, and, *avyayam,* imperishable'. That is My true nature. And these *mahātmas* understand that that Reality sometimes appears as a human being. Therefore, they worship Me in spirit and in truth.

In the 14th verse, Śrī Kṛṣṇa explains how they worship. When we have a *sāttvika* mind, our worship of God becomes constant; there is not a particular time for it. When we begin our spiritual life, we fix some time for going to the temple, or for sitting in prayer and meditation, etc. But when the mind becomes *sāttvika,* when we achieve that kind of purity inside, then it becomes a constant worship of the Divine. Even in the midst of work and all human relations, that worship will go on. That is being expressed in the 14th verse.

सततं कीर्तयन्तो मां यतन्तश्च दृढव्रताः ।
नमस्यन्तश्च मां भक्त्या नित्ययुक्ता उपासते ॥१४॥

*Satatam kīrtayanto mām yatantaśca dṛḍhavratāḥ;*
*Namasyantaśca mām bhaktyā nityayuktā upāsate* — 9. 14

'Glorifying Me always and striving with firm resolve, bowing down to Me in devotion, always steadfast, they worship Me.'

The *nityayuktas,* 'those who are always *yogīs*', not those half-an-hour-*yogīs,* but all through they are *yogīs. Nityayukta,* 'constantly in a spiritual mood'. How do such people 'worship Me', *upāsate*? *Satatam kīrtayanto mām,* 'constantly singing My glory', singing mentally or orally My divine glory; *yatantaśca dṛḍhavratāḥ,* 'striving with steady practice', i.e. full of effort, with the mind constantly oriented to the Divine. *Dṛḍha* means firm, *vratāḥ* means resolve; *dṛḍhavratāḥ* means 'of firm resolve'. *Namasyantaśca mām bhaktyā,* 'saluting Me with great devotion'. There may not be actual physical salutation. But the mind is in the mood of salutation all the time. There is that spirit of humility born of the understanding that the Divine is manifest in all beings. There is no pride. There is no small ego. So, that constant salutation of the Divine, not necessarily physical, but always mental. *Bhaktyā,* 'through great devotion'. *Nityayuktā upāsate,* 'that is how the *nityayuktas* worship Me'. Constant and spontaneous worship, adoration, prostration going on. They may or may not do it physically, but inwardly they are always in that mood—seeing the same Atman everywhere. So, what happens to that person? 'This state makes a person constantly salute the Divine everywhere, always feeling oneness with all.' What one practices with effort—practices like *śānta, dānta,* 'self-control, and control of the senses', etc., all such practices become natural in that state. The whole thing comes to him or her in a natural spontaneous way. There is a beautiful verse towards the end of the *Māṇḍūkya Upaniṣad Kārikā* (IV. 86). A person of spiritual realization is *naturally* pure, *naturally* humble, *naturally* concerned with others, because he or she feels oneness with all. *That concept and value of spontaneity and naturalness is expressed there.* Where do you find spontaneity in this world? You find it in children. They are spontaneous. This is the first type of spontaneity. That is why men of realization are compared to little children. There is no cleverness in them. Absolutely spontaneous, natural. When they say 'yes', it means 'yes'; when they say 'no', it means 'no'. That is childlike spontaneity. It is a very great state of mind. Sri Ramakrishna said: '*Paramahamsas* are like children of five years of age.' They are so natural, so spontaneous. There is no ego in them. That is the nature of the highest realization.

So, here, *namasyantaśca mām bhaktyā nityayuktā upāsate,* 'they salute Me with devotion constantly, all the time; they practice humility all the time'. This is the state of spiritual realization when the little 'I' vanishes forever. Something infinite, which is one with all, finds manifestation.

ज्ञानयज्ञेन चाप्यन्ये यजन्तो मां उपासते ।
एकत्वेन पृथक्त्वेन बहुधा विश्वतोमुखम् ॥१५॥

*Jñānayagñena cāpyanye yajanto mām upāsate;*
*Ekatvena pṛthaktvena bahudhā viśvatomukham — 9. 15*

'Others, too, sacrificing by the *Yajña* of knowledge (i.e. seeing the Self in all), worship Me, the All-Formed, as one, as distinct, as manifold.'

*Jñānayajñena cāpyanye yajanto mām upāsate*, 'other people worship Me through *jñānayajña*, sacrifice of knowledge.' This subject came up for discussion in the fourth chapter also. Through *jñānayajña* some devotees worship Me. How do they worship? *Ekatvena, pṛthaktvena,* 'either realizing oneness with all, or by realizing the separateness of God from human beings and becoming a servant of God.' That is the sense of *pṛthaktva.* A *bhakta* takes God as separate, and himself or herself as a devotee worshipping the Divine. That is the attitude in *bhakti. Jñāna* is the attitude, 'I am Brahman', 'I am the ultimate Reality'. Both are very high states of spiritual experience. *Bahudhā,* 'in various forms'; *viśvatomukham,* that Reality which is everywhere, 'whose face is turned everywhere'. That is the nature of the highest Reality.

One day, Sri Ramakrishna asked Narendra: 'what kind of realization do you like to have? Suppose there is honey in a bowl; do you want to get into the honey and get merged in it, or do you want to sit on the edge and drink a little?' Narendra replied, 'Of course, I want to sit on the edge and drink.' 'Why?' asked Sri Ramakrishna. Narendra said, 'If I get in, I will die!' Then Sri Ramakrishna smiled and said: 'But this is not the usual honey. This is the immortal *Saccidānanda* honey in which if you are well immersed you are not going to die! You will get fuller life. Don't fear like a worldly person.' A *bhakta* desires to enjoy that honey, to enjoy the love of God. He or she does not want to become one with God. That is the nature of *bhakti.* Therefore, in *jñāna* one will say, '*Śivo'ham*'. A *bhakta* will say, 'I am a *dāsa* or servant of Śiva, I am a child of Śiva.' He or she wants Śiva to be separate to enjoy him, to taste the love of God. 'I am *viśvatomukha*'; you can worship Me in any way. That is why there is no fixed standard. 'I am everywhere.' Every worship comes to Me. That is the Hindu conception out of which has come the spirit of tolerance and understanding in our culture for all these thousands of years.

अहं क्रतुः अहं यज्ञः स्वधाहं अहं औषधम् ।
मन्त्रोऽहं अहमेवाज्यं अहमग्निरहं हुतम् ॥१६॥

*Aham kratuḥ aham yajñaḥ svadhāham aham auṣadham;*
*Mantro'ham ahamevājyam ahamagniraham hutam* — 9. 16

'I am the *kratu,* I am the *yajña,* I am the *svadhā,* I the *auṣadha,* I am the *mantra,* I am the *ājya,* I the fire, and I the oblation.'

It is I who manifest myself as the various ingredients of worship and sacrifice. They are all one and the same reality. *Aham kratuḥ,* 'I am the sacrifice'; *kratu* is the Vedic sacrifice. *Aham yajñaḥ,* 'I am the *yajñaḥ*'; that is also another form of Vedic sacrifice. *Svadhāham,* 'I am that *mantra, svadhā*'. When you offer something you will say, *svāhā* or *svadhā;* both are *mantras* used for offering oblations. *Aham auṣadham,* 'I am also *auṣadha,* medicine'. Then, *mantro'ham,* 'I am the *mantra,* which you recite'. *Aham eva ājyam,* 'I am also the ghee that is poured into the fire'. That is called *ājyam. Aham agniḥ,* 'the fire into which one pours the ghee, that also is Myself'. *Aham hutam,* 'I am the oblation'. The act of oblation also is Myself. This idea had come in verse 24 of the 4th chapter:

*Brahmārpaṇam brahma havirbrahmāgnau brahmaṇā hutam;*
*Brahmaiva tena gantavyam brahmakarmasamādhinā* —

What a beautiful idea! How true it is! 'The offering is Brahman; the one who offers is Brahman; the fire is Brahman; the result is Brahman'; everything is Brahman. That is the truth, but we do see differences, and so, we observe these differences. But the truth is they are all essentially one infinite pure Consciousness appearing in these various forms.

Let us take the example of solar radiation. 'The Sun Is our Mother' was an article that appeared in the American *National Geographic* magazine some years ago. There you will find this statement: the sun is our mother. We eat the sun in our food; we wear the sun in our cloth; we burn the sun in our coal; we digest our food through the sun in the stomach as digestive energy. Everything is sun. Life and light are intertwined, says that article. Life and light, i.e. radiation, they are intertwined. All these, whatever you see in the solar system, are only various condensations of that solar radiation. You go still further; the infinite Atman or Brahman alone exists in all these various forms. That is the message conveyed by this sixteenth verse. I am all these; Brahman alone is all these. *Sarvam khalu idam brahma,* 'certainly, everything that is in this manifested Universe, is Brahman'. *Vāsudeva sarvam iti,* 'everything in this world is Vāsudeva'. That is the Advaitic vision. Everything has come from the One. Therefore, it is all that One. The cause is in the effect. So, you can say, whatever you see in the effect is nothing but the cause. There is nothing new in this universe. You can find in this universe nothing other than that primordial stuff out of which the universe, according to modern cosmology, evolved. And we have conservation laws: conservation of energy. The same energy, the totality of it, exists. Nothing is added to it, nothing is taken out of it. But, it is manipulated in different ways. So, this is the idea of absolute unity: 'from the One the universe has come; unto the One the universe will return.' This is the truth upheld in Vedanta long ago, and in essence, by modern science in our time. This is the Advaitic vision. We see our oneness with everything. We feel our oneness with nature also. If we treat it as separate, we try to exploit it, we try to destroy it. But when we know we are all essentially one, we know how to treat nature in a beneficent way. That is what is lacking in today's civilization. In older civilizations we had this concept: our intimate relationship with nature. And we are now trying to gain that understanding once again, in modern Western culture. Śrī Kṛṣṇa says further:

पिताहं अस्य जगतो माता धाता पितामहः ।
वेद्यं पवित्रं ओङ्कार ऋक् साम यजुरेव च ॥१७॥

*Pitāham asya jagato mātā dhātā pitāmahaḥ;*
*Vedyam pavitram omkāra ṛk sāma yajureva ca —* 9. 17

'I am the Father of this world—the Mother, the Sustainer, the Grandfather, the (one) thing to be known, the Purifier, (the syllable) *Om*, and also the *Ṛk, Sāman,* and *Yajus*.'

I am all these: first, *pitā aham asya jagato,* 'I am the Father of this universe'. This Fatherhood of God you can see in Judaism, Christianity and also in Islam. *Mātā,* 'I am also the Mother of the universe'. God as the Mother, *Mātā,* that you will find only in Indian religion, and in primitive religions. *Dhātā* is 'the one who sustains'. Then, *pitāmahaḥ,* 'Grandfather'. *Vedyam pavitram omkāra,* 'I am the one truth to be known, the Purifier, and I am the Om'. If you try to know anything in this world, that knowledge will eventually take you to that supreme Divine. Trace all these various entities in the universe to the root, and you will see God or Brahman there. So, *vedyam,* 'the greatest truth to be known' is the Origin and Sustenance of the universe. *Pavitram,* 'supremely pure', holy, sacred. *Omkāraḥ,* 'the syllable *Om*'. This *pavitram,* pure, is a beautiful concept for today's civilization, because everything that is *pavitram* has been eliminated from it. There is nothing *pavitram* today; nothing holy, nothing towards which we have to show reverence. Everything is matter of fact. That is the great weakness of modern civilization. Say, when you respect your mother you associate your mother with something special, a certain sentiment, something holy. And in today's civilization it is not there, especially, even in the language used: 'she is a good guy'. No sentiment. So, whatever is sacred has gone away. Even in married life, there is nothing sacred. Everything is just worldly. So, this kind of erosion of all sacredness from life has made life very very prosaic and of a low level. Here the importance of the word 'sacred' comes. There is one focus of sacredness in everything in this universe. Never eliminate it, never try to forget it. If neglected, the culture will become very poor. So, *pavitram omkāraḥ,* 'the supremely sacred syllable *Om*'. *Ṛg sāma yajureva ca,* 'and I am the three Vedas, *Ṛg Veda, Sāma Veda* and *Yajur Veda*'. Originally, we had three Vedas: *Ṛg, Sāma* and *Yajur.* A little later came the fourth Veda, *Atharva Veda.* Then it became four Vedas. All this happened in very ancient times.

गतिः भर्ता प्रभुः साक्षी निवासः शरणं सुहृत् ।
प्रभवः प्रलयः स्थानं निधानं बीजं अव्ययम् ॥१८॥

*Gatiḥ bhartā prabhuḥ sākṣī nivāsaḥ śaraṇam suhṛt;*
*Prabhavaḥ pralayaḥ sthānam nidhānam bījam avyayam*—9. 18

'The Goal, the Supporter, the Lord, the Witness, the Abode, the Refuge, the Friend, the Origin, the Dissolution, the Substratum, the Storehouse, the Seed immutable.'

Now the Supreme Divinity is described in many ways in this verse. *Gatiḥ,* 'the Goal'; the whole universe has That as the *gatiḥ* or goal. *Bhartā,* 'the Supporter'; *bhartṛ* means to protect, to cherish, to support; so *bhartā* means Supporter. *Prabhuḥ,* 'the Lord', Master. *Sākṣi,* 'the Witness'. What is the sun? He is the witness of the solar system. He can see everything happening in the solar system. He is called *jagatsākṣi,* 'witness of the world'. God is called the Witness of the whole universe. Sun is a witness of the solar system and we are also, as the Self, the witness of our little activities here. We call it *buddhisākṣi,* 'witness of the intellect'. The Atman in us watches the activities of the *buddhi.* That is called *sākṣi. Sākṣi* is a wonderful concept in our Vedanta philosophy. In fact, whenever you develop the capacity for objective judgement, you are a *sākṣi.* An event is taking place. If you are carried away by attachment, your judgement will be wrong. If your mind is free from attachment, you will be able to see things as they are. That capacity comes from being a *sākṣi* of our own nature. See things as they are. Don't colour it with attachment or aversion. So, this Self in us has the capacity to become a *sākṣi* of our activities within this body itself. And all impartial judgements, all such objective valuations come from the point of view of *sākṣi.* Ego cannot do so. Ego is highly motivated and is under the control of the genetic system. So, *sākṣi* is a beautiful concept in our Vedantic psychology as well as philosophy. Develop a *sākṣi-bhāva* or witness attitude. That means you are able to view things dispassionately. *Sākṣi*-consciousness is a wonderful idea. You can see your own mind, your own attachments and aversions, your own foolishness, everything from behind, whereas the ego cannot see all this. Ego can see the fault of others; not one's own. Only when the ego develops the *sākṣi* awareness, then you are able to find even your own faults. So, a little *sākṣi* awareness makes for a higher type of life, a higher type of consciousness. That is how the concept of *sākṣi* comes in. And God is considered to be *buddhisākṣi,* the *sākṣi* of all *buddhis* in this world. That is a beautiful conception. There is one who is the *sākṣi* of all these: your mind, my mind, and all these other minds. That is the Divine Being. So, one aspect of the divine is as *sākṣi.* And one aspect of man is also as *sākṣi. Nivāsaḥ,* 'the Abode', our abode is God himself. *Śaraṇam,* 'the final Destination', where we can take our refuge. And then, *suhṛt,* 'real Friend'. He is the only friend we have. The divine is the only friend we have. *Suhṛt* is the word used to mean 'constant friend'. How intimate God becomes when you consider him as *suhṛt* or friend! In the fifth chapter, the second line of the last verse referred to this:

*Bhoktāram yajñatapasām sarvalokamaheśvaram;*
*Suhṛdam sarvabhūtānām jñātvā mām śāntimṛcchati —*

Then, *prabhavaḥ pralayaḥ sthānam,* 'I am the place of Origin and the place of Dissolution of the whole universe'. From Me the universe comes, that is *prabhavaḥ;* into Me the universe merges later, that is, *pralayaḥ sthānam. Nidhānam bījam avyayam; nidhānam,* 'the Storehouse'; *avyayam bījam,* 'the immutable seed' of the universe. A normal seed cannot be immutable. They are all mutable. Seed decays when the plant comes out. That is why a seed is called mutable. But, here is a Seed which is 'immutable', *avyayam.* This is the verse which is highly commented upon by saints in India. Sri Ramakrishna's disciples like Swami Turiyananda used to very much appreciate this verse.

This Divine Reality is what you find operating in this universe. How?

तपाम्यहमहं वर्षं निगृह्णाम्युत्सृजामि च ।
अमृतं चैव मृत्युश्च सदसच्चाहमर्जुन ॥१९॥

*Tapāmyahamaham varṣam nigṛhṇāmyutsṛjāmi ca;*
*Amṛtam caiva mṛtyuśca sadasaccāhamarjuna* — 9 .19

'(As sun) I give heat; I withhold and send forth rain; I am immortality and also death; being and non-being am I, O Arjuna!'

Arjuna, I am all these: What are they? *Tapāmi aham,* 'I send out heat'. Solar heat comes from Me. Also, *varṣam,* 'rain'. By proper manipulation in the sky, it begins to rain. *Nigṛhṇāmi utsṛjāmi ca,* 'I give forth heat and rain, I can also withdraw them'. When the season is over all these are withdrawn. When the season is bright, they come out once again. So, going out and taking back, both are from Me. *Amṛtam caiva mṛtyuśca,* 'I am immortality as well as death'. That supreme Reality is both immortality and death. Death is not something else. The same Reality is both immortality as well as death. This is also from the *Ṛg Veda samhita* (X. viii. 121): *Yasya chāyā amṛtam yasya mṛtyuḥ,* 'whose shadow is death as well as immortality'. That is the *Ṛg Vedic* verse. So, we don't have two realities: one for life and another for death. *There is no devil in the whole of Hindu tradition.* This is all one only. That is a wonderful idea. 'All evil belongs to the devil, all good belongs to God'; we have no such conceptions. Evil and good are only relative terms. The same thing is evil, and the same thing can be good also. Nothing is all evil; nothing is all good. Today what is evil can be good tomorrow. Just like poison in a snake; it is evil. But for the snake itself, it is not evil. It is part of its nature. It isn't dying from its own poison! And we take that poison and inject it to stop bleeding. Therefore, it is no more evil. So, there are any number of occasions where what you treat as evil becomes good. What you treat as good becomes evil. Therefore, there is a relativity: the same thing appears as good in one context and as evil in another context. We never had that duality of good and evil in our tradition. In normal life, we make distinction: this is evil, this is good. Perfectly right. If we see a snake, and if someone says, 'it is all good to catch it', we don't do so. We stand at a distance because the snake is capable of doing some evil to us. But the truth is, what is evil is also good. Today or tomorrow, they exchange places. This understanding must come as a background. Then handle the world in a particular way. Therefore, Sri Ramakrishna said: 'the divine is in all beings, also in the tiger. That doesn't mean you go and embrace the tiger, because that tiger, in this particular context, can become an evil to you and may also destroy you. But the truth is, the same divine spark is there in the tiger also. So, from a distance you worship the tiger. Another tiger, a small cub, you can take it on your lap, and also play with it. It doesn't harm you. Water is divine; but some water is meant for washing feet, some meant only for bathing and drinking. All water is not good for every usage.' So, these differences are there, behind which there is the unity also. That is what our sages discovered: unity behind the diversities of nature. *Sat asat ca aham arjuna,* 'I am both *sat* and *asat,* O Arjuna'. *Sat* means 'being', *asat* means 'non-being'. I am both. *Sat* also means 'effect', *asat* means 'cause'. In different contexts, these meanings change. What you see is an effect. That is *sat.* And what you cannot see behind this effect is the cause, the *asat;* that you do not see. So we call it *asat* in one context. In the other context, that which is, and that which is not. *Sat* means 'being'; *asat* means 'non-being'. I am both. That is the language, because everything is one. Absolute unity behind this world of multiplicity.

Then, the *Gītā* says: those who worship various gods with a view to going to heaven, they are very ordinary type of devotees:

त्रैविद्या मां सोमपाः पूतपापा
यज्ञैः इष्ट्वा स्वर्गतिं प्रार्थयन्ते ।
ते पुण्यं आसाद्य सुरेन्द्रलोकं
अश्नन्ति दिव्यान् दिवि देवभोगान् ॥२०॥

*Traividyā mām somapāḥ pūtapāpā*
*yajñaiḥ iṣṭvā svargatim prārthayante;*
*Te puṇyam āsādya surendralokam*
*aśnanti divyān divi devabhogān —* 9. 20

'The knowers of the three Vedas, worshipping Me by *yajña,* drinking the *soma,* and (thus) being purified from sin, pray for passage to heaven; reaching the holy world of the Lord of the *devas,* they enjoy in heaven the divine pleasures of the *devas.*'

People, who sacrifice to gods with a view to going to heaven, enjoy the pleasures there for a limited period. A limited cause cannot create an unlimited effect. A limited cause will create a limited effect. So, you may go to heaven, enjoy all the pleasures there, but, later on, you will have to return. The next *śloka* says:

ते तं भुक्त्वा स्वर्गलोकं विशालं
क्षीणे पुण्ये मर्त्यलोकं विशन्ति ।
एवं त्रयीधर्मं अनुप्रपन्ना
गतागतं कामकामा लभन्ते ॥ २१ ॥

*Te tam bhuktvā svargalokam viśālam*
*kṣīṇe puṇye martyalokam viśanti;*
*Evam trayīdharmam anuprapannā*
*gatāgatam kāmakāmā labhante —* 9. 21

'Having enjoyed the vast *svarga*-world, or heaven, they enter the mortal world, on the exhaustion of their merit; thus, abiding by the injunctions of the three (Vedas), desiring desires, they (constantly) go and return.'

*Te tam bhuktvā svargalokam viśālam,* 'there, they, having enjoyed the extensive *svargaloka*'; *viśālam,* 'extensive'; *kṣīṇe puṇye,* 'when all the *puṇya* or merit is exhausted', your capital is exhausted; *martyalokam viśanti,* you have to 'come back again to the same earthly life', taking a new body, struggling again. This is the nature of human life at the level of spiritual ignorance, not knowing the truth. *Evam trayīdharmam anuprapannā,* 'thus those who follow the *dharma* taught in the three Vedas', i.e. the *karma-kāṇḍa* or the ritualistic portion of the Vedas. Such people go on offering sacrifices to this or that god with the attitude only to build up *puṇya* and go to heaven. Śrī Kṛṣṇa has already referred to this in the second chapter, that such people can never get that steadiness of mind which is the fruit of the highest spiritual realization. *Kṣīṇe puṇye,* 'when the *puṇya* is exhausted': *puṇya* is a finite quantity; how many good things can you do? How many sacrifices can you perform to build up a little capital of *puṇyam*? Yes, go there and enjoy. Then, when it is over, you cannot continue there; *martyalokam viśanti,* 'they come back to this *martyaloka* or mortal world'. *Evam trayīdharmam anuprapannā,* 'those who thus follow the *dharma* of the three Vedas'; *trayī, tri,* means 'three' Vedas: *Ṛg Veda, Yajur Veda, Sāma Veda,* these three. Those who depend upon these three Vedas and sacrifices mentioned therein, what happens to them? *Gatāgatam,* 'they keep going and returning all the time', but why? *Kāmakāmā,* because they are 'full of sensory desires', desires after desires: I must enjoy this, I must enjoy that; that is *kāmakāmā. Gatāgatam labhante,* 'constantly they will go and return'. This is not a very happy state of life, say the Upaniṣads. In the Upaniṣads, therefore, they developed *jñāna-kāṇḍa,* 'knowledge portion' dealing with how to understand the truth?, where is that heaven?, and all that. In *you* is the infinite heaven. This infinite you reject, and you desire to go here and there for a little pleasure; that is not correct. So, heaven became very very much reduced in value in the Upaniṣads; and the *Gītā* also has done so. Make a heaven here by realizing your immortal Atman. And all the *Purāṇas* also said the same thing. The development of *jñāna* and *bhakti* teachings in later times, reduced the importance of this heaven-going-business. You can have it here, be a devotee of the Divine, worship Him, serve people in that spirit, and here itself you can create a heaven. And so, in the *Viṣṇu Purāṇa* and the *Śrīmad Bhāgavata Purāṇa,* there is mention of the reverse process: Gods in heavens are eager to be born in India as citizens of this country, Bharata, a very holy land. So, in one conference of gods in heaven, they passed one resolution: when we end our life in this heaven, along with the exhaustion of the *puṇya* that has brought us here, with whatever little *puṇyam* remains, let us get birth in this holy land of India. Gods are eager to be born in India, this *puṇya-bhūmi.* This came through the philosophy of *bhakti* and *jñāna.* These great *jñānis* and *bhaktas*, they make this land holy and pure, and so we call it *puṇyabhūmi*. Bharata is a *puṇyabhūmi*. So many sages, so many holy people, have lived here. Every particle of dust is holy here. That interjection developed through the *Purāṇas*. So, the opposite is there. Gods are eager to be born as citizens of India, and some of our people are eager to go to heaven, not knowing that this is better than that! *Gatāgatam kāmakāmā labhante*, 'they get this constant ding dong march up and down because they are full of sensory desires'. This is how the Vedas, towards the end, in the Upaniṣads, very much reduce the value of heaven-going. 'Here itself', *ihaiva, ihaiva*, in this very body, in this very world, you can realize the highest. Why go here and there? Heaven is within you, 'the kingdom of God is within you', said Jesus. The infinite and immortal Atman is your true nature. Try to manifest it. See the same Atman in every being. Make a heaven of your own country. That is what we were taught by the *bhakti* and *jñāna* traditions of India, and that continues even today. The idea of going to heaven has become so little, though some sections of people may still be holding on to that idea. So, Sri Ramakrishna in our time, said: *'there, there' is ignorance; 'here, here' is knowledge*. In Bengali: *'Śekhāne, śekhāne, ajñān; Ekhāne, ekhāne, jñān.'* *Śekhāne* means 'there'; *ekhāne* means 'here'. Śrī Kṛṣṇa said in the second chapter, *vedavādaratāḥ pārtha nānyadastīti vādinaḥ*, 'those who remain engrossed in the (ritualistic) utterances of the Vedas and declare that nothing else exists', and *bhogaiśvaryaprasaktānām*, 'those whose minds delight in sensory enjoyment and affluence', for such people, *vyavasāyātmikā buddhiḥ samādhau na vidhīyate*, 'they will never get that steady mind, steady intellect, by being established in *samādhi*, in the infinite Atman'. And the Upaniṣads also speak very disparagingly of this running after heaven. The *Muṇḍaka Upaniṣad* says: 'fools only think so'; that is the language used there. Realize the truth here itself, *ihaiva tairjitaḥ sargo*, *Gītā* said: 'here itself they have conquered relativity, finitude', realizing the same Atman in every being. So, this *jñāna* and this *bhakti* are two profound teachings that came later influencing all our religions in India.

And now it has got a tremendous strength through Sri Ramakrishna and Swami Vivekananda. Here itself make a heaven. Sri Ramakrishna came to establish *Satya yuga* in this world. That is the language. A revolutionary Bengali Muslim poet, late Kazi Nazrul Islam of Bengal, composed two songs on Sri Ramakrishna and Swami Vivekananda. In the song on Sri Ramakrishna he mentions *Satya yuger puṇya smṛti kalite ānile tumi tāpas*, 'Hey *Tapas*! You brought the memory of *Satya yuga* in this *Kali yuga*.' What a beautiful expression! And about Swami Vivekananda he wrote: *Bhārate ānile tumi nava Ved, mūcchidile jāti dharmer bhed*, 'you brought to Bharata a new Veda and wiped away the differences based on castes and religions.' So, great teachers come, purify this earth, and they give us a message so that we can make a heaven here itself by our character transformation. Through developing *bhakti* and *jñāna* we can develop heaven here itself. That is the goal which Vivekananda has placed before all of us in the modern period. Everything is here, here, here. The highest reality is here. Why go far away? This is how the Upaniṣads gave us the profound message of the greatness and uniqueness of the human being. Human beings are greater than gods, greater than angels. In Islam also there is the story: when God created man, he asked all the angels to go and salute him. One angel did not salute. God cursed him and he became the devil. So, the human being's greatness is emphasized thereby. The very fact that God incarnates in a human frame, also raises the human being to a high pedestal. What a divine personality is a Ramakrishna, a Jesus, a Buddha. But, they are human beings like us and yet something wonderful. So, from now onwards the stress will be on how to make life in this world pure, holy, and oriented towards the divine, towards establishing happy inter-human relationships. That is the purpose of the *Gītā;* intense practicality of pure religion. Inter-human relationship becomes happy because one sees the spark of the divine everywhere. Love alone can come from the heart then. If all people can love each other, and if high character comes, then the world becomes a heaven. What else is heaven? This is heaven. The other is only a mere pleasure garden, with more and more of pleasure; that is all. There is no development there. In fact, it is emphasized that one does not acquire new *karma* in heaven. Only whatever *karma* you have done, whatever *puṇyam* you have acquired, that only you can enjoy; you cannot accumulate further *puṇyam* there. So, the earth is called *karmabhūmi;* heaven is called *bhogabhūmi.* That is why Śri Kṛṣṇa said: *gatāgatam kāmakāmā labhante,* 'people full of sensory desires, will experience repeated going and coming'. This is a profound observation of ancient Hindu thought and modern American experience.

In the post World War period, the American Hoover Committee's Report upon recent economic trends in the U.S. contains the following significant confession:

'The survey has proved conclusively what has long been felt theoretically to be true that desires are almost insatiable, that one desire makes way for another. The conclusion is that economically we have a boundless field before us; that there are no new desires which will not make way for newer desires as soon as they are satisfied.'

A human being becomes an utter slave of things. That is called *samsāra.* That is what is very much present in society today. That has to change. Where is our freedom then? We are being taken like a horse or a bull with a nose ring to various places. What is that due to? That is called unrestrained sensory desire for sense objects. That is how modern Western thinking is slowly trying to grasp this glory of the human being, who has something within, attaining which makes one fulfilled, makes one realize one's nature as the Atman, as *sat*, *cit*, and *ānanda,* 'Existence, Consciousness, and Bliss'. When you realize the Atman, or get on the road to realize it, these things become utterly childish.

One of the *ślokas* composed by Swami Vivekananda and which devotees recite during Sri Ramakrishna's *ārati* or the evening service has the line: *sampada tava śrīpada bhava goṣpada vāri yathāy;* this is one of the most profound utterances just like the Upaniṣadic utterances. *Sampada tava śrīpada,* 'when we get the treasure of your holy feet', then what happens to us? *Bhava,* 'the whole *samsāra*', *goṣpada vāri yathāy,* 'becomes like a mud puddle' in value. When you get a place at the feet of the Lord, all the attractions of the world, will be as insignificant as a mud puddle. When a cow passes by a muddy road, the hoof makes a mark on the ground. In that mark you find collected a little water. That is called *goṣpadavāri.* So, Vedanta says, *brahmāṇḍam goṣpadāyate,* 'the whole *Brahmāṇḍa* or universe becomes like a *goṣpada.*' That is the Vedantic teaching. And you can actually see it in the life of people. They have realized the highest, and these things never attract them. These are nothing; they have achieved something very great. How can you compare it with all these things? Like that Christian saint whose rich magistrate friend told another friend of the saint that when he dies he would donate all his money to that Christian saint. Hearing this the friend went and told the saint what the magistrate friend had told him. The saint answered: 'Does he not know that I have already died before he will die!' That is the language. *Brahmāṇḍam goṣpadāyate.* What a wonderful vision it is! How big you become when you are able to say that! These pleasures, power, name, fame are nothing. But at the beginning, we cannot do so. We are after these; no harm. Begin from where you are. But remember, there is that state also. When that is recognized, one can treat these like straw. That is the Vedantic teaching. It doesn't say, do not run after power, pleasure, etc. No. Run after these, but keep your eyes open. A time will come when you will know these are nothing. Something higher will attract you. At that time be ready to respond. Live in the world, but don't get immersed in worldliness. That is the Vedantic warning to every human being.

A reassessment of the whole ritualistic religion took place in the Upaniṣads and there they found that this ritualism and seeking to go to heaven are childish. They took to *jñāna,* the knowledge of the infinite Atman, the divine spark in every one of us, which is the birthright of every one. That is one stream of spiritual development; and very soon came the other stream, *bhakti,* pure love of God—God, the most beautiful person, the divine Person, who is full of auspicious qualities, *ananta-kalyāṇa-guṇa-sampannaḥ,* as Śri Rāmānujācārya has expressed it. Love of that Divine is love of the same infinite Brahman, but in its *saguṇa* or personal aspect. And therefore, *bhakti* became centred in the *saguṇa* aspect of the *saguṇa-nirguṇa* Reality. So, both these strands of spiritual development, *jñāna* and *bhakti,* helped to devalue not only the heaven concept but even the importance of too many rituals. This *bhakti* religion liberalised the whole concept of spiritual life, opening the door to salvation to everyone.

Such is the evaluation of this heaven-going concept and practice by the philosophy of the Upaniṣads and the *Gītā*. Therefore, the next verse, verse 22, considered to be a very remarkable verse in the *Bhagavad Gītā*, says that *the highest type of bhakti can be had here and now, in this very life*. A devotee begins with a good deal of self, ego, and yet he is a devotee. But, as he advances in spiritual life, the ego becomes thinner and thinner. Ultimately, the ego vanishes. 'Not I, but thou.' 'Thy will be done', as the New Testament puts it. That is the last stage of a devotee's life. Everything is the Lord's. I am nothing. The ego has vanished and the Lord fills the heart of such a devotee. At that stage something great happens to the devotee. We work for ourselves, we earn money, we look after our own interests, we take care of our bank accounts, we have to do all these and many more, because we have still the sense of ego. But a time will come when this genetically-controlled ego will vanish and the heart will be filled with the Divine. Then the Lord does everything for you. You have nothing to do for yourself. But that is a very high state of spiritual realization. The world's mystics—Hindu, Christian, Muslim—all have shown that high development in some people or the other. But very few can reach that highest level. That level is being expounded in verse 22:

अनन्याश्चिन्तयन्तो मां ये जनाः पर्युपासते ।
तेषां नित्याभियुक्तानां योगक्षेमं वहाम्यहम् ॥२२॥

*Ananyāścintayanto mām ye janāḥ paryupāsate;*
*Teṣām nityābhiyuktānām yogakṣemam vahāmyaham* — 9. 22

'Persons who, meditating on Me as non-separate, worship Me through everything they do, to them, who are thus ever zealously established in *yoga*, I provide what they lack and preserve what they already have.'

A very rare statement! A similar statement you get in the *Śānti Parva* of the *Mahābhārata* also from Bhīṣma. Here Śrī Kṛṣṇa says: *ananyāścintayanto mām,* 'those who think of Me and nothing else'; that means, exclusively, one-pointedly devoted to the Divine, that type of people. They are *ananyāḥ; anya* means 'another', somebody else; *ananyāḥ,* 'there is nobody else'. 'The Lord alone is my everything'—such people. *Ye janāḥ paryupāsate,* 'those who worship Me with that attitude', with that one-pointed mind; *teṣām,* 'to them'; *nityābhiyuktānām,* 'who are *nitya abhiyuktāḥ,* constantly in a spirit of *yoga*'; the Lord alone is, my self has gone away; only the Lord is present within me. *Yogakṣemam vahāmyaham,* 'I protect what they have and I supply what they need,' I look after their needs, their wants, etc. I do this for them. The Lord becomes the servant of the devotee. Devotee has nothing to worry about.

This is the state of the highest type of *bhakti.* There have been, as I said, *bhaktas,* devotees, in every religion, who had risen to this high level of complete self-surrender. In the end of the *Gītā,* in the eighteenth chapter, this will be the supreme closing song: complete surrender to the divine. At present it refers only to a few people. But it will be everybody's possibility when we become sufficiently mature in spiritual life. So, the sixty sixth verse of the last chapter of the *Gītā*—we call it *carama śloka,* 'the final message'—refers to this idea of complete self-surrender. Sri Ramakrishna used to say, when a five year old child is invited for dinner, it has not to worry at all; he or she is taken care of, given a particular seat, given food, and he or she is fed. He or she has nothing to do by oneself. Similarly, when you become a spiritual child, where the ego has completely disappeared, the Lord Himself does what is good for you, protects what is with you already. That is this great *śloka.* Many Indian saints have commented upon this particular verse. *Yogakṣemam vahāmyaham,* 'I carry *yogakṣema* to such people'. *Yogakṣema* are two meaningful words: *yoga* means, 'to get what you need and have not got'; and *kṣema,* 'to protect what you have'. So, *yogakṣema* is a wonderful word in Sanskrit. 'I look after the *yogakṣema* of such people.' The Lord becomes the servant of the devotee. The Lord has said this at several places. I am the servant of nobody, but I am the servant of the devotee. That is the statement of Lord Viṣṇu and Śrī Kṛṣṇa also. So, this is a great idea.

We have, in modern times, only one instance where this truth becomes very very prominently manifested. That is in Swami Vivekananda's life. Those who have read his biography by the Eastern and Western disciples will have come across this: He was travelling in the desert of Rajasthan area, with the hot sun scorching above, without a pie in his pocket, a wandering monk whom somebody had put in a first class compartment. He had nothing else with him and he became thirsty and hungry. When the train halted, he got down. There was also somebody else travelling in the same compartment—a rich man. He made fun of Vivekananda: 'you did not care to earn money and therefore you suffer'. When Swamiji got down, the rich man also got down and sat on a bench in the railway platform which was a covered area. Swamiji could not sit there because he was very ordinarily dressed. So, he sat outside under a tree, hungry. Then took place a wonderful event. From a distance, a man came onto the platform. Pointing to Swamiji with the finger, he said: 'Babaji, babaji, I have brought food for you.' He came closer and closer. Then Swamiji thought that he had made a mistake. So, he told him: 'I don't know you. You must have made a mistake. You must have meant to meet somebody else.' 'No, no, no', replied the man, 'I mean you. I am a sweetmeat seller here. I am a devotee of Śrī Rāma. I was taking my afternoon rest after my worship and lunch. Śrī Rāma came to me in a dream and said, "My devotee is in distress. You go and serve him." First, I slept without caring. I didn't listen to that dream instruction. But again I was pushed. "Go soon, go soon." Then I immediately got up, prepared sweets and *luchis* and all that, took water, and then came to the platform. And from a distance I could identify you. You have been shown to me in the dream. So, please take these.' Swami Vivekananda was touched by this experience and, with tears in his eyes, he took the food and blessed him. Swamiji himself narrated this story later on.

येऽपि अन्यदेवता भक्ता यजन्ते श्रद्धयाऽन्विताः ।
तेऽपि मामेव कौन्तेय यजन्ति अविधिपूर्वकम् ॥२३॥

*Ye'pi anyadevatā bhaktā yajante śraddhayānvitāḥ;*
*Te'pi māmeva kaunteya yajanti avidhipūrvakam* —9. 23

'Even those devotees, who endued with *śraddhā*, worship other gods, they too worship Me alone, O son of Kuntī, (but) by the wrong method.'

*Ye'pi anyadevatā bhaktā yajante śraddhayānvitāḥ*, if there are some 'people who worship with faith other gods and goddesses', so many divinities which we have; *te'pi māmeva kaunteya yajanti avidhipūrvakam*, 'even they are actually worshipping Me, but not in the correct form, not in the proper way'. *Avidhipūrvakam,* 'not according to *vidhi.*' *Anyadevatā bhaktā yajante śraddhayānvitāḥ,* that faith is there but they do not know that there is only One infinite Divine, they don't know that truth, so 'they worship individual deities here and there'. But all that worship eventually comes to Me only. But they are doing it not understanding the truth.

अहं हि सर्वयज्ञानां भोक्ता च प्रभुरेव च ।
न तु मां अभिजानन्ति तत्त्वेन अतश्च्यवन्ति ते ॥२४॥

*Aham hi sarvayajñānām bhoktā ca prabhureva ca;*
*Na tu mām abhijānanti tattvena ataścyavanti te* — 9. 24

'For, I alone am the Enjoyer, and Lord of all *yajñas;* but, because they do not know Me in reality, they return (to the mortal world).'

*Aham hi sarvayajñānām bhoktā ca prabhureva ca,* 'I am the one enjoyer and master of all worship, of all ritual, of all sacrifice and worship.' I am the centre of all this. There is only one infinite Divine to which all this worship will go. Some do not know that truth. Therefore, they are carried away by a deity here or a deity there. *Na tu mām abhijānanti,* 'this truth', that there is the One Divine, Myself, behind all these deities and divinities, etc., 'these people do not know'; *tattvena ataḥ cyavanti te,* and 'therefore, they fall down from the *tattva.*' What is the *tattva?* There is only one infinite Divine behind all these various divinities. Over four thousand years ago, the *Ṛg Veda* had proclaimed this Truth: *Ekam sat, viprā bahudhā vadanti,* 'Truth is one; sages call it by various names.' That they forgot, and invented hundreds of gods and goddesses, and ran after this god or that god. And therefore, Śrī Kṛṣṇa said in the previous verse: *avidhipūrvakam,* 'they are doing that kind of worship not according to *vidhi* or teaching of the Vedas. Even if I worship a particular divinity, I must have the conviction that this is only an expression of that supremely Divine Person.

यान्ति देवव्रता देवान् पितॄन्यान्ति पितृव्रताः ।
भूतानि यान्ति भूतेज्या यान्ति मद्याजिनोऽपि माम् ॥ २५ ॥

*Yānti devavratā devān pitṝnyānti pitṛvratāḥ;*
*Bhūtāni yānti bhūtejyā yānti madyājino'pi mām* —9. 25

'Votaries of the *devas* go to the *devas;* to the *Pitṛs* go their votaries; to the *bhūtas* go the *bhūta* worshippers; and, My votaries too come unto Me.'

*Yānti devavratāḥ devān,* 'those who are devoted to the *devas,* they go to the *devas.*' Similarly, *pitṝn yānti pitṛvratāḥ,* 'people who are devoted to ancestors, to spirits, they go to them.' Similarly, *bhūtāni yānti bhūtejyāḥ,* 'those who worship the various *bhūtagaṇas,* they will go to those *bhūtagaṇas.*' And many others you find in Saṅkarācārya's commentary. Their worshippers go to them. *Yānti mat yājinaḥ api mām,* 'but those who worship Me, come unto Me.' The one infinite Self in all beings is speaking, 'those who worship Me, they come unto Me.' Whatever *śraddhā* we have in whatever form of the divine, we will get it. But, the result will be poorer and poorer. If you concentrate on the highest, then naturally, the result will also be the highest. Worship of that one Divine, the Infinite, the Immortal Divine Personality, is simple. Worship of gods and other powers is extremely complicated, costly and difficult to perform. But, in many cases you will find, where there is pure *bhakti,* you don't have to spend much money for worship. But, to please these gods and goddesses, you need lot of money, lots of priests are needed. So, Śrī Kṛṣṇa says that the worship of this Divine Reality, the Divine Person, who is in the heart of all, is extremely simple; nothing can be simpler than that. That is the theme of the next verse.

पत्रं पुष्पं फलं तोयं यो मे भक्त्या प्रयच्छति ।
तदहं भक्ति उपहृतं अश्नामि प्रयतात्मनः ॥ २६ ॥

*Patram puṣpam phalam toyam yo me bhaktyā prayacchati;*
*Tadaham bhakti upahṛtam aśnāmi prayatātmanaḥ* —9. 26

'Whoever with devotion offers Me a leaf, a flower, a fruit, or water, that I accept—the devout gift of the pure-minded.'

The difference between little divine powers here and there and the one infinite Divine is this: the latter one is full of love; the other ones may sometimes love, and at other times they may be motivated by dislike also. You may displease a particular divinity, and therefore, you get contrary result. Your mind also begins to worry you. Have I done correctly? But in the case of this one Divine, who is all love, there is no question of contrary result. He is all love. So, Śri Kṛṣṇa puts it in a verse which is so often recited all over India. *Patram,* while worshipping just give a *tulasi* 'leaf'; *puṣpam,* just 'a flower'; *phalam,* a small 'fruit'; *toyam,* a glass of 'water'; *bhaktyā prayacchati,* 'those who give Me any one of these with devotion'; I see that devotion only. I don't see the quantity of offering. This offering, *bhaktyupahṛtam,* 'given out of devotion'; *tadaham aśnāmi,* 'I eat it, I consume it', because the devotee has given it who is *prayatātmanaḥ,* 'one with a pure heart full of love', full of satisfaction. This is the devotion I like to see, not the quantity of offering. But, whatever is given with pure love has infinite value.

The path of *Bhakti* therefore, reduces ritual, reduces expenditure, reduces show. That is the greatness of *bhakti.* And it brings you closest to the Divine. This verse is the maximum expression of that type of devotion. *Prayatātmanaḥ,* 'of a pure-minded devotee'. A sincere devotee does not have to offer many things to the Divine. When you are very intimate with somebody, you need not give any kind of formal offering or gift to that person, because your heart is one with his or her heart. Similarly, a devotee, who is one with the Divine, has not to perform formal worship in any big or costly way. He or she has already overcome that need. So, he or she uses the simplest worship, the material used is so very little, money spent is so little, but behind all this there is the immense pure love of the Divine, and the Divine sees that pure love in the heart, not the bigness of the offering in your hand. This is what Śrī Kṛṣṇa wants to convey to all devotees. Therefore, He further says:

यत्करोषि यदश्नासि यज्जुहोषि ददासि यत् ।
यत्तपस्यसि कौन्तेय तत्कुरुष्व मदर्पणम् ॥ २७ ॥

*Yatkaroṣi yadaśnāsi yajjuhoṣi dadāsi yat;*
*Yattapasyasi kaunteya tatkuruṣva madarpaṇam* — 9. 27

'Whatever you do, whatever you eat, whatever you offer in sacrifice, whatever you give away, whatever austerity you practice, O son of Kuntī, do that as an offering unto Me.'

That is a very beautiful exhortation. In two or three places in the *Gītā,* similar exhortations come. *Yat karoṣi,* 'whatever you do', any action you do; *yad aśnāsi,* 'whatever you consume by way of food'; *yat juhoṣi,* 'whatever you offer as a sacrifice'; *dadāsi yat,* 'whatever you give as *dāna,* charity or offering'; *yat tapasyasi,* 'whatever *tapas* or austerity you perform'; *tat kuruṣva,* 'do all these'; *kaunteya,* 'O Arjuna'; *mad arpaṇam,* 'as an offering unto Me'. That is how the whole of life becomes a worship of the Divine. Your actions, your human relations, all the worship that you do, everything becomes an offering to the Divine. That is Śrī Kṛṣṇa's blessed guidance to the devotees. He will give it in a stronger language in the last verse of the eleventh chapter where this message will be conveyed, and Śaṅkarācārya will say, commenting on it, that here you have the essence of the spiritual message of the *Gītā*. Here, in the present verse also, it is similar. What is the need for all types of showy religion and worship? True religion and worship is such a simple thing in which the whole of life can become a dedication to the Divine. We can live in Him. He will live in us. This is what we can do. There you have *pure* spirituality. This is a wonderful development. When people understand the nature of *bhakti,* more and more of such people will appear in our society, reducing the current noisy, showy, costly worship. The whole of life becomes religion, as Vivekananda said, as quoted by Sister Nivedita in her Introduction to the *Complete Works of Swami Vivekananda:* 'Life itself is religion'.

शुभाशुभ फलैरेवं मोक्ष्यसे कर्मबन्धनैः ।
संन्यासयोग युक्तात्मा विमुक्तो मां उपैष्यसि ॥२८॥

*Śubhāśubha phalairevam mokṣyase karmabandhanaiḥ;*
*Sannyāsayoga yuktātmā vimukto mām upaiṣyasi* — 9. 28

'Thus, freed from the bondage of actions bearing good and evil results, with the heart steadfast in the *yoga* of renunciation, and liberated, you shall come unto Me.'

When you become liberated by following this kind of spiritual practice, 'You will attain to Me'. How? *Sannyāsa yoga yuktātmā,* 'one who is practising the *yoga* of *sannyāsa,* complete renunciation'. And therefore, the whole life becomes divinized; eating, drinking, human relationships, everything becomes divinized. That is the real *sannyāsa yoga* in the path of *bhakti. Śubhāśubha phalairevam mokṣyase karma bandhanaiḥ,* 'by this you become freed from the bondage of *karma* based on pure and impure results'. What kind of bondage? *Śubha, aśubha,* sometimes 'good', sometimes 'bad'. Just living in the house, living in society, and yet you become *sannyāsa yoga yuktātmā,* because one offers all one's work to the Divine. *Vimukto mām upaiṣyasi,* 'such a devotee becomes freed and comes unto Me'.

Śrī Kṛṣṇa says in the next verse:

समोऽहं सर्व भूतेषु न मे द्वेष्योऽस्ति न प्रियः ।
ये भजन्ति तु मां भक्त्या मयि ते तेषु चाप्यहम् ॥२९॥

*Samo'ham sarva bhūteṣu na me dveṣyo'sti na priyaḥ;*
*Ye bhajanti tu mām bhaktyā mayi te teṣu cāpyaham — 9 .29*

'I am the same in all beings; to Me there is none hateful or dear. But those who worship Me with devotion are in Me, and I too am in them.'

'I am equal to all beings', *samo'ham,* there is no partiality in the Divine. This is a very important point. You can ask that question: Has He someone special?, some favourite? He sees no such differences. *Na me dveṣyo'sti na priyaḥ,* 'I have no enemy and no friend'. I am equal to all. Just like the sun which shines equally on the sinners and the saints, the good and the bad, on all. So also is the Divine. But what is the difference then? *Ye bhajanti tu mām bhaktyā mayi te, teṣu cāpyaham,* 'those who worship Me with devotion, they are in Me and I too am in them'. They have come close to Me on their own. They get the benefit of My presence more than anyone else. And Śaṅkarācārya gives a beautiful illustration. In winter season, we light a fire to warm ourselves. Now, if you sit near the fire, you get the blessing of the fire; if you sit far away, you won't get that blessing of the fire. Fire has done no harm to you nor any good to that person sitting near by. Fire is impartial in every way. But, it is for you to go and sit near the fire. Then you will get all the blessings of that fire. Similarly, these devotees who have got this blessing, they have got it because 'they are in Me', *mayi te,* and also 'I am in them', *teṣu cāpyaham'*. Therefore, it is for us to approach the Divine and get the benefit of that great Reality that is in you, in me, in all people. But the truth is *samo'ham sarva bhūteṣu,* 'I am equal in all beings'. It is the same case with the sun also. Everyone will get the blessing of the Divine. Even the worst human being will get this blessing. This *bhakti* message goes to everyone: sinners, saints, ordinary devotees, and very pure devotees. So, in the next *śloka* you find this wonderful statement:

**अपि चेत् सुदुराचारो भजते मां अनन्यभाक् ।**
**साधुरेव स मन्तव्यः सम्यक् व्यवसितो हि सः ॥३०॥**

*Api cet sudurācāro bhajate mām ananyabhāk;*
*Sādhureva sa mantavyaḥ samyak vyavasito hi saḥ* — 9. 30

'If even a very wicked person worships Me, with one-pointed devotion, he or she should be regarded as good, for he or she has very rightly resolved.'

Even if 'a person is extremely wicked', *sudurācāraḥ; durācāraḥ* means 'wickedness'; *sudurācāraḥ,* 'perpetrator of extremely wicked deeds'; even then, *bhajate mām ananyabhāk,* 'if such a person worships Me with one-pointed devotion'; *sādhureva sa mantavyaḥ,* 'then he or she must be considered a *sādhu* only', he or she must be considered as good; *samyak vyavasito hi saḥ,* 'because he or she has resolved rightly'. That person has decided to go closer to the Divine. Though that person was wicked, such a one is trying to be different hereafter. *Api cet sudurācāraḥ,* 'even if the person is extremely wicked', God is the purifier of everyone. The most sinful, the most wicked, all will be saved by the love of the Divine. And many cases have been reported in our spiritual literature of how great sinners became saints by a touch of the Divine. That is the beauty of *bhakti.* Very often a sinner becomes saintly, but society doesn't recognize it. Society will continue to hunt that sinner, because society sees only that sinner; it does not see that change inside. That is the theme in that famous French book by Victor Hugo, *Les Miserables,* a beautiful story of Jean Val Jean, a thief who stole from a Bishop's house many golden and silver items. He was being chased by the police. When he returned everything, the Bishop had no anger against him. The Bishop blessed him saying, it is yours, you take it. But the police took him to be a criminal. The Bishop had forgiven him. And the rest of his life was a play of this misunderstanding that he had become changed by the touch of the Bishop but the police did not recognize it; society did not recognize it. So, Jean Val Jean goes on constantly being shadowed by the police. Inspector Javert, one character, comes there. Very interesting story is the *Les miserables*. So, here also, the truth is very strongly put: *sādhureva sa mantavyaḥ*, 'he or she must be considered as a *sādhu* only'; *samyak vyavasito hi saḥ*, 'his or her mind has been well resolved to be good'. The mind has been yoked to the Divine. The past is finished, left behind. Now a new life has started. That is the great power of *bhakti*, love of God.

क्षिप्रं भवति धर्मात्मा शश्वत् शान्तिं निगच्छति ।
कौन्तेय प्रतिजानीहि न मे भक्तः प्रणश्यति ॥ ३१ ॥

*Kṣipram bhavati dharmātmā śaśvat śāntim nigacchati;*
*Kaunteya pratijānīhi na me bhaktaḥ praṇaśyati* — *9. 31*

'Soon does he or she become righteous, and attain eternal peace, O son of Kuntī; boldly can you proclaim that My devotee will never be destroyed.'

A profound promise of Śrī Kṛṣṇa you get in this verse. *Kṣipram*, 'very soon', *bhavati dharmātmā*, that person 'will become a *dharmātmā*, an ethical, moral person'; *śaśvat śāntim nigacchati*, 'very soon he or she will get supreme peace of mind'. Then Śrī Kṛṣṇa turns to Arjuna and says: *Kaunteya pratijānīhi*, 'Arjuna, make this promise to everyone': *na me bhaktaḥ praṇaśyati*,. 'My devotee will not perish'. You can take it for granted; it is the truth. Proclaim it from the housetops. That is what Śrī Kṛṣṇa is telling to Arjuna and to all else: *Kaunteya pratijānīhi*. In spite of being a criminal, in spite of doing so many bad things, devotion to the Divine has brought a big change in the person, and that change is a thorough change, not piecemeal. But it takes a little time for people to understand. A very puritan society will judge the weaknesses of men and women with great harshness, but a *bhakti*-oriented society will never do so. Members of that society will have sympathy. Who knows, tomorrow he or she may change. In the New Testament, you will find the story of the condemnation of a sinner only by other sinners. Saintly people never condemn sinners. That is the language. In the story of Jesus, you will find this. 'Where are your accusers?', he asked a woman taken in adultery. 'They have gone away, Sir,' she replied. 'They didn't find any fault with you?', Jesus asked. She said, 'No, they did not, because you told them: "he who had not done any sin, let him cast the first stone."' Hearing this, one by one all melted away. Then, Jesus said: 'So, they have left you? I also say, "I leave you. You are free. You can go. Go and sin no more."' That is the language. So, how does a holy mind view human failings and weaknesses? With tremendous compassion, not in a harsh way. Generally, in all these orthodox societies, there is too much of that harsh judgement. Our own society is full of such harsh judgement. That is the type of a prudish society. But, where there is real *bhakti,* there will never be that kind of harsh judgement. Today's sinner can become tomorrow's saint. As Dr. S. Radhakrishnan used to say, behind every saint there was a sinner and in front of every sinner there is a saint. So, let us not forget that these are all changeable, nothing is fixed, as it were. This we should constantly remember.

In Karachi in Pakistan, I saw a sentence written on the table of a newspaper editor: 'there is so much good in the worst of us and so much bad in the best of us that it ill behoves any of us to speak ill of the rest of us.' That impressed me. A society which doesn't judge human weakness very harshly is a healthy society. Weakness is there; it will come. But, show sympathy, that is what the world needs. The world needs sympathy, not harsh judgement. That is possible in a society where *bhakti* is current coin. Today or tomorrow, people can become devotees of God. They will never judge harshly any human weakness. They will make people aware that there are people here to help you. What a beautiful idea! Not throwing a man or woman down because he or she has some weakness. The whole society tells you, we are here to help you. That is the healthy society. We never had it for several centuries. Extremely harsh has been our society. That has to change. When pure religion will come, that change will come. That humanist feeling will come. Human response to human situations will come. Here Śrī Kṛṣṇa says, 'My devotee will not perish.'

Girish Chandra Ghosh was a drunkard and a great dramatist; and he had confessed all the evils of the world he had done. But Sri Ramakrishna loved him immensely. In spite of all these, he could see genius and goodness in that person, and had infinite faith in Girish Chandra Ghosh. Girish himself did not have so much faith in himself, as Sri Ramakrishna had in him! And eventually, Girish became a saint. And he said, 'This is the miracle of Sri Ramakrishna. He never asked me to give up this or that evil. He stimulated the positive element in me and I have become completely transformed.' That is the story of Girish Chandra Ghosh. Even girls, acting in Girish Ghosh's theatre in those days, were all treated as low-class women. There also Sri Ramakrishna blessed the good actresses. Slowly, their lives changed and, later on, one of them wrote a book on how her life was changed by the blessings of Sri Ramakrishna. So, this is an incident of our own times. We have plenty of such stories coming to us from olden days in our *Purāṇas*. It is good for us to know this truth conveyed by Śrī Kṛṣṇa: *Kaunteya pratijānīhi na me bhaktaḥ praṇaśyati*. The next verse says:

मां हि पार्थ व्यपाश्रित्य येऽपि स्युः पाप योनयः ।
स्त्रियो वैश्यास्तथा शूद्राः तेऽपि यान्ति परां गतिम् ॥३२॥

*Mām hi pārtha vyapāśritya ye'pi syuḥ pāpa yonayaḥ;*
*Striyo vaiśyāstathā śūdrāḥ te'pi yānti parām gatim* — 9. 32

'For, taking refuge in Me, they also, O son of Pṛthā, who might be of inferior birth, as well as women, *vaiśyas*, as well as *śūdras*—even they attain to the supreme Goal.'

This particular verse has been translated differently by different scholars. *Mām hi pārtha vyapāśritya*, 'truly those who take refuge in Me', let them be anybody; *pāpayonayaḥ*, 'those who are of sinful birth', let them be people of such types; or *striyaḥ vaiśyāḥ tathā śūdrāḥ*, 'women, *vaiśyas*, as well as *śūdras*', let them be any one of these; *te api yānti parām gatim*, 'they also go to the highest Goal' when they take refuge in Me. The main stress is: those whom society has neglected, whom society has condemned, My *bhakti* is there to lift them up, *every one of them.* That is the main theme. But, in our traditional interpretation, the word *pāpayonayaḥ* means 'those who are born of sin'. According to orthodoxy, women and *śūdras* are all born of sin. That was the medieval concept. Women, even *brāhmaṇa* women, are also thus born of sin! But nowhere in the *Mahābhārata* will you find that kind of statement. Śrī Kṛṣṇa's teaching, the teaching of the Upaniṣads also is that, all are capable of being redeemed; nobody is just born in sin. The Upaniṣads proclaim all human beings, Indian or foreign, as *amṛtasya putrāḥ,* 'children of Immortality', as re-proclaimed by Swami Vivekananda in his address at the 1893 Chicago Parliament of Religions. You can call some *pāpayonis* because they did some crime. But, even they will be saved. And the other three are separated from this *pāpayoni* category. *Striyaḥ vaiśyāḥ tathā śūdrāḥ,* 'women, *vaiśyas,* as well as *śūdras*'; *te api yānti parām gatim,* 'they also attain to the highest spiritual level.' That is the greatness of the *bhakti* centred in Me, says Śrī Kṛṣṇa here. The idea of *pāpa yoni,* 'born in sin', has been with us for several centuries in our *Smṛtis.* As I said, even our women were treated as *pāpa yoni.* That is the old medieval idea. The whole thing has been cast away today. Absolutely without any Vedantic basis, this evil belief was there. We have now thrown away that belief, we have gone back to the Upaniṣads. The same Atman is in every being; who then can be a *pāpa yoni?* So, a few centuries of social stagnation and social contraction of heart and mind have condemned many sections of people. That chapter is now finished. It has no more any place in our society, nor in the global society. The Negroes were treated as *pāpa yonis* by the Americans. Today, nobody will do so. Individuals here and there may still do it. But the whole tendency today is to see man and woman in their own real light. The same humanity is there in every human being. From every section, the highest development can come. That is the language which the world understands today and that is what was very much strengthened by Sri Ramakrishna, Holy Mother Sarada Devi, and Swami Vivekananda in our time.

Each soul is potentially divine. That divinity can be manifested in any human being. That is the true meaning of human life and religion. So, *mām hi pārtha vyapāśritya,* 'those who take refuge in Me, O Arjuna,' let them be all *pāpa yonis,* let them be women, let them be *vaiśyas* or *śūdras,* let them be anybody, they will all achieve the highest goal. The stress is not on *pāpa yoni,* the stress is on: whatever may be the priestly judgement of a section of people, when they come to *bhakti,* all of them will be raised to the highest level. That is the beautiful idea in this particular section. *Bhakti* doesn't make any distinction between caste, creed, sex, etc. In the last chapter of the *Nārada Bhakti Sūtras,* you find that *sūtra* which says that *bhakti* doesn't discriminate between men, women, high class, low class, etc. Why? The next *sūtra* (*sūtra* 73) gives the answer *yataḥ tadīyāḥ,* 'because they all belong to Him'. That is the wonderful language. Everyone belongs to the Divine. How can you condemn one or two or some of the groups? Never! *Yataḥ tadīyā.* 'They all belong to Him'. Everybody is a child of the Divine, children of Immortality, as I referred to earlier as what the Upaniṣad said, *amṛtasya putrāḥ.* Everyone of us is a child of immortality. *Śṛṇvantu viśve amṛtasya putrāḥ.* That is the great gospel or good news given by the Upaniṣads. So, based on that, this *bhakti* and this *jñāna* of Vedanta are there to redeem humanity, not to push people down. So, all of them attain the *parām gatim,* 'the supreme state'. What to talk of *brāhmaṇas* and *kṣatriyas.* That is the theme of the next verse. They have all this capacity. If only they turn to the Divine, practise *bhakti,* how much more quickly will they get it! They have got a cultural asset already with them which others have to struggle hard to get. If even these others can achieve, then why not these upper level people, and that too much more easily?

किं पुनः ब्राह्मणाः पुण्या भक्ता राजर्षयस्तथा ।
अनित्यं असुखं लोकं इमं प्राप्य भजस्व माम् ॥३३॥

*Kim punaḥ brāhmaṇāḥ puṇyā bhaktā rājarṣayastathā;*
*Anityam asukham lokam imam prāpya bhajasva mām—9. 33*

'What need to mention holy *brāhmaṇas*, and devoted *rājarṣis!* Having obtained this transient, joyless world, you worship Me.'

Holy devoted *brāhmaṇas* or *rājarṣis*, 'sage-like *rājas* or *kṣatriyas*'; *lokam imam prāpya*, 'having come to this world' which is *anityam*, 'impermanent' and *asukham*, 'joyless', if they worship Me, what doubt is there? They will also attain to the highest level. The concept of *rājarṣi* has been more fully expounded in chapter 4 of volume 1 of this book.

Śrī Kṛṣṇa first referred to the neglected section, and then referred to the pampered section in society. And therefore, He says in the last verse of this chapter:

मन्मना भव मद्भक्तो मद्याजी मां नमस्कुरु ।
मां एव एष्यसि युक्त्वैवं आत्मानं मत्परायणः ॥ ३४ ॥

*Manmanā bhava madbhakto madyājī mām namaskuru;*
*Mām eva eṣyasi yuktvaivam ātmānam matparāyaṇaḥ*—9. 34

'Fill thy mind with Me, be My devotee, sacrifice unto Me, bow down to Me; thus having made your heart steadfast in Me, taking Me as the supreme Goal, you shall come to Me.'

*Manmanā bhava*, 'let your mind be fixed on Me'; *madbhakto*, 'be My devotee'; *madyājī*, 'whatever ceremonies, rituals and sacrifices you do, do it to Me'; *mām namaskuru*, 'salute Me', all your salutations and adorations must be directed to the Divine Person. *Mām eva eṣyasi yuktvā evam*, 'by this type of *yoga*, you will reach Me only'; *matparāyaṇaḥ*, 'those who are fully devoted to Me'. This is the great exhortation in this chapter. As I said, this type of exhortation will come again once or twice in other areas also. *Mat parāyaṇaḥ; parāyaṇaḥ* means 'supreme goal'; when preceded by *mat* it means, 'Me as the supreme Goal'. In a Bengali song they say, *Tomāke koriyāchi jīvaner dhruvatārā*, which Sri Ramakrishna used to sing: 'I have made Thee alone the Pole-star of my life.'

When you have a little water in the river, you have to take the water out with great difficulty; and when the water overflows the banks, wherever you want you can get water.

Here it is a flood of *bhakti*. This is what must come to humanity in course of time when it understands the spiritual nature of human life which finds expression in love of God, love of human beings, more of compassion and the spirit of service; these are the fruits of that pure type of *bhakti*.

I have a deep feeling that, in this modern period within the next two-three centuries, people will understand this profound philosophy of Vedanta combining *bhakti* and *jñāna*, and which will find expression in every religion in the form of love and service of the people. Take for example, the Sufi woman saint Rābia of the eighth-ninth century AD. What did she do? 'Rābia, do you love God?', somebody asked her. Rābia said, 'yes, I love God, with a tremendous love, I love God.' Then she was asked, 'Rābia, do you hate the devil?' 'Love of God doesn't give me time to hate the devil!', she said. That type of mind will come more and more. Rābia was a great inspiration for all the Sufi saints thereafter. Eight hundred AD is very early. Later Sufis all got inspiration from this slave woman. She was a slave girl and became so high in spiritual dimension. In every religion you will find such examples. My feeling is: when people understand this truth, they will conduct their life and their activity surcharged with that devotion, full of love of God flowing out as love and service of the human beings. There will be a great sense of joy. This kind of *bhakti* will spread in society in course of time when we understand pure religion, as pure spiritual growth. For that, plenty of sources are there, like *The Gospel of Sri Ramakrishna*, where religion is expressed in a very simple form. When that *bhakti* will come, a big revolution will take place in human affairs, and I fully believe that such changes will come in India and the rest of the world also. In foreign countries also, I have seen that people are hungry for this kind of bread of pure spirituality, not the stones of dogmas and creeds. So, when they get this, then they also will turn in that direction. Then the promise in that great book, *Padma Purāṇa,* dealing with *Bhāgavata Māhātmyam*, 'the glory of the book *Śrīmad Bhāgavatam*', expressed there, will be implemented:

*Jñāna-vairāgya-yuktā yā bhaktiḥ premarasāvahā;*
*Prati geham prati janam tataḥ krīḍām kariṣyati —*

This is a prophetic utterance. 'This great *bhakti* strengthened by *jñāna* and *vairāgya*', *Jñāna-vairāgya-yuktā yā bhaktiḥ;* what is the nature of this *bhakti? Prema rasāvahā*, 'flow of *prema rasa*, pure love', that is the nature of this *bhakti*. Eventually, *krīḍām kariṣyati*, this *bhakti* 'will have its play'; *prati geham*, 'in every home'; *prati janam*, and 'in every heart' in this world. Today there is every possibility of humanity trying to *understand* this idea of religion, and in *living it*. It is the most practical. It is meant for everyone. That is why in the beginning of this chapter we studied the second verse, on which I spent a whole day:

*Rāja vidyā rāja guhyam pavitram idam uttamam;*
*Pratyakṣāvagamam dharmyam susukham kartum avyayam —*

*Rāja vidyā*, 'this is *rājavidyā*, king of sciences'; *rājaguhyam*, 'king of all mysteries'; *pavitram idam uttamam*, 'extremely purifying is this message'. How much of character change will come through this kind of *bhakti*! Purity, devotion, spirit of service, dedication, all these will come. *Pratyakṣāvagamam*, 'can be realized in day-to-day life', not in some far away forest retreat or in some heaven. You can have this experience while cooking in the kitchen, or working in a factory or office. *Dharmyam*, 'strengthens the fabric of society'; integration of the human being with other human beings in society will be strengthened. *Susukham kartum*, 'easy and happy to do', so simple it is. But, *phalam avyayam*, 'the fruit is infinite'. That is what you heard in the second verse in the beginning of this chapter. And we end this chapter with the special exhortation of Śrī Kṛṣṇa in the last verse,

Dealing with human problems in the world after the Second World War, the agnostic, late Bertrand Russell pleaded for love in the human heart, and with an apology, said Christian love—though he was an anti-Christian all through and knew no other religion—as a solution to solve these problems (*The Impact of Science on Society,* Chapter 6: 'Science and Values', p. 105):

'The root of the matter is a very simple and old fashioned thing, a thing so simple that I am almost ashamed to mention it, for fear of the derisive smile with which wise cynics will greet my words. The thing I mean—please forgive me for mentioning it—is love, Christian love or compassion. If you feel this, you have a motive for existence, a guide in action, a reason for courage, an imperative necessity for intellectual honesty. If you feel this, you have all that anybody should need in the way of religion. ...'

The science and technique of religion is really simple; we make it complicated. That should change. The greatest truths are simple. That kind of change will come in the human mind. I have every hope that, in this modern period, a tremendous revolution will take place all over the world, for I am seeing everywhere great spiritual hunger. Hungry to know what is this, what is that. What is higher life? It will take a little time for people to remove the antiquated dogmas and to understand all this, and it will slowly manifest in their life. That is why this chapter has got special significance for that one single expression, *pratyakṣa avagamam,* not 'there, there', but 'here, here'; here itself, where I am, I can be spiritual. I need not go here and there. The Lord is your own infinite Self. He is all love, all bliss. That is how we can deal with this great subject of science of religion, science of spirituality, in the light of *Bhagavad Gītā. Śrī Kṛṣṇa* is a universal teacher. That is the significance of this three-volume book bearing the title of *Universal Message of the Bhagavad Gītā.*

इति राजविद्या-राजगुह्य-योगो नाम नवमोऽध्यायः ।

*Iti rājavidyā-rājaguhya-yogo nāma navamo'dhyāyaḥ —*

Thus ends the ninth chapter called *The Way of the Kingly Knowledge and the Kingly Secret.*

# BHAGAVAD GĪTĀ

## CHAPTER 10

### VIBHŪTI-YOGA
### GLIMPSES OF THE DIVINE GLORY

The word *vibhūti* is used to describe the tenth chapter; *vibhūti yoga. Vibhūti* means 'power of manifestation', God in the manifested state. He is unmanifested, He is also manifested. Both are aspects of the Divine—the Impersonal and the Personal. They are one and the same, but two different approaches, as Sri Ramakrishna would say: 'A snake coiled up is that Impersonal state; the same snake, when it starts moving, is the Personal aspect of the Divine.' They are not two, but one. And because of this we can live and work in the world and yet attain spiritual realization. That is the philosophy developed in the ninth chapter. In fact, throughout the *Gītā*, that is the basic philosophy, though this idea comes only a little in the beginning, and a little reference to it in the twelfth chapter. The transcendental, beyond the sensory level, the Unmanifest, that path is also mentioned; but the main stress is on the path to God through the world of manifestation.

God is the Pole star of our life. He is manifested in this universe. We are never away from Him at any time. Only if we can see clearly, we can see Him *in* everything here. In some of the highest poetry of world's literature, this idea is expressed again and again. Even in purely nature poet's poetry you find, as William Wordsworth says in 'Tintern Abbey',

> ...I have learned
> To look on nature, not as in the hour
> Of thoughtless youth; but hearing oftentimes
> The still, sad music of humanity,

Nor harsh nor grating, though of ample power
To chasten and to subdue. And I have felt
A presence that disturbs me with the joy
Of elevated thoughts; a sense sublime
Of something far more deeply interfused,
Whose dwelling is the light of setting suns,
And the round ocean and the living air,
And the blue sky, and in the mind of man:
A motion and a spirit, that impels
All thinking things, all objects of all thought,
And rolls through all things. Therefore am I still
A lover of the meadows and the woods,
And mountains; and of all that we behold
From this green earth; of all the mighty world
Of eye, and ear,—both what they half create,
And what perceive; well pleased to recognise
In nature and the language of the sense
The anchor of my purest thoughts, the nurse,
The guide, the guardian of my heart, and soul
Of all my moral being.

Purely through nature poetry, you get this wonderful idea, this type of a vision, and William Wordsworth also speaks about a state in which 'we are laid asleep in body, and become a living soul'. When Swami Vivekananda was a student in Calcutta, the English Professor Hastie was teaching Wordsworth. There he referred to this experience of *samādhi* described by Wordsworth. And the professor said, 'This is a high state of mind. Very few achieve it. I know only one who has achieved it; that is Ramakrishna of Dakshineswar.' That is a reference Vivekananda, then known as Narendra, heard for the first time about Sri Ramakrishna (*Life of Swami Vivekananda by His Eastern & Western Disciples*, Vol. 1, pp. 47-48). That is the basis of *bhakti* in every religion. Christian *bhakti,* Hindu *bhakti,* Sufi *bhakti,* and Buddhist *bhakti*—in all these you will find this teaching of a profound Divine experience. That possibility is what gives meaning to human life.

So, coming now to the tenth chapter, we get this description of the world of manifestation; that One Divine has become the many. How has He become the many? Through His *yoga* power. He has got a wonderful power that, though He is one, He can also be the many—that is the language that will be used hereafter. So, it is called *vibhūti yoga*, 'the *yoga* of God's *vibhūtis*', various powers of manifestations. And this chapter begins with Śrī Kṛṣṇa's own statement. Sometimes, Arjuna questions and the chapter begins with that question. Sometimes Śrī Kṛṣṇa Himself continues. Here, Śrī Kṛṣṇa Himself opens the chapter.

**श्रीभगवान् उवाच –**

*Śrībhagavān uvāca —*

*'Śrī Bhagavān said:'*

**भूय एव महाबाहो शृणु मे परमं वचः ।**
**यत्तेऽहं प्रीयमाणाय वक्ष्यामि हित काम्यया ॥ १ ॥**

*Bhūya eva mahābāho śṛṇu me paramam vacaḥ;*
*Yat te'ham prīyamāṇāya vakṣyāmi hita kāmyayā* — 10. 1

'Again, O mighty-armed, do you listen to My supreme word, which I, wishing your welfare, will tell you who are delighted (to hear Me).'

Again, listen to Me, O Arjuna. *Bhūya* means 'again'; *śṛṇu me paramam vacaḥ*, 'please listen to My supreme word'. A word which contains a tremendous meaning, that is called *paramam vacaḥ*. Speeches can be empty, 'mere sound and fury signifying nothing', as Shakespeare says, or it can be profound; just like a beautiful beehive which is full of honey inside. Similarly, we can have words full of profound meaning. *Yatte'ham prīyamāṇāya*, 'I am conveying this to you because you are dear to Me'; *vakṣyāmi hita kāmyayā*, 'I am telling you in order to ensure your own welfare'.

**न मे विदुः सुरगणाः प्रभवं न महर्षयः ।**
**अहं आदिर्हि देवानां महर्षीणां च सर्वशः ॥ २ ॥**

*Na me viduḥ suragaṇāḥ prabhavam na maharṣayaḥ;*
*Aham ādirhi devānām maharṣiṇām ca sarvaśaḥ* — 10. 2

'Neither the hosts of *Devas*, nor the great *Ṛṣis*, know My origin, for in every way, I am the source of all the *Devas* and the great *Ṛṣis*.'

Neither the gods nor the *maharṣis*, great sages, know My origin. I am prior to all of them. That is a beautiful idea expressed first in the *Ṛg Veda* in the *Nāsadīya Sūkta:* How could the gods, who are subsequent to creation, know Him? That is the language. He is beyond all these. So Śrī Kṛṣṇa says, they do not know Me; even the earliest gods and various sages do not know My origin.

यो मां अजं अनादिं च वेत्ति लोक महेश्वरम् ।
असंमूढः स मर्त्येषु सर्वपापैः प्रमुच्यते ॥ ३ ॥

*Yo mām ajam anādim ca vetti loka maheśvaram;*
*Asammūḍhaḥ sa martyeṣu sarvapāpaiḥ pramucyate*—10. 3

'One who knows Me, the birthless and beginningless One, the great Lord of the universe—such a one, among mortals, is undeluded, and is freed from all sins.'

*Yo mām vetti,* 'those who know Me'; *ajam anādim ca,* 'I am *ajam* and *anādim*'; *ajam* means 'unborn'. There is no birth for the supreme Divine; other things have birth, change and death. This one is immortal, changeless, birthless. *Anādim* means, 'beginningless'. *Vetti lokamaheśvaram,* 'one who knows Me as the supreme ruler of the universe'. The one guide and ruler of the universe is He; by His power the world moves. In the *Bṛhadāraṇyaka Upaniṣad,* Yājñavalkya tells Maitreyī and Gārgī, particularly Gārgī, 'By the power of that imperishable Reality, the sun and the moon go in their respective courses, all the streams flow in the direction towards the ocean, ... ' Here also Śrī Kṛṣṇa is referring to this, *lokamaheśvaram,* 'the supreme Lord of the universe'. *Asammūḍhaḥ sa martyeṣu,* 'that person is certainly *asammūḍhaḥ* among all human beings'; *mūḍha* means 'a fool', a deluded person; *asammūḍhaḥ* means 'a non-deluded person'. In Sanskrit, *mūḍha* is the only abusive word we have: 'he is a fool', we say like this, that is all. But, the other is *asammūḍhaḥ,* 'absolutely free from delusion, foolishness'; *sarva pāpaiḥ pramucyate,* 'such a one becomes freed from all sins', all weakness, because he or she has understood this profound truth, the Truth of all truths.

बुद्धिर्ज्ञानं असंमोहः क्षमा सत्यं दमः शमः ।
सुखं दुःखं भवोऽभावो भयं च अभयं एव च ॥४॥

*Buddhirjñānam asammohaḥ kṣamā satyam damaḥ śamaḥ;*
*Sukham duḥkham bhavo'bhāvo bhayam ca abhayam eva ca—10. 4*

'Intellect, knowledge, non-delusion, forbearance, truth, restraint of the external senses, calmness of heart, happiness, misery, birth, death, fear as well as fearlessness,'

अहिंसा समता तुष्टिस्तपो दानं यशोऽयशः ।
भवन्ति भावा भूतानां मत्त एव पृथग्विधाः ॥५॥

*Ahimsā samatā tuṣṭiḥ tapo dānam yaśo'yaśaḥ;*
*Bhavanti bhāvā bhūtānām matta eva pṛthagvidhāḥ— 10. 5*

'Non-injury, equality, contentment, austerity, benevolence, good name, (as well as) ill-fame—(these) different kinds of qualities of beings arise from Me alone.'

In two verses Śrī Kṛṣṇa gives in summary that, the good, bad, the indifferent, and everything have come from the One. Vedanta does not have good things coming from a God and bad things coming from a devil. Everything has come from one infinite Source. So, what are the items that have come from that Source? *Buddhiḥ,* 'intellect'; *jñāna,* 'knowledge'; *asammūḍhaḥ,* 'non-delusion'; similarly, *kṣamā,* 'forgiveness' comes from the divine; *satyam,* 'truth'; *damaḥ,* 'restraint of the external senses'; *śamaḥ,* 'calmness of heart'; *sukham,* 'happiness'; *duḥkham,* 'misery'; *bhavaḥ,* 'birth'; *abhāvaḥ,* 'death'; *bhayam,* 'fear'; *abhayam,* 'fearlessness'; *ahimsā,* 'non-injury or nonviolence'; *samatā,* 'sense of equality'; *tuṣṭiḥ,* 'contentment'; *tapaḥ,* 'austerity'; *dānam,* 'benevolence'; *yaśaḥ,* 'good name'; and *ayaśaḥ,* 'ill-name or ill-fame'. *Bhavanti bhāvā bhūtānām matta eva pṛthagvidhāḥ*, 'these different kinds of qualities of all beings arise from Me only.' That is the bold statement in Vedanta. Not only the good but also what you call the evil also come from the same source. Very often people shout, how can evil come from God?, as if evil and good are two absolute things. They are relative things only. What is good to one may be evil to another. What is good to you now may be evil to you a little later. So, Vedanta never made an absolute distinction between good and evil. They are relative values. And we are seeing it everyday today. Say, for example, we have carbon dioxide going out of us; it is evil to us. But, it is very useful to the plants and the trees. Similarly, poison in a snake is no evil to the snake; it is evil only to the one whom the snake bites. In the snake, it is part of itself, its own nature. And, if you take a bit of it, it may stop your bleeding also. So, in this way, we discovered ages ago, that good and bad are relative. There is only one absolute, God himself. These good and evil are in the course of manifestation; the One assumes different aspects as now good, then bad, etc. The fire that burns a human being, can also give you warmth when it is a cold winter. Fire is neither good nor bad. So, everything in this world has its own status. Everything is mentioned here in these two verses as coming from Me, the Lord.

I gave the example some two Sundays ago of the article in America's *The National Geographic Magazine*, with the title, 'Sun is Our Mother', where the writer says that everything in the solar system is condensation of solar radiation—the good, the bad, everything. That doesn't make the sun bad at all! Bad in the manifested is not bad in the original source. And so, the cloth you wear, the food you take, the dirt you find around you, the digestive power in you, all these are nothing but manifestations of solar energy. This is a wonderful idea. This is the basis of the Advaitic vision—of the One behind the many. No two. No physical science can accept two behind the universe. Nor can Vedanta accept two behind the universe. There is only One. If you find the many here, you must derive the many from the One itself. That is boldness! These two verses give you that bold statement. *Matta eva,* 'they have come from Me only'; *pṛthagvidhāḥ,* 'in various forms'.

महर्षयः सप्त पूर्वे चत्वारो मनवः तथा ।
मत् भावा मानसा जाता येषां लोक इमाः प्रजाः ॥६॥

*Maharṣayaḥ sapta pūrve catvāro manavaḥ tathā;*
*Mat bhāvā mānasā jātā yeṣām loka imāḥ prajāḥ —10. 6*

'The seven great *Ṛṣis*, the previous four, as well as the Manus who had their thoughts fixed on me, were born of My mind and from whom are these creatures in the world.'

This verse contains allusions to our ancient mythology, i.e. the beginning of creation. First Brahmā appeared; then from that Brahmā came the four Kumāras; then the Manus; then all the various Rudras; all these things came from there. Those things find mention in these verses. So, a little of that background one has to know. But, essentially it means that the whole universe has come from the One divine source. Here Śrī Kṛṣṇa says, *maharṣayaḥ sapta,* 'the seven *maharṣis*'; the idea of the seven *maharṣis* is so well known to all of us in India, what you call the 'Great bear', the seven stars in the sky. They (in west) call it the 'Great bear' in modern language. They are called the *sapta ṛṣis,* 'seven *Ṛṣis*'. *Pūrve catvāro,* 'the previous four'. In interpreting 'the previous four', several interpretations have been given which are not satisfactory at all. *Manavastathā,* 'also seven Manus'; out of fourteen Manus in the present day of Brahmā, there have been past seven Manus and seven more are yet to come.

Bal Gangadhar Tilak has said, after thorough investigation, that 'the four ancient', *catvāro pūrve,* means the four *vyūhas: Vāsudeva, Saṅkarṣaṇa, Pradyumna* and *Aniruddha*—the four manifestations of the Divine. They are called the four *vyūhas.* In the *Nārāyaṇīya* section of the *Mahābhārata,* which is the inspiration for the *Gītā,* you find these four *vyūhas* mentioned. They are the four, nothing else can answer to these four. So, *catvāro pūrve* means, 'the four previous ones', these four *vyūhas*. *Manavastathā,* 'also the Manus'. Fourteen *Manvantaras* make for one particular age of the universe. So, we had Svāyambhuva Manu, the first Manu. Then, after the intermediate five Manus comes the Vaivasvata Manu. The seventh Manu is Vaivasvata. We are now living in the age of the Vaivasvata Manu. Each Manu's age will be millions of years. So, *manavastathā,* these are the seven Manus (from Svāyambhuva to Vaivasvata), namely, the seven Manus of the past. These are immense ranges of space and time calculations in our philosophy and theology. *Mat bhāvā,* 'they had their minds fixed on me'; *mānasā jātā,* and were 'born out of My mind', a projection of My mind. Brahmā himself is a projection of the Divine Nārāyaṇa. So also, are these Manus, the four *vyūhas* and the seven *Maharṣis.* All of them are divine mental projections. That is how the earliest creation has been mentioned. Absolutely subtle realities they were. Later on, creation became more and more concrete, until it came to this manifested level.

Now, in dealing with creation, this is nearly the way modern astronomy also adopts: that, in the beginning, it is all absolutely subtle; no differences are there between things in the beginning. Later on, every second, it becomes more and more concrete; more and more differences appear, until you get this fixed universe which you experience everyday. There is such a diversity now, whereas in the beginning there was absolute unity. The scientists call it the point of singularity—the technical term in astro-physics today. From there the explosion took place, and one by one it began to manifest. These differences were not there in the beginning; atoms, molecules and even electrons, protons—none of these were there. Just condensed energy; that was all that existed. Later on, they became concretized into this and that. And the whole universe has come from that One; and also it will return to that One towards the end of this experience of manifestation. So, Śrī Kṛṣṇa says, 'I am the beginning of all these *devas* and *maharṣis.* Those who know Me as the origin of all this universe, they become free from delusion.' And so manifestations begin with *maharṣayaḥ sapta pūrve catvāro manavaḥ tathā, mat bhāvā mānasā jātā.* They are called 'mental creations'; a wonderful idea. In fact, the whole universe was only a pulsation of the Divine mind: pure consciousness pulsation. They didn't have differences. Later on, they underwent condensation. Even in our day-to-day life, you act; behind your action, there is mental pulsation. First we think, we decide, we desire, and then we execute it into action. The house that you see built, is a solid house. Where was it before? In your mind; in your conception that, 'this house must come'. Then you prepare the plan. Then you build it up. So, in all these experiences you will find, 'the subtle precedes the gross'; and later on, the subtle will follow the gross in the inverse process when the world is being wound up. Evolution becomes involution, going backwards as it were. Just like in today's physics we say, a primordial explosion made for the manifestation of the universe; implosion will make for the return of the many into the One once again.

एतां विभूतिं योगं च मम यो वेत्ति तत्त्वतः ।
सोऽविकम्पेन योगेन युज्यते नात्र संशयः ॥७॥

*Etām vibhūtim yogam ca mama yo vetti tattvataḥ;*
*So'vikampena yogena yujyate nātra samśayaḥ* — 10. 7

'One who in reality knows these manifold manifestations of My being and (this) *yoga* power of Mine, becomes established in the unshakeable *yoga*; there is no doubt about it.'

Such a person who knows this truth, he or she develops *avikampa yoga*, '*yoga* which cannot be shaken'; *kampa* means 'shaking'; *avikampa* means 'unshakable', absolutely steady. That is what we seek; a steady mind, a steady *buddhi*, a steady life, not shaking. We are going to be strong and steady. So, such persons achieve *avikampa yoga*, 'unshakeable *yoga*'. How? *Etām vibhūtim yogam ca mama yo vetti tattvataḥ*, 'those who know *truly*, as it is in itself, My *vibhūti* and *yoga*, this manifestation of Mine as the universe and the power that made for that manifestation'. *Vibhūti* means 'power of manifestation'; *yoga* means 'the power that made for that manifestation'. *Yo vetti*, 'those who understand' this truth; *tattvataḥ*, 'truly'; *saḥ*, 'such a person'; *avikampena yogena,* 'by this unshakeable *yoga*'; *yujyate nātra saṁśayaḥ,* 'there is no doubt at all that he or she achieves' that *avikampa yoga,* 'the steady mind'. A steady mind is reflected in one aspect of the human physical individuality, namely, the eye. When the eye is steady, you can take for granted that the mind also is steady. If the eye is unsteady, mind also is unsteady. The eye is the index of the mind. The face itself is the index of the soul, according to Shakespeare, and we all accept it. And the eye is a great index of the state of the mind. Calm and steady eyes mean calm and steady mind. So, we can achieve this *avikampa yoga* by this kind of understanding. We become absolutely steady. *Nātra saṁśayaḥ,* 'there is no doubt about it.' So, it is good for us to struggle to develop that kind of steadiness, and make the eyes also calm and steady. It is a wonderful achievement. It doesn't come by itself; you have to work for it. That is how we try to bring fulfilment in our life. So, this is an important verse: *yo vetti tattvataḥ,* 'those who understand it truly'; *saḥ avikampena yogena yujyate, na atra saṁśayaḥ,* 'he or she becomes endowed with that unshakeable *yoga;* there is no doubt about it.'

अहं सर्वस्य प्रभवो मत्तः सर्वं प्रवर्तते ।
इति मत्वा भजन्ते मां बुधा भाव समन्विताः ॥८॥

*Aham sarvasya prabhavo mattaḥ sarvam pravartate;*
*Iti matvā bhajante mām budhā bhāva samanvitāḥ — 10. 8*

'I am the origin of all; from Me everything evolves—thus thinking, the wise worship Me with loving consciousness.'

*Aham sarvasya prabhavo,* 'I am the Origin of everything in this universe'. Whatever you see in a tree—leaves, twigs, branches, then flowers and fruits—all of them originate from the seed. So, this is the origin of everything—Myself, the infinite Divine. *Mattaḥ sarvam pravartate,* 'from Me emanate all things'; *pravartate,* 'manifests or emanates'. *Iti matvā,* 'knowing thus'; *bhajante mām budhā,* 'wise people worship Me' with this knowledge. What kind of wise people? *Bhāva samanvitāḥ,* 'people with loving consciousness'. *Bhāva* means 'emotion, love, *bhakti*'; this is the nature of *bhakti.* You can also have a non-*bhakti* consciousness and also worship. But, in this path of *bhakti,* this kind of loving consciousness is essential. It makes you rich with feeling. This is the difference between an austere philosophy and *bhakti*. Take for example, the philosophy of Marcus Aurelius, a Roman emperor; a very austere philosophy it is. In our country also there are plenty of such austere schools of philosophy. The other is very very human, full of emotion, capacity to love and to receive love. That is a richer human personality. That music of life is sweeter than the other music which is rather dry at a certain level, though at the highest level it may be perfectly fine. But at the lower levels it appears to be more dry. Comparing between these two, Sri Ramakrishna used to give an illustration. You can take that illustration and make your own meaning out of it. He said, 'in the temple of Dakshineswar, they play music. One man takes a pipe and simply goes on making a sound; the drone as we call it in musical language. Just the drone, the background music. The other man has another musical instrument with seven holes. And he produces certain notes out of it. The former produces only one note; this man produces seven notes. Which is sweeter? The seven-note is sweeter; you don't like to hear the drone for a long time; for a short time it is okay. So here you have this *bhakti* as the fulfilment of *jñāna,* manifesting in action. You get that complete human life here. There is joy in it. There is variety in it. That is why Sri Ramakrishna compares it with the *sapta-svara* instrument. The other is *eka-svara* instrument called the drone. So, a *jñāni*, as usually understood in our Vedantic tradition, is of that nature; very dry, can't feel any joy for anything. If such a one looks at a baby's face, he or she will say, it is all *māyā*. He or she does not find anything worthwhile in it. Such a one will say, 'I can't enjoy the smile of a child, the beauty of the sun, beauty of the earth. Why? All these things are delusions. The one transcendental Reality alone is real'. There you will find this kind of drone music. The other is *sapta-svara,* beautiful music, rich and fine. The best *bhakti* of India and the best *bhakti* of all religions belong to this category. Richness, diversity and intense humanity—that is the religion the *Gītā* expounds; intensely human. Śrī Kṛṣṇa himself was such a person. He had a very rich heart, rich human feelings, responding to human situations.

Today, Sri Ramakrishna, full of joy, conveys a religion of joy. You cannot go near an austere person; you are afraid of him. In our homes we have generally two types of people: perhaps an uncle, very austere; people are afraid of him, and won't go near him. There are other people to whom children go because they are very pleasing, with a smile and all that. Two types you can see. In this case, this *bhakti* will draw out millions and millions of people, intensely human, with a capacity to love and be loved. That is the description given in this chapter, and the whole of the *Gītā* is based upon that kind of outlook: intensely human. And we can dig affection in others and make others dig affection in us. This is the type of *bhakti* Śrī Kṛṣṇa is preaching, and yet it is based on the highest *jñāna,* the supremely divine principle behind this universe. And so *jñāna, bhakti* and *karma,* all combined together—that is the integrated *yoga* of the *Gītā.* Śrī Kṛṣṇa had referred to this: *Jñānam vijñāna sahitam,* '*jñāna* along with *vijñāna*'. *Vijñāna* means experience, day-to-day experience. That *jñāna* which finds expression in day-to-day experience in human relationships etc., that is what Śrī Kṛṣṇa said He was going to expound in the ninth chapter. So, the *Vibhūti Yoga* chapter has importance from this point of view. What is called *Māyā* in the school of Vedanta, is called here the 'glory of the Divine', the manifestation of the Divine in the form of this nature around us.

In the *Ṛg Veda,* this idea was started very early. There is a beautiful *mantra* which says: *Yasyaite himavanto mahitvā,* 'Whose glory these Himalayas proclaim'. See the poetic approach. The glory of the Himalayas; whose glory does it proclaim? Of that supreme Divine Reality behind this universe.

Śrī Kṛṣṇa, towards the end of this chapter will say in the last but one verse, in verse 41, that 'wherever you see extraordinary power manifesting and uplifting humanity, know My power is manifest there'. He gives you complete freedom to see the Divine in any type of manifestation, in any part of the world. That is going to be a joyous conclusion of this chapter of *Vibhūti Yoga*.

For example, you see a Gandhiji manifesting enormous power to lift up humanity, to release humanity from slavery, and to increase love and nonviolence in society. Millions were moved by his single utterance. That power is 'Mine', says Śrī Kṛṣṇa. 'My' power is there. We can see the same thing in a person like Abraham Lincoln. It can be in any one, in any part of the world. These are the people who show that the supreme Divine power that underlies the universe is manifested through a few individuals here and there. Salute them as the Divine power is manifest in them. That way Śrī Kṛṣṇa will conclude this chapter.

Here Śrī Kṛṣṇa says, *aham sarvasya prabhavo,* 'I am the origin of all this universe'; *mattaḥ sarvam pravartate,* 'everything comes from Me'; *iti matvā bhajante mām,* 'knowing this they worship Me'; *budhā,* 'the wise people'; *bhāva samnvitāḥ,* 'full of love in their hearts'; divine love is in their hearts. They are not dry, that is one thing we must remember. A living human personality, full of concern for others; you can go near and feel happy in his or her company. That kind of a rich human personality, emotionally rich, attracts others. Any system that destroys the emotions of a human being will destroy humanity itself. Without emotion there is no meaning to human life.

The famous neurologist of England, Sir Charles Sherrington, said, 'can a bird build its nest without the power of emotion?' Consider a bird just building a nest: What is impelling it to bring small pieces of wood or leaves, put it in a corner, again bring another, and yet another to make a nest? What is impelling it to do that? That emotion directed towards the baby that is to come for which a house is to be provided. That emotion makes the bird do all that work. You remove the nest, again she does it. That is where you can see the power of emotion. In fact, the best work you do is when you have emotion impelling you to work. If you merely have dry intellectual knowledge, you can't do any great work efficiently. Efficiency and energy come from emotion, not from intellectual knowledge, which can only direct that emotional energy. But the real impulse comes from the emotion. It makes you work at your highest and best. Take that emotion away and you become callous, absolutely callous and unresponsive. In fact, that is what we call, in ordinary language, the development of the heart. Brain and the heart—the brain you may develop; but you will be a very dry person if there is no heart along with the brain. That has been our misfortune in India for a few centuries. We developed the brain; we left the heart just as it was—a very very contracted heart, with no concern for others. Even now you find millions of us without any concern for others. There is no heart at all. Only 'I', 'I', 'I'. Such a person gets a modern education; and that makes him or her much worse. Without education he or she would have been much less troublesome. With education it becomes a mere nuisance to society. So, Swami Vivekananda said, 'develop the heart'; expand your heart. Then your emotions will function; there will be a sense of concern for others, love and care for others, a spirit of service; and with the intelligence behind all this, it will make for a wonderful personality. In this *Gītā bhakti,* you get both intelligence and emotion fused together. That is the nature of *buddhi;* in *buddhi,* emotion, intelligence and will, become fused together to give a highly efficient character. Śrī Kṛṣṇa will tell us a few verses later, *dadāmi buddhi yogam tam,* 'those whom I wish to bless, I give them that *buddhi*'; *yena mām upayānti te,* 'by which they find their way to Me.' I do not have to help them further. 'I have given them the best instrument, the *buddhi,* to make for success in life in any department.' That is the language that he will use some verses later.

मच्चित्ता मद्गत प्राणा बोधयन्तः परस्परम् ।
कथयन्तश्च मां नित्यं तुष्यन्ति च रमन्ति च ॥९॥

*Maccittā madgata prāṇā bodhayantaḥ parasparam;*
*Kathayantaśca mām nityam tuṣyanti ca ramanti ca — 10. 9*

'With their minds wholly in Me, with their senses absorbed in Me, enlightening each other, and always speaking of Me, they are satisfied and delighted.'

Such people who have that purified *buddhi*, whose emotion, intellect and will have been fused together, they are a special type of people. *Maccittāḥ*, 'their *citta* or mind has been fixed on Me'; *madgata prāṇā*, 'their whole bio-energy and psychic energy have also been directed towards Me'; *bodhayantaḥ parasparam*, 'enlightening each other'. When two such people meet, one will enlighten the other; that is the nature of their acquisition, and not pull each other down. *Kathayantaśca mām nityam*, 'constantly speaking about Me', the One behind the many. They are dealing with the many; they talk about the One behind the many to give value to the many. Then, *tuṣyanti ca ramanti ca*, 'they enjoy side by side with satisfaction'. Their life is a continuous satisfaction, a continuous delight, *tuṣyanti ca ramanti ca*; a wonderful idea! Joy becomes a permanent feature of human life. How?, by this method.

In *The Gospel of Sri Ramakrishna*, you will find mentioned that Sri Ramakrishna's room was a mart of joy. That is the language 'M', the author, has used there. Full of joy, always radiating joy. In Bengali it is called, *majār kuṭi*, 'the *kuṭi* for *majā*', 'the hut of joy', or 'the mart of joy'. In one of the spiritual books of India, namely, *Pāṇḍava-gītā*, there is a verse. I like it very much and I found it to be the best description of Sri Ramakrishna of our time. That *śloka* says,

*Nityotsavam bhavatyeṣām nityam śrī nityamaṅgalam;*
*Yeṣām hṛdistho bhagavān maṅgalāyatano hariḥ —*

A profound verse. Hari is the supreme Divine Reality that is present in the heart of all beings, but unmanifest. Hari is also called Nārāyaṇa, Śrī Kṛṣṇa, etc. All these words refer to the same Divine Reality. These are merely different names of the one Divine Reality from whom the whole universe has come. Naturally, He is in everything in this universe. If you can manifest that Hari, what will happen? Hari is the abode of 'all that is good and auspicious', *maṅgalam*. If that Hari manifests in your heart, what happens to your life? *Nityotsavam bhavatyeṣām,* 'their lives become a perpetual *utsava* or festival'; *nityam śrī,* '*śrī,* prosperity and welfare, manifests at every moment in their lives'; *nityamaṅgalam,* 'everything auspicious also manifests always in their lives'; when? *Yeṣām hṛdistho bhagavān maṅgalāyatano hariḥ,* 'in whose hearts, *Bhagavān* Hari, who is *maṅgala āyatana* or embodiment of auspiciousness, has manifested'. Then life will be one of joy every minute. Some of the mystics have shown that continuous joy, as if something is welling up from within. You can read the life of Sufi mystics, Christian mystics, our own mystics, and you will find this type of Divine manifestation in them. That is why they were full of joy. They radiated joy all round. Vedanta describes the ultimate Reality as *sat,* 'truth', *cit,* 'Pure Consciousness', and as *ānanda,* 'bliss'. This is a profound experience; a few attain it; but many can try to achieve it and come more and more close to having that experience. But it is possible that this human life can be made really joyous and beautiful when Lord Hari manifests in the heart of men and women. At present He is not manifest; only our own ego is manifest in us. We have to shed this ego through a spirit of service. Service is the best means to shed the ego. It is a wonderful teaching. By leading a life of service, we reduce the ego to thin proportions. And as the ego becomes less and less, the divine becomes more and more manifest in the heart of a human being.

Somebody said that in the Bible it is written: 'let Thy kingdom come'. Everyday we pray, 'let Thy kingdom come'. We go on repeating it hundreds of times; yet that kingdom doesn't come at all. What is the reason? And he gave the reason; the corollary has not been achieved. What is that? 'Let *my* kingdom go!' Then only His kingdom will come. The little 'I' must go. Then the Divine will manifest Himself in the heart. But somehow or other, in our day-to-day religious life, it is 'my' kingdom all the time; no place for 'His' kingdom at all. Even when you go to the temple, you lecture to God there all the time. You don't hear what God has to say! Noise, noise, noise. How can His kingdom come unless the conditions are satisfied? When you go to any temple, immediately become silent, inward, try to listen to what the Lord has to say to you. Learning to listen is a great thing in spiritual life. 'The first doorway to *yoga*,' says Śaṅkarācārya, in his *Vivekacūḍāmaṇi*, 'is control of speech', *yogasya prathamam dvāram vāṅnirodhaḥ*. That is what we have lost for centuries together. It has to change now. We must be endowed with more thinking, more feeling, less talking, and more working with the hands. So, this idea, that we can expose our heart to the manifestation of the Divine within and experience that fullness of joy, that fulfilment, is something wonderful.

Vedanta presents religion in the most rational way, studying human possibilities. In a hunger for food, the hunger is satisfied by taking food. In a hunger for knowledge, we satisfy it by education, by study, by thinking. It is a palpable hunger. Similarly is the hunger for the Divine. No amount of books can give you satisfaction. An experience of the Divine alone can satisfy that hunger. That is a wonderful hunger. So, our scriptures place before humanity all these possibilities and invite each one to go from one possibility to the next. Never be stagnant at one level. Even at the intellectual level, do not be stagnant. There is still one step more to go. Then you will achieve real joy, real fulfilment in the true sense of the term. So, in the next *śloka*, Śri Kṛṣṇa says something unique:

तेषां सतत युक्तानां भजतां प्रीतिपूर्वकम् ।
ददामि बुद्धियोगं तं येन मां उपयान्ति ते ॥१०॥

*Teṣām satata yuktānām bhajatām prītipūrvakam;*
*Dadāmi buddhiyogam tam yena mām upayānti te* — 10. 10

'To them, ever steadfast and serving Me with affection, I give that *buddhiyoga* by which they come unto Me.'

What do 'I' do to all such people who are struggling to rise to this higher level of experience of joy? I bless them, I encourage them. How? *Teṣām satata yuktānām*, 'to those who are constant *yogīs*'. *Yukta* is the word for *yogī*. One who is a *yogī* is also a *yukta*. These are all different forms of the same root word with the same meaning of 'union with God'.

Lokamanya Tilak has said in his *Gītā Rahasya* that the word *yoga* and its various other forms have appeared over eighty times throughout the *Gītā*. So, here is a *yukta*, but a very special type of *yukta*, *satatayukta*, 'constantly in a *yoga* state of mind'. *Satata* means 'always, constant'. *Bhajatām prītipūrvakam*, 'those who worship Me, adore Me, with great love'; what do I do to them? *Dadāmi buddhiyogam tam*, 'to them I give *buddhiyoga*'. A wonderful *yoga*, the *yoga* of reason, of 'equable reason', as Tilak translates it. Mind is always calm, steady; it is full of luminosity; that kind of *buddhi* is the best guide in human life. *Yena mām upayānti te*, 'with the help of that *buddhi*, they find their way to Me'. I give them the right attitude, the right reason, by which they find their way towards Me. This is a very great utterance. How does God help a human being? In many ways; but the best way is by helping him or her to develop the right attitude. One of the great teachings of Buddha's eightfold path is 'right attitude'. That is the greatest thing in life: right attitude. So, Śrī Kṛṣṇa says, 'I give them *buddhiyoga*.' This was already stated in the second chapter. The best we can have in life is *buddhiyoga*. We can live at the physical level like any creeping creatures on the earth. We can live at the sensory level like all animals on earth. We can live at the mental-intellectual level like all the intellectuals of the world. We can also live at the high spiritual level, which is the deepest reality that is within all; that is the fullest life. These are the various levels wherefrom Consciousness functions. When Consciousness functions at the sensory level, we are happy, we are miserable, we can be good, we can be bad, we can be wicked; all these we can be. No prediction is possible there. The sense organs have no direction. At the intellectual level also it is the same. You can be good, you can be bad; you can be extremely wicked also. But once you touch the deeper spiritual level, you become a completely positive individual. Love, concern, dedication, spirit of service, etc., become a by-product of that spiritual development that has taken place in you. You don't have to struggle for it. A rose doesn't struggle to send out its beautiful scent; it naturally goes out. So also, a human being becomes naturally good, naturally *dhārmic*, naturally moral and ethical. In all these, a higher nature than the external physical nature is involved. So, Śrī Kṛṣṇa says here, 'I give him or her *buddhiyoga*', *yena mām upayānti te*, 'with the help of that *yoga buddhi*, he or she finds the way to Me'; comes to Me by himself or herself. The best blessing that we can get from the Divine is that kind of clear thinking and pure reason, with the touch of the Atman behind. *Buddhiyoga* means that. That is why it is said in the *Mahābhārata:* when gods want to destroy a person, they turn away his or her *buddhi* in a bad direction. Then he or she will destroy oneself. So, here, Śrī Kṛṣṇa speaks of the positive side: 'I bless people with this *buddhiyoga, yoga* of *buddhi*'. *And that is the central teaching of the Gītā.* Character-efficiency comes from *buddhiyoga*, the *yoga* of *buddhi*. That was also the teaching of the second chapter: *buddhau śaraṇam anviccha*, 'take refuge in that *buddhi*'. Then all life will be wonderful. High character will manifest in a person. So, that is the blessing we have to seek from the Divine. Give me pure *buddhi*. That is all what I need. Everything will come through that one single instrument. That is why the *Ṛg Vedic* prayer, the *Gāyatrī*, has become the greatest universal prayer. There we pray for that *buddhi*. That is the central theme of the *Gāyatrī*. Why is it so great? Because of this: the greatest prayer is the prayer for an illumined *buddhi*. *Dhiyo yo naḥ pracodayāt*, 'endow us with that *dhī*', i.e. *buddhi*, that *yogabuddhi* referred to here. The full *Gāyatrī* is: *Tat savitur vareṇyam, bhargo devasya dhīmahi, dhiyo yo naḥ pracodayāt*—a three line prayer coming in the *Ṛg Veda*, five thousand years ago, with such universal relevance. That is the beauty of that prayer. Here, Śrī Kṛṣṇa reiterates that kind of prayer.

One more important message that Śrī Kṛṣṇa gives in verse eleven:

तेषां एव अनुकम्पार्थं अहं अज्ञानजं तमः ।
नाशयामि आत्मभावस्थो ज्ञानदीपेन भास्वता ॥११॥

*Teṣām eva anukampārtham aham ajñānajam tamaḥ;*
*Nāśayāmi ātmabhāvastho jñānadīpena bhāsvatā* — *10. 11*

'Out of mere compassion for them, I, abiding in their hearts, destroy the darkness (in them) born of ignorance, by the luminous lamp of knowledge.'

Another wonderful verse. *Teṣām eva,* 'to all such people'; *anukampārtham,* 'out of compassion to them'; what do I do? *Ahaṁ ajñānajam tamaḥ nāśayāmi,* 'I destroy their darkness and delusion born of ignorance'; *aham nāśayāmi,* 'I destroy'. How do I do that? *Ātma bhāvastho,* 'by establishing Myself in their hearts' or 'I begin to manifest in their hearts, helping them to achieve this tremendous transformation'. All that is dark, all that is delusive, are washed away. The bright light of knowledge comes. Everything becomes clear. 'That is the blessing that I confer on the devotee without his or her knowledge; silently, quietly, I do that.' How? *Ātma bhāvastho,* 'by entering into them'. What do I do there? That is a wonderful idea conveyed by the next phrase. *Jñāna dīpena bhāsvatā,* 'by the lamp of knowledge, brightening up everything'. This is the service the Lord does to His devotee, to the spiritual seeker. Then, he or she will be always on the right path, moving always towards the Divine and towards friendship and love for all beings in the world. That is the type of human transformation that takes place through this type of *bhakti* combined with *jñāna* as was taught earlier in the ninth chapter, and as taught now in the tenth chapter.

This is a very great verse: lighting the *jñānadīpa.* Now these are all spiritual ideas. We have symbolic acts to express these great ideas. You enter a house; you light a lamp. What a great spiritual significance we attach to it! For a Hindu home, lighting a lamp in the front is of a great significance. Its counterpart is here: light *within*. This—lighting the outside—is what we can do now. That is a symbol of a greater light we have to get lit in our own hearts. Nobody loves darkness. We want light; the heart also cries for light and not for darkness. And therefore, in the *Bṛhadāraṇyaka Upaniṣad,* another universal prayer of the human heart is found: *asato mā sad gamaya,* 'lead me from the unreal to the Real'; *tamaso mā jyotir gamaya,* 'lead me from darkness to Light'; *mṛtyor mā amṛtam gamaya,* 'lead me from death to Immortality'. This is the prayer from the human heart not only from the *Bṛhadāraṇyaka Upaniṣad* but also from many spiritual books of the world—this human craving for life, light and knowledge. Light up *jñānadīpa;* it is our own responsibility; we struggle, and at the last point, the Lord comes and helps us. Only when we struggle, can He help. If we are careless, it means that we don't know its value. Suppose God lights the lamp in our hearts and if we say, 'we don't want it', then it means we are not fit for it, we are not ready for it. But when we become sensitive, we struggle, then this great help comes from the Divine. So, grace comes from being grace-worthy. We prepare ourselves for the touch of that grace. But grace comes. That is how the higher religions of the world have expressed human progress in spirituality: your own effort, and the grace of the Divine, blending beautifully in all high spiritual developments.

Till now it was Śrī Kṛṣṇa who was speaking. Arjuna now begins to speak in praise of Śrī Kṛṣṇa in this verse:

**अर्जुन उवाच –**

*Arjuna uvāca —*

*'Arjuna said:'*

**परं ब्रह्म परं धाम पवित्रं परमं भवान् ।**
**पुरुषं शाश्वतं दिव्यं आदिदेवं अजं विभुम् ॥१२॥**

*Param brahma param dhāma pavitram paramam bhavān;*
*Puruṣam śāśvatam divyam ādidevam ajam vibhum—10. 12*

'You are the supreme Brahman, the supreme Abode, the supreme Purifier. The Eternal, the Self-luminous *Puruṣa,* the Primordial *Deva*, Birthless, and All-pervading.'

*Param brahma,* 'you are that supreme Brahman'; *param dhāma,* 'you are that supreme Abode'; *paramam pavitram bhavān,* 'you are the supremely purifying thing' in this world; *puruṣam śāśvatam divyam,* 'that eternal divine Person' you are; *ādidevam,* 'that primordial divine Person'; *ajam,* 'unborn'; and *vibhum,* 'all-pervasive'. Saying this Arjuna continues:

आहुस्त्वां ऋषयः सर्वे देवर्षिः नारदः तथा ।
असितो देवलो व्यासः स्वयं चैव ब्रवीषि मे ॥१३॥

*Āhustvām ṛṣayaḥ sarve devarṣiḥ nāradaḥ tathā;*
*Asito devalo vyāsaḥ svayam caiva bravīṣi me* — 10. 13

'So say all the *ṛṣis,* the *deva-ṛṣi* Nārada as well as Asita, Devala, and Vyāsa; You also say so unto me.'

Arjuna is quoting the sages here. 'All the sages speak about You in this way', *Āhuḥ tvām ṛṣayaḥ sarve;* including *devarṣiḥ nāradaḥ tathā,* 'as also the great *devarṣi,* Nārada'. He also speaks of You in this way: *puruṣam śāśvatam divyam ādidevam.* Other sages like Asita, Devala, and Vyāsa, speak of You in this way. Even the greatest sages speak of You in this way. If anybody is honoured by great people, that honoured person is certainly a supremely honoured person. Ordinary people can praise anybody, but here extraordinary people are also praising the Divine. That is the greatness of God Himself. *Svayam caiva bravīṣi me,* 'and You also say the same to me'. You are only confirming what the sages have said about You. All this is true, affirms Arjuna.

सर्वं एतत् ऋतं मन्ये यन्मां वदसि केशव ।
न हि ते भगवन् व्यक्तिं विदुः देवा न दानवाः ॥१४॥

*Sarvam etat ṛtam manye yanmām vadasi keśava;*
*Na hi te bhagavan vyaktim viduḥ devā na dānavāḥ* —10. 14

'I regard all this that you say to me as true, O Keśava. Verily, O *Bhagavān,* neither the *devas* nor the *dānavas* know your personality.'

*Ṛtam* means 'true'. *Sarvam etat ṛtam manye,* 'I consider all this to be true'; *yat mām vadasi keśava,* 'what you tell me, O Keśava'. I accept it, I consider it as true. *Nahi te bhagavan vyaktim viduḥ,* 'O *Bhagavan,* they do not know Your personality'; *devā na dānavāḥ,* 'neither *devās* or gods, nor *dānavas* or *asuras* can really understand' the true dimension of Your personality. You are infinite in every sense of the term.

स्वयं एव आत्मना आत्मानं वेत्थ त्वं पुरुषोत्तम ।
भूत भावन भूतेश देवदेव जगत्पते ॥१५॥

*Svayam eva ātmanā ātmānam vettha tvam puruṣottama;*
*Bhūta bhāvana bhūteśa devadeva jagatpate — 10. 15*

'Verily, You Yourself know Yourself by Yourself, O supreme Puruṣa or Person, O Source of beings, O Lord of beings, O *Deva* of *devas,* O Ruler of the world.'

Nobody can understand You, but You can understand Yourself, *svayam eva ātmanā ātmānam vettha tvam,* 'by Yourself You know Yourself'; *puruṣottama,* 'O Supreme Puruṣa'; *bhūta bhāvana,* 'the one nourisher of all beings in the world'; *bhūteśa,* 'the Master of all beings in the world'; *devadeva,* 'the God of gods'; *jagatpate,* 'O Master of this universe'. These are various adjectives which Arjuna uses to refer to the greatness of Śrī Kṛṣṇa.

वक्तुं अर्हस्यशेषेण दिव्या ह्यात्मविभूतयः ।
याभिः विभूतिभिः लोकान् इमान् त्वं व्याप्य तिष्ठसि ॥१६॥

*Vaktum arhasyaśeṣeṇa divyā hyātmavibhūtayaḥ;*
*Yābhiḥ vibhūtibhiḥ lokān imān tvam vyāpya tiṣṭhasi—10. 16*

'It behoves You to speak, without reserve, about Your divine attributes by which, filling all these worlds, You exist.'

You must tell me of all Your divine attributes, divine manifestations; I will be very happy to listen to this from Your own mouth; *aśeṣeṇa,* 'entirely'. *Vaktum arhasi,* 'it is fit that You tell me all this'; what kind of thing? *Divyā hi ātmavibhūtayaḥ,* 'Your own divine manifestations'; *yābhir vibhūtibhir lokān imān tvam vyāpya tiṣṭhasi,* 'by which manifestations, You remain encompassing this universe'; what are they?, I would like to know. Arjuna is asking this question: God is transcendental; He is also immanent in the universe; what are those manifestations of the Divine Reality in this world?, I would like to know. And a devotee or *bhakta* is not interested in the transcendental dimension of the Divine. A *bhakta* is interested in the manifested dimension of the Divine, with whom he can communicate, establish love relationship, *bhakti* relationship; that is the nature of all *bhaktas*. The transcendental dimension of Brahman is a tremendous experience. But, as a rule, devotees all over the world—Hindu devotees, Christian devotees, Muslim devotees, all of them—like to enjoy God as one human being enjoys another human being. They want to establish a love-relationship with the Divine. Those glories by which You are enveloping the whole world, tell me all of them. 'All of them' are the words Arjuna has used here. Śrī Kṛṣṇa will say later on, 'how can I say "all of them"? A few as samples I can convey to you.'

कथं विद्यां अहं योगिन् त्वां सदा परिचिन्तयन् ।
केषु केषु च भावेषु चिन्त्योऽसि भगवन् मया ॥१७॥

*Katham vidyām aham yogin tvām sadā paricintayan;*
*Keṣu keṣu ca bhāveṣu cintyo'si bhagavan mayā* — 10. 17

'How shall I, O *Yogī*, meditating on You always, ever know You? In what things, O *Bhagavān*, are You to be thought of by me?'

*Katham vidyām aham yogin*, 'how can I understand you, O Yogin'; *sadā paricintayan*, 'by constantly meditating upon You', how do I come to understand Your true nature, O great Yogin? Śrī Kṛṣṇa is considered a great yogin. *Keṣu keṣu ca bhāveṣu cintyo'si bhagavan mayā*, 'which are the entities in the world in which I can think of or meditate upon You?'; because the whole world is Your manifestation, give me those forms in which I can meditate upon You.

विस्तरेणात्मनो योगं विभूतिं च जनार्दन ।
भूयः कथय तृप्तिर्हि शृण्वतो नास्ति मेऽमृतम् ॥१८॥

*Vistareṇātmano yogam vibhūtim ca janārdana;*
*Bhūyaḥ kathaya tṛptirhi śṛṇvato nāsti me'mṛtam* — 10. 18

'Speak to me again in detail, O Janārdana, of your *yoga*-powers and attributes, for I am never satiated in hearing the ambrosia (of your speech).'

'Please say once again all these various *vibhūtis* that You have. I am not at all satiated by listening to them.' *Yogam*, Your tremendous '*yoga*-power', by which the One has become the many; that is the greatest *yoga*-power. The Lord is one, but He has become the many in the universe. *Vistareṇa ātmano yogam*, 'extensively tell me about this *yoga*-power'; *vibhūtim ca janārdana*, 'through which, O Janārdana, You become manifested as the universe'; *bhūyaḥ kathaya*, 'tell me that again'; *tṛptirhi me nāsti*, 'I have no satisfaction (satiation)' in listening to your speech which is *amṛtam*, 'which is nectar to me'. To those who can appreciate it, it is nectar; if you have not the capacity to appreciate, then it is not nectar. A spiritual teaching is a nectar to those who are spiritually inclined. To all others it is nothing. There is such a thing as the capacity to appreciate greatness. It is a remarkable capacity in a human being. Whether it is art, literature, philosophy, or religion, the capacity for appreciation depends upon the cultural level of the individual concerned. We appreciate music, but some people do not appreciate music at all; they don't have that musical ear. Now, we know Indian music; suppose you find someone singing Western music, you can't appreciate it, because you don't know the nature of that music. So, appreciation comes from a certain cultural and educational level. Spiritual appreciation comes from a certain spiritual growth in the individual.

We in India have got a tremendous power of spiritual appreciation. When any spiritually great person appears in our midst, we watch and see how he or she behaves, find out if he or she is genuinely great, and appreciate him or her. We never kill or crucify a spiritual teacher in our country. In other countries that appreciation is lacking. A Jesus, if he were in India, do you think he would have been crucified? Not at all. Here it is not possible, because we see true religion in such persons. We appreciate a person who lives the spiritual life; not one who is merely a scholar or a priest. They are all needed, but are secondary. This is primary. Throughout our history, one of the greatest blessings imparted by our culture on our people is this capacity to appreciate a truly spiritual personality. Sometimes one may speak most unpalatable things; still if his or her character is high, we appreciate him or her. A Buddha: he denounced many of the religious practices of that time. And yet nobody harmed him. We all respected him at that time. He was treated as an enlightened one. Today, Vivekananda; he has criticised the foibles of the Indian society more fiercely than anybody. And yet we admire him. He is a great soul. In any other country, Buddha and Vivekananda would have been chopped off! Take it for granted. All over the world it is so. There is a reason behind it. The reason is twofold. One, we have been taught that religion is not mere belief; it is experience. Even an unbeliever has a status in our Vedanta. That is number one. Secondly, these great teachers showed in their lives high character. All of them were universal; there was nothing narrow, nothing parochial. Whatever they taught was universal. *Mānava dharma*, '*dharma* for human beings' and not anything sectarian.

This kind of blessing India has got from where? From the philosophy and spirituality of the Upaniṣads. That has been percolating down all these thousands of years until our people have been educated in this vision. Seek for the spiritual in a person, not for his or her showy ways, not for his or her sacerdotal office. We see only the quality of spirituality in the person. Now, this blessing on the Indian people, coming from our past, has been recognized by many thinkers and writers. But I specially mention the late Pope of the Catholic Church who visited India some years ago—not the recent Pope but the earlier Pope. In one of his observations in Bombay—this was reported in the Roman Catholic paper in Rome—he asked his assistant, 'Who are these thousands of people here? Are they Catholics?' 'No, sir.' 'Are they Christians?' 'No, sir.' 'That means they are all Hindus! Majority of them Hindus!' Then he said, 'that is what I see as the greatness of this country. These Hindus came to see in me not the head of the Catholic Church, not the head of the Christian religion, but a man of God. That is India.'

That is a wonderful tribute that he gave to India at that time. Literally true. And so, no great religious teacher is killed or persecuted in this country. Remember that. If that were not so, Vivekananda would not have lived at all. He would have been killed in the first year itself. So also Buddha. Śaṅkarācārya also was very radical in his own time. And this I call 'Indian Wisdom'. Nowhere else is it found. Why did that Bahavullah suffer martyrdom in Iran? If Bahavullah were here would he have been killed? Not at all. He started a reform. Yes, it is up to you. Show by your character that you are divine; and we will worship you, we will honour you. That is the attitude. That means, the Hindu has been taught to seek religion in experience, in character, not in profession or belief. That is why even unbelievers are respected here, if they have character. One may be an atheist, but if he or she has high character, capacity to serve people, then we respect him or her. We don't kill him or her here. Nowhere else is this attitude present; you can take it for granted. Study the history of the whole world. This is the uniqueness of India from the time of the Vedas up to this day. We have not departed from it, though, for want of knowledge of these central features of the Hindu tradition, sometimes we misbehaved in the modern period due to various circumstantial difficulties. But that is India. The eternal *Amar Bhārat,* we call it.

So, this wonderful sentence is uttered by Arjuna here: this immortal story of truth when I listen to, I am not satiated at all. I want to hear more and more and still more. The *bhakta's* reaction to the Divine is exactly like this, 'I want to hear more of it.' It is so inspiring. That is the food for our souls, because we have started to feel the hunger of the soul. Hunger of the body is secondary. Hunger of the intellect also is secondary. Hunger of the soul is primary. When that hunger comes, these two hungers fall into insignificance. That has been the experience of humanity all over. The Christian saint has the same feeling. He is hungry for the divine, a touch of the divine. He doesn't care for physical glory, physical pleasure, name or fame, nothing. He wants a marvellous touch of the soul. Sufi saints have the same experience all over. There you can see the universal dimension of what we call religion. India has recognized it. Therefore, it respects every religion. We shall preserve this attitude, strengthen it, and shall create a new India based upon it. That is the importance of this particular teaching.

श्रीभगवान् उवाच –

*Śrībhagavān uvāca —*

*'The Blessed Lord said:'*

हन्त ते कथयिष्यामि दिव्या ह्यात्मविभूतयः ।
प्राधान्यतः कुरुश्रेष्ठ नास्त्यन्तो विस्तरस्य मे ॥१९॥

*Hanta te kathayiṣyāmi divyā hyātmavibhūtayaḥ;*
*Prādhānyataḥ kuruśreṣṭha nāstyanto vistarasya me—10. 19*

'O yes, I shall speak to you now, O best of Kurus, of My divine attributes, according to their prominence; there is no end to the particulars of My manifestation.'

*Hanta te kathayiṣyāmi,* 'well, I am going to tell you'; *divyā hi ātma vibhūtayaḥ,* 'My *ātma vibhūtis*'; how? *Prādhānyatataḥ,* 'some essential ones only'; why? *Nāstyanto vistarasya me,* 'there is no end to My various manifestations in this world.' So, I will take a few samples and present them to you, says Śrī Kṛṣṇa. The idea of the glory of God manifested in the universe is a beautiful idea. High poetry has come out of that idea. High spiritual experience has come from that idea.

Earlier, I referred to Tennyson and Wordsworth. These two British poets were very much in touch with nature and through that they developed mystical experiences and they recorded it in their poems. This is another aspect. A poet's eye sees glory in this vast universe. Some divine glory is there. That is what they tried to express in poetic language. When Tennyson says you go into ecstasy by seeing this glory around you, how does he express it? Before this mystery of the world, what am I? He answers:

But what am I?
An infant crying in the night;
An infant crying for the light;
And with no language but a cry.

What a beautiful expression! So, in all parts of the world you will find that, through art and poetry, you pierce this crust of the external world and see some powers of the Divine all over there. That is the nature of the artistic mind. All art is something that penetrates the external crust of nature. But in spiritual life and experience, it is a complete achievement. And none can compare with those great sages and seers who have achieved this. No artist can be compared to a person of great spiritual experience. You can see it for yourself.

A Buddha came. What happened? His life and example produced thousands of artists, thousands of writers, authors, etc. Similarly, a Jesus. How many bumper number of artists came forth to express the Christ-experience! That is their primacy. The greatest human being is that Divine Personality who gives inspiration to writers, artists, dramatists, to represent them in their own works. They are very rare in world's history.

That high poetry is the language Śri Kṛṣṇa uses here. *Prādhānyataḥ kuruśreṣtha nāstyanto vistarasya me*, 'My *vistāra*, My spread or pervasiveness in the world, there is no end to it'. It is infinite, you can say. I shall select a few sample manifestations for the purpose of your meditation, says Śri Kṛṣṇa. And the first manifestation that Kṛṣṇa presents before us is highly significant.

अहं आत्मा गुडाकेश सर्व भूताशय स्थितः ।
अहं आदिश्च मध्यं च भूतानां अन्त एव च ॥ २० ॥

*Aham ātmā guḍākeśa sarva bhūtāśaya sthitaḥ;*
*Aham ādiśca madhyam ca bhūtānām anta eva ca* — 10. 20

'I am the Self, O Guḍākeśa, existent in the heart of all beings; I am the beginning, the middle, and also the end of all beings.'

Beautiful! I am the Self hidden in the hearts of all beings in this world. Not in the heart of Hindus only! Or *Vaiṣṇavas* only! No; *in the heart of all beings*, I am the Self, like the thread that runs through a garland of pearls, making for the unity of the pearls. That is what Śrī Kṛṣṇa described in the *Gītā* earlier (7. 7): *Mayi sarvam idam protam sūtre maṇigaṇā iva.* So, here He says that, 'I am the Self, the Atman, in the heart of all beings.' *Guḍākeśa* is Arjuna's name. *Aham ātmā sarva bhūtāśaya sthitaḥ,* 'I am in the heart of all beings', ants, worms, animals, human beings. There is not anything in the world in the heart of which the Divine spark is not there. That is a supreme truth which can be highly appreciated by unprejudiced physical scientists today.

As I cited in the example given earlier, in this solar system, we can definitely say there is nothing that is not impregnated by solar radiation. Everything—stones, flowers, leaves, food, digestion—is irradiated by solar radiation. Similarly, the world has come from Brahman, who is of the nature of *satyam-jñānam-anantam,* as the *Taittirīya Upaniṣad* said: 'Brahman is *satyam, jñānam, anantam*'; *yo veda nihitam guhāyām parame vyoman;* where shall you find Him? 'In your own heart', not somewhere in the skies, far away beyond the universe. *Nihitam,* 'hidden'; *guhāyām,* 'in the cavity of your heart'. *Nihitam,* 'hidden' and so, you have to *discover* it. That is why a little struggle is needed. *Parame vyoman,* 'in the innermost space of the heart', not on the surface, but in its depth. In many aspects of our literature, we find the concept of a cave. The whole inner life is like a cave in which this Atman is hidden. That is why, later on in our culture, these three, the Hindus, Jains, and the Buddhists, created so many caves everywhere. And you sit in a cave in meditation. The cave has a high value from that point of view. So, *parame vyoman,* 'in the supreme space of the heart', or the emptiness of the heart. The word *vyoma* means space; it also means the sky; it also means emptiness. What is space?, emptiness. That is the language: *parame vyoman* or supreme *vyoman.* That person, who so meditates, achieves the highest in this very life, said the *Taittirīya Upaniṣad.* Similarly, here also it is said:

*Aham ātmā guḍākeśa sarvabhūtāśayasthitaḥ;*
*Aham ādiśca madhyam ca bhūtānām anta eva ca —*

'I am the beginning, the middle and the end of all beings in this world.' That is the nature of the ultimate Reality. And repeating this point let me state that, the way Indian philosophy approaches this subject of cosmology can be perfectly acceptable to any astrophysicist of the modern period. They also trace everything to the one behind the many. Everything is here. But in the beginning it was undifferentiated; now it has become differentiated as the universe. That is astrophysics. That is also Vedanta. But the astrophysicist will call it 'a material something'. Vedanta calls it Pure Consciousness, infinite and non-dual—*satyam jñānam anantam brahma*, 'truth, knowledge or consciousness, and infinity—that is Brahman.' Behind this universe *that* is the truth. That is why you see consciousness in you and me. If it were not there in the cause, how can it come in the effect? That is a wonderful argument today against materialism. So, many scientists also like this idea.

I am quoting Prof. Capra, the famous writer of *The Tao of Physics* where he says:

'The Brahman of the Hindus, the *Dhammakāya* of the Buddhist, and the Tao of the Taoist, are more complete background realities of the universe than what physical science gives us today.'

Physical science explains only the material universe. What about the non-material aspect of the universe? They can't explain it. But, we can explain both. Therefore, he said that this is the comprehensiveness of the Indian approach to the nature of the cosmos. So, Śrī Kṛṣṇa says, 'I am the Atman in the heart of all beings; I am the beginning, middle and end of all beings.' From God we came, in God we exist, and to God we return, using the word God in the Vedantic sense of the term—not something extra-cosmic, but as the one primordial reality, as the infinite Consciousness, which has spread out in the vast universe in which you and I live. We are also parts of Itself. That is why there is complete oneness between us, even with nature outside. We are not separate; nature and we are part and parcel of the same Reality. So, we don't destroy nature according to our philosophy. In the West it was different: dualistic attitude; so, you destroy nature, you treat it as an enemy to be conquered. We don't accept that idea. And all those who speak of ecology today, they accept the Indian idea. Nature is not something foreign to us. We are all part and parcel of that infinite whole. That is why this teaching becomes very very relevant.

What a tremendous truth it is! This is a vast universe; you look out and study the immensity of the universe before you. Perfectly true. But the immensity of the Self that is hidden within you is far far superior to any immensity of external nature. Our Voyager, American spacecraft, after passing past Neptune is going into the outer space now. That is a wonderful thing. You experience the infinite expanse of the universe. But compared to the truth that is hidden within you, these external things are nothing! And when men and women realize this truth, they know the true glory and greatness of the human being. Both in physical science and in Vedanta, we have this concept of the human being's uniqueness. This was a subject on which I spoke at the Sir C.V. Raman Institute in Bangalore on 2nd October—a Gandhi Memorial Lecture—'Man's Uniqueness in the Upaniṣads and in Modern Science'. The audience accepted it with great joy. It is a wonderful subject. Later, I gave two lectures—late nuclear scientist Vikram Sarabhai Memorial Lectures at Ahmedabad, as 'The Science of Human Uniqueness' which has been published as a booklet by the Bharatiya Vidya Bhavan, Mumbai. The first lecture deals with human uniqueness according to modern physical sciences and the second one on human uniqueness according to Vedanta. One continues in the other; there is no conflict. If men and women know this uniqueness, they will certainly behave better than the way many of them behave today. Today we misbehave in a thousand ways. But when we come to know this uniqueness, we will try to understand it, try to realize it in the course of our life and work.

That is the development that will come in the future in the wake of this great Vedantic teaching given by Swami Vivekananda—Practical Vedanta. Vedanta coming to the marketplace, Vedanta coming to the home, Vedanta coming to the offices—not merely sitting in the Himalayas in a monastic institution. That is why this teaching has profound significance for all people. Men and women have been upgraded to a high level. What looks like a tiny physical organism contains some profound dimension. That must be realized. And nature has given us the organic capacity to investigate and realize this truth. Use that capacity, don't waste it. That is the exhortation of Vedanta to all humanity: *Tamevaikam jānatha ātmānam, anyā vāco vimuñcatha; amṛtasya eṣa setuḥ*. This is what the *Muṇḍaka Upaniṣad* said (II. ii. 5): 'try to realize that one single truth, the Atman; give up all other vain talking; this is the bridge to immortality'. The 'bridge to immortality' is to realize this truth, 'I am the Atman', ever free, ever pure, ever enlightened. That is my true nature. What a beautiful idea! Even in the worst sinner, that Atman ever remains pure. Nothing can make it impure. Its very nature is purity. This is the great view, elevated view of man and woman given in Vedanta. In no other literature will you find this view. That is why *ātmajñāna*, 'knowledge of the Atman', is the greatest thing that we can aspire for. Then, Śrī Kṛṣṇa continues:

**आदित्यानां अहं विष्णुः ज्योतिषां रविरंशुमान् ।**
**मरीचिः मरुतां अस्मि नक्षत्राणां अहं शशी ॥२१॥**

*Ādityānām aham viṣṇuḥ jyotiṣām raviramśumān;*
*Marīciḥ marutām asmi nakṣatrāṇām aham śaśī*— 10. 21

'Of the *Ādityas,* I am Viṣṇu; of luminaries, the radiant Sun; of the winds I am Marīci; of the asterisms, the Moon.'

These are enumeration from nature and from our own theology. Various entities are there; things are chosen and presented by Śrī Kṛṣṇa. So, the first is, *ādityānām aham viṣṇuḥ,* 'among the *Ādityas—āditya* is the Sanskrit word for sun—I am Viṣṇu.' There are twelve *Ādityas,* and Viṣṇu is one of the twelve *Ādityas*. 'I am Viṣṇu among the *Ādityas*'. And *jyotiṣām raviraṁśumān*, 'among the luminaries, I am the radiant sun.' *Marīciḥ marutām asmi*, 'of the winds, I am Marīci'. These are all various terms in our theology. *Nakṣatrāṇām aham śaśī*, 'of asterisms, I am the moon'. Among the many planets that are there, I am the moon, because in the night sky, the moon shines bright.

वेदानां साम वेदोऽस्मि देवानां अस्मि वासवः ।
इन्द्रियाणां मनश्चास्मि भूतानां अस्मि चेतना ॥ २२ ॥

*Vedānām sāma vedo'smi devānām asmi vāsavaḥ;*
*Indriyāṇām manaścāsmi bhūtānām asmi cetanā — 10. 22*

'I am the *Sāma Veda* of the Vedas, and Vāsava (Indra) of the gods; of the senses, I am the mind; and intelligence among living beings am I.'

*Vedānām sāma vedo'smi*, 'among the Vedas, I am *Sāma Veda*'. That is very interesting. In other places, *Ṛg Veda* or *Yajur Veda* is given prominence. Here *Sāma Veda* is given prominence. And, in fact, in the *Manu Smṛti* it is mentioned that the speech of *Sāma Veda* is impure. Here, *Sāma Veda* is highly praised! The best explanation of this difficult statement is given by Lokamanya Tilak in his *Gītā Rahasya*, second volume, where he says that the *bhakti* religion places great emphasis on *bhajan*, on music; so, among the Vedas, *Sāma Veda* is musical. The basis of Indian music is *Sāma Veda*. Naturally, the *Nārayaṇīya* section of the *Mahābhārata*, which concerns with *bhakti*, upholds the concept of *bhakti* and *bhajan*. And here, therefore, that *bhajan* idea comes prominently to make *Sāma Veda* the pre-eminent Veda.

*Devānām asmi vāsavaḥ*, 'among all the *devas*, I am Vāsava, that is, Indra, the Lord of the *devas*.' *Indriyāṇām manaścāsmi*, 'among the sense-organs, I am the *manas*'. Now, *manas* is a very unique entity in the psycho-physical system. We have the five sense-organs of seeing, hearing, etc. The sixth sense-organ is *manas*, which is not mind in its full state, but mind in its initial state; the indecisive state of mind is called by Swami Vivekananda as *manas*. When you see a thing, you begin to think, 'is it this?', or 'is it that?' That *saṅkalpa-vikalpātmikā* state of mind is called *manas* in Sanskrit. And *manas* is treated therefore as one of the sense-organs, a little more refined, which can coordinate the activities of the other five sense-organs. *Bhūtānam asmi cetanā*, 'the principle of intelligence, I am, among all the beings'. *Cetanā* or *caitanya* means intelligence, capacity to know, experience, etc.

रुद्राणां शङ्करश्चास्मि वित्तेशो यक्षरक्षसाम् ।
वसूनां पावकश्चास्मि मेरुः शिखरिणामहम् ॥२३॥

*Rudrāṇām śaṅkaraścāsmi vitteśo yakṣarakṣasām*
*Vasūnām pāvakaścāsmi meruḥ śikhariṇāmaham* — 10. 23

'Among the *Rudras*, I am Śaṅkara; of the *Yakṣas* and *Rākṣasas*, I am the Lord of wealth, that is, Kubera; of the *Vasus*, I am Pāvaka; and among mountains, Meru am I.'

*Rudrāṇām śaṅkaraścāsmi*, 'among the *Rudras* I am Śaṅkara, Śiva'. Now, these are all words with Vedic background. They have different meanings when you come to the later *Purāṇas*. But in the earlier stages, so many *Rudras* are mentioned in the Vedas. And Śaṅkara is one *Rudra* in that sense only. *Vitteśo yakṣarakṣasām*, 'among all the *Yakṣas* and *Rākṣasas*, I am Kubera, *vitteśa*, "the lord of wealth".' *Vasūnām pāvakaścāsmi*, 'among all the *Vasus*, a type of high beings, I am Pāvaka, meaning fire.' *Meruḥ śikhariṇām aham*, 'and among the mountains, I am Meru'. The Meru is a mythical mountain round which the whole universe moves; that is a concept in our mythology.

पुरोधसां च मुख्यं मां विद्धि पार्थ बृहस्पतिम् ।
सेनानीनामहं स्कन्दः सरसामस्मि सागरः ॥२४॥

*Purodhasām ca mukhyam mām viddhi pārtha bṛhaspatim;*
*Senāninām aham skandaḥ sarasāmasmi sāgaraḥ* — 10. 24

'And of priests, O son of Pṛthā, know Me as the chief, Bṛhaspati; of generals, I am Skanda; of bodies of water, I am the ocean.'

*Mām viddhi*, 'consider Me'; *bṛhaspatim*, 'as Bṛhaspati'; *purodhasām ca mukhyam*, 'the chief among the priests of the divine order'. Bṛhaspati is a great priest. I am he. *Senānīnām aham skandaḥ,* 'among the generals I am Skanda'. Subrahmaṇya is a great general. In fact, it was for his birth that we had poet Kālidās's *Kumārasambhava* depicting the story of Śiva marrying Pārvati out of which came Skanda or Kārtikeya. He is called the general of the *devas. Sarasām asmi sāgaraḥ,* 'among the reservoirs of water I am the ocean', infinite, expansive.

महर्षीणां भृगुरहं गिरां अस्मि एकं अक्षरम् ।
यज्ञानां जपयज्ञोऽस्मि स्थावराणां हिमालयः ॥ २५ ॥

*Maharṣīṇām bhṛguraham girām asmi ekam akṣaram;*
*Yajñānām japayajño'smi sthāvarāṇām himālayaḥ* — 10. 25

'Of the great *ṛṣis,* I am Bhṛgu; of words, I am the one syllable Om; of *Yajñas* I am the *Yajña* of *Japa* (silent repetition); of immovable things, the Himalaya.'

*Maharṣīṇām bhṛguraham,* 'among all the *maharṣis,* I am Bhṛgu'. In the Vedas you will find Bhṛgu, so also in the *Purāṇas,* one who was of very high status. So, among all the *maharṣis,* I am Bhṛgu. *Girām asmi ekam akṣaram,* 'among all words or speech, I am that single letter called Om'. *Yajñānām japayajño'smi.* That is very interesting. 'Among all the *yajñas* or sacrifices, I am *japa yajña*', repetition or Lord's name. What a beautiful status you get for *japa!* You may have *Aśvamedha, agnihotra,* and various types of sacrifices, *koṭi arcanas,* which people talk of today. These are all *yajñas*. But the greatest *yajña* is *japa yajña,* 'repeating the Lord's name'. So, among all *yajñas,* I am *japa. Sthāvarāṇām himālayaḥ,* 'among the immovable things of the world, I am the Himalayas'. *Sthāvara* and *jaṅgama*—the world has two types of things: one moving (*jaṅgama*), the other unmoving (*sthāvara*). Among the unmoving, I am the Himalayas.

अश्वत्थः सर्व वृक्षाणां देवर्षीणां च नारदः ।
गन्धर्वाणां चित्ररथः सिद्धानां कपिलो मुनिः ॥ २६ ॥

*Aśvatthaḥ sarva vṛkṣāṇām devarṣīṇām ca nāradaḥ;*
*Gandharvāṇām citrarathaḥ siddhānām kapilo muniḥ*—10. 26

'Of all trees, I am Aśvattha, and Nārada among *devarṣis;* Citraratha among *Gandharvas* am I; and the *muni* Kapila among the perfected ones.'

*Aśvatthaḥ sarva vṛkṣāṇām,* 'among all the trees, I am the pepul tree'. Aśvattha is a very holy tree. In the fifteenth chapter of this *Gītā,* you will get the world described as an aśvattha tree with roots upwards. That is there in the *Kaṭha Upaniṣad* also. So, that tree has become very sacred in India. Even before Buddha appeared, it was a sacred tree. Buddha sat under it and became spiritually enlightened, and this gave it a further sacredness. So, it is called *bodhi drumam,* 'the Tree of *Bodhi,* Illumination'. That is why people go around that tree. In many parts of India you will find that this aśvattha tree is held very sacred by people.

*Devarṣīṇām ca nāradaḥ,* 'among the *devarṣis,* I am Nārada'. There are three types of *ṛṣis—devarṣi, brahmarṣi* and *rājarṣi. Rājarṣi* is a person holding political power, but deeply spiritual—handling power for the good of all. Any politician, administrator, collector, any one of them, if he or she is spiritual and works for the good of the people, such a one is called a *rājarṣi. Rājānaśca te ṛṣayaśca,* 'king and sage in one', says Śaṅkarācārya, as I have mentioned in the fourth chapter. *Brahmarṣi* are *brāhmaṇas* who become great sages. And Nārada is a *devarṣi.* Three types of *ṛṣis* you find in our literature.

*Gandharvāṇām citrarathaḥ,* 'among all the *gandharvas*—they are divine musicians—I am Citraratha, one of the important *gandharvas.' Siddhānām kapilo muniḥ,* 'among the *siddhas*, spiritually perfect beings, I am Kapila, the great sage'. Kapila is highly praised in our literature as the father of philosophy, the father of psychology; that is Kapila, a sage of high spiritual development. That is the nature of Kapila. So, 'whatever Kapila says, is sacred' is an utterance in the Vedas. So, Kapila is mentioned here. So many Kapilas are mentioned in our literature, and we don't know whether they are the same. We don't have historical descriptions of these Kapilas. But the Kapila who created the Sāṅkhya philosophy, the Kapila who taught his mother, Devahūti, as given in the *Bhāgavatam,*

Book III—they are all highly developed beings, spiritual. They knew the depth of the human being. So, Kapila's status is very very high. Śrī Kṛṣṇa says, therefore, 'among all the sages, I am Kapila'.

उच्चैःश्रवसं अश्वानां विद्धि मां अमृतोद्भवम् ।
ऐरावतं गजेन्द्राणां नराणां च नराधिपम् ॥ २७॥

*Uccaiḥśravasam aśvānām viddhi mām amṛtodbhavam;*
*Airāvatam gajendrāṇām narāṇām ca narādhipam* — 10. 27

'Know Me among horses as Uccaiḥśravas, *amṛta*-born; among lordly elephants, (I am) Airāvata; and also of human beings, the king.'

*Uccaiḥśravasam aśvānām.* When the *samudramanthan,* 'churning of the ocean', by gods, demons and men took place, various things came out including Danvantari, the great science of medicine. This also came out, namely, Ucchaiḥśravas, the horse. 'I am the Ucchaiḥśravas which came out of this churning of the ocean of nectar', *amṛta*-born. Similarly, elephants and so many other things also came out at that time. Among *aśvas* or 'horses', I am Ucchaiḥśravas that came out of the *samudramanthan. Viddhi mām amṛtodbhavam,* 'know Me to be *amṛta*-born'. *Airāvataḥ gajendrāṇām,* 'Among all the *gajendras,* royal elephants, I am Airāvata'. Similarly, *narāṇām ca narādhipam,* 'among human beings, I am the ruler of humanity, the king'. In the king, or his equivalent in different political systems, all power rests. He has got a special status in society. Therefore, 'I am the *narādhipa* among the *naras.*' In fact, it is said that a king gets a small portion of whatever good his citizens do, whatever meditations they do, whatever spiritual practices they do, because he protects society, keeps up law and order, etc., so that his subjects can live peacefully. That is how the word king or *narādhipa* came into use. Today, it means sovereignty; he may not be a crowned individual. Crowned individuals are getting less and less. But, sovereignty continues. Sovereigns go away, sovereignty continues. When the British left India, the sovereign left. But sovereignty did not go. Sovereignty came to the new republic which we established in this country with a President as the symbol of that sovereignty. And every citizen also is a sovereign in a democracy and a republic.

आयुधानां अहं वज्रं धेनूनां अस्मि कामधुक् ।
प्रजनश्च अस्मि कन्दर्पः सर्पाणां अस्मि वासुकिः ॥२८॥

*Āyudhānām aham vajram dhenūnām asmi kāmadhuk;*
*Prajanaśca asmi kandarpaḥ sarpāṇām asmi vāsukiḥ—10. 28*

'Of weapons, I am the thunderbolt; of cows, I am Kāmadhuk; I am the Kandarpa among the cause of offspring; of serpents, I am Vāsuki.'

*Āyudhānām aham vajram,* 'among the various weapons, I am *vajra* the thunderbolt', that tremendous weapon created for Indra. *Dhenūnām asmi kāmadhuk,* 'among the cows, I am the Kāmadhenu'; whatever wish you want to be accomplished, that cow will help you to accomplish it. That is a mythical cow. *Prajanaśca asmi kandarpaḥ,* 'for generating new generations of men and women, I am Kandarpa, the God of Love', that famous Eros as we call it in Western language. *Sarpāṇām asmi vāsukiḥ,* 'I am Vāsuki among the serpents'.

अनन्तश्चास्मि नागानां वरुणो यादसामहम् ।
पितॄणां अर्यमा चास्मि यमः संयमतां अहम् ॥२९॥

*Anantaścāsmi nāgānām varuṇo yādasām aham;*
*Pitṝṇām aryamā cāsmi yamaḥ samyamatām aham — 10. 29*

'And Ananta among snakes am I; I am Varuṇa among water-beings; and Aryaman among *pitṛs* am I; I am Yama among controllers.'

Among the two types—one is the serpent and the other is the snake—I am, among the *nāgas* or snakes, Ananta on which Viṣṇu rests. *Varuṇo yādasām aham,* 'those who live by water, I am Varuṇa among them'. *Pitṝṇām aryamā cāsmi,* 'among the *pitṛs* I am Aryama'. *Pitṛ* means 'dead ancestors'. Among them Aryama is one of the gods mentioned in the Vedas. *Yamaḥ samyamatām aham,* 'among those who control, regulate and discipline, I am Yama, the god of death'. Yama, Kāla, Death, all these are commonly used. We say Kāla is Yama. Why? Time regulates everything. And all are subject to time. Nobody can transcend time. So, I am that Yama among regulating things.

प्रह्लादश्चास्मि दैत्यानां कालः कलयतां अहम् ।
मृगाणां च मृगेन्द्रोऽहं वैनतेयश्च पक्षिणाम् ॥ ३० ॥

*Prahlādaścāsmi daityānām kālaḥ kalayatām aham;*
*Mṛgāṇām ca mṛgendro'ham vainateyaśca pakṣiṇām*—10. 30

'And Prahlāda am I among Diti's progeny; of measures, I am Time; and of beasts, I am the lord of beasts, the lion; and Garuḍa among birds.'

*Prahlādaścāsmi daityānām,* 'among the *daityas* or *asuras,* I am Prahlāda', the greatest devotee of God among *mānavas* or human beings, *asuras,* and *devas.* Among all of them, Prahlāda stands supreme. So, I am the Prahlāda among the *daityas. Kālaḥ kalayatām aham,* 'among those that regulate and measure things, I am Time'. We measure everything by time. Everything is subject to Time. *Kālabhuktam,* 'eaten by time or Kāla'—that is the language used in the *Mahābhārata. Mṛgāṇām ca mṛgendro'ham,* 'among the animals, I am the Lord of the beasts', that is, the lion. *Vainateyaśca pakṣiṇām,* 'among the *pakṣis* or birds, I am Garuḍa, *vainateya*'. Garuḍa is highly respected in our tradition.

पवनः पवतामस्मि रामः शस्त्रभृतामहम् ।
झषाणां मकरश्चास्मि स्रोतसामस्मि जाह्नवी ॥ ३१ ॥

*Pavanaḥ pavatām asmi rāmaḥ śastrabhṛtām aham;*
*Jhaṣāṇām makarścāsmi srotasām asmi jāhnavī* — 10. 31

'Of purifiers, I am the wind; Rāma among warriors am I; of fishes I am the shark; of streams, I am Jāhnavi (the Ganga).'

*Pavanaḥ pavatām asmi,* 'of things that purify I am *pavana* or the wind'. Wind purifies, clears up everything. That is why we want the windows open. We want a little purifying air. *Rāmaḥ śastrabhṛtām aham,* 'I am Rāma among all warriors who hold weapons', i.e. Daśaratha's son Śrī Rāma. *Jhaṣāṇām makarścāsmi*, 'among all the fishes, I am the shark, *makara*.' *Srotasām asmi jāhnavī*, 'among flowing waters, I am the Ganga, Jāhnavi.' What a beautiful expression!

सर्गाणां आदिरन्तश्च मध्यं चैवाहं अर्जुन ।
अध्यात्मविद्या विद्यानां वादः प्रवदतां अहम् ॥ ३२ ॥

*Sargāṇām ādirantaśca madhyam caivāham arjuna;*
*Adhyātmavidyā vidyānām vādaḥ pravadatām aham*—10. 32

'Of manifestations, I am the beginning, the middle and also the end; of all types of knowledge, I am the knowledge of the Self; and *Vāda* among disputations.'

*Sargāṇām*, 'of the projection, maintenance, and dissolution of the universe'; *sarga* means creation. But Vedanta does not accept creation in the sense of something coming out of nothing. From Brahman the world comes out; so, we call it projection. That is the English word for *sṛṣṭi* in Sanskrit. *Sṛj* means to project. Not creation. Of this projected universe, *ādi, anta* and *madhya*, 'beginning, end and middle', am I. I am the beginning, the middle and the end of this whole projected universe. Then, *vidyānām*, 'among the sciences'; *adhyātma vidyā*, 'I am *adhyātma vidyā*'. This is another wonderful statement. There are many sciences. *Vidyā* means science. It means knowledge. And in English, science means knowledge and nothing else. Precise knowledge, which we can verify and communicate, is called science. So, *vidyā*, knowledge or science all mean the same thing; we speak of all of them as *vidyās*. Among the *vidyās*, there are many: *rasāyana vidyā* or chemistry, *bhūta vidyā* or physics, etc. Beyond these is *adhyātma vidyā* or the science of spirituality. Among all the sciences this is the pre-eminent science according to Vedanta—the science of human being in depth, the science of human possibilities, the Science of sciences. What is the use of knowing all about things? You don't know anything about yourself! That is the idea. So, among all the sciences, I am *adhyātma vidyā*. If you translate it merely as religion, then it will rather look ridiculous.

Among all the sciences, religion is the supreme science. That doesn't carry any conviction today, because religions of the world, Swami Vivekananda said, have become lifeless mockeries (*Complete Works of Swami Vivekananda*, vol. 7, p. 501). But when you speak of *adhyātma vidyā*, you recognize a profound dimension in this human being which creates all these physical sciences. The human being is unique and supreme. That is slowly coming to the understanding of modern physical science. The uniqueness of the human being, the one who creates physical sciences, naturally is superior to physical science. Therefore, the science that gives the knowledge of the human being is truly a supreme science. Therefore, Śrī Kṛṣṇa says, *adhyātma vidyā vidyānām*, 'among all the sciences, I am *adhyātma vidyā*'. This will be understood and accepted probably sometime in the next century. The physical sciences are moving in that direction. There is no other way. After you finish studying the external world, what are you going to study? You can study the world in more detail, that is all. Major studies are over because you cannot go deeper into the world than what you have gone. The whole of that study, Vedanta calls the world of *dṛśyam*, 'the seen', 'the object'. What about 'the seer', 'the observer', the *dṛk*? There, modern physical science will have to follow the footprints of India's ancient and ever fresh Vedanta.

Some years ago, I read an article in the Siemen's Journal—Siemen is a great German firm of X-ray. *Electromedica* was the name of the journal. There, a scientist has written a wonderful article. He says that the modern age started as a major work of exploration. We explored the world around, first sending our ships to the Atlantic Ocean and Indian Ocean, finding out various parts of the earth. Then we went to the north pole, then the south pole. Then we went into the ocean, to explore the depth of the ocean. Then we climbed Mount Everest and the Alps also. All this we did. Still we were restless. We wanted to explore more and more. Then we started sending rockets up into the sky. The first rockets went only fifty or sixty miles and fell down. Then slowly we developed powerful rockets and one went round circling the earth. Then, later on, we landed on the moon. And now, Voyager-II is going beyond the solar system!

Having said all this, the writer says that there is one exploration waiting to be undertaken by our men and women, namely, the hinterland of our own consciousness. What is behind this mind? What is behind this knowing process? What is the knower behind the known? That is waiting for you.

And *that* science is what India developed ages ago in the Upaniṣads. *Adhyātma vidyā* means that. Behind the body, behind the senses, behind the mind, we discovered the infinite Atman—ever pure, ever free, infinite in dimension. That is the supreme truth. *Tattvamasi, tattvamasi,* 'you are That, you are That', is the message of the *Chāndogya Upaniṣad* on this subject. So, based upon that, Śrī Kṛṣṇa is telling here: *Adhyātmavidyā vidyānām.* The modern world will accept this idea within a short time. Everything is going in that direction. The dilemma of men and women today is that the one who created a highly technical civilization has become a *creature* of that civilization, suffering from that civilization! What a poor state of humanity! Is there nothing else in men and women to make them the master of the whole show? When this question is taken up seriously, and it is being pressed upon the mind of men and women today, human beings will be driven to this wonderful science—the science of human beings in depth, not the surface human being. The human being revealed by the senses is a very truncated creature in the whole of creation. But behind that is a great reality, a great dimension. That is what the Upaniṣadic sages and seers tried to understand and succeeded in expounding it to humanity as an eternal message, a *Sanātana Dharma*. There is only one thing that is *sanātana*, eternal, and that is the infinite Atman. Everything else is subject to change. The whole world is subject to change. Sun and stars are all subject to time, subject to change. There is only one thing *sanātana,* 'eternal'; that is the Atman, the infinite Self behind all of us. So, that is the direction in which all sciences move today, gently but steadily. And Western psychology and neurology are going faster in that direction. We can expect great developments in the next century. And, Śrī Kṛṣṇa says here, 'among all the sciences, I am the science of the Atman.'

*Pravadana* means discussion, disputation, argument. There are, in our study of logic in India, three types of *pravadana.* When you discuss a subject with somebody, you can do it in three ways. They are called *vāda,* second, *jalpa,* and third comes *vitaṇḍa.* What a wonderful classification! In *vāda,* your objective is to find out the truth. So, you are discussing a subject with the motivation of finding truth. You are calm, quiet, and never getting into heated arguments. Such an argument is called *vāda;* what sciences do, also what is done in high spiritual life, that is called *vāda.* The second is *jalpa,* in which you forget the purpose for which you started your discussion. You want to get victory over your opponent without making an honest attempt to arrive at truth. And when it comes to *vitaṇḍa,* you try to win simply by refuting the others' position. You are not interested in the truth. You are only fighting with words. It is something like our democratic State and Union politics today—less *vāda,* and more of *jalpa* and *vitaṇḍa.* A Parliament is where one is supposed to engage oneself in *vāda.* We discuss with a view to doing good to the nation. That is the purpose of discussion in a democracy. That we forgot, and we got into *jalpa* and *vitaṇḍa.* Now we have to return to *vāda* once again since democracy is governance by discussion.

So, Śrī Kṛṣṇa says, 'among all these disputation methods, I am the first one, *vāda.*' If you are engaged in *vāda,* Śrī Kṛṣṇa is present there. In a Parliament, the Lord is present, if they discuss with a view to arriving at truth, and ensure the happiness and welfare of the people. This is the meaning of the statement, 'among all these disputation methods, I am *vāda.*'

अक्षराणां अकारोऽस्मि द्वन्द्वः सामासिकस्य च ।
अहमेवाक्षयः कालो धाताहं विश्वतोमुखः ॥३३॥

*Akṣarāṇām akāro'smi dvandvaḥ sāmāsikasya ca;*
*Ahamevākṣayaḥ kālo dhātāham viśvatomukhaḥ* — 10. 33

'Of letters, I am the letter A; and *dvandva* among all compounds; I alone am the inexhaustible Time; I am the Sustainer (by dispensing the fruits of actions), and the All-formed.'

*Akṣarāṇām akāro'smi,* 'among all the alphabets, I am *A;* in Sanskrit, it is the first letter, अ.' The first letter that the mouth can produce, the first sound is *A,* as heard in the word, *assurance,* because it comes from the deepest level in the throat. In Sanskrit, it is *a-kāra.* In Sanskrit, 'A' is not the first letter. 'A' in Sanskrit is, ए; it is the seventh letter. अ is the first letter. All *akṣaras* or alphabets come from *A,* i.e. अ, as the beginning. *Dvandvaḥ sāmāsikasya ca.* When you combine two words, we get what you call *samāsa* in Sanskrit, combination of words. In Sanskrit, there are three or four *samāsas,* of which *dvandva* means one word is added to another word. Say, *Rāma* plus *Kṛṣṇa,* how do you call it?, *Rāmakṛṣṇau.* That is called *dvandva samāsa.* Similarly, all other aspects of this *samāsa* system. This is a part of Sanskrit grammar where you combine words; the last portion of the first word, and the first portion of the second word undergo minor changes. That is what is determined both in *sandhi* as well as in *samāsa.* Another *samāsa* is the *bahuvrīhi samāsa.* Yet another is called *tatpuruṣa.* Very interesting *samāsas* they are. *Bahuvrīhi* means *anyapadārtha pradhāno bahuvrīhiḥ,* 'in *bahuvrīhi samāsa,* the meaning is something other than the two words combined.' The other is *tatpuruṣa,* meaning 'exactly of it'. A person met a king; the king did not know Sanskrit. So, he sang a Sanskrit verse for the king. He said, *aham ca tvam ca rājendra, lokanāthau ubhauvapi,* 'O king, I and you are both *lokanāthas,* masters of the world.' That is the real meaning of *lokanātha.* The king became angry. He alone is *lokanātha,* not the other man. But the second line clarified it: *Bahuvrīhi samāso'ham, ṣaṣṭhī tatpuruṣo bhavān. Bahuvrīhi samāso'ham,* 'I am *lokanātha* in the *bahuvrīhi samāsa.*' *Bahuvrīhiḥ* is *anya padārtha pradhāno.* So, according to *bahuvrīhi,* the meaning of *lokanātha* is *loko yasya nāthaḥ sa lokanāthaḥ*. '*Loka* is my master', I am not the master! That is called *lokanātha* according to *bahuvrīhi*. And the meaning of *lokanātha* according to *ṣaṣṭhi tatpuruṣa* is *lokasya nāthaḥ lokanāthaḥ*, 'you are the Lord of the world'. 'Therefore', he said, 'you are *tatpuruṣa*, I am *bahuvrīhi*.' 'Both are *lokanātha*,' he said. In Sanskrit you can make many such funny and beautiful combinations. And so these are the *samāsas*—*bahuvrīhi*, *tatpuruṣa* and *dvandva*. *Dvandva* is usually used as in *rāmaśca kṛṣṇaśca rāmakṛṣṇau*. You can mix up like that; the two combine together. So that is why that *au* will come in dual number *rāmakṛṣṇau*. Similarly other words also. It is called *dvandva*, because it combines *a*, *b* and *c*. Therefore, He (Lord) is one who unites people with each other. In the sense of 'uniting principle', He is *dvandva* among *samāsas*.

*Aham eva akṣayaḥ kālo*, 'I alone am inexhaustible Time'. Time goes on flowing, flowing; as far as you look forward, time is there; as far as you look backward, time is there. This flow of time is something very impressive. It is only a little civilized human being who can recognize the importance of time. When we were primitive, we were acted upon by time. We couldn't comprehend time. But, we studied time when we became a little more cultured. And therefore, India has spent a lot of time to understand the nature of time. Modern science is also trying to understand the nature of time, and that is how Einstein combined space and time into a space-time continuum. The whole world is nothing but space-time continuum. You can't separate space from time. A united space-time is the reality today, and every thing in that space-time is an *event*, not a thing or an entity. When you understand space-time as a continuum, entities vanish; only events remain. Everything becomes an event—just like a cinema picture. So many small small entities are put together and given time as the background. That time movement converts all entities into events. Time combined with the three dimensions of space is the reality of the world, the four-dimensional continuum according to Einstein's relativity theory. The arrow of time goes onwards, onwards. It can go on endlessly. Śrī Kṛṣṇa calls it therefore: *aham eva akṣayaḥ kālo,* 'I am this *akṣyaḥ* or endless *kāla* or time'. *Kālo'smi,* 'I am *kāla*', He will say in the eleventh chapter; I have come to consume everything here. The whole world will be consumed by Time. *Kālo sarvasya bhoktāḥ,* is a statement: 'Time eats up everything in the world'. Nothing will be left out; that is the primordial nature of Time, the tremendous reality. Further, Śrī Kṛṣṇa says here, *dhātāham viśvato mukham,* I am also 'the sustainer, *dhātā,* with face turned towards all sides.'

**मृत्युः सर्व हरश्चाहं उद्भवश्च भविष्यताम् ।**
**कीर्तिः श्रीः वाक् च नारीणां स्मृतिः मेधा धृतिः क्षमा ॥ ३४ ॥**

*Mṛtyuḥ sarva haraścāham udbhavaśca bhaviṣyatām;*
*Kīrtiḥ śrīḥ vāk ca nārīṇām smṛtiḥ medhā dhṛtiḥ kṣamā—10. 34*

'And I am the all-consuming Death; and the prosperity of those who are to be prosperous; of women, I am fame, prosperity, speech, memory, intelligence, endurance and patience.'

Again comes the word *mṛtyu;* the only difference between *kāla* and *mṛtyu* is that when you speak of *kāla* you are unemotional; when you speak about *mṛtyu,* you become emotional because it directly concerns you. That is called death. Everyday we are dying; we are not worried about it. But we are afraid of a final death. So, *mṛtyu* comes to you as a final act of *kāla. Mṛtyuḥ sarvaharaḥ ca aham,* 'I am death which swallows up everything'. Similarly, in the language of *bhukti* we say, those who touch the feet of the Lord, are not touched by death. That is a wonderful statement by Śrī Kṛṣṇa's mother, Devakī, in the *Śrīmad Bhāgavatam* regarding Śrī Kṛṣṇa who was born of her in Kamsa's prison. There you will find Devakī's hymn to Śrī Kṛṣṇa, her own son, but as a divine form lying before her. Among the verses of the hymn is one such on death. *Mṛtyuḥ sarvaharaścāham,* 'I am death which consumes everything', except anyone who is at the feet of the divine. That is the statement of Devakī in that hymn of praise (X. iii. 27):

*Martyo mṛtyuvyālabhītaḥ palāyan*
*lokān sarvān nirbhayam nādhyagacchat;*
*Tvat pādābjam prāpya yadṛcchayādya*
*Svasthaḥ śete mṛtyurasmād apaiti —*

She is telling, pointing to baby Śrī Kṛṣṇa with her own hand: 'As soon as the mortal being is born, death is after him or her, chasing everyone. Everyone wants to escape it.' One eats, gets education, gets a job, marries, does good work, even goes to heaven. Why? To avoid death. 'But death is always behind everyone', closely following everyone, going to consume that person. In this way a human being becomes restless. *Martyaḥ mṛtyuvyālabhītaḥ*, 'a mortal fearing the *mṛtyuvyāla*'; *mṛtyu* is compared to a snake, *vyāla*, creeping towards us. People generally 'fear', *bhītaḥ*, things creeping towards them. Here death is a creeping thing. *Palāyan*, 'one runs away'. Figuratively one runs away from that *mṛtyu*-snake chasing him or her. *Sarvān lokān*, 'goes to all parts of the world, even to higher worlds'. *Nirbhayam nādhyagacchat*, 'nowhere does he or she get security and peace'. *Tvad pādābjam prāpya yadṛcchayā adya*, 'but, getting, by chance, a place at Your lotus feet', O Kṛṣṇa, then *mṛtyu* cannot enter that magic circle. *Mṛtyu* comes nearby and 'quietly retreats', *mṛtyurasmād apaiti; svasthaḥ śete*, 'leaving you in peace'. That is the divine Person that You are; that is the language Devaki uses there.

So, this infinite Atman is the only centre where *mṛtyu* cannot come. Everything else is subject to *mṛtyu*. This has been repeated again and again in the Upaniṣads. *Sarvam anyat ārtam*, 'everything else is subject to death, full of sorrow and suffering'. This alone is free from suffering, from death etc. You find it repeated again and again. 'Those who see differences here, they go from death to death; those who see the One behind the many, they alone become immortal', is the language used in the Upaniṣads again and again. Here Śrī Kṛṣṇa says, 'I am *mṛtyu* consuming everything in this world'.

*Udbhavaśca bhaviṣyatām*. What is prosperity? I am that *udbhava*, prosperity, of those who are to be prosperous. This person is going to be prosperous; I am behind him or her as the principle of prosperity. *Kīrtiḥ śrīrvākca nārīṇām smṛtirmedhā dhṛtiḥ kṣamā:* In women there are so many beautiful virtues and graces. Śri Kṛṣṇa relates a few of these and says, I am these. What are they? *Kīrti,* 'good name'; *śrī,* 'prosperity'; *vāk,* 'sweet speech'; *smṛtiḥ,* 'memory'; *medhā,* 'intelligence', the capacity to understand things; *dhṛtiḥ,* 'tremendous endurance'; *kṣamā,* 'patience'. These various virtues in women am I, says Śrī Kṛṣṇa in this verse.

The Divine is not only transcendent but also immanent. That is the main theme of this and the next chapter.

बृहत्साम तथा साम्नां गायत्री छन्दसां अहम् ।
मासानां मार्गशीर्षोऽहं ऋतूनां कुसुमाकरः ॥३५॥

*Bṛhatsāma tathā sāmnām gāyatrī chandasām aham;*
*Māsānām mārgaśīrṣo'ham ṛtūnām kusumākaraḥ* — 10. 35

'Of *Sāmas* also, I am the *Bṛhat Sāma;* of metres, Gāyatrī am I; of months, I am *Mārgaśirṣa;* of seasons, the flowery seasons.'

*Bṛhatsāma tathā sāmnām,* 'among the *sāmagānas,* songs of the *Sāma Veda,* I am the *Bṛhat Sāma*'—one of the items of the *Sāma Veda. Gāyatrī chandasām aham,* 'and among all the metres, Vedic metres, poetic metres, I am Gāyatrī'. Gāyatrī is an oft-occurring metre in the Vedas. *Om tat savitur vareṇyam, bhargo devasya dhīmahi, dhiyo yo naḥ pracodayāt;* this three-line kind of poetry is called Gāyatrī in *chandas. Chandas* means this kind of expression in Vedic poetry. Various forms of *chandas* there are in Sanskrit as well as in English and in all the languages. This is one such, which is not very current today. In the Vedic literature you get it. *Māsānām mārgaśīrṣo'ham,* 'among the months, I am *Mārgaśīrṣa,* December-January, from the middle of December to the middle of January.' It is also called *Agrahāyaṇa;* during the period of *Mahābhārata,* the year was started from *Mārgaśīrṣa,* or *Agrahāyaṇa,* the beginning of the year. *Mārgaśīrṣa* is a very sacred month even today in India. *Ṛtūnām kusumākaraḥ,* 'among the seasons, I am spring'. The language used here is, that season when flowers sprout in nature, *kusumākaraḥ*. *Kusuma* is flower. After the death of nature in winter, in spring the whole nature bursts out in beauty and charm. That is why spring is always highly appreciated in poetry. So, I am that spring among all the seasons; *kusumākaraḥ*. They also call it *Vasanta* in Sanskrit; *vasanta ṛtu*. *Ṛtu* is the Sanskrit word for 'season'.

द्यूतं छलयतां अस्मि तेजस्तेजस्विनां अहम् ।
जयोऽस्मि व्यवसायोऽस्मि सत्त्वं सत्त्ववतां अहम् ॥ ३६ ॥

*Dyūtam chalayatām asmi tejastejasvinām aham;*
*Jayo'smi vyavasāyo'smi sattvam sattvavatām aham* —10. 36

'I am the gambling of the fraudulent; I am the power of the powerful; I am victory; I am effort; I am *Sattva* of the *sāttvika*.'

It is interesting. *Dyūtam chalayatām asmi*. I am *dyutam*, that kind of play of gambling. You have in *Mahābhārata* cheating in gambling done by Śakuni. And so, I am the gambling of the gambler, the deceitfulness of the gambler. Many people, specially those who are of the monotheistic attitude, cannot appreciate this thing. Their God is separate from this universe. But, in India God is not separate from the universe. From God the universe has come. So, there is nothing supernatural in Indian thought. Therefore, whatever happens here is an expression of the Divine. I repeatedly gave the example of the sun. Solar energy is condensed into all the things on this earth. Good, bad, indifferent, everything is solar energy. The dirt here is also solar energy. And therefore, a unifying philosophy will have to accept not only the good but also the bad as expression of the same reality. So, from that point of view, *dyūtam chalayatām asmi*, as also *tejas tejasvinām aham*, 'those who are brilliant, I am that brilliance in them'. *Jayo'smi*, 'I am victory' of the victorious; *vyavasāyo'smi*, 'I am the determined effort of those who have that attitude'; *sattvam sattvavatām aham*, 'among those who are calm and steady, the *sāttvik* type, I am that *sattva*'. *Sattva* is what gives calmness, the balanced attitude. There are three states of mind: *sāttvik*, *rājasik*, and *tāmasik*.

वृष्णीनां वासुदेवोऽस्मि पाण्डवानां धनञ्जयः ।
मुनीनां अप्यहं व्यासः कवीनां उशना कविः ॥३७॥

*Vrṣṇīnām vāsudevo'smi pāṇdavānām dhanañjayaḥ;*
*Munīnām apyaham vyāsaḥ kavīnām uśanā kaviḥ — 10. 37*

'Of the Vṛṣṇis, I am Vāsudeva; of the Pāṇḍavas, Dhanañjaya; and among the *munis*, I am Vyāsa; of the poets, Uśana, the sage.'

*Vrṣṇīnām vāsudevo'smi,* 'among the Vṛṣṇis, the Yādavas, I am Kṛṣṇā or Vāsudeva'. There He is only identifying Himself. He Himself is the universal Divine. Now He says, among the Yādavas I am that Kṛṣṇa. Vāsudeva is the son of Vasudeva, Kṛṣṇa's father. So, Vāsudeva becomes Kṛṣṇa. *Pāṇḍavānām dhanañjayaḥ,* 'among the Pāṇḍavas, I am Arjuna'. Arjuna is in front of him! *Munīnām apyaham vyāsaḥ,* 'among all the sages, *munis*, I am Vyāsa', that brilliant mind which has contributed so much to the culture of India, to the intellect of India. That is Vyāsa of the *Mahābhārata,* and of many *Purāṇas* also. *Kavīnām uśanā kaviḥ,* 'among the poets, I am the poet Uśana', an old Vedic poet.

दण्डो दमयतां अस्मि नीतिरस्मि जिगीषताम् ।
मौनं चैवास्मि गुह्यानां ज्ञानं ज्ञानवतां अहम् ॥३८॥

*Dando damayatāmasmi nitirasmi jigiṣatām;*
*Maunam caivāsmi guhyānām jñānam jñānavatām aham—10. 38*

'Of punishers, I am the sceptre; of those who seek to conquer, I am statesmanship; and also of things secret, I am silence; and the knowledge of knowers, am I.'

*Dando damayatāmasmi,* 'among those forces that discipline men and women in the political life, I am *daṇḍa,* the principle of punishment'. *Daṇḍa* means stick. You hold a stick; you don't punish actually. That stick is there. That itself makes for orderliness in society. So, this is the concept of political authority through law and law-enforcing power. Just like the mace in the British Parliament. That mace is the authority of the Parliament. It doesn't actually break the head of anybody, but the very principle of authority makes for even goals of life and whenever things go wrong the force acts. That is called a political state with a power to enforce law and order on society. In fact, the philosophy of a political state is called *daṇḍa-nīti* in our Sanskrit language. The science of *daṇḍa—daṇḍa* means punishment, a big stick to punish; that is all. Only the stick is there and because of that, people go in the right way. And it is very very true that almost 99 per cent of people need an external power to make them behave properly. Only those who are moral and highly spiritual do not need an external power. They have their own power of self-discipline; they will never go wrong in their attitude, never harm anybody else. But the majority is not like that. If there is no law and order, each will try to exploit the other. Therefore, we need a state. We need law, regulation, etc. What Schopenhauer, the German philosopher, said is so true in actual life: 'man is moral, not because he chooses to be so but because of the fear of the police and public opinion'. These two things keep us moral. Take these two things away, and most people will be at each others' throat. So, *daṇḍo damayatām asmi.* I am that sense of political power of the state which regulates the whole society, *damayatām,* 'which disciplines' the whole society. *Nītirasmi jigīṣatām,* 'I am justice in those who seek victory', because there is a famous belief that justice alone can win. Injustice can win temporarily, but real victory belongs to *dharma,* justice. So, here it is said, *nītirasmi jigīṣatām,* those who obtain victory do so because they follow *dharma,* righteousness. That is the belief of the best of thinkers in every country, though, very often, the world itself may show the opposite. The unjust sometimes win. But we must take a long-range view. Therefore, this is that long-range view. *Yato dharmaḥ tato jayaḥ,* 'where there is *dharma,* there is victory'. That is a Sanskrit statement in the *Mahābhārata. Maunam caivāsmi guhyānām.* Another beautiful idea! 'Among all mysteries, I am silence'. The ultimate Reality is described in the Upaniṣads as silence. When you speak, you bring down Reality. You try to catch It in terms and formulae, but It escapes. Only in silence can you truly express the nature of the ultimate Reality. So, the greatest mystery is silence. And the Upaniṣads said, *śānto'yam ātmā,* 'this Atman is pure silence'. A disciple went to a teacher and requested him to teach him the highest Reality. The teacher kept quiet. The disciple put the question a second time, a third time. And when he said, 'I have been asking three times and you have not replied at all. Why is it so?' Then the teacher said, 'I have been answering your question all the time. You couldn't understand it! The Atman is silence, quietness, *śānto'yam ātmā.*' That is a great idea in the Upaniṣads. Whenever you express a thing, you just bring it within the fold of thought and speech. You restrict Reality. So, you cannot really express Reality which is beyond speech, beyond thought, beyond ideation. It is 'pure is', 'pure being'. That is the language used in the Upaniṣads and yet we do need language for communication. So, we use the language with the understanding that language can only give you an approximation. Thought can give you only an approximation. Truth itself is beyond speech and thought. *Yato vāco nivartante aprāpya manasā saha,* this is the beautiful expression of the *Taittiriya Upaniṣad:* 'that Reality from which speech and thought recoil not being able to comprehend It'. That is why at higher levels of mental development, speech becomes less and less. Intellectual expression becomes less and less. More of experience is emphasized there. In the beginning of life you can use plenty of language. We can be chattering all the time. But the more you approach that highest Reality, your speech becomes less and less; your argumentation becomes less and less. It is pure experience. That is absolute silence.

Sri Ramakrishna compares it with the honeybee and its behaviour. It is humming all the time, hovering over the flower. Humming, humming, humming. As soon as it sits on the flower and begins to drink the honey, all humming is over. That is the nature of spiritual experience. One can indulge in any amount of talk, any amount of argumentation in the beginning. But as one approaches closer and closer to Reality, these become less and less. And in direct experience, they die down. Therefore, silence has a tremendous value and I think, in higher aspects of all mystical life, you find this silence more and more. So, 'among all the mysteries I am silence'. *Maunam* actually means mouth shut and even thought becoming quiet. There is a beautiful expression in William Wordsworth:

> ...that serene and blessed mood,
> In which the affections gently lead us on,—
> Until, the breath of this corporeal frame
> And even the motion of our human blood
> Almost suspended, we are laid asleep
> In body, and become a living soul:

So, you can see the beauty of this physical instrument of speech or the psychic instrument of thought. These are all good only for interacting with the external world; to name a thing, to label it with concepts and words. Both are needed. They call it percept and concept. A thing that you see is a percept, and, when you think about it, it becomes a concept. These are needed only for interaction with the external world. When you deal with the Self, these things drop away, collapse; they have no value there. And yet, in order to approach It, we do need to use these things, but with carefulness; don't run away with the words. Word is not anything here. 'The letter killeth', when Jesus said, this is what he meant. 'The letter killeth, the spirit giveth life'. Therefore, don't depend on the letter, nor the concept, go beyond both. That is called experience of Reality, experience of the Divine. That is the true dimension of religion.

*Jñānam jñānavatām aham,* 'I am that *jñāna* among those who have achieved *jñāna.*' *Jñāna* means spiritual knowledge. We know our true nature. I am that *jñāna* among those who have got *jñāna.*

यच्चापि सर्वभूतानां बीजं तदहं अर्जुन ।
न तदस्ति विना यत्स्यात् मया भूतं चराचरम् ॥३९॥

*Yaccāpi sarvabhūtānām bījam tadaham arjuna;*
*Na tadasti vinā yatsyāt mayā bhūtam carācaram* — 10. 39

'And whatsoever is the seed of all beings, that also am I, O Arjuna. There is no being, whether moving or unmoving, that can exist without Me.'

*Arjuna,* 'O Arjuna!' *Yaccāpi sarvabhūtānām bījam tadaham,* 'all the things of the world have, as their seed, Myself, that ultimate Reality.' Śrī Kṛṣṇa is speaking, identifying Himself with that ultimate Reality of pure Consciousness, infinite and non-dual. So, whatever there is in this world has its origin in that ultimate Reality of pure Consciousness. I am that seed of everything in the world; I am that; I am that. *Na tadasti vinā yatsyāt mayā bhūtam carācaram,* 'there is nothing in this world, whether moving or unmoving, that can exist without Me'. Take away My being from anything in the world and it becomes nonexistent. I give the value of existence to it. Sri Ramakrishna gives the example of zero: it has no value even if you put twenty thousand zeroes. But put a '1' before the zeroes and every zero gets value; every new zero adds to the value. That '1' is the Divine. Among the changing things of the world, there is One that is real. The One, the infinite, the immortal; that makes them real. Take that away and they become unreal.

Śaṅkarācārya refers to it in his Upaniṣad commentary saying, *tadātmanā vinirmuktaḥ jagat asat sampadyate,* 'take away the Atman from the universe, and the universe becomes absolutely a zero,' with no value at all. That is what the *Gītā* is stressing. Put the One behind the many; then the many get a value. Otherwise, they have no value. This is spiritual understanding, spiritual vision. So, this is an important teaching that whatever is real is Brahman. So, there is a classification in Vedanta: everything in the universe consists of five factors. It is a very important Vedantic study. What are the five factors? *Sat-cit-ānanda*—the first three: 'Truth or being, consciousness, and bliss.' These three plus two more: 'name and form', *nāma* and *rūpa.* All things in the world are composed of all these five items: *sat, cit, ānanda, nāma* and *rūpa.* All these differences are because of name and form. Everything is *sat cit ānanda.* And that *sat-cit-ānanda* portion is Brahman. And name-form portion is the world. The world is essentially *sat-*

*cit-ānanda,* but with a special name and with a special form. Just like the ocean. Ocean is absolutely one sheet of water; then you have a wave. What is that wave? The ocean *plus* a name and a form. That is called the wave. You describe it that way. You can't describe the ocean. Just the infinite ocean; that is all. But once it gets a shape, you are able to name it, you are able to describe it. That is *nāma-rūpa,* name and form. Take for instance, a gold ornament. What is that gold ornament? Gold *plus* name and form. That is all. A bangle or a garland, any name you can give, but actually it is gold plus name and form. So, Vedanta says Brahman or Atman plus name and form is this universe. Take away the name and form. What remains? Only Brahman. These Vedantic ideas influenced some of the Western poets in the last century. And there you find therefore a British poet like Shelley expressing this truth in *Adonais,* an elegy on the death of John Keats: 'the One remains, the many change and pass'. So, this is the teaching: we have to put One behind the many. There is a verse from our Upaniṣadic literature, in the *Īśā Upaniṣad,* and the first verse in it emphasizes this truth: *Īśā vāsyam idam sarvam. Idam sarvam,* 'this entire manifested universe' is nothing but the Divine, that infinite pure Consciousness.

What modern astrophysics calls the background material which exploded and made for the evolution of the universe, Vedanta calls that the infinite pure Consciousness, one and non-dual. That exploded and became this universe. Therefore, that Consciousness is there in nature and it is manifest in living beings. It is more manifested in the human being. And men and women can also discover the truth in themselves and in others. The idea 'within the universe and beyond the universe', comes a little later, in a verse in the *Śrīmad Bhāgavatam.* An elephant was caught by a crocodile; he was suffering terribly, and it praised the Divine by offering to the Lord a lotus from the pool he was in. And the Lord came and saved that elephant. That is the mythical story in the *Bhāgavatam.* It is well known as the myth of *Gajendramokṣa,* 'salvation of the lordly elephant'. I have seen it depicted very beautifully in art in Cambodia and Indonesia. There, the elephant praises the Divine and one *śloka* in that hymn is very famous for conveying this idea (*Śrīmad Bhāgavatam,* VIII. iii. 3):

*Yasmin idam yataścedam yenedam ya idam svayam;*
*Yo'smāt parasmāt ca paraḥ tam prapadye svayambhuvam —*

'I take refuge in the self-existing Reality', *tam prapadye svayambhuvam;* that is the first description. Then the next is, a series of utterances regarding the nature of that Reality. *Yasmin idam,* 'in Whom is this universe'; *yataścedam,* 'from Whom is this universe'; *yena idam,* 'by Whom is this universe'; *ya idam svayam,* 'Who Himself is this universe'; and then, *yo asmāt parasmāt ca paraḥ,* 'Who is also beyond this universe'; *tam prapadye,* 'in Him I take refuge'. The highest Vedantic ideas are expressed in that verse of the hymn of the elephant in the *Śrīmad Bhāgavatam.* So, Śrī Kṛṣṇa says here in the *Gītā,* 'everything moving and unmoving in this world has Me as the focus of their Reality.' Take Me away and they lose their sense of being.

नान्तोऽस्ति मम दिव्यानां विभूतीनां परन्तप ।
एष तूद्देशतः प्रोक्तो विभूतेः विस्तरो मया ॥४०॥

*Nānto'sti mama divyānām vibhūtīnām parantapa;*
*Eṣa tūddeśataḥ prokto vibhūteḥ vistaro mayā* — 10. 40

'There is no end to My Divine powers, O scorcher of foes; but this is a brief statement by Me of the particulars of My Divine powers or attributes.'

*Nānto'sti mama divyānām vibhūtīnām parantapa,* 'there is no end to My Divine manifestations or powers, O Arjuna'. There is no end to it. Infinite they are. *Eṣa tūddeśataḥ prokto vibhūtervistaro mayā,* 'I have told you only just a few of the infinite powers of the Divine as the universe, as a sample.'

Then comes a very great utterance of the *Gītā* which has educated the people of India to bow down before greatness wherever it occurs, in any country, in any community, in any religion. If they see greatness, they bow down. That sanction comes from this verse:

यद्यद्विभूतिमत्सत्त्वं श्रीमदूर्जितमेव वा ।
तत्तदेवावगच्छ त्वं मम तेजोंऽशसम्भवम् ॥४१॥

*Yadyadvibhūtimatsattvam śrīmadūrjitameva vā;*
*Tattadevāvagaccha tvam mama tejo'mśasambhavam*—10. 41

'Whatever being there is great, prosperous, or powerful, you know that to be produced from a part of My splendour.'

Very beautiful verse. Wherever you find, *vibhūtimat*, 'endowed with a tremendous power of manifestation'; *sattvam*, 'pure energy and power'; *śrīmat*, 'good fortune'; *ūrjitam eva vā*, 'or with tremendous energy'. Wherever you find any such manifestation, uplifting humanity by doing great works, great thinking, Śrī Kṛṣṇa says, 'please know that a portion of My glory is present there', *tat tat eva avagaccha tvam mama tejo'mśa sambhavam.* Don't think that I am far away from you. When the concept of God is an item among items outside this universe, which is called monotheism, this subject, this idea, can never come under that theology. This Reality is infinite, universal, present in everyone—in some with a greater force, in some in a lesser way. An Indian sees in Jesus, a wonderful life, holy and pure, uplifting humanity; he or she sees the manifestation of the Divine there. Immediately, he or she will bow down there. So also, anybody else. For example, we respect American President, Abraham Lincoln. He did wonderful work against Negro slavery in America. We see a touch of the Divine in that kind of action. So, this applies all over the world. We have been educated to respect greatness which uplifts humanity wherever it happens, because this teaching is there. *Mama tejo'mśa sambhavam*, 'it is an aspect of My Divine energy manifesting there'. That is the importance of both this concept of Reality and the idea of its universal manifestation in the universe. On this subject, somebody asked this question to Sri Ramakrishna. That somebody was not an ordinary person; he was Pandit Iswar Chandra Vidyasagar. He asked this question, 'Sir, is there partiality in the Divine that He manifests more in one and less in the other?' 'Yes,' said Sri Ramakrishna. 'In this universe there is the manifestation, but there is also the difference in the quantum of manifestation. In some it is more, and in some it is less.' Then came the question; 'Is God partial then?' Immediately Sri Ramakrishna asked, 'what do you mean by partial? Why do I come to see you? I see a greater manifestation in you than in others, and therefore I come to see you. Many others also come and honour you. Have you developed two horns for us to come and see you?' He asked this question in Bengali: *Duṭo singh beriyeche?*, 'have you developed two horns so that people come and see you?' 'You have got a high character. Your intellect is clear, your heart is full of compassion, so the Divine energy is manifested more in you than in others. So, we come to see you.' That is a fact of experience. There is no question of partiality or any such thing. It is up to you to manifest more. Just like what you see in the human body: this skin cannot manifest light, but the eye ball can manifest light. The same skin, but it manifests light. There is difference between the two. So, behind differences in the manifestation are grades of manifestation, some more and some less. That is why this world is a world. If it is all one type, it will be no world at all. Differences make the world a real experience. So, Śrī Kṛṣṇa expounded this wonderful idea of Divine manifestation in the universe. This universe is 'essentially Divine': *īsāvāsyam.* Our eyes cannot reveal this truth, but when the mind is pure, it is able to penetrate deep and discover that One behind the many in yourself and then, when you look out, you find the same One manifested as this universe. This is the hint that is sung in the *Kaṭha Upaniṣad* in one or two beautiful verses. Scientist, Sir J.C. Bose of Calcutta, discovered the unity of the living and the non-living. He was a great physicist. First he was dealing with radio waves—the first one to discover radio waves in his own laboratory in Calcutta. Then he started studying the living plants. He studied that little plant, *Mimosa pudica*. It also has experience. Then he turned over to the study of metals, ordinary metals. He found that there is sensation in metals also; he found, in all these, response to stimulus. So, he expounded the theory of the unity of all nature: that this kind of response comes not only in the living but also in the non-living. With his own experiments, with his own experimental apparatus which he had designed, he could magnify various little events into a million times. Then he went to England. There he spoke before the Royal Society of England and in one or two other places. Distinguished scientists were there. He demonstrated; some were sceptical, some were very much taken by this wonderful demonstration. All this was described in *The Times* paper at that time. And *The Times* paper wrote, 'when we in the West were lost in the multitudinous things of the world, the Eastern sage went beyond and discovered a One behind the many'. And Bose's own speech at the end of the demonstration was:

'When I saw these beautiful events taking place unifying the living and the non-living, I understood the meaning of the utterance of my great ancestors in the Vedas on the banks of the Ganges when they proclaimed this truth: "he who sees the One in the many, to him belongs eternal peace, eternal happiness, and to none else, and to none else".'

That is a verse from the *Kaṭha Upaniṣad*. We see differences; we are not able to penetrate these differences to see the unity that is there. The whole function of human knowledge is to penetrate the surface and see the One behind the many. Every science does this. Now we are trying to unify the whole of nature in physics through a unifying field theory. Whenever one sees differences, a question arises, 'is this true?'. 'Is it true that they are entirely different? There must be a unity behind diversity.' Like biology telling us today, there are varieties of human racial types. But, as homo sapiens, they are one. There is only one human species among human beings—not two or more—with capacity of inter-breeding and inter-thinking. Now, this is the discovery of modern biology. Similarly, also in other departments of science. Vedanta took up the whole of experience and discovered the unity behind the diversity, and broke down barriers to neighbourliness. We are all essentially one. We may have differences in colour, in educational status, in cultural level, but we are all spiritually one. And this is the Vedantic language of ages ago. So, finally Śrī Kṛṣṇa concludes the tenth chapter with the verse:

अथवा बहुनैतेन किं ज्ञातेन तवार्जुन ।
विष्टभ्याहं इदं कृत्स्नं एकांशेन स्थितो जगत् ॥४२॥

*Athavā bahunaitena kim jñātena tavārjuna;*
*Viṣṭabhyāham idam kṛtsnam ekāmśena sthito jagat—10. 42*

'Of what avails you to know all this diversity, O Arjuna? I exist supporting this entire universe by a portion of Myself.'

'What is the use of further elaboration, O Arjuna? The truth is, I sustain this whole universe with a small portion of Myself.' *Idam kṛtsnam,* 'this entire universe'; *viṣṭabhyāham,* 'I sustain'. How? *Ekāmśena,* 'from a small portion of Myself'. That is the nature of this manifestation. You find the same utterance by the sages of the old *Ṛg Veda,* in the beginning itself of the *Puruṣa Sūkta: pādo'sya viśvā bhūtāni tripādasyāmṛtam divi,* 'a quarter of the Reality is manifested as the universe; the rest is all beyond manifestation and is immortal'. This universe is a product of a bit of that Divine energy manifesting as this multiplicity. The same *Puruṣa Sūkta* says, *etāvān asya mahimā,* 'this is His glory as seen in this universe'; but, *ato jyāyāmśca pūruṣaḥ,* 'the Real Self is beyond this manifestation'. So, there is one common feature between modern science and Vedanta, and that is the unity behind this diversity. And every science also accepts that eventually all this diversity will go back to that unity. In Vedanta and modern science these two truths are fully accepted. The world came from the One, and will go back to the One. Therefore, Śrī Kṛṣṇa says here, 'what is the need to know in more detail about this truth?' The truth is, 'I sustain this whole universe with a portion of Myself'. That is the idea.

Śrī Kṛṣṇa had said earlier: 'This is My *māyā*. Those who come and take refuge in Me, they will overcome this *māyā*', which produces this notion of separateness. Why this war? Why this crime? Why this violence? From a sense of separateness only they come. Therefore, all these troubles come. If we are all essentially one, how can troubles come? That knowledge has to come. Then only peace will come to the world. Basic knowledge is: we are essentially one. Therefore, we can express ourselves in acts and moods of love and service to each other. No hatred can ever come from that experience. This is the verdict of the Upaniṣads. Here, in the last *śloka* Śrī Kṛṣṇa says therefore, that 'I manifest Myself as the universe, but with only a portion of Myself.'

The solar energy manifested as the solar system is only an infinitesimal portion of solar energy. The rest is all still there as the sun. So, from all these points of view, we developed the concept of Reality, and we never made a separation between the world and God. The infinite One is manifested as this universe. The spark of the Divine is there in everything. In order to realize this truth, we need to train our minds, train our knowledge-process, first by studying external nature, seeing unity there, then turning over to the study of the science of human possibilities which is Vedanta, and discover the unity behind the multiplicity of beings in this world. This is the Vedantic concept of human knowledge in its two dimensions, physical and super-physical, as expounded earlier in chapter seven.

When the body consciousness goes away, we realize this truth. That is referred to in a famous small book of Vedanta, *Dṛk-dṛśya-vivek*, 'Discrimination between the observer and the observed or the seer and the seen', in the opening verse and in a later one. Till now, physical science studied only the seen. Now, science is turning towards the seer, the observer. When Vedanta studied both together, it came to the following conclusion.

The first verse says:

*Rūpam dṛśyam locanam dṛk*
*tat dṛśyam dṛktu mānasam;*
*Dṛśyāḥ dhīvṛttayaḥ sākṣī*
*dṛgeva na tu dṛśyate —*

'Form is the seen, eye is the seer; eye is the seen, mind is the seer; ideas in the mind are the seen, the *sākṣi* or witness is ever the seer and never the seen.'

*Dehābhimāne galite vijñāte paramātmani;*
*Yatra yatra mano yāti tatra tatra samādhayaḥ* —

'When the elation that you are (only) the physical body is removed and you realize the Supreme Atman,' then what happens to you?, 'wherever the mind goes, it attains *samādhi*.'

When the body-consciousness that makes us separate from each other goes away, we are able to achieve this universal vision. This is highly praised in many works of poetry, art, and drama all over the world. At a higher level, this is what you are going to achieve: complete unity. In the heart of nature there is unity. On the surface, all differences are there. That knowledge will come to human beings only when the body-consciousness goes away. It is the body that makes us separate from each other. I am this psychophysical system—I am separate from you and you are separate from me—when this awareness goes away, pure Consciousness comes in and we find we are all essentially one. Actually body-consciousness is behind most of the evils in human society, including racial conflicts. The UNESCO has, in its conference in Moscow, discovered this truth and proclaimed it in a series of propositions that racial superiority has no scientific basis (vide *UNESCO Courier*, April 1965). Any race can attain high levels of development provided you give it proper nourishment. Today's understanding of the world is based on declarations of this kind. All these differences were coming from prejudice, ignorance and delusion. We cultivated these in the earlier ages. Now they have no value. Ten or twelve paragraphs of the Moscow declaration are there. I quoted a few of them in my book, *Message of the Upanishads*, where the Upaniṣads themselves say, teach every child the ultimate unity of things. These differences are on the surface. We don't deny the differences. But that is the surface view. The deeper view is that they are essentially one, says the *Kaṭha Upaniṣad* (II. i. 11):

*Manasaivedam āptavyam neha nānāsti kiṃcana;*
*Mṛtyoḥ sa mṛtyum gacchati ya iha nāneva paśyati* —

This truth has to be grasped not through the senses but by the mind. Senses cannot grasp unity; mind can. So, *manasā eva idam āptavyam,* 'through mind alone you must realize this truth'. What is the truth? *Neha nānā asti kiṃcana,* 'there are no differences here'. But if you still go on living with the idea of these differences, you will experience death after death, *mṛtyoḥ sa mṛtyum gacchati.* Wars, violence, crime, all sorts of evils come because of these racial and other differences. So, the Upaniṣads said four thousand years ago, *mṛtyoḥ sa mṛtyum gacchati ya iha nānā iva paśyati.* And life and more life comes only from the knowledge that we are essentially one. Mind must be trained in this awareness. Minds of our children must be trained in the vision of the oneness of all. Even with nature we are one; not only among human beings is there unity. We are one with the animals, one with the plants, everything. There is a basic oneness in this universe. Conduct your life in the light of this. That is the language of Vedanta.

In this tenth chapter, Śrī Kṛṣṇa has given us this vision of divine manifestations as the universe. This is how the tenth chapter closes, opening the eleventh chapter, in which we meet Arjuna desiring to see the universal Form of the Divine, the *viśvarūpa* as it is called. That is the beauty and power that is going to be expressed in the eleventh chapter. Śrī Kṛṣṇa accepts Arjuna's question and shows him His universal Form, *viśvarūpa darśana.* That is a very famous chapter. We shall enter into that chapter next Sunday when we meet here again.

इति विभूति-योगो नाम दशमोऽध्यायः ।

*Iti vibhūti-yogo nāma daśamo'dhyāyaḥ* —

'The end of the tenth chapter, designated, *Glimpses of the Divine Glory.*'

# BHAGAVAD GĪTĀ

## CHAPTER 11

### VIŚVARŪPA DARŚANAM
### THE VISION OF THE UNIVERSAL FORM

We finished the study of chapter ten of the *Gītā,* known as *Vibhūti yoga,* 'the Lord manifested as the universe', last Sunday. There we heard in the last but one verse this great summing up:

*Yadyad vibhūtimat sattvam śrīmad ūrjitam eva vā;*
*Tat tat eva avagaccha tvam mama tejo'mśa sambhavam* —

'Wherever you find a great manifestation of energy, beneficial and uplifting humanity, know that I am present there. A portion of My own infinite nature is present in that particular event or person.'

This is the teaching that made we Indians respect greatness wherever it came. Not a communal greatness, national greatness, racial greatness, but just human greatness. We could see the spark of the divine in that greatness. I don't know any other nation or followers of religion being educated in this attitude. But in India this was the education given to us. So, we bow down to greatness wherever it occurs. Our great writers also have said that there are sages among *mlecchas,* sages among other communities also. And this evening we enter the great chapter, the eleventh, known as the *Viśva rūpa darśana* chapter—The Vision of the Universal Form of the Divine. Many sages and saints and devotees consider this chapter as very very important in the *Gītā: The Vision of the Universal Form of the Divine.*

**अर्जुन उवाच –**

*Arjuna uvāca—*

*'Arjuna said:'*

**मदनुग्रहाय परमं गुह्यं अध्यात्म संज्ञितम् ।**
**यत् त्वयोक्तं वचस्तेन मोहोऽयं विगतो मम ॥१॥**

*Madanugrahāya paramam guhyam adhyātma samjñitam;*
*Yat tvayoktam vacastena moho'yam vigato mama — 11. 1*

'By the supremely profound words on the subject known as spirituality, that have been spoken by You out of compassion towards me, this my delusion is gone.'

*Madanugrahāya paramam yat tvayā uktam,* 'whatever You have spoken till now out of love and blessing for me'; *guhyam adhyātma samjñitam*—what did You speak on? *Adhyātma samjñitam,* 'bearing the name of spirituality'. That is what You spoke, and whatever You spoke, as a consequence of that, what has happened to me? *Yattvayoktam vacastena,* 'through those words spoken by You'; *moho'yam vigato mama,* 'this, my delusion, has gone away'. I now realize that it is Your infinite Self that manifests as this universe everywhere. The distinction between 'I' and 'you', which is due to delusion, has vanished now. This is what Arjuna is confessing here: 'This *moha,* delusion, of mine is gone.' In the eighteenth chapter, *śloka* 73, he will repeat it again: 'I have lost all my delusion and ignorance. I will do what you ask me to do.' That is Arjuna's last statement in response to what Śrī Kṛṣṇa had said earlier in verse 63 of the eighteenth chapter, 'What you think proper, you do, after considering what all I have said. I am not going to *decide* for you. You decide for yourself.' That is a beautiful idea. You do not become dependent upon a teacher. You depend upon yourself. Take whatever the teacher has said, think deeply about it, come to your own decision, and take the responsibility for your decision. That is mature manhood and womanhood. That is what Śrī Kṛṣṇa wants. So, here, in the first sentence, Arjuna says, 'what all I have heard from You is the subject of spirituality', *adhyātmasamjñitam,* 'by the name *adhyātma'*; *samjñā* means name. 'That has removed my delusion.'

भवाप्ययौ हि भूतानां श्रुतौ विस्तरशो मया ।
त्वत्तः कमलपत्राक्ष माहात्म्यं अपि चाव्ययम् ॥ २ ॥

*Bhavāpyayau hi bhūtānām śrutau vistaraśo mayā;*
*Tvattaḥ kamalapatrākṣa māhātmyam api cāvyayam — 11. 2*

'From Yourself, O lotus-eyed one, I have heard at length of the origin and dissolution of beings, as well as of Your inexhaustible greatness.'

The origin and dissolution of this universe, *bhava* and *apyaya; bhava* means *prabhava*, 'origin'; *apyaya* means 'dissolution' of this universe; *śrutau vistaraśo mayā*, 'I have heard from you extensively'. *Tvattaḥ*, 'from You'; *kamalapatrākṣa*, Śrī Kṛṣṇa is addressed as one 'with lotus leaf eyes'. *Māhātmyam api ca avyayam*, 'and Your own infinite *māhātmyam*, glory', that also I have heard from you.

एवं एतत् यथात्थ त्वं आत्मानं परमेश्वर ।
द्रष्टुं इच्छामि ते रूपं ऐश्वरं पुरुषोत्तम ॥ ३ ॥

*Evam etat yathāttha tvam ātmānam parameśvara;*
*Draṣṭum icchāmi te rūpam aiśvaram puruṣottama— 11. 3*

'So it is, O Supreme Lord! You have declared Yourself. (Still) I desire to see Your *Īśvara*-form, O Supreme Person.'

I am not satisfied with whatever You have spoken about Yourself. I am not satisfied with hearing only; I want to see that Universal Form of Yours. It is not enough to hear. It should be audio and visual. Both must be there. So, Arjuna is very eager to see that Universal Form of the Divine. In Śrī Kṛṣṇa's life, there are about three or four occasions when He showed His Divine Form. One was in the court of Dhṛtarāṣṭra or the Kauravas, where Śiśupāla did some mischief, uttered some very bad words. At that time Śrī Kṛṣṇa showed His Divine form and killed Śiśupāla also. And Śrī Kṛṣṇa's minister, Akrūra, had a similar experience. Just a few such occasions are there, including the occasion in His childhood. He had eaten some mud, denied it, and mother Yaśoda asked Him to open His mouth. He did it and His mother saw the whole universe and herself in it. But the outstanding one of all such occasions is this Kurukṣetra experience of Arjuna where Arjuna has been shown the Infinite Form of *Bhagavān* Śrī Kṛṣṇa. *Evam etat yathā āttha tvam ātmānam parameśvara,* 'whatever You have said are all true; I accept them'. But, *draṣṭum icchāmi te rūpam aiśvaram puruṣottama,* 'I desire to see Your "Divine" Form, *aiśvaram.*'

**मन्यसे यदि तच्छक्यं मया द्रष्टुं इति प्रभो ।**
**योगेश्वर ततो मे त्वं दर्शयात्मानं अव्ययम् ॥४॥**

*Manyase yadi tacchakyam mayā draṣṭum iti prabho;*
*Yogeśvara tato me tvam darśayātmānam avyayam — 11. 4*

'If, O Lord, You think me capable of seeing it, then, O Lord of *Yogīs*, show me Your immutable Self.'

If You consider me fit to see that Form, *mayā draṣṭum,* 'to be seen by me'; *manyase yadi,* 'if You think'; *tat śakyam,* 'I am fit for it'; then, *yogeśvara,* 'O Master of *yoga*'. See the title! Śrī Kṛṣṇa is called *Yogeśvara.* Not only here, but also towards the last sentence of the *Gītā* the word *'yogeśvara'* will come. *Tato me tvam darśaya ātmānam avyayam,* 'please therefore, show me Your infinite Form, O Yogeśvara'. This is the concept of *yoga.* Here, Master of *yoga* means: 'how did He make the One become many in this universe?' That is the *yoga* power. That is the great *yoga* of the Divine: the One becoming the many, appearing as the many, and yet remaining perfectly okay as the One Infinite Divine. That is called the *yoga* power of the Divine, *yoga-śakti,* and He is the Master of that *yoga.* That, the *Gītā* repeatedly emphasizes; other passages in the *Mahābhārata* also repeat this *yoga* power of the Divine.

**श्रीभगवान् उवाच–**
*Śrībhagavān uvāca—*

*'Śrī Kṛṣṇa answered:'*

**पश्य मे पार्थ रूपाणि शतशोऽथ सहस्रशः ।**
**नानाविधानि दिव्यानि नानावर्ण आकृतीनि च ॥५॥**

*Paśya me pārtha rūpāṇi śataśo'tha sahasraśaḥ;*
*Nānāvidhāni divyāni nānāvarṇa ākṛtīni ca— 11. 5*

'Behold, O son of Pṛthā, by hundreds and thousands, My different forms celestial, of various colours and shapes.'

Arjuna, see My infinite Forms. He says, *paśya*, 'behold'; *śataśo'tha sahasraśaḥ*, 'hundreds and thousands'; *nānā vidhāni divyāni*, 'different forms celestial'; *nānāvarṇa*, 'of various colours'; *(nānā) ākṛtīni ca*, 'and of various shapes'. Whatever can be expressed in language is expressed in these words. But it will be given in greater detail as we proceed. So, here Śrī Kṛṣṇa says, 'Come and see! O Arjuna!' Sañjaya will say later on, 'Śrī Kṛṣṇa showed His Divine Form.'

पश्यादित्यान् वसून् रुद्रान् अश्विनौ मरुतस्तथा ।
बहून्यदृष्टपूर्वाणि पश्य आश्चर्याणि भारत ॥६॥

*Paśyādityān vasūn rudrān aśvinau marutastathā;*
*Bahūnyadṛṣṭapūrvāṇi paśya āścaryāṇi bhārata— 11. 6*

'Behold the *Ādityas*, the *Vasus*, the *Rudras*, the twin *Aśvins*, and the *Maruts;* behold, O descendent of Bharata, many wonders never seen before.'

See all these various Divine forms. What are they? *Ādityas* etc. In our mythology, there are twelve *Ādityas*, eight *Vasus*, eleven *Rudras*, two *Aśvins*, and *Maruts*. Behold, O Arjuna, many wonders never before seen on this earth. That is the language: *āścaryāṇi, adṛṣṭapūrvāṇi*, visions: wonders that these human eyes have not been able to see before. We can see the manifested universe. That itself is a great wonder. But still greater wonders are there which I, Śrī Kṛṣṇa, am going to show to you. But then a change in you is needed, which will be mentioned in verse 8. Now, Śrī Kṛṣṇa says,

इहैकस्थं जगत् कृत्स्नं पश्याद्य सचराचरम् ।
मम देहे गुडाकेश यच्चान्यत् द्रष्टुं इच्छसि ॥७॥

*Ihaikastham jagat kṛtsnam paśyādya sacarācaram;*
*Mama dehe guḍākeśa yaccānyat draṣṭum icchasi— 11. 7*

'See now, O Guḍākeśa, in this body of Mine, the whole universe centred in one—including the moving and the non-moving—and all else that you desire to see.'

*Iha*, 'here, in this very spot'; *mama dehe*, 'in this body of Mine'; and *adya*, 'now'; 'here and now, in this person of Mine', you can see manifested *jagat kṛtsnam*, 'the entire universe'; *sa carācaram*, 'consisting of moving and unmoving entities'; *guḍākeśa*, 'O Arjuna'; *yat ca anyat draṣṭum icchasi*, 'and other things also which you want to see'. You will see all these things.

There are beautiful paintings and sculptures in Indonesia and other places, of the event narrated in the *Śrīmad Bhāgavatam* of Śrī Kṛṣṇa as a child, eating mud. Mother Yaśoda asks Him to open His mouth and becomes frightened by what she sees there: What is this? Here is my child, and what am I seeing in his mouth! Infinite dimension! That is one of the great events in Śrī Kṛṣṇa's childhood life depicted in art in many places.

न तु मां शक्यसे द्रष्टुं अनेनैव स्वचक्षुषा ।
दिव्यं ददामि ते चक्षुः पश्य मे योगं ऐश्वरम् ॥८॥

*Na tu mām śakyase draṣṭum anenaiva svacakṣuṣā;*
*Divyam dadāmi te cakṣuḥ paśya me yogam aiśvaram—11. 8*

'But, you cannot see Me with these eyes of yours; I give you Divine or super-sensory sight; behold My supreme *yoga*-power.'

With these fleshy eyes, you can't see that Divine glory. There is a profound truth about it. *Divyam dadāmi te cakṣuḥ*, 'I give you the Divine eye.' With these Divine eyes, then *paśya me yogam aiśvaram*, 'see My *aiśvaram yogam*, Divine *yoga* power': see how I am the universal Self and yet am manifested as this universe; that, though manifested, yet I am just the same, the Divine, infinite Reality. That particular mysterious appearance of One as the many is through the power of *Māyā, Yogamāyā*.

सञ्जय उवाच–

*Sañjaya uvāca—*

*'Sañjaya said:'*

एवमुक्त्वा ततो राजन् महा योगेश्वरो हरिः ।
दर्शयामास पार्थाय परमं रूपमैश्वरम् ॥९॥

*Evamuktvā tato rājan mahā yogeśvaro hariḥ;*
*Darśayāmāsa pārthāya paramam rūpamaiśvaram*— 11. 9

'Having spoken thus, O King, Hari, the great Lord of *Yoga*, showed unto the son of Pṛthā His supreme *Īśvara*-Form.'

King Dhṛtarāṣṭra was in Hastināpura, in his palace, and Sañjaya was reporting to him, what was happening in the battlefield of Kurukṣetra, in these words: 'O King, Śrī Kṛṣṇa is *mahā yogeśvara,* the great Lord of *yoga*'. He is *Hariḥ;* Hari or Viṣṇu or Kṛṣṇa, all these are the same. *Darśayāmāsa pārthāya,* 'He showed to Pārtha', *parmam rūpam aiśvaram,* 'His supreme divine Form'. That is what is going to be described in the following verses:

अनेकवक्त्रनयनं अनेकाद्भुतदर्शनम् ।
अनेकदिव्याभरणं दिव्यानेकोद्यतायुधम् ॥१०॥

*Anekavaktranayanam anekādbhutadarśanam;*
*Anekadivyābharaṇam divyānekodyatāyudham*— 11. 10

'With numerous mouths and eyes, with numerous wondrous sights, with numerous celestial ornaments, with numerous celestial weapons uplifted.'

He is giving a little detail in this verse. Whatever is possible to describe in words, Sañjaya is describing: with numerous mouths and also eyes, numerous wondrous sights, with numerous celestial ornaments, with numerous celestial weapons uplifted. When you see the whole world in one single look, if you can do that, you will see all these things there. Consider, for example, any particular point of time; say, just now: in various parts of the world, somebody is dying, somebody is born, somebody is fighting, somebody is doing good work; all these are going on at the same time in millions of forms. You can't get a synoptic view of *all* of them with these normal eyes. But with the divine eye, you can. Many events are going on all over the world. What a wonderful mystery is this universe! *Mysterious Universe,* that is the language used by Sir James Jeans for his book on modern science. Highly mysterious is it!

You can just think, as I said, how many wonderful things are simultaneously going on in the world. Many more things, which are subtle, are going on too. We can't see these subtle things with these eyes. So, Śrī Kṛṣṇa said in the 8th verse, 'I am going to give you a divine eye to see that mystery.' With these fleshy eyes we can see a good deal of that mystery, but not enough. There are profound dimensions which these eyes cannot reveal. So, I give you that divine eye to see all these things in Me.

**दिव्य माल्याम्बरधरं दिव्य गन्धानुलेपनम् ।**
**सर्वाश्चर्यमयं देवं अनन्तं विश्वतोमुखम् ॥११॥**

*Divya mālyāmbaradharam divya gandhānulepanam;*
*Sarvāścaryamayam devam anantam viśvatomukham*—11. 11

'Wearing celestial garlands and apparel, anointed with celestial-scented unguents, the all-wonderful *Deva*, resplendent, boundless, and all-formed.'

Wearing celestial garments and dress, anointed with celestial-scented unguents, all-wonderful, resplendent, boundless and all-formed. *Sarvāścaryamayam,* 'all highly wonderful'; *devam,* 'the Divine Being, shining, resplendent'; *anantam,* 'infinite, without end'; *viśvatomukham,* 'looking at all directions', 'with the capacity to see everywhere', 'of universal face', like the sun, for example. I compare that kind of capacity to the sun. The sun looks in all directions. An example is nearby. Sun is not looking only in the front. It looks everywhere. If that is so with regard to this celestial phenomenon, how much more wonderful must be that Reality from which millions of suns have come into the universe! So, that is the language. This extraordinary phenomenon which only the Divine eye can see, is described in the next verse, the famous verse 12, which was the verse that came to the mind of the nuclear scientist Openheimer, when he first exploded the atom-bomb in USA just before the end of the Second World War. This is that *śloka.* When he saw the brilliance of the huge explosion rising up to the sky, deafening and even blinding the eye, he repeated to himself this verse.

दिवि सूर्यसहस्रस्य भवेत् युगपदुत्थिता ।
यदि भाः सदृशी सा स्यात् भासस्तस्य महात्मनः ॥१२॥

*Divi sūryasahasrasya bhavet yugapadutthitā;*
*Yadi bhāḥ sadṛśī sā syāt bhāsastasya mahātmanaḥ* —11. 12

'If the splendour of a thousand suns were to rise up simultaneously in the sky, that would be like the splendour of that mighty Being.'

That *mahātma's bhāsa* or glory or brilliance can be compared to a thousand suns rising simultaneously on the sky. *Divi sūrya sahasrasya,* 'a thousand suns in the sky'; one sun itself is tremendously brilliant. But a thousand suns rising there! *Yadi bhavet yugapat,* 'if it were to occur together', *utthitā,* 'rising' on the horizon; *sā bhāḥ,* 'that brilliance', *syāt bhāsastasya mahātmanaḥ,* 'would be like this Divine manifestation of Śrī Kṛṣṇa which has that glory'. Openheimer had studied the *Gītā,* and so, this *śloka* of the *Gītā* came to his mind: nearest to that extraordinary event which ushered in the Atomic Age in our modern history. That *mahātman's bhāsa* means 'brilliance of that mighty Being' can be compared only to a thousand suns dazzling in the sky at the same time. Therefore,

तत्रैकस्थं जगत्कृत्स्नं प्रविभक्तं अनेकधा ।
अपश्यत् देवदेवस्य शरीरे पाण्डवस्तदा ॥१३॥

*Tatraikastham jagatkṛtsnam pravibhaktam anekadhā,*
*Apaśyat devadevasya śarīre pāṇḍavastadā* — 11. 13

'There in the body of the God of gods, the son of Pāṇḍu then saw the whole universe resting in One, with its manifold divisions.'

Then Arjuna saw, *tatraikastham,* 'in one single spot'; *jagatkṛtsnam,* 'the entire universe'; *pravibhaktam anekadhā,* 'divided into multiple manifestations'—One single Reality divided into infinite manifestations. *Apaśyat devadevasya śarīre pāṇḍavaḥ tadā,* 'Arjuna then saw in the body of *devadeva,* the God of gods, in the supremely Divine, namely, Śrī Kṛṣṇa.'

ततः स विस्मयाविष्टो हृष्टरोमा धनञ्जयः ।
प्रणम्य शिरसा देवं कृताञ्जलिः अभाषत ॥ १४ ॥

*Tataḥ sa vismayāviṣṭo hṛṣṭaromā dhanañjayaḥ;*
*Praṇamya śirasā devam kṛtāñjaliḥ abhāṣata — 11. 14*

'Then Dhanañjaya, filled with wonder, with his hairs standing on end, bending down his head to the *Deva* in adoration, spoke with joined palms.'

*Dhanañjayaḥ,* 'Arjuna'; *vismayāviṣṭaḥ,* 'filled with wonder'; *hṛṣṭaromā,* 'with his hairs standing on end'; *praṇamya śirasā devam,* 'saluting, with bent head, that Divine Person'; *kṛtāñjaliḥ,* 'with joined palms'; *saḥ abhāṣata,* 'he said'. Now comes Arjuna's hymn of praise of this Divine Reality. This has been very often recited as prayer by devotees for all these hundreds of years. There are passages in other literature also—very few, but still there are some—dealing with this Universal Vision of the Divine. The Psalms in the Old Testament contain very beautiful ideas, moral and spiritual. I particularly like one beautiful passage (*The Holy Bible*, Psalms, 138. 8-10, published by Harwin press Ltd. 1959):

'If I go up to the heavens, You *are* there; if I sink to the nether world, You *are present there.*

'If I take the wings of the dawn, if I settle at the farthest limits of the sea;

'Even there Your hand shall guide me, and Your right hand hold me fast.'

We find in this Psalm, the conception of the Universal Form, though it is not found in any monotheistic religion. Monotheistic religions separate God and the world. But, when it becomes mystical experience in these religions, they break down this barrier. One Infinite Divine, everywhere—that is the realization that comes to these great mystics. We must separate mystics from ordinary creed-bound religious people. The latter have got a God separate from the world and far away. They have got dos and don't s written down. Do this, don't do this, like that. That is their religion. They have no experience of the Divine. But, when you begin to experience the Divine, many new dimensions come. In India there was no restriction by any clerical body on the type of experience one should get in one's spiritual practice. All were accepted. So, various descriptions are there of devotees and of their realizations of the Divine. No clerical body in India suppressed any particular vision. But, other countries had that difficulty. The religious authority stipulated that only this way should you go; only this type of realization you should have. A track has been laid; don't go beyond this. So, even if they get something higher, the saints have to express it very cleverly, mildly, so that they may not be persecuted. That is the story of a great Roman Catholic saint like Meister Eckhart, the 12th century German mystic. He realized the Impersonal aspect of God behind the Personal God. But in theology, only Personal God is given; no place for anything impersonal. So, he was called up by the Inquisition in Rome to be punished. Fortunately, he died before he could go to the Inquisition. Similarly, many Muslim Sufi mystics have realized the infinite dimension of the Divine, have realized that they are one with the Divine. *An al Haq*, 'I am God', is the famous statement of the Sufi mystic who was killed for saying this. You are God!, how can you say so? The Islamic priests could not understand or tolerate that dimension.

Whereas in India, from the ordinary to the most extraordinary, every type of these experiences has been accepted and respected. We don't kill away spiritual people who have had various types of spiritual experiences. In such experiences, we can go deeper and still deeper. So, the idea of killing away a person who went beyond the creed-based limit of religion never happened in India. In all other countries it has happened, including secular Greece and secular Rome. *Remember this—the uniqueness of the country in which we live, the uniqueness and comprehensiveness of the philosophy that has been guiding us all these hundreds of years.* So, any experience of the

Divine, we respect. Show the beauty of it in your character. If you are pure, if you are noble, we will accept it; these visions must find their expression in one's altered character. That is the test of a vision. And so, we watch and see. This person is truly genuine; his or her vision is genuine. Then we worship and salute that person. Otherwise, we ignore him or her. When people claim many visions, and if we do not find any impact of the visions on their life, we then just ignore them. But, still we won't kill anybody. This is the Indian tradition because of the influence of the Upaniṣads, the profound scientific approach to religion. That science had proclaimed that *experience* is the test of religion and *not mere creed or dogma.*

We find, in this verse of the *Gitā,* Arjuna filled with wonder, filled with amazement. You can imagine what it is to be amazed seeing this Universal Form.

**अर्जुन उवाच–**

*Arjuna uvāca —*

*'Arjuna said:'*

**पश्यामि देवांस्तव देव देहे**
**सर्वांस्तथा भूत विशेषसङ्घान् ।**
**ब्रह्माणं ईशं कमलासनस्थं**
**ऋषींश्च सर्वान् उरगांश्च दिव्यान् ॥१५॥**

*Paśyāmi devāmstava deva dehe*
*sarvāmstathā bhūta viśeṣasaṅghān;*
*Brahmāṇam īśam kamalāsanastham-*
*ṛṣīmśca sarvān uragāmśca divyān — 11. 15*

'I see all the *devas, O Deva,* in Your body, and hosts of all grades of beings; Brahmā, the Lord, seated on the lotus, and all the *Ṛṣis* and celestial serpents.'

O Lord, I see in You all these wonderful manifestations. What are they? All the *devas,* 'the luminous beings', Brahmā, the creator of this world, who sits on the lotus that issues from the navel of Viṣṇu, all the *Ṛṣis* or sages, and celestial serpents like Vāsuki. All these are in You. In other cultures, some other things may be considered divine. However, in Hindu culture, these things were considered as divine, as being beyond the physical or natural order of things—a higher order of things. Therefore, these things are mentioned here.

अनेकबाहूदरवक्त्रनेत्रं
पश्यामि त्वां सर्वतोऽनन्तरूपम् ।
नान्तं न मध्यं न पुनस्तवादिं
पश्यामि विश्वेश्वर विश्वरूप ॥१६॥

*Anekabāhūdaravaktranetram*
*paśyāmi tvām sarvato'nantarūpam;*
*Nāntam na madhyam na punastavādim*
*paśyāmi viśveśvara viśvarūpa* — 11. 16

'I see You of boundless form on every side, with manifold arms, stomachs, mouths, and eyes; neither the end nor the middle, nor also the beginning of Yourself do I see, O Lord of the universe, O Universal Form.'

Here Arjuna tries to express that tremendous wonder in a few words. Very often you cannot say anything. When you see anything very wonderful, you simply stand quiet, but a little expression is given by Arjuna by showing his reverence towards the Divine Form that he is experiencing in front of him. Then he says,

किरीटिनं गदिनं चक्रिणं च
तेजोराशिं सर्वतो दीप्तिमन्तम् ।
पश्यामि त्वां दुर्निरीक्ष्यं समन्तात्
दीप्तानलार्कद्युतिं अप्रमेयम् ॥१७॥

*Kirīṭinam gadinam cakriṇam ca*
*tejorāśim sarvato dīptimantam;*
*Paśyāmi tvām durnirīkṣyam samantāt*
*dīptānalārkadyutim aprameyam* — 11. 17

'I see You with diadem, club, and discus; a mass of radiance shining everywhere, very hard to look at, all around blazing like burning fire and sun, and immeasurable.'

You find in Lord Viṣṇu's image, a diadem or crown on the head, a conch shell, a discus, a club and a lotus, *śaṅkha-*

*cakra-gadā-padma*—these are the four things in the four hands of Lord Viṣṇu. A mass of radiance emanates, so brilliant that it is very hard to look at. Even one sun, we cannot look at! How can you look at a thousand suns? That is the language—very hard to look at. All around it is blazing like fire and sun, and is immeasurable. This is what I see everywhere, said Arjuna.

त्वं अक्षरं परमं वेदितव्यं
त्वं अस्य विश्वस्य परं निधानम् ।
त्वं अव्ययः शाश्वत धर्म गोप्ता
सनातनस्त्वं पुरुषो मतो मे ॥१८॥

*Tvam akṣaram paramam veditavyam*
*tvam asya viśvasya param nidhānam;*
*Tvam avyayaḥ śāśvata dharma goptā*
*sanātanastvam puruṣo mato me* — 11. 18

'You are the Imperishable, the supreme Being, the One thing to be known. You are the great Refuge of this universe; You are the undying Guardian of the Eternal *Dharma,* You are the ancient *Puruṣa,* I ween.'

This is a very beautiful spiritual expression. *Tvam akṣaram,* 'You are the imperishable'; *kṣara* means perishable, *akṣara* means imperishable. *Paramam,* 'supreme'; *veditavyam,* 'subject that is to be known'; if there is anything worth to be known, it is You—the highest subject that the human being has to know is God Himself who is the Self of all and of the universe. *Tvam asya viśvasya param nidhānam,* 'You are the supreme support and refuge of this whole universe', because in God alone this universe rests. So, God is called the 'refuge', *nidhānam.* Similarly, *tvam avyayaḥ śāśvata dharma goptā,* 'You are the imperishable, *avyaya*'; *vyaya* means 'spending' and *avyaya* means 'no spending'. Go on spending and yet the fund is full! That is called *avyaya;* it is not possible to exhaust it. So, *avyaya* is a great word in Sanskrit. *Śāśvata dharma goptā; goptā* means 'protector'; protector of what?, *śāśvata dharma,* 'Eternal Religion', which means *sanātana dharma,* the impersonal name that India gave to her religion. For example, cosmic law is one example of that eternal *dharma.* Sun is there, planets move around the sun. The earth also has a rotation on its own axis. In this way, the galaxies also move about. The whole universe has its various movements regulated. *Śāśvata dharma,* means 'cosmic or celestial *dharma*'. When you come to human life also, there is *śāśvata dharma* or eternal *dharma*. Other *dharmas* come and go; these scientifically-based *dharmas* remain. That is called *sanātana dharma.*

We have two aspects of *dharma* in our tradition: one is *sanātana dharma* and the other is *yuga dharma.* A *dharma* for a particular age, for a particular country, for a particular people, is called *yuga dharma*. They will be changing. One age changes and another age comes. So, you have got different *dharmas,* but within all this, there is one set of universal *dharma.* It never changes and it is called *sanātana,* 'eternal'. The other is called *yuga dharma*. Because we understood this distinction, and because we allowed changes in the *yuga dharma* as *yugas* changed, we are a living culture. We never die away. We know how to adjust to new situations. About a hundred years ago, every male Hindu wore a *śikhā* or tuft of hair on the head. *Śikhā* is essential for a Hindu. Then came the modern age and we began to cut away the *śikhā.* So, some traditional people thought that *Sanātana Dharma* was getting destroyed by cutting away the *śikhā.* They used to say like that, not knowing the distinction between *Sanātana Dharma* and *Yuga Dharma*. That is something profound. These are changeful; so change them. 'Don't cross the sea!', is a *Yuga Dharma*. That *yuga* is over, and we now cross the sea.

In this way, hundreds of changes have come in our *Yuga Dharma.* A new *yuga* has come. The old practice has no relevance today. New things must take the place of the old. And Sri Ramakrishna gave us the entire *Sanātana-Dharma*-wisdom on the subject when he said, 'The Mogul coins have no currency under the (East India) Company's rule.' What a beautiful idea! It has gold value, but no currency value. You have to mint it in a new mint. That exactly is the nature of *Yuga Dharma*. It *must* change. If it doesn't change, it will distort the human society, because new ideas have come now, new economic situations have come. You have to adapt to the new ways. In this way, changes must take place around you. But, in the midst of changes, there are eternal values which do not change.

For example, take truth. There is no question of truth and truthfulness undergoing change. 'Truthfulness is an Eternal *Dharma*', *eṣa dharmaḥ sanātanaḥ*. *Gītā* will say, 'the Eternal Atman, our true nature, that is also *sanātana*'. Our relationship with the Divine is *sanātana*. I may not know, but that relationship *is* there and it is *sanātana;* it cannot change. So, we have *Sanātana Dharma* and *Yuga Dharma*. *Sanātana Dharma* is centred in the Upaniṣads, or the Vedas. *Yuga Dharma* is represented by the *Smṛtis* and the *Purāṇas*. They can be changing, must be changing; so many times they have changed. The *Smṛti* rule for many centuries was: 'no low-caste person should enter a Hindu temple.' That is not *Sanātana Dharma*. That was a *Yuga Dharma*. That *yuga* has gone. So, we opened the temple to all people, to people of low and high caste alike. And nobody suffered here; no civil war was here. In any other country, there would have been a civil war on account of that change. So, remember, because of this distinction between *Sanātana Dharma* and *Yuga Dharma,* we could make changes without upheavals in society. A little bit of shouting here and there will be there. That cannot be escaped. But no serious upheaval, because we know that *that* is primary and *this* is only secondary. *That* is *sanātana* and *this* is *yuga,* meant for a particular time. And, therefore, the Upaniṣads remain eternal, from which you can always draw inspiration. They don't deal with *Yuga Dharma*—marriage, inheritance, food, drink, etc. These come in the *Smṛtis* and in the *Purāṇas*. There you find 'what you should do', 'what you should not do'. In the *Śrutis,* only beautiful ideas and great truths about the true nature of God, of human beings, of the relationship between the two, are given; and that is what Vedanta teaches. So, today, in India, a tremendous social change is taking place at the peripheral level, in our external life. More of such changes will come. We welcome them, but we will continue to hold on to those eternal values contained in the *Śruti*, in the Upaniṣads or Vedanta. A new India based on Vedantic inspiration is taking shape in India today, for the first time.

Look at our Republican Constitution. You will find beautiful Vedantic ideas, eternal values embedded there, whereas, all the discriminatory *Smṛti* values, which we had cultivated long, have been abrogated by the Constitution. Untouchability has been banned, casteism has been banned; all that you can see in the Constitution. So, the new Constitution gives you a new *Yuga Dharma,* a new *Smṛti* as it were. Follow *that!* The old rules are not to be followed hereafter. The day you adopted your Democratic Constitution, many of the old *Smṛtis* became absolutely irrelevant. They cannot function against the dictates of the Constitution. *That is the greatness of the culture and philosophy developed in this blessed country.* We know how to change according to time. What a social change has taken place from the *Ṛg*-Vedic India up to this day! And yet, we are the same people. One single current of unity runs through all of them. That is what all of us should understand. Many more changes will come. Within the next fifty years, tremendous changes will come. The status of women will be tremendously changed. Perfect equality, mutual respect, no subordination, will be there hereafter. Working class people will be given very high status. Working people are the noblest people—not the feudal lord sitting over there, smoking *hookah* and enjoying nicely. These, the latter, are not going to continue to dominate the Indian society. So, be prepared for further social changes to come. But the whole thing comes gradually, without violence, without hatred. This is the nature of Indian society, and Indian wisdom dealing with social matters. Our orthodox national tradition itself says: *Śruti smṛti virodhe tu śrutireva garīyasi,* 'in a conflict between the *Śruti* and *Smṛti,* the *Śruti* alone shall prevail.' We will have the same India, we will have the same spiritual continuity, along with these socio-economic changes. That is the beauty—unity in diversity, change and eternity, both going on together.

So, *śāśvata dharma goptā*, 'you are the protector of this *śāśvata dharma*, this perennial *dharma*' going on ages after ages, still fresh! Imagine this country, 5000 years old, so young today! India is very young, democratically as well as ideologically. Quite young and yet it is 5000 years old. Therefore, the statement of that famous Bengali intellectual, Dr. Brajendranath Seal, is so true: 'India is ever ageing, but never old.' That is what 'Young India' is. We say 'Young India' today; it is not a mere saying. Swami Vivekananda started using that word—Young India—we are all young. There is a supreme Divine who protects this *śāśvata dharma*. That *śāśvata dharma* is there in the *Koran*, in the *Bible*, in every scripture. Only they did not make any distinction between *śāśvata dharma* and *aśāśvata dharma* or *yuga dharma*. They mixed them up all together. Here, we understood the distinction. That is the only difference. *Śāśvata Dharma* and *Smṛti Dharma*, you will find both these in the *Bible*, *Koran*, everywhere. But, India has something very special. We understood the distinction between the two. We had the boldness to change these *Yuga Dharmas*. No fear! Most wonderful changes we have effected. And we are perfectly fine. We are better and still better. That is the one lesson the rest of the world can learn from *Sanātana Dharma* experience. Islam must learn this lesson one day or the other. There, both are mixed together, combined together. That is why they say, our religion and politics are one; they have no separate existence. Therefore, religion becomes politicised. Islamic *Sanātana Dharma* becomes subordinate to its *Yuga Dharma*. In all such religions you will find this. But in India, our *Sanātana Dharma* controls and guides all *Yuga Dharma*. This is one lesson you must particularly mark. You will understand India better, when you understand this distinction.

A Constitution without any provision for amendment will be a very difficult Constitution. That is the difficulty which other religions will learn slowly to cross over, and I am sure that the followers concerned will also adopt this Indian wisdom and make for necessary changes in the external life of its followers. But, its pure religious core will never suffer.

Truth will never suffer. Islamic *sanātana dharma* will never suffer. The Sufis of Islam understood this distinction. But, they had to pay a heavy price. Many of them had to face death at the hands of orthodox priests who were not spiritual. The concept of change is not a modern conception; it is not a result of modern education. This is the accepted idea in the most orthodox *Sanātana Dharma* tradition. Today, we say, therefore, that untouchability has no sanction in the *Śruti;* it is only in the *Smṛti.* The *Śruti* says everybody is the same Atman. So, the whole nation, especially the educated section, voted for the removal of untouchability. They did not say, we will be destroying religion thereby. Our people must know these things. Then great strength will come. This one single expression in the *Gītā* is beautiful in this context: The Lord is the protector of *Śāśvata Dharma*—not only of Hindu, but of Muslim, Christian, all. He protects it. Nobody can destroy it. But, there are the peripheral aspects of religion—what dress you should wear, what food you should take, etc. In a particular climate, say in Kerala, even the Maharaja of Cochin used to wear only a single *dhoti* on his body! You can imagine a Maharaja in a *dhoti!* Whereas if you go to Kashmir, you have to put on so many garments. There is a different climate there. You can't make a law of this nature for all people for all time for all places. That is called *Yuga Dharma.* It must change. So, this is what the Indian mind, its great sages, understood ages ago, and so they put this wonderful wisdom in our culture. One *Yuga Dharma* will conflict with another *Yuga Dharma.* That is one trouble. But, *Sanātana Dharma* never conflicts with any other *dharma*—Islamic *Sanātana Dharma,* Christian *Sanātana Dharma,* Hindu *Sanātana Dharma.* But, *Yuga Dharmas* will always be in conflict with each other. All the distinctions come there. Our people received this wisdom from the past. That is why we are still alive all these five thousand years, in spite of so many political upheavals and socio-economic challenges. These are profound pieces of wisdom coming from ancient times to modern times. So, the Lord is the infinite protector of the Eternal Religion, perennial religion.

*Sanātanastvam puruṣo,* 'You are also the *sanātana,* eternal Person'; the eternal Truth alone can protect the eternal religion. 'You are that *sanātana puruṣa,* Eternal Person', who protects this world, who protects the spirituality of the world. There are passages in the *Śrīmad Bhāgavatam* where it is mentioned that the Divine Person is protecting the spiritual life of the whole earth. And, in India, that Divine Person protects India's spirituality by doing *tapas* at Badrinath temple in the Himalayas. That is a statement in the *Śrīmad Bhāgavatam.* Nārāyaṇa is doing constant *tapas* at Badri to protect the spirituality of this great country. You will find such statements there.

*Sanātana* and *Śāśvata* mean the same thing. *Sanātanastvam puruṣo,* 'You are that *sanātana puruṣa*' and *Śāśvata dharma goptā,* 'You are the protector of the Eternal Religion'. *Mato me,* 'that is my understanding', said Arjuna.

Religions or sects come and go, but there is one Eternal Religion, whose protector is God Himself. Human-made religions come and go. God-made religions remain. That is the meaning of *Śāśvata Dharma* or *Sanātana Dharma.* In India, we have that distinction of human-made religion versus pure religion, ever-existing religion, based on the truths of the inner life. Dogmas and creeds can come from a human being; they cannot satisfy the heart of all human beings. If today they satisfy humanity, tomorrow they will not. So, they come and go. Many religions have come and gone. But there is a continuing religion based on truths about human beings, based on the science of human possibilities. That is what we call the *Sanātana Dharma.* This *Sanātana Dharma* is present in every world religion today. Only they do not recognize what is *sanātana* and what is temporary. We recognize that all the temporary aspects of our religion belong to the *Yuga Dharma, dharma* for a particular age, for a particular people; they come and go. We don't weep when they go. But the *Sanātana Dharma* remains. *Yuga dharma* deal with the most minute details of human life, binding each with rules and regulations. Such *dharmas* have changed again and again. But, the one Eternal

Religion remains because it consists of a set of verified Truths about human beings and is protected by the Divine Himself. That is the meaning of *śāśvata dharma goptā,* 'protector of the Eternal Religion'. That is the divine protector. All others are human-made.

Dealing with the term *śāśvata dharma goptā,* 'protector of the spiritual life of all human beings by the Supreme Being', and the concept of Bhārata as a *Puṇya bhūmi* or sacred land, the sixth century book, the *Śrīmad Bhāgavatam* says (V. xvii.14):

'In all these nine *varṣas* (continents), *Bhagavān* Nārāyaṇa (also known as Hari) is even today manifested in different forms in order to bless the inhabitants of these continents.'

Again (V. xix. 9):

'In the Bhārata Varṣa, the Lord, assuming simultaneously the twin form of Nara-Nārāyaṇa (the Human Being and the Supreme Divine Being) moves about unknown to any one. For the blessing of pious human beings out of mercy, He will live till the end of the *Kalpa* (one day of Brahmā, the Cosmic Person) revealing the true nature of the Atman through a life of austerity characterized by the highest morality, enlightenment, renunciation, power, self-control, and freedom from egoism.'

Again (V. xix. 21):

'So, the Divine beings (in heaven) sing as follows about the greatness of birth in Bhārata Varṣa:

'Is it because the auspicious acts done by them are of such transcendent merits, or is it because Śrī Hari has bestowed on them His unconditional grace, that these *jīvas* (souls) have obtained a birth in Bhārata Varṣa, where conditions are propitious for the practice of devotion to Śrī Hari? Would that we too obtain such birth in Bhārata!'

Again (V. xix. 28):

'If any more meritorious deeds remain in store for us after these enjoyments in heaven, may we, by virtue of these, be born in the blessed Ajanābha (an earlier name of Bhārata Varṣa) with our minds devoted to Thee.'

In the next verse of the *Gītā*, Śrī Kṛṣṇa says:

अनादिमध्यान्तं अनन्त वीर्यं
अनन्त बाहुं शशि सूर्य नेत्रम् ।
पश्यामि त्वां दीप्त हुताश वक्त्रं
स्वतेजसा विश्वं इदं तपन्तम् ॥१९॥

*Anādimadhyāntam ananta vīryam*
*ananta bāhum śaśi sūrya netram;*
*Paśyāmi tvām dīpta hutāśa vaktram*
*svatejasā viśvam idam tapantam — 11. 19*

'I see You without beginning, middle or end, infinite in power, of manifold arms; the sun and the moon are Your eyes, the burning fire, Your mouth, heating the whole universe with Your radiance.'

Arjuna is praising that Universal Divine Form, *viśva rūpa*, shown by Śrī Kṛṣṇa. *Anādi-madhya-antam,* I see You 'without beginning, middle or end'; *ananta vīryam,* 'infinite in power'; and *ananta bāhum,* 'of manifold arms'; *śaśi sūrya netram,* 'the sun and the moon are Your two eyes'; *dīpta hutāśa vaktram,* 'the burning fire, Your mouth'; *svatejasā viśvam idam tapantam,* 'heating up the whole universe with Your radiance'.

द्यावापृथिव्योरिदं अन्तरं हि
व्याप्तं त्वयैकेन दिशश्च सर्वाः ।
दृष्ट्वाऽद्भुतं रूपं उग्रं तवेदं
लोकत्रयं प्रव्यथितं महात्मन् ॥२०॥

*Dyāvāpṛthivyoridam antaram hi*
*vyāptam tvayaikena diśaśca sarvāḥ;*
*Dṛṣṭvā'dbhutam rūpam ugram tavedam*
*lokatrayam pravyathitam mahātman — 11. 20*

'This space betwixt heaven and earth and all the quarters are filled by You alone; having seen this, Your marvellous and awful Form, the three worlds are trembling with fear, O Great-souled One.'

Your Form is filling up everything; from the earth to far off space. And all the quarters are filled by You alone. Having seen this marvellous and awful Form of the Divine, the three worlds are trembling with fear.

अमी हि त्वां सुरसङ्घा विशन्ति
केचिद्भीताः प्राञ्जलयो गृणन्ति ।
स्वस्तीत्युक्त्वा महर्षि सिद्ध सङ्घाः
स्तुवन्ति त्वां स्तुतिभिः पुष्कलाभिः ॥ २१ ॥

*Amī hi tvām surasaṅghā viśanti*
*kecidbhītāḥ prāñjalayo gṛṇanti;*
*Svastītyuktvā maharṣi siddha saṅghāḥ*
*stuvanti tvām stutibhiḥ puṣkalābhiḥ* — 11. 21

'Verily, into You enter these hosts of *Devas;* some extol You in fear with joined palms; "May it be well!" thus saying, bands of great *Ṛṣis* and *Siddhas* praise You with splendid hymns.'

Similarly, *amī hi tvām surasaṅghā viśanti,* 'into Your mouth enter all these hosts of *Devas*'. 'They are entering into Your mouth' means that they are getting swallowed up by death. *Kecit bhītāḥ prāñjalayo gṛṇanti,* 'some extol You in fear with joined palms'. *Svasti iti uktvā maharṣi siddha saṅghāḥ,* 'May it be well! May it be well! Saying so, bands of great *Ṛṣis* and *Siddhas*'; *stuvanti tvām stutibhiḥ puṣkalābhiḥ,* 'praise You with splendid hymns'.

रुद्रादित्या वसवो ये च साध्या
विश्वेऽश्विनौ मरुतश्चोष्मपाश्च ।
गन्धर्व यक्षासुर सिद्धसङ्घा
वीक्षन्ते त्वां विस्मिताश्चैव सर्वे ॥ २२ ॥

*Rudrādityā vasavo ye ca sādhyā*
*viśve'śvinau marutaścoṣmapāśca;*
*Gandharva yakṣāsura siddhasaṅghā*
*vīkṣante tvām vismitāścaiva sarve* — 11. 22

'The *Rudras, Ādityas, Vasus, Sādhyas, Viśva-devas,* the two *Aśvins, Maruts, Uṣmapās,* and hosts of *Gandharvas, Yakṣas, Asuras,* and *Siddhas*—all these are looking at You, all quite astounded.'

We have in our theology all these divine entities—*Rudras, Ādityas, Vasus, Sādhyas, Viśva-devas,* the two *Aśvins, Maruts, Uṣmapās.* These are all divine entities. Also there are hosts of *Gandharvas, Yakṣas, Asuras,* and *Siddhas. Vīkṣante tvām,* 'they all look on You', *vismitāścaiva sarve,* 'with wonder, amazement'.

रूपं महत्ते बहु वक्त्र नेत्रं
महाबाहो बहु बाहु उरु पादम् ।
बहूदरं बहु दंष्ट्राकरालं
दृष्ट्वा लोकाः प्रव्यथिताः तथाहम् ॥२३॥

*Rūpam mahatte bahu vaktara netram*
*mahābāho bahu bāhu uru pādam;*
*Bahūdaram bahu damṣṭrākarālam*
*dṛṣṭvā lokāḥ pravyathitāḥ tathāham* — 11. 23

'Having seen Your immeasurable Form—with many mouths and eyes, O mighty-armed, with many arms, thighs, and feet, with many stomachs, and fearful with many tusks—the worlds are terrified, and so am I.'

'So am I'! Arjuna is also adding himself as one terrified on looking at the world as a unity. Since we have two eyes each, and there are many billions of people, there are many billions of eyes. So, it is said 'many mouths, many eyes', etc. The whole universe is seen as one. And there is one Reality, the universal Form, the *Virāṭ svarūpa* as we call it in Sanskrit. *Virāṭ* means the universal. The other is *vyakti,* 'individual'. We see only *vyakti;* we see a few *vyaktis.* Our vision cannot comprehend the totality of the universe. Here is that vision given to Arjuna and ultimately it frightens him. What a terrible thing it is! The whole world in this Form. 'I am also frightened', says Arjuna. *Dṛṣṭvā lokāḥ pravyathitāḥ,* 'seeing which the whole world is frightened'; *tathā aham,* 'so am I'. 'I am also very much frightened'.

नभःस्पृशं दीप्तं अनेक वर्णं
व्यात्ताननं दीप्त विशाल नेत्रम् ।
दृष्ट्वा हि त्वां प्रव्यथितान्तरात्मा
धृतिं न विन्दामि शमं च विष्णो ॥ २४॥

*Nabhaḥspṛśam dīptam aneka varṇam*
*vyāttānanam dīpta viśāla netram;*
*Dṛṣṭvā hi tvām pravyathitāntarātmā*
*dhṛtim na vindāmi śamam ca viṣṇo* — 11. 24

'On seeing You touching the sky, shining in many a colour, with mouths wide open, with large fiery eyes, I am terrified at heart, and find no courage nor peace, O Viṣṇu.'

*Nabhaḥspṛśam,* 'touching the sky'. This particular phrase from the *Gītā* has been adopted by the Indian Air Force as its motto. *Dīptam,* 'brilliant'; *aneka varṇam,* 'with many colours'; *vyātta ānanam,* 'with mouth wide open'; *dīpta viśāla netram,* 'with vast and shining eyes'; *dṛṣṭvā hi tvām pravyathita antarātmā,* 'seeing You, the inner self is frightened'; *dhṛtim na vindāmi,* 'I am not getting any courage'; *śamam ca,* 'I am not getting also peace'; *viṣṇo,* 'O Viṣṇu!'.

दंष्ट्राकरालानि च ते मुखानि
दृष्ट्वैव काल अनल सन्निभानि ।
दिशो न जाने न लभे च शर्म
प्रसीद देवेश जगन्निवास ॥ २५॥

*Daṃṣṭrākarālāni ca te mukhāni*
*dṛṣṭvaiva kāla anala sannibhāni;*
*Diśo na jāne na labhe ca śarma*
*prasīda deveśa jagannivāsa* — 11. 25

'Having seen Your mouths, fearful with tusks, (blazing) like *Pralaya*-fires, I know not the four quarters, nor do I find peace; have mercy, O Lord of the *Devas,* O Abode of the universe.'

'Blazing like *Pralaya*-fires' is an important idea. At the time of dissolution, there will be a tremendous fire. The whole world will be enveloped in that fire. In today's astrophysics, this sun will become expanded and still expanded, and then it will swallow all the planets of the solar system. That is one of the theories there. Similarly, other systems also. At the time of dissolution, there will be *kāla anala*, 'the Fire of Time'. That will envelope all things of the universe. 'I know not the four quarters', north, east, west or south. 'Nor do I find peace; have mercy.' Arjuna is frightened and he is asking for peace from the Divine.

अमी च त्वां धृतराष्ट्रस्य पुत्राः
सर्वे सहैवावनिपालसङ्घैः ।
भीष्मो द्रोणः सूतपुत्रस्तथासौ
सहास्मदीयैरपि योधमुख्यैः ॥२६॥

*Amī ca tvām dhṛtarāṣṭrasya putrāḥ*
*sarve sahaivāvanipālasaṅghaiḥ;*
*Bhīṣmo droṇaḥ sūtaputrastathāsau*
*sahāsmadīyairapi yodhamukhyaiḥ* — 11. 26

'All these sons of Dhṛtarāṣṭra with hosts of monarchs, Bhīṣma, Droṇa and Sūtaputra, with the warrior-chiefs of ours…'

वक्त्राणि ते त्वरमाणा विशन्ति
दंष्ट्राकरालानि भयानकानि ।
केचिद्विलग्ना दशनान्तरेषु
संदृश्यन्ते चूर्णितैरुत्तमाङ्गैः ॥२७॥

*Vaktrāṇi te tvaramāṇā viśanti*
*daṃṣṭrākarālāni bhayānakāni;*
*Kecidvilagnā daśanāntareṣu*
*saṃdṛśyante cūrṇitairuttamāṅgaiḥ* — 11. 27

'Enter precipitately into Your mouth, terrible with tusks and fearful to behold. Some are found sticking in the interstices of Your teeth, with their heads crushed to powder.'

A very important statement comes here. What is to happen in the war ahead is being told here. The host of monarchs and warrior chiefs are rushing towards Your mouth to be swallowed up; that is the language. *Daṃṣṭrākarālāni*, 'full of tusks' and other teeth; *bhayānakāni*, 'fearful to behold', and these teeth will be chewing everything. Nothing will be left. It is put here in human language. *Kecit vilagnā daśanāntareṣu samdṛśyante cūrṇitaiḥ uttamāṅgaiḥ,* 'some of them have been chewed. They are just left in between the teeth. Here and there some pieces are remaining, pieces of some of these mighty warriors'—meaning thereby that they are all entering into death. That is put in a blazing language. Even their best forms are being pounded and chewed and caught up between the teeth. That is the picture given.

Earlier, just before the war began, in the *Mahābhārata,* there occurs a verse (*Udyoga Parva,* 126. 31, Bhandarkar edition). Bhīṣma, seeing the critical condition, tells Śrī Kṛṣṇa, 'Kṛṣṇa, I find that the whole of these Kauravas and all others are rushing into the mouth of Time, mouth of Death. They can't escape, it so appears to me.' Probably, today's Delhi Duradarshan *Mahābhārata* serial also made this remark—Bhīṣma telling Dhṛtarāṣṭra that the whole Kaurava race is going to be ruined. We have sent these Pāṇḍavas to the forest. And this ruin of the Kaurava race is going to happen. And he became very much upset. Dhṛtarāṣṭra's blind attachment for his son Duryodhana, blinds him to everything. Bhīṣma says there, *Kālapakvam idam manye sarva kṣatram janārdana,* 'Janārdana! The whole of the *kṣatra, kṣatriya* groups, is *kālapakvam,* ready or ripe for Time', to be eaten up by Time.

यथा नदीनां बहवोऽम्बुवेगाः
समुद्रं एव अभिमुखा द्रवन्ति ।
तथा तवामी नर लोक वीरा
विशन्ति वक्त्राणि अभिविज्वलन्ति ॥ २८ ॥

*Yathā nadīnām bahavo'mbuvegāḥ*
*samudram eva abhimukhā dravanti;*
*Tathā tavāmī nara loka vīrā*
*viśanti vaktrāṇyi abhivijvalanti — 11. 28*

'Verily, as the many torrents of rivers flow towards the ocean, so do those heroes in the world of men enter Your fiercely flaming mouths.'

Just like rivers with tremendous flow rush to get lost in the sea, similarly, these heroes in the world are entering Your fiercely flaming mouths. This is what is happening just now. None can stop it. It just goes on.

यथा प्रदीप्तं ज्वलनं पतङ्गा
विशन्ति नाशाय समृद्ध वेगाः ।
तथैव नाशाय विशन्ति लोकाः
तवापि वक्त्राणि समृद्ध वेगाः ॥ २९ ॥

*Yathā pradiptam jvalanam pataṅgā*
*viśanti nāśāya samṛddha vegāḥ;*
*Tathaiva nāśāya viśanti lokāḥ*
*tavāpi vaktrāṇi samṛddha vegāḥ* — 11. 29

'As moths precipitately rush into a blazing fire only to perish, even so do these creatures also precipitately rush into Your mouth only to perish.'

Another example is taken. Moths, when they see fire, rush into it only to get destroyed there. Similarly, these creatures also rush into Your mouth to perish. God has two aspects, the protecting aspect and the destroying aspect. Both are the same, life and death. Both are parts of the Divine. We forget one part. We think it is only life. But life *and* death constitute Reality. So, all these living creatures are now rushing towards death. Nobody can resist it.

लेलिह्यसे ग्रसमानः समन्तात्
लोकान् समग्रान् वदनैर्ज्वलद्भिः ।
तेजोभिरापूर्य जगत् समग्रं
भासस्तवोग्राः प्रतपन्ति विष्णो ॥ ३० ॥

*Lelihyase grasamānaḥ samantāt*
*lokān samagrān vadanairjvaladbhiḥ;*
*Tejobhirāpūrya jagat samagram*
*bhāsastavogrāḥ pratapanti viṣṇo* — 11. 30

'Swallowing all the worlds on every side with Your flaming mouths, You are licking Your lips. Your fierce rays, filling the whole world with radiance, are burning, O Viṣṇu.'

A most gruesome description is given: *grasamāṇaḥ samantāt lokān samagrān,* 'swallowing all the worlds on every side'; *vadanaiḥ jvaladbhiḥ lelihyase,* 'with Your flaming mouths, You are licking Your lips.' It is just like licking the blood on the lips when one bites one's lips. Further, *tejobhirāpūrya jagat samagram bhāsaḥ tava ugrāḥ,* 'Your fierce rays, filling the whole world with radiance'; *pratapanti viṣṇo,* 'are burning, O Viṣṇu'.

**आख्याहि मे को भवान् उग्ररूपो**
**नमोऽस्तु ते देववर प्रसीद ।**
**विज्ञातुं इच्छामि भवन्तं आद्यं**
**न हि प्रजानामि तव प्रवृत्तिम् ॥३१॥**

*Ākhyāhi me ko bhavān ugrarūpo*
*namo'stu te devavara prasīda;*
*Vijñātum icchāmi bhavantam ādyam*
*na hi prajānāmi tava pravṛttim* — 11. 31

'Tell me who You are, fierce in form. Salutation to You, O supreme *Deva,* have mercy. I desire to know You, O Primeval One. I know not indeed Your purpose.'

Arjuna is in a very humble state of mind. He is asking the Lord, *ākhyāhi me ko bhavān ugrarūpo,* 'who are You, O Lord, please tell me about this wonderful fierce form of Yours.' *Namo'stu te devavara prasīda,* 'salutations to You, O Great among gods; be peaceful or gracious.' *Vijñātum icchāmi bhavantam ādyam,* 'I would like to know Your origin.' *Na hi prajānāmi tava pravṛttim,* 'I am unable to understand Your activities.' Your actions are something beyond comprehension.

Now comes Śrī Kṛṣṇa's own words.

**श्रीभगवान् उवाच–**
*Śrībhagavān uvāca —*
*'Śrī Bhagavān said:'*

**कालोऽस्मि लोकक्षयकृत् प्रवृद्धो**
**लोकान् समाहर्तुं इह प्रवृत्तः ।**
**ऋतेऽपि त्वां न भविष्यन्ति सर्वे**
**येऽवस्थिताः प्रत्यनीकेषु योधाः ॥३२॥**

*Kālo'smi lokakṣayakṛt pravṛddho*
*lokān samāhartum iha pravṛttaḥ;*
*Ṛte'pi tvām na bhaviṣyanti sarve*
*ye'vasthitāḥ pratyanīkeṣu yodhāḥ* — 11. 32

'I am the mighty world-destroying Time, here made manifest for the purpose of infolding the world. Even without you, none of the warriors arrayed in the hostile armies shall live.'

I am Time that comes to consume everything. *Lokakṣayakṛt,* 'that which consumes the entire world'; that is called *Kāla.* Now, *pravṛddhaḥ,* 'it has become very active'; *iha pravṛttaḥ,* 'is functioning here'; *lokān samāhartum,* 'to destroy this world'. *Ṛte'pi tvām na bhaviṣyanti sarve,* 'even without you none will survive'; *ye'vasthitāḥ pratyanīkeṣu yodhāḥ,* 'these hostile armies present here.' They are all marked for consumption by death.

तस्मात् त्वं उत्तिष्ठ यशो लभस्व
जित्वा शत्रून् भुङ्क्ष्व राज्यं समृद्धम् ।
मयैवैते निहताः पूर्वं एव
निमित्तमात्रं भव सव्यसाचिन् ॥ ३३ ॥

*Tasmāt tvam uttiṣṭha yaśo labhasva*
*jitvā śatrūn bhuṅkṣva rājyam samṛddham;*
*Mayaivete nihatāḥ pūrvam eva*
*nimittamātram bhava savyasācin* — 11. 33

'Therefore, do you arise and acquire fame. Conquer the enemies, and enjoy unrivalled dominion. Verily, by Myself have they been already slain; be you merely an instrument, O Arjuna.'

Remember, Śrī Kṛṣṇa is telling this just before the battle begins, in the midst of the battlefield. Arjuna wanted to withdraw from battle. He became weak, grief-stricken, as we saw in the last verse of the first chapter and Śrī Kṛṣṇa's immediate response in the second and third *ślokas* of the second chapter. Here is Śrī Kṛṣṇa again giving Arjuna a message of strength: *tasmāt tvam uttiṣṭha,* 'therefore, you raise yourself', don't lie down, weak, helpless. Stand up, Arjuna! *Yaśo labhasva,* 'acquire the glory' which belongs to every true human being. Facing obstacles, facing difficulties, facing death itself, try to achieve something great in life. That is the message of the *Gītā.* When you do great things, you get glory. You might have to fight against death itself; what does it matter? We know there is death. We are going to fight it. We shall fight and get destroyed, but by so doing we shall acquire the great glory of manliness. This is the philosophy that will create heroes in a society—not any goody-goody philosophy leading to comfort, pleasure and laziness. This is called the greatness of tragedy. Life is a tragedy. A tragic hero will face extreme pressures and difficulties. But, he or she will face them and will face death courageously, doing something great. This is called heroic philosophy. The world is a world of death. It is a battlefield. Every day there is dying here, dying there. If we have to die at all, why not die doing some great work? That is the challenge. Why die in a bed? A *kṣatriya* is not expected to die in a bed. That was the rule in ancient India. Die in the battlefield; die in the field of work, in the struggle for serving weaker sections. We had been given this heroic philosophy which we, except a few, forgot during the last few centuries. We sought for a cosy, comfortable life. That made us low and almost dead. One death is there, and before that death comes another death. That is what the great Shakespeare referred to in *Julius Caesar* (Act II. Scene II):

'Cowards die many times before their deaths; The valiant never taste of death but once.'

That valiant attitude is the central message of the *Gītā.* Be a hero in every department of life. You need not be a soldier in the army to be a hero. An average citizen can be a hero. Great works one can do. Take a boy who rescues another boy from drowning. And the Government of India gives a prize to him. It is really beautiful. He has done a really heroic act. So, there are hundreds and thousands of occasions when our life can show that heroic impulse. We had rejected this philosophy long ago, became very small, petty-minded. We wanted only a cosy, comfortable life. That has ruined us. So, death comes to us in a thousand ways. But, if you are a hero, it will come only once. You are fighting against death itself. That makes a tragic hero. The Greek tragedies speak of this tragic hero. Even in the *Mahābhārata*, there are many tragic heroes. They knew things were going bad, but they would face them. 'We will die, we don't care. We will stick to our own ideas.' That kind of thinking was there. Karṇa, a great hero, knew towards the end that he was a brother of the Pāṇḍavas. But being brought up by Duryodhana, his determination was, 'I belong to his side. I will fight only for him and for nobody else. I don't mind dying.' There are so many occasions when one will be called upon to show the real strength that is within.

A very ordinary life—eating, drinking, begetting and passing away one day—is an animal life. It does not bear that heroic touch. Swami Vivekananda always emphasized that India should develop that heroic touch. 'Your country needs heroes. Be heroes,' he had said. And in that heroic philosophy, suffering is no problem. We are prepared to face suffering. A soldier faces death every second, and that spirit must come to the citizen also; it is not merely for the soldier. This is how we develop greatness as a people. Leading a comfortable life cannot make any nation great.

So, if Śrī Kṛṣṇa's words are put into today's context, this will be the meaning. *Tasmāt tvam uttiṣṭha,* 'all of you, citizens of India, stand up.' *Yaśo labhasva,* 'develop that manliness which is the glory of humanity.' Without that manliness, there is no glory. Our lives would then be like that of petty animals, like sheep, bleating all the time. That is not what we need. We want that lion which roars, full of strength. The whole forest can feel the touch of one lion. How to do that? *Jitvā śatrūn,* 'overcome your enemies.' Arjuna's enemies were the Kauravas. Our enemies are different. Our enemies are poverty, backwardness, injustice in society. These are our enemies. Fight them. Every citizen must rise up, face them, and then overcome them. And then? *Bhuṅkṣva rājyam samṛddham,* 'enjoy life in this prosperous country of ours.' If we overcome poverty, backwardness, insanitary conditions, if all villages are fine and clean, and if we are economically healthy, what a pleasure it would be to live in such a society! All the slums have gone, the dwellers have all been rehabilitated, and they have work to do. If we achieve this kind of development by our united efforts, what a joy it will be to live on this earth! *Bhuṅkṣva rājyam samṛddham,* 'enjoy your prosperous country'. That is called happy, glorious, human life on earth; it is far better than life in a heaven, as has been repeatedly mentioned in the *Gītā*. Then, Śrī Kṛṣṇa adds: *mayaivete nihatāḥ pūrvam eva,* 'I have already destroyed these enemies' of the nation. India will become great in the modern age—that is the message of the time spirit. *Nimittamātram bhava savyasācin,* 'you be merely the instrument for that actual achievement.' Destiny says, 'India shall be great. India shall overcome its poverty and backwardness.' That is the dictate of the modern age. The Lord has already spoken that way. You only be the instrument for achieving it for your own greatness and glory. *Nimittamātram bhava savyasācin,* can apply to every one of us. Be an instrument for this great purpose—to build up India, its economy, its society, its politics, and develop a progressive, social system and democratic state, and work devotedly for international peace. What a happy life we will have then! What happy human relationships we shall have. No crime, no corruption, everybody healthy. You can keep your doors open all the time. Nobody will touch anything with the idea of stealing. These are not utopian ideas. Sometimes our nation had achieved this. It is the dictate of the age. You be the instrument for bringing about this situation. This is what the destiny of India whispers to every citizen.

This applies to the international field as well. This modern age is whispering to everyone of us, 'We shall break down barriers to neighbourliness. We shall create a one-world where humanity will feel oneness with each other. A happy world we shall have.' This also is the meaning of the statement of Śrī Kṛṣṇa uttered five thousand years ago, to men and women of today. Don't say it is my fate to live in a disorganised country or the world. Never! *Uttiṣṭha!* 'Stand up!' Śrī Kṛṣṇa always uses this word. Get up! Don't remain lying down, weeping all the time. Stand up! Why did our *satyāgrahis* go and face the bullets of the foreign power and got injured or killed? That is glory. We very much respect them today. Where is that spirit gone? Your main enemies are not outside. But, there are plenty of enemies within. How much injustice, how much top to bottom corruption, how much of cheating, how many similar evil things we are now having! We have to expose all of them, correct them, create a healthy public opinion to face and overcome them. How can there be a free democracy, if a woman cannot move freely and fearlessly in the streets at night and work freely in offices, without being molested, without their honour being protected? Where is freedom then? Freedom will be only for the powerful. That will be a bad India. If people do not protest against these things, you will have worse conditions coming in the future. Here is a *Mahābhārata* verse giving one aspect of a healthy society (*Śānti Parva*, 12. 68. 32, Bhandarkar Edition):

*Striyaścāpuruṣā mārgam sarvālaṅkāra bhūṣitāḥ;*
*Nirbhayāḥ pratipadyante yadā rakṣati bhūmipaḥ —*

'Where there is a healthy political state'—remember that expression, *a healthy political state*—'in that state, women, with many ornaments on the body, can pass fearlessly through the lanes and streets of cities, towns and villages of that state, without being accompanied by a male member'.

That is called a healthy society. Woman is to be treated as a person recognising her rights. Without her consent, nothing can be done on her. If you have number of people with this attitude filling a society, that society is healthy. But, today it is not so. We are far, far away from that condition, because many in India are inactive, without value awareness, and feudal in outlook. 'Let the trouble come to me and then I shall see. When the trouble comes to others, I do not mind.'

This is the way in which we have been thinking for a thousand years. When a foreigner invaded one of our states, we thought, 'Let him come to my state and then I shall attend to it', instead of joining together to expel the foreign invader. We never did that. Once or twice, small attempts have been made. Soon it fizzled out. So, this attitude is destructive. We have already suffered plenty. Now there is the awakened, democratic, political conscience. If there is any injustice, we have to join together immediately, and protest against it. And injustice becomes less and less. Without protest, no injustice can be destroyed. Don't think that the government alone will be able to destroy injustice. Government, as it is now, is inclined more often to protect the evil doers and the corrupt ones. Our democracy must become more alive, more alert, and more active. Then we will get a healthy government.

In many countries this problem has been there. Once the people become awake, very few governments can withstand that pressure. In Western democracies, because people are educated, nobody can do that much evil to the people as we find here in India. So, they are much more free from this kind of feudal power exercised by a government. We have also to get general education for all our people; at least up to class 8. Then they will understand their inner strength, their own power, their own political personality status. Then governments cannot do whatever they like, good or evil. But now they can do whatever they like because there is no strong, widespread, independent public opinion. Therefore, Śrī Kṛṣṇa is giving this message to all the people, even of today. Conditions are different now. Arjuna had only one single war, but here it is a day-to-day war against corruption, injustice and oppression. But the message is the same: Awake and overcome your enemies and enjoy life in a prosperous India—*jitvā śatrūn bhuṅkṣva rājyam samṛddham.*

Śrī Kṛṣṇa's message is always strengthening and purifying. The whole Vedantic message is of fearlessness and strength. In no other philosophy will you find this wonderful idea of fearlessness and strength as a central note. That is

Vedanta—*abhayam,* 'fearlessness'. In the later chapters of the *Gītā,* when Śrī Kṛṣṇa describes the *daivī sampat,* 'divine qualities of the human being', He lists *abhayam,* 'fearlessness' as the first *sampat* or wealth.

द्रोणञ्च भीष्मञ्च जयद्रथञ्च
कर्णं तथान्यानपि योधवीरान् ।
मया हतांस्त्वं जहि मा व्यथिष्ठा
युध्यस्व जेतासि रणे सपत्नान् ॥३४॥

*Droṇañca bhīṣmañca jayadrathañca*
*karṇam tathānyānapi yodhavīrān;*
*Mayā hatāmstvam jahi mā vyathiṣṭhā*
*yudhyasva jetāsi raṇe sapatnān — 11. 34*

'Droṇa, Bhīṣma, Jayadratha, Karṇa as well as other brave warriors—these, already killed by Me, do you kill. Be not distressed with fear; fight, and you shall conquer your enemies in battle.'

Śrī Kṛṣṇa is finally telling Arjuna: this Droṇa, this Bhīṣma, this Karna—pointing out to them—and then Jayadratha, a very powerful ruler of Sind who had done a lot of wicked deeds. A hundred sons and one daughter were born to Dhṛtarāṣṭra. Jayadratha was the husband of that only daughter in the Kaurava family. That ruler of Sind, Jayadratha, had abducted Draupadi in the forest and had got punished by the Pāṇḍavas.

*Tathānyānapi yodhavīrān,* 'and all other great heroes of battle'; *mayā hatān,* 'they have already been killed by Me.' I, the supreme Divine as Time, have already consumed them. *Tvam jahi,* 'do you conquer them'; *mā vyathiṣṭhā,* 'be not distressed with fear'; *yudhyasva,* 'fight on!' *Jetāsi raṇe sapatnān,* 'in this battle, you will win all these enemies eventually.'

सञ्जय उवाच–

*Sañjaya uvāca —*

*'Sañjaya said:'*

Sañjaya is repeating the story.

एतच्छ्रुत्वा वचनं केशवस्य
कृताञ्जलिर्वेपमानः किरीटी ।
नमस्कृत्वा भूय एवाह कृष्णं
सगद्गदं भीतभीतः प्रणम्य ॥३५॥

*Etacchrutvā vacanam keśavasya*
*kṛtāñjalirvepamānaḥ kirīṭī;*
*Namaskṛtvā bhūya evāha kṛṣṇam*
*sagadgadam bhītabhītaḥ praṇamya* — 11. 35

'Having heard this speech of Keśava (i.e. Śrī Kṛṣṇa), the diademed one (Arjuna), with joined palms, trembling, prostrated himself, and again addressed Śrī Kṛṣṇa in a choked voice, bowing down, overwhelmed with fear.'

*Etat śrutvā vacanam keśavasya,* 'hearing these words of Śrī Kṛṣṇa'; *kṛtāñjaliḥ vepamānaḥ kirīṭī, 'kirīṭī* or Arjuna, shivering as it were, and with hands saluting Śrī Kṛṣṇa'; *namaskṛtvā,* 'and also bowing to Him'; *bhūya eva āha kṛṣṇam,* 'again spoke to Śrī Kṛṣṇa'; *sagadgadam,* 'with a voice full of emotion'. That gurgling sound comes whenever you are emotionally charged. Your speech will then be *sagadgadam. Bhītabhītaḥ,* 'full of fear'; *praṇamya,* 'saluting him.'

अर्जुन उवाच–
*Arjuna uvāca —*

*'Arjuna said:'*

स्थाने हृषीकेश तव प्रकीर्त्या
जगत् प्रहृष्यत्यनुरज्यते च ।
रक्षांसि भीतानि दिशो द्रवन्ति
सर्वे नमस्यन्ति च सिद्धसङ्घाः ॥३६॥

*Sthāne hṛṣīkeśa tava prakīrtyā*
*jagat prahṛṣyatyanurajyate ca;*
*Rakṣāṃsi bhītāni diśo dravanti*
*sarve namasyanti ca siddhasaṅghāḥ* — 11. 36

'It is quite proper, O Hṛṣīkeśa, that the world is delighted and rejoices and praises You, that *Rākṣasas* fly in fear to all quarters and all the hosts of *Siddhas* bow down to You in adoration.'

Arjuna said, 'it is only proper, O Śrī Kṛṣṇa, that the world is delighted and rejoices in Your praise. *Rākṣasas* fly in fear in all directions'. *Rākṣasas* are types of human beings with no moral sense. They have energy, they have power, but they have no moral sense. They can do any evil. That is the nature of *Rākṣasa* type. So, human beings are *Rākṣasas* when they have these qualities—trying to destroy others, their welfare, their power. So, *Rākṣasas* are mentioned here as flying in all directions out of fear. And all the hosts of *Siddhas* bow down to You in adoration. *Siddhas* are another type of semi-divine beings, who are well disposed, and so they are bowing down to You in adoration.

कस्माच्च ते न नमेरन् महात्मन्
गरीयसे ब्रह्मणोऽप्यादिकर्त्रे ।
अनन्त देवेश जगन्निवास
त्वं अक्षरं सदसत्तत्परं यत् ॥३७॥

*Kasmācca te na nameran mahātman*
*garīyase brahmaṇo'pyādikartre;*
*Ananta deveśa jagannivāsa*
*tvam akṣaram sadasattatparam yat* — 11. 37

'And why should they not, O Great-souled One, bow to You, greater than, and as the Primal Cause, of even Brahmā, O Infinite Being, O Lord of the *Devas*, O Abode of the universe? You are the Imperishable, the Being and the non-Being, (as well as) That which is beyond (them).'

*Kasmācca te na nameran*, 'O, why should not they adore You?' asks Arjuna. *Mahātman*, 'O Great Soul!' *Garīyase*, 'You are superior to'; *brahmaṇopi ādikartre*, 'and the Primal cause of even that Brahmā who is the original creator of this universe'. *Ananta deveśa*, 'Infinite Lord of all beings, of all *devas*'; *jagannivāsa*, 'Abode of the universe'. He is not only outside, He is also inside. The universe lives in You, O Kṛṣṇa. *Tvam akṣaram,* 'You are the imperishable One', *sat asat tatparam yat,* 'You are the cause and the effect and also what is beyond cause and effect'; *sat* is effect, *asat* is cause. What cannot be seen is called *asat.* The cause cannot be seen and so it is *asat. Sat* is what can be seen, the effect. So, 'You are the effect and cause, and what is beyond both of them'.

त्वं आदिदेवः पुरुषः पुराणः
त्वमस्य विश्वस्य परं निधानम् ।
वेत्ताऽसि वेद्यं च परं च धाम
त्वया ततं विश्वं अनन्तरूप ॥ ३८ ॥

*Tvam ādidevaḥ puruṣaḥ purāṇaḥ*
*tvamasya viśvasya param nidhānam;*
*Vettāsi vedyam ca param ca dhāma*
*tvayā talam viśvam anantarūpa* — 11. 38

'You are the primal *Deva,* the ancient *Puruṣa.* You are the supreme Refuge of this universe, You are the Knower, and the (One Thing to be) Known. You are the supreme Goal. By You is the universe pervaded, O You of boundless Form.'

*Tvam ādidevaḥ puruṣaḥ,* 'You are the primal divine Person'; the first among all the gods, *ādideva,* 'primary, primordial divine Being'; that *puruṣa,* 'Person', You are. *Purāṇaḥ,* 'most ancient'. *Tvamasya viśvasya param nidhānam,* 'You are the supreme refuge of this *viśva,* i.e. this universe'; *vettāsi vedyam ca,* 'You are the Knower, and You are the Known'. See the language! *Vettā* means 'Knower'. *Vedyam* means 'the Known'. You are the Knower and the Known. Only in that state this experience can come. I am the Knower of this world, but I am *not* the world. But in my true nature, I am *both* the Knower and the Known. *Param ca dhāma,* 'that supreme State also You are'. *Tvayā tatam viśvam,* 'by You is the whole universe pervaded'. *Anantarūpa,* 'of infinite Form'—that is Your true nature.

वायुर्यमोऽग्निर्वरुणः शशाङ्कः
प्रजापतिस्त्वं प्रपितामहश्च ।
नमो नमस्तेऽस्तु सहस्रकृत्वः
पुनश्च भूयोऽपि नमो नमस्ते ॥ ३९ ॥

*Vāyuryamo'gnirvaruṇaḥ śaśāṅkaḥ*
*prajāpatistvam prapitāmahaśca;*
*Namo namaste'stu sahasrakṛtvaḥ*
*punaśca bhūyo'pi namo namaste* — *11. 39*

'You are Vāyu or air, Yama, Agni or fire, Varuṇa, the Moon, Prajāpati, and the Great-grand-father. Salutation, salutation to You, a thousand times, and again and again salutation, salutation to You!'

You are Vāyu, Yama, Agni, Varuṇa, the Moon, Prajāpati, and the Great-grand-father. Brahmā is the grand father, and the Divine Lord is called *prapitāmahaḥ*, 'the Great-grand-father'. Salutations, salutations to You! Again and again, salutations, salutations to You. A thousand times salutations, and again and again, salutations! Full of divine fervour! Arjuna is not able to express his devotion enough through words. So, he says merely, 'a thousand salutations to You!'

नमः पुरस्ताद् अथ पृष्ठतस्ते
नमोऽस्तु ते सर्वत एव सर्व ।
अनन्तवीर्य अमितविक्रमस्त्वं
सर्वं समाप्नोषि ततोऽसि सर्वः ॥४०॥

*Namaḥ purastād atha pṛṣṭhataste*
*namo'stu te sarvata eva sarva;*
*Anantavīrya amitavikramastvam*
*sarvam samāpnoṣi tato'si sarvaḥ* — *11. 40*

'Salutations to You before and behind, salutation to You on every side, O the All! You, infinite in power and infinite in prowess, pervade all; wherefore You are All.'

*Namaḥ purastād*, 'salutations to You in front' of me. But, He is not only in the front. *Atha pṛṣṭhataste*, salutations 'to You behind also'. *Namo'stu te sarvata eva sarva*, 'salutations to You everywhere, and the All'. *Anantavīrya amita vikramastvam*, 'You are endowed with *ananta vīrya*, infinite energy, and *vikramaḥ*, of heroic actions.' *Sarvam samāpnoṣi*, 'You envelop everything'; *tato'si sarvaḥ*, 'therefore, You are everything'. See the language! You envelop everything, therefore, You are everything. This manifested universe is the adorable Brahman only. That is based on the verse (II.ii.11) of the *Muṇḍaka Upaniṣad: Brahmaivedam viśvamidam variṣṭham.*

The next verse is a beautiful one. Arjuna is now feeling that he has not been fully aware of the greatness of Śrī Kṛṣṇa; till now he had taken Him to be His friend only. But now he finds Him to be an extraordinary person, so great, so divine. So, he is expressing his repentance in the next two verses.

सखेति मत्वा प्रसभं यदुक्तं
हे कृष्ण हे यादव हे सखेति ।
अजानता महिमानं तवेदं
मया प्रमादात् प्रणयेन वापि ॥४१॥

*Sakheti matvā prasabham yaduktam*
*he kṛṣṇa he yādava he sakheti;*
*Ajānatā mahimānam tavedam*
*mayā pramādāt praṇayena vāpi* — 11. 41

'Whatever I have presumptuously said from carelessness or affection, addressing You as "O Kṛṣṇa, O Yādava, O friend", regarding You merely as a friend, unconscious of this Your greatness.'

I have been related to You all these years as a friend. I 'treated You as a friend'—*sakheti matvā*. Thinking of You as a *sakhā* or friend, what did I do? *Prasabham yaduktam,* 'carelessly have I said'; *he kṛṣṇa, he yādava, he sakhe,* 'O Kṛṣṇa, O Yādava, O Friend!' How could I do so? *Ajānatā mahimānam tavedam,* 'not knowing Your *mahimā* or greatness of this nature'. I was utterly ignorant of this tremendous majesty of Yours. I took You to be like myself; or, *mayā pramādāt,* 'through my delusion'; or *praṇayena vāpi,* 'out of love', comradely love, I have taken liberties with You.

यच्चावहासार्थं असत्कृतोऽसि
विहार शय्यासन भोजनेषु ।
एकोऽथवाप्यच्युत तत्समक्षं
तत्क्षामये त्वां अहं अप्रमेयम् ॥४२॥

*Yaccāvahāsārtham asatkṛto'si*
*vihāra śayyāsana bhojaneṣu;*
*Eko'thavāpyacyuta tat samakṣam*
*tat kṣāmaye tvām aham aprameyam* — 11. 42

'In whatever way I may have been disrespectful to You in fun, while walking, reposing, sitting, or at meals, when alone (with You), O Acyuta, or in company—I implore You, O immeasurable One, to forgive all this.'

*Tat kṣāmaye tvām*, 'please forgive me' for all this, says Arjuna. What are these? *Yat ca avahāsārtham asatkṛto'si*, 'what I have spoken to You in fun and in frolic'; sometimes making fun of You, merely without knowing Your greatness, I have been disrespectful to You. A very interesting admission at this stage—*vihāra śayyā āsana bhojaneṣu*, 'while walking, reposing, sitting, or at meals'; *ekaḥ athavā api*, 'also when alone with You'. In all these situations, I took You to be my friend. That is all. And I behaved accordingly. Now I find that the whole thing was wrong. You are so great, so majestic, and I was ignorant of it till now. Please forgive me, O immeasurable One, for all these childish pranks of mine towards You. Arjuna is great, but Śrī Kṛṣṇa is the greatest. But, Arjuna behaved with Śrī Kṛṣṇa as friends equal in age. That is also very interesting. In the *Mahābhārata*, you find many passages of that friendly nature. Arjuna and Śrī Kṛṣṇa mean one soul in two bodies. That is the nature of their relationship. Now Arjuna finds that the whole thing is different.

पितासि लोकस्य चराचरस्य
त्वमस्य पूज्यश्च गुरुर्गरीयान् ।
न त्वत्समोऽस्त्यभ्यधिकः कुतोऽन्यो
लोकत्रयेऽप्यप्रतिमप्रभाव ॥४३॥

*Pitāsi lokasya carācarasya*
*tvamasya pūjyaśca gururgarīyān;*
*Na tvatsamo'styabhyadhikaḥ kuto'nyo*
*lokatraye'pyapratimaprabhāva* — 11. 43

'You are the Father of the world, moving and unmoving; the object of its worship, greater than the great. None else exists who is equal to You in the three worlds; who then can excel You, O You of power incomparable?'

*Pitāsi lokasya carācarasya,* 'You are the Father of this universe of moving and unmoving things'; *tvamasya pūjyaśca,* 'You are also the most adorable One' in the universe; *gururgarīyān,* 'highly venerable *Guru* of this world'. *Na tvat samo asti,* 'there is none equal to You'; *abhyadhikaḥ kuto'nyo,* 'who else can be superior to You?' There is none equal to You; how then can there be anyone superior to You? *Lokatraye'pi,* 'in the three *lokas* or worlds', You are supreme. *Apratima-prabhāva,* 'Your energy, Your glory is incomparable'. There is no second one of this nature.

Arjuna is understanding this dimension of Śrī Kṛṣṇa. Now you are reading all this in this eleventh chapter. And actually Arjuna is seeing this vision. Later on, Śrī Kṛṣṇa will withdraw this vision. And the old relationship will continue. Here is an interval, an interregnum as it were. In fact, you are just about to see the beginning of the Kurukṣetra war in the *Udyoga Parva* of the *Mahābhārata.* And, just when Śrī Kṛṣṇa was to go as the ambassador of the Pāṇḍavas to the Kaurava court to plead for peace between the two parties, Sañjaya was sent by Dhṛtarāṣṭra to go to the Pāṇḍava camp and see how things were going on. Sañjaya entered Arjuna's camp and he was surprised to see Arjuna lying down with his legs in the lap of Śrī Kṛṣṇa. What sign could be more illustrative of the intimate relationship that existed between them than that! As soon as he saw it, Sañjaya returned and said to Dhṛtarāṣṭra, 'your Duryodhana has no hope of winning this war. He is gone. If Arjuna can place his feet on the lap of Śrī Kṛṣṇa with such intimacy, and as Śrī Kṛṣṇa is so powerful, how can the Kauravas win?'

You get such illustrations even hereafter. This is just an interregnum. Because he wanted to see the divine Form, Śrī Kṛṣṇa showed it to him. And Arjuna will say a little later, 'I don't want to see this Form any more! I want to see that familiar form of Yours.' Then, Śrī Kṛṣṇa shows His familiar form. Very often, when we are not fit to have a divine experience or vision, we begin by wanting to see it, and once we get it, we are fed up with it, and we say, 'please take it back!' Even today, people do not know this and they say, 'I want the vision of God.' But, if the vision of God comes to you, you will have to wind up all your business. You can't do anything in that state. That is quite possible. The manager of the Dakshineswar temple, Mathur Babu, prayed to Sri Ramakrishna: 'Please give me the divine vision. I have been serving you as the manager of the temple, and of the big estate of its creator, Rāṇi Rāsmaṇi.' Sri Ramakrishna consoled him saying, 'it will come in the right time'. But again and again, Mathur Babu requested him. Then, Sri Ramakrishna said, 'Mother, let him have some vision.' Within a short time, Mathur Babu was beyond himself in some divine experience—always going about weeping, smiling, always having mystical experiences. One day, two days, three days passed in this way, with his business at a standstill. No work was proceeding. And he felt this. Then he came to Sri Ramakrishna and said, 'Please take back all these visions. All my business is suffering. I cannot have this anymore.' Sri Ramakrishna said: 'I told you so. Spiritual experience will come at the right time. Don't press for it.' And he took back that vision from him. So, you can see this kind of thing happening in spiritual life, which people do not realize and they say: 'I want this, I want that.' It will come in time. We have to build up our spiritual life step by step. The nervous system must get the capacity to bear these experiences. Otherwise, there will be a breakdown. These are all truths about spiritual life. So, a steady development is the best. Somebody got 'it', I also must get 'it'—that is not correct. So, here Arjuna is in that condition: 'There is none equal to You in the three worlds', says Arjuna.

तस्मात् प्रणम्य प्रणिधाय कायं
प्रसादये त्वां अहं ईशं ईड्यम् ।
पितेव पुत्रस्य सखेव सख्युः
प्रियः प्रियायार्हसि देव सोढुम् ॥४४॥

*Tasmāt praṇamya praṇidhāya kāyam*
*prasādaye tvām aham īśam īḍyam;*
*Piteva putrasya sakheva sakhyuḥ*
*priyaḥ priyāyārhasi deva soḍhum* — 11. 44

'So prostrating my body in adoration, I crave Your forgiveness, Lord adorable! As a father forgives his son, a friend a dear friend, a beloved one (forgives) his object of love, even so should You forgive me, O *Deva*.'

Finally, he submits with this statement: 'Prostrating my body in adoration, I crave Your forgiveness, O Lord adorable. As a father forgives his son, a friend forgives his dear friend, a beloved forgives his beloved one, even so should You forgive me, O Lord.' That is a beautiful expression of Arjuna.

अदृष्टपूर्वं हृषितोऽस्मि दृष्ट्वा
भयेन च प्रव्यथितं मनो मे ।
तदेव मे दर्शय देव रूपं
प्रसीद देवेश जगन्निवास ॥४५॥

*Adṛṣṭapūrvam hṛṣito'smi dṛṣṭvā*
*bhayena ca pravyathitam mano me;*
*Tadeva me darśaya deva rūpam*
*prasīda deveśa jagannivāsa* — 11. 45

'Overjoyed am I to have seen what I never saw before; yet my mind is distracted in terror. Show me, O *Deva,* only that (familiar) Form of yours. Have mercy, O Lord of *Devas,* O Abode of the universe.'

*Adṛṣṭapūrvam hṛṣito'smi dṛṣṭvā*, 'I am overjoyed to have seen what I have never seen before'; *bhayena ca pravyathitam mano me,* 'yet my mind is distracted with fear'. The whole thing is causing fear. *Tadeva me darśaya deva rūpam,* 'show me that old divine Form alone'; *prasīda deveśa jagannivāsa,* 'O Lord of the Universe, be gracious.' *Deveśa* means 'Lord of all the *devas*.' *Prasīda* means 'have mercy.' What kind of form does Arjuna want to see again?

किरीटिनं गदिनं चक्रहस्तम्
इच्छामि त्वां द्रष्टुं अहं तथैव ।
तेनैव रूपेण चतुर्भुजेन
सहस्रबाहो भव विश्वमूर्ते ॥४६॥

*Kirīṭinam gadinam cakrahastam*
*icchāmi tvām draṣṭum aham tathaiva;*
*Tenaiva rūpeṇa caturbhujena*
*sahasrabāho bhava viśvamūrte — 11. 46*

'Diademed, bearing a mace and a discuss, I desire to see You as before. Assume that same four-armed Form, O You of thousand arms and of universal Form.'

*Viśvamūrte,* 'O You of universal Form'; *sahasrabāho,* 'O one with thousand arms'. Please withdraw this Form and show me the old Form. What is that old Form? *Kirīṭinam gadinam cakrahastam,* the usual picture of Viṣṇu with *kirīṭa, gada* and *cakra,* 'with crown, and with mace and discus in hand'. *Icchāmi tvām draṣṭum aham tathaiva,* 'this is what I like to see'. *Sahasra bāho,* 'O one of thousand hands!' *Tenaiva rūpeṇa caturbhujena,* 'show Yourself to me in that divine Form with four hands'.

श्रीभगवान् उवाच–
*Śrībhagavān uvāca —*

*'The Blessed Lord said:'*

मया प्रसन्नेन तवार्जुनेदं
रूपं परं दर्शितमात्मयोगात् ।
तेजोमयं विश्वं अनन्तं आद्यं
यन्मे त्वदन्येन न दृष्टपूर्वम् ॥४७॥

*Mayā prasannena tavārjunedam*
*rūpam param darśitam ātmayogāt;*
*Tejomayam viśvam anantam ādyam*
*yanme tvadanyena na dṛṣṭapūrvam — 11. 47*

'Graciously have I shown to you, O Arjuna, this Form supreme, by My own *yoga* power, this resplendent, primeval, infinite, universal Form of Mine, which hath not been seen before by anyone else.'

Through My *ātma-yoga*, I have shown you this, My divine Form. I was pleased with you; *mayā prasannena*, 'out of My grace' I have shown this to you. *Tejomayam*, 'full of brilliance'; *viśvam anantam ādyam*, 'the universal, infinite, primordial'. *Yat me tvat anyena na dṛṣṭapūrvam*, 'nobody else other than you has seen this before'.

न वेद यज्ञाध्ययनैः न दानैः
न च क्रियाभिः न तपोभिरुग्रैः ।
एवं रूपः शक्य अहं नृलोके
द्रष्टुं त्वद् अन्येन कुरुप्रवीर ॥४८॥

*Na veda yajñādhyayanaiḥ na dānaiḥ*
*na ca kriyābhiḥ na tapobhirugraiḥ;*
*Evam rūpaḥ śakya aham nṛloke*
*draṣṭum tvad anyena kurupravīra* — 11. 48

'Neither by (the study of) the Vedas and *Yajña*, nor by gifts, nor by rituals, nor by severe austerities, am I, in such Form, seen in the world of human beings, by any other than you, O great hero of the Kurus.'

Nobody has been able to see this before. No kind of sacrifice, ceremony, ritual, can help you to realize Me in this Form. Śrī Kṛṣṇa is telling Arjuna, 'Neither by (the study of) the Vedas, nor by *Yajñas*, nor by gift, nor by ritual, nor even by severe austerities, am I in this Form seen in this world, by anyone other than you, O great hero of the Kurus.' You are a unique person to have seen this Form.

मा ते व्यथा मा च विमूढ भावो
दृष्ट्वा रूपं घोरमीदृङ्ममेदम् ।
व्यपेतभीः प्रीत मनाः पुनस्त्वं
तदेव मे रूपं इदं प्रपश्य ॥४९॥

*Mā te vyathā mā ca vimūḍha bhāvo*
*dṛṣṭvā rūpam ghoramīdṛṅmamedam;*
*Vyapetabhīḥ prīta manāḥ punastvam*
*tadeva me rūpam idam prapaśya* — 11. 49

'Be not afraid nor bewildered, having beheld this Form of Mine, so terrific. With your fears dispelled and with gladdened heart, now see again this former Form of Mine.'

*Mā te vyathā,* 'don't have fear or sorrow.' *Mā ca vimūḍha bhāvo,* 'also don't be deluded'. *Dṛṣṭvā rūpam ghoram īdṛṅ-mamedam,* 'by seeing this type of *ghora rūpa* of Mine', this terrible Form of Mine. Give up all fear and delusion. *Vyapetabhīḥ,* 'free from all *bhaya* or fear'; *vyapeta* means 'without'; *prīta manāḥ,* 'with mind pleased'; *punaḥ,* 'again'; *tadeva me rūpamidam tvam prapaśya,* 'do you see this, that former Form of Mine', which you wanted to see.

**सञ्जय उवाच–**
*Sañjaya uvāca —*

*'Sañjaya said:'*

**इत्यर्जुनं वासुदेवः तथोक्त्वा**
**स्वकं रूपं दर्शयामास भूयः ।**
**आश्वासयामास च भीतं एनं**
**भूत्वा पुनः सौम्यवपुः महात्मा ॥५०॥**

*Ityarjunam vāsudevaḥ tathoktvā*
*svakam rūpam darśayāmāsa bhūyaḥ;*
*Āśvāsayāmāsa ca bhītam enam*
*bhūtvā punaḥ saumyavapuḥ mahātmā — 11.50*

'So, Vāsudeva, i.e. Śrī Kṛṣṇa, having thus spoken to Arjuna, showed again His own Form; and the Great-souled One, assuming His gentle Form, pacified him who was terrified.'

So, Vāsudeva, that is Śrī Kṛṣṇa, having thus spoken to Arjuna, again showed him His own Form. And the Great-souled One, assuming His gentle Form, pacified him who was terrified. He showed him, *saumyavapuḥ,* 'that pacified Form', that gentle Form.

**अर्जुन उवाच–**
*Arjuna uvāca —*

*'Arjuna said:'*

दृष्ट्वेदं मानुषं रूपं तव सौम्यं जनार्दन ।
इदानीं अस्मि संवृत्तः सचेताः प्रकृतिं गतः ॥५१॥

*Dṛṣṭvedam mānuṣam rūpam tava saumyam janārdana;*
*Idānīm asmi samvṛttaḥ sacetāḥ prakṛtim gataḥ* — 11. 51

'Having seen this Your gentle human Form, O Janārdana, my thoughts are now composed, and I am restored to my natural state.'

*Dṛṣṭvedam mānuṣam rūpam tava saumyam*, 'seeing this, Your gentle human Form'. See the beauty! For a human being, if God comes in a human Form, it will be easier to appreciate. A human being will not be able to appreciate at all some divine or terrible Form. That is why God takes, once in a while, a human Form called a Divine incarnation for the satisfaction of devotees. 'O Janārdana, my thoughts are now composed. I am restored to my original state.' That is Arjuna's reply: 'I see a human form now. All fear is gone.'

श्रीभगवान् उवाच–
*Śrībhagavān uvāca* —

*'The Blessed Lord said:'*

सुदुर्दर्शमिदं रूपं दृष्टवानसि यन्मम ।
देवा अप्यस्य रूपस्य नित्यं दर्शन काङ्क्षिणः ॥५२॥

*Sudurdarśamidam rūpam dṛṣṭavānasi yanmama;*
*Devā apyasya rūpasya nityam darśana kāṅkṣiṇaḥ* —11. 52

'Very hard indeed it is to see this Form of Mine which you have seen. Even the *devas* or gods ever long to behold this Form.'

*Sudurdarśam idam rūpam*, 'extremely difficult is it to see this Form' which I showed to you. 'Even gods in heaven are hankering to see that Form', *devā api asya rūpasya nityam darśana kāṅkṣiṇaḥ*.

नाहं वेदैर्न तपसा न दानेन न चेज्यया ।
शक्य एवं विधो द्रष्टुं दृष्टवान् असि मां यथा ॥५३॥

*Nāham vedairna tapasā na dānena na cejyayā;*
*Śakya evam vidho draṣṭum dṛṣṭavān asi mām yathā* — 11. 53

'Neither by the Vedas, nor by austerity, nor by gifts, nor by sacrifice can I be seen as you have seen Me.'

Śrī Krṣṇa is now telling: *Nāham vedaiḥ,* 'Neither by the study of the Vedas'; *na tapasā,* 'nor by austerity'; *na dānena,* 'nor by gifts'; *na ca ijyayā,* 'nor by sacrifice'; *śakya evam vidho draṣṭum,* 'can I be seen like this'; *dṛṣṭavān asi mām yathā,* 'as you have seen Me.' Then by what means can one see You? The next *śloka* makes this clear.

भक्त्या त्वनन्यया शक्य अहं एवंविधोऽर्जुन ।
ज्ञातुं द्रष्टुं च तत्त्वेन प्रवेष्टुं च परन्तप ॥५४॥

*Bhaktyā tvananyayā śakya aham evamvidho'rjuna;*
*Jñātum draṣṭum ca tattvena praveṣṭum ca parantapa* —11. 54

'But by single-minded devotion I may be known in this Form, O Arjuna—and to know, to see, and truly to enter into (Me), O scorcher of foes.'

Only through *Bhakti* can one realize Me in this Form. What kind of *bhakti? Bhaktyā ananyayā,* 'through one-pointed devotion'. *Jñātum draṣṭum ca,* 'to know Me, to see Me'; *tattvena,* 'as I am truly'; *praveṣṭum ca,* 'and to enter into Me', to become one with Me. Only that *bhakti* can help you in this matter. That is why Śrī Krṣṇa has said earlier, *teṣām jñāni nitya-yukta,* 'among them, the *jñāni* is *nitya-yukta,* ever devoted to the Divine'; his or her knowledge is fixed on the Divine. So also, the *bhakta's bhakti,* this kind of *ekānta-bhakti, ananya-bhakti,* is fixed in the Divine. There is no other way.

Now comes the last verse of this chapter. And this verse is introduced by Śaṅkarācārya with a beautiful remark in his commentary:

> *Adhunā sarvasya gītā śāstrasya sārabhūto artho niḥśreyasārtho anuṣṭheyatvena samuccitya ucyate;*

*Ucyate,* 'it is said' by Śrī Kṛṣṇa; *adhunā,* 'now', in this last verse of this chapter; *sarvasya gītā śāstrasya sārabhūto artho,* 'the essential meaning of the whole *Gītā śāstra*'; *niḥśreyasārtho,* 'that is capable of taking us to the highest *mokṣa* or spiritual liberation'; *anuṣṭheyatvena,* 'a thing one has to practise and live by'; *samuccitya,* 'by summing it up'.

It is said that the *Gītā* is the essence of all the Upaniṣads. And this *śloka* is the essential meaning of the *Gītā,* to be practised in day-to-day life. If only we keep to these few practical instructions of this 55th verse, nothing more is needed. And it is so simple. *Bhakti* is always simple. Our misfortune is that many people do not want simple things. The more complicated you make things, the happier they are. Anybody can follow these simple teachings. What are they?

मत्कर्मकृत्मत्परमो मद्भक्तः सङ्गवर्जितः ।
निर्वैरः सर्वभूतेषु यः स मामेति पाण्डव ॥५५॥

*Matkarmakṛtmatparamo madbhaktaḥ saṅgavarjitaḥ;*
*Nirvairaḥ sarvabhūteṣu yaḥ sa māmeti pāṇḍava* —11. 55

'One who does work for Me alone and has Me for his or her goal, is devoted to Me, is free from sensory attachment, and bears no enmity towards any being—he or she attains to Me, O Pāṇḍava.'

A very simple *śloka. Mat karma kṛt,* 'a doer of actions for Me'; whatever actions you do, do it as an offering for Me. You are working in an office, treat that as serving the Lord. Working in the household, you are serving the Lord. It is a fact. If the whole universe is His Form, any work that one does is service to Him. *Mat paramo,* 'keep Me as the supreme Goal'; everything else is secondary, and God is the primary goal. That is why those who keep God as the supreme Goal, don't go to ecstasy when they get a little remark of appreciation, a little title, a little promotion; these are nothing. The greatest thing is this *bhakti. Mad bhaktah,* 'be My devotee'; the only relation between you and Me is pure love. *Saṅga varjitaḥ,* 'free from any sensory attachment'; free the mind from various attachments. Attachments will go, but love will remain. You may be detached from your friend, but you will be loving your friend; detached from the wife, but will love and serve the wife. That distinction we must know. Detachment does not mean becoming apathetic to things around you. That is not the meaning of detachment. 'I don't care. Children are weeping there, I don't care. I have no attachment.' That is not detachment. Love is there, but no attachment is there. My child and another child—both are the same. I am going to look after that child also if necessary. So, it is an expansion, not a contraction. Without any attachment, but with only pure love. *Then comes an important teaching of jñāna and bhakti: Nirvairaḥ sarvabhūteṣu,* 'with no hatred towards any beings'. There is no difficulty about it. Why should I hate? There is the same Self in all beings. A little thinking will give us that conviction. *Yaḥ,* 'he or she who is such'; *saḥ mām eti pāṇḍava,* 'such a person attains to me, O Arjuna'. This is Śrī Kṛṣṇa's promise, and is also the essence of all the teachings in the *Gītā.*

This is what Indians and people all over the world must learn today—a religion which finds expression in high character. No hatred towards anybody; only love for all; with a detached mind. What a beautiful idea! Good work we do, but offer it to the Divine. I don't claim anything for myself. So, in this way, these are all practicable things and I wish more and more people will understand and practise religion as given in this *śloka.* This is the greatest *śloka* of a great chapter. *Bhagavān* Himself expresses it. So, the whole chapter ends with this note of *bhakti* in this last *śloka.* And the next chapter is all on *bhakti.* It is the *Bhakti-yoga* chapter. A little bit of *bhakti* you get in the 15th chapter also. Finally, you get *bhakti* again, in the 18th chapter.

**इति विश्वरूपदर्शन-योगो नाम एकादशोऽध्यायः ।**

*Iti viśvarūpadarśana-yogo nāma ekādaśo'dhyāyaḥ —*

'So, this is the eleventh chapter named, *The Vision of the Universal Form* of *Bhagavān* Śrī Kṛṣṇa.'

# Index


*A Midsummer Night's Dream*, 228.
*A Pilgrim Looks at the World*, 50.
*Abhayam*, 498. *See also* Fearlessness.
*Abhyāsa & vairāgya*, 159–164.
*Abhyāsa yoga*, 289.
Action. *See* Work.
*Adhibhūta*, 273, 275, 278, 279; what is, 277.
*Adhidaiva*, 273, 275, 278; what is, 277.
*Adhiyajña*, 273, 275, 278; what is, 277, 279.
*Adhyātma*, 268, 275, 464, 465; what is, 276, 278–279.
*Adhyātma vidyā*: among *vidyās* God is, 439; what is, 439–442.
*Adhyātma vikāsa*, 33. *See also Ātma-vikāsa.*
Ādi Śaṅkarācārya. *See* Śaṅkarācārya.
*Āditya(s)*, 467, 486; God is Viṣṇu among the, 431.
*Adonais*, 321, 454.
Advaita: comprehensive philosophy of human unity & service, 14; true, 13.
Advaitic: importance of, vision, 459–460; vision, 367–368, 404.
*Agni*, 502.
*Agnihotra*, 434.
Agnosticism, 199.
*Agrahāyaṇa*, 447.
Airāvata, 436.
Ajanābha (Bhārata varṣa), 484.
*Ajñā cakra*, 301.
*Ajñāna*: according to Sri Ramakrishna, 334, 344, 376; *jñāna* hidden by, 54.
*Akāmaḥ*, 110.
*A-kāra*: among the alphabets God is, 443.
*Ākāśa*, 28, 229; God compared to, 350.
Akrūra, 465.
Ali, Mohammed, 56.
Allah, 252.
Aloneness: importance of, 129–130.
American: joint manoeuvre of, & British navy—an incident, 184.
American Hoover Committee Report, 304, 378.
American youth movement, 49.
*An al Haq*, 473.
*Anāhata cakra*, 301.
*Ānanda. See also* Joy; God is of the nature of, 342; source of, 150; three levels of, 83–86.
Ananta: among the snakes God is, 437.
*Anāsakti*, 108. *See also* Detachment.
Anger: control of, 140.
Animals: do not have the capacity to seek knowledge, 56; have no sense of ethical responsibility, 59; live only at sensory level, 57.
*Aniruddha*, 405.
*Antaryāmī*, 271.
*Anubhava*, 178, 293, 295. *See also* Experience; beginning of, in evolution, 212–213.
*Aparā prakṛti*, 195–196, 271. *See also Prakṛti*; is *jaḍa*, 203.
*Aparā Vidyā*, 195, 196, 219.
*Aparigrahaḥ*, 130.
*Āraṇyakās*, 198.
*Arctic Home of the Vedas*, 328.

Arjuna. *See also* Dhanañjaya; could see the Universal form of God due to God's grace, 509; delusion of, destroyed, 464; describes what he saw in the Universal form of God, 474–476, 484–491; dilemma of, regarding *karma sannyāsa* & *karmayoga*, 7; finds *dhyānayoga* very difficult, 157–158; frightened by the vision of God's universal form, 486–487; intimate friendship of, with Śrī Kṛṣṇa, 505; Kṛṣṇa agrees to reveal His Universal form to, 467–468; Kṛṣṇa bestows, with the Divine eye, 468; Kṛṣṇa exhorts, to become His instrument, 492–498; Kṛṣṇa reveals His Universal dimension to, 469–471; prays to Śrī Kṛṣṇa to show His familiar form, 507; repents for having treated Śrī Kṛṣṇa merely as his friend, 503–504, 507; request of, to Śrī Kṛṣṇa to reveal his divine Universal form, 465–466; request of, to Śrī Kṛṣṇa to tell about his divine manifestations, 421–423; sings the glory of Śrī Kṛṣṇa—the God, 500–502, 505.

*Ārtaḥ*, 241, 244, 247.

*Arthārthī*, 241, 247.

*Ārurukṣoḥ*, 114.

Aryaman: among the *pitṛs* God is the, 437.

*Āsana*, 131.

Asceticism, 27, 135; utility of, 183.

Asita, 420.

Astronomy, 351. *See also* Creation; concept of singularity in western, 60; modern, 406–407; western, moving towards Vedantic conclusions, 60.

Astrophysics. *See also* Astronomy; background material of the universe, 429, 454.; sun will swallow the planets in due course, 487.

*Asuras*, 438, 486.

*Āsurī sampat*, 240, 363; effect of, 361–362.

*Aśvamedha*, 434.

Aśvattha: among the trees God is, 435.

*Aśvin*, 467, 486.

*Atharva Veda*, 369.

Atheism, 199.

*Ātmabalam*, 123; importance of, 296–298.

Atman, 33, 37, 53, 76, 98, 109, 133, 147, 167, 220, 247, 252, 272, 279, 431, 441, 446. *See also* Brahman; capacity of *buddhi* to perceive, 142–143; description of, 269, 270; different meanings of, 124; has left footprints on human experience, 349; indestructibility of, 270; is Brahman, 72–73; is realised when body consciousness is dissolved, 461; is silence, 451–452; knowledge of, found only in Upaniṣads, 340–341; nature of, 38; our true nature, 56; pure *buddhi* & pure *manas* are same as, 148; result of realising, 67–70, 141–144; simple to realise, 340; source of infinite bliss, 81–87, 88; state of being established in, 141–144; undivided, appears to be divided, 28; value of the world without, 295, 453; vision of a *yogi* established in, 152; who realises, 123–125.

*Ātma śraddhā*, 21, 163, 251. *See also* Faith.

*Ātmavikāsa*, 32. *See also Adhyātma vikāsa.*

Aurelius, Marcus, 409.
Austerity, 230; right type of, 134–135.
*Avaśaḥ* (helpless), 316, 317, 322; human beings are, 352–353.
*Avatāra*, 257, 356, 358. *See also* Incarnations.
*Avidvān*, 11.
*Avidyā Māyā*, 59, 241, 362. See also *Māyā*.
*Avikampa yoga*, 407–408.
*Avimāra*, 30.
*Avyakta*, 316, 317, 347, 348, 351. See also *Prakṛti*; state of, 314; supreme & imperishable, 318–320, 321–322; universe comes from the, and dissolves back in to it, 311–315.

Bahavullah, 425.
*Bāhubalam*, 122, 296. *See also* Strength.
*Bahuvrīhi samāsa*, 443.
Belief: place of, in spiritual life, 177–178.
*Bhāgavatam*, 15, 239, 272, 323, 375, 435, 468; creation, 325–326; God is protecting India's spirituality, 482–483; on how God attracts the hearts of great devotees, 324–325; on how men become God's devotees, 242–243; on nature of desire, 112; on the source of the universe, 455; on uniqueness of man, 248; story of Nāradā's spiritual attainment, 181; story of Prahlāda's love for God, 244; two types of people who are happy according to, 52; who overcomes death, 445.
*Bhajan*, 84, 85.
*Bhakta(s)*, 127. *See also* Devotees; attitude of a, 366; God takes care of the highest type of, 380–383; God's, will never perish, 390–392; likes to enjoy God, 422; on how men become God's, 242–243; who is the supreme, 244.
*Bhakti*, 104, 185, 186, 188, 244, 313, 331, 332, 418, 432; *ahaituki*, 324–325; *ananyā*, is the means to realise God, 322–324, 512–514; can make all—even the most wicked & sinners—attain God, 392–394; easiest path for Self realisation is, 156; future of, in coming centuries, 396; highest, & highest *jñāna* are same, 242, 246; highest, expresses itself in the form of simple worship, 385–386; highest type of, 380–383; makes no distinction between men, 394; richer than austere *jñāna*, 408–411; supreme, 395; the way to ecstatic life, 341–342.
*Bhakti yoga*, 162; how does a man become a candidate to the path of, 242–243.
Bhāsa: makes a comparison between the wise & the foolish, 30.
Bhīṣma, 331, 381, 488, 489, 498.
Bhṛgu: among the *ṛṣis* God is, 434.
*Bhūta vidyā*, 439.
*Bible*, 154, 174, 414, 472, 480.
*Bījam* (seed): God is the, of everything, 453.
Biology, 77, 348; goal of evolution in modern, 114–115; human beings according to modern, 75; modern, moving towards Vedanta, 200, 202; on unity, 458.
Bliss, 104, 150. *See also* Happiness; source of highest, 81–87.
Bondage: how to be free from, 18.

Books: *A Midsummer Night's Dream*, 228; *A Pilgrim Looks at the World*, 50; *Arctic Home of the Vedas*, 328; *Avimāra*, 30; *Bhāgavatam*, 15, 52, 112, 181, 323, 324, 325, 375, 435, 445, 455, 482; *Bible*, 154, 174, 414, 472, 480; *Brahma Sūtras*, 38, 218, 270, 330; *Bṛhadāraṇyaka Upaniṣad*, 38, 150, 215, 226, 278, 331, 341, 402, 418; *Chāndogya Upaniṣad*, 75, 213, 328, 329, 330, 441; *Complete Works of Swami Vivekananda*, 8, 11, 32, 44, 103, 197, 252, 306, 387, 440; *Devī Māhātmyam*, 56, 57, 58, 59, 61; *Dialogues of Plato*, 282; *Eastern Religions and Western Thought*, 190; *Evolution: A New Synthesis*, 200; *Faust*, 61, 94, 111; *Gītā Rahasya*, 303, 328, 432; *Gospel of Sri Ramakrishna*, 68, 137, 191, 248, 396, 413; *Greek View of Life*, 270, 282; *Guru Granth Sāhib*, 299; *Hitopadeśa*, 25, 345; *Īśā Upaniṣad*, 243, 284, 290, 454; *Impact of Science on Society*, 200, 336, 398; *Integrative Action of the Nervous System*, 210; *Intelligent Universe*, 60, 202, 274; *Karmayoga*, 24, 306; *Kaṭha Upaniṣad*, 27, 43, 86, 98, 142, 146, 170, 216, 291, 299, 323, 435, 457, 458, 461; *Kena Upaniṣad*, 8; *Koran*, 106, 174, 480; *Kumārasambhava*, 434; *Lectures from Colombo to Almora*, 8; *Les miserables*, 390; *Life of Ramakrishna*, 257; *Life of Swami Vivekananda by His Eastern & Western Disciples*, 400; *Living Brain*, 35; *Māṇḍūkya Kārikā*, 160, 365; *Māṇḍūkya Upaniṣad*, 272; *Mahā Nārāyaṇa Upaniṣad*, 12; *Mahābhārata*, 15, 110–111, 296, 304, 309, 312, 331, 381, 393, 405, 417, 432, 438, 448, 449, 450, 466, 489, 494, 496, 504, 505; *Manu Smṛti*, 21, 97, 109, 432; *Masnavi*, 202; *Meghadūta*, 87; *Message of the Upaniṣads*, 320, 461; *Modern Man in Search of A Soul*, 47; *Muṇḍaka Upaniṣad*, 13, 74, 98, 195, 204, 212, 217, 227, 266, 376, 431, 503; *Mysterious Universe*, 469; *Mystery of Mind*, 211; *Myths and Symbols of the Hindu Religion*, 325; *Nārada Bhakti Sūtras*, 244, 323, 394; *New Testament*, 78, 194, 201, 380, 390; *Old Testament*, 472; *Pāṇḍava-gītā*, 413; *Parabola*, 326; *Positive Sciences of the Ancient Hindus*, 292; *Rāmāyaṇa*, 15; *Reincarnation: An East-West Anthology*, 169; *Republic of Plato*, 148; *Ṛg Veda*, 189, 198, 269, 327, 328, 369, 372, 375, 384, 402, 410, 417, 432, 459; *Ṛg Veda samhita*, 281; *Saint John's Gospel*, 300; *Secret Life of Plants*, 274; *Śakuntala*, 61; *Śivānandalahari*, 162; *Śvetāśvatara Upaniṣad*, 89, 201, 214; *Sutta Nipāta*, 359; *Taittirīya Samhitā*, 279; *Taittirīya Upaniṣad*, 73, 81, 205, 221, 293, 342, 428, 451; *Tao of Physics*, 326, 429; *Uniqueness of Man*, 248; *Utilitarianism*, 304; *Viṣṇu Purāṇa*, 375; *Viṣṇu Sahasranāma*, 273; *Vivekacūḍāmaṇi*, 83, 269; *Yoga Sūtras*, 130, 156, 159.

Bose, J. C: studies of, on plants & metals, 457–458.

*Brāhmaṇa*, 395.

*Brahma Sūtras*, 38, 218, 263, 330; on nature of Atman, 270.

*Brahma vidyā*, 204, 217; easy & simple, 340; is *dharmyam & amṛtam*, 338–339; nature of, 337–341.

Brahmā, 252, 306, 311, 315, 316, 317,

351, 405, 406, 474, 483, 500, 502; age of present, 310; day & night of, 308–310; is also subject to rebirth, 306–307; life span of, 313; only one temple of, in India, 319; the first born, 313; why, is called *Vedamūrti*, 325–326.

Brahmananda, Swami, 86.

*Brahmacarya*, 299.

Brahman, 28, 36, 68, 167, 193, 215, 275, 429; all this is, 13, 367–368; alone is, 224–227, 247–248; definition of, 73, 221; described, 205; is Atman, 72–73; is *sama* (equal), 72, 76, 105; is the Light of all lights, 291; *jñāni*'s realisation of, 191; knower of, becomes Brahman, 98; meaning of, 293; *śakti* or *māyā* and, are one, 59, 61; source of infinite joy, 150–151; traits of a person established in, 77, 128; *vijñāni*'s realisation of, 191; what is, 205, 276, 278; where to seek, 428; who realizes, 97–98, 100, 268–272; why, is called omniscient, 290.

*Brahmarṣi*, 435.

Brahmo Samaj Movement, 243.

Brain, 215; mind and, 208–212; should be developed along with the heart, 412.

*Bṛhadāraṇyaka Upaniṣad*, 38, 215, 278, 331, 402, 418; *antaryāmi brāhmaṇa*, 226; *aupaniṣadam puruṣa*, 341; criticizes the worship of gods, 250–251; on the source of joy, 150.

Bṛhaspati, 433.

*Bṛhat Sāma*, 447.

British: joint manoeuvre of, & American navy—an incident, 184.

Browning, Robert, 56, 94, 321.

Buddha, 33, 56, 78, 81, 101, 115, 134, 136, 137, 138, 196, 204, 257, 260, 357, 377, 416, 424, 427, 435; combine Śaṅkara's intellect with the heart of, 18; conclusion of, regarding asceticism, 183; dialogue of, with Dhaniya, 359–360; on middle path, 135; parable of a man struck by an arrow, 23; view of, on service & meditation—an incident, 10; why Indians do not kill a, 424–425.

*Buddhi*, 146, 173, 230, 288, 298, 412; capacity of, to perceive the highest truth, 141–143; nearest to Brahman, 297–298; pure, mind & Atman are one, 148; what is, 143.

*Buddhibalam*, 122, 296, 297.

*Buddhiyoga*: greatest blessing that one can receive from God is the blessing of, 415–417.

*Cakras*, 301.

*Candālas*: two types of, 70.

Capra, Fritjof, 326; on the background material of the universe, 429.

Cause, 205; definition of, 221.

Cell, 226; *anubhava* begins with the living, 212–213; what is a living, 207.

Cerebral system: role of, in human life, 126.

*Cetanā* (intelligence): in all beings God is, 433.

*Chandas* (metre): what is, 447.

*Chāndogya Upaniṣad*, 75, 328, 329, 330, 441; *tat tvam asi*, 213.

Chandrasekhar, Dr. 223.

Character, 185; building, of child-

ren, 120–123; how to build, 118–123.
Christian, 481.
Christianity, 369; concept of *Omkāra* entering Indian, 300; orthodoxy in, 177, 178, 179.
*Cit*, 203, 204.
*Cit & acit*: universe is comprised of, 205–208.
*Cit & jaḍa*, 210; mixed up, 220.
*Cit-jaḍa-granthī*, 210, 213.
Citraratha: God is, among the *gandharvas*, 435.
Civilization, 48; consumerist, 82; healthy, 97; problem of modern, & its solution, 90; value of purity getting eroded from modern, 369.
Clarke, James Freeman, 169.
*Complete Works of Swami Vivekananda*, 8, 11, 32, 44, 103, 197, 252, 306, 387, 440.
Consciousness: being accepted by modern science, 207–212; different levels through which, functions, 416; is non-dual, 272; is the background material of the universe, 429; mixed up with matter, 220; no plurality in, 73; pervades everything, 347; place of, in modern physical science, 197, 202, 347–348; role of, in evolution, 203, 206–207, 212–213; role of, in the universe, 206; universe sustained by, 196–197, 203, 205-208; western scientists are slowly accepting, 73, 319.
Consumerism, 82, 214, 346.
Cosmology, 368. *See also* Astrophysics; background material of the universe according to Indian, 429, 454; cosmos exists in two states, 309; creation in Indian mythology, 325–326; creation in modern, 406–407; *eko'ham bahusyām*, 313; evolution of the universe, 309; how the universe comes into being, 60; imploding of the solar system, 312; Indian, 233; relevance of, to human life, 312–313; same universe helplessly gets manifested & dissolved, 315–318; scale of time in Indian, 308–310; universe comes from the *avyakta* and dissolves back in to it, 311–318; universe comes from the *prakṛti* and dissolves back in to it, 350–352; universe pervaded by the background material, 347; western, 217; western versus Indian, 217.
Cranston, S. L, 169.
Creation, 60, 277, 405–407, 439. *See also* Cosmology; in Indian mythology, 325–326; is the, original?, 317; like a spider projecting its web, 351; meaning of, 206; same beings are manifested in every, 316–318; two aspects of, 312; what is, 217.
Creativity, 316–318; depends on *tapas*, 326.
Culture: Indian, needs to be combined with Greek culture, 285.

*Daivī sampat*, 240, 362, 363, 498.
*Dakṣiṇāyanam*, 329, 330, 331, 332.
*Daṇḍa* (sceptre), 449.
*Daniya Sutta* (of *Sutta Nipāta*), 359.
Danvantari (science of medicine), 436.
Darwin Centenary (1959), 222.
Das, Tulsi, 302.
Death, 168–169, 173, 198, 276, 278,

279, 292, 438, 485, 489; a patient dying with God's vision—an incident, 283; everything is subject to, 445–446; God is the all consuming, 445, 492; how God is realised at the time of, 279–286, 286–289, 292–298; how to face, 270, 493; how to fix the mind on God at the time of, 280; how to overcome, 268–272; illustration of how everything enters the mouth of, 489–490; journey of the soul after, 327–333; meaning of, 280–285; never understood by the Greeks, 282–283; who escapes, 445–446; who succeeds in giving up the body with the knowledge of God, 273.

Debendranath, Tagore: how his life changed, 242–243.

Definition: of Brahman, 73, 221; of cause, 221; of *kavi*, 227; of *Māyā*, 234; of *paṇḍita*, 69; of philosophy, 192, 199; of *purāṇaḥ*, 292; of religion, 39, 64; of theology, 199; of *yoga*, 332.

Delusion: Arjuna's, destroyed, 464; experiential knowledge alone dispels, 63; twofold, 261–264.

Democracy, 15, 17, 497; how, functions in India today & its future, 70; how to create a healthy, 496–498; in Scandinavian nations most developed, 71; means to achieve true, 152; *samadarśitva* is the very soul of, 70.

Desire, 375, 378; *dhārmik*, not condemned, 231; makes us lose our discriminative faculty, 249–252; nature of, 112; ratio of enjoyment of happiness &, for happiness, 304; role of, in human life, 112; root of work is, 108–109; *saṅkalpa* is the root of, 110–111.

Desire & aversion: result of overcoming, 264–266; the twofold delusion of, 261–264.

Desirelessness: true, 109–110; two types of, 109–110.

Detachment, 35–36, 40, 44, 354, 514. *See also Anāsakti*.

Determination, 160.

*Deva*, 384, 402, 420, 438, 470, 472, 474, 485, 500, 501, 511; concept of, taken up by western thinkers, 274; God is Vāsava among the *devās*, 432.

*Devadeva*, 472.

Devahūti, 435.

Devakī, 445.

Devala, 420.

*Devarṣi*, 435.

*Devayāna*, 328, 332.

*Devī Māhātmyam*, 57, 58, 59, 61; animals live only at sensory level according to, 56–57.

Devil: no concept of, in Indian philosophy, 12.

Devotees. *See also Bhakta(s)*; God destroys the darkness from the hearts of, 418–419; how do, remain absorbed in God, 413–415.

*Dhammakāya*, 429.

Dhanañjaya: among the *pāṇḍavas* God is, 449.

Dhaniya, 359.

*Dharma*, 374, 424, 450; distinguishes human beings from animals, 345–346; importance of distinguishing *sanātana*, from *yuga-dharma*, 476–482.

*Dharmyam & amṛtam*, 338–339.

Dhṛtarāṣṭra, 465, 469, 488, 489, 498, 505.

*Dhṛti*, 447.

Dhruva: story of, 323–324.

*Dhyāna*, 156.
*Dhyāna yoga*: is very difficult, 157–158; way to success in, 159–164.
*Dialogues of Plato*, 282.
Dickinson, Lowes, 270, 282.
Dignity, 24.
Discipline. *See also* Self-discipline; importance of, 50; of animal energy in man, 95; of raw human energy, 92–97; of sensory system—its results, 118–123; of the self, 124.
Discrimination, 220; is lost due to desire, 249–252.
Divine: why the, manifests differently in different men, 456–458.
Divine eye, 468, 470.
Divine Mother, 130, 137; concept of, 57–61.
Dogma, 267; what is, 221.
*Dṛk & dṛśyam*, 440. *See also* Subject & object.
*Dṛk dṛśya viveka*, 460.
Droṇa, 488, 498; how, was insulted by Drupada, 361.
Drupada, 361.
Duryodhana, 489, 494.
*Dvandva*, 305; among the compounds God is, 443.
*Dvandva samāsa*, 443–444.
*Dyūtam* (gambling), 448.

*Eastern Religions and Western Thought*, 190.
Eckhart, Meister, 473.
Ecstasy: in daily life, 341–342.
Eddington, Sir Arthur Stanley: on the true spirit of science & religion, 176.
Education, 9, 43, 90, 497; total, 297; training the mind is, 266–267; true, 31, 99.
Efficiency: two dimensions of, according to *Gītā*, 149.
Ego, 192; best means to shed our, 414; true dimension of, 53.
Einstein, Albert, 56; theory of relativity, 444.
*Electromedica* (journal), 440.
Emotion (s): control of anger, 140; *icchā, bhaya & krodha*, 102; *kāma & krodha*, 91–97, 100; place of, in human life, 411–412.
Energy: all energies are the manifestation of the Primordial, 57; channelization of human, 92–97; psychic, 143; two directions of human, 100.
Eros, 437.
Eschatology, 327–333; validity of eschatological statements, 330–333; verdict of the *Gītā* on, 332–333.
Evolution, 277, 309, 355–356; according to Vedanta, 203–204; beginning of *anubhava* in, 212; criteria of quantity & quality in, 222; direction of Human, 33; Events and Issues in Evolution-100 Years of Evolution, 222.; goal of human, 65, 90, 114-115; of religious ideas, 327; of universe, 309; psychosocial, 200; role of consciousness in, 203, 206–207, 212–213; role of pain & pleasure in spiritual, 305–306; three levels of, 213; what is, 213, 217.
*Evolution: A New Synthesis*, 200.
Experience, 474; beginning of, in evolution, 212–213; gives knowledge, 306; psychophysical fitness required to sustain spiritual, 506.

Faith, 160, 163, 251, 253, 254; in oneself, 21, 117.
Fanaticism: cause of, 189–190.
*Faust*, 61, 94, 111.
Fearlessness, 133, 498.
Fenwick, Mr. 50, 51.
Force, Canon Wilber, 72.
Freedom, 125, 496. *See also Nirvāṇa*; here itself, 67; how to attain, 65–66; human beings alone can seek, 352–353; importance of, 65; man bestowed with the, to choose between *parā* & *aparā prakṛti*, 58–59; men have limited, in this world, 316, 352–353; spiritual, 308; what is, 35, 81, 97, 213; while alive, 334; who attains, 97–98, 100, 101–102.
*Freedom* (drama), 148.
Freud, Sigmund, 119.
Fulfilment, 77, 90; goal of human life is, 114–115.

*Gajendramokṣa*, 327, 454.
*Gandharva*, 486.
Gandhi, Mahatma, 72, 99, 118, 256, 411; his method of deciding the propriety of an action, 17.
Ganga, 438.
Gārgī, 278, 402.
Garuḍa, 438.
Gāyatrī, 178, 417; among the *chandas* God is, 447.
Gauḍapāda, 160.
Ghosh, Girish Chandra, 392.
Gibbon, Edward, 96.
*Gitā*: all-comprehensive nature of the *yoga* of the, 157, 182; all states of *guṇas* proceed from God yet God remains unaffected, 231–232; *aparā prakṛti*, 195–196; Arjuna describes what he saw in the Universal form of God, 474–476, 484–491; Arjuna prays to Śrī Kṛṣṇa to show His familiar form, 507; Arjuna repents for having treated Śrī Kṛṣṇa merely as a friend, 503–504, 507; Arjuna sings the glory of Śrī Kṛṣṇa—the God, 500–502, 505; Arjuna's delusion dispelled, 464; Arjuna's prayer to Śrī Kṛṣṇa to reveal His divine Universal form, 465–466; Arjuna's request to Śrī Kṛṣṇa to tell him about His divine manifestations, 421–423; Arjuna frightened by the vision of God's universal form, 486–487; attainment of spiritual goal preceded by several births of spiritual struggle, 246–248; attitude of the, towards the wicked persons, 389–392; *avyakta* which is supreme & imperishable, 318–321, 321–322; best book on practical Vedanta, 17; beings in all *lokas* are subject to rebirth, 306–307; cause of delusion, 54; central theme of the, 333; *carama śloka* of the, 381; comprehensive spirituality of, 188; concept of time in the, 308–310; creation, 405–407; deals with scientific classification of religion, 145; demoniac men deluded by *māyā* do not worship God, 240; description of God, 290–292, 419–421; different aspects of God, 368–373; dilemma of Arjuna regarding *karma sannyāsa* & *karma yoga*, 7; doer of good deeds never comes to grief, 166; eschatology in the, 327–333; essence of the, 343; essence of, according to Śa-

*Gītā (contd.)*
ṅkara, 512; evaluation of heaven-going concept in the, 374–380; fate of a *yogabhraṣṭa*, 165–175, 180–181; fate of men seeking heavenly enjoyment, 374–380; fate of those who don't have *śraddhā* in *brahmavidyā*, 345–346; four types of men worship God, 241–245; God alone is, 224–227, 367–373; God as the Self is the beginning, middle & end of all beings, 427–429; God destroys the darkness of our heart, 418–419; God exhorts Arjuna to become His instrument, 492–498; God is impartial, 388; God is the all consuming death, 492; God is the source of good as well as bad, 403–404; God never bound by his actions, 353–354; God pervades the universe & yet remains detached & free, 347–350; God projects the universe by animating His *prakṛti*, 352, 355; God realisation is for all—even the most wicked & sinful, 392–394; God sustains the universe, 459; God takes care of the highest type of *bhaktas*, 380–383; God's brilliance compared to thousand suns, 471; God's devotees will never perish, 390–392; God's divine manifestations, 426–427, 431–449; gods do not know the origin of the God, 402; greatest blessing that one can receive from God, 415–417; greatness manifest in the world is all caused by the manifestation of an infinitesimal power of God in them, 456–458; highest *bhakti* expresses itself in the form of simple worship, 385–386; how & where does the *yogi* (*vaśī*) dwell, 44; how & why do *yogis* work, 37, 39–40; how do devotees remain absorbed in God, 413–415; how do *nityayuktas* worship God, 364–367; how does a wise man worship God, 408–411; how God is realised at the time of death, 279–286, 292–298; how one is freed from all sins, 402; how should a *yogi* meditate, 129–130; how the *yogi* of the, attains God, 333; how to fix the mind on God, 288; how to get over Lord's *Māyā*, 233–239; how to go beyond the wheel of birth & death, 64–66; how to meditate, 132–135; how to realise God, 287–289, 322–324, 387–388, 395, 512–514; how to remain inactive in midst of all action, 44–46; how to work without being tainted, 32–36; *jñāna* & *vijñāna*, 191–192; *jñāna* along with *vijñāna* frees us from all evil, 335–336; *jñāni* is the best among the worshippers of God, 243–244; *kāma* according to, 231; *krama mukti*, 329; Kṛṣṇa agrees to reveal His Universal form to Arjuna, 467–468; Kṛṣṇa re-assumes His ordinary form, 510; Kṛṣṇa reveals His Universal dimension to Arjuna, 469–471; means of success in *yoga* of meditation, 159–164; mentality of foolish people, 359; mentality of great souls endowed with *daivī sampat*, 363–365; middle path prescribed by the, 135–138; nature of *brahma vidyā*, 337–341; nature of sense enjoyment, 87; nature of spiritual life & success

*Gītā (contd.)*
in it, 193–194; no rebirth for one who realises God, 303, 307–308, 321–322; obstacles to God realisation, 261–264; *Om*—the supreme state to be attained, 299–300; on self dependence—raise yourself by yourself, 116–118; *parā prakṛti*, 196–197; people deluded by the *guṇas* remain ignorant of God, 232–233; posture of the body in meditation, 132; preliminary steps to meditation, 101–102; respective results of worshipping gods & The God, 255, 383–384; result of being established in *yoga*, 141–144; result of meditation, 134, 147–154; result of *samadarśitva*, 71–72; *samadarśitva* —the result of self realisation, 67–70; same universe helplessly gets manifested & dissolved, 315–318; *sannyāsa* difficult to attain without *karmayoga*, 29; secret of an integrated life, 149; secret of true happiness, 79, 91; seeing God in all & in oneself, 153; *śraddhā*, 253–254; solution of the, to the dilemma of *karma sannyāsa* & *karmayoga*, 10, 20, 23; source of the universe, 205–208, 214–224; spiritual practitioner goes beyond the dos & don'ts of the religion, 174–180; spirituality of, is *dharmyam* & *amṛtam*, 338–339; spiritualizing everyday life, 386; status of work according to, 184; technique of meditation, 145–147; totality of knowledge, 189–192; traits of a person established in Brahman, 77, 128; two dimensions of efficiency according to, 149; uniqueness of the *yogi* of the, 332–334; universe comes from the *avyakta* and dissolves back into it, 311–318; universe comes from the *prakṛti* and dissolves back into it, 350–352; verdict of the, on the eschatological phenomenon, 332–333; vision of a *yogi* established in Self, 151–152; ways in which God is manifested in the universe, 229–231; what is Brahman, *adhyātman*, *adhibhūta*, *adhidaiva*, *karma* & *adhiyajña*, 275–279; what is the state of *yoga*, 141–144; what is true *sannyāsa*, 110; when is a *yogi* said to be abiding in God, 153; when is a *yogi* said to be established in *yoga*, 125–127, 138; when is God realized, 55; who attains freedom, 97–98, 100; who attains peace, 103; who gets established in *yoga*, 407–408; who is a *sannyāsi*, 18–19, 107–108; who is a *yogārūḍha*, 116; who is a *yogi*, 91, 107–108; who is eligible for action & who for inaction, 114–115; who is our friend & who is our enemy, 116–117, 118–123; who is the agent of all actions in the universe, 47; who is the greatest *yogi*, 154; who is the supreme *yogi* according to, 186; who realises God easily, 302; who realises the supreme Self, 123–125, 264–266, 268–272; who succeeds in giving up the body with the knowledge of God, 273; why divine incarnations are not recognized, 256–260, 356–358; why do men worship mythical gods, 249–252; *yoga* of *dhyāna* is only a part of the wider *yoga* of,

*Gītā (contd.)*
140, 156; *yoga* of meditation is very difficult, 157–158; *yogi's* subdued mind compared to a steady flame of a lamp, 139; *yogi* of the, superior to *jñānis, tapasvis* & *karmis*, 181–184; *yuktas* and *ayuktas*—their respective fates, 40.

*Gītā Rahasya*, 328, 432.

God, 109, 182, 278; alone is, 224–227, 367–373; amongst the methods of disputation, is *Vāda*, 442; among the alphabets, is *A-kāra*, 443; among the birds, is Garuḍa, 438; among those who are brilliant, is *Tejas* (brilliance), 448; among the cause of offspring, is Kandarpa, 437; among the *chandas*, is Gāyatri, 447; among the compounds, is *Dvandva*, 443; among the controllers, is the Yama, 437; among the cows, is Kāmadhuk, 437; among the *daityas*, is Prahlāda, 438; among the elephants, is Airāvata, 436; among the fishes, is Makara, 439; among the flowing waters, is Jāhnavi (Ganges), 438; among the fraudulent, is *Dyūtam*, 448; among the horses, is Uccaiḥśravas, 436; among the measurers, is the *Kāla*, 438; among the months, is *Mārgaśīrṣa*, 447; among the *munis*, is Vyāsa, 449; among the *nara*, is Narādhipa, 436; among the *pāṇḍavas*, is Dhanañjaya, 449; among the persevering, is *Vyavasāya*, 448; among the *pitṛs*, is the Aryaman, 437; among the poets, is Uśana, 449; among the purifiers, is *Pavana*, 438; among the *sāma* songs, is *Bṛhat Sāma*, 447; among the seasons, is *Kusumākara*, 447; among the sense organs, is the mind, 432; among the serpents, is Vāsuki, 437; among the snakes, is the Ananta, 437; among the syllables, is *Om*, 434; among the warriors, is Rāma, 438; among the water beings, is Varuṇa, 437; among the weapons, is the Vajra, 437; among the *yādavas*, is Vāsudeva, 449; among the *yajñās*, is *japa-yajñā*, 434; among *vidyās*, is *Adhyātma vidyā*, 439; an illustration how of, takes care of his devotees, 382; Arjuna could see the Universal Form of, out of God's grace, 509; Arjuna describes what he saw in the Universal form of, 474–476; Arjuna frightened by the vision of God's universal form, 486–487; Arjuna sings the glory of Śrī Kṛṣṇa—the God, 500–502, 505; as *sākṣi*, 370; as the Self is the beginning, middle & end of all beings, 427–429; brilliance of, compared to thousand suns, 471; compared to *ākāśa*, 350; demoniac men deluded by *māyā* do not worship, 240; described as a *kavi* (poet), 227–228; description of, 290–292, 380, 419–421; destroys the darkness of our heart, 418–419; devotees of, will never perish, 390–392; different aspects of, 367–373; divine manifestations of, 426–427, 431–449; exhorts Arjuna to become His instrument, 492–498; fate of men worshipping, desiring heaven, 374–380; fatherhood of, 369; four

*God (contd.)*
types of men worship, 241–245; friend of all, 103–106, 185; gods do not know the origin of the, 402; greatest blessing that one can receive from, 415–417; greatness manifest in the world is all caused by the manifestation of an infinitesimal power of God in them, 456–458, 463; highest form of worship of, is the simplest, 385–386; how, attracts the hearts of great devotees, 324–325; how do devotees remain absorbed in, 413–415; how do *nityayuktas* worship, 364–367; how does a wise man worship, 408–411; how, is realised at the time of death, 279–286, 292–298; how the *yogi* of the *Gītā* attains, 333; how to fix the mind on, 288; how to fix the mind on, at the time of death, 280, 286–289; how to realise, 287–289, 322–324, 387–388, 395, 512–514; importance of knowing, in totality, 189–192; in the form of the manifested world, 399–401; Indian & western concept of, 319–320; inside as well as outside, 12; is *ānanda svarupa*, 342; is Bhṛgu among the *ṛṣis*, 434; is Bṛhaspati among the priests, 433; is Citraratha among the *gandharvas*, 435; is directly realisable & verifiable, 337, 343–344; is impartial, 388; is Kapila among the *munis*, 435; is Kubera among the *yakṣas*, 433; is Meru among the mountains, 433; is Nārada among the *devarṣis*, 435; is our only friend, 371; is our own Self, 104–106; is, partial that he manifests differently among different men?, 456–458; is Pāvaka among the *vasus*, 433; is *Sāma Veda* among the Vedas, 432; is Śaṅkara among the *rudras*, 433; is Śaśi among the asterisms, 432; is Skanda among the generals, 434; is the all consuming death, 445, 492; is the Aśvattha among the trees, 435; is the *bījam* (seed) of all, 453; is the *cetana* in all beings, 433; is the Himālaya among the immovables, 434; is the inexhaustible Time, 443, 444; is the Sāgara among the reservoirs of water, 434; is the source of good as well as bad, 403–404; is Vāsava among the *devas*, 432; is Viṣṇu among the *ādityas*, 431; *jñāni* is the best among the worshippers of, 243–244; knowing, as it is, 193; men appreciate, in human form, 511; never bound by his actions, 353–354; no rebirth for one who realises, 303, 307–308, 321–322; of the *jñānis*, is *jñāna*, 452; of the *sātvikas*, is *sattva*, 448; of the secrets, is *maunam*, 450; of the victorious, is *jaya*, 448; of those who are to be prosperous, is *udbhava*, 446; of those who seek victory, is *nīti*, 450; of the rulers, is *daṇḍa*, 449; philosophically developed concept of, as Mother is purely an Indian product, 62; projects the universe by animating His *prakṛti*, 352, 355; protects India's spirituality, 482–483; psycho-physical fitness required to sustain vision of, 506; realisation, 151–153; realisation of, is for all—even the most wicked & sinful, 392–394; realisation of, preceded

*God (contd.)*
by several births of spiritual struggle, 246–248; remains unknown due to the delusion caused by the *guṇas*, 232–233; respective results of worshipping gods & The, 383–384; reveals His Universal dimension to Arjuna, 469–471; seeing, in all, 68; seeing, in all & in oneself, 153; source of infinite joy is, 150; sustains the universe, 459; takes care of the highest type of *bhaktas*, 380–383; universe is pervaded by, and yet God remains detached, 347–350; value of world when, is realised, 378–379; ways in which, is manifested in the universe, 229–231; what happens when, manifests in our heart, 413–414; who realises, 264–266, 268–272; who realises, easily, 302; who succeeds in giving up the body with the knowledge of, 273.

gods & goddesses, 253; crave to be born in India, 375, 483; do not know the origin of the God, 402; do not like men transcending them, 251; human beings greater than, 377; respective results of worshipping, & The God, 255, 383–384; why do men worship mythical, 249–252; worship of, criticized, 250–251.

Goethe, Johann Wolfgang von, 61, 94; nature of desire according to, 111.

Goldsmith, Oliver, 43.

Good: and evil are relative, 372–373, 404; as well as bad come from the same source, 403–404; doer of, deeds never comes to grief, 166.

*Gospel of Sri Ramakrishna*, 68, 137, 191, 248, 396, 413.

Grace, 240, 419, 509.

Greek, 270; culture needs to be combined with Indian culture, 285; never understood death, 282–283; thought, 268.

*Greek View of Life*, 270, 282.

*Gṛhastha*: status of, 21.

*Gṛhastha āśrama*, 21.

*Guṇās*: all states of, proceed from God & yet God remains unaffected, 231–232; deluded by, men remain ignorant of God, 232–233; role of the three, 238–239.

*Guru Granth Sāhib*, 299.

*Hādith-e-Suidsi*, 202.

*Hādith-e-Urufi*, 202.

Hanumān, 127.

Happiness. *See also Ānanda*; ratio of enjoyment of, & desire for happiness, 304; secret of true, 79–87, 88, 91, 97; supreme, 141, 148, 150–151.

Hari, 324, 325, 413, 483.

Hastie, Prof. William, 400.

Hastināpura, 469.

Head, Joseph, 169.

Heart: what is, 301.

Heaven, 472; concept of going to, 374–380; is within us, 376.

Himālaya, 434.

Hindu, 481; who is a, according to Swami Vivekananda, 294.

*Hiraṇyagarbha*, 307.

Hiraṇyakaśipu, 244.

Hitler, Adolf, 319; victim of unchecked ambition, 94.

*Hitopadeśa*, 25, 345.
Hoover Committee Commission Report, 112.
Householder: not inferior to *sannyāsin*, 23–24; status of, 20–21.
Hoyle, Fred, 60, 202, 274.
Hugo, Victor, 389.
Human (beings): Atman has left footprints on, experience, 349; according to modern biology, 75; alone can seek freedom, 352–353; *amṛtasya putrāḥ*, 214; *aparā prakṛti* of, 196; appreciate God in human form, 511; architects of their own destiny, 52; are combination of two natures—*cit jaḍa granthi*, 48; are helpless, 352–353; are helplessly born, 316–318; attitude of the *Gītā* towards the wicked, 389–392; be self-dependent, 116–118; behaviour of, cannot be explained by brain alone, 208–212; bestowed with the freedom to choose between *parā* & *aparā prakṛti*, 58–59; bestowed with the freedom to choose between *vidyā māyā* & *avidyā māyā*, 362; beware of stagnation, 26–27, 88; brain should be developed along with the, heart, 412; capacity of, to detach, 35–36; cause of misery and pain in, life, 87; channelization of, energy, 92–97; deluded by *āsurī sampat*, 361–362; deluded by *guṇās* remain ignorant of God, 232–233; deluded by *icchā* & *dveśa*, 261–264; demoniac men deluded by *māyā* do not worship God, 240; destroying nature, 346; direction of, evolution, 33; ecstasy in daily life, 341–342; fate of those, who don't have *śraddhā* in *brahma vidyā*, 345–346; fate of, who seek heavenly enjoyment, 374–380; few, succeed in spiritual life, 193–194; four types of, 41; four types of, worship God, 241–245; generally, seek mysterious religion, 339–340; goal of, evolution, 65, 77, 90; goal of, life, 114–115, 322; God destroys the darkness of our hearts, 418–419; God exhorts, to become His instrument, 492–498; greater than gods, 377; greatest blessing that a, can receive from God, 415–417; have limited freedom in this world, 316; highest attainment in, life, 143; how can, attain happiness, 91; how do *sāttvika*, worship God, 364–367; how, are freed from all sins, 402; how to build character strength, 118–123; how to face death, 493; how to face the battle of, life, 492–498; how to judge a, 257–258, 262–263, 356–358, 361; how to look upon, weaknesses & failures, 391–392; how to make joy a permanent feature of, life, 413–414; how to overcome *sarga*, 71–72; importance of control of mind in, life, 139–140;. importance of controlling the sense organs in, life, 126; importance of positive thinking in, life, 288; importance of raising, life above sensory level, 79–87; importance of spiritual realisation in, life, 201–202; influence of advertisements on, 113; are playgrounds for the forces of *prakṛti*, 58; are *cit-jaḍa-granthi*, 204, 210, 213, 220; are not servants of the

Human (beings) *(contd.)*
matter, 213; life is full of pain and is ephemeral, 303–306; live in the city of nine gates, 44–45; meaning of death of a, 168–169, 173; mentality of foolish people, 359; mentality of great souls endowed with *daivi sampat*, 363–365; message of Śrī Kṛṣṇa to all, 183–184; mind in the state of *yoga*, 139; morality in case of ordinary, depend on external force, 449–451; on how, become God's devotees, 242–243; place of *abhyāsa & vairāgya* in, life, 159–164; place of emotions in, life, 411–412; profoundest truth about, 37–38; purpose of, life, 345–346; quest for Truth in, life progressed in two directions, 197–199; ratio of pain and joy in, life, 303–306; relevance of cosmology to, life, 312–313; role of cerebral system in, life, 126; role of desire in, life, 112; role of pain & pleasure in, life, 305–306; secret of an integrated, life, 149; should carry on the battle of life with mind fixed on God, 287; six enemies of, 93; six fold changes in, life, 269; spiritualizing everyday, life, 25–27, 386; three levels of, personality, 167; three sources of strength in, 122, 296–298; three types of persons according to Śrī Kṛṣṇa, 11; true dimension of, 53, 89; true nature of, 220; two directions of, energy, 100; two stages of, development, 29; uniqueness of, 56, 58, 248, 345–346, 377, 430–431, 440–442; value of purity getting eroded from, life, 369; wants versus needs of, 111–112; what happens when God manifests in, heart, 413–414; what should be the foundation of, life, 78; when should, take to spiritual life, 136–137; who escapes death, 445–446; who is our friend & who is our enemy, 116–117, 118–123; why do, worship mythical gods, 249–252; why the Divine manifests differently in different, 456–458; worshipping gods are like cattle to gods, 250–251.

Huxley, Aldous Leonard, 229.

Huxley, Sir Julian, 14, 77, 88, 200, 248; on criteria of quantity & quality in evolution, 222; on goal of human life, 114–115; on God, 320.

*Icchā & dveśa*, 261, 264, 266.

*Impact of Science on Society*, 200, 336, 398.

Incarnations, 511; why, are not easily recognised, 255–260, 356–358.

India: ageing but never old, 480; ancient yet new, 292; cause of her ruin, 8; future of, 268; God protecting India's spirituality, 482–483; gods are eager to be born in, 375; has always accepted change and has thus survived, 477–483; how to make, prosperous, 494–498; how to overcome the enemies of, 494–498; is the *puṇyabhūmi*, 375, 483; needs citizen-*yogis*, 42; needs *samadarśitva*, 69–70, 152; needs scientific temper, 258; new *yuga dharma* for, 479; role of scientific

India *(contd.)*
thinking & search in, 261; scientific exploration of nature in, 197–199; secret of its inner strength, 189.
Indian (s): cause of evil in, society, 155; concept of nature, 195; culture needs to be combined with Greek culture, 285; know to respect greatness wherever they may see it, 456, 463; need to awaken desires in the minds of, people, 109; no concept of devil in, philosophy, 12, 372; people need training of mind, 264; scale of time in, cosmology, 308–310; uniqueness of, religious tradition, 179, 189, 192, 225, 327, 423–425, 473–474; uniqueness of, religious tradition—distinction between *sanātana & yuga dharma*, 477–482; western &, concept of God, 319–320; wisdom, 425.
Indian Air Force: motto of, 487.
Indra, 274, 432, 437.
Infinite: inexhaustibility of the, 190.
*Integrative Action of the Nervous System*, 210.
*Intelligent Universe*, 60, 202, 274.
*Īśā Upaniśad*, 243, 284, 290, 454.
Islam, 369, 481; human being greater than gods & angels according to, 377; orthodoxy in, 177, 178, 179; *sanātana & yuga dharma* are mixed up in, 480; *sanātana dharma* in, 481.
Islam, Kazi Nazrul, 155, 377.

*Jaḍa*, 203, 204.
Jāhnavi (Ganges), 438.
*Jalpa*, 442.
*Japayajña*, 434.
*Jaya*: of the victorious God is, 448.
Jayadratha, 498.
Jean, Val Jean, 389.
Jeans, James, 470.
Jesus, 33, 78, 92, 115, 177, 194, 201, 258, 259, 357, 358, 376, 377, 390, 423, 427, 452, 456.
*Jijñāsuḥ*, 241, 247.
*Jīva*: service of, is worship of Śiva, 12–13.
*Jīvanmukti*, 67, 334.
*Jnāna*, 64, 125, 156, 188, 249, 331, 418. *See also* Knowledge; according to Sri Ramakrishna, 334, 344, 376; of the *jñānis* God is, 452; destroys all impurities instantly, 66–67; gets obscured by desires, 249–252; hidden by *ajñāna*, 54; highest, & highest *bhakti* are same, 242, 246; *puruṣa tantra*, 263; *vastu tantra*, 263, 266, 330; what is, 336.
*Jñāna & vijñāna*, 191–192, 216, 410; frees us from evil, 335–336.
*Jñāna Kāṇḍa*, 198, 375.
*Jñāna yajña*, 366.
*Jñāna yoga*, 162.
*Jñānadīpa*, 418.
*Jñāni* , 182, 241, 247, 512; attitude of a, 366; best among the worshippers of God, 243–244; dry in nature, 409–410; his method of realization, 191.
Joy. *See also* Bliss; derived from Brahman, 150–151; God is the source of all, 342; how to make, a permanent feature of our life, 413–414.
Judaism, 369.
*Julius Caesar*, 493.
Jung, Carl, 47.

*Kāla*, 282, 284, 311, 438, 445.
*Kāla anala*, 488.
*Kālarātriḥ*, 58.
Kālidāsa, 30, 61, 87, 434.
Kālī, 61.
*Kalpa*, 309, 350–351.
*Kāma*. *See also* Desire; status of, in Vedanta, 231.
*Kāma & Krodha*, 100; result of withstanding the current of, 91–97.
Kāmadhuk: among the cow God is, 437.
Kamsa, 445.
Kandarpa, 437.
Kant, Immanuel, 49.
Kapila, 435.
*Kāraṇa śarīra*, 167.
*Karma*, 149, 268, 275, 278; what is, 276, 277, 279.
*Karma Kāṇḍa*, 198, 374.
*Karmayoga*, 8, 46; is an independent path, 140; *sāṅkhya* (path of *jñāna*) &, are non-different, 20, 23, 25; *sannyāsa* difficult to attain without, 29; superior to *karma sannyāsa*, 9–14, 18.
*Karmayoga* (book), 24, 306.
*Karmayogī*: how a, works without being tainted, 32–36.
Karṇa, 494, 498.
Kārtikeya, 434.
*Kaṭha Upaniṣad*, 98, 142, 170, 216, 291, 299, 323, 435, 457, 458, 461; 'arise awake….', 27, 43, 86; chariot-horse imagery from, 146.
Kaurava, 505.
*Kavi*: definition of, 227; God described as, 290–291.
Keats, John (English poet), 87, 454.
*Kena Upaniṣad*, 8.
*Kīrti*, 447.
Kiruna, 328.
Knowledge, 125. *See also Jñāna*; covered by ignorance, 54; destroys ignorance & reveals the Supreme Truth, 55; experiential versus theoretical, 62–63; knowing tends to being in inner life, 98; leads to unity, 68; obstructions to right, 261–264; role of pain & pleasure in attainment of, 305–306; should evolve into wisdom, 200–201; totality of, 189–192, 217; who attains, & how, 264–266.
Knowledge & experience, 191–192.
*Koran*, 106, 174, 480. *See also Shariyat*; on nearness of God, 333.
*Krama mukti*, 329.
Kṛṣṇa, Śrī: addressed as *Yogeśvara*, 466; agrees to reveal His Universal form to Arjuna, 467–468; Arjuna could see the Universal form of, out of His grace, 509; Arjuna repents for having treated, merely as his friend, 503–504, 507; Arjuna's request to, to reveal his divine Universal form, 465–466; bestowing Arjuna with the Divine eye, 468; had revealed His universal form only a few times in his life, 465–466; intensely active but detached & free, 354; intimate friendship of Arjuna with, 505; message of, to all, 183–184; re-assumes His ordinary form, 510; reveals His Universal dimension to His mother, 468; reveals His Universal dimension to Arjuna, 469–471; three types of people in the world according to, 11.
*Kṛtakṛtya*, 78, 115.
*Kṛtārtha*, 78, 115.
*Kṣamā*, 447.

*Kṣatriya*, 395, 493.
Kubera, 433.
*Kumārasambhava*, 434.
*Kusumākara*, 447.

*Lectures from Colombo to Almora*, 8.
*Les miserables*, 390.
Life: & death, 168–169, 268–272, 279–285; attitude towards those who surpass us in spiritual, 184–185; beginning of spiritual, 80; carry on the battle of, with mind fixed on God, 287–289; cause of misery and pain in, 87; comprehensive philosophy of, 16; distinction between wants & needs in human, 111–112; ecstasy in daily, 341–342; goal of human, 77, 322; greatest blessing one can receive in human, is of *buddhiyoga*, 416–417; highest attainment in human, 143; how to face the battle of, 492–498; how to make joy a permanent feature of human, 413–414; human, is full of pain and is ephemeral, 303–306; importance of control of mind in human, 139–140; importance of positive thinking in human, 288; importance of raising human, above sensory level, 79–87; importance of spiritual realisation in human, 201–202; is a centre of education, 31; men have limited freedom in their, 316; middle path in spiritual, 135–138; nature of spiritual, & success in it, 193–194; place of *abhyāsa & vairāgya* in human, 159–164; place of belief in spiritual, 177–178; place of emotions in human, 411–412; purpose of human, 345–346; ratio of pain and joy in human, 303–306; reincarnation, 168–171; relevance of cosmology to our, 312–313; right type of austerity in spiritual, 134–135; role of desire in human, 112; role of pain & pleasure in human, 305–306; secret of an integrated, 149; six fold changes in human, 269; spiritualizing everyday, 25–27, 386; today qualitative richness of, is stressed more, 105; two stages in spiritual, 114; value of purity getting eroded from human, 369; what should be the foundation of human, 78; when to take up spiritual, 136–137.
*Life of Ramakrishna*, 257.
*Life of Swami Vivekananda by His Eastern & Western Disciples*, 400.
Lincoln, Abraham, 411, 456.
*Living Brain*, 35.
*Loka*, 196.
*Lokasamgraham*, 11.
*Lokottara*, 196.
Love, 40, 76, 514.

Madhavananda, Swami, 250.
*Madhya panthā*, 135. *See also* Middle path.
*Madhyama pratipāda*, 183.
*Mahā Nārāyaṇa Upaniṣad*, 12.
*Mahābhārata*, 15, 296, 304, 309, 312, 331, 381, 393, 405, 417, 432, 438, 448, 449, 450, 466, 489, 494, 496, 504, 505; gods do not like men transcending them, 251; how Droṇa was insulted by Drupada, 361; root of desire according to,

110–111.
*Mahārātriḥ*, 58.
Maitreyī, 402.
Makara, 439.
*Māṇḍūkya Kārikā*, 365; verse on firm determination, 160.
*Māṇḍūkya Upaniṣad*, 272.
Manliness, 120, 229, 494; how to gain, 493.
Manu, 405, 406.
*Manu Smṛti*, 432; desire is the root of action according to, 109; on *gṛhastha āśrama*, 21; on secret of true happiness, 97.
*Manvantaras*, 405.
*Mārgaśīrṣa*, 447.
Marīci, 432.
Marut, 467, 486.
*Masnavi*, 202.
Materialism: is a dogma, 219.
Mathur, Babu, 506.
Matter: mixed up with consciousness, 220.
*Maunam*, 450. *See also* Silence.
*Māyā*, 241, 244, 260, 318, 349, 353, 355, 410, 459, 468; definition of, 233-234; demoniac men deluded by, do not worship God, 240; how to get over Lord's, 233–239; story of how Lord Viṣṇu was caught up in, 237–238; story of Nārada getting deluded by Lord's, 236–237; two aspects of, 59, 362; two dimensions of, 234–235.
*Medhā*, 447.
Meditation, 10, 11, 107, 301, 339; difficult to attain, 157–158; how should a *yogi* meditate, 129–130; how to meditate, 132–135; nature of a steady mind in, 139; place of sense organs in, 142; posture of the body in, 132; prayer (meditation) versus work, 12; preliminary steps to, 101–102; result of, 134, 147–154; seat for, 131; self-realised person is always in, 100; state of mind established in *yoga* of, 141–144; technique of, 145–147; way to success in, 159–164; *yoga* of, is only a part of the wider *yoga* of *Gītā*, 140, 156.
*Meghadūta*, 87.
Meru (the mythical mountain): among the mountains God is, 433.
*Message of the Upaniṣads*, 320, 461.
Middle path, 135–138, 183.
Mill, John Stuart, 304.
Mimosa pudica, 121, 457.
Mind, 215; a prayer to God to control the, 162; being accepted by modern neurology, 208–212; cause of restlessness of, 148; concentration of, 129–130; control of, & its result, 118–123; control of, very difficult, 157–158; desire & aversion, 261–264; eye is the index of, 408; filled with jealousy not fit to receive truth, 335–336; highest state of, according to Plato, 148; how to fix the, on God at the time of death, 280, 286–289, 292–298; illustration of how a part of, should be fixed on God, 287–288; importance of control of, 139–140; in meditation, 145–147; nature of a steady, established in *yoga*, 139; pure, *buddhi* & Atman are same, 148; result of, being successful in meditation, 147–154; role of a positive frame of, in human life, 288; scientific, 258, 261–264, 267; state of, being established in *yoga*, 141–144; steady, 124, 128,

Mind *(contd.)*
408; train the mind in & through work, 31; training of, 25–26, 264–267; two states of, 139; way to control the, 159–164; what is, 432; when is the, said to have achieved *yoga*, 138.
Misery: cause of, 87.
*Modern Man in Search of A Soul*, 47.
Mohammad, Prophet, 106, 202.
*Moharātriḥ*, 58.
*Mokṣa*. *See also* Freedom; who attains, 64–66.
Monotheism, 456.
Moral sense: what is, 49.
Morality: in case of ordinary men, depends on external force, 449–451.
*Mṛtyu*, 445.
*Mukti*, 212.
Muller, Prof. Max: on why the west has lagged behind in spiritual science, 223.
*Muṇḍaka Upaniṣad*, 98, 195, 204, 212, 217, 227, 266, 376, 431, 503; every thing is Brahman, 13; universe is Brahman, 74.
*Mysterious Universe*, 469.
*Mystery of Mind*, 211.
Mystics: religion of the, 472–473.
Mythology: interpretation of, 325–326.
*Myths and Symbols of the Hindu Religion*, 325.

Naidu, Mrs. Sarojini, 256.
Nanak, Guru, 299.
Nandi (the bull): meaning of Śiva riding the bull, 326.
Napoleon, Bonaparte, 94.
Nārada, 420; among the *devarṣis* God is, 435; how, achieved highest realisation, 181; story of, getting deluded by Lord's *māyā*, 236–237.
*Nārada Bhakti sūtras*, 394; who is the supreme *bhakta*, 244, 323.
Narādhipa, 436.
Narasimha, 244, 323.
*Nārāyaṇa*, 247, 406, 483.
Narendra, 366.
*Nāsadīya Sūkta*, 402.
Naṭarāja: meaning of Śiva's dance as, 326.
*National Geographic*, 367, 404.
Nature. *See also Prakṛti*; according to Indian & Western thought, 195; control of lower, 48–52; doer of all works, 47–49; human beings destroying, 346.
Neurology: future of modern science & cosmology if consciousness gets acceptance in, 217–218; modern, realising the importance of mind & consciousness, 208–212.
*Neurology and What Lies Beyond* (a lecture), 211.
*New Testament*, 78, 194, 201, 380; knowing God according to, 193; story of a woman taken in adultery, 390.
Nietzsche, 319.
*Niḥśreyasa*, 10.
*Nirvāṇa*, 134. *See also Mokṣa*.
*Nirvāṇa Śatakam*, 216.
*Nirvikalpa samādhi*. *See Samādhi*.
*Nīti* (justice), 450.
Nivedita, Sister, 387.
*Nivṛtti*, 113, 157.
Non-attachment, 108.

Obstinacy: different from will, 22.
*Ode to Melancholy* (a poem), 87.
*Old Testament*, 472.
*Om*, 229, 301, 369; among the syllables God is, 434; entering Indian Christianity, 300; the supreme state to be attained, 299–300.
Openheimer, 470.
Oracle of Delphi, 268.

*Padma Purāṇa*, 396.
Pāṇḍavas, 494, 505.
*Pāṇḍava-gītā*, 413.
*Paṇḍita*, 67; definition of, 69.
*Pāpayonī*: even a, can attain God, 392–394.
*Parā prakṛti*, 196–197, 207, 271, 274. *See also Prakṛti*; is *cit*, 203.
*Parā Vidyā*, 195, 196, 219.
Parables/stories: of a Christian saint, 379; of a diamond being assessed by different persons, 257; of a man struck by an arrow, 23; of a woman taken in adultery, 390; of an ant and the sugar mound, 190; of Brahmā giving boon to a man, 313–314; of fishes caught in a fisherman's net, 41; of the philosopher & the boatman, 63; of three robbers, 238–239; of two men building their houses on sand & rock respectively, 78; on urge for spiritual life, 137.
*Parabola*, 326.
*Paracelsus* (a poem), 56.
*Parāk*, 293.
*Paramātman*, 124.
Pātañjali, 130, 136, 139, 156, 159, 182.
*Pāvaka*, 433.
*Pavana*, 438.
Peace, 128, 186. *See also* Happiness; how to attain, 124, 134; who attains, 40, 103.
Penfield, Wilder: accepts mind behind the brain, 209–211.
Philosophy: advaita—the comprehensive, for mankind, 14; defined by a Western theologian, 199; definition of, 192; impulse release, 49; of equality, 17; should study both life & death, 281; speculative, 199; west in need of a comprehensive, of life, 16.
Physics: modern, moving towards Vedanta, 200.
*Pitṛyāna*, 328, 332.
Plato, 15, 270; high state of mind according to, 148.
Politics: what is true, 17.
Pope: appreciation of the, for Indian's outlook towards spirituality & religion, 424.
Portland radio talk, 50–52.
*Positive Sciences of the Ancient Hindus*, 292.
Practical Vedanta, 16, 184, 431; *Gītā* is the best book on, 17.
*Pradyumna*, 405.
Prahlāda, 244, 325; among the *daityas* God is, 438; his devotion to God, 323–324.
Prajāpati, 502.
*Prakṛti*, 349, 361. *See also* Nature; *aparā*, 195–196; *avyakta & vyakta*, 311–315; control of *aparā*, 48–52; God projects the universe by animating His, 355; *mohini* (deluding) power of, 362; *parā*, 196–197; *parā & aparā*, 47–50, 57–61, 194–195, 203, 271; *parā & aparā*,

*Prakṛti ( contd.)*
—their role in evolution, 212–213; *parā & aparā*, is the source of the universe, 205–208, 214–224; universe comes from the, and dissolves back into it, 350–352.
*Pralaya*, 60, 309, 312, 487; what is, 312.
*Praṇava*, 299, 300.
*Pratīka*, 299.
*Pratimā*, 299.
*Pratyagātman*, 293.
*Pratyak*, 293.
*Pravṛtti*, 113, 149, 157.
Prayer: versus work, 12.
Process, 277, 279.
*Psalms*, 472.
Psychic: energy, 143.
Psychology, 209.
Psychosocial: two steps in, evolution, 200.
*Purāṇa* (scripture), 292, 309, 311, 323, 343, 376, 434, 449, 478.
*Purāṇaḥ*, 501; definition of, 292.
Purandara, Dāsa (the saint), 358.
*Puruṣa*, 341, 501; how to attain the, 322–324.
*Puruṣa Sūkta*, 459.
*Puruṣa tantra jñāna*, 263.

*Quran. See Koran.*

Rābia (the sufi saint), 396.
Radhakrishnan, Dr. S, 324, 391; defines toleration, 190.
*Rāga*, 299.
Rahiman, Abdul III, 303.
*Rājarṣi*, 395, 435.
*Rajas*, 235, 236, 238; cause of restlessness, 148.
*Rākṣasa*, 433, 500.
Rāma, Śrī, 127, 357, 382; among the warriors God is, 438.
Ramakrishna, Sri, 9, 11, 60, 61, 68, 82, 155, 157, 245, 246, 248, 249, 259, 260, 280, 281, 292, 342, 357, 362, 365, 366, 371, 373, 377, 378, 381, 392, 393, 395, 400, 410, 456, 457, 477, 506; a song sung by, 130; advaita of, 12–13; as an experimenter of science of religion, 180; best description of, 413; compares *bhakti* to a music played on seven holed instrument, 409; compares *māyā* to the magic of a magician, 234; described by Romain Rolland, 257; four types of men according to, 41; how, practised even-mindedness, 126–127; how, transformed Girish Ghosh, 392; illustration given by, of how a part of mind should be fixed on God, 287–288; Kazi Nazrul Islam on,.377; meditation & work reconciled by, 12; narrates the story of how Lord Viṣṇu was caught up in His own *māyā*, 237–238; narrates the story of Nārada who was deluded by Lord's *māyā*, 236–237; on asceticism, 27; on discrimination (an illustration), 220; on experiential versus theoretical knowledge, 63; on fasting, 137; on *gāyatri & sandhya*, 178; on how to live in the world with mind fixed on God, 289; on inexhaustibility of the spiritual knowledge, 190; on *jñāna & vijñāna*, 191–192; on knowledge & ignorance, 334, 344, 376; on the extent of freedom that man has in this

Ramakrishna, Sri *(contd.)* world, 316; on the jurisdiction of Divine *Prakṛti*, 58; on the nature of spiritual experience, 451; on three levels of bliss, 83; on totality of reality—an illustration, 216; on two dimensions of *Māyā*, 234–235, 362; on urge for spiritual life, 137; on utility of *sattvaguṇa* in overcoming *māyā*, 236; parable of a diamond being assessed by different persons, 257; parable of three robbers, 238–239; pure mind, *buddhi* & Atman are same says, 148; teaches Naren not to condemn other's religious practices, 253; two aspects of Reality according to, 355.

Ramaṇa, Maharṣi, 115.

Rāmānujācārya, 227; describes God, 380.

*Rāmāyaṇa*, 15.

Ranganathananda, Swami: experience of, in Paris, 55; experience of, meeting a person seeking mysterious religion, 339–340; Gandhi memorial lecture of, 430; how a week boy from Rangoon gained strength and confidence, 163; how to keep up one's self respect—an incident, 24; in Sweden & Holland, 328; meeting of, with Fred Hoyle, 202; *Neurology and what lies beyond*—a lecture by, 211; observation of, regarding democracy in Scandinavian countries, 71; Portland radio talk, 50–52; regarding a person who was a member of many religious bodies, 265; speaks at Moscow & West Berlin, 214; Vikram Sarabhai memorial lecture of, 430; visiting a school teacher, 356; with Dr. Chandrashekar, 223.

*Rasāyana vidyā*, 439.

Rāṣmaṇi, Rāṇi, 506.

Reality: alone is, 224–227; beyond speech & thought, 450–452; importance of knowing, in its totality, 189–192; is philosophically ultimate but spiritually intimate, 105; knowing, in its totality, 194–195, 197, 216–217, 220–221, 271, 310; life plus death make for totality of, 284–285, 372, 490; name of the, 215; nature of, 293; nature of highest, 215; no word can indicate the highest, 72, 105; of the world, 444; the best symbol of the highest, is *Om*, 299–300; two aspects of, 311, 355–356.

Rebirth: beings in all *lokas* are subject to, 306–307; no, for one who realises God, 303, 307–308, 321–322.

Reductionism, 208.

Reductionists, 203.

Reincarnation, 167–171. *See also* Rebirth.

*Reincarnation: An East-West Anthology*, 169.

Relativity: how to overcome, 71–72.

Religion: cause of intolerance in, 189–190; cheap, of today, 16; definition of, 39, 64; differentiated from spirituality, 294–295; evolution of religious ideas, 327; generally men seek mysterious, 339–340; is realization, 179; is simple & easy, 339–340; no magic & mystery in, 339–340; of the mystics, 472–473; science of, 175–177; spiritual practitioner goes

beyond the dos & don'ts of, 174–180; true, 11–12; true spirit of, according to Eddington, 176; two classifications of, 145, 175; uniqueness of Indian religious tradition, 423–425, 473–474; uniqueness of Indian religious tradition—distinction of *sanātana & yuga dharma*, 477–482.
Renunciation: true, 29.
*Republic of Plato*, 148.
*Ṛg Veda*, 198, 328, 369, 375, 432, 459; *'ekam sat viprāḥ...'*, 189, 327, 384; *gāyatri mantra*, 417; *Nāsadīya Sūkta*, 402; on life & death, 269, 372; *'yasyaite himanvanto mahitva'*, 410.
*Ṛg Veda samhita*, 281.
Rolland, Romain: describes Sri Ramakrishna, 257.
Roman empire: cause of its fall, 96.
Roy, Raja Rammohan, 243.
*Ṛṣis*, 485; three types of, 435.
*Rudra*, 467, 486; among the, God is Śaṅkara, 433.
Rumi, Jalaluddin, 202.
Russell, Bertrand: on the need of wisdom, 200–201, 336; solution prescribed by, for human problems, 397.

*Śabdabrahma*, 174, 300.
*Sādhya*, 486.
*Ṣaḍripu*, 93.
*Sāgara*, 434.
*Saint John's Gospel*, 300.
Sainthood, 29.
*Sākṣi*, 271–272; concept of, 370.
*Śakti*, 58, 234, 319, 355. *See also* Divine Mother; universe is manifestation of, 59.
Śakuni, 448.
Śakuntala, 61.
*Samabuddhiḥ*, 128.
*Samadarśitva*, 17, 67–70, 128, 152.
*Samādhi*, 191, 192, 400; *nirvikalpa*, beyond the domain of Divine *Prakṛti*, 58; when is, attained, 461.
*Samadṛṣṭi*, 151–157.
*Śamaḥ*, 115.
*Samāsa*, 443–444.
*Samatva*, 17, 106, 107, 129, 151–157; when is, attained, 126.
*Sāma Veda*, 369, 375; God is, among the Vedas, 432.
*Samsāra*, 378; how to get out of, 64–66; is *tāpatraya*, 305; what is, 27; who gets trapped in, 345–346.
*Samsāri*: who is a, 27.
*Samudramanthan*, 436.
*Sanātana Dharma*, 167, 229, 267; importance of distinguishing, from *yuga dharma*, 476–482.; spiritual practitioner goes beyond dos & don'ts of religion, 175–180.
*Sandhyā vandana*, 178.
Sañjaya, (prince) 304.
Sañjaya, 469, 505.
*Saṅkalpa*, 116; root of desire, 110–111.
Śaṅkara (a *rudra*), 433.
Śaṅkarācārya, 9, 62, 65, 69, 83, 133, 176, 204, 205, 216, 220, 226, 250, 251, 261, 263, 266, 269, 270, 273, 277, 292, 293, 294, 298, 299, 320, 330, 340, 341, 342, 347, 358, 359, 361, 384, 387, 415, 425, 435; defines cause, 221; defines *kavi*, 227; describes *buddhi*, 297–298; describes the nature of Atman, 38; essence of *Gītā* according to, 512; gives an illustration of God's impartial nature, 388; intellect of,

to be combined with Buddha's heart, 18; on how the highest Reality can be denoted, 215; on nature of highest reality, 215; on self effort, 95; prayer of, to Śiva to control the mind, 162; types of students according to, 8; value of the world without Atman according to, 295, 453.
*Saṅkarṣaṇa*, 405.
*Sāṅkhya* (path of *Jñāna* ): *karmayoga* &, non-different, 20, 23, 25–26.
Sāṅkhya (philosophy), 60, 205, 233, 311.
*Sannyāsa*, 108; difficult to attain without *karmayoga*, 29; *karmayoga* superior to *karma*, 9–14, 18; of *karma*, 8; true, 19, 110.
*Sannyāsi*, 116; householder not inferior to, 23–24; who is a, 18–19, 108.
*Śānti Parva*, 312, 381; criteria of a healthy society, 496.
*Sapta ṛṣis*, 405.
Sarada, Devi (The Holy Mother), 155, 393.
*Sarga*: how to overcome, 71–72.
*Śaśī* (moon): God is, among the asterisms, 432.
*Śāśvata dharma. See also Sanātana dharma*; importance of distinguishing, from *yuga dharma*, 476–482.
*Sattva*: of the *sātvika* God is, 448; utility of, *guṇa* in overcoming *māyā*, 235–236, 238–239.
*Satya Yuga*, 155.
Satyajit, 260.
Scepticism: cause of, 199.
Schopenhauer, Arthur: on morality of men, 450.
Schrodinger, Erwin, 73, 213, 272.
Science, 266; difference between physical, & spiritual science, 222; future of, 223–224; future of modern, & cosmology if consciousness gets acceptance in neurology, 217–218; future of spiritual, 398; higher & lower, 196; modern, gradually accepting consciousness, 207–212, 319; modern, moving towards Vedanta, 200, 202, 208–209, 219, 440–442; nature of spiritual, 337–341; of human possibilities, 14, 56, 88, 115, 177; of meditation, 131; of religion, 175–177; of sciences, 204, 217, 439–442; of values links physical & spiritual sciences, 200; place of consciousness in modern physical, 197, 347–348; revolutionary changes in modern, can be expected in the 21st century, 217–218; spiritual, is easy & simple, 339–340; study of, in India, 261; true spirit of, according to Eddington, 176; western, has threatened Western philosophy & theology, 199; what is, 212, 262.
Scientific: attitude, 258, 261–264, 267; exploration of nature in India, 197–199; place of desire & aversion in, investigation, 261–264; verification of Truth, 343.
Seal, Dr. Brajendranath, 292, 480.
*Search for Truth in Science*, (a lecture) 223.
*Search for Truth in Vedanta*, (a lecture) 223.
*Secret Life of Plants*, 274.
Self, 125, 128; God as the, is the beginning, middle & end of all beings, 427–429; nature of mind established in, 139; result of being established in the, 141–

144; state of being established in the, 141–144; vision of a *yogi* established in, 151–152; when is the mind said to be established in the, 138; who realises the, 123–125.
Self-confidence, 21. *See also Ātma śraddhā*
Self-dependence: raise yourself by yourself, 116–118.
Self-discipline, 450. *See also Discipline.*
Self realisation, 252; at the time of death, 279–286; attainment of, preceded by several births of spiritual struggle, 246–248; here itself, 333–334, 376–379; how to attain, 287–289, 322–324, 395; is for all—even for the most wicked & sinful, 392–394; *karmayoga* is an easier path for, 29; obstacles to, 261–264; result of, 67–70, 71; role of silence in, 451–452; through meditation, 134; traits of a person established in, 77, 128; two paths for, 20, 23; value of world when, is attained, 378–379; when does, take place, 55; who attains, 97–98, 100, 123–125, 264–266, 268–272.
Self-respect, 23–24.
Sen, Keshab Chandra, 259.
Sense organs: among the, God is mind, 432; control of, 145–146; importance of controlling the, 126; place of, in meditation, 142; speed of nervous impulse, 141.
Service: importance of, to man in spiritual life, 10-14.
Śeṣa (the serpent), 325.
Shakespeare, William, 401, 408; greatness of, 227–228; on death, 493.
Shankar, Pundit Ravi 50.
*Shariyat*, 175. *See also Koran.*
Shelley, Percy Bysshe (British poet), 94, 290, 321, 454.
Sherrington, Sir Charles, 210, 411.
*Siddha*, 485, 486, 500.
Silence, 451–452. *See also Maunam.*
Śiśupāla, 465.
Śiva, 33, 58, 252, 319, 324, 355, 366, 434; meaning of, riding the bull (Nandi), 326; meaning of his dance as Naṭarāja, 326; service of *jīva* is worship of, 12–13.
*Śivānandalahari*, 162.
Skanda, 434.
*Smṛti*, 175, 478, 479, 481.
*Smṛti* (memory), 447.
Society: cause of evil in our, 155; cause of evils in, & its solution, 74; criteria of a healthy, 496; fate of a, devoid of spiritually realised men, 247; real social progress, 43; stable, 97.
Socrates, 15, 268, 270, 282, 302, 304; scene of his death, 282.
soul, 168–169, 283. *See also Sūkṣma śarīra*; journey of the, after death, 327–333.
Space-time continuum, 444.
*Sparśa* (sense of touch): how to go beyond, 80–87.
Spiritual: attainment of, goal preceded by several births of struggle, 246–248; attitude towards those who surpass us in, life, 184–185, 194; beginning of, life, 80; capacity of Indians for, appreciation, 423–425; experience is best expressed in silence, 451; experience is super sensory, 142; freedom, 308, 352–353; future of, science, 398; how does a man enter the, life, 242–243; import-

ance of, realisation in human life, 201–202; middle path in, practice, 135–138; nature of, life & success in it, 193–194; nature of, science, 337–341; place of belief in, life, 177–178; practitioner goes beyond the dos & don'ts of religion, 174–180; psychophysical fitness required to sustain, experience, 506; realisation, 247–248; right type of austerity in, life, 134–135; role of pain & pleasure in, evolution, 305–306; science is *dharmyam & amṛtam*, 338–339; science is easy & simple, 339–340; strength, 121, 122, 123; truth should be given to whom?, 335–336; two stages in, life, 114; when to take up, life, 136–137.

Spirituality, 464; can be expressed in several ways, 327; differentiated from religion, 294–295; God protecting India's, 482–483; pure, 387; science of, 439–442; tremendous capacity of Indians for appreciating, 423–425; true, 11–12.

Spontaneity, 365; two levels of, 51.

*Śrāddha*, 327.

*Śraddhā*, 163, 165, 186, 253–254, 383. *See also Ātma śraddhā*; fate of those who don't have, in *brahma vidyā*, 345–346.

*Śrī* (prosperity), 447.

*Śrīmad Bhāgavatam. See Bhāgavatam.*

*Śṛuti*, 293, 479, 481; prevails over *Smṛti*, 479.

*Sthūla Śarīra*, 167, 170.

Strength, 231, 492, 494; developing inner, 117, 118–123; three sources of, 122, 296–298.

Subject & object. *See also Dṛk & dṛśyam*; mixed up in living beings, 212–213, 220.

Subrahmaṇya, 434.

Subtle body, 167–170, 173.

*Śūdra*: even a, can attain God, 392–394.

Sujātā, 135.

Śuka, 324, 325.

*Sūkṣma śarīra*, 167–170, 173. *See also* soul.

*Sun Is our Mother* (an article), 367, 404.

Sūtaputra, 488.

*Sutta Nipāta*, 359.

*Svārājya-siddhi*, 65.

Svāyambhuva Manu, 406.

*Svabhāva*, 54, 55, 276, 279. *See also Prakṛti*; doer of all works, 47–49; significance of, 57–61.

*Śvetāśvatara Upaniṣad*, 201, 214; on our true nature, 89; vision of a realised sage in, 227.

*Syāmantaka* (the gem), 260.

Tagore, Rabindranath, 242.

*Taittirīya Samhita*, 279.

*Taittirīya Upaniṣad*, 73, 205, 293, 342, 428, 451; defines Brahman, 221; on bliss, 81.

*Tamas*, 235, 236, 238.

Tao, 429.

*Tao of Physics*, 326, 429.

Taoist philosophy, 150.

*Tapas*, 230, 512; of *jñāna*, 326; what is, 27.

*Tat tvam asi*, 213, 441.

*Tatpuruṣa samāsa*, 443.

*Tejas* (brilliance), 448.

Tennyson, Lord Alfred, 94, 426.

Theology: defined by a Western philosopher, 199.

*Three Lectures on the Vedanta Philosophy*, 223.
Tilak, Lokmanya, 118, 328, 405, 432; on ratio of pain and joy in life, 303–304.
Time, 282, 284, 285, 438, 488; concept of, 308–310; concept of *truṭi*, 351; God is the all consuming, 492; God is the inexhaustible, 443, 444.
*Time Magazine*, 320.
*Times* (News paper), 458.
Tintern Abbey, 399.
Truth: explored in two directions, 197–199; importance of knowing, in its totality, 189–192; is directly realizable & verifiable, 337, 343–344; is one but has different names, 327, 384; knowing, in its totality, 220–221; obstacles to knowing, 261–264; spiritual, should be given to whom?, 335–336; who attains, & how, 264–266.
*Truṭi* (fraction of a second), 351.
*Turīya*, 272.
Turiyananda, Swami, 371.

Uccaiḥśravas, 436.
*Udbhava*, 446.
*Udyoga Parva*, 304, 489, 505.
*UNESCO Courier*, 461.
*Uniqueness of Man*, 248.
Universe: comes from the *avyakta* and dissolves back in to it, 311–318; creation of the, 405–407; God pervades the entire, 225–227, 347–350; God projects the, by animating His *prakṛti*, 352, 355; God sustains the, 459; interconnectedness of everything in the, 313; is Brahman, 247–248; is space-time continuum, 444; made of five factors, 453–454; made of three *guṇās* which hide the Truth, 232–233; manifestation of the Divine Mother is the, 57–58; pervaded by consciousness, 347; pervaded by the background material, 347; proceeds from God & yet God remains unaffected, 232; pulsation of *Śakti* is, 59–60; same, helplessly gets manifested & dissolved, 315–318; source of the, 205–208, 214–224, 454–455; sustained by consciousness, 196–197, 203, 205–208; value of the, without Atman, 295, 453; value of world when God is realised, 378–379; ways in which God is manifested in the, 229–231; whole, is one's own family (a *śloka*), 245.
Upaniṣad, 15, 179, 198, 199; *Bṛhadāraṇyaka*, 38, 150, 215, 226, 278, 331, 341, 402, 418; *Chāndogya*, 75, 213, 328, 329, 330, 441; creation in, 206; full of poetry, 291; *Īśā*, 243, 284, 290, 454; *Kaṭha*, 27, 43, 86, 98, 142, 146, 170, 216, 291, 299, 323, 435, 457, 458, 461; *Kena*, 8; knowledge of Atman found only in, 340–341; *Māṇḍūkya Kārikā*, 160, 365; *Māṇḍūkya*, 272; *Mahā Nārāyaṇa*, 12; *Muṇḍaka*, 13, 74, 98, 195, 204, 212, 217, 227, 266, 376, 431, 503; preach *abhaya* & *śakti*, 252; reduced the value of heaven-going concept, 376–380; *Śvetāśvatara*, 89, 201, 214; *Taittirīya*, 73, 81, 205, 221, 293, 342, 428, 451.
*Ūrmis* (waves of change): six, 269.
Uśana, 449.

*Uśmapā*, 486.
Utilitarianism, 304.
*Uttarāyaṇam*, 329, 331.

*Vāda*, 442.
*Vaiśya*: even a, can attain God, 392–394.
Vaivasvata Manu, 406.
*Vajra*, 437.
*Vāk*, 447.
Vāmadeva, 250.
Varuṇa, 274, 502; among the water beings God is, 437.
Vāsava, 432.
*Vastu tantra jñāna*, 263, 266, 330.
Vāsudeva, 247, 510; among the *yādavas* God is, 449.
*Vāsudeva*: one of the *vyūhas*, 405.
Vāsuki, 474; among the serpents God is, 437.
*Vasus*, 467, 486; among the, God is Pāvaka, 433.
Veda (s), 198, 229, 307, 326, 333, 374, 434, 435, 437, 447, 509, 512; spiritual practitioner goes beyond the dos & don'ts of the, 174–180; treats the world as one family, 245; what is, 228.
*Vedamaya*, 326.
*Vedamūrti*, 326.
Vedanta: background material of the universe according to, 454; comprehensive philosophy of, 14; different meanings of Atman in, 124; evolution according to, 203–204; five factors constitute the world, 453–454; highest reality according to, 193; highest vision according to, 152; influences even the communists today, 15; modern science moving towards the conclusions of, 208–209, 219; nature of Reality according to, 293; no creation in, 206; place of freedom in, 65; place of, in modern thought world, 267; practical. *See* Practical Vedanta; preaches fearlessness & strength, 497; the clarion call of, 26.
*Vibhūtiyoga*, 399, 401, 410.
Vidula, Queen, 304.
*Vidvān*, 11.
*Vidyā*, 196, 439–442; nature of *brahma*, 337–341; *parā & aparā*, 195.
*Vidyā Māyā*, 59, 241, 362. *See also Māyā*.
Vidyasagar, Iswar Chandra, 456.
*Vijñāna*, 125. *See also* Wisdom; what is, 336.
*Vijñāni*: vision of a, 191.
*Vikāsa*, 32, 316. *See also Adhyātma vikāsa*.
*Vikṛti*, 311.
*Virāt*, 486.
*Visargaḥ*, 277.
Vision: of the Universal form of God, 469–471.
Viṣṇu, 247, 252, 273, 277, 279, 280, 324, 362, 437, 474, 475, 487, 490, 508; cosmic dimension of, 326; God is, among the *ādityas*, 431; meaning of, lying on śeśanāga, 325; story of how Lord, was deluded by in His own *māyā*, 237–238.
*Viṣṇu Purāṇa*, 375.
*Viṣṇu Sahasranāma*, 273, 279.
*Vitaṇḍa*, 442.
*Viveka*, 220. *See also* Discrimination.
*Vivekacūḍāmaṇi*, 83, 269; on self effort, 95; on Vedantic concept of God, 320; the first doorway to

*yoga* according to, 415.
Vivekananda Society: in Moscow, 14.
Vivekananda, Swami, 9, 12, 17, 27, 70, 71, 86, 154, 155, 204, 214, 259, 268, 284, 285, 292, 293, 296, 305, 324, 358, 378, 387, 393, 400, 412, 424, 431, 440, 480, 494. *See also* Narendra; an anecdote from the life of, regarding *samadarśitva*, 69; an incident from life of, illustrating how God carries *yogakśema* of his devotees, 382; belonged to the *nityamukta* class, 42; combine Śaṅkara's intellect and Buddha's heart says, 18; communists have started accepting, 15; defines *Māyā*, 233–234; defines religion, 39; education according to, 99–100; *karmayoga* is an independent path according to, 140; Kazi Nazrul Islam on, 377; literature of, stresses the idea of 'don't condemn', 253; on eschatology, 330; on faith in oneself, 251; on India as a great national ship, 43; on meditation, 103; on modern science moving towards vedantic conclusions, 219; on role of consciousness in universe, 206; on scientific exploration of nature in India, 197–199; on society devoid of spiritually realised men, 247; on the central teaching of Upaniṣads, 252; on the rising India, 8–9; on the status of householders & *sannyāsins*, 24; on true sainthood, 29; on uniqueness of Indian tradition, 189; regarding our attitude towards those who surpass us in life, 184–185; religion according to, 11, 64; who is a Hindu according to, 294; why Indians do not kill a, 424–425.
Voyager, 430.
Vyāsa, 420; among the *munis* God is, 449.
*Vyavasāya*, 448.
*Vyūhas*, 405, 406.

Walter, Gray (neurologist), 35.
West: in need of a comprehensive philosophy of life, 16; why the, has lagged behind in spiritual science, 223.
Western: astronomy moving in the direction of Vedantic conclusions, 60; concept of nature, 195; concept of reincarnation in, culture, 169; concept of singularity in, astronomy, 60; cosmology, 217; Indian &, concept of God, 319–320; philosophy, 199; science has threatened western theology & philosophy, 199; scientists accepting consciousness, 73.
Whitman, Walt, 61.
Will: different from obstinacy, 22.
Wisdom, 125, 336; Indian, 425; knowledge should evolve into, 200–201.
Women: even, can attain God, 392–394.
Wordsworth, William, 94, 399, 400, 426; on silence, 452.
Work. *See also Karma*; as a centre of education, 30; becomes no-work, 149; desire is the root of, 108–109; how & why does a *yogi*, 37, 39–40; how to be inactive in midst of action, 44–46; how to, without being tainted, 32–36;

prayer (meditation) versus, 12; purpose of, 30; role of emotion in efficient, 411–412; status of, according to *Gītā*, 183–184; who is eligible for action & who for inaction, 114–115; without attachment, 354.

World: welfare of, 11, 99–100, 101.

Worship: four types of men, God, 241–245; highest *bhakti* expresses itself in the form of simple, 385–386; how do *nityayuktas*, God, 364–367; how does a wise man, God, 408–411; respective results of worshipping gods & The God, 255, 383–384; spontaneous, 364–365; who can truly, God, 264–266; why do men, mythical gods, 249–252.

*Yajña*, 273, 277, 279, 333, 509; among the, God is *japayajñā*, 434.; of knowledge, 366.

Yājñavalkya, 226, 278, 402.

*Yajur Veda*, 369, 375, 432.

*Yakṣas*, 486; among the, God is Kubera, 433.

Yama, 284, 502; among the controllers God is the, 437.

Yaśoda, 468.

*Yati*, 130.

Yayāti, 112.

*Yoga*, 129, 133, 292, 468, 508; all-comprehensive nature of the, of *Gītā*, 182; *avikampa*, 407–408; concept of, 466; definition of, 332; divine, 349; fate of a *yogabhraśṭa*, 165–175, 180–181; how to give up the body in, 301–302; how to meditate, 132–135; importance of middle path in, 135–138; means for attaining the state of, 114; means of success in, of meditation, 159–164; of *abhyāsa*, 289; of Meditation, 107; of meditation is only a part of the wider *yoga* of *Gītā*, 140, 156; of meditation is very difficult, 157–158; posture of body in meditation, 132; practitioner of, goes beyond the dos & don'ts of religion, 174–180; purpose of, 140; result of, 125, 128, 138; result of being established in, 141–144; result of, of meditation, 134, 147–154; state of, 301; state of, compared to a steady flame of a lamp, 139; the first doorway to, according to Śaṅkara, 415; true, same as true *sannyāsa*, 110; vision of a *yogi* established in, 151–152; what is, 127, 149; what is the state of, 141–144; when is a *Yogi* said to be established in, 125–127; when to take up the practise of, 136–137; who gets established in, 407–408; who is a *yogārūḍha*, 116; *yogi* steadfast in, realises God easily, 302.

*Yogabalam*, 123. *See also* Strength; importance of, 296–298.

*Yogabhraśṭa*: fate of a, 167–174, 180–181; two types of birth for the, 170–172.

*Yogakṣema*, 382–383; an illustration of, 382.

*Yogamāyā*, 259–260, 468. *See also* *Māyā*.

*Yoganidra*, 325.

*Yogārūḍha*, 114, 115; who is a, 116.

*Yoga Sūtras*, 130, 156, 159.

*Yogeśvara*, 133; Śrī Kṛṣṇa addressed as, 466.

*Yogī*: fate of a, fallen from the path of *yoga*, 165–175, 180–181; goes beyond the dos & don'ts of religion, 174–180; greatest blessing that a, can receive from God, 415–417; how & why does a, work, 37, 40; how does a *nitya*, worship God, 364–367; how should a, meditate, 129–130; how the, of the *Gītā* attains God, 333; is not deluded by the eschatological paths, 332–333; means for becoming a, 114; nature of the mind of a, established in *yoga*, 139; of the *Gītā* superior to *jñānis, tapasvis* & *karmis*, 181–184; result that a, attains in meditation, 147–154; should follow the middle path, 135–138; steadfast in *yoga* realises God easily, 302; subdued mind of a, compared to a steady flame of a lamp, 139; uniqueness of *Gītā*'s, 332–334; vision of a, established in Self, 151–152; when is a, said to be abiding in God, 153; when is a, said to be established in *yoga*, 125–127, 138; Who is a, 91, 108, 111; who is the greatest, 154; who is the supreme, according to *Gītā*, 186.

*Yuga*, 310.

*Yuga dharma*: importance of distinguishing *Sanātana dharma* from, 477–482; new, for India, 479.

*Yukta*: who is a, 126.

*Yukti*, 293.

Zen Buddhism, 150.

Zimmer, Prof. 325.